ENCYCLOPEDIA of the HOLOCAUST

ENCYCLOPEDIA of the HOLOCAUST

Israel Gutman, Editor in Chief

Volume 3

Yad Vashem
The Holocaust Martyrs' and Heroes'
Remembrance Authority
Jerusalem

Sifriat Poalim Publishing House
Tel Aviv

MACMILLAN PUBLISHING COMPANY
NEW YORK

Collier Macmillan Publishers
LONDON

Macmillan Publishing Company
866 Third Avenue
New York, New York 10022
Collier Macmillan Canada, Inc.
Library of Congress Catalog Card Number: 89-13466
Printed in the United States of America

printing number
2 3 4 5 6 7 8 9 10

Library of Congress Cataloging-in-Publication Data

Encyclopedia of the Holocaust / Israel Gutman, editor in chief.
p. cm.
Includes bibliographical references.
ISBN 0–02–896090–4 (set)
Trade edition ISBN 0–02–546705–0 (set)
1. Holocaust, Jewish (1939–1945)—Dictionaries. I. Gutman, Israel.
D804.3.E53 1990 89-13466
940.53'18'-03—dc20 CIP

Acknowledgments of sources and permissions to use previously published materials are made in Acknowledgments, page xix.

LABOR SERVICE SYSTEM IN HUNGARY. *See* Munkaszolgálat.

LABOR ZIONIST ORGANIZATION OF AMERICA. *See* American Zionist Emergency Council.

LACHVA (Pol., Lachwa), town in the Belorussian SSR. In the interwar period, Lachva belonged to Poland, and in September 1939 it was occupied by the Red Army and incorporated into the Soviet Union. At the end of World War I, Jews constituted a third of the town's population of 3,400, and on the eve of World War II their number was 2,300. The Germans entered Lachva on July 8, 1941, two weeks after they had launched the invasion of Russia. On their orders a JUDENRAT (Jewish Council) was set up, headed by Dov Lopatyn. A ghetto was established on April 1, 1942, consisting of forty-five houses.

The Zionist YOUTH MOVEMENTS in Lachva created an underground, whose moving spirit was Itzhak Rochczyn, a member of one of the groups, Betar. There was cooperation between the underground, the Judenrat, and the Jewish police, with some members of the underground serving in the police. At one underground meeting, a Judenrat member promised to provide funds for the purchase of arms. Two events served as warnings to the Jews of the fate in store for them: the murder by the Germans of seven Jewish girls who had been roaming the villages in search of food for their families in the ghetto, and a report on the killing of the Jews of nearby Mikashevichi.

On September 2, 1942, Rochczyn and Lopatyn received word that pits were being dug in the town's vicinity. By late afternoon of that day the ghetto was surrounded by a force of 150 Germans and 200 local policemen, who had first been given generous allotments of hard liquor. The underground's plan was to organize twenty-two groups that at midnight would attack the police guarding the ghetto fence; in the ensuing confusion the Jews would break out and make for the forest area.

The leaders of the uprising decided to postpone the attack on the fence until morning. When the German commander came at 9:00 a.m. on September 3 to tell Lopatyn that he was going to liquidate the ghetto but that thirty persons, all of whom were skilled laborers, would be left behind, Lopatyn's answer was "Either we all stay alive or we all perish." When the underground gave a signal, the ghetto fence was breached. Lopatyn set fire to a house; Rochczyn attacked a German with an ax, splitting his skull, but was himself shot and killed as he was about to jump into the river that flowed near the fence. The other members of the underground launched an attack, fighting with axes or with their bare hands, and many were killed or wounded; Lopatyn was wounded in both hands.

The Jews, running out through the ghetto fence, were met by German fire and many were killed. About 1,000 fled; of these, 600 reached the Pripet marshes. Some 500 persons, women and old men, were taken to the pits that had been dug and were executed

there. Many of those who had made their escape were betrayed by the local inhabitants, and only 120 managed to assemble in the forest. A group of 25 escapees, with two rifles in their possession, were accepted into the ranks of a Soviet partisan unit. Lopatyn joined the "Stalin" partisan unit; on February 21, 1944, he was killed when he stepped on a mine. In July of that year, Lachva was liberated by the Red Army. Only a few dozen of its Jews survived.

BIBLIOGRAPHY

Michaeli, H. A., et al. *First Ghetto to Revolt—Lachva: Memorial Library of Jewish Communities.* Jerusalem, 1957. (In Hebrew.)

SHALOM CHOLAWSKI

LAMBERT, RAYMOND-RAOUL (1894–1943), Jewish leader in Vichy FRANCE. Born in a suburb of Paris, Lambert was raised and schooled in French culture, and received a minimal Jewish education. After serving in the French army in World War I, he entered the French civil service, where he held several minor positions, maintained some contacts with the Jewish community, and preserved his penchant for literary creativity. In the 1930s his involvement in Jewish affairs became more pronounced as he edited the leading French Jewish newspaper, *L'Univers Israélite,* and was active in the Comité d'Assistance aux Refugiés (CAR), which aided German Jewish refugees. Always a most patriotic Frenchman and deeply attached to French culture, Lambert was convinced that the Jews of France had successfully integrated into French society.

Released from active duty in the army with the fall of France, Lambert immediately reassumed his communal involvement in CAR-Marseilles, while he closely followed Vichy's withdrawal from the egalitarian principles of the French Revolution. In September 1941 he was summoned to Vichy to meet Xavier VALLAT, the commissioner for Jewish affairs in the Vichy government, to discuss the creation of a compulsory Jewish organization, the UNION GÉNÉRALE DES ISRAÉLITES DE FRANCE (UGIF). It was eventually established on November 29, 1941, and Lambert became its central personality. The UGIF functioned as an overall JUDENRAT (Jewish Council) in France. It had eighteen council members, nine for the occupied zone in the north and nine for the unoccupied zone (Vichy France) in the south. Throughout the war, the northern and southern councils had little to do with each other. Although Lambert was strongly criticized by leading Jewish figures in the unoccupied zone for his negotiations with Vallat, he proceeded to organize UGIF-South into a federative system in order to provide maximum autonomy for the participating welfare societies.

During the deportations from the French internment camps in the south that took place in August and September of 1942, Lambert strongly protested to the French authorities and helped arrange the relief extended to the deportees. Having a legalistic turn of mind, he directed the UGIF council into legal operations, hoping thereby to preserve the efficacy of welfare to the community. After the wide-scale deportations from Marseilles in late

January of 1943, which included native French Jews and UGIF employees, Lambert gravitated toward supporting resistance activity, although he remained at the head of the council and refused both to put an end to the UGIF's open-door policy and to encourage the Jewish population of Marseilles to disperse.

During the last months of his activity in the UGIF, Lambert succeeded in thwarting an attempt to unify it into an authoritarian body under the northern council. He closed ranks with his former antagonists in the CONSISTOIRE CENTRAL DES ISRAÉLITES DE FRANCE and preserved the federative character of UGIF-South. After a heated protest made in mid-August 1942 to Prime Minister Pierre LAVAL regarding confiscations of Jewish property, Lambert was arrested and, together with his wife and four children, was deported to DRANCY and four months later to AUSCHWITZ. His private wartime diary, published as *Carnet d'un témoin, 1940–1943* (edited by R. Cohen; Paris, 1985), provides a fascinating look into the life of an acculturated French Jew during the cataclysmic days of the Holocaust.

BIBLIOGRAPHY

Cohen, R. I. *The Burden of Conscience: French Jewish Leadership during the Holocaust.* Bloomington, 1987.

RICHARD COHEN

LAMMERS, HANS HEINRICH (1879–1962), Nazi official. A career civil servant, Lammers joined the Nazi party in 1932, and was appointed by Adolf Hitler to be his chief of chancery on January 30, 1933 (on November 26, 1937, Lammers was raised to the rank of *Reichsminister*). The chancery was the German head of government's main center of communication with the government departments, and Lammers's influence and power grew rapidly with Hitler's increasing power. When Cabinet meetings became less frequent and, in consequence, there were fewer occasions on which votes were taken on government bills, the chief of chancery's regular presentation to the Führer became the most important means of approach to Hitler. All draft legislation, including every anti-Jewish measure, passed through Lammers's hands. In the face of growing anarchy, Lammers sought to run the chancery in accordance with established administrative principles and on the basis of legal norms, but as time went on he had to make more and more ideological concessions, and, after 1941, the influence he had wielded passed increasingly into the hands of Martin BORMANN. In the 1949 *Wilhelmstrasse-Prozess* (Ministries Trial), Lammers was sentenced to twenty years' imprisonment for formulating and authorizing antisemitic legislation, which culminated in the "FINAL SOLUTION." The sentence was reduced to ten years by the United States High Command in 1951, and in December 1954 he was pardoned and released from prison.

BIBLIOGRAPHY

Adam, U. *Judenpolitik im Dritten Reich.* Düsseldorf, 1972.

Speer, A. *Inside the Third Reich.* London, 1970.

UWE ADAM

"LANGUAGE REGULATION." *See* Sprachregelung.

LATVIA. [*This entry consists of an overview of Latvian history that focuses on the Soviet and German occupations during World War II, followed by a review of the Holocaust era in Latvia.*]

General Survey

Latvia is a Soviet republic on the Baltic Sea, situated between ESTONIA to the north and LITHUANIA to the south. Between 1918 and 1940 it was an independent republic. Latvia's main regions are Livonia (central Latvia), with the capital, RIGA; Kurland in the southwest, with the city LIEPĀJA; and Latgale in the east, with DVINSK (now Daugavpils). During the course of World War II, Latvia experienced three occupations. In accordance with the terms of the NAZI-SOVIET PACT of 1939, the Soviet Union occupied Latvia in June 1940. The Germans invaded Latvia in June 1941, and in 1944 the Soviet

army expelled the Germans, retaking Latvia.

During its period of independence between the two world wars, Latvia had close economic ties with Germany, fostered by an influential German minority. In 1934 the veteran politician Karlis Ulmanis led a right-wing revolution, relying on the Aizsargs paramilitary organization. The democratic regime was ended, and among the casualties was the extreme rightist and nationalist organization Pērkonkrust (Thundercross), which was dismantled.

On October 5, 1939, Latvia was forced to allow the Soviet army to establish bases in its territory. In June 1940 the Soviet army took over Latvia, and a month later the country was declared a Soviet republic. During this occupation, Latvia was subjected to measures to make it conform to the Soviet pattern. National and local civilian administrative organs were destroyed, the military and civilian leadership was eliminated, and Latvia's economy was nationalized. All farms over 74 acres (30 hectares) were divided into lots of 25 acres (10 hectares) as a preparatory step toward collectivization, and on June 14, 1941, about nineteen thousand Latvians, among them five thousand Jews, were deported to Siberia.

While the Soviet occupation was undoubtedly imposed by force, the Soviets did manage to enlist the sympathy, if not the outright support, of about one-tenth of the population. The overwhelming majority of those who served in the Soviet-controlled civil administration and police were Latvian gentiles. Although the number of Jews working in the Soviet administration in the cities, especially those of Latgale, was considerable, it was less than their percentage in the general population.

On the same day that the Germans invaded the Soviet Union, June 22, 1941, they crossed the Latvian frontier. Riga was occupied on July 1, and it took the Wehrmacht until July 10 to clear Latvia of Soviet troops. Under the command of Gen. Franz Walter STAHLECKER, Einsatzgruppe A entered Latvia along with the Wehrmacht. Within hours, Stahlecker's troops began organizing the killing of Latvia's Jews and other "enemies" of the Nazi regime, Communists and GYPSIES. Latvia became an integral part of REICHSKOMMISSARIAT OSTLAND and was called Generalbezirk Lettland (General Commissariat Latvia). The *Generalkommissar* (general commissioner) appointed by the Germans for Latvia was Dr. Heinrich Drechsler. He headed a local administration composed of Latvians, which had a degree of independence.

Nevertheless, the German occupation of Latvia was brutal. Although numerous Latvians, especially those who had suffered under the Soviets, greeted the German forces as liberators, the Germans entered Latvia with plans to exploit Latvian economic and labor resources. Figures for gentiles killed or victimized are difficult to assess, but it may be said that as many as two thousand of Latvia's four thousand Gypsies, as well as the patients of all the mental hospitals, were killed. According to estimates made by a Latvian resistance organization, as many as twenty thousand Latvian Communists and members of the national resistance also lost their lives. In addition, tens of thousands of Latvians were incarcerated or deported to Germany, and throughout the period of German occupation Latvia's jails were filled to capacity. Eighty thousand Latvian men served in the Latvian SS Legion, and an additional thirty thousand men in the Latvian police corps were deployed against the Soviet army.

Initially, it was not planned to use Latvian troops against the Soviets. Part of Heinrich HIMMLER's and Reinhard HEYDRICH's plan, however, was to enlist Latvians in the murder of Jews and Communists. Although the commanders of Einsatzgruppe A supervised the killing of Jews, local and national Latvian police units were integrated into the implementation of the "FINAL SOLUTION," and they frequently carried out the killings themselves. The major Latvian killing unit, which took part in numerous operations in Riga and in the provinces during the war, was led by Viktor Arajs (who was sentenced in 1979 to life imprisonment and died in 1988). His unit, known as the Arajs Commando, numbered about four hundred men; it played a major role in the killings in the Bikernieki Forest near Riga, the Latvian provincial areas, the Ukraine, Belorussia, and Russia. Perhaps as many as thirty thousand Latvian Jews were killed by the Arajs Commando. The Latvian commanders of provincial police forces that carried out or participated in the killing operations included Petersons and Bluzmanis of Dvinsk, Captain Macs of Rēzekne, Fricons of Liepāja, Vagulens of Jelgava, Runka of Valmiera, Vaczemnieks of Ventspils, Lietuvietis of Smiltene, Janis Cirulis of Alūksne, and Janis Niedra of Tukums. The total number of Latvians who actively participated in the killing operations is impossible at present to determine; however, it is clear that more than two thousand Latvians served the SD (Sicherheitsdienst; Security Service) in various capacities.

BIBLIOGRAPHY

Benton, P. *Baltic Countdown*. London, 1984.

Bilmanis, A. *A History of Latvia*. Westport, Conn. 1970.

Bilmanis, A., comp. *Latvian-Russian Relations: Documents*. Washington, D.C., 1978.

ANDREW EZERGAILIS

The Fate of Latvian Jewry

Jews first arrived in Kurland and Livonia in the sixteenth century. At the beginning of the twentieth century about 200,000 Jews lived there, but expulsions, emigration, and the World War I military campaigns cut their numbers to less than half. During the first years of Latvian independence, the Jews, who then constituted about 5 percent of the population, enjoyed equal rights in almost every sphere. Like the other minorities in Latvia, they were granted broad educational and cultural autonomy. The 1934 revolution of Karlis Ulmanis, however, brought about a certain deterioration in the Jews' situation. The hardships and the difficulties in earning a living during the second half of the 1930s drove many young Jews from the villages to the large cities of Riga, Liepāja, and Dvinsk, where two-thirds of the Jews lived at the end of the decade.

According to a 1935 census, 94,000 Jews lived in Latvia; however, at the time of the German invasion in June 1941, only some 70,000 remained in the country. About 4,000 had left Latvia before the Soviet occupation, 5,000 (heads of the Jewish community and members of the cultural and economic elite) had been deported to Siberia by the Soviets, and up to 15,000 managed to escape to the Soviet interior ahead of the advancing German army. Of the 70,000 remaining Jews, it is estimated that not more than 3,000 survived the Nazi massacres. In addition to native Latvian Jews, about 20,000 Jews from Austria, Czechoslovakia, and Germany were deported to Latvia. Of them, only about 1,000 survived the war.

The murder of the Jews in Latvia was carried out in three main stages. The first was from July to October 1941, when about 30,000 Jews from Latvia's provincial towns and about 4,000 more Jews from Riga were killed. The second stage was from November to December 1941, during which most of the Jews living in the ghettos of the larger cities—Riga, Dvinsk, and Liepāja—were annihilated. In October 1941, a change in command of the SD (Sicherheitsdienst; Security Service) took place. The main force of Einsatzgruppe A left Latvia for Leningrad, and the police duties for Latvia were taken over by the *Höherer SS- und Polizeiführer* (Higher SS and Police Leader), SS-Brigadeführer Friedrich JECKELN, who had excelled in the killing operations in the Ukraine. Jeckeln, like all the Higher SS and Police Leaders, had been given special authority by Heinrich HIMMLER, and he arrived in Riga with a plan to "empty the ghetto." In the so-called Jeckeln Aktion, which took place on November 30 and December 7, 1941, about 25,000 Jews from the Riga ghetto were killed in the RUMBULA Forest. (In 1946 Jeckeln was convicted and hanged in Riga for his part in this operation.)

The third stage lasted from January 1942 until July of that year, and during this period as many as 14,000 of the 20,000 Jewish deportees from Austria, Czechoslovakia, and Germany were killed. Most of these Jews were killed in the Bikernieki Forest and at other locations in the vicinity of Riga. At the beginning of 1943 only about 5,000 Jews remained in the ghettos of Riga, Dvinsk, and Liepāja, and in a few labor camps, the largest of which was KAISERWALD. Starting in the fall of 1943, the remaining Jews in the cities were moved to Kaiserwald. Sporadic killings continued until the end of the war. The largest burial grounds of the massacred Jews are in the Rumbula and Bikernieki forests. Altogether, there are perhaps as many as sixty sites of mass graves of murdered Jews in Latvia.

During the late summer of 1944, as the Soviet forces were approaching Riga, the remaining Jews in Latvia were transported to Germany, mostly to the STUTTHOF camp. Thereafter their fate varied; most were marched to work in the German interior under blizzard conditions in early 1945 as the Soviet army closed in on the German forces. Numerous people died on the way from hunger and exposure. Out of the entire Latvian Jewish community only about 150 survived by hiding with the help of Latvian gentiles, and several dozen Jews who had fought with partisan units also survived. No more than 1,000 Latvian Jews returned from camps in Germany.

After the war some 13,000 Jews who had been refugees and exiles in the Soviet interior returned to Latvia. They were joined by another 20,000 Jews from other parts of the Soviet Union. In 1970 there were 36,592 Jews in Latvia, and by 1987 about one-third of them had emigrated to Israel.

BIBLIOGRAPHY

Bobe, M., et al., eds. *The Jews in Latvia.* Tel Aviv, 1971. (In Hebrew.)

Levin, D. *With Their Backs to the Wall: The Armed Struggle of Latvian Jewry against the Nazis.* Jerusalem, 1978. (In Hebrew.)

Schneider, G. *Journey into Terror: The Story of the Riga Ghetto.* New York, 1979.

ANDREW EZERGAILIS

LAVAL, PIERRE (1883–1945), French politician and collaborator; head of the Vichy government from 1942 to 1944. A republican politician of the Center, Laval was twice pre-

Pierre Laval, premier of Vichy France, receiving an earful from Göring. [National Archives]

mier (in 1931–1932 and 1935–1936) before becoming vice-premier of the Vichy government immediately after its establishment in 1940. Dismissed on December 13 of that year by the premier, Philippe PÉTAIN, Laval was recalled to office in May 1942 with the help of Hitler. He formed a new cabinet and served as chief of government, continuing in that position to the end of the war.

Laval was known as a pragmatist rather than an ideologue, and he championed an agreement with Hitler and the Germans. French fortunes, he argued, were linked with those of the victorious Reich. Consequently, he attempted to comply with Nazi requests on matters he felt were not crucial to French national interests. Among these was the Jewish issue. Believing that he could win the confidence of the occupation authorities by satisfying their demands for foreign Jews, Laval agreed in 1942 to assist the Germans in rounding up their victims and dispatching them from France. It was he who meshed the apparatus of the French police and administration with the Nazis' machinery of destruction. When faced with protests such as those of the Protestant leader Pastor Marc Boegner, who said that the Jews were being murdered, Laval adhered rigidly to the story agreed upon with the SS: the Jews were being sent to work camps in the east. He began to drag his heels in 1943, when the failure of his policies was becoming evident, the outcries against the deportations were growing, and the most cruel measures increasingly involved native French Jews. He attempted, without much exertion, to limit the deportations to foreigners. Although he gradually lost control of events, Laval clung, almost to the end, to his illusions about the efficacy of his program.

Tried after the war for plotting against the security of the state and for conducting intelligence with the enemy, Laval was sentenced to death after a short, poorly run trial. Having failed in a suicide attempt, he was executed in October 1945.

BIBLIOGRAPHY

Kupferman, F. *Laval, 1883–1945*. Paris, 1987.
Laval, P. *The Diary of Pierre Laval* (1948). Reprint, New York, 1976.

Marrus, M. R., and R. O. Paxton. *Vichy France and the Jews*. New York, 1981.
Warner, G. *Pierre Laval and the Eclipse of France, 1931–1945: A Political Biography*. London, 1968.

MICHAEL R. MARRUS

LAW AND JUDICIARY IN NAZI GERMANY. The perversion by the Nazis of the legal system in Germany was based on the racist-"folkish" concepts (*völkisch* derives from *Volk* [nation], which in Nazi terminology is applicable to "pure" Germans only) formulated in the Nazi party platform, paragraphs 4 and 5.

> Para. 4: Only those who are our fellow Germans [*Volksgenossen*] shall be citizens of our state. Only those who are of German blood can be considered as our fellow Germans, regardless of creed. Hence no Jew can be regarded as a fellow German.
>
> Para. 5: Those who are not citizens of the state must live in Germany as foreigners and must be subject to the law of aliens.

Three methods were applied to effect the perversion of the rule of law: (1) the enactment of ANTI-JEWISH LEGISLATION; (2) the reinterpretation, by the German courts, of the existing laws in accordance with racist concepts; (3) the taking of measures based on anti-Jewish laws without legal standing, or even in contradiction to existing laws.

The Nazi regime actually abrogated the civil-liberal state based on the rule of law ("normativism") by subordinating it to a supralegal racist-*völkisch* authority ("blood, folk, and race") and the supreme authority of the Führer. (The Nazi party program decreed that interpretation of all sources of law must be based on Nazi ideology, especially as explained in the party program and in the speeches of the Führer.) Nevertheless, the Nazis also sought to subvert the constitutional state and its laws through "legal" means, by using the existing laws to obtain a pseudolegal carte blanche for the legislation they wanted, especially that directed against the Jews. This is the only way to explain the *Reichstagsbrand-Verordnung* (Reichstag Fire Decree), the emergency decree signed by President Paul von HINDENBURG on February 28, 1933, for the "Protection of the People and the State." This decree conformed, in formal terms, with the Weimar Constitution, even though it suspended basic civil rights. The same approach accounts for the *Ermächtigungsgesetz* (Enabling Law) of March 24, 1933, the Law for the Removal of Distress of the People and the State, under which the government (that is, Hitler) was given the "legal" power to promulgate laws on its own, even if such laws deviated from the constitution.

This opened the gates to a flood of laws, decrees, and ordinances, increasingly radical in form and content, that inundated the German Reich and were intended to eliminate racial and political opponents of the Nazis from the political, professional, social, and cultural life of the country. The main target of this destructive legislative policy was the Jews, the Nazis' "major enemy," and the resulting legislation sentenced the Jews to "civil death," with the state organs losing no time in carrying out the sentence.

The Law for the Restoration of the Professional Civil Service, of April 7, 1933, under which non-Aryan state officials were eliminated from the civil service, was only the beginning of an extensive series of legislative acts that so restricted the possibilities for Jews to train for and practice a profession as to virtually impose a total ban on Jewish professionals. The *Reichsfluchtsteuer* (emigration tax) law of May 18, 1934, deprived the Jews of any assets they might have retained after losing their livelihood and being forced to seek emigration.

The Reich Citizenship Law (reminiscent of an ancient Teutonic "law of aliens") and the Law for the Protection of German Blood and German Honor (i.e., the NUREMBERG LAWS), both of September 15, 1935, made the Jews aliens in what had been their own land—disenfranchising them, removing any remaining obstacles to their total dispossession and their expulsion from the country, and abolishing their rights with regard to personal status, all by "legal" means.

Under the Eleventh Supplementary Decree of the Reich Citizenship Law, enacted on November 25, 1941, a German Jew whose regular place of residence was, or came to be, abroad was deprived of his citizenship, and this in turn led to the confiscation of his property by the Reich. This meant, among other things, that the Jews who were deported to AUSCHWITZ or MAJDANEK were *eo ipso* stripped of their property: a joint act of robbery and murder, ordered and executed by the state. The Jews who stayed behind, temporarily or permanently, were also stripped of all their rights, even of the protection of the labor laws, under ordinances passed on October 7 and October 31 of 1941.

Even in civil law the Jews were subject to special legislation, although, on the face of it, the racist-*völkisch* ideology was neutral. Thus, under a rent law for Jews, dated April 30, 1939, rent control as far as Jews were concerned was reduced to such an extent as to be in fact totally lifted.

In criminal law, the laws on the amendment of the criminal code and procedure, of June 28, 1935, and the numerous decrees and ordinances based thereon, deprived the Jews of any protection they had left under the law. Jews were liable to punishment merely on the basis of having violated the racist-*völkisch* idea underlying a criminal law and its popular interpretation, even in the absence of any specific sanction in the law. Under the Thirteenth Supplementary Decree of the Reich Citizenship Law of July 1, 1943, "punishable offenses" committed by Jews were no longer prosecuted by the courts and came under the exclusive jurisdiction of the police; in practice this meant automatic deportation to concentration camps.

Although there was enough anti-Jewish legislation to condemn the Jews to "civil death," the courts time and again found themselves confronting legal norms still in force that, if interpreted under the established principles of the rule of law, would have had to lead to verdicts in favor of the Jewish party in a trial. This problem, too, was overcome, in a variety of ways: by using a formula based on racist policy, by reinterpreting existing law on the basis of changing (that is, Nazi) legal concepts, and by filling in gaps existing in the law by analogy with subsequent (Nazi) anti-Jewish legislation.

The racist formula was expressed as follows, in a statement on behalf of the Reich minister of justice, defining the status and duty of judges, before the 1936 national jurists' convention:

> Legal provisions promulgated prior to the National Socialist revolution must not be applied in cases where such application would be an insult to the sound insight presently held by the German people.

Reinterpretation of the laws was to be carried out on the basis of the reformed political ideology, that is, in accordance with racist theory and the "sound insight" of the German people.

The filling in of legal gaps by analogy with Nazi anti-Jewish legislation was to be used only if the existing traditional law did not lend itself to bending, to the extent required to obtain the desired result. For all three methods, the overriding principle was "The law is that which is good for the [German] *Volk*," to which, under the Reich Citizenship Law, the Jews no longer belonged. "It is the Führer's will that determines what is good for the German people; and the Führer's will is the supreme law."

These rules of interpretation applied to the entire legal sphere—civil, criminal, and public law—but only to "prerevolutionary" (pre-Nazi) laws. Laws promulgated from 1933 on were "the expression of the common will as expressed in the Führer" and had to be obeyed to the letter. A survey of legal decisions, by lower courts as well as by the supreme court, shows that these racist-*völkisch* principles of legal interpretation were generally observed.

The perversion of justice reached its peak in what Ernst Fraenkel, in his book *The Dual State: A Contribution to the Theory of Dictatorship*, defines as the "Prerogative State," which replaced the "Normative State" in all legal spheres, but especially where Jews and the criminal law were involved, in a case that was classified as "political." For example:

1. In a letter to the president of the People's Court, dated September 9, 1942, the Reich minister of justice stated: "In criminal proceedings against Jews the decisive fact is their Jewishness, rather than their culpability."
2. A decree issued by the REICHSSICHERHEITSHAUPTAMT (Reich Security Main Office; RSHA) dated March 11, 1943, orders: "Jews who have been sentenced to a term in prison and have completed serving

their term are to be sent to the Auschwitz or Lublin concentration camps, for life imprisonment, irrespective of the length of the original prison term to which they were sentenced."

The Nazi leaders' racist-*völkisch* delusions had systematically transformed a state based on the rule of law into a state based on illegality and injustice.

[*See also* Arierparagraph; Entjudung.]

BIBLIOGRAPHY

Fearnside, W. W. "Three Innovations of National Socialist Jurisprudence." *Journal of Central European Affairs* 16/2 (1956): 146–155.

Fraenkel, E. *The Dual State: A Contribution to the Theory of Dictatorship.* New York, 1969.

HELGE GRABITZ

LAWS PUNISHING NAZIS AND NAZI COLLABORATORS. The trials of Nazi war criminals that followed the NUREMBERG TRIAL, which was conducted by the International Military Tribunal (IMT) at Nuremberg, were based on the principles adopted and the judgments made by that tribunal, in the spirit of its charter and in the letter of its verdict. The various countries amended their existing legislation to conform with the dispositions in the IMT judgments. New laws were enacted and new courts were established for this purpose that took into account the developments in international law generated by the IMT (as well as the far-reaching changes that had taken place in military technology).

Outstanding among the new international and municipal legislation in this sphere were the laws on the crime of GENOCIDE passed by various countries in 1949 and later; the abolition of the statute of limitations on war crimes and crimes against humanity (1968); and the Geneva and other international conventions and documents. For the most part, these conventions deal with humanitarian law—the codification and further development of the laws and customs of war, including the prohibition of new advanced weapons and the steps to be taken to prevent nuclear, biological, and chemical warfare. Some conventions also relate to the continuous struggle against discrimination on grounds of race, religion, sex, age, and political views. They emphasize the need for the extension of human rights, as a vital element in the preservation of peace among nations; and the need for respect of humanity in relations among individuals.

In occupied Germany, the Allied Control Commission, on December 20, 1945, enacted Control Council Law No. 10, which faithfully reflects the principles then being formulated in preparation for the IMT. It also deals in detail with the punishment of members of organizations that the law defines as criminal. Law No. 10, by its application, reinforced the postulate that the punishment of Nazi war criminals was not to be regarded as an act of revenge, but as a contribution to peace and justice. The trials held in accordance with Law No. 10 clearly show the impact of the proposals that were being drafted for the IMT and that were to guide its procedure and judgments. This aspect was prominent in the trials held in the American zone, but it also influenced the trials held in the British and French zones. In the British zone, the formal basis for the trials was the *Manual of Military Law,* which had been in force long before the Nazi aggression, and also a Royal Decree Incorporated in the Order to the Armed Forces No. 81/45. In the French zone the formal legal basis for the trials was a decree dated August 28, 1944, that incorporates the relevant passages from the French code of military law and the principles of criminal law in force before the war.

All of these laws and decrees had in common the emphasis on the validity and applicability of the laws and customs of war as defined in the various Hague and Geneva conventions and of the principles of humanity and conscience formally accepted by all civilized nations. The impact of the IMT principles, and the emphasis on the Hague Convention and the accepted norms of civilized behavior, are also evident in the trials of war criminals by Canadian courts, the legal basis for which was a law passed on August 30, 1945, and by Australian courts, for which Law 48/1945 provided the legal basis. In all these courts, and also in the courts of Norway, the Netherlands, and Belgium, the issue of retroactive legislation did not arise in any of the Nazi war-crimes trials. This was because these courts, like the IMT itself, based their proceedings on declarative and universal principles that had been developed since time immemorial and formally put into force particularly since the nineteenth century.

In contrast to the very effective role of the IMT and Law No. 10, the DENAZIFICATION law enacted by the Allied Control Commission on March 5, 1946, turned out to be a failure, when Nazis who were suspected of having a criminal past were reappointed to high posts, in both West and East Germany. Little evidence is available as to how Law No. 10 was applied in the Soviet zone of occupation, and even less about how the denazification process was carried out there.

In Austria, the provisional government, on June 26, 1945, enacted the Constitutional Law on War Crimes and National Socialist Crimes, which is also based on the fundamental principles of the Nuremberg Tribunal. In practice, the Austrian performance in this respect has been disappointing.

The principles of the Nuremberg Trial are to be found in appropriate form in most of the special legislation enacted by the other countries that were part of the anti-Nazi alliance, among them Poland (in a decree of December 11, 1946), Czechoslovakia (by regulations issued on January 24, 1946), Norway, and the Netherlands (*see* TRIALS OF WAR CRIMINALS: THE NETHERLANDS). Such legislation was also enacted against collaborators, even by former Axis countries (Bulgaria, Romania, and Hungary) and by countries that had been neutral during the war. These laws contributed to the spread and acceptance of the principles embodied in the IMT charter and judgment. They aided in increasing worldwide recognition of the need to prevent international conflicts, and, if these should break out, to settle them by peaceful means; they led to a deeper understanding of humanitarian principles and their overriding significance.

BIBLIOGRAPHY

United Nations War Crimes Commission. *History of the United Nations War Crimes Commission.* London, 1948.

United Nations War Crimes Commission. *Law Reports of Trials of War Criminals.* Vols. 1, 3, 4. London, 1947, 1948.

MARIAN MUSHKAT

LEADERSHIP PRINCIPLE. *See* Führerprinzip.

LEAGUE OF JEWISH WORKERS IN RUSSIA, LITHUANIA, AND POLAND. *See* Bund.

LEBANON. *See* Syria and Lebanon.

LEBENSRAUM ("living space"), a basic principle in Nazi foreign policy. Stemming originally from the fields of political geography and geopolitics, the concept of *Lebensraum* was developed in the works of Sir Halford Mackinder, Friedrich Ratzel, and Karl Haushofer, who gave a pseudoscientific basis to the drive for conquest and the expansionist ambitions of the Nazis. Hans Grimm's book *Volk ohne Raum* (A People without Space; 1926) became a classic in the literature on Germany's need for vital space.

There was, however, a difference between the understanding of this concept in the writings of the geopoliticians and Hitler's interpretation of it. The geopoliticians spoke of military conquest to achieve autarky and acquire foodstuffs, and of military self-sufficiency and defensibility as a solution of Germany's political and social problems. Although Hitler accepted and disseminated this line of thought, he added a mythological conception related to his blood-and-soil mystique, with antisemitic and anti-Bolshevist characteristics. He believed that the east had to be conquered in order to establish a vast continental empire settled by Germans, so as to secure for the Aryan race its place in the world as a *Herrenvolk* ("master race"). The expansion to the east would achieve territorial continuity, augment the population, infuse the nation's body with new blood, and also serve as a basis for the supply of food and raw materials. The policy toward the conquered populations would eventually include the physical annihilation of their leading political and intellectual strata, the extermination of the Jews, and the exploitation of the masses through slave labor, as well as the transfer to Germany of those children of Czechs, Poles, and other Slavs who appeared Aryan in their physical and physiognomic traits and who would improve the quality of the Aryan race and strengthen it demographically.

BIBLIOGRAPHY

Bracher, K. D. *The German Dictatorship: The Origins, Structure and Effects of National Socialism.* New York, 1971.

Hillgruber, A. "Die 'Endlösung' und das deutsche Ostimperium als Kernstück des rassenideologischen Programms des Nationalsozialismus." In *Hitler, Deutschland und die Machte,* edited by F. Funke, pp. 94–114. Düsseldorf, 1976.

Hitler, A. *Hitler's Secret Book.* New York, 1961.

Tal, U. "Territory and Space (*Raum*) in the Nazi Ideology." *Zemanim* 1 (Autumn 1979): 68–75. (In Hebrew.)

Wistrich, R. W. *Hitler's Apocalypse: Jews and the Nazi Legacy.* New York, 1985.

DAVID BANKIER

LECCA, RADU (c. 1902–c. 1980), official in charge of "Jewish questions" in ROMANIA; a double agent serving the Nazis and the Ion ANTONESCU government at the same time. Lecca had ties to the Nazis as early as 1935; he was the correspondent in Romania for the Nazi party newspaper, the *Völkischer Beobachter,* and for the Deutsches Nachrichtenbüro, the German news agency. He was a member of the antisemitic National Democratic Party, headed by Alexandru CUZA, until its dissolution on orders of King Carol II in 1938.

In September 1940, when the joint Antonescu and IRON GUARD government was established, Lecca was appointed section chief in the prime minister's bureau, by virtue of his Nazi ties. For a while he served as director of the Romanian security services; following the Iron Guard's attempted coup and its suppression, in January 1941, he became Antonescu's liaison officer with the German legation in Bucharest.

Lecca was charged in October 1941 with "settling the Jewish question in Romania," an appointment that he retained until the downfall of the regime in August 1944. Until October 1943 his office was a section in the prime minister's bureau, whose acting head was Mihai ANTONESCU. At that time, Lecca's title was changed to *Comisar General Pentru Promlemele Evreesti* (Commissar for Jewish Questions), and his office was relocated to the Ministry of Labor—a change indicative of the decreasing significance of the "Jewish question" and the regime's dissociation from the "FINAL SOLUTION." As commissar, Lecca controlled the CENTRALA EVREILOR (Jewish Center) and supervised the execution of the regime's antisemitic policy, in both legislative and administrative matters. He collaborated with the German legation and with Gustav RICHTER, its adviser on Jewish affairs, with whom he established a close friendship. Lecca also devoted some of the funds that accumulated in his office—from bribes and special levies that the Jews were forced to pay—to cover expenses incurred by the legation staff.

Lecca supported German plans for the deportation of all the Jews of Romania to the EXTERMINATION CAMPS in Poland. He also did his best to comply with Antonescu's demands to strip the Jews of their assets, and he drafted Jews into forced-labor battalions. He made ample use of all opportunities to pocket bribes, received for exempting Jews from punitive measures, such as deportation to TRANSNISTRIA or assignment to labor battalions engaged in dangerous work in remote areas. In the spring of 1942 he collaborated with the Germans in preparing for the deportations, arranging for a census of "persons of Jewish blood," and drawing up plans for the establishment of ghettos.

In the summer of 1942, Lecca was invited to Berlin to participate in further planning for the deportation of Romanian Jews to the extermination camps. This visit was to have been the climax of Lecca's collaboration with the Nazis, but in fact it proved to be a turning point in his attitude, because he felt that his reception was not the kind that he had a right to expect. Moreover, Ion Antonescu was reluctant to go along with the Nazi plans to deport the Jews to their deaths in Poland. Nevertheless, Lecca continued to keep the German legation, and Richter, informed about the Romanian government's misgivings over its original consent to the deportation of the Jews; about the changes that were taking place in Romanian policy; and, at a later stage, about the projected immigration to Palestine of tens of thousands of Romanian Jews. The information that Lecca provided to the Nazis helped them foil the Romanian plans. Some of Lecca's reports to the Germans were authorized by his superiors, and in these Lecca appears to have succeeded in misleading Richter on Romania's policy toward the Jews, following the cancellation of the plans for their deportation to Poland.

In his capacity as de facto chief of the Centrala Evreilor, Lecca impoverished Romanian Jews by extorting huge sums from them. The money was channeled to the state treasury, but some of it was diverted to Antonescu's wife, who headed a welfare and rehabilitation institution for Romanian war veterans. In this way, Lecca was able to ward off the many complaints lodged against him by his colleagues, who envied him for the personal riches that he was accumulating. Occasionally, the Jews were able to exploit Lecca's greed to gain concessions (for example, the provision of assistance to certain communities) or to prevent the implementation of certain severe measures, as in the case of the Zionist pioneers who were about to be deported to Transnistria.

When the Antonescu regime was deposed, Lecca was arrested and was found to be in possession of Romanian and foreign currency, valuables, gold, and commercial goods. He was tried and sentenced to death, but his past services were not forgotten; his sentence was commuted to life imprisonment, and after a few years he was set free. He spent the last years of his life in Bucharest, living off the pension he received as a retired government official.

BIBLIOGRAPHY

Ancel, J., ed. *Documents concerning the Fate of Romanian Jewry during the Holocaust.* Vols. 4, 7, 8. Jerusalem, 1986.

Cristian, S. C. *Patru ani de urgie: Notele unui evreu din Romania.* Bucharest, 1945.

Lavi, T. *Romanian Jewry in World War II.* Jerusalem, 1965. (In Hebrew.)

JEAN ANCEL

LE CHAMBON-SUR-LIGNON, French town in the Haute-Loire department in southern FRANCE that served as a focal point for the sheltering of thousands of Jews during most of the Nazi occupation. The town's overwhelmingly Protestant population responded to the call of Pastor André Trocmé to extend aid to fleeing Jews and sheltered them in private homes and outlying farmsteads, as well as in public institutions in Le Chambon and nearby localities. Pastor Trocmé, who with his wife, Magda, initiated and presided over this vast rescue operation (with the help of interdenominational organizations), has been described as the "charismatic leader" and "living spirit" of Le Chambon, and his wife as the "motor" of the large operation. Trocmé always responded to calls for help to hide Jews in danger of detection by the German police, even if this jeopardized not only his own life but those of his wife and children and members of his community. Refugee Jews were housed in public institutions and children's homes or with local townsmen and farmers, for various periods of time. Then, with the help of others, such as Pastor Edouard Théis, director of the Collège Cévenol, some were taken on dangerous treks through French towns and villages and under assumed French names to the Swiss frontier. They were surreptitiously smuggled across it and into the waiting hands of other Protestant supporters on the Swiss side (the Swiss authorities invariably drove Jews back across the border and therefore had to be avoided).

Daniel Trocmé, a cousin of André Trocmé, directed the children's home Maison des Roches at Le Chambon. He was betrayed, reportedly by a German officer staying at a military convalescent home in Le Chambon, and was arrested on June 29, 1943, and taken to Moulins for interrogation. He readily admitted his role in the rescue of Jewish children, and was sent to the BUCHENWALD concentration camp, where he perished in April 1944. André Trocmé was also arrested, by Vichy authorities, but he was released, although he refused to sign a statement agreeing to desist from further aiding of Jews. It is estimated that some three thousand to five thousand Jews found shelter in Le Chambon and its environs at one time or another between 1941 and 1944.

Survivors celebrate the liberation (June 1944) in the village square of Le Chambon. [Eli Ben-Gal]

Asked about his motivations in extending aid to Jews, one Le Chambon resident responded: "We were doing what had to be done. . . . It was the most natural thing in the world to help these people." The rescue operation was unique in that an entire community banded together to rescue Jews, seeing this as their Christian obligation.

Pierre Sauvage, born in Le Chambon to Jewish parents who were refugees there, produced a documentary film, *Weapons of the Spirit,* about the rescue operation. André Trocmé, Daniel Trocmé, and Edouard Théis, as well as thirty-two other residents of Le Chambon and its environs, have been recognized by YAD VASHEM as "RIGHTEOUS AMONG THE NATIONS."

BIBLIOGRAPHY

Hallie, P. P. *Lest Innocent Blood Be Shed: The Story of the Village of Le Chambon and How Goodness Happened There.* New York, 1979.

Rittner, C., and S. Myers, eds. *The Courage to Care.* New York, 1986. See pages 99–119.

MORDECAI PALDIEL

LEḤI. *See* Loḥamei Ḥerut Israel.

LEMBERG. *See* Lvov.

LEMKIN, RAPHAEL (1901–1959), Jewish jurist. Lemkin was born into a Jewish farming family in an Eastern Galician village, and studied philosophy and law at the University of Lemberg (Lvov) and at universities in Germany, France, and Italy. He settled in Warsaw, but when World War II broke out, he fled to Vilna, and from there made his way to the United States, by way of Sweden, the USSR, Japan, and Canada. He taught law, first at Duke University and then at Yale University.

While serving as a state attorney in Warsaw, Lemkin took a special interest in crimes of mass murder and the persecution of minorities, and his preoccupation with this subject grew when Hitler came to power in Germany. In 1933 Lemkin submitted to the League of Nations Law Committee meeting in Madrid a draft proposal for an international convention on barbaric crimes and vandalism.

During his stay in Sweden, Lemkin began to collect documentation on discriminatory legislation, particularly on the racist legislation introduced by the Nazis. In 1944, by which time he had arrived in the United States, Lemkin published his book *Axis Rule in Occupied Europe, Laws of Occupation—Analysis of Government, Proposals for Redress,* and it is there that the term GENOCIDE was used for the first time. To this day the book remains the basic work for the study of racist legislation, in its general as well as its Nazi manifestations. Lemkin was appointed special counsel to the United States Economic Warfare Commission, and later served as counsel to Supreme Court Justice Robert Jackson, when the latter became United States chief counsel for the prosecution at the NUREMBERG TRIAL of Nazi war criminals. Lemkin was also appointed counsel to the war-crimes section of the United States military headquarters in Germany, and to the prosecution in other war crimes trials conducted by the Americans at Nuremberg.

Lemkin had an important share in drafting the United Nations convention on the prevention of genocide and the punishment of the organizers of the crime of genocide. His contribution has become a cornerstone of international law, especially in its modern criminal aspect and in the protection of the human rights and liberty of peoples, religious communities, and other groups. Lemkin's other key writings include "Genocide" (in *The American,* March 1946) and "Responsibility of Persons Acting on Behalf of States in the Crime of Genocide" (in *The American,* April 1946).

BIBLIOGRAPHY

Maza, H. *Neuf meneurs internationaux.* Paris, 1965.

MARIAN MUSHKAT

LENARD, PHILIPP (1862–1947), Nobel prize–winning physicist, honored by the Nazis for his contribution to "German physics." Born in Bratislava to a family with pan-German nationalist sympathies, Lenard was a professor of physics in Kiel (1898) and then in Heidelberg (1907–1931). He began experimenting with cathode rays in the 1890s as assistant to the Jewish-born physicist Heinrich Hertz, and in 1905 was awarded the Nobel prize for physics. Lenard's research provided some of the prerequisites for the theories of Albert EINSTEIN, whose work, however, Lenard rejected as a "Jewish fraud."

During World War I Lenard espoused the German nationalist cause, and after the war he became increasingly racist. His antisemitism alienated him from the German scientific community, especially when he began to express open support for Adolf Hitler and Erich LUDENDORFF in the mid-1920s. In his *Grosse Naturforscher* (Great Naturalists; 1929) and *Deutsche Physik* (German Physics; 1936–1937), Lenard sought to establish a racist basis for the understanding of natural phenomena and to make science an integral part of Nazi philosophy. Alfred ROSENBERG, in presenting Lenard with a new Nazi prize for scholarship, eulogized his struggle for an "Aryan" physics. Lenard withdrew completely from public life in the later years of the Third Reich. There were suggestions after the war that he be tried in a denazification court, but the acting rector of the University of Heidelberg dissuaded the authorities from taking this course.

BIBLIOGRAPHY

Beyerchen, A. D. *Scientists under Hitler: Politics and the Physics Community in the Third Reich.* New Haven, 1977.

LIONEL KOCHAN

LEO BAECK INSTITUTE. *See* Documentation Centers: Leo Baeck Institute.

LES MILLES, internment camp situated a few miles from Aix-en-Provence, in the south of FRANCE. The camp of Les Milles was founded in September 1939, after France's declaration of war on Germany, for the internment of German and Austrian nationals. Originally a tile works, it was requisitioned by the French army, and was ill adapted to receive a population that by the end of 1940 had risen to three thousand prisoners. The majority of the inmates were of Jewish origin, including many intellectuals: writers (Lion Feuchtwanger, the author of *Jud Süss*), scientists (Otto Meyerhof, recipient of the Nobel prize for physiology), painters (Max Ernst), musicians, and politicians. After the armistice between France and Germany in June 1940, certain anti-Nazis were delivered by the French to the Germans and imprisoned at the camp.

By the end of November 1940, Les Milles became a transit camp for emigration, and many relief organizations, both Jewish and non-Jewish, struggled to find ways to liberate the internees. At the beginning of August 1942, after the agreement between the Vichy government and the Nazi authorities in France concerning the deportation of Jews "to the east," the camp, still in the unoccupied zone, was sealed off, and nearly 2,000 of its inmates were deported to DRANCY, from where 1,511 were evacuated to the extermination camps. On December 10, 1942, the camp of Les Milles was finally closed, leaving as a memento only the huge frescoes in the tile works painted by the interned artists.

BIBLIOGRAPHY

"Les camps en Provence, 1933–1942." *Revue Ex* (1984): special issue.

Feuchtwanger, L. *Der Teufel in Frankreich*. Rudolstadt, East Germany, 1954.

Fontaine, A. "Le camp des Milles: Historique provisoire." *Cahiers d'Etudes Germaniques* 5 (1981): 287–322.

ALAIN MICHEL

LEVI, PRIMO (1919–1987), Italian Jewish author. Levi was born in Turin, to a family that had been living in the Piedmont region for many generations. In October 1938, when Levi was a first-year student of chemistry, the leadership of the Italian Fascist party decided to adopt a policy of racism, and by November, racial laws had been enacted in the country. Until then, being Jewish had been for Levi "a slight and insignificant difference," and this was the first time that he felt a wall of separation rising between him and the environment in which he was living. In September 1943 he earned a doctorate in chemistry, despite the difficulties he encountered as a Jew. Following Mussolini's downfall and the Pietro BADOGLIO government's surrender to the Allies, the Germans seized control of the greater part of Italy. Levi fled to the mountains in the north, planning to join an anti-Fascist partisan unit, but in December 1943, before his group was consolidated, he was caught by the Fascist militia. Under questioning, Levi admitted that he was Jewish, and he was imprisoned in the Fossoli transit camp; in February 1944 he was deported to AUSCHWITZ.

Levi spent ten months as a prisoner in Auschwitz, an experience that was to leave an indelible imprint upon his view and way of life. By pure chance, he was one of the few Jews from Italy to survive Auschwitz: an Italian civilian working in the camp provided him with some extra food; Levi knew some German; and at one point he was taken on to work as a chemist in the Buna Works synthetic-rubber factory, an Auschwitz satellite camp, thanks to which he was spared many of the vicissitudes of camp life. In the latter part of January 1945, on the eve of the evacuation of the Auschwitz camp complex, Levi fell ill; he was not put on the death march (*see* DEATH MARCHES) and was liberated by the Soviet forces that entered the camp on January 27. On his release from Auschwitz, Levi did not go straight back to his home in Italy but for nine eventful and difficult months wandered through Poland, the Ukraine, and Belorussia. His account of his experiences in Auschwitz and his observations about life there were published in English as *Survival in Auschwitz: The Nazi Assault on Humanity* (1961). The book's original title was *Se questo è un uomo* (If This Is a Man).

When he finally returned to Turin, Levi took up his profession, working in an industrial plant. He raised a family and lived in his ancestral home. He was haunted, however, by the experience of Auschwitz; as he described it, Auschwitz "had been, first and foremost, a biological and social experiment of gigantic dimensions." Levi was one of the few survivors of the concentration camps who was intellectually equipped to observe and analyze the behavior of human beings in the reality of Auschwitz.

Survival in Auschwitz, written in 1947, was Levi's first book on his life in the camp. It was not well received, and a prominent Italian publisher had, in fact, rejected it. It took several years for Levi's talent to be appreciated: his ability to perceive the inhumane with human eyes and to present the horror authentically, in a language that avoided angry outbursts and generalizations. In 1963 he published *La tregua* (The Lull; published in English as *The Reawakening*, 1965). This is a picaresque story rich in detail, with colorful characters and adventures that the author had gathered in his encounters with people from many lands. Levi's pleasure at being able to communicate what he observed comes through in the book and is accompanied by a delicate humor; clearly, the experience of meeting with simple people of various origins was part of a rehabilitation process that enabled him to resume living.

As time went on, Levi's Jewish identity also came to be fully developed and found its expression in *Il sistema periodico* (The Periodic Table; 1984), in which the different chemical elements, which played such an important role in Levi's mind, meet with the world of his forefathers and with his own experience as a man and as a Jew.

Slowly but surely, Levi came to be widely acknowledged as an outstanding writer. His books were translated into many languages, and he was regarded as one of the great Italian writers of his time. But in April 1987 he committed suicide, without leaving behind any explanation for this step.

BIBLIOGRAPHY

Hughes, H. S. *Prisoners of Hope: The Silver Age of the Italian Jews.* Cambridge, Mass., 1983.

Levi, P. *The Drowned and the Saved.* New York, 1988.

Rosenfeld, A. *A Double Dying.* Bloomington, 1980.

ISRAEL GUTMAN

LÉVITTE, SIMON (1912–1970), leader of the ECLAIREURS ISRAÉLITES DE FRANCE (French Jewish Scouts). Born in Saint Petersburg, Lévitte emigrated in 1920 with his parents to France, where he studied agricultural engineering and joined the Eclaireurs, becoming its secretary-general in 1939. When Paris was occupied by the Germans in June 1940, Lévitte transferred the movement's headquarters to Moissac, in southern France, where he also established a scout leaders' training institute. In May 1942, in Montpellier, he formed the Mouvement de la Jeunesse Sioniste (Zionist Youth Movement; MJS); he subsequently established branches of it in all the major French cities and developed its educational functions. When the movement went underground soon after its founding, Lévitte enlisted dozens of its activists in a rescue organization, a separate network called Education Physique (Physical Training). On his initiative, Education Physique produced and distributed thousands of forged identity cards, provided clandestine lodging and means of livelihood to hundreds of families, and played a leading role in efforts to smuggle Jewish children into Switzerland. In 1943, Lévitte was appointed to the command of the ARMÉE JUIVE, the French Zionist resistance movement, and he recruited to its ranks many graduates of the MJS. After the war he was appointed chief administration and supply officer of the YOUTH ALIYA institutions in France.

BIBLIOGRAPHY

Hammel, F. C. *Souviens-toi d'Amalek: Témoignage sur la lutte des Juifs en France (1938–1944).* Paris, 1982.

Kappel, S. R. *The Struggle of the Jews of Occupied France: In Internment Camps and in the "Jewish Fighting Organization."* Jerusalem, 1971. (In Hebrew.)

Lazare, L. *La résistance juive en France.* Paris, 1987.

Michel, A. *Les Eclaireurs Israélites de France pendant la seconde guerre mondiale.* Paris, 1984.

LUCIEN LAZARE

LEY, ROBERT (1890–1945), Nazi leader. Ley studied chemistry and earned a doctorate in natural science. In World War I he was a fighter pilot, and was shot down and taken prisoner by the French. From 1920 to 1928 he was employed by I.G. FARBEN. Ley joined the

Nazi party in 1923, and in June 1925 was appointed *Gauleiter* of Rhineland South, in which capacity he founded the *Westdeutscher Beobachter* (West German Observer), a Nazi-party political journal concentrating on antisemitic propaganda. In 1930 he was elected to the Reichstag on the Nazi slate. He became Gregor Strasser's deputy in the latter's capacity as the Nazi party's chief of organization, succeeding Strasser in that post in December 1932. In May 1933, after the trade unions were broken up, Ley established and headed the Deutsche Arbeitsfront (German Labor Front; DAF), into which the trade unions were incorporated. Under his direction, the DAF became the Third Reich's largest mass organization, with 25 million members and a huge administrative staff.

Ley was the prototype of a Nazi caricature—loud, coarse, and propagating the crudest kind of antisemitism. More often than not in an alcoholic haze, Ley (whose nickname was *Reichstrunkenbold,* "the Reich drunkard") gave vent to his antisemitic feelings in articles and speeches. Charged as a major war criminal, he committed suicide in his cell in Nuremberg.

BIBLIOGRAPHY

Smelser, R. *Robert Ley: Hitler's Labor Front Leader.* Marietta, Ga., 1988.

UWE ADAM

LIBAU. *See* Liepāja.

LIBYA. [*This entry consists of a survey of the history of Libya and Libyan Jewry in the Fascist era, followed by a review of the Italian forced-labor and internment camps on Libyan soil during World War II.*]

General Survey

Libya, in east-central North Africa, was under Italian rule from 1911 to 1943; it achieved independence as a kingdom in 1951. In 1969 a group of military officers overthrew the monarchy and established a republic.

Jews lived in the city of Cyrene (in the province of Cyrenaica) at least from the second century B.C. The first report on Jews in Tripoli dates from the fourth century A.D.

In modern times, the largest and most important Jewish community in Libya was that of Tripoli; the next in size was that of Benghazi in Cyrenaica, which was a separate political and administrative unit. The Jewish community of Libya was the smallest among the countries of North Africa, although in proportion to the size of the local population, it was the largest. In 1931 it numbered twenty-one thousand, equivalent to 4 percent of the total population. On the eve of World War II it had grown to thirty thousand; over half of the Jews lived in Tripoli, 10 percent in Benghazi, and the rest in various small towns.

Under Italian rule, the Jews of Libya had an educational system sponsored by Italian Jewry. The Italian influence on the Libyan Jews was less than that of the French regime on the Jews of French North Africa; Italian rule was much briefer, in relative terms, and it was only in 1931 that the Italians gained full control of the country. The Italians also failed to work out a clear policy on the Jews, vacillating between an approach that called for their political and social advancement and one that opposed their receiving preferential treatment that might arouse the anger of the Muslim population.

In 1935 a Sabbath Decree was issued that obliged the Jews to keep their shops open on their Sabbath. This was not based on a policy dictated by Rome, but rather on the initiative of local Italian officials who did not want Tripoli's economic life to come to a standstill

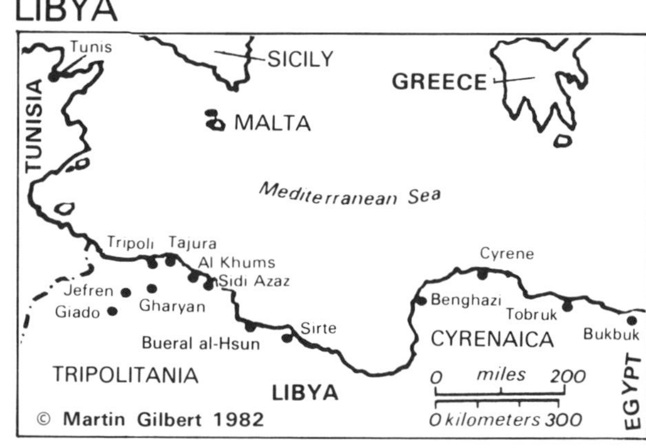

every Saturday. When Benito MUSSOLINI visited Libya in 1937, he agreed to meet with representatives of the Jewish community. He promised the chief rabbi, Aldo Lattes, that the Fascist regime would respect the Jewish tradition, and indeed the penalties imposed on Jews under the Sabbath Decree were revoked later that year.

Following ITALY's rapprochement with Nazi Germany in 1938, the local authorities in Libya, headed by the governor, Marshal Italo Balbo, sought to refrain from applying the anti-Jewish line newly adopted by the Italian government. On the ground of having to preserve public order, they did not disseminate the anti-Jewish diatribes that Radio Bari in Italy was broadcasting to the Arabs in the North African countries. In 1938 Italy also passed racial laws against the Jews, but in Libya, Balbo managed to blunt their edge and to neutralize the local Fascist Blackshirt organizations, which advocated a more aggressive anti-Jewish policy.

The Jews of Libya had less to fear from local Fascist elements than they did from the Muslim population, which displayed hostility toward them and harassed them, influenced by reports of the Arab riots in Palestine. Ironically, the only Jews affected by the racial laws were those of Italian nationality who held civil-service posts, from which they were dismissed. Although the Jewish students were expelled from the public-school system, Balbo established parallel elementary-school classes for the Jewish children in the same school buildings. He also arranged for the Jewish community to look after the continued schooling of the Jewish students who had been expelled from high school. The provision in the race laws under which Jews of foreign nationality were barred from Italian-controlled territory was disregarded, and until Italy's entry into the war on June 10, 1940, hundreds of Jews who were French or British nationals continued to live in Libya. After that date, the authorities in Libya received instructions from Rome to detain all foreign Jews in the Giado (Jadu) concentration camp, 93 miles (150 km) southwest of Tripoli, but this order, too, was only partially obeyed.

The situation of the Jews in Libya took a turn for the worse after Marshal Balbo died in an airplane accident on June 28, 1940, and the Fascists accused the Jews of hoarding food and spying for Britain. On December 9 of that year, the British launched an attack on the Italian forces on the Egyptian front, and within two months they had captured Cyrenaica, including its capital, Benghazi. The Italian defeats at the hands of the British led to more incitement against the Jews. Hitler's response to the British advance was to send German forces to Libya in February 1941. In April and May of that year the Afrika Korps, under Gen. Erwin Rommel, drove the British back into Egypt.

The Italians returned to Cyrenaica, reestablished their control, and accused the Jews of collaboration with the British, arresting some and punishing them severely. The French nationals among the Jews were moved to Tunisia, and the British nationals, numbering some three hundred, were transferred to Italy and interned in concentration camps. These included Civitella del Tronto in central Italy, 8 miles (13 km) north of Teramo; Bagno a Ripoli, 2 miles (3.2 km) southeast of Florence; and Bassano del Grappa, 18 miles (29 km) north-northeast of Vicenza, on the Brenta River. In 1944 the Germans, who were then in control of northern Italy, sent the British Jews to BERGEN-BELSEN.

In December 1941 and January 1942 the British reconquered Cyrenaica, only to be driven out again in May and June. At this point the Italians instituted harsher and more numerous anti-Jewish measures. On Mussolini's orders, three thousand Jews of Cyrenaica were interned in the Giado camp and in the Tigrinna and Gharyan camps, 46.5 miles (75 km) south of Tripoli (see below). From June to December 1942, many more anti-Jewish decrees were issued. Jewish economic activity was strictly controlled, and real-estate transactions with "Aryan" Italians or with Muslims were forbidden. Jews were not allowed to engage in the import and export of goods with Italy, the retail trade, or any activity associated with Libya's military defense. This was followed by a decree ordering the drafting of all male Jews aged from eighteen to forty-five for forced labor, and for this purpose a general census of the Jewish population was taken. In August a labor camp was established at Sidi Azaz, near Al Khums, 62 miles (100 km) east of Tripoli (see below). On the eve of the final attack by the British (October 23, 1942), three hundred and fifty Jews were brought to the Tobruk area.

A decree issued on October 9, 1942, stated that the Italian racial laws were to be enforced in Libya and that Jews could not own or manage banks or insurance and transport companies, and could not belong to cooperative societies. They were also forbidden to publish anything except religious texts. This decree was scheduled to go into effect on December 17 of that year but was never applied, because by then the battle for Libya was in its final stages, all of Cyrenaica had been liberated, and the British were advancing toward Tripolitania. Tripoli was liberated on January 23, 1943. This was the end of Italian rule in Libya, and all the racist legislation was rescinded.

Jewish units from Palestine were among the British forces that entered Libya. With the permission of the British authorities, the Jewish soldiers organized relief operations for the Libyan Jews returning from the camps and helped restore the Jewish community institutions. In the autumn of 1944, most of the Jewish units were posted away from Libya, and Muslim-Jewish relations deteriorated. This was exacerbated by Libyan nationalists who, having returned after the Italians and Germans had been driven out, incited the Arab masses against the "Zionists" and the British. From November 5 to 7, 1945, a pogrom took place against the Jews of Libya, one of the worst in their history, in which 121 Jews were murdered, many more were injured, synagogues were destroyed, and hundreds of residences and businesses were pillaged and ruined. It was only on the third day that the British forces intervened to quell the riots. These events came as a great shock to the Jews and led to a fundamental change in their relations with the Muslims. Jewish identity was reinforced, as was the desire of the Jews to leave Libya and settle in Palestine. Riots broke out again in 1948, but this time the Jews defended themselves and killed several of the attackers. In 1950 and 1951, over thirty thousand Jews left Libya to settle in Israel. Following the 1967 Six-Day War between Israel and its Arab neighbors, riots once more took place. Many of the Jews left the country, most of them for Italy, and only a few Jews remained.

BIBLIOGRAPHY

Ageron, C. R. "Les populations du Maghreb face à la propagande allemande." *Revue d'Histoire de la deuxième Guerre Mondiale* 29/14 (1979): 1–39.

Felice, R. de. *Jews in an Arab Land: Libya, 1835–1970.* Austin, 1985.

Juarez, P., et al., eds. *Jews of Libya.* Tel Aviv, 1960. (In Hebrew.)

United Restitution Organization. *Judenverfolgung in Italien, den italienisch besetzten Gebiete und in Nordafrika.* Frankfurt, 1962.

MICHEL ABITBOL

Forced-Labor and Internment Camps

During World War II, Jews in Libya were imprisoned in two types of camps: (1) internment camps for enemy nationals suspected of hostile activity, which functioned from September 1940 until the British occupation in January 1943, and in which Jews and non-Jews were imprisoned; and (2) forced-labor camps for Jews only, which functioned from May 1942 until the British occupation of Libya.

The main internment camps for enemy subjects established in Libya itself were at Tajura in the Sidi abd el-Krim fort, some 11 miles (18 km) east of Tripoli; at Bueral al-Hsun, about 54 miles (87 km) west of Sirte in Tripolitania; and at Hun, about 141 miles (227 km) south of Sirte. Small detention camps were established on the outskirts of Benghazi and Tripoli.

Detention conditions were not severe, and the Italian guards treated the prisoners humanely. Families were allowed to visit the prisoners and give them food and money. Difficulties were greater for those detainees who were poor. The camp authorities sometimes supplied food staples that the prisoners cooked themselves, and at times food could be purchased in the neighboring villages. The frequent transfers from camp to camp and the distance from their families were onerous for the prisoners.

Forced-labor camps for Jews alone were established in 1942. The army commands were in urgent need of manpower for labor, in view of the situation on the front. The main forced-labor camps established in Libya in 1942 were Sidi Azaz and Bukbuk for the Jews of Tripolitania, and Giado (Jadu) for the Jews of Cyrenaica. Some Jews from Cyrenaica were also sent to the villages surrounding Giado, and were housed outside the camp, at Gharyan, Jefren, and Tigrinna.

Giado. This was the worst camp in Libya. Out of the twenty-six hundred Jews sent there, more than five hundred died, of weakness and hunger, and especially from typhoid fever and typhus. Water shortages, malnutrition, overcrowding, and filth intensified the spread of contagion. Giado was a former army camp, surrounded by a barbed-wire fence. Its commandants were Italian, and the guards were Italian and Arab policemen. There was a machine-gun emplacement on the hill overlooking the camp, for shooting down fugitives. A hut in the camp served as a confinement cell for minor offenders. Prisoners committing more severe offenses were transferred to the prison in Tripoli.

The Jews lived in ten long huts without internal partitions. Three hundred to three hundred and fifty people were crammed into each hut; families created partitions with blankets and sheets to obtain some privacy. Sanitary conditions were extremely poor. Initially, the Jews lived on the food they had brought with them. Later they had to manage with the poor food supplied in the camp: about 3.5 to 5.25 ounces (100–150 g) of bread daily, and a further small weekly supply of rice, macaroni, oil, sugar, tea, and coffee. Those with means supplemented these meager supplies with food purchased from Arab peddlers who were allowed to come to the fence. Some assistance came from Tripoli.

The prisoners were employed in removing garbage, cleaning lavatories, and moving gravel and rocks from place to place. In general there was no daily work quota. Each hut had a KAPO in charge of the work. The Kapos also set up a synagogue in one of the huts and saw to burying the many dead in a cemetery on a hill outside the camp.

Sidi Azaz. Here there were about one thousand Jewish males aged eighteen to forty-five, from Tripoli and its vicinity. Most were skilled workers recruited for forced labor,

Jewish survivors from Libya who were British nationals. They were first interned in concentration camps in Italy and were then sent to Bergen-Belsen in 1944, returning to Tripoli (in Libya) in August and September 1945.

principally for railway construction and road repairs. The commandants were Italians, but uniformed German officers held a weekly inspection. There were almost no permanent buildings in the camp, apart from two or three shacks housing the Jewish Kapos. The other Jewish detainees lived four or five to a tent. The camp was located in an open desert area near the town of Homs, and a few months after its establishment it was enclosed by a barbed-wire fence. All the prisoners were divided into small groups of fifty to sixty, each group headed by a Jewish Kapo responsible for ensuring that the daily work quota was met. After the morning roll call, the prisoners left the camp to work at digging up stones and transporting gravel. The working day was from 6:00 a.m. to 4:00 p.m.

The daily food supply consisted of approximately one pound (0.5 kg) of bread, and rice or macaroni at midday. Occasionally canned food was brought. Here too, the better-off prisoners supplemented the food quota from the Arab peddlers in the vicinity.

Bukbuk. About three hundred and fifty prisoners were transferred from the Sidi Azaz camp to this one, situated beyond the eastern border of Libya, in order to repair roads. The camp was headed by a Jewish engineer, Moshe Hadad, who recruited the men in Sidi Azaz and then supervised the work in the camp. He also ordered his men to dig pits for protection, in view of the frequent British air raids. The Jews worked from 7:00 a.m. until the evening, excavating rocks and digging up and cutting stones for reinforcing roads along the Egyptian border. Supervision was extremely haphazard, with the regional Italian commander making an inspection tour only once every few weeks. In the absence of supervision, the Jews attempted to sabotage the Axis forces by closing part of the road for repairs, thus compelling the vehicles retreating from Egypt to leave the road and sink into mud. The relations with the Italian command were strained, but no Jews were harmed by this.

In general, food at the camp was sufficient. The problems were shortage of water and absolute isolation from the population. The camp was not fenced, but there was nowhere to escape. Those who fell ill left the camp with the permission of the Italian camp doctor, and the number of workers gradually fell to about two hundred. The Jews remained at Bukbuk for only about two months, and on November 6, 1942, with the retreat of the Italians and the Germans, they received orders to make their own way back to Tripoli.

BIBLIOGRAPHY

Felice, R. de. *Jews in an Arab Land: Libya, 1835–1970.* Austin, 1985.

Simon, R. "The Jews of Libya on the Verge of Holocaust." *Pe'amim* 28 (1986): 44–77. (In Hebrew.)

IRIT ABRAMSKI-BLIGH

LICHTENBERG, BERNHARD (1875–1943), German Catholic priest. Lichtenberg was born in Silesia and became a priest in 1899. After World War I he served on the Berlin city council as representative of the Catholic Zentrum (Center) party. In 1938 he was appointed *Dompropst* (chief priest) of Saint Hedwig's Cathedral in Berlin.

In 1941, in a letter to Leonardo Conti, the Nazi *Reichsärztefühier* (Reich Chief of Civilian Health Services), Lichtenberg protested against the EUTHANASIA PROGRAM, following the lead set by the bishop of Münster, Clemens von GALEN. That same year, he offered a public prayer for the Jews who were being deported to the east, calling on the congregants to observe the biblical commandment "Love thy neighbor" with regard to the Jews. Lichtenberg was denounced to the authorities and arrested, put on trial, and sentenced to two years in prison. On his release in October of 1943, when Lichtenberg was sixty-eight years old and a sick man, the Gestapo sent him to DACHAU; he died on the way there.

BIBLIOGRAPHY

Leber, A., ed. *Conscience in Revolt: Sixty-four Stories of Resistance in Germany, 1933–1945.* London, 1957.

Weisenborn, G. *Der lautlose Aufstand.* Hamburg, 1953.

ZVI BACHARACH

LIDA, city in the Novogrudok district, in the west of the Belorussian SSR. Between the two world wars Lida was in independent Poland, and in September 1939 it was included in the territory occupied by the Red Army and annexed to the Soviet Union. Jews lived in the city from the fifteenth century. On the eve of the German invasion of the Soviet Union in 1941, the Jewish population numbered nine thousand.

On June 30, 1941, the Germans occupied Lida. About three thousand Jews from the surrounding towns, in addition to refugees from VILNA, were speedily assembled there. On July 8, eighty Jewish intellectuals were put to death. A ghetto was created, comprising four separate quarters. The chairman of the JUDENRAT (Jewish Council), Kalman Lichtman, helped about one thousand refugees from Vilna to obtain identity cards, but members of the underworld in the ghetto informed on him and he was put to death, together with seven other members of the Judenrat.

On May 8, 1942, an *Aktion* was carried out in Lida, and 5,670 Jews were killed. Afterward, the Germans assembled the 3,500 survivors of the ghettos of Voronovo, Biniakon, and Solechniki in Lida. It was then that the idea of contacting the partisans and amassing arms matured. Contacts were made with the BIELSKI and "Iskra" partisan units; young people smuggled twenty guns from the Ger-

man arms supplies into the ghetto; others prepared arms in the ghetto workshops. Despite the appeals of the workshop directors, people began to escape to the forests; they included the group of Barukh Levin, comprising eleven men and eleven guns. Emissaries came from the forest to the ghetto three times and took out groups of Jews. In this they were aided by Lazar Stolitski, head of the Jewish police in Lida. Those who escaped assembled in the Naliboki, Lipiczany, and Nacha forests. In addition to the men, a printing press, medicines, and clothing were taken out of the Lida ghetto.

On the evening of September 17, 1943, a group of Jewish partisans again came to the ghetto to take Jews out to the forest, but the group was caught in the liquidation *Aktion.* On the following day, September 18, the Jews of the Lida ghetto were assembled and sent to MAJDANEK. Only a few managed to escape at the last minute. Altogether, about five hundred Jews fled from Lida to the forests, some three hundred of them reaching the partisan units, and approximately one hundred were still alive when Lida was liberated in mid-July 1944.

BIBLIOGRAPHY

Damesek, E. *In Leaden Letters: Memoirs of a Partisan.* Tel Aviv, 1983. (In Hebrew.)

Levin, B. *In the Forests of Vengeance.* Tel Aviv, 1968. (In Hebrew.)

Manor, A., et al., eds. *Sefer Lida: The Book of Lida.* Tel Aviv, 1983. (In English, Hebrew, and Yiddish.)

SHALOM CHOLAWSKI

LIDICE, village in Czechoslovakia, 10 miles (16 km) from Prague, that was destroyed by the Germans during World War II. On October 9, 1940, on Hitler's decision, the Nazi plan for the final disposition of the Protectorate of BOHEMIA AND MORAVIA was formulated. The Protectorate was to become part of the German "living space" (LEBENSRAUM), with about half of the Czech people to be integrated into the German nation and the other half to be expelled. In September 1941 Reinhard HEYDRICH was appointed acting *Reichsprotektor* (governor) in place of Konstantin von NEURATH, who was officially declared "ill." Heydrich's task was to rid the Protectorate of elements seen as harming the interests of the Reich, namely, the underground movement, which was gaining in strength and increasing the incidence of sabotage acts; the growing impact of the London-based propaganda; and, most importantly, the decline of industrial production, which was of vital necessity to Germany.

Heydrich arrived in Prague on September 27, and the following day a state of emergency was declared in seven districts, with the support of Karl Hermann FRANK, the Protectorate's secretary of state. The same day, Alois Elias, head of the Protectorate government (whose removal from office had been postponed on three previous occasions), was sentenced to death by a People's Court (*Volksgerichtshof*). In the next two months more than 4,000 Czechs were arrested, and of these 404 were executed. President Emil Hácha of Czechoslovakia was forced to give his approval to the appointment of a new Czech government that was completely subservient to the Germans.

Even before Heydrich's arrival, the underground organizations had suffered heavy blows. The underground organizations that were loyal to the Czech government-in-exile in London had set up an umbrella organization, Ústredňi Vedeni Odboje Domaciho (Central Committee for the Internal Struggle). The underground movement Obrana Narodu (People's Defense), which relied on veterans, collapsed when thousands of its members were arrested. Another important body was the Peticni Vybor: Verni Zustaneme ("Forever Faithful"; PVVZ), which was based on Social Democrat circles (including Jewish intellectuals, who played an important part in its operations) and which served as an important channel of communications with London.

In the summer of 1940 the Gestapo had seized the PVVZ records, and after Heydrich's appearance on the scene, the information found in the records enabled mass arrests to be carried out. The number of persons arrested rose from 1,298 in August 1941 to 2,744 in October, among them 1,772 underground members. This blow put the underground organization out of action, except for

Bodies of the murdered inhabitants of the Czech village of Lidice.

the Communist underground. The latter group had become much stronger after the German invasion of the Soviet Union; it stressed the unity of the national struggle and was thus able to attract non-Communist circles to its activities. This was one reason why Heydrich made overtures to the working class. He raised the workers' food rations slightly and made a considerable improvement in the social-security provisions. The effect of these measures on the workers was negligible and temporary, but it did result in a more relaxed atmosphere in the Protectorate.

The Czech government-in-exile in London was alarmed by this development, and circles close to the government, after much deliberation and grave warnings from the home front, decided to make an attempt on Heydrich's life. On October 4, 1941, several two-man teams of parachutists were dropped into the Protectorate. Some of the teams did not succeed in performing their specific tasks in the mission, but of those that did, one established a radio link and another carried out the assassination itself. This latter team, code-named "Anthropoid," consisted of Jan Kubis and Jozef Gabcik, and had the support of the small "Sokol" underground organization. The attack took place on May 27, 1942. Heydrich was on his regular trip to Prague that morning, and at 10:30 a.m. Gabcik and Kubis, who had been hiding at a bend in the road, lobbed hand grenades at his car. Heydrich was severely wounded, and a few days later, on June 4, he died of his wounds.

The Germans immediately declared a state of emergency and within twenty-four hours raided five thousand towns and villages. By September 1, 1942, 3,180 persons had been arrested and 1,344 sentenced to death. Two hours after the attack took place, Hitler had ordered the execution of ten thousand Czechs, increasing that number threefold when Heydrich died of his wounds; when the assassins and the other teams of parachutists were caught, Frank was able to have Hitler's order postponed and then canceled. On June 9, 1942, Hitler warned the Protectorate government: "Nothing will prevent me from expelling millions of Czechs, if they are not prepared for a peaceful life together."

Early in the morning of June 10, 1942, all the inhabitants of the village of Lidice were taken out of their homes, and all the men in the village—192 in all—were killed, as were 71 women. The remaining women, numbering 198, were imprisoned in the RAVENSBRÜCK concentration camp, and of these, 143 returned to the village after the war. Of the 98 children who had been "put into educational institutions," no more than 16 survived. In the presence of Frank and of Ernst KALTENBRUNNER (who was Heydrich's successor), as well as of photographers, Lidice was razed to the ground, the official reason being that the villagers had helped the assassins—an allegation that had no basis in fact—and that two men from Lidice serving with the Czech forces in Britain had assured the parachutists that they could trust the villagers. In Hitler's eyes, at any rate, the punishment was a mild one.

The assassins and the other parachutists, who had taken refuge in the Saints Cyril and Methodius Church in Prague, were killed when their hiding place was divulged, but not before putting up desperate armed resistance. Even worse was the fate of Lezaky, a village near Pardubice, east of Prague, where the radio transmitter was discovered. The entire adult population of the village was murdered, and the children were handed over to be "reeducated" as Germans. Only two of them, however, were accepted for such "reeducation" and grew up as Germans, and they were the only Lezaky children to survive the war.

The Czech population was deeply shocked. The resistance movement—which to Heydrich's surprise had recovered (as he had recorded two weeks before the assassination)—was now put out of action. The government-in-exile denied that it had been involved in the assassination and claimed that the attack on Heydrich had been a protest against the wave of terror the Germans had launched.

Lidice was rebuilt after the war and became a symbol both of the Nazi terror regime and of the heroism of the Czech resistance movement. German sources—especially the Gestapo officer Kriminalrat (Criminal Investigator) Heinz Pannwitz, who prepared a comprehensive report on the whole affair for Hitler—reveal that, in addition to "Operation Lidice" (which, according to Pannwitz, had been the brainchild of the Security Police chief in Prague, Josef Böhme), there was another German revenge operation. On orders given by the *Reichsführer*-SS, Heinrich HIMMLER, 252 persons who were relatives or friends of the inhabitants of Lidice were killed at the MAUTHAUSEN camp on October 24, 1942; the victims included 130 women who were gassed and a large number of youths.

BIBLIOGRAPHY

Berton, S. F. "Das Attentat auf Reinhard Heydrich vom 27 Mai 1942: Ein Bericht des Kriminalrats Heinz Pannwitz." *Vierteljahrshefte für Zeitgeschichte* 33/3 (July 1985): 668–706.

Bradley, J. *Lidice: Sacrificial Village.* New York, 1972.

Wittlin, T. *Time Stopped at 6:30.* Indianapolis, 1965.

SEEV GOSHEN

LIEBEHENSCHEL, ARTHUR (1901–1948), senior SS officer; commandant of concentration camps. Born in Posen (now Poznań), Liebehenschel studied public administration and economics, and after World War I served as a sergeant major in the Reichswehr. In

Arthur Liebehenschel at his trial in Kraków.

February 1932 he joined the Nazi party and in August 1934, the SS, where he served in the TOTENKOPFVERBÄNDE (Death's-Head Units).

Liebehenschel served as an adjutant in the COLUMBIA HAUS (in Berlin) and Lichtenburg (near Prettin) camps. He then held senior administrative posts in the Totenkopfverbände headquarters, in the Inspectorate of Concentration Camps, and, as a senior director, in the SS WIRTSCHAFTS-VERWALTUNGSHAUPTAMT (Economic-Administrative Main Office; WVHA). On November 10, 1943, Liebehenschel was appointed commandant of the AUSCHWITZ extermination camp, and on May 19, 1944, commandant of MAJDANEK. When that camp was evacuated, he was given a senior post in the SS-Personalhauptamt (Manpower Main Office).

After the war, Liebehenschel was arrested by the Americans and extradited to Poland. He was put on trial in Kraków, sentenced to death, and executed on January 24, 1948.

SHMUEL SPECTOR

Aharon Liebeskind.

LIEBESKIND, AHARON ("Dolek"; 1912–1942), underground fighter; leader of the HEHALUTS HA-LOHEM group in KRAKÓW. Born in Zabierzow, a village near Kraków, Liebeskind studied law at Kraków University. In 1938 he became secretary of the Akiva movement, which he had joined at the age of fourteen. In early 1939 he was appointed national secretary of Akiva and went to live in Warsaw, although he retained his home in Kraków and continued to lead the movement there; he also managed to complete his doctoral dissertation. His job kept him in Warsaw until the outbreak of the war.

From the onset of the German occupation of Poland, Liebeskind was convinced that the Jews would not be able to live under the occupation regime, and he did all he could to get the members of his movement out of Poland. A charismatic figure, much admired by his fellow members and disciples, he did not accept an immigration certificate to Palestine for himself, so as not to abandon his family and followers in time of trouble.

In December 1940 Liebeskind was put in charge of an agricultural and vocational training program in the Kraków area, sponsored by the Jewish Self-Help Society, which had its head offices there. He utilized his position to promote the activities of the Jewish underground in the city, which he had founded and which he led. Using the society's official stationery, he distributed leaflets and arranged money transfers to the members of the underground. Liebeskind also arranged for the financing of the Kopaliny training farm, headed by Shimshon DRAENGER, which served as a cover for underground operations. His post enabled him to move around and thereby to maintain and strengthen contact with fellow members in various locations.

The deportation of Jews from the Kraków ghetto in June 1942 convinced Liebeskind that the only way left was that of armed struggle, even though it did not hold out much hope of survival. He is credited with saying that "the Jewish fighters are fighting for three lines in history." He initiated the establishment of a broadly based fighting organization in Kraków, forging ties with the other leaders of the He-Haluts (pioneer) youth organizations in the city. An especially close tie existed between Liebeskind and Avraham Leibovich ("Laban") of the Dror movement, and the two became the commanders of the resistance organization, the Fighting Organization of the Pioneering Jewish Youth (He-Haluts ha-Lohem).

When the authorities began to pursue him, in November 1942, Liebeskind and the organization's headquarters moved to the "Aryan" part of the city. From there he renewed contact with the Polish Communist Workers' party (PPR)—which had been broken off in the wake of an abortive attempt made in September 1942 to leave the ghetto and take refuge in the forests—and with its Jewish unit, commanded by Heshek (Zvi) BAUMINGER. Liebeskind's aim was to launch a large-scale attack on the Germans inside Kraków. On December 22, 1942, He-Haluts ha-Lohem and the Jewish unit of the PPR attacked German targets in Kraków. They inflicted many casualties on the Germans, but following the attack, the headquarters and most of the members of He-Haluts ha-Lohem fell into German hands. On December 24 Liebeskind was caught in the headquarters bunker and killed in a hand-to-hand fight.

BIBLIOGRAPHY

Dawidson, G. *Justina's Diary.* Tel Aviv, 1978. (In Hebrew.)

YAEL PELED (MARGOLIN)

LIEPĀJA (Ger., Libau), port city in LATVIA, on the Baltic Sea. In 1935 Liepāja had a Jewish population of 7,379, out of a total population of 57,098. In August 1940, as part of Latvia, it was annexed to the Soviet Union. On June 29, 1941, a week after the invasion of Russia, the Germans occupied the city and only a few Jews managed to escape in time.

On July 5, 1941, the local German military governor issued a number of anti-Jewish decrees, among them decrees ordering the wearing of the yellow badge (*see* BADGE, JEWISH) and a draft for FORCED LABOR. Jewish males aged sixteen to sixty were required to report daily at the city square, ostensibly for work. Of those who reported, some were sent on forced labor, and others were taken to prison. Jewish men who failed to report as ordered were arrested in the street or in their homes. On July 8 and 9, all Jewish prisoners were taken to the Baltic seashore and shot to death there. In the last ten days of July the same pattern of arrests and murder was repeated, on a larger scale. At least a thousand Jewish men were murdered in that first month of German occupation.

In August 1941 the wave of arrests and mass murder was halted, and in the following two months the daily reporting to the city square also ceased. Most of the Jews had by then been dismissed from their posts, and they were now issued work permits and put to work, mainly for the German army and police units in the city. Many Jews had their money, furniture, household goods, and valuables confiscated, and were expelled from their homes. A Jewish Ältestenrat (Council of Elders) was set up (the Jews referred to it as "the community"), headed by a businessman by the name of Izraelit, with a lawyer named Kagansky acting as his deputy. A Jewish home for the aged was in operation, as was the Linat Tsedek Hospital, the latter staffed by four doctors and a team of nurses and administrative helpers. The killing of Jews, however, did not come to a stop, most of the victims being persons who were unfit for work. According to the reports submitted by the local detachment of the German Sicherheitspolizei (Security Police), 658 Jews were murdered in the period from September 22 to December 13, 1941. Of these, 454 were Jewish men and women unfit for work; that figure included the inmates of the Jewish home for the aged, the institution itself having been liquidated. In November 1941 the German military administration reported that 3,890 Jews were left in the town.

On December 13, 1941, a decree was issued ordering the Jews to stay at home on December 15 and 16. The Sicherheitspolizei issued new work permits for Jews, but only to skilled technicians working in the German police stations, a few artisans whose work was essential for the German army, the officers of the Ältestenrat, and the staff of the

A series of photographs found after the liberation in May 1945, among Gestapo papers in the city of Liepāja, depicted the massacre of 2,800 Jews of Liepāja between December 15 and 17, 1941. The victims were taken to Skeden, a fishing village north of Liepāja, to a site where trenches about 197 to 328 feet (60 to 100 m) long and 10 to 13 feet (3 to 4 m) deep had been dug. Ordered to undress in a temperature of 23° F (−5° C), they were then led in groups of ten to the edge of the trenches, where they were shot by firing squads of twenty men, Latvians and Germans; two gunmen aimed at one victim. Women were told to hold their babies against their shoulders to make them easier targets. Here, a group waits at the edge of the trench to be shot. In the trench are bodies of those already shot.

hospital—a total of no more than 300 to 350 permits. On the night of December 14, Latvian police rounded up Jews in their homes and took them to prison. The holders of the new work permits and their families were released, but all the other Jews were taken to Skeden, a fishing village on the Baltic, north of Liepāja, to be killed there. The massacre began on the morning of December 15, at which time the roundup of Jews in the city was in full swing, and it continued until noon on December 17. During those three days, 2,700 to 2,800 Jews, including women and children, were murdered. About 1,000 Jews were left in Liepāja.

Two more *Aktionen* took place, one at the end of February 1942 and the other in April of that year. Twenty-two Jews succeeded in escaping from the sleds in which they were being taken to Skeden; 150 were murdered. After these *Aktionen* 805 (or 829) Jews were left in Liepāja, and in July 1942 they were confined to a ghetto, consisting of a dozen apartment houses, that provided 43 square feet (4 sq m) of space per person. The Ältestenrat provided an employment office and the Jewish police, as well as several workshops, for the ghetto's own requirements. Several dozen Jews were murdered in the ghetto for a variety of reasons during its existence.

On October 8, 1943, the eve of the Day of Atonement, the Liepāja ghetto was liquidated and its inhabitants taken to the KAISERWALD camp, near RIGA. Several Jews, with some children among them, were taken in by peasants, and eleven Jews found refuge in the home of a Latvian farm storehouse keeper by the name of Saduls, in a bunker that had been prepared in advance and properly equipped, underneath his own house. The Jews in hiding worked at various jobs, such as repairing electrical appliances, and in return their needs were provided for. Saduls was their contact man with the outside. When he was killed in an air raid, one of his associates took over the dangerous mission.

When the Red Army entered Liepāja, on May 9, 1945, twenty to thirty Jews were left in the city.

BIBLIOGRAPHY

Levin, D., ed. *Latvia and Estonia.* In *Pinkas Hakehillot; Encyclopaedia of Jewish Communities.* Jerusalem, 1988. (In Hebrew.)

ESTHER HAGAR

LIETUVIU AKTYVISTU FRONTAS (Lithuanian Activist Front), nationalist Lithuanian organization set up in Berlin on November 17, 1940, by Lithuanian nationalists who had fled LITHUANIA shortly after the Soviets seized control of the country in August of that year. The moving spirit in the organization was Lt. Col. Kazys Škirpa, who had been Lithuanian ambassador to Germany and had stayed on in Berlin as a political refugee. Cooperating closely with the ABWEHR (the WEHRMACHT intelligence service) and the Nazi security organizations, the Front activated underground cells in Lithuania for intelligence and sabotage operations against the Soviet regime. These operations were stepped up in the spring of 1941, on both sides of the German-Lithuanian border, as part of the preparations for the German invasion of the Soviet Union.

In anticipation of the invasion, the Front smuggled into Lithuania propaganda material that contained detailed instructions on staging an armed uprising at the outbreak of war and on seizing control and settling accounts with those who had collaborated with the Soviets. A flyer put out close to the invasion date was headlined "The Time Has Come to Settle Accounts with the Jews." In it the Jews of Lithuania, "all of them, without a single exception," were warned to "leave the soil of Lithuania without delay."

On June 22, 1941, when the Nazis invaded Lithuania, and in the days that followed, armed bands of Lithuanians went on a bloody rampage against Jews all over the country and killed them by the thousands. Front members, as well as others who called themselves partisans, helped the German forces seize control of Lithuania by attacking the retreating Soviet units and occupying points of strategic importance. The Germans, however, did not fulfill the Lithuanians' hopes for the restoration of the country's independence. On July 28, the Provisional Lithuanian Government, which had been established under the Front's auspices, was ordered by the Germans to cease functioning. It suspended its activities on September 22, 1941, after only six weeks of existence. Many Front members, however, found places for themselves in the civil administration, or enlisted in Einsatzkommandos 2, 3, and 9 and in police units that engaged in the killing of Jews, in Lithuania and in other places.

BIBLIOGRAPHY

Jurgila, C. *Lithuania: The Outpost of Racedom.* Saint Petersburg, Fla., 1976.

Kaslas, B., ed. *The USSR-German Aggression against Lithuania.* New York, 1973.

DOV LEVIN

LIPKE, JANIS (d. 1987), Latvian who saved many Jews from the RIGA ghetto. On December 1, 1941, Lipke and his eight-year-old son witnessed a particularly brutal massacre of thousands of Jews in Riga. From then on, Lipke resolved to do everything in his power to save Jews from the Germans and their

Janis Lipke, a "Righteous among the Nations."

Latvian collaborators. He left his job as a dockworker and joined a Luftwaffe (German air force) civilian enterprise as an overseer, so as to be able to enter the ghetto to fetch Jews for work in various Luftwaffe installations in and around the city. He then arranged for trusted Latvian confidants to replace those Jews who failed to return to the ghetto, so that the final count would match the number of workers who left each morning. These Latvian friends entered the ghetto with Jewish badges on their coats, then removed them and left the following morning with other Latvian contractors who came to fetch Jews for work.

Lipke also arranged for Jews to escape from labor camps in the Riga vicinity. By visiting Jews inside labor camps or whispering coded messages to them across barbed-wire fences, he coordinated their escape. To some he provided jewelry and money left in his care by relatives of imprisoned Jews, so that they could bribe the gate guards if necessary. Some he brought to his home, with the help of a Latvian named Karlis who transported them on his truck, hidden beneath a heap of lumber and other items. At first, Lipke kept them in a specially constructed shelter, with the help of his wife, Johanna, and their eldest son. He then devised a plan to transfer Jews across the Baltic Sea to Sweden and drew on his dock-working experience to prepare a boat that he hoped to launch for this purpose. But the plan had to be abandoned, since suspicions arose and the authorities intervened. Lipke was able to talk himself out of it and was freed. A Jewish fellow conspirator, Perl, was executed.

Lipke then arranged for fleeing Jews to be taken to a farm in Dobele, which he had purchased for this purpose. They were hidden by friendly Latvians in an underground shelter and other hiding places outside Riga. Lipke maintained close links with all those under his care for extensive periods of time; when danger threatened, he arranged their transfer to safer locations. He was active in the rescue of Jews from December 1941 up to the country's liberation by the Russians in October 1944.

In 1966, Janis and Johanna Lipke were recognized by YAD VASHEM as "RIGHTEOUS AMONG THE NATIONS."

BIBLIOGRAPHY

Levin, D., ed. *Latvia and Estonia.* In *Pinkas Hakehillot; Encyclopaedia of Jewish Communities.* Jerusalem, 1988. (In Hebrew.)

MORDECAI PALDIEL

LITERATURE ON THE HOLOCAUST. [*This entry consists of six articles on Holocaust literature in different linguistic and cultural settings:*

France
Germany
Hebrew Literature
Poland
United States
Yiddish Literature

See also Diaries, Holocaust, *and the biographies of individual authors.*]

France

Non-Jewish French authors have produced little work dealing with the Holocaust. Writers who fought Nazism and saw many of their comrades shot or deported failed to realize the unique nature of the Holocaust. The extermination of the Jews added nothing to the portrait of the antisemite drawn by Jean-Paul Sartre as early as 1939, and the solution he advocated for the Jewish problem owed nothing to it. *La peste* (1947; *The Plague,* 1957), by Albert Camus, is an allegory not of the Holocaust but "of the struggle of the Résistance against Nazism," as Camus stated to Roland Barthes. When the Christians Julien Green and François Mauriac wished to pay homage to the victims of Auschwitz, they chose converted Jewish women. Antisemitism soon reappeared in French literature, which, starting in 1950, began to distance itself from recent history.

As a rule, non-Jewish writers have left writing on the Holocaust to their Jewish colleagues or to non-Jewish survivors, who sometimes compose gripping passages relating their own experience to the fate of the Jews. A mass grave unearthed and the rumble of rolling trains reveal to the narrator of Pierre Gascar's *Le temps des morts* (1953; *Beasts and Men and the Seed,* 1960) the terrible fate of the Jews. The murder of children torn to pieces by dogs, to the great merriment of the executioners, as described in Jorge Sempron's *Le grand voyage* (1963; *The Long Voyage,* 1964), powerfully summarizes the cruelty of the Nazis. With the exception of a few works, the major literary productions on the Holocaust appeared at the end of the 1950s or later. Survivors of death camps and ghettos relived an experience in which spiritual and moral man confronted the human who had yielded to his bestial instincts.

The works of Elie WIESEL are totally dedicated to the fight against oblivion. From *La nuit* (1958; *Night,* 1964) to *Entre deux soleils* (1970; *Between Two Suns,* 1981), through *La ville de la chance* (1962; *The Town beyond the Wall,* 1967) and *Les portes de la forêt* (1964; *The Gates of the Forest,* 1966), the author pursues his interrogation of man and God. In *La nuit,* an autobiographical tale of his Holocaust experience in the form of a novel, Wiesel suggests the unthinkable by juxtaposing the traditional meaning of Hasidic and kabbalistic terms and metaphors with the reality of Auschwitz. His later works transcend the real-life experience and create a poetic universe rooted in Jewish tradition.

The same need to bear witness so as to "let others know the meaning of human wickedness and blindness" drove Anna Langfus, an assimilated Jew, to write *Le sel et le soufre* (1960; *The Whole Land Brimstone,* 1962). This realistic and ironic novel depicts, through the adventures of the heroine, the tragedy of the Polish Jews—their loneliness, their misery, and their dignity. Langfus's *Saute, Barbara* (Jump, Barbara; 1965) deals with hatred and revenge, which, as in works by Primo LEVI and in Wiesel's *Le cinquième fils* (1983; *The Fifth Son,* 1985), do not find release.

Authors who had no concentration camp experience but who had lived through the war attempted to explain the Holocaust by interpreting it. *Le dernier des justes* (1959; *The Last of the Just,* 1961), by André Schwarz-Bart, is a rich, dense, sometimes tragic and sometimes ironic work blending history and legend. Ernie Levy is one of the thirty-six righteous men who traditionally have lived in every generation. He is the last of a line of such persons, whose origin goes back to the Middle Ages. An "exemplary individual," he embodies the fate of the religious Jews whose greatness he describes. By viewing the Holocaust as the culmination of persecutions borne ever since medieval times, the author endows it with historical perspective. Belief in martyrdom as the sanctification of God's name explains the behavior of the victims and gives the extermination a religious meaning. In the face of evil, Ernie chooses to oppose the violence of Christians with spiritual resistance. He elects to join his family and share their death in the gas chamber.

Obsession with the extermination is felt in the entire work of Romain Gary, from *L'éducation européenne* (1945; *A European Education,* 1960) to *La vie devant soi* (The Life ahead of Him; 1975). *La danse de Genghis Cohn* (1967; *The Dance of Genghis Cohn,* 1968) is a philosophical novel that describes the mad epic of humanity bent on its own destruction. Its narrator, Moshe Cohn, alias Genghis Cohn, a comic by trade, embodies love of life and of men, joy, and Jewish consciousness, which the author opposes to Western consciousness. Cohn was exterminated in 1944 in the Polish forests by the Nazi Schatz, whom he has been haunting ever since. The presence of this ghost, whose philosophical and historical reflections make up the bulk of the narrative, leads to an ongoing confrontation between the present time and the Holocaust. A critique of the trends responsible for the extermination denounces the cult of death, of force, and of idealization of the flesh. To all these, Gary contrasts the truth of the Jew and his love of mankind. Gary's narrative starts out as an absurd imaginary story, continues as an allegory, and ends up as a nightmare. By way of contrast, in the extermination scene, factual material and authentic historical details overwhelm the reader with the reality of the genocide. Humor and derision underscore the unacceptable and reveal the perversion in Nazi language and thought.

Jean-François Steiner, seeking to understand the passivity of the Jews during the Holocaust, wrote a fictionalized history, *Treblinka* (1966; *Treblinka,* 1976). Whereas Schwarz-Bart merely imagined the journey, the selection, and the gas chamber, Steiner went inside the camp, depicted characters, created dialogues, and set up situations deriving from documents and oral testimony. At the end of his investigation he found the explanation he was seeking, that "the highest value of Judaism is not heroism, but rather life." The failure of the mind, incapable of conceiving and understanding; of the imagination, incapable of imagining; and the impossibility of writing coupled with the necessity to write about the Holocaust—these are some of the dilemmas posed in *Un cri sans voix* (A Cry without a Voice; 1985), by Henri Raczymov, a beautiful novel written in a clear style.

BIBLIOGRAPHY

Fine, E. "New Kinds of Witnesses: French Post-Holocaust Writers." *Holocaust Studies Annual* 3 (1985): 121–136.

Haft, C. *The Theme of Nazi Concentration Camps in French Literature.* The Hague, 1973.

Wardi, C. "L'oubli du génocide." *Les Nouveaux Cahiers* 58 (1979): 4–9.

CHARLOTTE WARDI

Germany

Literature concerning the fate of the Jews under the National Socialist regime represents a borderline situation, both in the sphere of human behavior and in its expression as literature. It may be asked whether it is at all possible to portray, in a meaningful and aesthetic form, the trauma of the events that constituted the destruction of a people, and in particular, whether this can be done by German writers, in the language used by the Nazis. The trend in Germany to deny or forget the Holocaust means that attempts to confront the memory of the past are relatively rare; that very trend sometimes constitutes the background or the theme of literary creations. *Kollektivschuld* (collective guilt) or *Kollektivscham* (collective shame), as it came to be called after a while, is one of the forms of *Vergangenheitsbewältigung* (coping with the past). This is a term that has been widely used since the 1950s, and as time went on it was exploited as a justification for repressing the memory of what had happened in that past. The demand was therefore made that the term be emended to *unbewältigte Vergangenheit* (failure to cope with the past)—the imperative need to recall the past, as a means of shocking people into recognition of that need. This has been characteristic of the treatment of the subject in German literature ever since the fall of Nazism.

German Holocaust literature deals with various layers of memory and guilt feelings: the juridical aspect (that is, the nature of the crime and the punishment); the aspect of moral responsibility, whether applied to the individual or to the entire community; and the attempt to arrive at a metaphysical conceptualization of the Holocaust.

Some works emphasize the Holocaust as a demonization process of the German people in the Nazi era; others trace the roots of the Holocaust to the sociopsychological condition of the German petite bourgeoisie and its provincialism. A number of works concentrate on the fate of an individual as "representative" of the general course of events; others seek to document specific events as experienced by survivors. Most of the authors are inclined to describe both victim and executioner in stereotyped form. There are literary works that lie somewhere between personal and "literary" testimony, such as *Jenseits von Schuld und Sühne* (1966; *At the Mind's Limit,* 1980) by Jean Amery, an Auschwitz survivor; or *Mützen ab* (Hats Off; 1948), by Zenon Rosanski. This kind of documentation aspires to remain faithful to the personal experience, even though there is also an awareness of the need to communicate that experience. The problem with such descriptions is that they are fragmentary, based on the perspective of a single individual, and hence provide only a limited perception of the overall historical reality.

First and foremost among the testimonies, albeit in literary form, are those written in German by Jews who personally experienced the Holocaust—as emigrés, in hiding, as children, or as the offspring of mixed marriages. Outstanding among the works whose subject is Nazism, its background and manifestations, are those of Nelly Sachs, primarily her poems and the 1964 play *Eli: Ein Mysterienspiel vom Leiden Israels* (*Eli: A Mystery Play of Jewish Suffering*; 1968); the poems of Paul Célan, the most famous of which is *Todesfuge* (1948; *Death Fugue,* 1980); and Peter Weiss's work on Auschwitz, *Die Ermittlung* (1965; *The Investigation,* 1966). A work of a special character, in which tragic, comic, and grotesque elements alternate, is Jurek Becker's *Jacob der Lügner* (1969; *Jacob the Liar,* 1974), a description of life in the ghetto. Works by Jews and by the offspring of mixed marriages, in which childhood memories are used in fictional form to uncover the roots of Nazism and antisemitism, include Christa Wolf's *Kindheitsmuster* (1968; *A Model Childhood,* 1976), Anna Seghers's *Der Ausflug des toten Mädchens* (The Excursion of the Dead Girls; 1946), and Johannes Bobrowski's *Levins Mühle* (1964; *Levin's Mill,* 1970). In the works of Wolf and Seghers (and, to a lesser degree, also in Bobrowski's book) the story becomes a "representative situation" and, to some extent, takes the Holocaust out of history.

Heinrich Böll's *Wo warst du, Adam?* (1951; *And Where Were You, Adam?,* 1974) presents the stereotype of a concentration camp commandant who finds relief for his frustrations in the extermination of Jews. In Günter Grass's famous novel *Die Blechtrommel* (1959; *The Tin Drum,* 1971), Oscar the dwarf, as narrator, tells the story of his life. The main theme is his decision to rebel against the Nazi lower middle class and to be the odd man out in the society and era in which he lives. The book is written in a realistic-fantastic style that also describes the fate of the Jews. Markus, the Jewish toy merchant, commits suicide as he is about to be deported to a concentration camp, and Herr Feingold comes back from TREBLINKA after the war and relives as a dead man the memory of his living-dead relatives who were murdered there.

In Germany the drama *The Diary of Anne Frank,* by Frances Goodrich and Albert Hackett (1965), caused a great stir, as did Erwin Sylvanus's play *Korczak und die Kinder* (Korczak and the Children; 1957). In the latter, the author seeks to create the impression that he was looking for a playwright and actors, so as to indicate in dramatic form the audience's lack of interest in the issue and the reluctance to face it in present-day Germany. These and other works again convey the dialectic between telling the story of the individual victims and the overall story, and the problem of how to relate contemporary indifference to that which prevailed during the Holocaust. A dramatic effort to connect the horrors of the past to contemporary repression of its memory through evidence submitted by survivors and their torturers is Rolf Hochhuth's *Der Stellvertreter* (1963; *The Deputy,* 1964).

Other literary works, in addition to those that use documentation or personal memories (authentic or imaginary) in a realistic or realistic-fantastic style, take the form of parables, which depict events that are supposed to be analogous to those associated with antisemitism and the persecution of the Jews. Examples are two plays by Max Frisch, *Andorra* (1961) and *Bidermann und der Brandstifter* (Bidermann and the Arsonist; 1958). The parable used in these and other plays is based on the assumption that antisemitism and the Holocaust can be compared to aspects of any totalitarian regime, or to an existential situation in which the individual faces the threat of losing his identity by having to conform to the existing totalitarian rules of behavior; such generalization, however, has a diminishing effect, as far as the Holocaust is concerned.

Despite Theodor Adorno's well-known assertion that to write poetry after Auschwitz is "barbaric," the silence cried out and demanded its artistic expression; this, despite the fact that the events of the extermination and the guilt feelings it evoked represent a questionable background for literary creativity and perhaps constitute its opposite. On the one hand, there is the demand that "historical truth" be respected and that it not be distorted, even though realistic means of description cannot faithfully reflect that truth. On the other hand, expressions of a "literary" sort (comparison, Brechtian alienation, grotesquery, parables, and so on) may divert the emphasis from the true facts to their aesthetic description and thereby dilute the facts. The demand that the literary description of the Holocaust should remain true to the facts or to their meaning is a central issue in the discussion of Holocaust literature in general, and of German Holocaust literature in particular.

The treatment of the Holocaust in German literature is either comprehensive, encompassing the entire background and development of the Nazi era, or it is restricted to the persecution of the Jews. In the latter case, it either describes the persecution of the Jews in all its manifestations, or confines itself to the concentration camps, the ghetto, or the surviving remnant. It may consist of the story of a murderer or of a victim, and may be told by the protagonist or by his offspring. It may be written by German or German-speaking authors who were witnesses to and participants in Nazism, the war, and the extermination; who experienced them as children; or who knew about them from hearsay. Each of these possibilities for the background of the writer or for the literary embodiment of some manifestation of Nazism may have its own fictional specialty.

The killings that took place in the ghettos and in the concentration camps was thought to be unsuitable for literary treatment, yet it gained wide expression (particularly after the EICHMANN TRIAL) in the form of testimonies submitted in courts of law and recorded in reports of court trials, and also through the publication of documents—the memoirs of survivors and victims, such as the diary of Anne Frank. In the 1970s and 1980s, when the younger generation sought to establish its identity by searching its own childhood memories and its parents' attitudes during the Nazi era, literary works emerged that refer directly or indirectly to the extermination of the Jews. They express the intergenerational confrontation in which the son seeks his own identity and feels his way to his parents; in the process he is caught up between a sense of rejection and guilt on the one hand and a craving to belong and understand on the other. Peter Handke's *Wunschloses Glück* (1972; *Sorrow beyond Dreams*, 1974) evokes the memory of his mother, who throughout her life had no means of expressing her miserable fate in action or in words. The autobiographical *Die Reise* (The Journey; 1971), by Bernard Vesper, is a bitter and cynical confrontation between the author and his father, the Nazi writer Will Vesper. There are similar situations in which the narrator, in the first person singular, searches for his identity by trying to discover the truth about his parents' Nazi past. He is torn apart by his alienation from them and his desire to accept them as parents. Such situations are also described in Elisabeth Plessen's *Mitteilungen an den Adel* (Message to the Nobility; 1976), Ruth Rehmann's *Der Mann auf der Kanzel* (The Man at the Pulpit; 1979), and Christoph Meckel's *Suchbild: Über meinen Vater* (Hidden Picture: About My Father; 1980).

This literary dialogue between Germans and their past has just begun. It remains to be seen whether it will continue and where it will become stabilized between documentation and fiction. Helmut Heissenbüttel, in his *Kalkulation über das was alle gewusst haben* (Reckoning about What Everybody Knew; 1965), referred to the Holocaust as it is treated in German literature: "Of course everybody knew; one knew one thing, the next another, and the third yet another. But nobody knew more, and one really should have asked one question after another, and added question to question. That is, if one could do so, but this was far from easy."

BIBLIOGRAPHY

Brettschneider, W. *Zorn und Trauer.* West Berlin, 1979.

Durzak, M. *Deutsche Gegenwarts Literatur.* Stuttgart, 1981.

Jaspers, K. *Die Schuldfrage: Ein Beitrag zur deutschen Frage.* Zurich, 1946.

Mitscherlich, A., and M. Mitscherlich. *Die Unfähigkeit zu trauern.* Munich, 1967.

Schmelzkopf, C. *Zur Gestaltung jüdischer Figuren in der deutschsprachigen Literatur nach 1945.* Hildesheim, 1983.

Wagener, H., ed. *Gegenwartsliteratur und Drittes Reich: Deutsche Autoren in der Auseinandersetzung mit der Vergangenheit.* Stuttgart, 1977.

LEAH HADOMI

Hebrew Literature

Hebrew Holocaust literature seeks to give meaning to the recorded evidence of the most traumatic event in the history of the Jewish people. It wrestles with the horror by trying to give expression to ordeals and situations that are "beyond words," moving freely between fact and fiction and between the concrete and the mythical. This applies primarily to fictional writing, where it appears in two forms. In the first, the writer seeks to put superhuman terror into words from a historical point of view, a method that is based on rational cause and effect and historical principles; this form may be classified under the heading "historical fiction." Historical realism is found in Naomi Frankel's *Sha'ul ve-Yohanna* (Saul and Joanna) and in Yonat and Alexander Sened's novel *Ben ha-Metim u-ven ha-Hayyim* (Between the Dead and the Living). Combined with naturalist realism, it appears in the series of works by K. Zetnik (Jehiel Dinur), *Salamandra* (Salamander), *Bet ha-Bubbot* (House of the Dolls), *Piepel,* and *Ha-'Immut* (Confrontation). Such naturalist "art of revulsion" also shows up in Shammai Golan's works, such as *Be-Ashmoret Aḥaronah* (On the Last Shift), and, expanded into a grotesque form, in Yoram Kaniuk's *Adam Ben-Kelev* (Son of a Dog). In a more refined form, realism is used in Uri Orlev's *Hayyalei 'Oferet* (Tin Soldiers), and, in lyrical form, in Itamar Ya'oz-Kest's novel *Ba-Ḥalon ha-Bayyit ha-Nosea'* (In the Window of the Moving House).

In the second form of Hebrew fiction on the Holocaust, the element of lyrical realism predominates; this group may be subsumed under the heading "trans-historical fiction." These works do not purport to rest upon established historical facts, but rather on internal principles that draw their inspiration from a world in which mythical forces hold sway. This kind of fiction, in Aharon Appelfeld's version, is concerned mainly with migration and persecution, as in *Ashan* (Smoke). His descriptions of the postwar world are filled with terrible memories. The "time of horror" is dealt with in *Adnei ha-Nahar* (River Banks), *Shanim ve-Sha'ot* (Years and Hours), and *Kutonet ha-Passim* (Coat of Many Colors). In essence, this is "Jewish existentialist fiction," and it is also to be found in the works of the younger generation of writers, such as *'Ayyen 'Erekh Ahava* (See Entry "Love"), by David Grossman.

The Holocaust has also made its imprint on the Hebrew drama, for example, Lea Goldberg's play *Ba'alat ha-Armon* (Lady of the Manor); Yehuda Amichai's sketch *Pa'amonim ve-Rakavot* (Bells and Trains), based on his novel *Lo me-Askhshav, Lo mi-Kan* (Not of This Time, Not of This Place); Ben-Zion Tomer's drama *Yaldei ha-Tsel* (Children of the Shadows); and Shmuel Hasefari's *Kiddush,* Yehoshua Sobol's *Ghetto,* and Moti Lerner's *Kasztner.* These Hebrew playwrights, belonging to different generations, have brought the tension between fact and fiction before the reader and theatergoer of the post-Holocaust world by means of the drama's conflict. Their plays, based on the trauma of Jewish experience in World War II, have added yet another artistic and literary dimension to Hebrew Holocaust literature.

Hebrew poetry on the Holocaust has been created by three generations of poets. The first generation—the poets of the 1940s, such as Uri Zvi Greenberg, Nathan Alterman, Lea Goldberg, and Avraham Shlonsky—were far from the scene. They composed their poems on the basis of what they sensed of the dread of the Holocaust and the marginal effects that they experienced. They approached the subject in a variety of ways. Nathan Alterman addressed it directly, in his weekly feature in the newspaper *Davar,* in *Ha-Tur ha-Shevi'i* (The Seventh Column), and by means of symbols, as in *Shirei Makkot Mitsrayim* (Poems on the Plagues of Egypt) or *Simhat 'Aniyyim* (Joy of the Poor), which some interpret as poems on the Holocaust. In Uri Zvi Greenberg's poetry, a metaphoric expressionism prevails. Thematically the emphasis is on dirges and lamentations, which reach their highest point in his *Reḥovot ha-Nahar* (Streets of the River); these are elegies on the "extermination of the Jewish communities," on the murdered brothers and sisters, and on the fate in store for the survivors. Elegies are also characteristic of Ezra Sussman's poetry on the Holocaust, whereas Sh. Shalom (Shalom Shapira) links the elegiac motif to the world of Jewish mysticism.

The second generation of Israeli poets of the Holocaust belong to the "generation of the State" that witnessed the creation of the state of Israel. Most of these poets abandoned the direct approach, the outcry and the lamentation, and searched for indirect means of expressing the horror, to such an extent that a poetic language of "codes" came into being. This is a language based on expressions coined in the concentration and extermination camps, on biblical archetypes, and on images of the European landscape. Such poets as Abba KOVNER, Dan Pagis, Itamar Ya'oz-Kest, and Yaakov Besser, who had had personal experience of World War II in their early childhood or youth, express both the personal and the national trauma. Prominent in their work is the genre of the epic poem, which enables them to relate to historical events of national importance. The epic poem, such as Kovner's *Aḥoti ha-Ketanna* (My Little Sister), Pagis's *'Akevot* (Imprints), Ya'oz-Kest's *Nof be-Ashan* (Landscape in Smoke) and *Mul Germania* (Facing Germany), and Besser's *Ḥoref Elef Tesha Me'ot Arba'im ve . . .* (Winter Nineteen-Forty . . .), made it possible, in a way, to mythicize the events on "the other planet." The short lyric poem, on the other hand, enabled the poet to give concrete expression to the horror by concentrating on commonplace situations that do not lend themselves to intensification, projection, or abstraction.

Those poets of the "generation of the State" who, in contrast to the Holocaust survivors, had not experienced the horror themselves and had only observed it from afar, write about it as though they had witnessed it indirectly. Thematically, these poets revert to the anguish, the outcries, and the lamentations that marked the poets of the 1940s, but the form they use is that of the "new poem." The pain is to be found in the poems composed by Amir Gilboa and Haim Gouri, which represent the transition from Holocaust to rebirth; the outcry is typical of Aryeh Sivan's and Asher Reich's poems; and the lamentations, in "elegiac spirit," characterize the poems of Tuvya Rubner, Shlomo Tanai, David Rokach, and Israel Har, among others.

The third generation of poets who write about the Holocaust are the children of Holocaust survivors. In the 1970s and 1980s, Oded Peled, Rivka Miriam, Tanya Hadar, and Dudu Barak published poetry in which, in a mixture of empathy, identification, and rejection, they give expression to the trauma they inherited. In the late 1980s another group of young poets emerged, children of the survivors of Salonika and other Jewish communities of Greece, such as Margalit Matityahu and Avner Peretz. Their poems express the suffering inherited by the descendants of their families' parents, most of whom were murdered in the crematoria of Auschwitz.

BIBLIOGRAPHY

Kohn, M. *The Voice of My Blood Cries Out: The Holocaust as Reflected in Hebrew Poetry.* New York, 1979.

Mintz, A. *Hurban: Response to Catastrophe in Hebrew Literature.* New York, 1985.

Silberschlag, E. "The Holocaust in Hebrew Literature." *Jewish Spectator* 43/4 (Winter 1978): 16–23.

Yaoz, H. "The Heritage of Trauma in Hebrew Poetry on the Holocaust." In vol. 2 of *Remembering for the Future,* pp. 1643–1649. Oxford, 1988.

Yaoz, H. *The Holocaust in Hebrew Literature as Historical and Trans-Historical Fiction.* Tel Aviv, 1980. (In Hebrew.)

Yaoz, H. *The Holocaust in Modern Hebrew Poetry.* Tel Aviv, 1984. (In Hebrew.)

Yuter, A. J. *The Holocaust in Hebrew Literature: From Genocide to Rebirth.* Port Washington, N.Y., 1984.

HANNAH YAOZ

Poland

The sufferings of the Jews, their struggle, and their destruction in World War II are among the motifs of the literature produced in Poland during and after the war. Each of these themes constitutes an organic part of the vast and ongoing body of literature written on the war and the Jews of Poland. In works on the Holocaust—written in Yiddish and occasionally in Hebrew, in addition to

Polish—the borderline between literature and documentation is blurred. The Holocaust motifs have not yet been clearly defined, nor have they been thoroughly analyzed by literary criticism. There is no complete and up-to-date bibliography. A 1963 biographical guide to Polish literature for the first eight postwar years lists 112 important literary works, diaries, testimonies, documents, and adaptations. But even without precise information on the subject, it can be stated that Polish literature on the tragedy of the Jews consists of at least several hundred items.

Polish Holocaust literature began to emerge during the Holocaust itself. Works originating in the ghettos included Itzhak KATZENELSON's "Song of the Murdered Jewish People" (translated into Polish by Jerzy Ficowski in 1982), Władysław Szlengel's *Co czytałem umarłym* (What Did I Read to the Dead; 1979), and works by Zuzanna Ginczanka, Henryka Lazowertowna, Stefania Ney-Grodzienska, Izabela Gelbard, and Michał Borwicz.

There were also testimonies and chronicles, among them Janusz KORCZAK's *Diary*, Emanuel RINGELBLUM's *Notes from the Warsaw Ghetto*, Jakub Poznański's *Pamiętnik z getta łódzkiego* (Łódź Ghetto Diary), and Adam CZERNIAKÓW's *Warsaw Ghetto Diary*. Much original writing was done by Jews—letters, prose descriptions, and poems on the suffering experienced. Testimonies written by children included the diaries of Roza Gold and Krystyna Gold (1945), the *Diary of Dawidek Rubinowicz* (1960), David Sierakowiak's *Diary* (1960), Janka Hescheles's *Oczyma dwunastoletniej dziewczyny* (In the Eyes of a Twelve-Year-Old Girl; 1946), and Mary Berg's *Warsaw Ghetto Diary*.

The Holocaust, with extraordinary power, gives to the written word its most basic function: existence beyond death. The largest collection of testimonies was preserved as a result of the efforts made by the ONEG SHABBAT Archive in the Warsaw ghetto, which was founded on the initiative of the historian Emanuel Ringelblum. Other writings often passed from hand to hand and were discovered, years later, in hiding places in concentration camps and prisons, in cellars and attics.

During the Holocaust, when Jews were writing in the ghettos, Polish poets outside the ghetto walls (some of them Jews who had gone into hiding on the "Aryan" side) were doing the same, among them Mieczysław Jastrun, Czesław Miłosz, Tadeusz Sarnecki, Jan Kott, Flora Bienkowska, Helena Wielowieyska, and Roman Bratny. Some of these poets were living abroad, including Władysław Broniewski, Józef Wittlin, Antoni Słonimski, Stanisław Balinski, Julian Tuwim, Kazimierz Wierzyński, and Lucjan Szenwald.

A special vitality is to be found in the lines written by Miłosz in *Biedny chrześcijanin patrzy na getto* (The Poor Christian Stares at the Ghetto), which speak of the "solitude of the dead" and foresee that as time goes on "rebellion will light up the poet's message." Plays were also written during the war, such as *Wielkanoc* (Easter) by Stefan Otwinowski and *Smocza 13* by Stefania Zahorska. Other works were *Wielki tydzień* (The Great Week), a long story by Jerzy Andrzejewski, and two major chronicles, *Kronika lat wojny i okupacji* (Chronicle of the Years of War and Occupation) by Ludwik Landau, and *Dziennik z lat okupacji* (Diary of the Years of Occupation) by Zygmunt Klukowski. Under the impact of the main *Aktion*, of the summer of 1942, Antoni Szymanowski wrote *Likwidacja getta warszawskiego* (The Liquidation of the Warsaw Ghetto); the WARSAW GHETTO UPRISING inspired Maria Kann's pamphlet *Na oczach świata* (For All the World to See). It was also at this time that Julian Tuwim wrote his famous manifesto *My, Żydzi polscy* (We, the Jews of Poland), about the many assimilated Jews who had returned to Judaism on account of the suffering. A theme of these works was an appeal for the saving of lives. Included in this category is the anthology of Polish Jewish poems *Z otchłani* (From the Abyss; 1944), which was published in New York that same year under the title *Poezja Getta* (Poetry from the Ghetto).

After the war the writing of works about the Holocaust accelerated. The flood of compositions included many documents from the Ringelblum archive, writings by survivors of the camps and the ghettos, and new testimonies: Ludwik Hirszfeld's *Historia jednego życia* (Story of a Life), Władysław Szpilman's *Śmierć miasta* (Death of a City), Noemi Szac-Wajnkranc's *Przeminęło z ogniem* (Gone with the Fire), Krystyna Zywulska's *Przeżyłam Oświęcim* (I Survived Auschwitz), Krystyna Nowakowska's *Moja walka o życie* (My Struggle for Life), Tova DRAENGER's *Pamiętnik Justyny* (Justina's Diary), and Kopel Holzman's *Ziemia bez Boga* (Land without God). The documents also include Marek EDELMAN's *Getto walczy* (The Ghetto Fights), dating from 1945. In 1947 Michał Borwicz published an anthology of poems about Jews under the German occupation, *All the Poetry Will Survive,* which contains works from the war years and the years that followed.

In the Polish literature on World War II there are few important works of which the fate of the Jews is not an integral part. This is true of the classical creations *Noc* (Night) by Jerzy Andrzejewski, *Pożegnanie z Maria* (Farewell to Maria) and *Kamienny świat* (The Stone World) by Tadeusz Borowski, *Czarny potok* (The Black Stream) and *Pierwsza świetność* (First Light) by Leopold Buczkowski, *Pokolenie* (The Generation) by Bogdan Czeszko, *Przygody człowieka myślacego* (Adventures of a Thinking Man) by Maria Dąbrowska, *Sława i chwała* (The Name and the Glory) by Jarosław Iwaszkiewicz, *Bestia* (The Beast) by Władysław Kowalski, *Niemcy* (The Germans) by Leon Kunczkowski, *Medaliony* (Medallions) by Zofia Nalkowska, *Dymy nad Birkenau* (Smoke over Birkenau) by Seweryna Szmaglewska, *Romans z ojczyzna* (Romance with the Fatherland) by Jerzy Zawieyski, and *Z kraju milczenia* (From the Land of Silence) by Wojciech Zukrowski.

Some of the literary works also dealt specifically with the Holocaust. In the immediate postwar period the outstanding examples were the works of Adolf Rudnicki, a Polish writer of Jewish origin: *Ucieczka z jasnej polany* (Flight from a Clearing in the Forest; 1949) and *Złote okna* (Golden Windows; 1963). These works were republished in various collections, such as *Żywe i martwe morze* (A Living Sea and a Dead Sea). Also noteworthy were Kazimierz Brandys's *Samson* and *Antygona* (Antigone), *Oczekiwanie* (The Expectation) by Jerzy Broszkiewicz, *Śmierć liberala* (Death of a Liberal) by Artur Sandauer, and *Bomby i myszy* (Bombs and Mice) by Mina Tomkiewicz.

Holocaust literature written soon after the war is extraordinarily powerful, colorful, and emotion-laden, and of great documentary value. The manifold sufferings and crimes described in this literature have no counterparts in previously recorded experience and do not follow accepted conventions. Above all, Polish postwar literature spoke through "ghetto, Gestapo, camp" (Borowski's formula). In Nalkowska's and Borowski's prose, and in Tadeusz Różewicz's poetry, this literature describes total crime and draws its conclusions. The effort to penetrate into the darkest core, and the rejection of all embellishment and sermonizing, characterized Polish Holocaust literature; it confronts the stark and uncompromising truth of totalitarianism and of the merciless crushing of masses of human beings. Two approaches clash in this literature: the martyrological and romantic tendency of Rudnicki's work, and the stark and unmitigated denunciation represented by Borowski. But this outburst of feeling and penetration into the Holocaust universe was soon suppressed. The Socialist Realism that was forced upon Polish literature by the advent of Stalinism charged these writers with "catastrophism" and "antiaestheticism"; when that period passed from the scene, only the few writers most faithful to the subject of the Holocaust again took up its motifs.

Since the end of Stalinism in Poland in October 1956, new works, both literary and documentary, have appeared. They include *Ocalil mnie kowal* (A Blacksmith Saved Me) by Izabella Stachowicz-Czajka, *Gwiazda Dawida* (Star of David) by Maria Czapska, *To jest morderstwo* (This Is Murder) by Mieczysław Frenkel, *Skrawek czasu* (A Fragment of Time) by Ida Fink, *Apteka w getcie krakowskim* (A Pharmacy in the Kraków Ghetto) by Tadeusz Pankiewicz, *Kartki z dziennika Doktora Twardego* (Pages from the Diary of Dr. Twardy) by Julian Aleksandrowicz, *Pusta woda* (Empty Water) by Zofia Zywulska, *Do Edenu* (To Eden) by Ryszard Klys, *Jak Święty Franciszek przyniosł chleb do getta* (How Saint Francis Brought Bread into the Ghetto) by Roman Brandstaetter, and *W kotlinie* (In the Mortar), *Koncert życzen* (A Concert of Congratulations), and *O świcie* (At Dawn) by Stanisław Wygodzki.

At this point, however, Polish literature on the Holocaust had entered a new phase, because of the passage of time and the appearance on the scene of new writers who were too young to have experienced the Holocaust. The influence of contemporary events also made an impact on Holocaust literature and its development: the emergence and development of the state of Israel; the attitude toward Jews in Poland, especially the sudden recrudescence of official antisemitism in 1968; and the subsequent expulsion from Poland of Holocaust survivors and of many of the Holocaust authors.

In this period, Polish literature devoted greater attention to the subject of Jewish-Polish relations during the Holocaust, which until then had been dealt with only on a factual basis. A common history extending over many centuries, and the tolerance and cooperation that had existed, failed to overcome ignorance, alienation, and lack of sympathy, and these came to the fore when the Poles faced the test of Hitler's crime. Polish literature denounces the Poles who informed on the Jews for money (the *szmalcownicy*) and the profiteers who lay in wait to seize Jewish property. Primarily, it exposes the abandonment of the Jews and the morally destructive indifference to their fate. Works devoted to these themes are Antonina Zabinska's *Ludzie i zwierzęta* (Men and Beasts) and Halina Balicka-Kozlowska's *Mur miał dwie strony* (The Wall Had Two Sides). The literature of this period also describes manifestations of Polish solidarity with the Jews, and displays of heroism, as in *Ten jest z ojczyny moje: Polacy z pomoca Żydom* (He Belongs to My Country: Poles Who Helped Jews), edited by Władysław Bartoszewski and Zofia Lewin. The moral aspects of these issues are clearly expressed in the poems of Anna Kamienska and those of Anna Swirszczynska, by Wiesława Szymborska in her poem *Jeszcze* (Still), and by Zbigniew Herbert in *Pan Cogito szuka rady* (Mr. Cogito Wants Advice).

Young writers who remember the Holocaust from their childhood include Henryk Grynberg, Bogdan Wojdowski, and Hanna Krall. Wojdowski and Grynberg deal almost exclusively with the Jewish theme. Wojdowski's most ambitious work is *Chleb rzucony umarłym* (Bread Thrown to the Dead; 1971), which records the destruction of a people in the Warsaw ghetto. Using contemporary literary devices, Wojdowski recalls from limbo not only the Jewish people, but also the culture of the Polish Jews, which was lost with them and is not known in Poland today. Grynberg's work, which he began in Poland and continued in the United States after 1968, traces the history of his family, in *Ekipa Antygona* (The Antigone Group), *Żydowska wojna* (The War of the Jews), and *Kaddish*. In his 1984 volume of essays, *Prawda nieartystyczna* (The Non-Artistic Truth), Grynberg comes to the conclusion that the truth about the Holocaust is more dreadful than anything that has been written about it, and in his poems and prose writings he seeks to penetrate to the uncompromising truth. Grynberg also believes that, contrary to Nalkowska's thesis that the Holocaust was something that "people did to people," it was what "people did to Jews." In this he stands alone in Polish literature.

The major figure that has preoccupied Polish Holocaust literature is that of Janusz KORCZAK. Its treatment of Korczak has gone through a development of its own: as a defender of Jewish honor (Gelbard, Szlengel), as an outstanding doctor, educator, and writer (Hanna Mortkowicz-Olczakowa), and, finally, as a secular saint. In Igor Newerly's book *Żywe wiązanie* (The Living Link), Korczak's saintliness is portrayed as continuing the ethical tradition of the Polish Left as it existed in the early twentieth century. Another writer venerated by Polish Holocaust literature is Bruno Schulz, who was murdered in the town of Sambor. Around Schulz a veritable cult has developed, in literary criticism (Artur Sandauer) and biography (Jerzy Ficowski).

In poetry, wide interest has been aroused by Ficowski's poems on Jews, which were collected and published in *Odczytanie popiołów* (Deciphering the Ashes; 1979). Prominent among them is *List do Marka Chagalla* (Letter to Marc Chagall). Based on the diaries of murdered children, it was illustrated by Chagall and has been translated into many languages. In these poems the author seeks to reawaken forgotten sentiments, "to try to catch up, even if it is too late."

Hanna Krall's *Zdążyć przed Panem Bogiem*

(Beat God to It; 1977), which combines prose writing and historical research, links two motifs in the person of Dr. Edelman, the book's hero. It presents an antiheroic, nonartistic story of the Warsaw ghetto uprising, and tells of a way of life that has survived from the past. This book illustrates a development in Polish Holocaust literature as a whole, namely, that the truth about the Holocaust affects all the problematic aspects of Jewish existence. One is the attitude toward tradition, as seen in the works of Julian Strjykowski, or in Stanisław Vincenz's *Tematy żydowskie* (Jewish Themes; 1977). Another is the relative significance of moral values, as depicted in Rozewicz's 1982 play *Pułapka* (The Trap). The life of the survivors is described in Artur Sandauer's *Zapiski z martwego miasta* (Notes from a Dead City), Henryk Vogler's *Autoportret z pamięci* (Self-Portrait from Memory; 1987), Wojdowski's *Kręte drogi* (Curved Ways; 1987), and Stanisław Benski's *Ocaleni* (The Survivors; 1986). The Holocaust remains on the Polish literary scene not only as a subject whose memory stays alive. It is also present when other subjects of a general nature are the theme, even if only as a ghostly apparition, as in Tadeusz Konwicki's *Bohinia* or in Pawel Huell's *Weiser Dawidek.* This perspective is also found in the latest and most comprehensive anthology, *Męczeństwo i zagłada Żydów w zapisach polskiej literatury* (The Holocaust and Destruction of the Jews in Works of Polish Literature; 1988), edited by Irena Maciejewska.

Thus, the tragedy of the Jews plays a unique role in Polish literature. As the critic Andrzej Kijowski stated in a discussion of Polish literature in the journal *Twórczość* (Creation) in 1957, "The Jewish motif has sharpened the Poles' awareness of their own fate by showing them that living together with the Poles in the same country were human beings who were condemned to suffer more than the rest, more than the majority. This motif arouses a new sense of responsibility."

BIBLIOGRAPHY

Grynberg, H. "Holocaust w literaturze polskiej." In *Prawda nieartystyczna.* Berlin, 1984.

Maciejewska, I., ed. *Męczeństwo i zagłada Żydów.* Warsaw, 1988.

TADEUSZ DREWNOWSKI

United States

As a collective, the American people have confronted the Holocaust only vicariously— although the soldiers who fought in the European theater and the refugees who adopted America as their place of refuge certainly brought their personal experiences to bear on the American encounter with the ravages of a war fought elsewhere. But since neither the American language nor American soil had been polluted by the Nazi presence, the terms of the American engagement with the subject are less a function of the actual experience of war and mass murder than of other factors.

The shifts in sensibility toward the Jewish catastrophe that can be traced in the long aftermath of the war reflect changing perceptions of the place of the Jew in the Western mind, as well as changing definitions of the American self in relation to its European origins. Distinctions should, of course, be made between specifically Jewish literature in America and literature written by Americans with neither direct nor indirect connections with the civilization that was destroyed. Although American identity was—and continues to be—carved out in juxtaposition with the European past and European culture, the specifically Jewish culture of central and eastern Europe began to be an ingredient in American consciousness only from the beginning of the twentieth century, with the massive migration westward of Jews from Russia and Poland. An ethnically specific, almost "regional" Jewish literature evolved in America in the following decades, nourished by memories of the European homeland, by the flourishing of Yiddish culture in large urban centers, and by the drama and conflicts of the immigrant experience. By the mid-1940s, a first generation of native sons and daughters had emerged to claim their literary birthright. So distinctive was their stake in American culture—and so estranged had many of them become from Jewish communities in other parts of the world—that in February

1944 the editors of the journal *Contemporary Jewish Record* could conduct a symposium on the centrality of Jewish writing in the United States without any direct reference to the mass murder that had already reached its final stages in Nazi Europe. In response to the questions posed by the editors of the symposium, the writer Delmore Schwartz insisted that "the fact of being a Jew became available to me as a central symbol of alienation," and the poet Isaac Rosenfeld wrote that the Jew is a "specialist in alienation." Both the editorial presumption that the children of Jewish immigrants had reached the "front ranks of American literature" and the Jewish writer's assumption of what would become the rather fashionable posture of "alienation" were a far cry from any identification or even empathy with the actual suffering of the Jew as, quite literally, *alien* and outcast in all the countries of Europe. It seems to have been a generic memory rather than an active historical consciousness that fostered a sense of Jewish marginality among these writers—rather more of an existential dilemma, a voluntary moral stance, than a historically determined condition. "Antisemitism" was noted in passing by the editors of this 1944 symposium as if it were a kind of social disease. Jewish fiction of the immediate postwar years evinces a similar psychosocial approach to racial prejudice as an indwelling but abstracted threat: Arthur Miller's *Focus,* Saul Bellow's *The Victim,* and Laura Hobson's *Gentleman's Agreement* all revolve around the Jew who, having been identified (or misidentified) primarily by his appearance, is isolated as a social scapegoat. Two of the themes that dominate this fiction of the 1940s will reemerge later: that of the mistaken (or ambiguous) identity of the Jew based on external traits and that of the social role of the Jew as victim or sacrifice.

Specific literary responses to the Holocaust would eventually be shaped by three processes that related only tangentially to the events that had taken place in Europe: the return of the American soldiers who had participated in the defeat of Germany and the liberation of the extermination camps, the arrival and growing impact of large numbers of survivors, and the EICHMANN TRIAL, which took place some sixteen years after the war.

The first historically specific encounter with the fate of the Jews of Europe can be found in the stories and poems of returning American soldiers who stumbled upon traces of starvation, disease, torture, and mass murder as they participated in the liberation of the concentration camps at the end of the war (William Hoffman's *The Trumpet Unblown;* Stefan Heym's *The Crusaders*). The horror of the sight of piles of mutilated, undifferentiated corpses so exceeded the grasp of the imagination of even the soldier hardened to death and disfiguration on the battlefield that the poetic language which tried to contain it was often stretched to its limits; in Randall Jarrell's poem "A Camp in the Prussian Forest" (1948), the very syntax is mutilated in the effort to convey unprecedented reality: "Here men were drunk like water, burnt like wood." In much of this writing the shock of the encounter is so great as to preclude the normal empathetic response to tragedy. The soldier-literature did succeed in placing the camps on the map of American consciousness, but it would take many years for the subject to achieve human scale in the imagination.

In the decade or so following the war, while the historical evidence mounted, a certain cultural numbness continued to prevail, approximating in its effect a conspiracy of silence. *The Diary of Anne Frank* provides an interesting test case for the slowly evolving sensibility and the elaborate defensive apparatus brought to bear on this subject throughout the 1950s. At first rejected by several editors in the United States who were convinced that there would be no market for the book because the "public shie[s] away from such material" and by potential producers of the dramatic adaptation who claimed that audiences would not "come to the theater to watch on the stage people they know to have ended up in the crematorium; it would be too painful" (Levin, *The Obsession*), both the book and the play eventually reached audiences numbering probably in the millions. But it may be that the published version of the *Diary*—and to an even greater extent the American-written and American-produced play based upon it—enjoyed the popularity they did precisely because of the *absence* in them of any scenes of horror or computation of loss, because of their comfortable affirmation of the ultimate triumph of the forces of good over evil. Ten years after the liberation of the concentration camps, audiences who should have known better were eagerly applauding Anne's final statement that "it will all come right," and embracing a drama that had largely sanitized the story of its Jewish particularity (see Bruno Bettelheim's "The Ignored Lesson of Anne Frank" in *Surviving*). A satiric example of how Anne Frank has entered the myths of American culture in the most benign way can be found in Philip Roth's *The Ghostwriter* (1979). The narrator, an aspiring Jewish writer, has fallen in love with a beautiful refugee whom he believes to be Anne Frank (somewhere in the American imagination, that is, she is still alive). He brings his fiancée home to meet his parents, who ask the natural question: "Is she Jewish?" "Yes, she is," he answers sheepishly. "But who is she?" "Anne Frank." It is in the parodic Hollywood fantasy of such a happy ending that the implications of the refrain "it will all come right" can be appreciated.

The trial of Adolf Eichmann in Jerusalem in 1961 marked a watershed in worldwide Jewish consciousness and had a two-pronged impact on the American imagination. In the first place, psychopolitical interpretations of Eichmann's character and of his function in the Nazi machine made available to the writer material that had been, up to that point, cast into the safe realm of a demonic otherness. Additionally, survivor testimony at the trial revealed the poetic potential of the individual's struggle against the collective fate.

Through the mediation of Hannah Arendt's theory of the banalization of evil (*Eichmann in Jerusalem*), a new literary strategy evolved whereby Nazi evil could be domesticated and incorporated into the human drama. In the two decades following the Eichmann trial, a kind of "fascination with Nazism" (see Saul Friedländer's *Reflections of Nazism*) came to inform both popular and serious culture in America and in Western Europe. At the level of lowbrow fiction and film, it fed sensationalist, sadomasochistic fantasies (see Alvin Rosenfeld's *Imagining Hitler*); at the level of serious literature and drama, it probed the capacity for evil in Everyman. A number of European-produced movies and plays that explored the average citizen's collaboration with Nazism as a natural social phenomenon—an indictment of the system rather than of any of the individuals serving it—were very well received by American audiences (Klaus Mann's *Mephisto;* C. P. Taylor's *Good*). Several American novelists and playwrights expressed variations on that motif through an elaborate confusion of identities. In William Styron's *Sophie's Choice,* the presumption of the banality and universality of the Nazi mentality crystallizes in the person of Nathan, a Jew whose sadistic conduct toward Sophie, the (non-Jewish) concentration camp survivor, is undifferentiable from that of any of Hitler's henchmen; in fact, in the same novel, the historical Nazi, Rudolf Höss, commandant of Auschwitz, appears as rather affable and eminently human. Along similar lines, Robert Shaw's *The Man in the Glass Booth,* modeled after the Eichmann trial, confounds and universalizes Nazi identity by presenting the main character as a Jew posing as a Nazi posing as a Jew. This principle of interchangeable identities dissolves the gap between victims and victimizers, between the human and the demonic (see also Arthur Miller's *Incident at Vichy*).

Whereas the sensational appearance of the Nazi has a primarily titillating effect in pornographic literature, the admission of the Nazi bureaucrat into the family of man resonates quite differently in the serious work of the imagination. Consistent with the twentieth-century American tendency to approach behavior on psychological rather than moral grounds, this strategy leaves nothing out of bounds or unapproachable. The most extreme expression of this theme may be Jerzy Kosinski's novel *The Painted Bird,* in which a child—normally represented as the last bastion of innocence, even in a war-torn world—is so utterly corrupted by his environment that, as an act of revenge or gratuitous violence, he derails a trainload of peasants. Whatever humanizing effects it is meant to have on the encounter between the self and its darkest impulses, the leveling of the human propensity for evil also contributes to a blurring of the lines of historical accountability.

Parallel and in some respects contrary to these developments has been the emergence, also in the wake of the Eichmann trial, of survivor voices out of the silence into which they had fallen after their arrival on American shores. The procession of witnesses who testified at the trial seemed for the first time to rescue the individual from the statistical anonymity to which the Nazi machine had reduced him and to highlight the pathos of his lonely struggle for survival. Elie Wiesel's was one of the first and most enduring of the survivor voices. Although he writes in French, the impact of his novels and his public presence is most keenly felt in the United States, which he made his home after leaving Europe. Wiesel's first book, *Night,* is both an act of confession and commemoration and a claim for the historical foundation of all the fiction to come. As autobiography, it stretches the genre to its very limits, tracing not the growth but the utter collapse of the integrity of all life-support systems surrounding the young adolescent. In *Night* the American reader encountered the kind of text that Anne Frank might have written had she survived Bergen-Belsen; it is not a story in which it "all comes right."

The narratives of survival, autobiographical and fictional, proliferated and reached wide audiences in America in the decades following the Eichmann trial; the survivor—as writer and as persona—began to emerge as a new kind of hero against a landscape of mass murder. This literature is a far cry from the stories of successful immigrants that make up the melting-pot saga of early twentieth-century America, the Horatio Alger tales of impoverished new Americans who reconstruct their lives in the land of freedom and promise; nevertheless, they owe much of their impact to the American elevation of the individual in his or her struggle against circumstance. A few of these narratives were written in English by survivors who had mastered the language of their adopted country (Ilona Karmel's *An Estate of Memory*); the others reached American readers in translation. American-born Jewish writers may have found in these autobiographical fictions a set of literary conventions that would enable them to enter hitherto uncharted regions (E. L. Wallant's *The Pawnbroker;* Saul Bellow's *Mr. Sammler's Planet;* Susan Fromberg-Schaeffer's *Anya*). *The Pawnbroker* (1961) is one of the earliest fictional attempts to reconstruct the postwar life of the survivor in America; the way in which the embittered Sol Nazerman is finally able to confront his repressed memories of torture and loss and to enter a space normally reserved for heroes in American fiction is to become, along with his assistant ("Jesus"), a kind of expiatory Christ figure. The Jew as sufferer and as sacrificial victim thus reemerges schematically in the 1960s and 1970s in the portrait of the survivor or refugee (see also the fiction of Bernard Malamud).

Over the years the events in Europe, which had been, for most American Jews, just beyond the orbit of their own experience and had in fact tested the boundaries of their own identity (see, for example, Philip Roth's early story "Eli the Fanatic"), became a focus of identification with the remnants of Jewish collectives elsewhere. After a generation or two of deliberate disengagement from the European motherland, the idea of "peoplehood" is reaffirmed partly through the imaginative return to ruined communities in Eastern Europe.

But all these processses are disciplined by the larger context in which the minor dramas of an ethnic subculture are being played out. American culture has largely resisted sectarian efforts to mythicize the Holocaust—primarily through monumental acts of commemoration—as a cluster of events somehow central to the American ethos or collective memory. Unlike the Israeli context, in which the narratives by and about survivors encounter and are subsumed in a powerful national myth of catastrophe and regeneration, the survivors and their dead are assimilated into American culture primarily as individuals whose stories are read as object lessons in the power and limits of the human spirit in the face of adversity.

BIBLIOGRAPHY

Ezrahi, S. D. "History Imagined." In *By Words Alone: The Holocaust in Literature.* Chicago, 1980.

Fussell, P. *Wartime: Understanding and Behavior in the Second World War.* New York, 1989.

Rosenfeld, I. "The Meaning of Terror" (1949). In *An Age of Enormity: Life and Writing in the Forties and Fifties,* edited by T. Solotaroff. Cleveland, 1957.

Rosenfeld, I. "Terror beyond Evil" (1948). In *An*

Age of Enormity: Life and Writing in the Forties and Fifties, edited by T. Solotaroff. Cleveland, 1957.

Sontag, S. "Fascinating Fascism." In *Under the Sign of Saturn.* New York, 1980.

SIDRA DEKOVEN EZRAHI

Yiddish Literature

In the period that followed the 1917 Russian Revolution and the demise of the classic authors of Yiddish literature (Mendele Moikher Seforim, Isaac Leib Peretz, and Sholem Aleichem), newly independent Poland and its capital, Warsaw, were lively centers of Yiddish literature and culture. Most of the literature appeared in contemporary Yiddish periodicals; in the 1920s and 1930s, up to the outbreak of World War II, more than seventeen hundred Yiddish periodicals and daily newspapers were being published in ninety-one places in Poland alone.

This flowering of modern Yiddish literature was halted by the Holocaust, at the point when a new generation of writers and editors were about to join its ranks. By a cautious estimate, at least 266 Jewish writers of fiction, most of them born in the twentieth century, lived in Poland under the Nazi regime. By 1939, most of the Polish-Hebrew writers had left for Israel, and many of the Yiddish writers had also emigrated from the country. That same estimate puts the number of bilingual writers (writing in both Hebrew and Yiddish) of fiction at 20 percent of the total.

During the Holocaust. The list of bilingual authors who wrote in the Holocaust period includes Israel-Dov Itzinger (Alter Shnur) of the Łódź ghetto; Peretz Opoczinski, Haim Yitzhak Bunin, Meir Czudner, Malkiel Lusternik, and Hillel ZEITLIN of the Warsaw ghetto; Hirsh GLIK of the Vilna ghetto; Eliezer Heyman of the Kovno ghetto; Avraham Eliezer Lerner of the Lvov ghetto; and Itzhak KATZENELSON of Łódź, who moved to the Warsaw ghetto during the war. Apart from a few writers who used both Yiddish and Polish, such as Ida Grodzianowski of the Vilna ghetto, Hinde Grin-Neiman (Helena Grin) of the JANÓWSKA (Lvov) camp, and Golda Mira (Lydia) of the Kraków ghetto, most of the Yiddish literature composed in the Holocaust was the work of authors who wrote in Yiddish only.

Yiddish literature continued to be written in the ghettos and camps despite the prevailing conditions and, indeed, reached new heights of expression and influence. An examination of 315 poems in Yiddish composed in the Holocaust and published in several collections reveals that they were the work of ninety authors and were created in over forty different places in eastern Europe—in ghettos, camps, and forests. There were at least six main centers of Yiddish literary creativity: Białystok, Warsaw, Vilna, Łódź, Kovno, and Kraków. This also indicates continuity from the prewar period: before the war, these cities were the leading centers of Yiddish newspapers and other periodical publications. The underground newspapers that were published in the Warsaw ghetto reflected the moods and opinions of a large part of the Jewish population. Many contributors, among them Katzenelson, Yehiel Lerer, and Hersh Danielowicz (Hershele), did not sign their names, using pseudonyms instead.

Like the underground press in Warsaw, which served as an indispensable source of information on world events, Yiddish literature played an important public role in providing spiritual sustenance to the ghetto population. This was not literature that could be put away and forgotten, nor was it a flight from reality into a world of fantasy. Yiddish literature in the Holocaust was usually a direct outgrowth of the cultural and social context in which it was conceived, seeking to face reality and to cope with it. Hardly any work by Katzenelson failed to reach the public in one way or another—through the underground press, theater performances, or public readings. The same was true of many of Abraham SUTZKEVER's literary creations in the Vilna ghetto, of Isaiah (Yeshayahu) SPIEGEL's songs, which were sung in the Łódź ghetto, and of the songs of many other poets that were sung in public in the ghettos and camps, as borne out by existing evidence. One striking example is Hirsh Glik's "Song of the Partisans," which gained popularity beyond the confines of the Vilna ghetto, was copied time and again, and underwent many changes before it became a folk song and the partisans' anthem, "by an unknown author," and was sung in the camps and the forests.

A close look at component parts of Yiddish literature in the Holocaust—the complete works of such writers as Katzenelson, Spiegel, Sutzkever, Simha Bunim Shaiewicz, and Joseph Zelikowicz, from the Łódź ghetto, and Yehoshua Perle, from Warsaw—reveals that this literature is intimately connected with the events of the time and the author's own biography; it cannot be fully grasped without knowing the historical background and the circumstances of the author's life. It is also an integral part of the internal life of the ghetto, and, together with mutual aid, the underground press, and preparations for an armed uprising, represents a further facet of the resistance offered by wide circles of the population. Yiddish literature is therefore a rich lode of information on the history of Jewish culture in the Holocaust.

Little is known about the Yiddish literature created in the extermination camps; it is a subject very difficult to document. It was hard to find a hiding place for literary works in these camps, and even those authors who survived came back empty-handed. This was true of Zami Feder, Mordecai Strigler, Hava Rosefarb, and Rivka Kwiatkowski, among other surviving writers. Some of Isaiah Spiegel's manuscripts were taken away from him in AUSCHWITZ; most of Hirsh Glik's manuscripts were lost. Still, a few of the works created in the camps were saved, such as Zalman Gradowski's *In Harts fun Gehenem* (In the Heart of Hell) and literary descriptions of Auschwitz. The texts of songs sung in CHEŁMNO, TREBLINKA, Auschwitz, and other extermination camps were published by Nahum Blumenthal.

The work of collecting and researching Yiddish literature in the Holocaust was begun while the ghettos were still in existence, and many of the extant literary documents were saved for posterity in underground archives in the Warsaw, Vilna, and Białystok ghettos and in other places where the initiative was taken to collect and copy them. In the ghettos the first steps were taken to research the lives of the authors and their works in the Holocaust, and articles were written on Yiddish literature, such as Zalman Kalmanowicz's comprehensive essay on Peretz, or Katzenelson's articles on the works of Seforim, which were published in the Warsaw ghetto underground press.

The corpus of Yiddish literature in the Holocaust, together with Jewish literature from that period in Polish, Hebrew, or any other language, has the force of a last will and testament. It is a literary heritage expressing emotions and thoughts that were intended not only for the time in which they were recorded.

YEHIEL SZEINTUCH

After the Holocaust. The Holocaust is the heart of post–World War II Yiddish literature. The destruction of European Jewry is the major subject of the Yiddish novel, short story, drama, poem, and chronicle.

The historian and sociologist seeking to unfold the multi-dimensional story of eastern European Jewry up to the end of World War II, in the large city and the shtetl (small town), will find in Yiddish literature a rich depository of scholarly data, intellectual treasure, and emotional outpouring. By 1950 alone, over ten thousand literary items had been published on the subject of the Holocaust (Yi., *khurbn*); tens of thousands more have since appeared, and a complete bibliography remains to be compiled.

Yiddish literature may be said to contain the entire tragic record of the Holocaust, in all its various manifestations. Among its writers are people of outstanding sensitivity, such as Abraham Sutzkever, Chaim Grade, Jacob Glatstein, Uri Zvi Greenberg, Aaron Zeitlin, Itzhak Katzenelson, Isaiah Spiegel, and K. Zetnik. The Yiddish they write is the language of the twelve million Jews who spoke it before World War II.

In poetry, the following works stand out: Zusman Segalowicz's two highly esteemed epics, *A Boym in Poyln* (A Tree in Poland) and *Dort* (There); H. Leivick's *In Treblinke Bin Ikh Nit Geven* (I Was Not in Treblinka); Itzik Manger's *Volkns afn Dakh* (Clouds on the Roof); *Iker Shokhakhti* (I've Forgotten the Main Point) by Melech Ravitch; *Ringen in Shtam* (Rings in the Tree Trunk) by Aryeh Shamri; *Kh'tu Dermonen* (I Recall) by Jacob Glatstein; *Lider fun Khurbn un Lider fun Gloybn* (Poems of Destruction and Poems of

Faith) by Aaron Zeitlin; *Der Melekh Dovid Iz Aleyn Geblibn* (King David Remained Alone) by Kadia Molodowsky; *Fun Heysn Ash* (From Hot Ashes) by Abraham Zak; *A Yid afn Yam* (A Jew on the Sea) by A. Leyeles (pseud. of Aaron Glanz); *Libshaft* (Love) by Yakow Frydman; *Di Gnod fun Vort* (The Mercy of the Word) by Rachel Korn; *Aroys fun Gan-Eydn* (Out of Paradise) by Eva Rosenfarb; *Yetsies Eyrope* (Exodus from Europe) by Joseph Rubinstein; *In der Velt fun Akeydes* (In the World of Sacrifices) by Hirsh Osherowitch; *Af Yener Zayt Vunder* (On the Other Side of Wonder) by Isaac Ianasovitch; *Likht fun Mayn Gas* (Light from My Street) by Iaacov Zvi Shargel; *Tsvishn Itst un Keynmol* (Between Now and Never) by Lajser Ajchenrand; *Mayne Intime Minutn* (My Intimate Minutes) by Moshe Berenshtein; *Tseshotene Kreln* (Scattered Beads) by Rivka Basman; *In Varshaver Geto in Khoydesh Nisn* (In the Warsaw Ghetto in the Month of Nisan) by Binem Heller; *Regnboygn Tsukopns* (Rainbow at My Head) by Moses Yungman; *Baym Pinkes fun Lublin* (From the Lublin Community Annals) by Moses Shulstein; *Mir Zaynen Do: Lider fun di Getos un Lagern* (We Are Here: Poems from the Ghettos and Camps), edited by Chana Gordon Mlotek and Malka Gordon Gottlieb; *Dos Letste Lid* (The Last Poem) by Moshe Broderson; *In Vaytn Elter* (In Old Age) by Joseph Papiernikow; *Papirene Zeglen* (Paper Sails) by Alexander Spiegelblatt; *In Shayn fun Brenendikn Dorn* (In the Light of the Burning Thornbush) by Nahman Rapp; *Yomer Gezang* (Song of Lament) by Solomon Warzager; *Lider* (Songs [of the Holocaust]) by Mordecai GEBIRTIG; *Dos Gezang fun Vilner Geto* (Songs of the Vilna Ghetto) by Shmaryahu (Shmerke) KACZERGINSKI; *Der Mames Nign* (The Mother's Melody) by Shloime Roitman; *Fun Mentsh tsu Mentsh* (From Man to Man) by Hadasa Rubin; and *Ariel in der Alter Heym* (Ariel in the Old World) by Yisrael Chaim Biletzky. Also noteworthy is the poetry of Abraham Reisin, in his book *Dortn* (There); Mani Leib's *Lider un Baladn* (Poems and Ballads); *Lider* (Poems) by Leizer Wolf; and *Megiles Rusland* (Scroll of Russia) by Joseph Rubinstein.

Yiddish poets in the Soviet Union have a special place in Holocaust literature. After the October Revolution the Jewish past had to be disavowed, and there could be no communication with the preceding Jewish generations. By the end of World War II this situation had undergone a change, which was expressed in the works of Yiddish poets.

Peretz Markish's great 600-page epic *Milkhome* (War) represents the moral stocktaking of a Jew in the Soviet Union; in his *Tsu a Yidisher Tentserin* (To a Jewish Dancer) a Jewish girl seeks a place to dance in; his *Roytarmeyishe Balades* (Red Army Ballads) celebrate the bravery of the Jewish soldier and Jewish partisan, individually and in groups; his novel *Dor Oys Dor Ayn* (Generations Come and Go) was translated into Hebrew (*Dor Holekh ve-Dor Ba*) by Eliyahu Meytes. David Hofstein's poems signify a return to Jewish tradition. To Hofstein, his paramount duty as a poet was to encourage the survivors, the motto of his poems being "Lo amut ki ekhye" ("I shall not die, but live"). One of his poems is based on a verse from Ezekiel (16:6): "When I passed by you and saw you wallowing in your blood I said to you, 'Live.' " In *Foter Komandir* (Father Commander) by Aaron Kushnirov, published in Moscow in 1948, one hears the echo of the battles in which the Jewish soldier has participated, on all the fronts. (Kushnirov was a frontline high Soviet army officer.) Leib Kvitko's book *Fayer af di Sonim* (Fire at the Enemy) and Izi Kharik's poem *Af der Vakh* (On Guard) are also based on Holocaust motifs. Even Itzik Fefer, who had been an unreserved supporter of the October Revolution, made his way back, in the poem *Shotns fun Varshaver Geto* (Warsaw Ghetto Shadows) and in his book *Shayn un Opshayn* (Light and Reflection), which has as its themes Rabbi Akiva, the Jewish homeland, and the shores of Haifa. A lyrical note is struck in Zelig Aksel'rod's *Heybene Shtilkeyt* (Sublime Silence) and in Arn Vergelis's *Oyg af Oyg* (Eye to Eye).

The poetic works of Shmuel Halkin abound with Jewish themes and a yearning for the Jewish past, in the wake of the Hitler horror. His poems are an expression of contemplation, emotion, and thought, devoted to the question of the future of the Jewish people. Halkin gives his own answer, in his book *Mayn Oytser* (My Treasure): "As long as the candle is still burning, the opportunity is still here." This saying, attributed to the nineteenth-century Hasidic rabbi Menachem Mendel of Kotsk, is frequently expressed in Halkin's poetry.

To sum up: the central theme of Yiddish poetry in the Soviet Union—man struggling for the realization of socialism the world over—gave way to that of the struggle of the Jewish people for its continued existence. The poetry returned to its Jewish national values, stressing the will to survive and demanding that a flowering Jewish culture and life be made available to the Jewish people.

This change of direction was not confined to poetry but also affected Yiddish prose. The two giants among the Soviet Yiddish writers, David Bergelson and Der Nister (pseud. of Pinchas Kahanovitch), openly returned to their Jewish origins. Bergelson's *Lo Amut ki Ekhye* (I Shall Not Die, but Live) and his play *Prints Ruveni* (Prince Ruveni) both contain the message that every people, including the Jews, has the right to a piece of land of its own. His *Geven Iz Nakht un Gevorn Iz Tog* (Night Became Day) and *Naye Dertseylungen* (New Stories) are lessons on the Holocaust. Der Nister's books *Flora* (Flora), *Vidervuks* (New Growth), and *Korbones* (Sacrifices) reveal a great Jewish author who, using Jewish metaphors, depicts aspects of the Holocaust on a broad epic canvas. Hirsh Orland, an activist of the JEWISH ANTIFASCIST COMMITTEE, in his *Ukrainishe Erd* (Ukrainian Soil) provides insight into a Jew who builds his life on the soil of the Ukraine. Samuel Godiner, in his story *Eyner Aleyn in Feld* (All Alone in the Field), describes the loneliness of the Jew during the war. Samuel Gordon, in *Milkhome Tsayt* (Time of War), reveals that the major theme of his stories is *bitokhn* (trust) in the Almighty; Noakh Lur'e, in *Bay der Ofener Grub* (At the Open Grave), mourns over his people; Samuel Persov, in *Dayn Nomen Iz Folk* (Your Name Is People), describes the life of Jewish partisans. Itzik Kipnis wrote *Di Tsayt Geyt* (Time Passes) and *Tsum Nayem Lebn* (To a New Life), and after the war took to wearing a Star of David emblem on the lapel of his jacket; Iosif Rabin wrote *Mir Lebn* (We Are Alive), a proclamation of a new life; Natan Zabare, in *Af Gekirtste Vegn* (On Shortened Roads), recalls Jewish historical figures, mainly the medieval philosopher Maimonides, implying that nothing must be consigned to oblivion.

The documentary writings of Yiddish literature record the trials and tribulations of the Jewish people and the individual Jew, as depicted by Yehiel Brogin in *Fun Vilne biz Yisroel* (From Vilna to Israel); Sh. Bar-Ozi in *Mayn Yesurim Veg: Zikhroynes fun di Turme un Lagern Yorn in Sovyet Rusland* (My Path of Suffering: Recollections of the Prison and Camp Years in Soviet Russia); Hersh Smoliar in *Sovyetishe Yidn unter Geto Parkn* (Soviet Jews under Ghetto Parks); Salomon Strauss-Marko in *Poylishe Yidn in di Velder* (Polish Jews in the Forests); Aharon Rozin in *Mayn Veg Aheym: Memoarn fun Asir-Tsiyon in Ratnfarband* (My Way Home: Memoirs of a Prisoner of Zion in the Soviet Union); Adolf Abraham Berman in *Vos der Goyrl Hot mir Bashert: Yidn in Varshe, 1939–1942* (What Fate Had in Store for Me: Jews in Warsaw, 1939–1942); Rachel Auerbach in *Varshaver Tsavoes* (Warsaw Testaments); Mordecai Strigler in *Verk "Tse"* (Factory "C") and *Maydanek* (Majdanek); Szie Czechewer in *Neshome-Likht* (Memorial Candle); Zivia LUBETKIN in *In Umkum un Oyfshtand* (In Defeat and Resistance); Esther Rosenthal-Schnaiderman in *Af Vegn un Umvegn: Zikhroynes, Gesheenishn, Perzenlikhkeytn* (On Ways and Byways: Recollections, Events, Personalities; 2 vols.); Berl Mark in *Megiles Oyshvits* (Auschwitz Scroll); Symcha Polakiewicz in *Inem Poylishn Zhungl* (In the Polish Jungle); Jonas Turkow in *Der Sof fun Iluzyes* (The End of Illusions); Toni Solomon-Maaravi in *Teg un Veg: A Khronik fun Yetsies Rumenye nokh der Hitler-Mapole* (Days and Ways: A Chronicle of the Exodus from Romania after Hitler's Defeat); Levi Shalit in *A Yid in der Velt* (A Jew in the World); Mark Dworzecki in *Yerushelayim de-Lite in Kamf un Umkum* (The Jerusalem of Lithuania [Vilna] in Struggle and Defeat); and Abraham Zak in *Geven a Yidish Poyln* (There Was a Jewish Poland).

In Yiddish fiction, the following are some of the outstanding works: *Borves iber Shney* (Barefoot on the Snow) and *Der Prayz fun Yenem Broyt: Dertseylungen* (The Price of That Bread: Stories) by Meir Yelin; *Gzar Din* (Fateful Judgment) by Mordechai Tsanin (part of a series); *Fremde Velder—Eygene Erd* (Foreign Forests—Our Own Soil) by Jechiel

Granatsztajn; *Erev* (Evening), a novel by Elye Shekhtman; *Di Yidishe-Poylishe Milkhome: Otobiografishe Dertseylungen* (The Jewish-Polish War: Autobiographical Stories) by Mendel Mann; *In Vayser Farfalnkeyt: Roman fun Sovetish Lager far Tsvangsarbet* (In the White Hopelessness: Novel of a Soviet Forced-Labor Camp) by Jechiel Hofer; *In Dayn Blut Zolstu Lebn* (In Your Blood, May You Live) and *Mit Blinde Trit iber der Erd* (Over the Earth with Blind Steps) by Leib Rochman; *Ash-Shtern* (Star of Ashes) by K. Zetnik; *Der Khurver Dor* (The Destroyed Generation) by Leib Fininberg; *Di Antloyfers* (The Escapees) and *Fun Gsise tsu Lebn* (From the Deathbed to Life) by Rachmil Bryks; *Ven Poyln Iz Gefaln* (When Poland Fell) by Joseph Opotashu; and *Der Boym fun Lebn* (The Tree of Life) by Eva Rosenfarb.

A special chapter is constituted by the YIZKOR BOOKS (memorial books) of the communities destroyed in the Holocaust; 800 such books, commemorating as many destroyed communities, had been published by 1982. Between the two world wars many Jews emigrated from eastern Europe to other countries, taking along photographs, newspapers, letters, and a variety of documents and souvenirs; all of these contain material of important historical value. The *Landsmannschaften* (organizations based on common origin from a particular place or region) have sponsored many of these memorial books, which have served to commemorate the destroyed communities.

Yiddish literature in its varied artistic forms records a Jewish life that no longer exists and the terrible conditions of the Holocaust years. It has proved an inspiration to succeeding generations, providing insights into the culture and heroism of a world that is no more.

YSRAEL CH. BILETZKY

BIBLIOGRAPHY

Lahad, E., Y. Szeintuch, and Z. Shinnur, eds. *Literary Creations in Yiddish and Hebrew in the Ghetto.* Naharia, Israel, 1985. (In Hebrew and Yiddish.)

Leftwich, J., ed. *The Golden Peacock: A Worldwide Treasury of Yiddish Poetry.* New York, 1961.

Niger, S. "Yiddish Poets of the Third Destruction." *Reconstructionist* 13/10 (27 June 1947): 13–18.

Szeintuch, Y., ed. *List of Diaries and Manuscripts in Yiddish That Were Published between the Two World Wars.* Jerusalem, 1986. (In Hebrew and Yiddish.)

LITHUANIA, southernmost of the Baltic states; since 1940 the Lithuanian SSR. In the thirteenth century the Lithuanians, who fought the Slavs and the German Teutonic Order, founded a strong state. During the course of the thirteenth to fifteenth centuries Lithuania became a great power, extending from the Baltic Sea to the Black Sea and encompassing what is today Belorussia, most of the areas of the Ukraine, and broad expanses of western Russia. The majority of the inhabitants of Lithuania were then Slavs. In the late fourteenth century Lithuania became allied with Poland, and in 1569 the two countries united, with Lithuania as the lesser partner in the united state. In the third partition of Poland, in 1795, Lithuania was annexed to Russia. Between the two world wars it was an independent country.

Lithuania was in conflict with Poland (which in 1920 occupied Vilna, the historic capital) and later with Germany, because Lithuania controlled MEMEL (Klaipėda), most of whose inhabitants were Germans and which had a special status as an autonomous territory. Independent Lithuania suffered from economic and social problems, had many national minorities (constituting about a fifth of all the inhabitants), and was politically unstable. After a military coup in 1926, Antanas Smetona became president and leader of the fascist Gelezinis Vilkas (Iron Wolf) organization, and Augustinas Voldemaras was prime minister. In 1929 Voldemaras was dismissed, and Smetona became sole ruler.

Jews lived in Lithuania beginning in the fourteenth century, and from the seventeenth century the country's yeshivas (rabbinical academies) attained worldwide fame. In the nineteenth century Lithuania was a center of many Jewish religious and cultural trends, and from the end of the nineteenth century, of Zionism and the BUND. In the wake of the tsarist-instigated pogroms of 1881 and 1882, many Lithuanian Jews emigrated, principally to the United States and also to South Africa. Of the masses of Jews who were expelled from Lithuania to Russia during World War I, many never returned. About 150,000 Jews lived in independent Lithuania at the time of its establishment after World War I.

In the first years of Lithuanian independence the Jews enjoyed national and cultural autonomy within the structure of the government, and a Jewish minister was responsible for their affairs. Even after this autonomy was repealed in 1924, the Jews continued to maintain their own Hebrew and Yiddish educational network. However, the authorities excluded the Jews from various sectors of the economy, and there was strong antisemitism in the country. Between the two world wars more than twenty thousand Jews left Lithuania, almost half of them emigrating to Palestine.

On March 23, 1939, Germany annexed Memel. The agreements between Germany and the Soviet Union in the wake of the NAZI-SOVIET PACT placed Lithuania in the Soviet sphere of influence, and on October 10 of that year, Lithuania was compelled to permit the establishment of Soviet bases on its territory. Vilna, together with a surrounding area of about 3,475 square miles (9,000 sq km), was restored to Lithuania (from Poland) on October 30. On June 15, 1940, the Soviet army assumed control of Lithuania, and about seven weeks later the country was officially annexed to the Soviet Union as the Lithuanian SSR.

Among the underground groups formed in reaction to the Sovietization of the country and of the different aspects of life were extremist nationalist groups such as the LIETUVIU AKTYVISTU FRONTAS (Lithuanian Activist Front), which strongly supported Nazi Germany. On June 14, 1941, the Soviets exiled tens of thousands of Lithuanians, who were defined as "enemies of the people" and politically or socially unreliable. About a week later, on June 22, the Germans invaded the Soviet Union and occupied all of Lithuania; Lithuanian underground activists followed in the wake of the retreating Soviet army. In the few days it took to occupy Lithuania, most of the leaders and activists of the Soviet rule and of the Lithuanian Communist party fled into the Soviet Union, together with multitudes of citizens who did not wish to remain under Nazi occupation. From their numbers the Lithuanian Rifle Division (No. 16) was formed in the Soviet army, with Jews constituting more than 50 percent of its membership. In various branches of the Lithuanian partisan movement, the percentage of Jews was far greater than in the general population.

Most of the Lithuanians welcomed the Germans, and many collaborated with them. Nonetheless, their hope of renewed political independence was disappointed. Lithuania became part of the REICHSKOMMISSARIAT OSTLAND (Reich Commissariat for Ostland), and its name was changed to Generalbezirk Litauen (General District of Lithuania). It was headed by a German *Generalkommissar* who had a kind of ministerial council (*Generalrat*), consisting of well-known Lithuanian personalities under Gen. Petras (Peter) Kubiliunas, and supporters of Voldemaras. The Lithuanian national army was not reconstituted, and several of its former officers and soldiers were incorporated into the Lithuanian police battalions. In the wake of the German collapse on the Stalingrad front, the relations of the Lithuanians with the Nazi occupation authorities deteriorated. When the Soviet army returned to Lithuania in the summer and fall of 1944, however, many Lithuanians fled to Germany. With the German expulsion from Memel in January 1945, Nazi rule in all parts of Lithuania came to an end, and Lithuania became once more a Soviet republic.

When Vilna and its vicinity were returned to Lithuania in October 1939, the Jewish population of the country grew by about one hundred thousand. This number included some fifteen thousand refugees from occupied Poland. The Jews of Lithuania then totaled approximately a quarter of a million, about 10 percent of the overall population.

Frustrated by the 1939 Nazi agreement with the Soviet Union, which took away Lithuanian sovereignty, the Lithuanian populace greatly increased attacks on Jews and Jewish property. Certain incidents, as when windows were shattered in several towns on the same day, were obviously organized on a national scale. With the entry of the Lithua-

Between June 25 and July 8, 1941, thousands of Jews from Kovno were rounded up by Lithuanian militiamen and taken to the "Seventh Fort," one of a number of old forts on the outskirts of Kovno that served as prisons. Every day Lithuanian guards removed groups of Jews, beat them, raped the women, and then shot the Jews. Here, the militiamen watch the arrival of a contingent of Jewish women.

nian army into Vilna, pogroms were conducted against the Jews with the blessing of the new government, and about two hundred Jews were injured.

The situation of Lithuanian Jewry changed dramatically when the country became a Soviet republic. On the one hand, the Jews were given appropriate representation in the government bodies, the institutions of higher education were opened to them unrestrictedly, and they were allowed to join the local and central official establishment, previously closed to them. On the other hand, they were affected more than others by several of the processes of Sovietization, particularly in the economic sphere: 83 percent of the commercial establishments and 57 percent of the factories that were nationalized belonged to Jews; the Hebrew educational system, encompassing 80 percent of the Jewish pupils, was abolished; the renowned rabbinical academies of Telz, Slobodka, Kelme, and other places were closed down; and Jewish workers were compelled to work on the Sabbath and on Jewish holidays. Political bodies were also closed, apart from the Communist organizations, and almost all the cultural and welfare institutions were shut down and many of their leaders and activists arrested. In the June 14, 1941, mass deportation of "enemies of the people," about seven thousand Jews were exiled to Siberia and other areas of Soviet Asia, 3 percent of all the Jews in Lithuania, as compared to only 1 percent of the rest of the population. Deported heads of families were interned in labor camps and many died as a result of the harsh conditions.

Although the Jews suffered greatly and were hard hit by Soviet rule, the Lithuanians regarded them as supporters of the Soviet regime that had enslaved their country. The Lithuanian Activist Front agitated against the Jews. The bulletins it circulated before the anticipated Nazi invasion contained concrete threats against the Jews, whose fate had already been decided. Upon the invasion in June 1941, many Lithuanian Jews desperately attempted to flee for their lives in the wake of the retreating Soviet army. However, because of German shelling, difficulties in crossing the old Soviet border, and attacks by Lithuanian underground groups, only about 15,000 Jews succeeded in reaching the Soviet Union. More than a third of these fought the Nazis actively. The overwhelming majority of Lithuanian Jewry, about 220,000 people, remained in their homes. Even before the arrival of the Germans, the Lithuanians carried out pogroms against the Jews. According to findings based on reliable testimonies from 214 localities, pogroms occurred in at least 40 places, in most of which Jews were killed and injured. In at least 25 localities, rapes took place, and in 36, rabbis were cruelly abused.

The wave of murders and assaults grew with the entry of the German forces, and principally of Einsatzkommando 3 of Einsatzgruppe A. Beginning on July 3, 1941, it implemented a systematic program of exterminating all of Lithuanian Jewry, in accordance with an exact timetable. Many of the stages of the extermination, such as confining and guarding the victims, and transporting them to the massacre sites, were carried out by Lithuanians, including soldiers and policemen. Before being killed the victims were made to perform physical exercises, to sing and dance, or to strike each other, in front of their Lithuanian neighbors, public figures, and heads of the local intelligentsia, who took great delight in this spectacle. In forty-eight localities, individual Jews offered concrete or symbolic resistance. But only in a few instances did any of the victims succeed in escaping from the murder site. In July and August 1941 the overwhelming majority of the Jews of the provinces were slaughtered. From September to November, most of the Jews in the large cities, who had been interned in ghettos, were liquidated in a similar fashion.

By late 1941 only forty thousand Jews remained in all of Lithuania, and they were concentrated in four ghettos—those of Vilna, KOVNO, ŠIAULIAI, and Švenčionys—and in several labor camps. About eight hundred Jews from the towns of western Lithuania were in a labor camp at Heidekrug, in the Memel district. In 1943 the survivors were transferred to AUSCHWITZ and from there to WARSAW, to work on clearing the ruins of the ghetto. In the summer and fall of that year the ghettos of Vilna and Švenčionys were liquidated, and those of Kovno and Šiauliai became concentration camps, with branches in their vicinities. Some fifteen thousand of the Jews were transferred to labor camps in LATVIA and ESTONIA, where they died, and about five thousand Jews, principally old people, women, and children, were sent to extermination camps. In the second half of 1943 and early in 1944 more than two thousand Jews escaped from the ghettos and camps. About half of them joined partisan units. The rest, mainly people with families, found hiding places in monasteries and in the homes of non-Jews in cities and towns. Shortly before withdrawing from Lithuania in the summer of 1944, the Germans transferred about ten thousand of the Jews of Kovno and Šiauliai to concentration camps in Germany. Many who attempted to resist were murdered. The retreating Nazis were accompanied by numerous Lithuanian collaborators and killers of Jews.

When Germany surrendered in May 1945, a few Lithuanian Jews, interned in the concentration camps, remained alive. The overall number of Lithuanian Jews who survived in the area under Nazi rule is estimated at eight thousand. In places under Soviet rule, about 10 percent of all the Jews living in Lithuania in early 1941 survived, including the fighters in the ranks of the partisans.

Soon after the liberation of Lithuania, in the second half of 1944, the Soviet authorities made great efforts to uncover mass-murder sites of prisoners of war and civilians, and through inquiry commissions to determine, insofar as possible, the circumstances of the slaughter and the number and identity of the victims. At some of the sites monuments were erected with inscriptions in Russian and Lithuanian. The victims were generally commemorated only as Soviet citizens, without mention of their ethnic affiliation. In a few places, after repeated requests to the authorities, Jewish survivors who had raised money were allowed to erect monuments with inscriptions in Yiddish and in Hebrew.

In the early postwar years and later, many of the Lithuanians who had collaborated with the Nazi occupation authorities were identified, including many killers of Jews. Some were tried and received sentences ranging from a defined period of imprisonment to execution. The Lithuanian and other killers who had fled to Germany and to countries overseas were tried *in absentia*. Some of them not only found refuge there but also integrated successfully into the life of these countries. Only in the 1980s did the American, Canadian, and Australian governments begin to pursue the killers of the Jews, and several were brought to trial. Lithuanian immigrants in these and other countries fiercely opposed these steps, raising money and making political and legal efforts to frustrate the bringing to trial of collaborators.

[*See also* Policiniai Batalionai.]

BIBLIOGRAPHY

Arad, Y. *Ghetto in Flames: The Struggle and Destruction of the Jews in Vilna in the Holocaust.* Jerusalem, 1980.

Levin, D. *Between the Hammer and the Sickle: Baltic Jewry under Soviet Rule during World War II.* Jerusalem, 1983. (In Hebrew.)

Levin, D. *Fighting Back: Lithuanian Jewry's Armed Resistance to the Nazis, 1941–1945.* New York, 1987.

Misiunas, R. J. *The Baltic States: Years of Dependence, 1940–1980.* London, 1980.

Myllyniemi, S. *Die Neuordnung der baltischen Länder 1941–1944: Zum nationalsozialistischen Inhalt der deutschen Besatzungspolitik.* Helsinki, 1973.

Neshamit, S. "Rescue in Lithuania during the Nazi Occupation." In *Rescue Attempts during the Holocaust.* Proceedings of the Second Yad Vashem International Historical Conference, edited by Y. Gutman and E. Zuroff, pp. 289–332. Jerusalem, 1977.

DOV LEVIN

LITHUANIAN ACTIVIST FRONT. *See* Lietuviu Aktyvistu Frontas.

LITHUANIAN POLICE BATTALIONS. *See* Policiniai Batalionai.

LITVINOV, MAKSIM MAKSIMOVICH (orig., Meir Walach; 1876–1951), Soviet diplomat. Born in Białystok into a bourgeois Jewish family, Litvinov joined the Russian Social Democrats in 1898. Arrested in 1901, he escaped from prison in 1902 and fled to Switzerland. In 1903 he joined the Bolsheviks, becoming, in 1908, the Bolshevik representative in the Socialist International and head of the Bolshevik party branch in London. His wife came from a middle-class English Jewish family.

From 1918 to 1921, Litvinov was a collegium member of the Commissariat for Foreign Affairs. In 1920 he signed the first Soviet international treaty (with Estonia) and became the first Soviet ambassador to Estonia. The following year he was appointed deputy to People's Commissar for Foreign Affairs Georgi Chicherin, whose chief rival he became and whom he replaced in 1930, with Stalin's support.

Litvinov championed the campaign for collective security; he played a key role in the United States' recognition of the USSR in 1933 and in the Soviet entry, in 1934, into the League of Nations, where he served as Soviet representative. He was the target of vicious Nazi attacks claiming that he, together with others, constituted the real Soviet leadership, and that Stalin was their puppet.

In May 1939 Litvinov was relieved of all his positions—a harbinger of the NAZI-SOVIET PACT. In February 1941 he was expelled from the party's Central Committee, narrowly escaping arrest. After the German invasion of the Soviet Union in June 1941, Litvinov was appointed Deputy People's Commissar for Foreign Affairs and also Soviet ambassador to the United States, a position he held until 1943.

Litvinov's activity ceased in 1943, although he formally retained his position as deputy commissar until 1946. According to Nikita Khrushchev, Stalin had considered the possibility of assassinating Litvinov.

BIBLIOGRAPHY

Bishop, D. G. *The Roosevelt-Litvinov Agreements: The American View.* Syracuse, N.Y., 1965.

Pope, A. U. *Maxim Litvinoff.* New York, 1943.

Roberts, H. L. "Maxim Litvinov." In *The Diplomats, 1919–1939,* edited by G. A. Craig and F. Gilbert, pp. 344–377. Princeton, 1953.

MIKHAIL AGURSKY

"LIVING SPACE." *See* Lebensraum.

ŁÓDŹ, city in POLAND, about 75 miles (121 km) southwest of Warsaw. In 1827 the population of Łódź was 2,800, of whom 400 were Jews. The city grew rapidly as a result of the development of industry, especially textiles. The Jewish population too grew considerably. Before long Łódź became Poland's second largest city, next only to Warsaw, and the city's Jews came to constitute the second largest Jewish community in Poland, after Warsaw. By 1857 the Łódź population was 25,000, including 2,900 Jews; by the end of the nineteenth century it had risen to 300,000, a third being Jews; and on the eve of World War II it was 665,000, of which 34 percent (223,000) were Jews. Nearly 55 percent of the population were Poles, but Łódź also had a sizable German population, amounting to 10 percent of the total.

The Jews contributed much to the growth of the city. Many of the industrial enterprises were founded by Jews, and more than 50 percent of the Jewish population derived their livelihood from industry. A Jewish proletariat came into being, a fact accounting for much of the Łódź Jewish community's unique character.

Łódź was also an important center of Jewish culture. Its network of Jewish schools included three Hebrew secondary schools (*Gymnasien*), one of them the first such school to be founded in Poland (in 1912); yeshivas (rabbinical academies); libraries; Jewish theaters; and sports clubs. Outstanding intellectuals and artists lived in Łódź, among them the poets and writers Itzhak KATZENELSON, Moshe Broderson, Jacob Cohen, and David Frischmann, and the painters Arthur Szyk, Maurycy Hirszenberg, Leopold Pilichowski, and Jacob (Yankel) Adler. The pianist Artur Rubinstein and the Israeli scientists Aharon Katzir and Ephraim Katzir (Kaczalski; the latter also served as Israel's fourth president) came from Łódź. Before the outbreak of World War II, the city had two Yiddish and two Polish daily newspapers. There was a great deal of political and social activity among Łódź Jewry; of special importance were the social-welfare programs, which established Jewish hospitals, orphanages, and other institutions.

Early Stage of Occupation. On September 8, 1939, the Germans occupied Łódź, making it part of the WARTHEGAU, which in turn was annexed to the Reich. On April 11, 1940, the occupiers renamed the city Litzmannstadt (after the German general Karl Litzmann, who had conquered it in World War I); most of the German documents concerning the Łódź ghetto refer to it as the "Litzmannstadt ghetto."

Brutal persecution of the Jews began as soon as the city was occupied. It was organized largely by Einsatzkommando 2, under Sturmbannführer Fritz Liphardt, joined by a Selbstschutz (Self-Defense) unit manned by

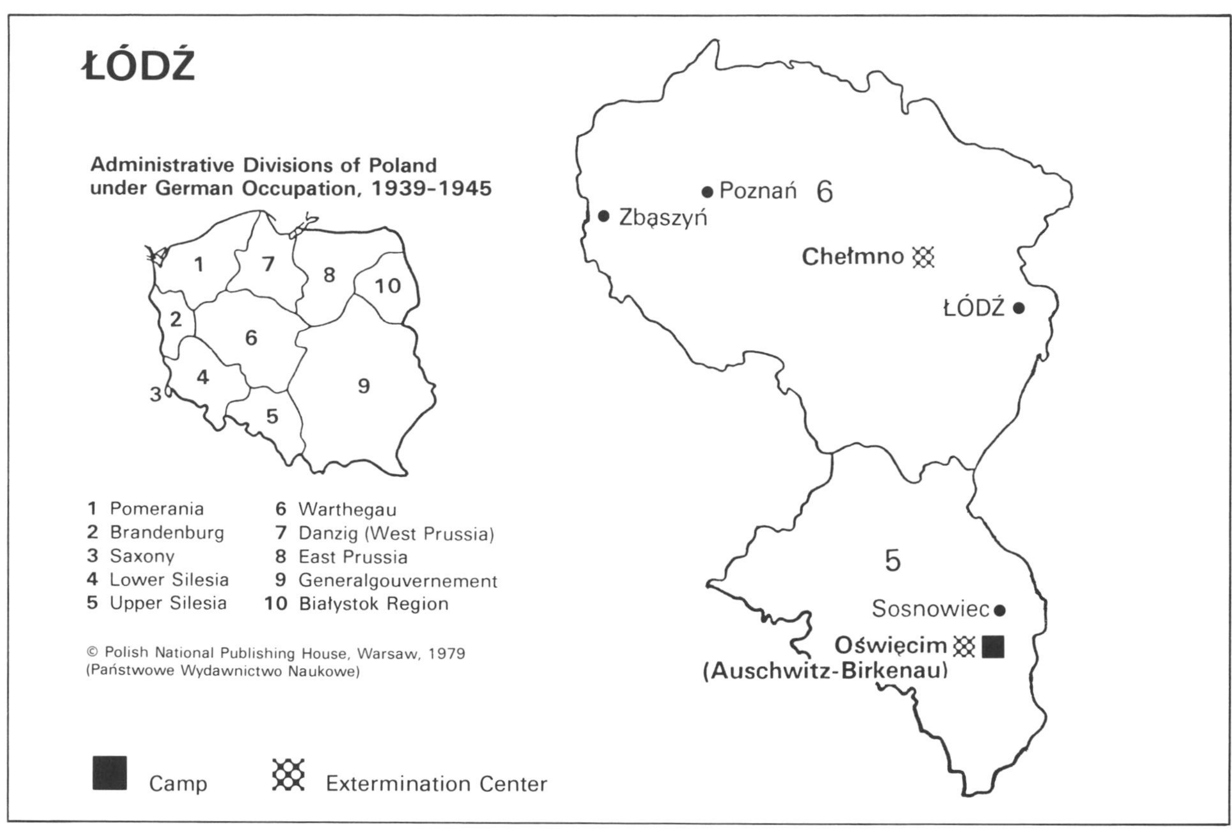

fifteen hundred local VOLKSDEUTSCHE (ethnic Germans) and organized under the command of a Standartenführer Teufel. The riots, the abduction of people for forced labor, and the harassment of passersby in the streets all soon led to the collapse of the economic and social life of the Jews in the city. Jewish public and cultural institutions were liquidated overnight. German soldiers and local German inhabitants entered Jewish shops and houses and walked off with whatever took their fancy, with no one to restrain them. The German authorities issued one decree after another designed to make life miserable for the Jews. Jews were confined to their homes from 5:00 p.m. to 8:00 a.m.

On September 18, 1939, a number of decrees were promulgated that struck at the heart of the economic life of the Jews. All Jewish-owned bank accounts were blocked, and Jewish cash holdings were restricted to 2,000 zlotys (the equivalent of $377 at the time). Jews could no longer engage in the textile business, and Jewish enterprises were put in the hands of commissars, meaning, in effect, that they were confiscated and taken over by Germans. Jews could no longer use public transportation, could not leave the city without special permission, and were not allowed to have cars, radios, and various other items in their possession. Synagogue services were outlawed, and Jews had to keep their shops open on Jewish holidays, including the New Year and the Day of Atonement.

On November 9, Łódź was officially annexed to the Reich, a step followed by an intensification of the German terrorization of the Jews and Poles. Several thousand Jews and Poles were arrested and taken to the Radogoszcz prison, on the outskirts of the city. Soon afterward some of them were killed there and others deported to concentration camps in Germany.

From November 15 to 17 the Germans destroyed all the synagogues in the city, among them the magnificent Reform Synagoga on Kościuszko Boulevard and the Altschule synagogue, dating from 1809, on Wolborska Street. On November 4 the Jews were ordered to wear a yellow armband. This instruction was amended on November 17, and Jews now instead had to wear yellow badges (*see* BADGE, JEWISH) on the right side of their clothing, front and back, in the form of a Star of David.

From the very beginning of the occupation Jews were subject to expulsions, which came in waves. In the first few weeks hundreds of Jewish apartments were confiscated and their tenants deported, without prior notice. On November 12, a decision was taken to launch mass deportations, which were to affect thirty thousand Jews and an equal number of Poles. By March 1940, seventy thousand Jews had left the city. Among them were those who fled of their own volition to the Soviet-controlled areas in the east, and others who believed that the situation of the Jews was better in Warsaw and other cities of the GENERALGOUVERNEMENT. However, most of the Jews were deported by the Germans, who intended to reduce the Jewish population substantially or even remove it completely.

In October and November 1941, about twenty thousand Jews were deported to Łódź from Germany (Berlin, Hamburg, Frankfurt, Düsseldorf, Cologne, and Emden and its environs) and from Luxembourg, Vienna, and Prague. Here, a woman deportee is "tagged" by a Jewish policeman upon arrival in Łódź.

On October 13 and 14, 1939, the Germans appointed a JUDENRAT (Jewish Council), which in Łódź was called an Ältestenrat (Council of Elders), with Mordechai Chaim RUMKOWSKI as its chairman. On November 11 all thirty-one members of the Ältestenrat, with the exception of Rumkowski, were arrested and put into the Radogoszcz prison. Eight were released after a time, and the others were all killed. Rumkowski was ordered to set up a new Ältestenrat, which was to operate under the strict supervision of the Gestapo.

Establishing the Ghetto. On December 10, 1939, Friedrich Übelhör, governor of the Kalisz-Łódź district, issued a secret order for the establishment of a ghetto in the northern section of Łódź, where the Jewish Baluty slum quarter was situated. Übelhör's order was addressed to the German authorities in the city, who were to take an active part in setting up the ghetto. After listing in detail the assignment that each Nazi authority was to carry out, the order stated, in its final passage: "Needless to say, the establishment of a ghetto is only a provisional phase . . . the ultimate goal must be the total purge of this scourge." On February 8, 1940, the chief of police in Łódź, SS-Brigadeführer Johannes Schäfer, issued a public announcement on the establishment of the ghetto. This was followed by the expulsion of the Jews from the other parts of the city and their removal to the ghetto area, a process accompanied by a further intensification of robbery, harassment, and murder.

The ghetto, blocked off on April 30, 1940, comprised an area of 1.54 square miles (4 sq km), of which only .96 square miles (2.5 sq km) was built up. Approximately 164,000 Łódź Jews were forced in. The density of population in the ghetto area was now seven times as great as it had been before the war. There were a total of 48,100 rooms in the ghetto area, most in wooden houses, with no running water and no sewers. The ghetto area was divided into three parts by two major thoroughfares that passed through it and served as the links between the ghetto and the other city quarters. The three parts of the ghetto were made accessible to one another

The bridge over Zgierska Street that connected the two parts of the Łódź ghetto. The street itself was not part of the ghetto. [Mendel Grossman]

by means of bridges that were constructed over the two thoroughfares.

In 1941 and 1942 some 38,500 Jews from outside Łódź were moved into the ghetto: 20,000 from Germany, Austria, Czechoslovakia, and Luxembourg, and 18,500 from provincial towns in the Warthegau. The total number of persons who passed through the ghetto was now 202,500, to which must be added the 2,300 babies born there, bringing the total to 204,800 men, women, and children.

Nazi Administration. The concerns of the Łódź ghetto were in the hands of a ghetto administration (Gettoverwaltung) headed by Hans BIEBOW. On May 25, 1940, Biebow issued orders for factories to be set up in the ghetto (called *Arbeitsressorte,* or work sections). Provided with very cheap labor, these factories were to serve the Nazis as a source of easy profits and exploitation. The Jews in the ghetto, cut off as they were from all other possible sources of livelihood, were prepared to work for no more than a loaf of bread and some soup. The exploitation of the Jews imprisoned in the ghetto yielded a profit to the ghetto administration estimated at 350 million reichsmarks ($14,000,000).

Guarding the ghetto and ensuring absolute order in it was the task of special SS units commanded by Standartenführer Walter Rudolf Keuck. A special KRIMINALPOLIZEI (Criminal Police) headquarters, called Kriminalpolizei Sonderkommissariat Ghetto, was set up inside the ghetto, under the command of Bruno Obersteiner and Wilhelm Neumann. This police unit, which was notorious for its brutal behavior, was primarily concerned with ferreting out Jewish possessions and confiscating them. The monetary value of the items it confiscated in 1941 and 1942 is estimated at 20 million reichsmarks ($800,000). The Gestapo section for Jewish affairs in Łódź (Section II B 4, later redesignated IV B 4, headed by Günther Fuchs and Gerhard Müller) was also involved in the administration of the ghetto.

The German authorities allowed the Ältestenrat, and primarily its chairman, Rumkowski, wide powers in the organization of

TABLE 1. *Factories in the Łódź Ghetto*

DATE	TOTAL GHETTO POPULATION (APPROXIMATE)	PRODUCTION UNITS (FACTORIES)	NUMBER OF EMPLOYEES
July 1942	102,000	74	68,986
August 1942	101,000	91	77,982
January 1943	87,000	96	78,946

the ghetto's internal life. The Ältestenrat's main task was to organize the operation of the factories. It regarded the establishment of factories as the only possible means of saving the ghetto population from unemployment and starvation, imprisoned and isolated as it was from the rest of the world, and the Ältestenrat approached the task with great energy. Ninety-six factories were established in the ghetto, the majority producing textiles; in 1942 and 1943 they employed over seventy thousand workers (*see* Table 1). Rumkowski greatly expanded the Ältestenrat offices, its staff growing from fifty-five hundred in February 1941 to thirteen thousand in August 1942. The services provided by the Ältestenrat involved housing and sanitation, as well as the distribution of the small quantities of food permitted by the German authorities. Until October 1941 the Ältestenrat also ran a school system, consisting of forty-five elementary schools and two secondary schools, which were attended by fifteen thousand pupils. Of special importance were the health services; five hospitals were in operation in the ghetto up until the summer of 1942. Internal order in the ghetto was maintained by the Ältestenrat's JÜDISCHER ORDNUNGSDIENST (Jewish ghetto police), whose maximum strength was 530. The Ältestenrat also administered a prison, on Czarnieckiego Street.

Living Conditions in the Ghetto. The Łódź ghetto had a high mortality rate owing to the extremely poor conditions there. Overcrowding and substandard sanitary facilities led to epidemics, especially of typhus fever. In winter, the severe shortages of fuel caused intolerable suffering from the cold. The population also lacked clothing, especially shoes, and most of the inmates had to wear wooden clogs. The worst affliction of all, however, was starvation, and this was the chief problem the ghetto had to contend with throughout its existence. The average daily food ration per person was less than 1,100 calories.

Some 43,500 persons—21 percent of all the inmates—died in the ghetto from starvation, cold, and disease. The mortality rate reached its peak in 1942. The smaller number of deaths from "natural" causes in 1943 was due to the fact that by then most of the children and elderly people had died or been deported. Even so, the 1943 mortality rate was six times that in the prewar period.

Deportations. More devastating than even the mass deaths and the hunger from which the ghetto population suffered were the deportations. In the first stage, deportations were to forced-labor camps outside the ghetto, and from there the Jews were sent on to extermination camps. Generally speaking, the Jews imprisoned in the ghetto were not aware of the final destination of the deportations. The first deportations were launched in December 1940 and continued until late June 1942. A total of seventy-two hundred men were deported to forced-labor camps in the Poznań area and were put to work on the construction of a highway from Poznań to Frankfurt an der Oder. Most of them perished

Jews of the Łódź ghetto on their way to the railway station to be deported (1942).

Lunch break in one of the Łódź ghetto workshops. [Mendel Grossman]

as a result of the intolerable working conditions.

Beginning on January 16, 1942, the deportations from the Łódź ghetto went directly to the CHEŁMNO extermination camp. The German authorities forced Rumkowski to draw up lists of candidates for deportation and to set up assembly points for the deportees on the edge of the ghetto. Rumkowski tried—in vain, as it turned out—to persuade the Germans to reduce the number of deportees. From the assembly points, reinforced German units accompanied the deportees to Chełmno; on the day of their arrival there, or on the following day, all were killed in GAS VANS. In the period from January to May 1942, fifty-five thousand Jews and five thousand Gypsies, who had been temporarily interned in Łódź, were deported to Chełmno. (The Gypsies had been temporarily accommodated in a block of buildings separated from the ghetto.)

Between September 5 and 12 of that year, a second deportation operation to Chełmno took place. This time the Germans did not require lists from the Ältestenrat: German forces entered the ghetto, blocked off one section after another, and dragged the Jews out of their homes, using extremely brutal methods in the process. This was followed by a *Selektion,* with the Germans choosing for deportation those who were less fit for work—children, the elderly, and the infirm. Nearly twenty thousand Jews (among them some who were young and physically fit) were then deported to Chełmno, where they were all killed. Indeed, hundreds were murdered on the spot, while the deportation was in progress. The Germans proclaimed a general curfew in the ghetto, a *Gehsperre* (ban on movement), and that week of bloody murder came to be known as the *Sperre* by the surviving ghetto inhabitants, a term that became deeply imbedded in their memory. The "Gehsperre" Aktion began with the liquidation of the ghetto hospitals, and their patients were its first victims.

Between September 1942 and May 1944, when the final liquidation of the ghetto was undertaken, there were no more deportations to extermination camps. While minor transports to forced-labor camps did occur from October 1942 to May 1944, this period is regarded as one of relative quiet in the ghetto. In effect, the ghetto had become a single large forced-labor camp: 90 percent of its population were employed in the factories, and only a few children and old people were still to be found. The ghetto population at the end of that period, in May 1944, was seventy-

Distribution of bread in the Łódź ghetto. [Mendel Grossman]

A street scene in the Łódź ghetto. [Mendel Grossman]

seven thousand.

Ghetto Activities and the Underground. Throughout its existence, the ghetto was the scene of animated illegal political, public, and cultural activities. When the ghetto was blocked off, all the Jewish political parties that had been active before the war organized into cells; the leaders who had left the city with the first wave of refugees were replaced by lesser-known figures. The youth organizations embarked on a particularly broad program of operations.

Public activities in the summer and fall of 1940 concentrated on a search for solutions to the enormous problems of unemployment and lack of food. The Zionist parties and the BUND initiated welfare operations and established soup kitchens, which developed into places for party meetings and public and cultural functions. Po'alei Zion Left, the Bund, and the Communists provided the strongest contingents for the mass demonstrations that were held to put pressure on the Ältestenrat and force it to find a solution for the distress. These demonstrations were brutally suppressed with the help of German police forces. Each incident was followed by an outbreak of major strikes in the factories, most taking the form of hunger strikes, or "soup strikes," the strikers refusing to accept the daily bowl of soup that was handed out to the workers. The aim of the strikes was to try to coerce the Ältestenrat staff to distribute the small amount of food supplied to the ghetto on a more evenhanded basis. These strikes went on as long as the ghetto existed.

The political parties and the youth organizations inaugurated an energetic program of cultural activities, in an effort to counter moral deterioration and help bolster the spirit in the ghetto. Clandestine classes and regular lectures were held, and underground libraries were in operation; the largest were maintained by Po'alei Zion Left and the Communists, with Meir Ber Gutman and Lolek Skopicki, respectively, acting as librarians.

Of great importance was the work of the radio-monitoring teams. The possession of radio receivers and the distribution of newspapers were outlawed in the ghetto: the only paper to appear was the Ältestenrat's *Geto-Zeitung* (Ghetto Journal), and the only news it published were the decrees issued by the German authorities. Clandestine radios were

A postage stamp (one of several denominations) issued by the Łódź Jewish Council (the city was renamed Litzmannstadt by the Germans). In the upper right-hand corner is a photograph of Mordechai Chaim Rumkowski, the chairman of the Ältestenrat (Council of Elders); in the center drawing is his signature and the implements of the various occupations in the ghetto.

therefore the only source of information on world developments and its dissemination in the ghetto. In early June 1944 the Gestapo uncovered a radio-monitoring team and made several arrests, followed by the execution of those arrested. The team leader, Zionist activist Chaim Nathan Widawski, committed suicide to avoid falling into Nazi hands.

Another significant underground activity was the cultural program run by the writers' group, headed by the poet Miriam Ulinower. Groups of religious people were also active in the ghetto, holding clandestine services and maintaining a program of religious studies.

The political and public organizations in the Łódź ghetto did not set up a unified underground organization, but some of them cooperated with one another. The youth or-

Jews from the Łódź ghetto boarding the freight cars that will take them to the Chełmno extermination camp.

ganizations also failed to organize a unified body, each operating on its own. The ghetto as a whole was isolated from the world and had no contacts with any outside organization, either with Jews in other ghettos or with the Polish underground.

The underground organizations in the ghetto were helpless in the face of the deportations to the extermination camps. Although no clear-cut information on the existence of such camps had come to their knowledge, the Jews of the Łódź ghetto sensed the danger faced by the deportees. The underground organizations sharply denounced the Ältestenrat, and Rumkowski in particular, for having drawn up the lists of candidates for deportation in the first half of 1942. Rumkowski's policy was condemned, but the Łódź ghetto underground was unable to come up with any alternative.

Liquidation. In the spring of 1944 the Nazis decided to liquidate the Łódź ghetto, and they reactivated the Chełmno extermination camp with this purpose in mind. On June 23 the deportations to Chełmno were resumed, on the pretext that they were forced-labor transports to Germany. The method used in early 1942 was revived, and the Ältestenrat was again forced to organize the transports and bring the deportees to assembly points on the edge of the ghetto. By July 15, 7,176 persons had been transferred to Chełmno under German escort, to be killed there. From July 15 to August 6, the deportations were at a standstill. They were renewed on August 7, their destination now being AUSCHWITZ. The transports were organized in haste, and the operation took on the form of an evacuation. It was handled by the Chełmno camp staff, headed by Hans BOTHMANN and SS Sonderkommando 1005. Section after section of the ghetto was cleared and searched for people in hiding; each section was then declared out of bounds, and anyone found there was sentenced to death.

The ghetto population resisted only passively, the Jews making desperate efforts to avoid deportation in the hope that the city would soon be liberated by the advancing Soviet army. In late July, however, the Soviet offensive came to a halt along the line of the Vistula River. It was difficult to construct hiding places in the ghetto, where most of the houses were made of wood; those who did go into hiding had no food supplies stored up. This made it easy for the Germans to seize them one by one.

The last transport left the Łódź ghetto on August 30; by then, 74,000 persons had been deported to Auschwitz. Twelve hundred Jews were left, held in two assembly camps. After a short while, 600 of them were transferred to forced-labor camps in Germany, mostly Dresden, where Hans Biebow was able to reactivate his manufacturing plants. The other 600 Jews were put into the Jakuba Street camp, where they were made to collect the possessions of the Jews who had been deported and prepare them for transmission to Germany. The camp came to be known as the Aufräumungskommando ("tidying-up detachment"); the original 600 prisoners were joined by an additional 230 Jews, who had been seized in the hideouts in which they had taken refuge in the ghetto.

In the fall of 1944 an average of forty to sixty freight cars a day left the Łódź ghetto for Germany, loaded with the possessions of the Jews who had been deported and with the equipment of the ghetto factories. This continued until the Nazis completed both the liquidation of the ghetto and the pillage of all the victims' property and possessions.

The Nazis planned to kill all the prisoners in the Jakuba Street camp before retreating from the area, and they had prepared pits for this purpose in the Jewish cemetery grounds.

The prisoners became aware of these plans and preparations, and at the appropriate moment they managed to escape and take refuge in the ghetto area, with which they were quite familiar. Numbering about eight hundred, these prisoners were finally liberated by the Soviet army, on January 19, 1945. No precise figures are available for the number of Łódź ghetto inmates who survived the concentration camps; estimates range from five thousand to seven thousand.

For several years after the war, Łódź contained the largest concentration of Holocaust survivors in Poland; in late 1945 it had a Jewish population of thirty-eight thousand. In that period, Łódź was also the leading center of the public and cultural activity of Polish Jewry. It was the site of the Centralna Żydowska Komisja Historyczna (Central Jewish Historical Commission) and had a Jewish theater, Jewish schools, and a variety of Jewish newspapers. In the waves of emigration that took place in 1946–1947, 1956–1957, and 1967–1969, however, nearly all the Jews left Łódź, and only a few hundred elderly Jews remained in the city.

BIBLIOGRAPHY

Dobroszycki, L., ed. *The Chronicle of the Lodz Ghetto, 1941–1944.* New Haven, 1984.

Hirshkovitch, B. "The Ghetto in Litzmannstadt (Lodz)." *YIVO Annual* 5 (1950): 85–122.

Jasni, W. *Di Geshichte fun Jidn in Lodz in di Jorn fun der Deitsher Jidn-Ojsrotung.* 2 vols. Tel Aviv, 1960, 1966. (In Yiddish.)

Trunk, I. *Ghetto Lodz: A Historical and Sociological Study.* New York, 1962. (In Yiddish, with English summary.)

Trunk, I. *Judenrat: The Jewish Councils in Eastern Europe under Nazi Occupation.* New York, 1972.

SHMUEL KRAKOWSKI

ŁÓDŹ GHETTO, CHRONICLES OF THE, chronological record of events in the ŁÓDŹ ghetto initiated and maintained by the archivists of the statistics section of the JUDENRAT (Jewish Council). The team responsible consisted of journalists, writers, and men of letters. Outstanding among them were a journalist, Julian Zucker (whose pen name was Stanisław Czerski); an engineer, Bernard Ostrowski; an ethnographer, Joseph Zelikowicz; and Dr. Abraham Shalom Kamenetzki, a biblical scholar. The chronicles were initiated in January 1941 and were kept up uninterruptedly until July 30, 1944. Until September 1942 the language used was Polish, but the chronicles' contributors, like other GHETTO inhabitants, fell victim to starvation and disease, and they were replaced by Jews who had been deported to Łódź from other European countries. As a result, at the end of 1942 Polish was replaced by German, the new team being made up of Jews from Czechoslovakia and Austria, headed by Dr. Oskar Rosenfeld and Dr. Oskar Singer.

Entries in the chronicles were based on documents and data transmitted to the archive by the various departments of the Jewish ghetto administration, on the instructions of Mordechai Chaim RUMKOWSKI, head of the Judenrat. The daily entries usually included a weather report, statistical data on births and deaths, a list of criminal arrests, a food distribution list, data on health conditions, official statements and announcements, and reports on places where Jews were employed, on raids, on expulsions, and on executions. From time to time the chronicles included articles on life in the ghetto and on the mood of the population, vignettes of everyday life, rumors, and even jokes.

While the chronicles are an important authentic source, encompassing nearly all aspects of life in the ghetto, they are not to be regarded as a document that contains the true history of the ghetto, and are not to be taken at their face value. The authors and contributors were subject to the supervision of Rumkowski's personal staff and lived in the shadow of the Nazi threat. They had to use cautious and restrained language, even when describing assaults and harassment, expulsions, robberies, and murders. Almost completely ignored was the social life of those Jews in the ghetto who did not belong to the official establishment.

The chronicles that were saved after the liquidation of the ghetto consist of some two thousand typewritten pages. They are now held in part by the Jewish Historical Institute (ŻYDOWSKI INSTYTUT HISTORYCZNY) in Warsaw and in part by the YIVO Institute for Jewish Research in New York; a photostatic copy is in the YAD VASHEM archives in Jerusalem. Parts of the chronicles were published in Poland in 1965 and 1966, and an extensive selection taken from all parts of the chronicles was published in English translation in the United States in 1984. In Israel, the first two of four volumes of a complete translation into Hebrew have appeared.

[*See also* Oneg Shabbat.]

BIBLIOGRAPHY

Dobroszycki, L., ed. *The Chronicle of the Lodz Ghetto, 1941–1944.* New Haven, 1984.

JOSEPH RAB

LOḤAMEI ḤERUT ISRAEL (Fighters for the Freedom of Israel; known by its acronym, Leḥi; also known as the "Stern Group" or, by the British, as the "Stern Gang"), one of the manifestations of Revisionist maximalism in Zionism (i.e., radical Zionism), a trend that originated in the late 1920s. Its continuation was the post-1937 Irgun Tseva'i Le'ummi (National Military Organization, or Irgun, with the acronym Etsel). Revisionist maximalism advocated that the Revisionist movement should not function as a parliamentary opposition to the Zionist movement, but instead should become a liberation movement fighting for independence without waiting for a Jewish majority to be achieved in Palestine. The innovation introduced by Abraham Stern ("Yair"), the Leḥi leader, was his attempt to put this ideology into practice by going over to active opposition against Britain, following the publication of the 1939 WHITE PAPER severely restricting Jewish immigration into Palestine, and the outbreak of World War II. Stern's approach was contrary to the policy of Vladimir JABOTINSKY, the Zionist Revisionist leader, of identifying with Britain in its war against Adolf Hitler.

Leḥi came into being after a stormy meeting of Etsel's commanders in mid-June 1940. At that time Stern advocated a policy of continued struggle against the British, in opposition to the unofficial truce with the British declared by Etsel's pro-British faction, led by David Raziel. In September, Stern's splinter group adopted the name Ha-Etsel be-Israel (The Irgun in Israel); later, to clarify the differences between the two positions, Stern changed its name to Leḥi. Leḥi existed in this condition until Stern was shot by detectives of the British Palestine Police in February 1942.

Leḥi had its ideological roots in the 1930s, and believed that in history it was the strong leaders—men like Benito MUSSOLINI, Józef Piłsudski, and Adolf Hitler—who prevailed. Like all the proponents of radical right-wing movements in Europe during the interwar period, Stern and his associates were influenced by the theory of Social Darwinism. They did not consider World War II an ideological struggle, regarding it instead as a fight for world hegemony. Yair was therefore opposed to participating in the war on Britain's side and looked for rapprochement with Britain's enemies, the Axis powers.

Stern propounded the idea that there was a difference between a "persecutor" and an "enemy." Persecutors, from Haman to Hitler, had sought to destroy the Jews throughout the ages; but an enemy is much more dangerous, because he occupies the Jewish homeland. This reasoning led Stern to see Britain as the principal enemy. Stern accepted Jabotinsky's view that there was a difference between Nazi antisemitism and Polish antisemitism, but he argued that since it had been demonstrated that a common language could be found with Polish antisemitism—by winning its support for Jabotinsky's plan for the "evacuation" of Polish Jewry and its secret support for a war of liberation—it followed that it might also be possible to reach an understanding with Nazi antisemitism.

At the end of 1940, Stern, with the backing of his Leḥi command, sent an emissary by the name of Naphtali Lubenchik to Beirut, then under the control of Vichy France, to establish contact with the Axis representatives there and broach the idea of establishing a Jewish state within the framework of the "New Order." Such an idea had apparently been discussed regarding Italy earlier in 1940, its principal element being that a Jewish protectorate would be set up in Palestine to which the Jews of Europe would be transferred. No permanent contact, however, had been established with Italy, and it seems that the "Italian option" was dropped in view of

Italy's military defeats in the Western Desert and in Greece.

In early 1941 Stern's emissary met with Otto Werner von Hentig, a German Foreign Ministry representative, and submitted a memorandum on "the community of interests between the German concept of the New Order in Europe and the true national aspirations of the Jewish people, as represented by the Irgun." Stern was not authorized to speak on behalf of the Irgun, but only in the name of his own group (which numbered up to two hundred members), and on its behalf he offered political, military, and intelligence support to Nazi Germany, in exchange for the creation of a Jewish state and the formation of Jewish military units in occupied Europe that would take part in the conquest of Palestine.

For a while, Stern and his associates in the Etsel command believed that Hitler was planning to concentrate all the Jews of Poland in the Lublin Reservation (*see* NISKO AND LUBLIN PLAN). When Hitler dropped that plan, they thought he was going to concentrate the Jews in Madagascar (*see* MADAGASCAR PLAN), an idea that was current in the late autumn of 1940. They assumed that what Hitler had in mind was a "territorialist," non-Zionist solution, and, since they believed in the possibility of reaching agreement with Hitler on a joint war against Britain in exchange for the establishment of Jewish statehood, they thought Hitler could also be persuaded to agree to the evacuation of the Jews of Europe to Palestine, instead of Madagascar. They also were under the impression that the situation of the Jews in the Polish ghettos was no different from that of Russian Jews during the Russian Revolution, and that these ghettos would one day become the source of underground fighters and liberators of the Jewish homeland.

Von Hentig's reply to Stern's emissary was that two schools of thought existed among German official circles. One, based on *Realpolitik,* favored the expulsion of the Jews from Europe; the other, based on *Idealpolitik,* wanted the Jews to be destroyed. Since no progress was being made on the expulsion solution, the danger was that the prospects for the other kind of solution were on the rise.

The failure of Lubenchik's mission led to a split in Ha-Etsel be-Israel, with its commanders quitting the group. Some of Stern's spiritual mentors warned him that he and his supporters were running the risk of being accused of treason, but Stern argued that Lenin had also pressed for an agreement with the Germans, at Brest-Litovsk in 1918.

Even when the war was over, Leḥi continued to consider Britain its number one enemy. Time and again it reiterated the charge that Britain was just as guilty of the slaughter of Europe's Jews as was Germany. It accused Britain of making new preparations for destroying the surviving remnants and the Jewish population of Palestine, because of the cold war then raging between the West and the Soviet Union. Leḥi further accused Britain of rehabilitating Germany so as to enable that country once again to take up the murder of the Jewish people. The Soviet Union, so Leḥi believed at that time, was the only power that could prevent this from happening, by helping to establish a Jewish state.

BIBLIOGRAPHY

Eliav, Y. *Wanted.* Tel Aviv, 1983. (In Hebrew.)

Loḥamei Ḥerut Israel. *Writings.* Vols. 1, 2. Tel Aviv, 1959, 1960. (In Hebrew.)

Orenstein, J. *Enchained.* Tel Aviv, 1973. (In Hebrew.)

Yisraeli, D. *The Palestine Problem in German Politics, 1889–1945.* Ramat Gan, Israel, 1974. (In Hebrew.)

JOSEPH HELLER

LOHSE, HINRICH (1896–1964), German politician and wartime *Reichskommissar* for the Baltic and Belorussian areas. Born at Mühlenbarbek, in Schleswig-Holstein, Lohse studied commerce and worked as a clerk in a savings bank. He took part in World War I. In 1925 he was appointed *Gauleiter* (regional leader) for Schleswig-Holstein, and was elected a member of the Prussian Landtag (Chamber of Deputies) in 1928 and of the Reichstag in 1932. In 1933 he was promoted to the Prussian State Council and to the presidency of the province of Schleswig-Holstein.

Hinrich Lohse (right) with Heinrich Himmler and Martin Bormann. [National Archives]

The following year he was made an SA-*Gruppenführer*. Between 1941 and 1944 Lohse functioned as *Reichskommissar* for the Ostland, with his headquarters in Riga. This was the period when, under his supervision, the "FINAL SOLUTION" was implemented in the Baltic and Belorussian areas.

Lohse instructed his subordinates that ghetto inmates were to receive the bare minimum of food rations necessary to sustain life, until the machinery for the "Final Solution" was fully operative. Nonetheless, the mass shootings in the Vilna ghetto and elsewhere led him to question whether "all Jews, regardless of age or sex, or their usefulness to the economy (for instance, as skilled workers in the Wehrmacht's ordnance factories), were to be liquidated." When he was informed that this was indeed the case, Lohse acquiesced.

He was arrested in 1945 and sentenced in 1948 to ten years' penal servitude, but was released in 1951 on grounds of ill health. The pension he drew from the local authorities of Schleswig-Holstein was withdrawn under pressure from the Bonn government, not because of the war crimes he had committed, but because of his record as an enemy of democracy during his political activity in Schleswig-Holstein.

BIBLIOGRAPHY

Arad, Y. *Ghetto in Flames: The Struggle and Destruction of the Jews in Vilna in the Holocaust.* Jerusalem, 1980.

Dallin, A. *German Rule in Russia, 1941–1945: A Study of Occupation Policies.* London, 1957.

LIONEL KOCHAN

LÖSENER, BERNARD (1890–1952), the "racial expert" (*Rassereferent*) of the German Interior Ministry from 1933 to 1943. In this post, Lösener took part in drafting twenty-seven anti-Jewish decrees. Most important among them were the NUREMBERG LAWS of 1935 and the subsequent legal definitions that distinguished among different kinds of partial Jews ("hybrids," or MISCHLINGE), in effect exempting quarter Jews and secularized half Jews from the full brunt of persecution. After the war, Lösener recalled how he was summoned at the last minute to bring his Interior Ministry files to the 1935 Nazi party rally, where the drafting of the Nuremberg Laws took place over a hectic weekend. His detailed firsthand account of this event has frequently been cited, especially by those historians who emphasize the unplanned and evolutionary nature of Nazi Jewish policy.

Lösener was the son of a minor judicial official. He served as a soldier throughout World War I, attended the University of Tübingen, and passed his civil service examinations, becoming a customs official in 1924. He joined the Nazi party in December 1930. In April 1933, when experienced officials with party credentials were in short supply, he was summoned from his obscure customs post to the Interior Ministry in Berlin.

By his own account, Lösener became quickly disillusioned with the Nazis, for two reasons: the inclusion of even one-quarter Jews among those banned from the civil service, and the party's intervention in the internal affairs of the Evangelical church. Like many others, Lösener claimed that he clung to his post to prevent worse from happening and to save those who could still be saved. By his own admission, this meant accepting the impossibility of doing anything for "full Jews," but doing everything possible to prevent quarter and half Jews, as well as the latter's parents living in mixed marriages, from being equated with full Jews. It also meant abjuring open opposition and framing his arguments on the basis of Nazi ideology, despite the "internal aversion" and "shame" he felt.

Two factors distinguish Lösener's apologia from those of others. First, he did in fact work consistently, tenaciously, and with considerable success to prevent *Mischlinge* and Jews in mixed marriages from being affected by the regime's anti-Jewish measures. According to his calculations, this saved from deportation as many as 100,000 of the former and 20,000 of the latter. Second, unlike others who clung to their posts allegedly to prevent worse, but in fact steadily accommodated themselves to the escalating violence, Lösener had a limit beyond which he would not go. When he learned of the December 1941 massacres of the first German Jews deported to Riga, he requested a transfer from his post as *Rassereferent*. Eventually, in March 1943, he was appointed as a judge.

Lösener was arrested in November 1944 for hiding a couple implicated in the July 1944 attempt to assassinate Hitler. He was expelled from the party for "treason," but survived his Berlin imprisonment until liberation. After two subsequent arrests—first by the Russians and then by the Americans—and submitting to denazification proceedings, he was briefly employed by the German mission of the American Jewish JOINT DISTRIBUTION COMMITTEE in 1949. He then resumed government employment until his death. A posthumous memoir was published about Lösener's activities in the Interior Ministry, "Als Rassereferent im Reichsministerium des Innern," *Vierteljahrshefte für Zeitgeschichte* 9/3 (1961), pp. 264–313.

BIBLIOGRAPHY

Hilberg, R. *The Destruction of the European Jews.* 3 vols. New York, 1985.

CHRISTOPHER R. BROWNING

LÖWENHERZ, JOSEF (1884–1946?), head of the Jewish community of VIENNA during the Nazi occupation of AUSTRIA. Löwenherz was born in Galicia and settled in Vienna, where he worked as a lawyer and Zionist activist. Beginning in 1929 he was elected each year as the deputy chairman of the city's Jewish community, as a General Zionist representative. Löwenherz showed organizational skill in his contacts with the American Jewish JOINT DISTRIBUTION COMMITTEE (JDC; known as the Joint) offices in Paris and in the United States, as well as with the Wanderfürsorge (Refugee Committee) in Vienna, formed in 1930. After the rise of the Nazis to power in Germany, Vienna became the European center of the latter. He was also active in the Arbeitsgemeinschaft der Kultusgemeinden Österreichs (Association of Jewish Communities in Austria), which began to function in 1936. Löwenherz was appointed the director of Vienna's Jewish community at the beginning of 1936. This appointment caused a crisis, for two reasons: the non-Zionists were angered that the post was given to a Zionist; and it was considered unacceptable that he was transferred from an honorary to a paid position.

The community's offices were closed down by the Germans on March 18, 1938, a week after the annexation of Austria (*see* ANSCHLUSS). Löwenherz was arrested, together with the members of the community executive and the leaders of the Zionist and Jewish organizations, but since he was a salaried official he was not sent with the others to DACHAU. At the beginning of May, Adolf EICHMANN, who was active in Austria at the time, instructed Löwenherz to reorganize the community. An advisory committee was set up to function together with him, but he was given sole responsibility for all decisions made. In actuality, he was totally dependent on the SS and the Gestapo.

In line with the main goal of Eichmann's policy, the endeavors of the Austrian Jews to emigrate increased between 1938 and 1940. Löwenherz and Alois Rothenberg, the chairman of the Palestine Office (an office that dealt with emigration), planned to set up a central bureau to provide information on emigration and guidance for members of the Jewish community, and at the same time to serve as an umbrella organization for all the relevant government organizations in Vienna. Eichmann, however, converted this positive plan into a tragedy for the Jews by turning the bureau into a center for the confiscation of their possessions. On the other hand, Eichmann released monies from the levy that the emigrating Jews were required to pay and from the community property that had been seized, equal to the amount that the Joint transferred to aid the emigrants. These monies, also forwarded by the COUNCIL FOR GERMAN JEWRY in London, were used to cover the emigration costs of poverty-stricken Jews, welfare projects that grew as the community became increasingly impoverished, and financing for the establishment of an educational and retraining network. With the Joint's support, Löwenherz succeeded in persuading Eichmann to renew Jewish emigration, which had ceased during the October 1939 expulsions of Jews to Nisko (*see* NISKO AND LUBLIN PLAN), and to continue it even during the expulsion to the KIELCE region in February and March of 1941. However, Löwenherz was forced to provide alternate candidates for deportation in place of essential officials and doctors and persons holding emigration certificates, whose names had been removed from the Gestapo lists received from Berlin. This was the first step of cooperation in expulsion, instead of the coordination of the emigration policy, which had been the case until then.

Eichmann and his successors developed this method even after the systematic expulsion of Jews from Vienna began in mid-October 1941. In 1941 and 1942, when the Jews of Vienna were concentrated in residential areas within a type of open ghetto, Löwenherz fought a losing battle for every essential official, in whose stead he was forced to provide other candidates for expulsion.

Löwenherz remained in Vienna until the liberation by the Soviet army in 1945. After the war he was arrested, interrogated, and released by his son, who was an officer in the United States Army. He emigrated with his wife to the United States, and died shortly thereafter.

BIBLIOGRAPHY

Fraenkel, J., ed. *The Jews of Austria*. London, 1967.

Rosenkranz, H. "Austrian Jewry: Between Forced Emigration and Deportation." In *Patterns of Jewish Leadership in Nazi Europe, 1933–1945*. Proceedings of the Third Yad Vashem International Historical Conference, edited by Y. Gutman and C. J. Haft, pp. 65–75. Jerusalem, 1979.

Rosenkranz, H. *Verfolgung und Selbstbehauptung: Die Juden in Österreich 1938–1945*. Vienna, 1978.

HERBERT ROSENKRANZ

LUBETKIN, ZIVIA (1914–1976), one of the leaders of the Jewish underground in Poland and a founder of the ŻYDOWSKA ORGANIZACJA BOJOWA (Jewish Fighting Organization; ŻOB). Born in Beten, in eastern Poland, Lubetkin joined Freiheit (Dror), the Zionist pioneering youth movement, and eventually became a member of HE-HALUTS HA-LOHEM's executive council. When World War II broke out, she was caught in the Soviet-occupied part of Poland, but in 1940 she made her way back to German-occupied WARSAW to take part in her movement's underground operations.

Lubetkin was one of the outstanding figures in the underground movement in Poland. In 1942 she was one of a small group of underground members who founded the Antifascist Bloc, the first organization to be established in the Warsaw ghetto whose purpose was to offer armed resistance to the Germans. In July of that year, when the great deportation from Warsaw was in full swing, Lubetkin took part in establishing the ŻOB, and from the outset played an important role in determining its character and policy. She was a member of the Żydowski Komitet Narodowy (Jewish National Committee), the political leadership of the ŻOB, and of the Coordinating Committee, which served as an intermediary between the Jewish National Committee and the BUND.

Lubetkin participated in the first armed resistance operation launched by the ŻOB, in January 1943, and in the WARSAW GHETTO UPRISING in April of that year. She spent the final days of the uprising in the organization's command bunker at 18 Mila Street, leaving the bunker on May 10 and, with a group of survivors, passing over to the "Aryan" side of Warsaw by way of the sewer system. Until the end of the war Lubetkin stayed in hiding in the Warsaw underground, and was in the ranks of the ŻOB units that joined the WARSAW POLISH UPRISING from August to October of 1944.

When the war was over, Lubetkin became active in the She'erit ha-Peletah (the "surviving remnant") organization and was one of the organizers of the BERIḤA. In 1946 she settled in Palestine and was among the founders of Kibbutz Loḥamei ha-Getta'ot (the Ghetto Fighters' Kibbutz) and of its memorial center, BET LOḤAMEI HA-GETTA'OT. Lubetkin held various leading public positions as the representative of the kibbutz movement, Ha-Kibbutz ha-Meuḥad, and was a witness in the EICHMANN TRIAL. She was married to Yitzhak ZUCKERMAN.

BIBLIOGRAPHY

Dror, Z., ed. *Testimonies of Survival: Ninety-six Personal Interviews from Members of Kibbutz Loḥamei ha-Getta'ot.* Vol. 1. Naharia, Israel, 1984. See pages 328–345. (In Hebrew.).

Lubetkin, Z. *In Days of Destruction and Revolt.* Naharia, Israel, 1980.

Syrkin, M. "Zivia: The Passing of a Heroine." *Midstream* 24/8 (October 1978): 56–59.

ISRAEL GUTMAN

LUBLIN, city in eastern POLAND and capital of the district bearing that name; a center of industry, communications, and culture. Jews lived in Lublin, one of Poland's oldest cities, from the fourteenth century, and in the sixteenth and seventeenth centuries it was the hub of Jewish learning in the country. During the nineteenth and twentieth centuries Lublin was the scene of important Hebrew and Yiddish cultural activities, and Jewish organizations and political parties flourished there. On the eve of World War II, the city had a Jewish population of some 40,000 out of a total of 122,000.

In the first few weeks of the war, thousands of Jews fleeing the German advance found refuge in Lublin. Some of these refugees and several hundred of the town's Jewish residents moved even farther east, into territory that was annexed to the Soviet Union shortly thereafter. The Jewish Community Council gave help to the refugees. From the beginning of September 1939 until the eighteenth of that month, when the city was occupied by the Germans, the Jews participated in resistance efforts against the invading German forces. Jewish groups removed the debris caused by German bombing, acted as firefighters, and dug defense trenches.

As soon as the Germans entered the city, they began seizing Jews for forced labor, inflicting bodily harm on them, and robbing them of their property. In November 1939 the Jews were driven out of the main street, Krakowskie Przedmieście, and their apartments were confiscated; they were ordered to wear the Jewish BADGE, and their movements in certain areas, both inside and outside the city, were restricted.

Lublin was linked to the Nazis' plan to create the Lublin Reservation, an enclave in which all the Jews of the GENERALGOUVERNEMENT and other parts of Poland annexed to

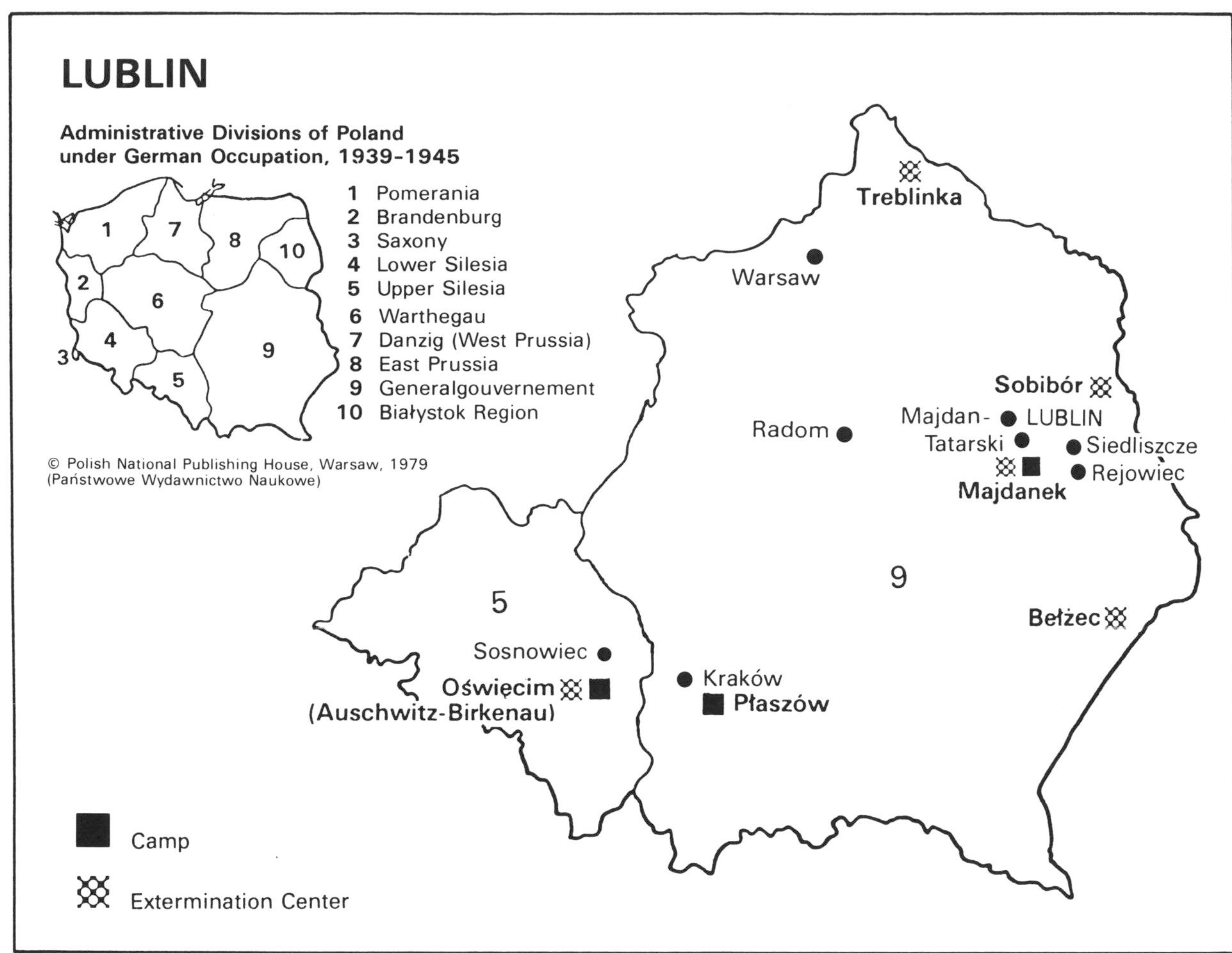

the Reich, as well as those from the Reich itself, were to be concentrated (*see* NISKO AND LUBLIN PLAN). By February 1940, sixty-three hundred deportees had arrived in Lublin under this program, including a group of thirteen hundred Jews from Stettin. But the plan was implemented in a haphazard fashion, lacking coordination with the various branches of the German administration, and in April 1940 it was dropped. Lublin, however, remained a center where the policy of mass deportation and extermination on Polish soil was carried out. It was the headquarters of Odilo GLOBOCNIK, the head of AKTION REINHARD, who was responsible for the operation of death camps in the eastern part of the Generalgouvernement; the MAJDANEK concentration and extermination camp was situated in a Lublin suburb.

Following the German occupation, the Jewish Community Council continued to function, with hardly any change from its prewar composition. Its range of activities was broadened in response to German demands and the new needs of the Jewish population. For the Germans, the council had to provide daily quotas of forced labor and to collect and surrender valuables, furniture, and other items of household equipment. In the Jewish community itself, the council provided aid to the needy and to refugees. On occasion, it intervened with the German authorities for the release of hostages and prisoners, and for the reduction of fines and easing other economic measures that had been imposed on individuals or on the entire Jewish population.

On January 25, 1940, the council officially became a JUDENRAT (Jewish Council), consisting of twenty-four members. Few changes in personnel were made; the membership continued to include people who before the war had belonged to a range of political parties, from Agudat Israel to the BUND.

German soldiers of the Leibstandarte-SS "Adolf Hitler" (Adolf Hitler SS Bodyguard Regiment), the earliest established SS militarized formation, humiliate an elderly Jew on a Lublin street by cutting his beard.

Heading the Judenrat was Henryk Bekker, an engineer, but its outstanding personality was the deputy chairman, Mark Alten. The Judenrat maintained the policy previously pursued by the Jewish Community Council; it built up a broad network of welfare institutions and soup kitchens and made special efforts to provide orphanages and institutions for abandoned children. It also invested much effort in providing health services, setting up two 500-bed general hospitals and a 300-bed hospital for contagious diseases, with outpatient clinics.

As German policy toward the Jews became harsher, however, the Judenrat had increasingly less room for maneuvering between compliance with German demands and taking care of the vital needs of the community. In 1940, the Germans stepped up their demands for forced labor, and there was an increase in the number of people seized on the streets for this purpose. Individual Jews and the Judenrat tried to find employment opportunities in factories that were important to the German economy, hoping in this manner to gain immunity from random capture. In this way, many Jews came to be employed in the workshops of the DEUTSCHE AUSRÜSTUNGSWERKE (German Armament Works), located in the prisoner-of-war camp at 7 Lipowa Street. In the summer of 1940, the Germans began rounding up Jews and taking them to work camps outside the city, mainly for labor on the Soviet border. The Judenrat was also ordered to provide laborers for these camps; its compliance led to tension between it and the Jewish population.

In preparation for the establishment of a ghetto in the spring of 1941, the Germans ordered part of the Jewish population of Lublin to be deported. Though they described the deportation as "voluntary evacuation," the Germans in fact exerted great pressure in order to achieve their goal. From March 10 until the end of that month, 10,000 Jews were expelled from Lublin; 1,250 were deported to Rejowiec, 2,300 to Siedliszcze, 3,200 to Sosnowiec, and the rest to other localities in the area. In these places the deportees faced enormous economic difficulties and suffered from appalling housing conditions.

The ghetto was established at the end of March 1941, with a Jewish population of over thirty-four thousand. On April 24 a decree was published forbidding Jews to leave the ghetto, except for those who had special passes or were part of work crews employed outside. In the summer of 1941, a typhus epidemic broke out in the ghetto. Medical teams and a special health service did what they could to control the disease, but they were severely hampered by the prevailing conditions—starvation, overcrowding, and a lack of medicines.

Lublin Jews were among the first selected to be the victims of the gas chambers at the BEŁŻEC extermination camp. Their deportation began on March 17, 1942, and proceeded at a rate of fourteen hundred per day, the quota fixed by the Germans. Some of the German units and their Ukrainian helpers were positioned on the ghetto perimeter to foil any attempt at escape, while others made house-to-house searches within the ghetto. The *Selektionen* for deportation took place at assembly points. In the initial stage of the *Aktion*, the passes held by Jewish skilled workers were honored by the Germans, but the workers' families were not exempt. Most of the Jews who had gone into hiding in the ghetto or had crossed over to the "Aryan" sector of the city—some five hundred persons—were caught by the Germans; all were murdered on the spot. The *Aktion* came to an end on April 20. Thirty thousand Jews had been deported from Lublin, most of them to their death at Bełżec, and the rest were killed in the forests near the city.

On March 31, while the *Aktion* was in full swing, the Germans reduced the size of the Judenrat by half, from twenty-four to twelve, and named Mark Alten as chairman. Some of those not reappointed were deported to Bełżec. Opinions differ concerning the conduct of members of the Judenrat, especially of Alten. Some informed persons have expressed understanding for the Judenrat's policy and emphasize its efforts on behalf of the community. Others have criticized the members for being out of touch with the people, for personal arrogance, and for capitulating

One of the deportations from Lublin.

too easily to the Germans. Some of the Jewish police as well have been sharply criticized for their behavior.

Following the *Aktion* of March and April 1942, the surviving members of the community, now numbering only four thousand, were moved to Majdan Tatarski, a suburb of Lublin. One section of the suburb was emptied of the Poles who lived there and was surrounded by a fence; in this area, dubbed the "small ghetto," the remaining Jews were interned. Conditions were intolerable; some of the prisoners did not even have a roof over their heads. From the first day of the existence of the "small ghetto," the Germans made *Selektionen* among the newcomers and went on a murder rampage. There were lineups and sporadic raids to identify those Jews who did not possess work passes, and many of these "illegals" were killed on the spot.

The population of the "small ghetto" was gradually destroyed. In an *Aktion* on September 2, 1942, a *Selektion* was made, following which two thousand Jews were dispatched to their death at the Majdanek camp. The pattern was repeated on October 25, when a further eighteen hundred Jews were sent to their death in Majdanek. In May 1943 several dozen craftsmen who had been employed by the Germans were murdered. In July 1944, shortly before their retreat from Lublin, the Germans killed the last remaining Jewish workers who had been held in Lublin Fortress, where they were employed in small workshops serving the German garrison troops.

Following the liberation of Lublin, on July 24, 1944, the city became an assembly point for survivors from the city and its vicinity, for Jewish partisans in the area east of Lublin, and for Jews who had taken refuge in the Soviet Union at the beginning of the war. Until the liberation of Warsaw in January 1945, Lublin was the provisional capital of Poland, and it was there that the central institutions of the surviving Jewish community established themselves. A branch of the Jewish Community Cultural Society, a national institution recognized by the Polish government, existed there until 1968. The Jewish community came to an end in the early 1970s, and only a few Jews continue to live in Lublin.

BIBLIOGRAPHY

Blumenthal, N. *Documents from the Lublin Ghetto: Judenrat without Direction.* Jerusalem, 1967. (In Hebrew.)

Blumenthal, N., and M. Korzen, eds. *Lublin.* Vol. 5 of *Encyclopedia of the Jewish Diaspora.* Jerusalem, 1957. (In Hebrew.)

Trunk, I. *Judenrat.* New York, 1972.

SHMUEL KRAKOWSKI and AHARON WEISS

LUBLIN-LIPOWA, prisoner-of-war (POW) camp for Jews. The Lublin-Lipowa camp was set up in December 1939 in a block of buildings at 7 Lipowa Street in LUBLIN, Poland. It was used to bring together in one place Jewish POWs of the Polish army who had been taken prisoner by the Germans in the September 1939 fighting and had first been interned in various POW camps in Germany. Some seven thousand Jewish POWs passed through the camp. The Germans treated them in the most brutal manner. At the end of December 1939 one thousand of them were taken out of the camp and put on a death march (*see* DEATH MARCHES) to the border between the German- and Soviet-occupied parts of Poland. During the march, most of the Jews were killed by the SS men who served as their escort in a unit under the command of Sturmbannführer Hermann Dolp.

In the spring of 1941, 3,200 POWs who came from German-occupied Poland were released, while the rest, more than 2,500 men whose homes had been in the Soviet-occupied area of Poland, continued to be held. The camp administration made strenuous efforts to strip the Jews of their rights as POWs and make them concentration camp prisoners. These attempts were strongly resisted by the prisoners, who united in a clandestine organization, led by Roman Fisher. In late 1942 and early 1943 the organization succeeded in smuggling 400 of its members out of the camp, in order to form partisan units in the area. However, before any partisan operations could be launched, 250 of the escaped POWs were caught by the Germans and killed. Another 50 were treacherously murdered by antisemitic Poles, who had first promised to give them help. Approximately 100 escapees managed to organize themselves into two partisan units, led by Shmuel Jegier and Shmuel Gruber, respectively. Later on they joined the GWARDIA LUDOWA (People's Guard) and fought in partisan operations until the final liberation of the area, in July 1944.

On November 3, 1943, when the forced-labor camps in the Lublin district were being liquidated during the "ERNTEFEST" *Aktion*, the Germans removed all the remaining prisoners from the camp, numbering over two thousand. The Germans took them to the nearby MAJDANEK camp, where they were all shot in front of prepared pits adjoining the camp crematoria.

BIBLIOGRAPHY

Krakowski, S. *The War of the Doomed: Jewish Armed Resistance in Poland, 1942–1944.* New York, 1984.

SHMUEL KRAKOWSKI

LUBLIN, LUCIEN (b. 1909), underground organizer in FRANCE. Born in Brest-Litovsk, Lublin received a degree in electrical engineering in Toulouse, France. At the outbreak of World War II he enlisted in the French army. Lublin was a Zionist Labor Movement activist, and in January 1942, together with Abraham POLONSKI, he founded a Jewish military underground, the ARMÉE JUIVE, and became a member of its supreme command. Lublin placed the underground under the authority of the YISHUV, the organized Jewish community in Palestine, and of the Hagana, the Yishuv's underground armed force. He obtained financial backing with the aid of the leaders of the Zionist Labor Movement in France, and recruited for the underground the cream of Zionist youth and members of the He-Haluts movement who slipped into France from the NETHERLANDS. In late 1943 and early 1944 about three hundred members of the Armée Juive, including He-Haluts members from the Netherlands, managed to flee over the border to SPAIN with the aid of the Armée Juive flight network; from Spain most immigrated to Palestine. Many other members fought in the partisan battles in France. After the war, Lublin founded the Oeuvre de Protection des Enfants Juifs (Society for Protecting Jewish Children), an organization for aiding children who had survived the Holocaust and helping them immigrate to Palestine.

BIBLIOGRAPHY

Kapel, S. R. *The Jewish Struggle in Occupied France: The Internment Camps and the Jewish Fighting Organization, 1940–1944.* Jerusalem, 1981. (In Hebrew.)

Knout, D. *Contribution à l'histoire de la résistance juive en France.* Paris, 1947.

Latour, A. *Jewish Resistance in France, 1940–1944.* New York, 1981.

Lazare, L. *La résistance juive en France.* Paris, 1987.

LUCIEN LAZARE

LUBLIN RESERVATION. *See* Nisko and Lublin Plan.

ŁUCK. *See* Lutsk.

LUDENDORFF, ERICH (1865–1937), German military leader and nationalist politician. Born in Posen, Ludendorff had an outstanding army career during World War I. At the outbreak of that war he was appointed *Oberquartiermeister* (Senior Quartermaster General) of the Second Army. He was promoted to *Generalstabschef* (Chief of Staff) of the Eighth Army under Gen. Paul von HINDENBURG, the army chief of staff, and, in 1916, to *Generalquartiermeister* (First Quartermaster General). His victories over the Russians at the battles of Tannenberg and the Masurian Lakes in 1914 contributed greatly to the "Ludendorff myth." When his 1918 summer offensive on the western front failed, he demanded an immediate armistice. He was dismissed in October 1918 and fled to Sweden, where he wrote his war memoirs.

Returning to Munich in 1919, Ludendorff identified himself with nationalist anti-republican groups and helped to propagate the DOLCHSTOSSLEGENDE ("stab-in-the-back" myth). In 1923 he was arrested for participating with Adolf Hitler in the abortive November *Putsch,* but was acquitted. He served in the Reichstag from 1924 to 1928 as deputy for the Nazi party. Ludendorff's candidacy for the Reich presidency in 1925 on behalf of the imprisoned Hitler was an ignominious failure, and the two men became increasingly estranged.

In 1926, influenced by his second wife, Mathilde Kemnitz (1877–1966), Ludendorff founded the Tannenbergbund, to whose "German God awareness" he devoted himself. This pseudoreligious body worshiped the ancient Norse gods and circulated countless pamphlets denouncing the "Jewish-Masonic-Bolshevik" international conspiracy in terms that were plainly paranoid and pathological. In 1933, Ludendorff warned Hindenburg that to appoint Hitler chancellor would "lead . . . our nation to an unprecedented catastrophe." In spite of this, Ludendorff went unscathed, and his death in 1937 was marked by a state funeral.

BIBLIOGRAPHY

Borst, G. *Die Ludendorff-Bewegung 1919–1961.* Munich, 1969.

Frentz, H. *Die unbekannte Ludendorff: Der Feldherr in seiner Umwelt und Epoche.* Wiesbaden, 1972.

Goodspeed, D. J. *Ludendorff: Soldier, Dictator, Revolutionary.* London, 1966.

LIONEL KOCHAN

LUDIN, HANS ELARD (1905–1946), Nazi diplomat; German ambassador to SLOVAKIA from 1941 to 1945. Ludin joined the Nazi party in 1930 and the SA (Sturmabteilung; Storm Troopers) in 1931. He was among a group of prominent SA men who survived the "Night of the Long Knives" of June 1934 and were appointed ambassadors to Germany's eastern European allies and satellites during World War II.

Ludin's duties in Slovakia were minimal, since before his appointment a system of German advisers had already been established. These German advisers, such as Dieter WISLICENY for Jewish affairs, received their instructions and salaries from their superiors in Berlin, and used the German embassy as little more than a convenient postbox.

In February 1942, however, Ludin conveyed to the Slovak government Heinrich HIMMLER's request for 20,000 strong, young Jews to work in the east, a request the Slovak government "eagerly snatched up," according to Ludin. In late March he again relayed a German request, for the deportation of all the remaining Slovak Jews, and reported back that the Slovak government had agreed "without any German pressure." When growing Slovak reluctance brought the deportations to a near standstill that June, the Slovak prime minister, Vojtech TUKA, requested additional German pressure to overcome internal opposition to the deportations. Ludin obtained a letter expressing German "surprise" at the halting of Jewish deportations, but there is no evidence that he used it.

Further negotiations concerning the deportation of Slovak Jews were left in the hands of the Jewish adviser, Wisliceny, and then of the Foreign Office troubleshooter, Edmund VEESENMAYER, in 1943, but without result. Following the SLOVAK NATIONAL UPRISING in 1944, however, the SS carried out further deportations, for which Ludin provided diplomatic support. Ludin was tried and executed in Czechoslovakia in 1946.

BIBLIOGRAPHY

Browning, C. R. *The Final Solution and the German Foreign Office.* New York, 1978.

Graml, H. "Die deutsche Gesandte in der Slowakei." In vol. 2 of *Gutachten des Instituts für Zeitgeschichte,* pp. 337–343. Stuttgart, 1966.

Hilberg, R. *The Destruction of the European Jews.* 3 vols. New York, 1985.

CHRISTOPHER R. BROWNING

LUDWIGSBURGER ZENTRALSTELLE (official name, Zentrale Stelle der Landesjustizverwaltungen zur Aufklärung von NS-Verbrechen Ludwigsburg, or Central Office of the Judicial Administrations of the *Länder* for Investigation of Nazi Crimes, Ludwigsburg; the *Länder* are the eleven states that make up the Federal Republic of Germany). Established on December 1, 1958, at Ludwigsburg, near Stuttgart, the Zentrale Stelle was given the task of investigating Nazi crimes in the period from 1933 to 1945 that were based exclusively or primarily on Nazi ideology and were punishable under existing legislation of the Federal Republic. The legal basis of the Zentrale Stelle's establishment was an agreement reached by the ministers and senators of justice of the several states; the office is staffed by prosecuting attorneys and judges.

At its inception, the Zentrale Stelle Ludwigsburg dealt only with crimes committed outside the present border of the Federal Republic. In 1964 the Zentrale Stelle's authority was extended to include all Nazi crimes, irrespective of the scene of the crime. It is not, however, authorized to deal with war crimes in the narrow sense of the term, that is, crimes committed in the course of the fighting that have no clear link to Nazi ideology. The task with which it was charged by the judicial administrations is to collect all available information and evidence on Nazi crimes, sort out the crimes, classify them into various categories, and establish the whereabouts of the criminals. Once a Nazi criminal's presence in the Federal Republic is established by the Zentrale Stelle, its task is to pass the case on to public prosecutors in the respective area for further action under the law.

By the end of 1985 the Zentrale Stelle had initiated more than twelve thousand cases for prosecution by the various public prosecution offices. In addition, the office coordinates the work of the public prosecutors in this field and in related judicial proceedings. To enable the Zentrale Stelle to carry out this coordination, the public prosecution offices forward to it all relevant material (such as protocols of court proceedings and other documents); the Zentrale Stelle in turn enters this material and information into a central card index and registry, which it puts at the disposal of all the public prosecutors and authorized investigative bodies.

BIBLIOGRAPHY

Hellendall, F. "Nazi Crimes before German Courts: The Immediate Post-War Era." *Wiener Library Bulletin* 24/3 (Summer 1970): 14–20.

Rückerl, A. *The Investigation of Nazi War Crimes, 1945–1978: A Documentation.* Hamden, Conn., 1980.

Rückerl, A. "Nazi Crimes Trials." In *The Nazi Concentration Camps: Structure and Aims; The Image of the Prisoner; The Jews in the Camps.* Proceedings of the Fourth Yad Vashem International Historical Conference, edited by Y. Gutman and A. Saf, pp. 505–518. Jerusalem, 1984.

Rückerl, A. *NS-Verbrechen vor Gericht.* Heidelberg, 1982.

ADALBERT RÜCKERL

LUTHER, MARTIN (1896–1945), Nazi official. As head of Abteilung Deutschland (Division Germany) of the German Foreign Office from 1940 to 1943, Luther was in charge of all business in the Foreign Office relating to internal and party affairs, including the Jewish desk (D III) of Franz RADEMACHER. His meteoric career was a not untypical manifestation of the destructive energies that the Nazi regime harnessed for its own purposes by opening up opportunities for advancement to the able and ambitious but professionally disadvantaged in Germany's tradition-bound society.

Born in Berlin, Luther joined the army in August 1914 without completing his high-school studies. After building up a furniture-moving business in the 1920s, he joined the Nazi party and the SA (Sturmabteilung; Storm Troopers) in March 1932. While active in party affairs in the Berlin suburb of Dahlem, he ingratiated himself with Joachim von RIBBENTROP and the latter's wife in the course of redecorating their villa. Luther gradually made himself indispensable to Ribbentrop, both as his major domo and as a political infighter against party rivals, and he was brought into the Foreign Office after Ribbentrop became foreign minister in 1938.

Luther rose rapidly to the rank of division chief in 1940 and under secretary in 1941, as he vigorously sought to build up a bureaucratic empire within the Foreign Office dedicated to Nazifying that institution from within while defending its position against party rivals on the outside. Thus, when it became clear to Luther in the fall of 1941 that the deportation and mass murder of European Jewry was a priority for the Nazi regime, he saw to it that the Foreign Office facilitated the deportations. Foreign Office cooperation with Adolf EICHMANN's office in the REICHSSICHERHEITSHAUPTAMT (Reich Security Main Office; RSHA) in this regard was finalized when Luther attended the WANNSEE CONFERENCE, initiated and chaired by Reinhard HEYDRICH, on January 20, 1942.

Tiring of Ribbentrop's obvious incompetence and gradually becoming estranged from him, Luther plotted to oust the foreign minister. The plot miscarried, and Luther was arrested in February 1943. He spent the rest of the war in the SACHSENHAUSEN concentration camp and died shortly after the collapse of the Third Reich.

BIBLIOGRAPHY

Browning, C. R. *The Final Solution and the German Foreign Office: A Study of Referat D3 of Abteilung Deutschland, 1940–1943.* New York, 1978.

CHRISTOPHER R. BROWNING

LUTSK (Pol., Łuck), city in the Ukrainian SSR; one of the most ancient cities in the Soviet Union. Between the two world wars, Lutsk was the capital of the Volhynia district in independent Poland; in September 1939 it was occupied by the Red Army and annexed with all of eastern Poland to the USSR. Jewish settlement had begun there in the late fourteenth century. On the eve of World War II, eighteen thousand Jews lived in the city, out of a total of forty-one thousand residents. During their rule over Lutsk, from September 1939 until June 1941, the Soviets nationalized the economy and liquidated the Jewish institutions and organizations.

From the first day of their invasion of the Soviet Union, on June 22, 1941, the Germans bombed Lutsk, and about 60 percent of its buildings were destroyed and many citizens killed, including a large number of Jews. On June 25 the Germans entered the city. The following day, Ukrainians conducted a pogrom during which they robbed the Jews, beat them, and killed several of them. Young Jews tried to organize a defense against the rioters. On June 27 an advance party of Einsatzkommando 4a reached Lutsk and found the corpses of many prisoners in the local jail, including numerous Ukrainians who had been killed by the Soviets prior to their retreat. The German military government and the heads of the nationalist Ukrainian community accused the Jews of murder. In reprisal, they seized three hundred Jews, whom they put to death on June 30. On July 2, Jewish men between the ages of sixteen and sixty were summoned for work; about two thousand of them were taken to the ruins of the Lubart fortress and murdered. German

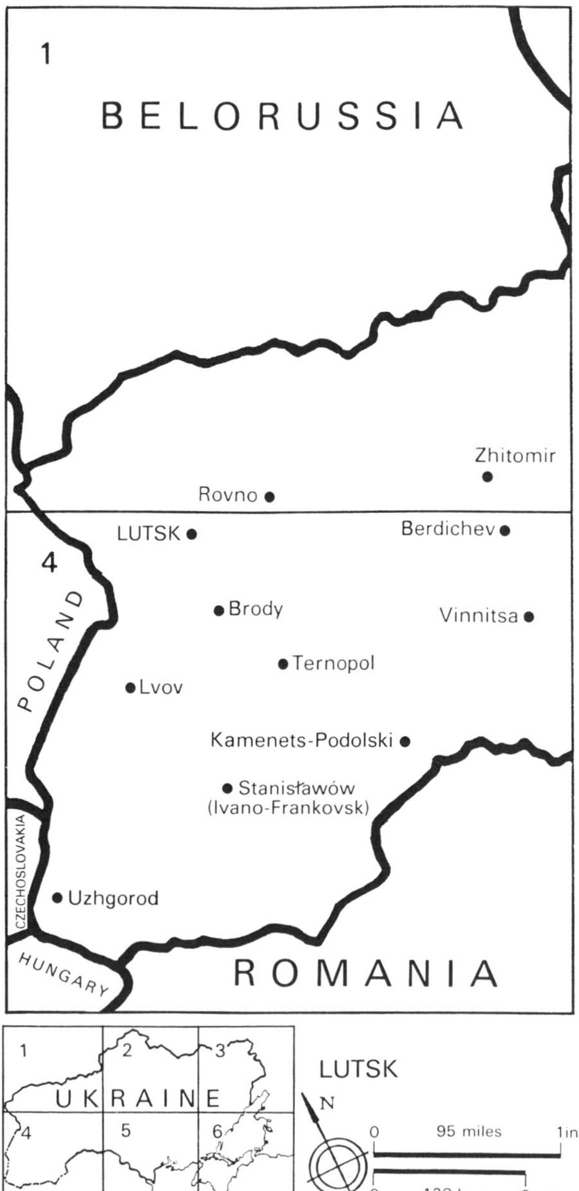

soldiers from rearguard units stationed in the city participated in the murder. In late July the Germans appointed a twelve-member JUDENRAT (Jewish Council), made up mainly of former communal workers. Valuables, radio receivers, and other items were confiscated, and the Jews had to pay fines in gold, silver, goods, and commodities.

On October 19 the SS created a labor camp in Lutsk where five hundred men were imprisoned. The Jews were moved on December 11 and 12 to a ghetto in the poorest part of the city, in conditions of great overcrowding and poor sanitation. On March 18, 1942, several hundred young Jews were sent to Vinnitsa to build Hitler's staff quarters. When the work was completed, all were killed, except for three who escaped to TRANSNISTRIA and were saved there with the help of Jews from Romania.

Between August 20 and 23 of 1942, 17,500 Lutsk Jews were taken outside the city and shot to death alongside pits prepared by a special SD (Sicherheitsdienst; Security Service) unit. On September 3 another 2,000 or so Jews, who were seized or found in hiding places, were murdered. The only Jews now remaining in the city were those in the labor camp. On December 11, 1942, the Jewish camp elder learned that they were to be put to death the next day. A revolt was quickly organized, led by the prisoner in charge of the carpentry shop and the tinsmith Moshe. In addition to several revolvers and sawed-off shotguns that were in their possession, the Jews prepared axes, knives, iron rods, bricks, and acid. On December 12 the Germans laid siege, but when they tried to enter the camp, they encountered a hail of bullets, bricks, and acid. Several of the attackers were wounded, and the face of the German commander was burned by acid. The Germans brought several armored vehicles and opened fire. After several hours, when most of the rebels had fallen, the Germans succeeded in entering the camp and murdered the remaining Jews, except for several who hid and escaped. The most prominent helpers of the Jews in this time of distress and in their flight from Lutsk were the Ukrainian Witold FOMENKO, several Poles, and some Czechs from the surrounding villages.

Lutsk was liberated on February 5, 1944. Since most of the city had been burned and destroyed, and since the front was not far away, most of the 150 survivors went to Rovno.

BIBLIOGRAPHY

The Lutsk Book. Tel Aviv, 1961. (In Hebrew.)

Spector, S. *The Holocaust of Volhynian Jews, 1941–1944.* Jerusalem, 1986. (In Hebrew.)

SHMUEL SPECTOR

LUTZ, CARL (Charles; 1895–1975), Swiss diplomat who heroically rescued Jews in HUNGARY in 1944. Born in Switzerland, Lutz studied in the United States, and in 1935 served as head of the Swiss consulate in Tel Aviv. At the outbreak of World War II in September 1939, he interceded on behalf of the twenty-five hundred German settlers in Palestine who were being deported as enemy aliens by the British. This stood him in good stead with German authorities in Hungary years later. On January 2, 1942, he arrived in BUDAPEST to represent the interests of the United States, the United Kingdom, and other countries that had severed relations with Miklós HORTHY's Hungary, a member of the Axis nations.

During the fall of 1942, in his capacity as the representative of British interests, Lutz, in coordination with Moshe (Miklós) Krausz (who represented the Jewish Agency in Budapest), drew up lists of children and gave them certificates of immigration to Palestine. Nearly two hundred children and their adult chaperons were able to leave for Palestine before the German occupation of Hungary.

When the Germans invaded Hungary on March 19, 1944, Lutz invited Krausz to move into a Swiss office on Szabadsag Ter and continue his work from there. Under Lutz's protection, from this office and later from the Glass House at 29 Vadasz Utca, Krausz continued to promote various schemes for immigration to Palestine and related rescue projects.

The protection of Hungarian Jews with documents that certified them as foreign nationals had begun somewhat before the German occupation. The Geneva representative of the El Salvador government, George Mantello, had granted papers to thousands of Hungarian Jews that certified them as Salvadoran nationals. Lutz, who also represented Salvadoran interests in Budapest, was responsible for the distribution of these certificates. Perhaps this is what inspired Moshe Krausz to urge the Jewish Agency and the Swiss to persuade the British to declare that all bearers of Palestinian certificates of immigration were to be treated as potential British nationals. By the end of June 1944, the British had accepted the proposal. In the meantime, various diplomats in Budapest and abroad, including Lutz, pressured the Hungarian government to stop the deportations that had begun in mid-May. Early in July, Horthy ordered the deportations stopped, and soon thereafter declared his government's willingness to allow some seventy-five hundred bearers of certificates to leave for Palestine. The stage was now set to bring these Jews under Swiss protection.

With the help of Krausz, a group of fifty Jews was assembled in the Glass House to work with Lutz. Photos were collected from four thousand persons, and Lutz issued four collective passports, each with one thousand names. Each person was then issued a "protective letter" (*Schutzbrief*) guaranteeing that person's safety until his or her eventual departure for Palestine. To add as many people as possible to these *Schutzbriefe,* Lutz interpreted the permits as representing family units and not individuals. Eventually, protective letters were drawn up for fifty thousand Jews.

At the same time, Lutz instructed the recently arrived Swedish diplomat Raoul WALLENBERG on the best uses of the protective passes, and gave him the names of persons in the government hierarchy with whom to negotiate. This idea served as a model for various types of protective letters issued by other neutral countries and by the International RED CROSS through Friedrich Born, its representative in Budapest. In addition, after the pro-Nazi ARROW CROSS PARTY came to power in mid-October of 1944, the Zionist youth underground manufactured and distributed tens of thousands of false documents, perhaps more than one hundred thousand, mostly in the name of Switzerland. Owing to

Carl Lutz.

the proliferation of false protective papers, the authorities pressured Lutz and Wallenberg to affirm the validity of the documents they had distributed. Lutz acquiesced so as to preclude the collapse of the entire rescue project. Late in November, he and his wife sorted out the bearers of legitimate passes from those holding forged papers at the assembly point in the Óbuda brickyard.

In the meantime, Lutz and other neutral diplomats, including Wallenberg and the papal nuncio, Angelo Rotta, interceded to have the new Hungarian government recognize the protective documents, using as bait the recognition of the regime by their governments. With the establishment of two ghettos, one for holders of protective passes and one for the rest of the Jews, Lutz procured twenty-five high-rise apartment buildings for concentrating the people under his protection. The Glass House and its annex also became a refuge for about three thousand Jews.

During the notorious death march (*see* DEATH MARCHES) of November 10 to 22, 1944, when over seventy thousand Jews were forcibly marched toward the Austrian border under the most inhumane conditions, Lutz and his fellow diplomats interceded on behalf of many Jews. Lutz made use of Salvadoran certificates still in his possession, following the deportees on their march and filling in many of their names on the documents. Those saved in this way were allowed to return to Budapest, which was already under siege by the Red Army. Ernst KALTENBRUNNER, the Gestapo head, in a dispatch to the German Foreign Ministry complained about the disappearance of many Jews on this march as a result of intervention by the Swiss legation, as well as by the representatives of Sweden, Spain, Portugal, and the Vatican.

With the tightening of the Soviet siege of Budapest in December 1944, all foreign representatives were ordered to leave the beleaguered capital. Maximilian Jaeger, the head of the Swiss legation in Budapest, had already departed on November 10. But Lutz, not willing to abandon his protégés, decided to remain behind. Over thirty thousand Jews (out of a total of some one hundred thousand) with various protective passes—Swiss, Swedish, Red Cross, and Vatican—were housed in the so-called international ghetto.

Lutz later related that a German diplomat revealed to him that the Arrow Cross had received instructions not to harm the protected houses so long as Lutz remained in Budapest, as a token of Germany's gratitude to him for having looked after the interests of German expatriates in Palestine in 1939 and 1940. For three months thereafter, Lutz, together with his wife and a group of Jewish refugees, lived a precarious existence in the basement of the abandoned, but bombarded, British legation, almost without food and water. When the Russians stormed the building, Lutz jumped through the window and managed to reach Buda, the section of the city occupied only in February 1945.

In 1965, Lutz was recognized by YAD VASHEM as a "RIGHTEOUS AMONG THE NATIONS."

BIBLIOGRAPHY

Grossman, A. *Nur das Gewissen: Carl Lutz und seine Budapester Aktion; Geschichte und Porträt.* N.p., Switzerland, 1986.

MORDECAI PALDIEL and ROBERT ROZETT

LUXEMBOURG, grand duchy in western Europe bordering on Belgium, France, and Germany, with an area of 999 square miles (2,586 sq km) and a population, before World War II, of about 300,000.

From the Middle Ages to the nineteenth century, the Duchy of Luxembourg was variously part of Germany or the Low Countries, and later (1815–1830) was joined to the Netherlands. In 1868 it gained recognition as an independent, neutral entity, a status that did not, however, prevent Germany from occupying it during World War I. Jews are mentioned in Luxembourg as early as the thirteenth century, but settled there in significant numbers only in the nineteenth; on the eve of World War II the duchy had a Jewish population of thirty-five hundred, of whom three-quarters came from eastern Europe, including one thousand to fifteen hundred refugees who arrived after 1933. Heading the Jewish establishment was a Consistoire, which financed religious functionaries and community institutions. Jewish welfare organizations helped the refugees obtain residence visas and provided them with economic support; as a result, the refugees' integration proceeded fairly smoothly, despite their relative large numbers and the differences in religious customs and way of life.

On May 10, 1940, the Germans invaded Luxembourg. Although they met with little resistance, they had the help of a fifth column, made up of VOLKSDEUTSCHE (ethnic Germans) who apparently wanted to see the duchy incorporated into the Third Reich. An ongoing effort was launched to gain the support of the population for this step. As soon as the invasion started, the grand duchess and her family fled, first to France and from there to the United States, and the cabinet (except for one minister) fled to London.

From early May to early August 1940, Luxembourg was under military administration. Some Jewish property was confiscated, but no conspicuous anti-Jewish legislation was enacted. Many Jews had fled to Belgium and France in the first phase of the occupation, and when it seemed to them that Jews were not being singled out for harassment, some returned. On August 2, 1940, a civilian administration was installed, headed by Gauleiter Gustav Simon, a former shoemaker and a member of the Luxembourg Nazi party. Simon made efforts to have Luxembourg "return" to the Reich, the emphasis being on return rather than annexation. On August 10, festivities were held to mark this "return," but the event met with a hostile reaction on the part of the local population. Attempts were made to incite the Luxembourgers to riot against the Jews from August 16 to 18—Jewish shops were marked with a yellow label for this purpose—but no excesses against Jews are reported to have taken place, and the population remained indifferent.

In September of that year a campaign was launched to induce the population to join the Nazi party; many of those who refused to do so were sent to Germany as forced laborers, and numerous arrests were made among the intellectuals. An additional campaign was conducted for Luxembourgers to join the Reich by becoming German citizens on an individual basis. The Germans preferred such individual "annexation" of Luxembourg nationals to the duchy's formal annexation, since the latter would have contradicted their claim that Luxembourg was simply coming back of its own will into the German fold. The effort continued until October 19, 1941, when a census was held and the inhabitants were called upon to declare themselves German nationals. Instead, 95 percent registered as Luxembourgers. This amounted to an all-out demonstration against the regime, and led to mass arrests.

On August 20, 1942, all male Luxembourg nationals of draft age were ordered to follow the example set by the *Volksdeutsche* and enlist in the German army. The order, affecting 14,500 persons, was met with mass resistance and a general strike, to which the Germans reacted with executions that lasted throughout the period of occupation. The Luxembourgers' resistance expressed itself in the publication of illegal placards, strikes, sabotage in the factories, and a few underground operations; there is, however, no evidence of Luxembourgers supporting Jews as a means of expressing their opposition to the Germans. In the week preceding their withdrawal from the duchy, in the fall of 1944, SS units engaged for the last time in a terror campaign against the population.

About a month after the installation of the civil administration under Gauleiter Simon, on September 5, 1940, the NUREMBERG LAWS were introduced in Luxembourg; at the same time, the Jews were put on forced labor. This was followed by more anti-Jewish decrees, and in September 1941 Jews were ordered to wear the yellow badge (*see* BADGE, JEWISH). In practice, the authorities encouraged the emigration of Jews from Luxembourg, permitting sixteen groups of Jews, including all the community leaders, to go to France and Portugal between August 1940 and May 1941. In the spring of 1941 the last two leaders of the community, Rabbi Robert Serebrenik and Louis Sternberg, attended a meeting in Berlin at which they were told by Adolf EICHMANN that the emigration of Jews from Luxembourg was being stopped. In May 1941 they themselves left for Portugal on the last convoy. On October 15, 1941, a Jew born in Metz, Alfred Oppenheimer—who had not previously belonged to the leadership of the community—was appointed chairman of the Consistoire (renamed in April 1942 the Ältestenrat der Juden, or Council of Jewish Elders). Oppenheimer affixed his signature to any instructions placed before him by the Gestapo.

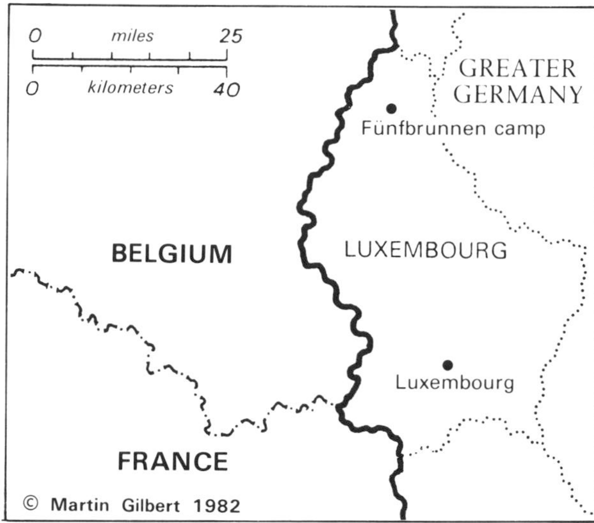

Two days previously, on October 13, the Consistoire reported that 750 Jews were left in Luxembourg, of whom only 13 were fit for work; 80 percent were aged fifty or above, and 60 percent were sixty or above. The Germans had begun rounding up the Jews two months earlier, placing them in the Fünfbrunnen camp, on a railway line near Ulflingen, at a site that up to 1938 had been a Jesuit monastery. The camp was organized along ghetto lines and became the point from which the Luxembourg Jews were deported to the east. The first transport (and the largest, comprising 324 persons) left for Łódź on October 16, 1941. Altogether, 674 persons were deported on eight transports, the last of which left on September 28, 1943. Only 36 persons out of those deported survived; all the rest perished.

Luxembourg became *judenrein* ("cleansed of Jews") except for a few Jews who had gone into hiding or were married to non-Jews. Once the deportations started, the chances of Jews' being saved were poor. The country was small; it had a relatively large German population; the Luxembourgers were indifferent to the fate of the Jews, and while there were few instances of open hostility or informing, neither were there many efforts to hide Jews or otherwise help them, despite the prevailing opposition to the occupying power. The splendid synagogue, dating from 1894, was destroyed in August 1943 by an Italian contractor—according to the Luxembourgers, no local contractor was prepared to take on the job of demolition. With the sizable emigrations and escapes, as well as deportations, finally only a small, leaderless, and mostly aged community was left, spared by the Germans, who presumably assumed that it would die out before long.

Allied forces liberated Luxembourg on September 9, 1944. Of the 3,500 Jews who had been living there in 1939, 1,555 were saved, by fleeing, hiding, or surviving in the camps; 1,945 were murdered, a third in the extermination camps to which they were deported, the rest in the duchy itself or in other occupied countries to which they fled or were deported for extermination. Only a few Jews returned to Luxembourg after the war.

BIBLIOGRAPHY

Bech, J. M., ed. *Luxemburg and the German Invasion, Before and After (The Grey Book).* London, 1942.

Cerf, P. *Longtemps j'aurai mémoire.* Luxembourg, 1974.

Friedrich, E. *Als Luxemburg entvölkert werden sollte.* Luxembourg, 1969.

Weber, P. *Geschichte Luxemburgs im Zweiten Weltkrieg.* Luxembourg, 1947.

RUTH ZARIZ

LVOV (Pol., Lwów; Ger., Lemberg), city in Eastern Galicia, now capital of an oblast (district) in the western part of the Ukrainian SSR. An industrial and cultural center, Lvov was founded in the thirteenth century. From 1772 to 1918 it was under Austrian rule, and in the interwar period it was a provincial capital in independent Poland. The population was 340,000 in 1939, when its Jewish population of 110,000 made it the third largest Jewish community in the country. Active antisemitism was widespread, one reason being that the Poles and the Ukrainians each accused the Jews of helping the other. On the eve of World War II, Jewish Lvov was a center of culture and education and of vigorous political activity by the Orthodox Jews (including Hasidim), Zionists, Bundists, and Communists.

Three weeks after the outbreak of the war, the Soviets entered Lvov and annexed it to the USSR, together with the rest of Eastern Galicia. The Soviet authorities disbanded the community institutions; outlawed political parties; nationalized factories, large holdings, and wholesale businesses; restricted the retail trade; and organized the artisans into cooperative societies. Cultural life, however, remained lively. Some 100,000 Jewish refugees from German-occupied western Poland crowded into the city; in the summer of 1940

During the Lvov pogrom of June 30 to July 3, 1941, a Ukrainian rabble rampaged through the city, ravishing, abusing, and murdering Jews. Here, German soldiers film the pogrom.

many of them were expelled to the remote regions of the USSR. Following the German invasion of the Soviet Union on June 22, 1941, about 10,000 Jews escaped from Lvov, together with the Red Army, which was retreating from the city.

On June 30, 1941, the Germans occupied Lvov. The killing of Jews began that same day, committed by Einsatzgruppe C (*see* EINSATZGRUPPEN), German soldiers, Ukrainian nationalists, and plain rabble. The Germans and the Ukrainians spread a rumor that the Jews had taken part in the execution of Ukrainian political prisoners whose bodies had been discovered in the dungeons of the NKVD (the Soviet political police). In four days of rioting, ending on July 3, 1941, four thousand Jews were murdered. On July 8, Jews aged fourteen and over were ordered to wear on their right arm a white badge with a blue Star of David (*see* BADGE, JEWISH). From July 25 to 27 the Ukrainians again went on the rampage, murdering two thousand more Jews. These pogroms became known as the PETLIURA DAYS. At the end of July 1941, a temporary Jewish committee was established, made up of five prominent community leaders. Within a short time the committee was enlarged and became a JUDENRAT (Jewish Council), with Dr. Joseph Parnes as chairman. Throughout the period he was in office, Parnes stood up for the interests of the community. That August, the Jews of Lvov were ordered to pay a ransom of 20 million rubles. Hostages were taken to ensure payment, and were killed even though the money was paid at the appointed time.

During the summer of 1941, Jewish property was plundered, the Jews were put on forced labor, synagogues were burned down, and Jewish cemeteries were destroyed. In the fall, the Germans intensifed their demands for Jewish forced labor for road work and for the construction of bridges and military camps. In September a Jewish police force was established, under the Judenrat. Its duties, in the initial period, consisted of keeping order and ensuring cleanliness in the streets

Ukrainian youths molest a Jewish woman during the pogrom of June 30 to July 3, 1941.

inhabited by Jews, confiscating valuables at the behest of the Germans, and escorting persons who were on their way to forced labor. Parnes, the chairman of the Judenrat, was killed by the Germans at the end of October, when he refused to hand over Jews who were to be moved to the JANÓWSKA camp, then being established. His place was taken by Abraham Rotfeld.

On November 8, 1941, the Germans published an order on the establishment of a ghetto, giving the Jews until December 15 to move into the area allocated for this purpose. In the course of the move to the ghetto, five thousand elderly and sick Jews were killed as they were about to cross the bridge on Peltewna Street. The move was not completed by the allotted time, but many thousands of Jews were herded into the Zamarstynów and Kleparów quarters, in which the ghetto was set up. During the winter of 1941–1942, the Germans began sending Jews to labor camps at Laszki Murowane, Hermanów, Vinniki, Jaktorów, Kamionka Strumilowa, and Skole. In February 1942 Abraham Rotfeld died, and the Germans appointed Henryk Landsberg to take his place as Judenrat chairman.

In March 1942, the Judenrat was ordered to prepare lists of Jews who were to be sent to the east, allegedly to work there. A delegation of rabbis appealed to Landsberg to refuse to cooperate with the Germans in preparing the lists and rounding up the people on them. Landsberg refused, claiming that if the Germans themselves were to carry out the deportation, far more people would be killed. In this *Aktion,* which began on March 19 and continued until the end of the month, fifteen thousand Jews were taken to the BEŁŻEC extermination camp.

In the spring of that year, the Jews of Lvov tried to find jobs in factories that performed an essential function for the German economy, hoping thereby to be exempt from future deportations. On July 8, seven thousand Jews who could not produce a certificate of employment were seized by the Germans and deported to the Janówska camp, where they were murdered. A month later, on August 10, the "Large *Aktion*" was launched, lasting until August 23, in the course of which fifty thousand persons were sent to Bełżec. At the beginning of September 1942 Jews who were still living outside the ghetto were herded inside, the ghetto area was greatly reduced, and what remained was sealed off. Landsberg and a group of Judenrat employees, as well as the Jewish policemen, were hanged by the Germans. Eduard Eberson was appointed Judenrat chairman in place of Landsberg.

In November, five thousand to seven thousand "unproductive" persons were removed from the ghetto, some of them to be sent to the Janówska camp and the rest to Bełżec. Toward the end of 1942, the ghetto came to resemble a labor camp. The inhabitants were assigned lodging in buildings according to their place of employment. Those who had no employment card in their possession were hunted down systematically and, when caught, were put to death in groups.

In January 1943 the ghetto officially became a labor camp, a *Julag* (*Judenlager,* or "Jewish camp"). At the beginning of that month, ten thousand Jews were executed, having first been classified as "illegals" because they could show no employment card. On January 30 the Judenrat was disbanded, and most of its members were murdered. An *Oberjude* (chief Jew) was appointed head of the *Julag* to serve as liaison "between the surviving inmates of the ghetto-camp and the authorities." On March 17, fifteen hundred Jews were murdered, most of them in the Piasky area near the city, and at the same time some eight hundred Jews were deported to AUSCHWITZ. In May 1943 the slaughter of the remnant of the community was speeded up. *Selektionen* were made at the places where the Jews were working, and only those classified as "vitally important" were permitted to stay; the rest were killed.

On June 1, 1943, the final *Aktion* was undertaken, to liquidate the ghetto-*Julag*. German and Ukrainian police units surrounded the ghetto and closed every avenue of escape. Additional police units entered the ghetto to round up all the inhabitants. At this point the Germans and their Ukrainian helpers encountered resistance; hand grenades and Molotov cocktails were thrown at them and they were fired on. Nine persons, Germans and Ukrainians, were killed, and twenty were wounded. The Germans did not dare enter the buildings; instead, they blew them up or set them on fire, in order to kill those who were inside or force them to come out of their hiding places and give themselves up.

In the course of liquidating the ghetto, the Germans seized seven thousand Jews, whom they deported to the Janówska camp, where they were soon put to death. In the ghetto area itself about three thousand Jews met their death. The liquidation process came to an end on June 2, 1943, but as late as July, searches were still being made for Jews hiding in the ghetto ruins.

As of mid-1942, and especially in the wake of the "Large *Aktion*," efforts were made in the ghetto to organize an underground. Groups of young people tried to obtain weapons so as to be able to offer armed resistance. Toward the end of 1942, one such group attempted to escape from the ghetto into the nearby forest, where they planned to set up resistance centers against the Germans and their helpers. The attempt failed, and most of the members of the group were killed en route. Nevertheless, more efforts were made to reach the forests situated in the BRODY area. In one such attempt the vehicle in which one of the groups was traveling was apprehended, and all of its passengers fell into German hands. The driver, a Pole who had undertaken to transport the group to their destination, was suspected of having informed on them to the Germans.

While there was no organized and consolidated resistance movement in the Lvov ghetto, in many instances various forms of action were taken against the Germans and their helpers. Attempts to organize resistance to the Germans were made in one of the Jewish police units. An organized resistance group headed by Tadek Drotorski was active in one of the labor camps, on Czwartakow Street, where hundreds of Jews were employed. When the Germans picked up the group's trail, in March 1943, Drotorski shot and killed a German policeman. An underground news sheet was published in the ghetto by Ha-Shomer ha-Tsa'ir followers and edited by Michael Hofman.

The month of March 1943 witnessed more and more attempts to break out of the *Julag* in order to reach the forest and establish contact with the partisans active in the area. Among those who made such attempts was the Yiddish poet Jacob Schudrych, who succeeded in reaching the forest, only to find his death there.

BIBLIOGRAPHY

Kahana, D. *Lvov Ghetto Diary*. Jerusalem, 1978. (In Hebrew.)

Lewin, E. "Zagłada lwowskiego getta." *Biuletyn Żydowskiego Instytutu* 17–18 (1965): 171–214.

Wells, L. *The Janowska Road*. New York, 1963.

Zadereczki, T. *When the Swastika Ruled in Lvov: The Destruction of the Jewish Community as Seen by a Polish Author*. Jerusalem, 1982. (In Hebrew.)

AHARON WEISS

M

MACEDONIA, region in southern YUGOSLAVIA; now one of the country's six federated republics. Jews lived in Macedonia as far back as Roman times. On the eve of World War II, it had a Jewish population of about 7,800, mostly Sephardim living in Skopje (3,800), Bitola (3,300), and Štip (550). In April 1941 Yugoslavia was invaded by Germany, and during the rest of the war it was occupied by German, Italian, Hungarian, and Bulgarian troops. Macedonia was annexed to Bulgaria, and the anti-Jewish legislation that had been introduced in that country in January 1941 was now also applied to Macedonia.

Initially, anti-Jewish legislation was enacted mainly in the economic sphere. Macedonian Jews, who had been quite poor to begin with, were hard hit by the new measures: shopkeepers lost their businesses, and Jewish professionals—lawyers, doctors,

The Macedonian partisan brigade. The four young women are Jewish; their names are Estreja Ovadia, Estreja Levi, Zamila Kalonymus, and Adela Faridi.

teachers, and so on—were prohibited from dealing with non-Jews. From time to time, fines were imposed on the Jewish communities, and various restrictions were laid down limiting the Jews' freedom of movement, the places where they could live, and the public facilities they could visit.

Further legislation, enacted in the fall of 1942, made a clear distinction between Jews and the rest of the population. The first such step was the withholding of Bulgarian citizenship from Macedonian Jews (it was automatically conferred on the rest of the population). Next, on September 4, 1942, Jews were ordered to identify their places of residence and their businesses, and, by the end of the month, all Jews aged ten and over had to wear a Star of David on their left breast (*see* BADGE, JEWISH).

At the end of 1941 the Germans entered into negotiations with Bulgaria concerning the deportation of Bulgarian Jews to extermination camps. These negotiations were conducted by the German ambassador in Sofia, Adolf Heinz Beckerle, and the Bulgarian minister of the interior, Petur Gabrovski. In the final stage, Adolf EICHMANN's special representative in Bulgaria, Theodor DANNECKER, and the Bulgarian commissar for Jewish affairs, Aleksander Belev, took matters into their own hands. On February 22, 1943, Bulgaria and Germany signed an agreement under which "twenty thousand Jews, irrespective of sex or age . . . would be expelled to the eastern provinces [of the Reich]; . . . the Bulgarian Ministry of the Interior would ensure that the transports would consist only of Jews." The figure of twenty thousand was more than the total number of all the Jews of Macedonia and northern THRACE, so in order to fill the entire quota, Bulgarian Jews were also to be included. The Bulgarian government wanted above all to get rid of the Jews in the newly annexed territories, Macedonia and Thrace.

On March 11, 1943, in a well-planned operation arranged and coordinated by the Bulgarian Commissariat for Jewish Affairs, all the Macedonian Jews were seized by the Bulgarian police and gendarmerie; the same fate also overtook the Jews of Thrace. In the operation, 7,341 Macedonian Jews were imprisoned in a temporary transit camp put up for this purpose in the government tobacco warehouses in Skopje. Eleven days later, 165 of the detainees, mostly doctors, pharmacists, and foreign nationals, were set free. The rest were deported to the TREBLINKA extermination camp (on March 22, 25, and 29), where they were all killed in the gas chambers, including more than 2,000 children below the age of sixteen. Only 200 Macedonian Jews survived the war.

BIBLIOGRAPHY

Chary, F. B. *Bulgarian Jews and the Final Solution, 1940–1944.* Pittsburgh, 1972.

Matkovski, A. "The Destruction of Macedonian Jews." *Yad Vashem Studies* 3 (1959): 203–260.

MENACHEM SHELAH

MACH, ALEXANDER (Saňo; 1902–?), Slovak leader; commander of the fascist HLINKA GUARD, head of the Slovak secret police and the propaganda office, and later minister for internal affairs in the Slovak puppet state. Mach was one of the chief advocates of the expulsion of the Jews from SLOVAKIA. In the summer of 1940 he succeeded Dr. Ferdinand Ďurčanský as minister of internal affairs. Along with President Jozef TISO and Prime Minister Vojtech (Bela) TUKA, he participated in a meeting with Adolf HITLER at Salzburg on July 28, 1940. There, the decision was made to establish a National Socialist regime in Slovakia. For most of the duration of the

Slovak state, Mach and Tuka headed a more extreme faction that opposed the somewhat less extreme Tiso faction in the government.

In September 1941, Mach and Tuka pressed for the evacuation of some ten thousand BRATISLAVA Jews to Saris-Zemplin in eastern Slovakia. The deportation of Slovak Jewry began on March 27, 1942, and the Slovak government agreed to pay the Germans a "carrying charge" of 500 reichsmarks per Jew (45 million reichsmarks, or $1.8 million, for what amounted to the deportation of nearly fifty-eight thousand Jews over a seven-month period). The deportations were implemented by the notorious Department 14, which was headed by Anton Vasek and was a part of Mach's ministry. At the beginning of the deportations, Mach announced over the radio that the Jewish problem was being solved in a "Christian" way, in that the Jews were being deported to work.

On February 7, 1943, Mach threatened to renew the deportations. His plans were thwarted, however, because the Germans were not pressing for the continuation of the transports at the time, and also because of the efforts of the PRACOVNÁ SKUPINA (Working Group) in Slovakia. Mach continued to serve as a minister until the Slovak government was reconstituted on September 5, 1944, during the time of the SLOVAK NATIONAL UPRISING.

After the war, Mach was condemned to thirty years' imprisonment by the National Tribunal in Bratislava.

Alexander Mach (front, right) with Prime Minister Vojtech Tuka next to him.

BIBLIOGRAPHY

Dagan, A., et al., eds. *The Jews of Czechoslovakia: Historical Studies and Surveys.* Vol. 3. Philadelphia, 1984.

Manatey, V. S., and L. Rudomir. *A History of the Czechoslovak Republic, 1918–1948.* Princeton, 1973.

ROBERT ROZETT

MADAGASCAR PLAN. The expulsion of the European Jews to Madagascar, an island off the southeast coast of Africa, was a notion of numerous antisemites that briefly dominated Nazi Jewish policy in the summer of 1940. Its ultimate impracticality helped pave the way psychologically among the Nazis for a "FINAL SOLUTION" to the Jewish question through mass murder rather than expulsion.

In the interwar years the idea of expelling Jews to Madagascar, then a French colony, was put forward in Britain by the antisemites Henry Hamilton Beamish and Arnold Leese, and in the Netherlands by Egon van Winghene. In 1937 the Poles, who wished to encourage the emigration of a large number of Jews, received permission from the French to send a three-man investigative commission comprised of Maj. Mieczysław Lepecki, Leon Alter, and Solomon Dyk to Madagascar to explore the possibility of settling Polish Jews there. Lepecki thought that 40,000 to 60,000 Jews could be supported in the cooler highlands, but Alter—the more optimistic of the two Jewish members of the team—felt the island could accommodate a maximum of only 2,000 Jews. In addition to the Polish and French governments, the British government and even the JOINT DISTRIBUTION COMMITTEE briefly toyed with the notion of resettling Jews in Madagascar. It is not surprising, therefore, that the idea appealed to the Nazis as well.

In early 1938, just ten days before the ANSCHLUSS, Adolf EICHMANN was instructed to collect material for a "foreign-policy solution" to the Jewish question (as was being negotiated by Poland with France concerning the possibility of transferring Polish Jews to Madagascar). Various Nazi leaders—Julius STREICHER, Hermann GÖRING, Alfred ROSENBERG, Hans FRANK, Joachim von RIBBENTROP, and even the fellow traveler Hjalmar SCHACHT

—mentioned the idea during the next years. However, it did not catch fire until the summer of 1940, when a conjuncture of factors made the Madagascar Plan a panacea eagerly grasped at by frustrated Nazis.

In the spring of 1940, Heinrich HIMMLER's cherished dream of expelling the Jews and Poles from the incorporated territories of western Poland into the GENERALGOUVERNEMENT clashed with the pragmatic econonic arguments of Hermann Göring and the governor general, Hans Frank, that population resettlement be subordinated to the interests of the war economy and the receptive capacity of the Generalgouvernement. The imminent victory over France, however, gave Himmler the opportunity of reviving his plan through a direct appeal to Hitler. Himmler's memorandum "Some Thoughts on the Treatment of the Alien Populations in the East" was discussed with Hitler on May 25, 1940, one week after German troops had reached the English Channel and trapped the best units of the Allied armies at Dunkerque. Himmler argued for removing all the "ethnic mush" of Germany to the Generalgouvernement, where it would be reduced to a denationalized helot status. As for the Jews in particular, Himmler wanted an even more drastic and comprehensive solution: "I hope completely to erase the concept of Jews through the possibility of a great emigration of all Jews to a colony in Africa or elsewhere." Concerning this systematic eradication of the ethnic composition of eastern Europe, Himmler concluded: "However cruel and tragic each individual case may be, this method is still the mildest and best, if one rejects the Bolshevik method of physical extermination of a people out of inner conviction as un-German and impossible." Hitler found Himmler's plans "very good and correct" and permitted Himmler to inform his rivals that the Führer had "recognized and confirmed" them as authoritative guidelines.

Himmler's vision of expelling the Jews to an African colony was made more plausible and attractive by several other factors. The expectation of imminent victory over France and Britain seemed to place the colonies of the former and merchant shipping of the latter at Germany's disposal. Occupation of additional territories in western Europe brought hundreds of thousands of additional Jews into the German sphere; meanwhile, resettlement of even the half-million Jews in the incorporated territories on a Lublin Reservation had proved unrealizable (*see* NISKO AND LUBLIN PLAN). The failure of this earlier expulsion scheme thus enhanced the attractiveness of expulsion overseas.

In late May 1940, Hitler approved Himmler's general idea of expelling the Jews to some African colony, but it was left to the Jewish expert of the German Foreign Office, Franz RADEMACHER, to turn the Madagascar Plan into a concrete proposal. Anxious to ensure that the racial question was not ignored by the more traditional elements of the Foreign Office when the peace treaty with France was drawn up, Rademacher proposed on June 3, 1940, that Germany exploit the victory over France to send at least some, if not all, Jews out of Europe—"to Madagascar, for example." The idea was almost immediately taken up by Hitler. At a conference on June 18 concerning the fate of the French empire, Hitler and Ribbentrop informed Benito Mussolini and the Italian foreign minister, Count Galeazzo Ciano, of Germany's intention to settle the European Jews in Madagascar. Hitler repeated this intention to Grand Adm. Erich Raeder two days later. Himmler's deputy, Reinhard HEYDRICH, quickly asserted his jurisdiction in "a territorial final solution" to the Jewish question. Henceforth work on the Madagascar Plan was to proceed in both the Foreign Office and the SS.

News of the plan rapidly spread to the German occupation authorities in the east. On July 1, 1940, the head of the JUDENRAT (Jewish Council) in Warsaw, Adam CZERNIAKÓW, recorded in his diary that an SS man had blurted out "that the war would be over in a month and that we would all leave for Madagascar." Governor General Frank was greatly relieved to receive word not only that the impending expulsion of Jews into his territory was now canceled, but that he would soon be rid of his own Jews as well. In the Generalgouvernement, ghetto construction was halted as pointless, in view of the Führer's plan. Moreover, the expulsion of the ŁÓDŹ Jews into the Generalgouvernement, repeatedly postponed and most recently rescheduled for August, was canceled once again, and the German authorities there faced the prospect of having to keep their Jews until victory over Great Britain opened the seaway to Madagascar.

Meanwhile, work went forward feverishly in Berlin under the auspices of both Rademacher in the Foreign Office and Eichmann, Heydrich's expert for Jewish affairs and evacuations, who had been working since the outbreak of war on expelling Jews and Poles from the Third Reich into the Generalgouvernement. Rademacher consulted various authorities and developed a plan involving numerous German agencies: the Foreign Office would handle negotiations with both France and Britain for the peace treaty, as well as with other European countries for regulating their participation; the Office of the FOUR-YEAR PLAN would coordinate the utilization of Jewish property; the Führer Chancellery would coordinate transportation; propaganda would be handled by Goebbels internally and by the Foreign Office abroad; and the SS would be in charge of collecting the Jews in Europe and administering the island "super-ghetto."

Eichmann also conducted extensive research, sending members of his staff to the Tropical Institute in Hamburg and the French colonial archives in Paris. He met with a group of German Jewish leaders in early July 1940 and ordered them to prepare within twenty-four hours a list of considerations that would have to be taken into account for evacuating four million Jews from Europe at the end of the war. Consultation with them came to an abrupt end, however, when they showed enthusiasm only for the destination of Palestine, which Eichmann explicitly ruled out. In contrast to the Foreign Office plan, which provided for broad participation, the SS version that emerged by the end of the summer placed the entire direction of the project—from finance to transport to security and even to diplomatic negotiations—under Heydrich.

The differences between Foreign Office and SS versions of the plan were never reconciled, for work on it came to an abrupt halt with Germany's failure in the Battle of Britain in September 1940. Born of hopes of imminent military victory over France, the Madagascar Plan died with Germany's unexpected setback in the skies over Great Britain. Hitler faced a new strategic dilemma, and Nazi Jewish policy would be inextricably caught up in his decision to break out of this dilemma through an attack on the Soviet Union. The ensuing "war of destruction" against the Soviet Union would unleash a war of destruction against the Jews as well.

The Madagascar Plan has sometimes been dismissed by historians as a misleading reflection of Nazi intentions because of its brief existence and its seeming fecklessness in contrast to the monumental horrors that followed. But in the summer of 1940, Nazi leaders were not engaged in an elaborate sham; they were making real decisions based on the Madagascar Plan as a reality of Nazi Jewish policy. Though not yet the "Final Solution"—the compulsive and comprehensive program to kill every Jew whom the Nazis could lay their hands on—the Madagascar Plan still implied massive losses among the Jewish population.

BIBLIOGRAPHY

Browning, C. R. *The Final Solution and the German Foreign Office: A Study of Referat D3 of Abteilung Deutschland, 1940–1943.* New York, 1978.

Friedman, P. "The Lublin Reservation and the Madagascar Plan: Two Aspects of Nazi Jewish Policy during the Second World War." *YIVO Annual of Jewish Social Studies* 7 (1953): 151–177.

Hevesi, E. "Hitler's Plan for Madagascar." *Contemporary Jewish Record* 5 (1941): 381–395.

CHRISTOPHER R. BROWNING

MAIN COMMISSION FOR INVESTIGATION OF NAZI CRIMES IN POLAND. *See* Documentation Centers: Main Commission for Investigation of Nazi Crimes in Poland.

MAIN TRUSTEESHIP OFFICE EAST. *See* Haupttreuhandstelle Ost.

MAJDANEK, concentration camp run by the Waffen-SS (*Konzentrationslager der Waffen-SS Lublin*). Majdanek was located in a suburb of LUBLIN, Poland, and was called the Majdan Tatarski camp, or Majdanek for short. It was established on the orders of Heinrich HIMMLER, following an agreement with the Wehrmacht under which some Soviet prisoners of war would be handed over to the SS and put at the disposal of the program for the "Germanization" of the east. The SS and Police Leader in the Lublin district, Odilo GLOBOCNIK, played a decisive role in the establishment of Majdanek. Until 1943 the camp's designation was *Kriegsgefangenenlager der Waffen-SS Lublin* (Prisoner-of-War Camp of the Waffen-SS Lublin). It was not, however, confined to any particular category of prisoners. Its function was to destroy enemies of the Third Reich and to take part in the extermination of the Jews and the deportation and "resettlement" of the inhabitants of the ZAMOŚĆ region. The Majdanek camp covered about 667 acres (2.7 sq km) of uncultivated land on the Lublin-Zamość-Chełm highway. It had a double barbed-wire fence connected to a high-voltage transmission line, with nineteen watchtowers, each 26.5 feet (8.8 m) high, equipped with mobile searchlights and 130 illumination fixtures.

The camp was divided into five sections, each serving a different purpose—one, for example, was for women prisoners and another for hostages. There were twenty-two prisoner barracks, two of which were used for administration and supplies. Majdanek also had seven gas chambers and two wooden gallows, situated in the area separating the camp's sections from one another, as well as a small crematorium. Adjoining the camp were workshops, storehouses, buildings for coal storage, laundries, and so on. In all there were 227 structures. In September 1943 a large crematorium, containing five furnaces, was added. The section reserved for the SS contained their barracks, a casino, and the camp commandant's offices. The plans for the camp provided for the eventual construction of barracks for 250,000 prisoners, the establishment of industrial plants, and the construction of additional gas chambers and a more efficient crematorium; but by the time the camp was liberated, only 20 percent of these plans had been put into effect.

Close to 500,000 persons, from twenty-eight countries and belonging to fifty-four different nationalities, passed through Majdanek. Of

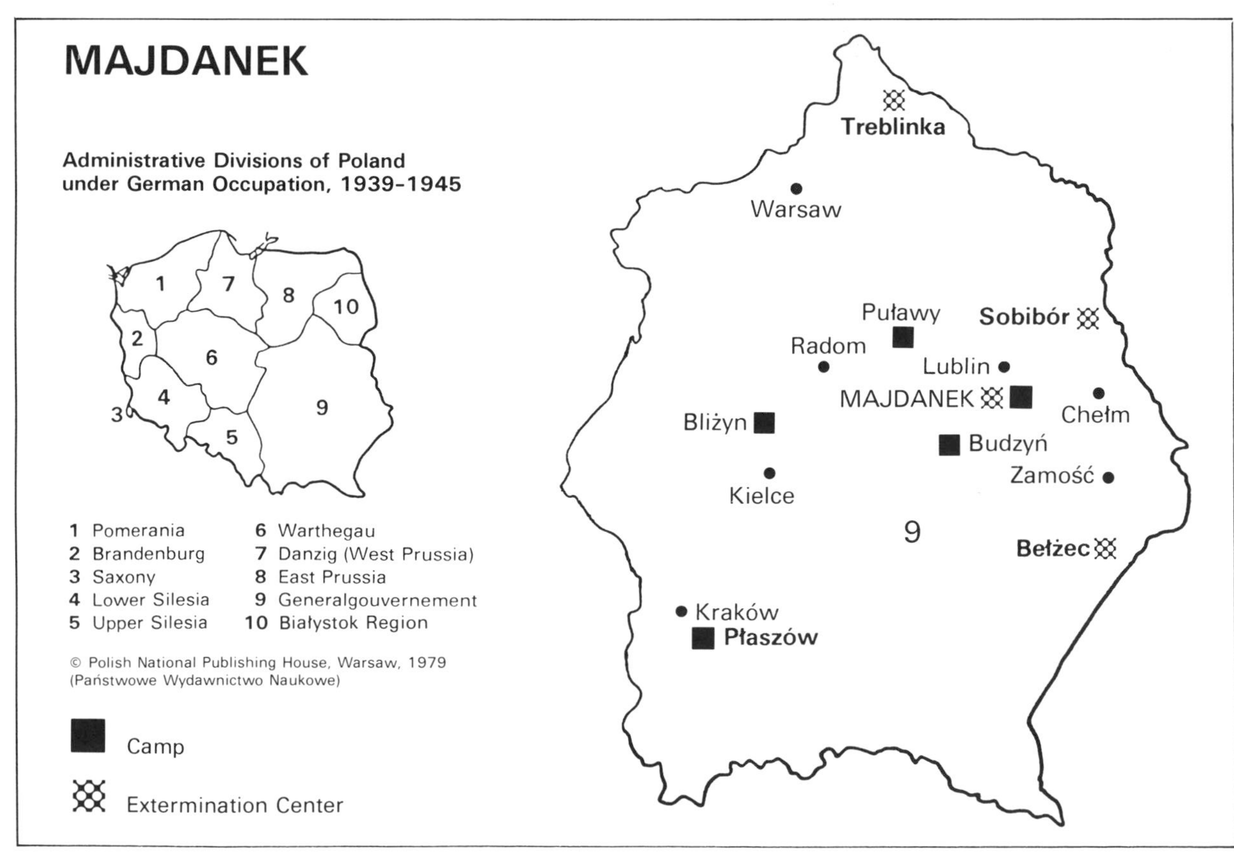

Survivors of the Majdanek concentration camp when it was liberated in July 1944.

these, according to current estimates, some 360,000 perished. Sixty percent of them died as a result of the conditions in the camp—starvation, exhaustion, disease, and beatings—and 40 percent were put to death in gas chambers or executed. Some of the prisoners were taken to the gas chambers on arrival; in this sense Majdanek was a camp of immediate extermination.

The first batch of prisoners arrived in the camp in October 1941. It was followed by groups from Soviet prisoner-of-war camps and from other concentration camps (SACHSENHAUSEN, DACHAU, AUSCHWITZ, BUCHENWALD, Flossenbürg, NEUENGAMME, GROSS-ROSEN, and GUSEN); by Poles who had been seized in raids or had been imprisoned elsewhere (in January 1944, for example, 10,000 persons arrived from Warsaw); by Jews from Czechoslovakia, Germany, Hungary, France, Belgium, Greece, the Netherlands, and Poland; by residents of Belorussia and the Ukraine; and by Polish farmers who had been expelled from the Zamość region. In April 1943 several tens of thousands of Jews from Warsaw and, later, from Białystok, were sent to the camp. Extant lists of prisoner transports reveal that the transports covered by these lists consisted of 250,000 persons, of whom 100,000 were Poles, 80,000 Jews, 50,000 Soviets, and 20,000 of other national origins. In addition to the mass murder in the gas chambers, mainly of Jewish inmates (with carbon monoxide and ZYKLON B gas), mass shootings were carried out in the camp and nearby areas. In 1941 and 1942, sick Soviet prisoners of war were shot to death; in April 1942, 2,800 Jews were murdered by this method, as were several thousand other prisoners of different nationalities that spring, 300 Soviet army officers in the summer of 1943, and another 18,000 Jews in November 1943, in the "ERNTEFEST" *Aktion*. Majdanek had numerous satellite camps: at Bliżyn, in the KIELCE district; at BUDZYŃ, near Kraśnik; in Lublin (two labor camps); in Puławy; in RADOM; and in WARSAW, on Gesia Street.

The commandants of the Majdanek camp were Karl KOCH (September 1941 to July 1942), Max Koegel (August to October 1942), Herman Florsted (October 1942 to September 1943), Martin Weiss (September 1943 to May 1944), and Arthur LIEBEHENSCHEL (May to July 22, 1944).

Resistance movements, among them the "Orzel" (Eagle) organization, were active in the camp at various periods, and several escapes were arranged by individuals and groups. Polish aid organizations, such as the Polish Red Cross and the RADA GŁÓWNA OPIEKUŃCZA (Central Welfare Council), as well as the Polish resistance movement, extended help to the Polish prisoners. In July 1944, in the face of the Red Army's advance, Majdanek was liquidated, and about a thousand prisoners were taken away, half of them reaching Auschwitz. Before abandoning the camp, the staff destroyed documents and set fire to the buildings and the large crematorium, but in their haste to withdraw, the Germans failed to destroy the gas chambers and the larger part of the prisoners' barracks.

In July 1944 a special Polish-Soviet Nazi Crimes Investigation Commission began to investigate the crimes that had been committed at Majdanek. On September 16, 1944, it published its report in Moscow, in Polish, Russian, English, and French. Only a few of the thirteen hundred staff members of the camp were brought to trial after the war. In November 1944, six SS men who had served at Majdanek were tried in Lublin; four were sentenced to death, and two committed suicide before sentence was passed. This was the first trial of the Majdanek camp staff.

From 1946 to 1948 a trial was held in Lublin of ninety-five SS men who had been at Majdanek, most of them as guards. Seven of the accused were sentenced to death, including the women's camp commandant, Else Ehrich, and the rest received long terms in prison. From 1975 to 1980, sixteen former Majdanek staff members, including six women, were tried in Düsseldorf, West Germany. The most important of those accused were Hauptsturmführer Hermann Kackmann, an officer at the camp headquarters; Hermine Braunsteiner, supervisor of the women's camp; Heinrich Schmidt, the camp physician; and an SS staff member, Hildegard Lachert, whom the prisoners had nicknamed "Blutige Brigide" (Bloody Brigide).

In October 1944 a national museum was established on the site of Majdanek. It maintains the remains of the camp as well as a permanent exhibition, administers an archive, publishes *Zeszyty Majdanka* (Majdanek Journal), and edits research works on the history of the camp. A Majdanek Preservation Society functions in support of the museum.

BIBLIOGRAPHY

Berenstein, T., and A. Rutkowski. "Żydzi w obozie koncentracyjnym Majdanek (1941–1944)." *Biuletyn Żydowskiego Instytutu Historycznego* 58 (1968): 3–57.

Gutman, Y., and A. Saf, eds. *The Nazi Concentration Camps: Structure and Aims; The Image of the Prisoner; The Jews in the Camps.* Proceedings of the Fourth Yad Vashem International Historical Conference. Jerusalem, 1984.

Lichtenstein, H. *Majdanek: Reportage eines Prozesses.* Frankfurt, 1979.

Marszalek, J. *Majdanek: Oboz koncentracyjny w Lublinie.* Warsaw, 1981.

ZYGMUNT MANKOWSKI

MALINES. *See* Mechelen.

MALY TROSTINETS, village in eastern Belorussia, 7.5 miles (12 km) east of MINSK; camp and site of mass murder. The village of Bolshoi Trostinets is two-thirds of a mile (1 km) north of Maly Trostinets, and in both of these villages, Jews from the final *Aktionen* in Minsk were murdered and buried, between July 28 and 31, 1942, and on October 21, 1943. Some of the Jews were brought in GAS VANS, and were dead on arrival.

During 1942, Jews from the Protectorate of Bohemia and Moravia, Austria, Germany, the Netherlands, and Poland were transported by train to Maly Trostinets, to be killed there. It is estimated that there are sixty-five thousand bodies at Maly Trostinets, including those of about thirty-nine thousand Jews from the final *Aktionen* in Minsk. The inmates of the camp were employed in sorting the victims' possessions, or in camp maintenance. From time to time they were subjected to *Selektionen,* which became more frequent during 1943.

Most of the victims were lined up in front of pits 164 feet (50 m) long and 10 feet (3 m) deep, and shot to death. After the executions, the pits containing the victims were leveled

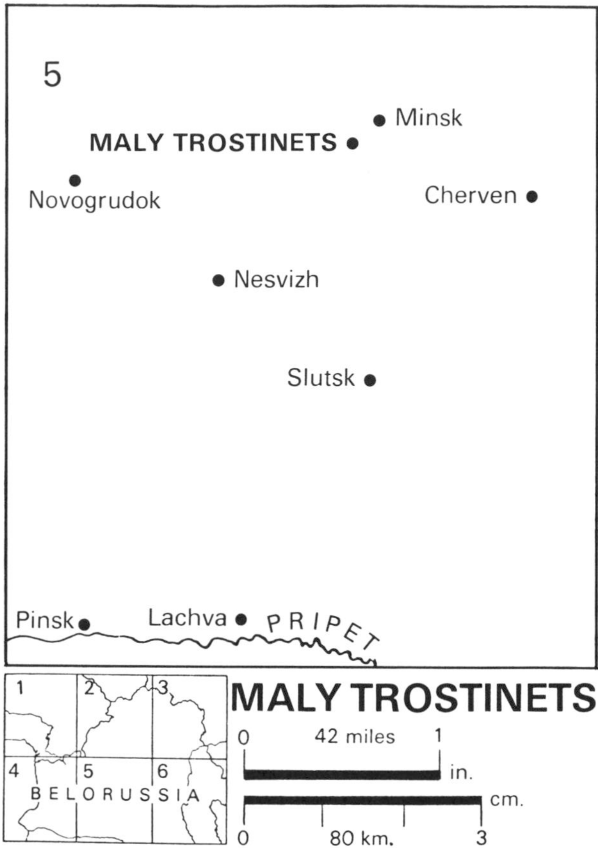

by tractors. The operation was conducted by a unit of thirty to one hundred SS men, commanded by an officer named Rider. A Soviet source estimates the number of persons killed and buried in the Trostinets area at over two hundred thousand.

In the fall of 1943 the Germans began to obliterate the traces of the mass murder by cremating the bodies in nearby Blagoveshchenie. There, a team of Soviet prisoners of war were made to sift the ashes in search of gold. During June 1944, as the Soviet forces approached, the Germans killed most of the remaining inmates. On June 30, the Germans burned the camp to the ground. When the Soviet forces arrived on July 3, they found a handful of the Jewish escapees alive.

A memorial has been erected at Bolshoi Trostinets, bearing the following inscription: "Here in the Trostinets area, the German invaders murdered and burned 201,500 people; peaceful citizens, partisans, and Red Army prisoners of war, 1941–1944." Jews are not mentioned on the memorial.

BIBLIOGRAPHY

Prestupleniia nemetsko-fashistskikh okupantov v Belorusii. Minsk, 1965.

Soobschchenie Cherezvychainoi Komissii . . . v gorode Minsk. Moscow, 1944.

SHALOM CHOLAWSKI

MANSTEIN, ERICH VON (orig., Erich von Lewinski, 1887–1973), German *Generalfeldmarschall* (General of the Army). Military historians and experts generally consider Manstein the most brilliant field commander in World War II. He had fought in World War I and afterward held various staff and regimental appointments. Upon the general mobilization of Germany in 1939, he became chief of staff of Army Group South in the attack on Poland, and in October 1939 he went in a similar capacity to the western front. Manstein designed the Sichelschnitt Plan for the defeat of France. In the campaign against Russia he served at first as a corps commander and then rose to command the Eleventh Army, which conquered the seashore area of the Ukraine, including the Crimea. Attached to this army was Einsatzgruppe (mobile killing unit) D. With the fall of Sevastopol in 1942, Manstein was promoted to the rank of field marshal. As army group commander he vainly attempted to free the German Sixth Army, which was encircled in STALINGRAD. At the end of March 1944 he was relieved of his command owing to his differences with Hitler over the conduct of operations in the east, and was not employed again.

Manstein was tried in 1949 by a British military tribunal in Hamburg, where he was defended by the British defense counsel Reginald Thomas Paget. During the war, he had issued an order calling the Jew "the liaison between the Red Army on the front and the enemy on the rear," elaborating even more extremely on Field Marshal Walter von REICHENAU's order of October 10, 1941, which called for "harsh countermeasures against Jewish subhumanity." Manstein was sentenced to eighteen years' imprisonment as a war criminal,

Field Marshal Erich von Manstein. [National Archives]

but by lying to the tribunal he was cleared of charges that he had been involved in carrying out massacres of Jews. He swore that he had no knowledge whatever that the SD (Sicherheitsdienst; Security Service) was killing Jews in the area under his command, and the court believed him.

In his memoirs, *Verlorene Siege* (English title, *Lost Victories*), written after his release from prison in 1953, Manstein tried to justify the German generals and troops and blamed the "dilettante" Adolf Hitler for Germany's defeat.

BIBLIOGRAPHY

Paget, R. T. *Manstein: His Campaigns and His Trial.* London, 1951.

Wallach, J. L. "Feldmarschall Erich von Manstein und die deutsche Judenausrottung in Russland." *Jahrbuch des Instituts für Deutsche Geschichte, Tel Aviv* 4 (1975): 457–472.

JEHUDA L. WALLACH

MÁRAMAROSSZIGET. *See* Sighet Marmaţiei.

MARCULEŞTI, Romanian internment camp for Jews, established in the village of that name on the bank of the Dniester River, close to the Bălţi-Soldanesti (Beltsy-Sholdaneshty) railway line, 28 miles (45 km) from Soroca (Soroki), the district center. The village was inhabited by Jewish farmers numbering 2,319, according to the 1931 census. For several days, beginning on July 9, 1941, Romanian peasants living in the vicinity robbed the Jews of their belongings; a Romanian army unit, which had previously taken part in the IAŞI pogrom, then murdered the village Jews. In the early part of July, hundreds of corpses were scattered over the village streets, attracting swarms of flies and thousands of rats.

The camp was set up on September 1, 1941, by the Romanian gendarmerie, on orders of the Romanian army. It was designed to detain Jews from BESSARABIA who had survived the first murder wave of July and August 1941, and it subsequently also served as a transit camp for Jews from BUKOVINA who were deported to TRANSNISTRIA beginning on September 14, 1941.

In the initial stage, eleven thousand Jews from the vicinity were taken to the Marculeşti camp, and in the three months of its existence, additional thousands of Jews were brought there, by train or on foot, on their way to Transnistria. On September 28, Jews from small camps that were being liquidated in the Bălţi district—Limbeni-Noi, Răutel, and Rascani—were brought to Marculeşti on orders of the Romanian army. The surviving remnants of the Jews of the CHERNOVTSY district were brought to the camp on October 22.

Three commandants from the VERTUJENI camp who were transferred to Marculeşti introduced a regime of terror, robbery, rape, and systematic torture. The prisoners were put to work on various forms of forced labor,

MARCULEŞTI

0 160 miles 1 in.
0 300 km. 3 cm.

Annexations from June to September 1940: (1) Bessarabia and (2) N. Bukovina to USSR; (3) N. Transylvania to Hungary; (4) S. Dobruja to Bulgaria.

were not permitted to rest on the Sabbath and Jewish holidays, and were forced to desecrate the Jewish cemetery and use the tombstones to pave the camp streets. When the deportations to Transnistria took place, the families were separated and taken there via the Cosauti forest and Rezina, and from there to Iampol in Transnistria. The deportees had to walk all the way, from the camp to the border at Rezina, in columns of one thousand to two thousand. Thousands of Jews were killed on the way by their escort, made up of gendarmes and an auxiliary force consisting of young men who were about to enlist in the gendarmerie.

The Marculeşti camp was liquidated on December 16, 1941. It was only in May 1948, four years after Romania's liberation, that the camp commandants were brought to trial. They were sentenced to long prison terms.

JEAN ANCEL

MAROS-VÁSÁRHELY. *See* Tîrgu-Mureş.

MARTYRDOM. *See* Kiddush ha-Shem.

MAURITIUS, tropical island in the Indian Ocean, approximately 496 miles (800 km) east of Madagascar. Now an independent country, Mauritius was still a British colony during World War II. In late December 1940, 1,580 Jews who had been seized by the British while trying to enter Palestine "illegally" were taken to Mauritius; most of these refugees were interned in a camp there until early August 1945.

In 1940 the British foreign and colonial offices, with the cooperation of the High Commissioner for Palestine, Sir Harold MacMichael, intensified their campaign against "illegal" immigration to Palestine. Among the deterrent measures considered was the deportation to a British colony of "illegal" immigrants who were captured.

In November of that year, three vessels reached the shores of Palestine, with more than thirty-six hundred refugees on board—veteran Zionists, relatives of Palestine residents, and pioneers from Germany, Austria, and Czechoslovakia. They had begun their journey in Bratislava, Slovakia. At the Romanian port of Tulcea, seven hundred boarded one of the ships, the *Milos*; over one thousand, the *Pacific*; and nineteen hundred, the *Atlantic*.

The British received word of the three ships in early October, and on October 15 the Colonial Office in London asked the governor of Mauritius whether he "could accommodate, at short notice, a substantial number of Jews who were attempting to enter Palestine illegally." The office added that the detention of the deportees would require the building of a camp, to be surrounded by a barbed-wire fence, that would be under permanent guard. In his reply, dated October 17, the governor agreed to accept fifteen hundred refugees at once and another twenty-five hundred within six months.

On November 1 the *Pacific* reached the shores of Palestine, followed, on November 3, by the *Milos*. Both ships were apprehended by the British coast guard and taken to Haifa, where the passengers were kept on board for two weeks. They were then transferred to another vessel, the *Patria*, which was being readied to take them to Mauritius. The Jewish Agency Executive in London discussed on November 11 the British plan to deport the refugees to Mauritius. On November 20 Winston CHURCHILL gave his consent to Colonial Secretary George Ambrose Lloyd's proposal to deport the refugees, provided that they were treated decently; Churchill also suggested that the decision be applied to future instances of refugees' trying to enter Palestine illegally.

In Palestine, the High Commissioner refused to receive a delegation of the Asefat ha-Nivharim (the elected assembly of Palestine Jewry), maintaining that the Jews of Palestine were not authorized to deal with the affairs of Jews who were not residents of the country. On November 24, the third vessel, the *Atlantic,* was brought to Haifa by a British warship. That same evening, some of its passengers were transferred to the *Patria,* with the rest scheduled to follow them the next day. On the morning of November 25, however, the underground Jewish army, the Hagana, sabotaged the *Patria* so as to prevent the deportation, placing a small explosive charge on the ship. Because the ship was old and rusty, a large hole opened up, and within fifteen minutes the *Patria* sank and was lying on its side. Over 250 refugees were listed as missing; most of them drowned, but a few apparently reached the shore without being apprehended. Following public protests in Britain and the United States, London instructed the Palestine authorities to permit the survivors on the *Patria* to stay in the country. The rest of the *Atlantic* passengers, however, who had not been transshipped to the *Patria,* were deported on December 9 to Mauritius, and arrived there on December 26. The order for their expulsion stated that they were to be barred from entry into Palestine even when the war was over. MacMichael's successor as High Commissioner, Lord Gort, who took up the post in 1944, eventually permitted the refugees to return from Mauritius to Palestine. On August 26, 1945, some 1,300 of the deportees sailed into the Haifa port; 124 had died in Mauritius and 212 young refugees had volunteered for service in the Allied forces. Most of them enlisted in the Czechoslovak army, and 56 in the JEWISH BRIGADE GROUP, which had been formed in 1944.

In Mauritius the 1,580 exiles—849 men, 635 women, and 96 children—were held in a camp near the town of Rose Hill (Beau Bassin). They suffered from the poor conditions prevailing in the camp and a typhus epidemic broke out. In the initial stage, the camp commandants kept the men and women apart, even the married couples. Otherwise, the attitude toward the detainees was correct, and during the epidemic, men and women of the local population gave them help. Many of the detainees found work, and they organized a busy schedule of cultural activities. Marriages took place and children were born to the detainees on the island.

[*See also* Aliya Bet; Yishuv.]

BIBLIOGRAPHY

Wasserstein, B. *Britain and the Jews of Europe, 1939–1945.* Oxford, 1979. See pages 56–76.

Zwergbaum, A. "Exile in Mauritius." *Yad Vashem Studies* 4 (1960): 191–257.

Zwergbaum, A. "From Internment in Bratislava and Detention in Mauritius to Freedom." In vol. 2 of *The Jews of Czechoslovakia,* edited by A. Dagan, pp. 594–654. New York, 1971.

LENI YAHIL

MAUTHAUSEN, concentration camp created shortly after the ANSCHLUSS of Austria in March 1938, near an abandoned stone quarry about 3 miles (5 km) from the town of Mauthausen in Upper Austria. On May 16, 1938, work began in the quarry, initially employing thirty civilian workers. The first prisoners were brought to the camp on August 8 of that year and were put to work in the construction of the camp and at the quarry.

Categories and Numbers of the Prisoners. Most of the prisoners brought to Mauthausen in the first year of its existence were criminal offenders, and the rest were "asocial elements." Almost all were transferred from DACHAU. The first consignment was accompanied by eighty-eight SS guards from the Dachau TOTENKOPFVERBÄNDE (Death's-Head

Facing page: Plan of the Mauthausen camp. (Adapted from a map in E. Le Chêne's *Mauthausen: The History of a Death Camp,* London, 1971.)

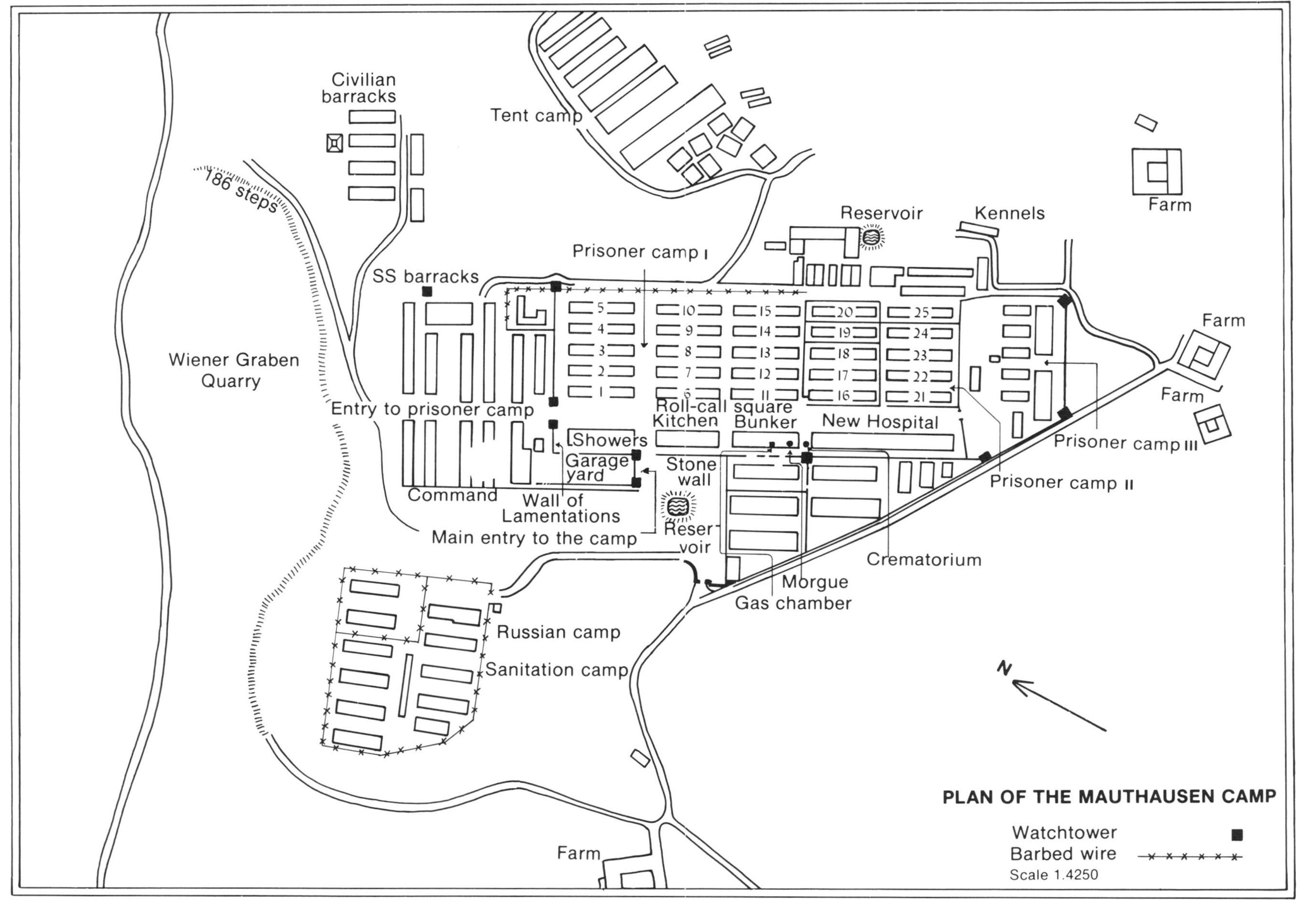
Civilian barracks
Tent camp
186 steps
Wiener Graben Quarry
SS barracks
Prisoner camp I
Reservoir
Kennels
Farm
Farm
Farm
Entry to prisoner camp
Roll-call square
Kitchen
Bunker
New Hospital
Prisoner camp III
Showers
Garage yard
Stone wall
Prisoner camp II
Command
Wall of Lamentations
Main entry to the camp
Reser voir
Crematorium
Morgue
Gas chamber
Russian camp
Sanitation camp
N
PLAN OF THE MAUTHAUSEN CAMP
Watchtower
Barbed wire
Scale 1.4250
Farm

Units). In 1938, a total of 1,100 prisoners arrived. The first political prisoners, also from Dachau, arrived in May 1939, and soon afterward groups of political prisoners were brought from jails in Czechoslovakia. Late in September the Dachau "Punishment Squad" arrived at the camp. In December 1939 there were 2,666 prisoners, almost all Germans, interned in Mauthausen.

In the course of 1940 about 11,000 new prisoners were recorded in the camp's "book of numbers," which served to record each new prisoner, together with his camp number. The minority were German prisoners from the camps of SACHSENHAUSEN (1,032) and BUCHENWALD (300), who were all transferred to GUSEN, the first Mauthausen subcamp. A further three consignments brought an unknown number of Spanish republicans who had fled from Franco's regime and been caught in France after its defeat by Germany. The number of prisoners in that year reached 3,833.

Seven consignments of Spanish prisoners arrived in 1941, and their number in the camp reached 7,241. Many Jews were also sent, together with groups of Czech prisoners. On May 12 the first Jews from the Netherlands arrived, and on October 20 an initial 4,205 Soviet prisoners of war, of whom about 2,000 were transferred to the Gusen camp. That year Mauthausen received a total of 18,000 new prisoners. The mortality rate was high, and the number of prisoners in both Mauthausen and Gusen reached only 11,135.

In 1942, in addition to Czech, Dutch, Soviet (civilians and prisoners of war), and Yugoslav prisoners, internees also arrived from France, Belgium, Greece, and Luxembourg. A new category of prisoners, those in "protective custody" (*Sicherheitsverwahrungs-Häftlinge*), were transferred from various prisons. A first dispatch of 218 such prisoners reached Mauthausen on November 26 from the Regensburg jail. Altogether, 13,000 new prisoners came to the camp in 1942.

On August 19, Reinhard HEYDRICH published an edict that divided the concentration camps into categories. Only Mauthausen and Gusen were placed in the most harsh classification, and all prisoners in protective custody who were considered incorrigible, who manifested negative behavior, and so forth, were to be sent there.

MAUTHAUSEN and Sub-Camps

The stream of prisoners of different nationalities continued throughout 1943, during which 21,028 new prisoners were recorded, of whom only a few were Jews. That year, 8,334 prisoners were entered in the records as having died in Mauthausen and Gusen, along with 147 prisoners of war. In addition, many victims were killed by order of the Gestapo immediately upon their arrival at the camp, and did not go through the registration procedures.

In 1944 the number of prisoners reaching Mauthausen increased considerably. Many subcamps were built (*see* Table 1), and the new prisoners were sent to them. A record 65,645 new prisoners were listed in the "book of the numbers." The maximum prisoner population at any one time in 1944 was 114,524. Beginning in May the camp received large transports of Jews from *Selektionen* in AUSCHWITZ, and in May and June four such transports brought a total of 7,500 prisoners. On August 10 a dispatch of 4,589 Jewish prisoners came from the PŁASZÓW camp, near Kraków. The last large transport in 1944 arrived in late September, bringing 6,449 prisoners, of whom half were Jews. According to the camp's records, a total of 13,322 Jewish males and 504 Jewish females entered Mauthausen in 1944. The number of Jews who died that year was 3,437.

On January 25, 1945, the first transport of Auschwitz evacuees reached Mauthausen. In

TABLE 1. *Mauthausen Subcamps in Which More than 250 Prisoners Were Held*

NAME	MAXIMUM NUMBER OF PRISONERS	DATE OF CREATION
Amstetten	2,966	March 1945
Amstetten (women)	500	March 1945
Ebensee	18,437	November 1943
Eisenerz	400	June 1943
Enns	2,000	April 1945
Grossraming	1,013	January 1943
Gunskirchen	17,000–20,000	March 1945
Gusen I	11,480	May 1940
Gusen II	12,537	March 1944
Gusen III	274	December 1944
Hartheim castle	over 250	1938
Hinterbrühl	2,737	September 1944
Hirtenberg (women)	459	September 1944
Leibnitz-Graz	655	February 1944
Lenzing (women)	565	November 1944
Linz I	790	February 1943
Linz II	285	February 1944
Linz III	5,615	May 1944
Loibl-Pass (north)	1,296	June 1943
Loibl-Pass (south)	over 250	1941
Melk	10,352	April 1944
Passau II	333	March 1944
Peggau	888	August 1944
Sankt Valentin	1,480	August 1944
Saurer-Werke	1,480	August 1944
Schlier-Redyl-Zipf	1,488	October 1943
Schwechat	2,568	August 1943
Steyr-Münichholz	1,971	February 1942
Ternberg	406	January 1943
Wagrein	300	June 1941
Wels I	1,500	December 1944
Wiener Neudorf	2,954	August 1943
Wiener Neustadt	1,000	August 1943

one week about 9,000 prisoners of various nationalities arrived, the majority of them Jews. Thousands of prisoners were also transferred from Sachsenhausen, from GROSS-ROSEN, and from other camps, and were absorbed in the Mauthausen satellite camps. In April another gigantic flow of Jewish prisoners, who had been transferred from their native Hungary to camps along the Austrian-Hungarian border, reached Mauthausen. A total of 24,793 new prisoners were recorded in the camp books in 1945. The number of the last prisoner, 139,157, was allocated on May 3, two days before the camp's liberation.

Structure of the Camp. The camp area was divided into three sections: (1) the prison camp; (2) the command area; (3) the SS dwellings. The prison camp occupied the main part of the camp area and had three sectors. Camp No. 1 was the residential camp, with twenty wooden huts. Four of these were quarantine huts, where the new prisoners lived for three weeks, after which they were transferred to other sections of the camp. The last hut, No. 20, was separated by a stone wall and initially housed the Soviet PRISONERS OF WAR. Camp No. 2, the workshop area, contained four huts; from early 1944 this was also a quarantine area. Camp No. 3, built in the spring of 1944, initially contained six huts. Beginning in the summer of 1944 the sick and debilitated prisoners were transferred here prior to being killed. Each hut was designed to hold 300 prisoners, but in most instances double that number and even more were packed into them.

Opposite the main gate was the assembly ground, where the prisoners had to stand for the morning and evening roll call, and where certain prisoners were taken to be killed in the presence of all the others. On one side of the parade ground were three stone buildings. Two were used for the camp services (kitchen, showers, and laundry). The third housed the prison (*Bunker*) and the gas chamber, which was disguised as a shower. Beneath the *Bunker* was the crematorium; in a nearby cell, prisoners were shot.

Outside the camp enclosure was the "Russian camp," which was converted into the camp hospital in the spring of 1943. About a month before the liberation, in April 1945, a tent camp was set up outside the camp enclosure, with fourteen large tents. It was designated for Hungarian Jews who had been brought from camps along the Austrian-Hungarian border, and for Jews from the entire network of Mauthausen camps to stay in until they were taken to GUNSKIRCHEN. The entire Mauthausen camp covered about 37 acres (150,000 sq m).

Regime. Until the outbreak of World War II, the regime in Mauthausen resembled that of other concentration camps in Germany. Most of the prisoners who arrived in 1938 were criminal offenders transferred from Dachau together with their SS guards, and they brought with them the regime prevailing in the camp of origin. Apart from the crushing labor, the conditions of Mauthausen were not so severe at that time. With the start of the war, the nature of the camp and its regime changed radically, and within a short time the number of prisoners increased from 994 in late 1938 to 2,666 in December 1939.

Mauthausen became a concentration camp and killing center for "undesirable political elements" in the Reich, as well as a liquidation center for opposition elements in the occupied countries. From mid-1940 the majority of prisoners were no longer German. The camp absorbed about 7,500 Spanish republican prisoners and members of the International Brigades who had fought alongside the republicans in the Spanish Civil War. Eight thousand Polish prisoners were also brought to the camp, principally from the intelligentsia, such arrests being part of the effort to paralyze the leadership stratum in occupied Poland. The same policy was adopted with the Czechs. With the change in the composition of the prisoners came a drastic worsening of conditions; their treatment and punishments became more severe. The food rations were cut and the prisoners were severely overcrowded, resulting in a deterioration of the sanitary conditons, a spread of typhus and dysentery epidemics, and a consequent marked increase in the mortality rate. In 1939, 445 dead were recorded, while in 1940, 3,846 prisoners died in the camps of Mauthausen and Gusen. The latter was set up in early 1940 about 3 miles (5 km) from Mauthausen as a branch of the main camp; its prisoners worked at cutting stone in the two Gusen quarries.

In 1942 another essential change occurred in the regime, following a decision to expand military industry in the camps. Because of the severe shortage in the labor force throughout the Reich, the need grew for efficient employment of the concentration camp prisoners. From the fall of 1943 most of the Mauthausen prisoners were engaged in work in the military industry in the region. They were employed principally in the construction of subterranean tunnels to house factories for rocket assembly and production of plane parts. In a short time the camp population increased dramatically: from March to December of 1943 the number of prisoners in Mauthausen and Gusen grew from 14,800 to 26,000. The maximum number, recorded in March 1945, was 84,000.

Command of the Camps. The first commandant of the Mauthausen camp was SS-Standartenführer Albert Sauer. In August 1939 he was replaced by SS-Standartenführer Franz Ziereis, who remained in office until the end of the war. Seven SS officers and heads of divisions served under him. Ziereis's deputy and the commandant of the prison camp was SS-Hauptsturmführer Georg Bachmayer, who had two deputies. Beneath them were the *Rapportführer* (recording officer), the *Arbeitsdienstführer* (labor-service officer), and the *Arbeitseinsatzführer* (officer responsible for roll calls and general administrative units), as well as *Blockführer* (block officers) and *Kommandoführer* (labor-gang officers). On September 30, 1944, there were ninety-one SS *Blockführer* and *Kommandoführer* in Mauthausen. The camp's political department, which was directly subordinated to the security police, was headed by SS-Hauptsturmführer Karl Schulz, who was in command of nineteen noncommissioned officers and many prisoners. The camp guard units, *Blockführer,* and *Kommandoführer* belonged to the Mauthausen SS-Totenkopfverbände.

Most of the prisoners in Mauthausen holding supervisory and other posts were criminal offenders, and the camp authorities encouraged them to treat the rank-and-file prisoners harshly. They had complete control over the lives of the prisoners under their command. The principal positions held by prisoners were those of *Lagerälteste* (camp elder) and his deputies, and *Lagerschreiber* (camp registrar). The work in the camp was supervised by the KAPOs, and the blocks were under the authority of the *Blockälteste* (block elder), the *Blockschreiber* (block registrar), and the *Stubenälteste* (room elder). All enjoyed a large number of privileges.

Prisoners by National Groups. The Poles were the largest national group at Mauthausen. The first Polish prisoners arrived on March 9, 1940, and in the same year another nine transports arrived. All were sent to Gusen. In 1944, after the suppression of the WARSAW POLISH UPRISING, the last groups of Poles arrived. Poles of German origin (VOLKSDEUTSCHE, or ethnic Germans) who declared their allegiance to the German race were released. The Polish students and members of the underground in the first transports were killed in the fall of 1940. The camp's record of the dead lists 30,203 Poles, including many Polish Jews. Altogether, there were nearly 50,000 Poles in the Mauthausen camps.

Czech prisoners arrived mainly in 1941 and 1942 and consisted principally of political

SS-Standartenführer Franz Ziereis, commandant of the Mauthausen concentration camp from August 1939 until the end of the war.

prisoners, including Jews, Communists, and intellectuals. In the first months of 1942 three transports arrived bringing 970 prisoners, who were soon killed by the block elders and the Kapos. After the assassination in Prague of Reinhard Heydrich by the Czech underground on May 29, 1942, 253 Czechs were brought to Mauthausen and killed. The women among them were taken in groups to the gas chamber. Most of the Czech prisoners were murdered in the three months following Heydrich's assassination. Altogether, about 5,200 Czechs arrived at the camp. The number who survived is unknown.

The majority of the Soviets were prisoners of war. They lived in separate huts set up in an area known as the "Russian camp." Of the five thousand who arrived in the first shipments, no more than eighty were still alive in March 1942. One group of Soviet inmates were the prisoners of Operation K, officers or noncommissioned officers who had escaped and been recaptured. Some five thousand of these prisoners were transferred to Mauthausen, where they were held under particularly harsh conditions, and within a few weeks many had died. In early February 1945 about five hundred of them rebelled and succeeding in breaking out of the camp enclosure and dispersing in the vicinity. In a rapid operation that took place with the participation of the local inhabitants, all the escapees were caught or killed except for eight, who survived the war.

In addition, there were large groups of French, Italian, and Yugoslav prisoners in the camp at different times, as well as German prisoners. Of the seventy-five hundred Spanish republicans, about forty-two hundred died in the camp in 1941 and 1942.

Fate of the Jews. Until the spring of 1941 only a few Jews arrived at Mauthausen; most died within a short time from the work at the quarry and from maltreatment. Beginning in 1941, groups of Jews began arriving. The first consisted of Czech Jews who were brought with the transports of Czech political prisoners. The SS officers, the Kapos, and the block elders treated this group of Jews harshly, and all soon perished. In 1941 a second group, consisting of about nine hundred Jews, arrived from the NETHERLANDS, as hostages taken after protests in the Dutch cities against the occupation. Late in that year only nine of this group remained alive, and not one of them survived until the liberation.

From mid-1944 on, far larger groups of Jews began to arrive. The six thousand Hungarian Jews brought to work in the Mauthausen camps after *Selektionen* at Auschwitz in May and June of 1944 were followed by forty-six hundred Jews from the Płaszów camp. These Jews too were treated far more harshly than the other prisoners, being employed in digging tunnels for the munitions factories. The work was conducted in three shifts, at an extremely accelerated pace. No effort was made to spare the labor force; after a month or two they were broken men who could hardly put one foot before the other. Each month thousands of new prisoners arrived to replace those who had died. The Jews subsisted in conditions far worse than those of other groups. Starvation and diseases caused by starvation accounted for more than 95 percent of the deaths.

From January 25, 1945, with the general evacuation of Auschwitz, a second wave of transports began to arrive at Mauthausen. The majority of the nine thousand new prisoners were Jews. Like their predecessors, they were sent to work principally in digging underground tunnels at various subcamps. The last large group consisted of Hungarian Jews. Beginning in the fall of 1944, tens of thousands of Hungarian Jews had been sent to build a line of fortifications along the border between Austria and Hungary. As the front drew near in March and April of 1945, the camps there were evacuated and the prisoners sent by foot to Mauthausen. Many died during the evacuation. They were housed in a tent camp, where they slept on the muddy earth in greatly overcrowded conditions, with no sanitation, no running water, and no toilets; they had to relieve themselves in pits that they dug. Food was supplied in small quantities. Mass epidemics of typhus and dysentery soon broke out, causing many deaths. On April 9, when there were already more than eighty-five hundred prisoners in the tent camp, the transfer to this camp of all the Jewish prisoners in the main camp and at Gusen was launched. An estimated three thousand prisoners died in the tent camp. On April 16, the first group of prisoners was

Six thousand Mauthausen prisoners being kept naked in the camp courtyard. After twenty-four hours, 140 had died.

taken from there to the Gunskirchen camp, about 37 miles (60 km) west of Mauthausen. The rest of the prisoners were transferred to Gunskirchen in two groups, a few days apart. They were taken by forced march, and all who fell by the way were shot down on the spot.

Liquidation Stage. In the second half of 1944, the stream of prisoners brought to Mauthausen increased. The mortality rate rose to maximal dimensions. According to the official camp records, 24,613 prisoners died between January and May 1945. The actual number of dead was far greater, however, since the frequent transfers made exact record keeping impossible. Transports arrived from the camps that had been evacuated: Gross-Rosen, BERGEN-BELSEN, ORANIENBURG, DORA-MITTELBAU, NEUENGAMME, Buchenwald, RAVENSBRÜCK, Sachsenhausen, and other small camps. In late March and in April of 1945 the prisoners from the satellite camps were marched to the main camp. All those who could not march were killed with phenol injections, and their corpses were buried in the camps.

The main camp was now full to overflowing and in total disorder. The severe overcrowding and reduced food rations hastened the death of many. In the hospital, cases of cannibalism were documented. The crematoria could not burn all the corpses, and a gigantic grave was dug near the camp enclosure for the concealment of ten thousand corpses. At the same time, in April 1945, the Germans began to burn documents and to release favored prisoners, particularly criminal offenders, inmates of long standing, and those holding posts in the camp. Prisoners of Norwegian, Danish, Dutch, Belgian, and French nationality were released and handed over to the International RED CROSS, which took them to Switzerland. The Jews were all transferred to Gunskirchen under the most severe conditions, an act interpreted by the prisoners as a step toward their slaughter.

On May 3 the guarding of the camp was handed over to a police unit from Vienna. The following day, May 4, work ceased and the SS officers left the camp. That same day, the officer in charge of the *Bunker* killed all the prisoners employed in the crematorium and in the *Bunker,* with a single exception. The next day, at 11:30 a.m., American army tanks entered Mauthausen. The prisoners opened the gates and the camp was liberated.

The number of prisoners who passed through Mauthausen is estimated at 199,404. It is believed that 119,000 of them died, of whom 38,120 were Jews. This number includes the victims at the Hartheim castle. From August 1941 to October 1942, and from April 1944 to the end of that year, sick and debilitated prisoners and "undesirable" prisoners, including Jews, were regularly sent from the network of Mauthausen camps to the Hartheim castle near Linz, to be killed in the gas chamber there.

The suffering of the Mauthausen internees has been expressed in the Greek composer Mikis Theodorakis's *Ballad of Mauthausen,* based on a work by the Greek Jewish poet Jacob Kambanelis.

BIBLIOGRAPHY

Eckstein, E. *Mauthausen: Concentration and Annihilation Camp.* Jerusalem, 1984. (In Hebrew.)

Le Chêne, E. *Mauthausen: The History of a Death Camp.* London, 1971.

Marsalek, H. *Die Geschichte des Konzentrationslager Mauthausen: Dokumentation.* Vienna, 1980.

Pingel, F. *Häftlinge unter SS-Herrschaft: Widerstand, Selbstbehauptung und Vernichtung im Konzentrationslager.* Hamburg, 1978.

Rabitsch, G. *Das KL Mauthausen: Studien zur Geschichte des Konzentrationslager.* Stuttgart, 1970.

BENYAMIN ECKSTEIN

MAYER, SALY (1882–1950), Swiss Jewish leader; representative of the JOINT DISTRIBUTION COMMITTEE (JDC). Mayer made his living as a lace manufacturer, and retired in the 1930s. He was elected a representative of a liberal-democratic party in his native Saint Gall in 1921 and was involved in the financial sector of municipal administration until 1933. Mayer was active in the Saint Gall Jewish community, founding a modern welfare organization there, and became secretary of the Schweizerischer Israelitischer Gemeindebund (Federation of Swiss Jewish Communities; SIG). He assumed the presidency of the SIG in 1936, and held it until late in 1942.

During his presidency, the SIG joined the WORLD JEWISH CONGRESS, and was actively involved in the negotiations regarding the partition of Palestine in 1937. In 1938, with the Austrian ANSCHLUSS, a stream of three thousand to four thousand Jewish refugees from that country began arriving in SWITZERLAND. Mayer became involved in negotiations with Dr. Heinrich Rothmund, head of the Alien Police, regarding their reception; he was later criticized for the restrictive Swiss policy on Jewish immigration. It is true that Mayer accepted the fiat of the government without public protest. The Swiss Jewish community numbered about eighteen thousand, and they were committed to looking after the refugees already staying in the country, whose well-being hinged on this financial commitment. Public opinion supported the anti-refugee stance of the government, and it may be questioned whether options were available to the Jewish leadership in these circumstances.

Help from the JDC enabled the SIG to look after the increasing number of refugees. This brought Mayer into close contact with the JDC, and he was appointed its representative in Switzerland in 1940, on a voluntary basis. In 1942 he was forced out of the presidency of the SIG, at least partly because of the above-mentioned criticism.

At first the sums at Mayer's disposal for help to Jews in occupied Europe were small: \$6,370 in 1940 and \$3,030 in 1941. His main tasks were to receive information from all over occupied Europe and transmit it to the JDC European office in Lisbon, and to look after the refugees in Switzerland. A lonely, very conservative, pedantic, and suspicious man, Mayer had bad relationships with other Jewish organizations in Switzerland, with the exception of the He-Haluts office under Nathan Schwalb.

Mayer's role changed with the entry of the United States into the war in 1941. In order to circumvent American restrictions on transferring funds to Nazi Europe, Mayer suggested (and the JDC agreed) that money be sent to support the increasing number of Jewish refugees in Switzerland, and that equivalent sums of Swiss Jewish money, freed from the obligation to keep the refugees alive, be sent to Nazi Europe. He received $235,000 early in 1942 and $1,588,000 late in 1943, but from the spring of 1942 to the fall of 1943 no money was received, since the Swiss refused to accept philanthropic dollars to be converted into Swiss francs in Switzerland. However, despite the arrangements for refugees in Switzerland, whose numbers increased until they reached about twenty-five thousand in 1944, much of the money had to go to support them. In effect, in 1942 and 1943, Mayer had $1,127,515 to spend outside of Switzerland. In 1944 he received $6,467,000, and between January and May 1945, another $4,600,000. Of these sums he had to spend $1,913,000 in Switzerland in 1944, and about another $1 million in the first months of 1945, so that he had in fact somewhat over $4.5 million to spend in Europe in these seventeen months. This was of course much more than he had had before, and it went largely to Hungary, Romania, France, and Shanghai. In the end it was far from adequate, and each country obtained much less for saving lives than it demanded. Even so, Mayer received an increasing proportion of the total JDC budget: in 1944, 42 percent ($15,216,000 was all the JDC could obtain that year from American Jews).

In the summer of 1942, Mayer was approached by the Slovak underground Jewish leadership (PRACOVNÁ SKUPINA, or Working Group) to provide ransom money to save Jewish lives. Later, in November and December, negotiations began in Slovakia for a larger ransom payment (the EUROPA PLAN), which was supposed to save western and southeastern European Jews from deportation. Mayer at first saw these offers as simple extortion demands, but he changed his mind in the spring of 1943 and sought to provide the money. The Lisbon office refused to accept his views, but he nevertheless sent Swiss money through He-Haluts (illegally) to Bratislava, and intervened with the Jewish Agency to provide money from Istanbul to Slovakia.

In 1944, after the failure of the Joel BRAND–Bandi Grosz mission from Hungary to Istanbul (the "Blood for Trucks" offer), the Hungarian Jewish negotiator with the Nazis, Rezső KASZTNER, suggested that Mayer negotiate with the Nazis for the ransom of Hungarian Jews. Mayer was told by the United States authorities that he should negotiate but not offer either money or goods, and that he had to report to the United States legation on his moves. The Swiss gave him identical instructions, and forbade the Nazis to cross into Swiss territory. The JDC told him he was not their representative in these talks. Mayer nevertheless engaged in the negotiations between August 21, 1944, and February 5, 1945, with SS-Obersturmbannführer Kurt BECHER and his representatives. Kasztner also attended most of these meetings. In the course of skillful negotiations, orders were obtained from Heinrich HIMMLER to abandon plans for the deportation of the Jews of BUDAPEST, and Mayer succeeded in arranging for a meeting between Becher and the representative of the American WAR REFUGEE BOARD in Switzerland, Roswell D. McClelland, on November 5, 1944. To assuage the Nazis and keep the negotiations going, Mayer, contrary to his instructions, arranged for the supply of a number of tractors to the Nazis.

After the war, Mayer was accused of not conducting these talks in conjunction with other Jewish organizations, and of not standing up for Jewish demands strongly enough. The Hungarian Jewish negotiators accused him of not supplying the money and goods that the Nazis demanded. While it is only human that these accusations should have been leveled against Mayer, they seem to have little substance. Mayer proved to be his own querulous self when he turned his Hungarian Jewish colleagues into bitter enemies because he suspected them—wrongly—of financial dishonesty. Approached after the war by Becher and other Nazis to help them escape American justice, he managed to evade them.

Mayer continued to serve as liaison for the JDC in central Europe after the war, and he sent food parcels to DACHAU and other places in south Germany immediately upon their liberation. He also intervened, not always felicitously, in the reconstitution of JDC committees in Hungary and Romania. Gradually, his role diminished, and although he was much praised by the JDC for his work, he retired. He died before he could write his memoirs.

BIBLIOGRAPHY

Bauer, Y. *American Jewry and the Holocaust: The American Jewish Joint Distribution Committee, 1939–1945*. Detroit, 1982.

Bauer, Y. *The Jewish Emergence from Powerlessness*. Toronto, 1979. See pages 7–25.

YEHUDA BAUER

MCDONALD, JAMES GROVER (1886–1964), League of Nations High Commissioner for REFUGEES from Germany. McDonald taught history and political science at the University of Indiana and in 1919 became chairman of the Foreign Policy Association in New York, serving in that capacity until 1933. He then became involved in the Jewish refugee problem, which brought him into conflict with officials of the State Department. Several visits to Nazi Germany convinced McDonald that the National Socialists were tending toward a radical solution of the "Jewish question." On April 3, 1933, following the Nazis' anti-Jewish BOYCOTT of April 1, he reacted to the events in the Reich in a speech before the Foreign Policy Association, expressing his dismay at the State Department's antisemitic perception of the Jewish plight.

James G. McDonald, the first American ambassador to Israel, presenting his credentials to President Chaim Weizmann (not in photo) on March 29, 1949.

McDonald's growing involvement with the refugee crisis placed him in contact with James Rosenberg, Felix Warburg, Mildred Wertheimer, and the Lehman brothers (Arthur and Herbert Henry). They were the financial bulwark of the private Jewish agencies in America, among which the AMERICAN JEWISH COMMITTEE and the JOINT DISTRIBUTION COMMITTEE in particular were active in behalf of German Jewry. It was partly their influence, together with that of Raymond Fosdick, president of the Rockefeller Foundation, that led to McDonald's appointment, in 1933, as head of the newly created League of Nations' Office of the High Commissioner for Refugees from Germany. The problem of Jewish refugees being predominant, a department of Jewish affairs was instituted in the office, headed by the British Zionist Norman Bentwich. McDonald designed a comprehensive plan of economic, legal, and political-aid activities.

But almost from the outset, the commissioner found himself beset with problems that made his office virtually impotent. The appointment of an American commissioner to a League agency was anomalous, since America did not belong to the world organization. The commission, unlike other humanitarian efforts of the League, found little support in the State Department. The British and French foreign offices proved singularly unsupportive. Germany, which had just left the League, claimed that McDonald's activity constituted interference with an internal issue, and did not welcome the commission's activities. Because of the lack of a budget, 90 percent of the administrative expenses were assumed by the Joint Distribution Committee. In 1935, when the NUREMBERG LAWS added potential new refugees to the problem, McDonald decided to resign, but in a dramatic fashion, so that the refugee problem would be highlighted. His widely publicized statement of resignation, delivered on December 3, 1935, accused the German government of planning racial extermination; he condemned the members of the League for their heartless indifference to the plight of the refugees. "I cannot remain silent. . . . When domestic policies threaten the demoralization of hundreds of thousands of human beings, consideration of diplomatic correctness must yield to those of common humanity." The entire document, with forty pages of supportive material, was printed in the *New York Times*.

The German annexation of Austria in March 1938 and the deteriorating refugee problem led to a change in the Roosevelt administration's policy. Thirty-two nations were invited to attend a conference on refugee problems, held at Evian in July of that year (*see* EVIAN CONFERENCE). Simultaneously, Franklin D. ROOSEVELT established a quasi-governmental agency, the PRESIDENT'S ADVISORY COMMITTEE ON POLITICAL REFUGEES (PAC), to serve as a link between the government and the numerous private agencies involved with refugees. McDonald was appointed its chairman, but with no budget or salary.

He soon discovered that the problems he had faced as High Commissioner were amplified on the American domestic scene. Virtually every suggestion funneled through the PAC to ease the plight of the refugees was rejected by the State Department, either on grounds of legality or practicality or, more commonly, on the ground that the security of the United States would be compromised by admitting spies. Finally, in the fall of 1940, McDonald clashed directly with the State Department, when the PAC's requests to grant special visas to prominent European labor, political, and cultural leaders were rejected. Discouraged, he turned down a vague offer to head the American delegation to the BERMUDA CONFERENCE, held in April 1943.

Particularly nettling for McDonald was the agreement between the governments of Britain and the United States to prevent large-scale immigration to the most logical haven, Palestine. Over the years, the Zionist experiment had won his grudging admiration. The fact that he was acceptable to leading American Zionists earned him a place on the Anglo-American Committee of Inquiry on Palestine, appointed by President Harry S. Truman in 1945 to examine the Palestine problem. The committee's recommendation that 100,000 displaced persons—Jewish survivors—be immediately admitted to Palestine was turned down by the Mandatory power, the British government. After the establishment of Israel in May 1948, McDonald became the first American ambassador to the Jewish state, a position he held until 1951.

BIBLIOGRAPHY

Feingold, H. L. *The Politics of Rescue.* New York, 1970.

Genizi, H. "James G. McDonald: High Commissioner for Refugees, 1933–1945." *Wiener Library Bulletin* 30/2 (1976): 40–52.

HENRY L. FEINGOLD

MECHELEN (Fr., Malines), city in BELGIUM, midway between Antwerp and Brussels. The population of Mechelen during World War II was about sixty thousand. In 1942 the German authorities took over the Général Dossin de Saint Georges barracks in the old city, dating back to the eighteenth century, to serve as an assembly camp for the Jews of Belgium, from which they would be deported to the east. The place seems to have been selected because of its location relative to the distribution of the Belgian Jewish population and because it could serve as a convenient rail link with the concentration and extermination camps in eastern Europe.

The barracks were close to the river, and the railway tracks led right up to them; at the same time, they were surrounded by the houses of local inhabitants. The barracks consisted of a single three-story building, which surrounded a courtyard on all its sides. The site was designated as a camp in the summer of 1942, in preparation for the "Final Solution," and had to be prepared to take in the Jewish prisoners. The first group of Jews to be arrested, on July 22, 1942, at the Antwerp railway station, was taken to the BREENDONCK camp and, five days later, transferred to the Mechelen camp. During its first weeks of existence, Mechelen took in groups of Jews (at the rate of some two hundred per day) who had been ordered to report for a "labor draft" by notices issued to them, beginning on July 25.

The Jews in the camp were divided into several groups: those designated for deportation, who were deported at the first opportunity; nationals of neutral countries or of Germany's allies, some of whom were not deported; *Entscheidungsfälle* (borderline cases and doubtful cases, such as persons of mixed parentage or Jews married to non-Jews), who were later sent to the DRANCY camp in France; and the politically "dangerous," who were passed on to prisons or punitive camps. In the final stage of the camp's existence, there were also contingents of GYPSIES.

Conditions in the camp underwent changes over the course of time. The first commandant of the camp, Philip Schmitt, left it in poor physical shape, but his successor seems to have made improvements. However, there was no change in the harassment of the prisoners and in the low food rations they received.

The camp at the Dossin barracks was under the command of the Breendonck camp, and since Philip Schmitt was the camp commandant at the latter, he also assumed responsibility for Mechelen when it was set up. The acting commandant was SS officer Rudolf Steckmann. Most of the camp staff was German, but a few Belgians (Flemish) were also employed. Jewish prisoners were appointed as room, shower, and sick-bay orderlies. Little is known of the life of the Jews in the camp; the subject has not been researched, and the survivors among the Belgian Jews did not, as a rule, write their memoirs of the period. The ASSOCIATION DES JUIFS EN BELGIQUE had a special department in charge of sending packages to the prisoners and maintaining contact with them. Except for this, there is no information on the existence of an ongoing contact between the Jews in the camp and those outside. However, from time to time some items were smuggled into the camp, mainly food parcels. Jewish underground activists also succeeded in smuggling in burglar's tools, which were useful in the recurring escapes from the transport trains. The main testimony about such escapes concerns Transport No. 20, of April 1943.

As of August 4, 1942, two transports of Jews left the camp weekly, each carrying some 1,000 persons. Later the rate was slowed down, but on some days two transports left the camp, with about 1,500 deportees. In 1943 deportation trains were sent out only in the months of January, April, July, and September. Between August 4, 1942, and July 31, 1944, a total of twenty-eight trains with 25,257 Jewish prisoners left Mechelen for the camps in the east, most going to AUSCHWITZ. In addition, several trainloads of Gypsies were dispatched from the camp at the end of 1943 and in early 1944.

BIBLIOGRAPHY

Hakker, J. *La mystérieuse caserne Dossin à Malines, le camp de déportation des juifs.* Anvers, 1944.

Klarsfeld, S., and M. Steinberg. *Mémorial de la déportation des juifs de Belgique.* Brussels, 1982.

Steinberg, M. *Le dossier Bruxelles-Auschwitz: La police SS et l'extermination des juifs de Belgique.* Brussels, 1980.

Steinberg, M. "Malines: Antichambre de la mort." *Regards* 128 (March 1979): 6–13.

DAN MICHMAN

MEDICAL EXPERIMENTS. Between September 1939 and April 1945, at least seventy medical-research projects of various kinds were conducted in Nazi concentration camps, consisting of medical experiments performed on human beings against their will. At least seven thousand persons were subjected to such forced experiments. This figure, based on existing documentation and testimonies, does not include numerous similar projects for which no documentation exists or on which no detailed testimonies have been submitted.

Though experiments on human beings are an accepted and recognized practice in medical research, they are generally subject to severe restrictions. They must not be intended for "pure" research, that is, for research that does not have the immediate purpose of developing a new medicine or a new kind of treatment; they must not have the sole purpose of advancing the researcher's career; human beings may be involved only in those phases of an experiment for which they are absolutely essential; and high-risk medicines and experimental medical treatments may be tried out only when no cure exists and where an illness is already fatal. Under no circumstances may a person in good health be deliberately infected with a dangerous disease in order to try out a new medicine or a new form of treatment. While low-risk experimental medicines and forms of treatment may be tried out on persons who are in good health, this may be done on a voluntary basis only, and the volunteer must be fully informed of all possible risks involved in the experiment. While accidents can occur in medical experiments on human beings, impairing the health of the subject or even causing his death (as happens in legitimate medical practice), under no circumstances must the induction of a disease or the death of the human being involved be a deliberate, essential element of the experiment.

In Nazi Germany, medical experiments on human beings were carried out in which these fundamental rules were disregarded. It is this kind of cruel and murderous experiment, carried out by qualified and experienced doctors, in cold blood and in the name of science, that is here under consideration.

The Nazi medical experiments were carried out by the established institutions of the Third Reich—the state and party civil medical services, the army medical corps, and the medical services of the SS. The fact that the entire medical complex of the country was subject to the control of the Nazi establishment played a major role in the adoption and implementation of a policy of conducting experiments and treatments that violated the established code of medical ethics and were designed to serve Nazi racist ideology. This ideology, despite its claim to have universal goals, was in fact a particularist and dehumanized ideology that based salvation on the exclusive advancement of the "Aryan" race and negated the equality and right to exist of other, "inferior" races, particularly the Jews, whom it also defined as a destructive race.

Medical ethics, a universalist ethic based on the equality of every being in human society, morally and personally obliges every medical doctor to safeguard the health and life of every human being: "Strengthen my body and soul so that they may at all times be ready for untiring efforts, on behalf of the rich and the poor, the good and the bad, the beloved and the hated; let me see in every patient man only, for man he is." Thus a passage from the "Doctor's Prayer," attributed to Maimonides (1135–1204), rabbi, codifier, philosopher, and physician.

The large-scale medical experiments carried out in Germany and the occupied countries during World War II fitted the ideological policy pursued by the Third Reich. Some of them directly served the regime's ideological goals, and all contained elements that violated the norms of medical research, reflecting the researchers' Nazi ideology and aiding them to put into effect, with great efficiency, the most inhuman objectives of Nazi racism.

Some two hundred German medical doctors were stationed in the Nazi concentration camps, conducting *Selektionen,* medical services, and research. Those engaged in research and experiments maintained close professional ties with the scientific medical establishment. It was the universities and research institutes in Germany and Austria that planned the research projects and advised the camp doctors in their work, and it was to their laboratories that the doctors transmitted blood samples and human tissue for examination.

It is impossible to differentiate between the medical and scientific establishments, on the one hand, and the political establishment, on the other. As soon as Adolf Hitler came to power, he put all the health and medical services in Germany under a single national authority. In June 1942 he appointed Karl Brandt, a member of his staff, as chief of all medical services in the country, including the military and the SS, and authorized him to plan, direct, and supervise them. Nazi ideology came to be applied to the practice of medicine in 1933, when racist-inspired measures relating to the field of medicine were introduced. That year a law was passed to prevent persons with genetic diseases from procreating, followed, in 1935, by a law for the protection of the German people's genealogical heritage and the Law for the Protection of German Blood and Honor. In compliance with such policy, German doctors and other medical personnel carried out the following measures:

1. The sterilization, between 1933 and 1937, of 200,000 young men and women who were found to be suffering from supposedly genetic diseases;
2. The killing of 90,000 mentally and chronically ill persons in the EUTHANASIA PROGRAM;
3. The establishment of departments for genetic research and for genetic, anthropological and genealogical surveys of the entire non-German population to which the Law for the Protection of German Blood and Honor was applicable. The purpose was to identify those individuals who qualified as being of "pure Aryan" blood.

In the period from 1942 to 1945, medical experiments were conducted in concentration camps, rather than in hospitals and research institutions. They were carried out on human beings regarded as racially inferior, in locations that were the most concrete expression of Nazi ideology. Every medical experiment had to have the approval of Heinrich HIMMLER, who took a personal interest in them, interfered in them, and allocated the resources required for their implementation. While at first every application had to be submitted directly to Himmler, from 1944 it was Dr. Ernst Robert GRAWITZ, chief medical officer of the SS, who first handled all applications, obtaining two expert opinions before passing them on to Himmler. One was from Dr. Karl Gebhardt, Himmler's personal physician and chief surgeon of the SS and police, on the medical aspect; and the other was from Richard GLÜCKS and Arthur NEBE, concerning the prospective victims to be chosen for the proposed experiment.

The medical experiments fell into two broad categories: (1) experiments whose objectives were compatible with professional medical ethics and the purposes of medical practice, but whose mode of implementation violated moral law; (2) experiments whose very purposes violated medical ethics and which were irreconcilable with the accepted norms of medical research.

Immorality of Implementation. The first category consisted of two groups: experiments related to survival and rescue, and experiments involving medical treatment.

Survival and rescue. Survival and rescue experiments related to physiology, their purpose being to test the human potential for survival under harsh conditions and adaptation to such conditions, and to determine the means required to save lives. Experiments involving high altitudes, freezing temperature, and the drinking of seawater were conducted by the German air force in cooperation with the SS, on prisoners in the DACHAU concentration camp.

High-altitude experiments had the purpose of determining the maximum altitude at which air crews of damaged aircraft could be

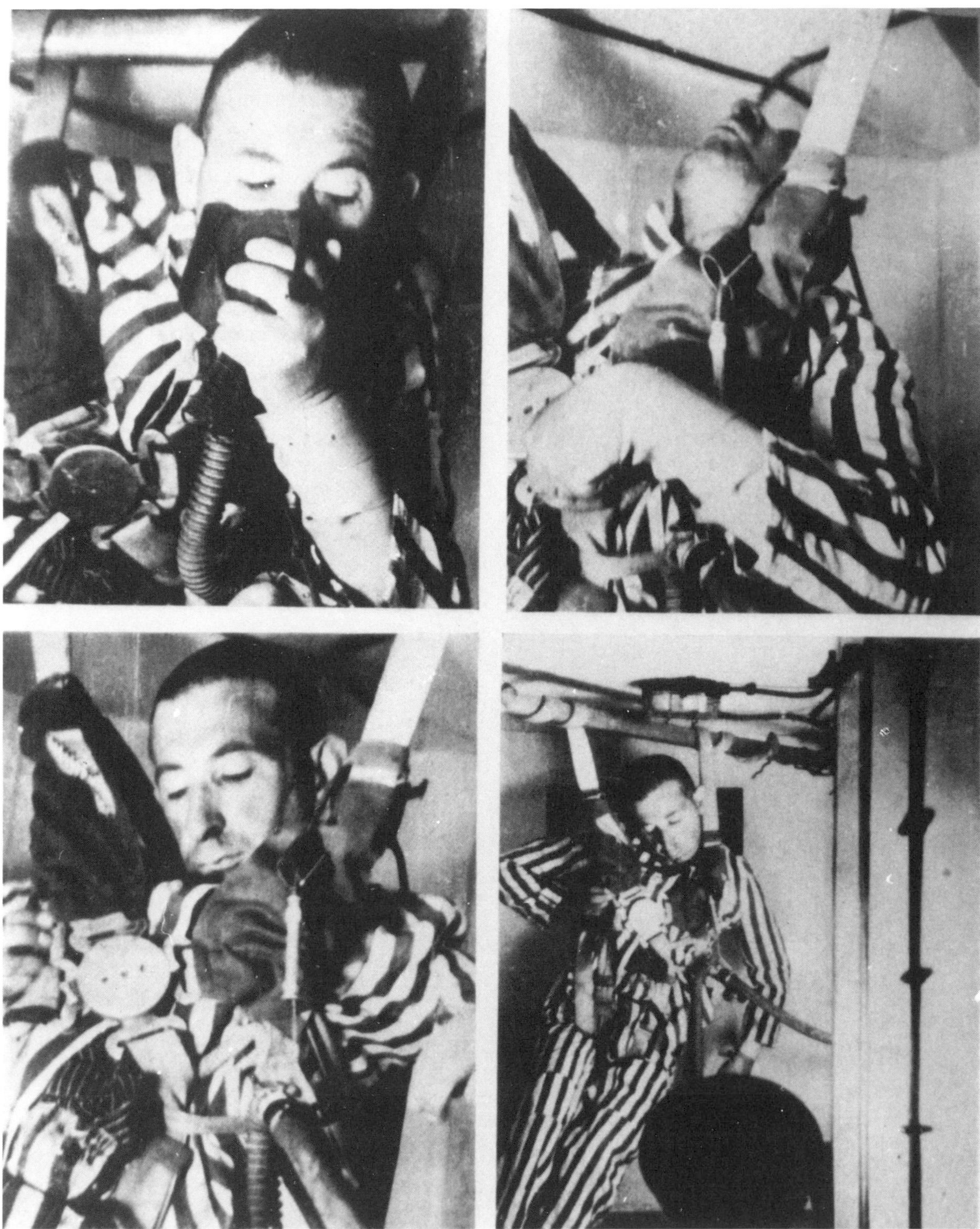

A prisoner in a parachute harness is deprived of oxygen in low-pressure experiments. Clockwise from top left: breathing through a mask in a decompression chamber; in convulsive seizures caused by anoxia (severe oxygen deficiency); limp stage; and unconscious in the chamber. The photographs are from the files of doctors at Dachau.

saved, and what equipment they required in order to save themselves at an altitude of 13 miles (21 km), the maximum altitude reached by Allied aircraft at the time. The victims of these experiments were put into pressure chambers that duplicated the conditions prevailing at 13-mile altitudes—low pressure and a lack of oxygen. The experiments were carried out with the knowledge that for the most part human beings cannot function properly at an altitude of 3.7 miles (6 km) and above without a supply of oxygen. Under conditions that simulated parachuting from an altitude of 8 miles (13 km) without an oxygen supply, spasms began and the victims lost consciousness. At 9 miles (15 km) they had breathing problems, and there were instances when they stopped breathing altogether. Nevertheless, the experiments, without an oxygen supply, went on to an altitude of 13 miles. Some two hundred Dachau prisoners were used for these experiments and seventy to eighty lost their lives as a result. The experiments were carried out by Dr. Siegfried Ruff and Dr. Hans Romberg, civilian doctors from the Deutsche Versuchsanstalt für Luftfahrt (German Experimental Institute of Aviation) in Berlin, and by Dr. Sigmund Rascher, an air force doctor and SS officer.

The freezing experiments were designed to establish the most effective method of treating persons who were in a state of shock following prolonged immersion in freezing seas or exposure to dry cold. The victims of the first of these experiments were put into a tank of ice water and kept there for seventy to ninety minutes or as long as it took for them to lose consciousness. At this critical stage they were taken out of the freezing water and attempts were made to restore their body temperature, by various means. No painkillers were used to relieve the victims' suffering. About three hundred persons were used in these experiments, eighty to ninety losing their lives.

In the experiments involving exposure to dry cold, the victims were put naked into the

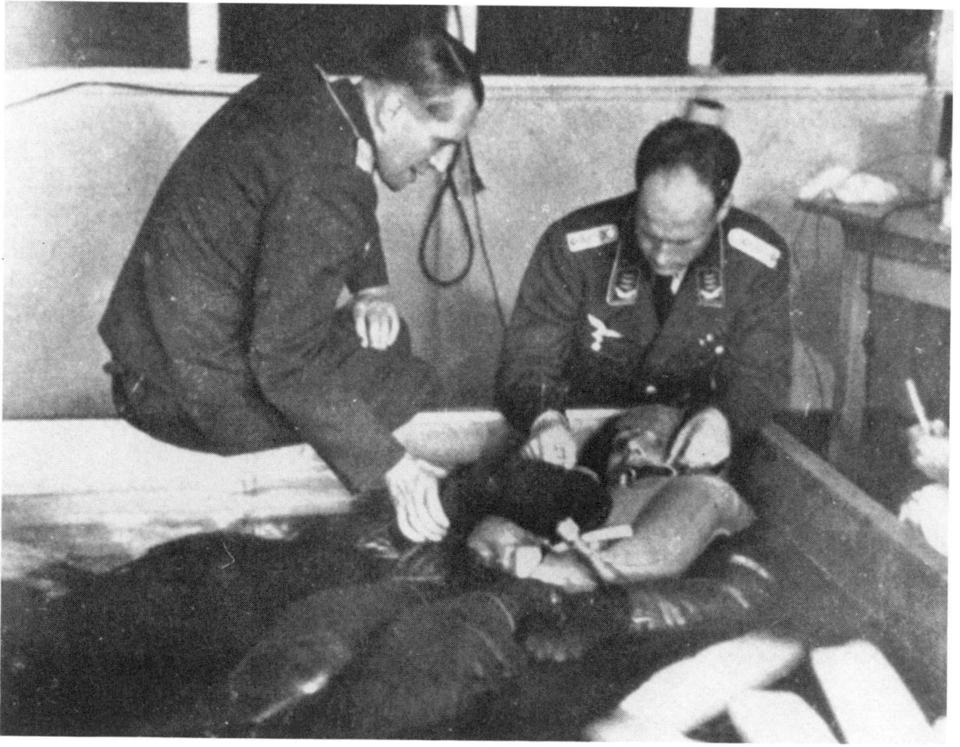

Dachau prisoner immersed in ice water to test an experimental exposure suit. Dr. Ernst Holzlöhner (left), a professor of physiology at the medical school of the University of Kiel, and Dr. Sigmund Rascher (right) observe the victim, a political prisoner. The photograph is from captured war records.

snow-covered courtyard of the experiment compound and kept there for nine to fifteen hours, from 6:00 in the evening to 9:00 the next morning, at a temperature of 8.4°F (−6°C). Though their terrible screams of pain were ignored and they were given no means of relief, their screaming had the effect of forcing these experiments at Dachau to be discontinued, because of their impact on the civilian population living in the vicinity. The dry-cold experiments were carried out by Professor Ernst Holzlöhner and Dr. E. Finke of Kiel University, who had been drafted to the air force for this purpose, and by SS Dr. Sigmund Rascher. Satisfactory results were achieved after experiments on sixty people, providing new information on the proper treatment of cold victims.

The experiment with salt water was designed to establish a reliable method of making seawater potable, in order to improve the chances for survival of air crew or naval personnel stranded in the sea and forced to spend several days under these conditions. The experiment was conducted on forty-four persons, forty-one of them GYPSIES. The main purpose was to establish the chances of survival when the only liquid available to drink was seawater, or seawater whose taste had been improved by a chemical agent (named Berkatite, after its inventor), without any change in the salt content. The experiment was conducted in series of fifteen-day periods, during which the victims were forced to drink .5 to 1.0 liters (.53–1.06 quarts) of seawater or Berkatite per day. Dr. Wilhelm Beiglböck, an air force adviser, was in charge. The experiment confirmed what was already known, namely, that there was no difference between seawater and Berkatite as far as their dehydrating effect on human beings was concerned.

Medical treatment. Experiments involving medical treatment took place in far greater numbers and consisted of three main categories: those relating to the treatment of battle injuries; those relating to the treatment of victims of gas attacks; and those testing immunization compounds or medicines, for the prevention or treatment, respectively, of contagious and epidemic diseases.

One of the experiments for the treatment of war wounds took place in the RAVENSBRÜCK camp; the victims were seventy-five female Polish political prisoners. Its purpose was to establish the effectiveness of sulfanilamide in preventing infection and putrefaction from taking place in limbs as a result of wounds. The doctor in charge of this experiment was Dr. Gebhardt. Gebhardt had been the attending physician of Reinhard HEYDRICH after the assassination attack on the latter, and when Heydrich died of his wounds it was hinted that he could have been saved if sulfanilamide had been available in sufficient quantities. Himmler asked Gebhardt to prove, by experiment, that sulfanilamide was not effective against putrefaction caused by gangrene (the immediate cause of Heydrich's death). Since this was the purpose of the experiment, a special effort was made to induce severe infections in the bodies of the victims. When Dr. Grawitz learned that there had as yet been no deaths in the experiment, he demanded that the virulence of the infections be further increased. In compliance with his demand, the wounds inflicted on the victims were infected more severely. As a result, five women died because they were not given proper surgical treatment, since the experiment demanded that only sulfanilamide be used. The remaining women were ill for a long time and remained disabled for life. Since infection by gangrene bacilli is a frequent occurrence in battle wounds, the purpose of the experiments was legitimate, but the methods used turned them into criminal acts.

Another series of experiments relating to war wounds involved the treatment of fractures and the transplanting of bones, muscles, and nerves. These were conducted at Ravensbrück by Dr. Gebhardt on Polish women prisoners, the purpose being to find solutions to problems in the treatment of severe wounds in the upper and lower limbs. The experiment, which involved breaking the leg bones of physically sound young women and giving them various treatments, later came to involve the extraction of entire bones and other tissues in order to transplant them into patients at the SS hospital in Hohenlychen. In fact, whole limbs were amputated from the prisoner victims for transplants into patients at the SS hospital. These amputations were carried out on mentally ill prisoners, who were then put to death. The experiment cost the lives of eleven out of the twenty-four victims; the rest were maimed for life.

Yet another war-wounds experiment involved the treatment of suppurative wounds, its purpose being to test the effectiveness of the biochemical treatment of infected wounds. In this experiment, pus was injected into the soft tissue of the victims in order to generate infected wounds. The experiment, which took place in the Dachau hospital, was carried out on twenty German prisoners and forty prisoners of other nationalities, all members of various churches, and cost the lives of nineteen. Experiments relating to second- and third-degree burns were conducted at AUSCHWITZ, while BUCHENWALD was the scene of experiments dealing with phosphor burns caused by incendiary bombs.

Another experiment in the treatment of wounds was designed to test the effectiveness of coagulating agents. This experiment, too, was carried out by Dr. Rascher at Dachau. The specific substance being tested was Polygal 10, which is taken orally to stop bleeding resulting from wounds or after surgery. To conduct the experiment, Dr. Rascher used four persons, shooting them point-blank in parts of the body that are prone to heavy bleeding, after first making them swallow a certain amount of Polygal. The victims died instantly. This bizarre experiment replaced the simple method, employed by hospitals, of determining the effectiveness of a coagulating agent by measuring the duration of bleeding and the time it takes for the blood to coagulate.

Experiments on the treatment of chemical-warfare victims were conducted under army auspices throughout the war. In March 1944, however, Hitler ordered Karl Brandt to intensify medical research on the effects of chemical warfare. As a result, all studies conducted in this field became part of the Reich's overall research program on gas warfare. In 1939, experiments on the use of mustard gas were carried out in the SACHSENHAUSEN concentration camp by Dr. Walter Sonntag and Dr. Heinrich Baumkötter. At the same time, Dr. August Hirt was conducting experiments in this field, on a larger scale, at the Ganzweiler camp; of the 220 persons he used as subjects, 50 died as a result. Ganzweiler was also the scene of experiments in the treatment of phosgene poisoning (phosgene is a gas that causes suffocation; if absorbed in large doses, it leads to death by asphyxiation). These experiments, which tested the effectiveness of hexamethylene tet-

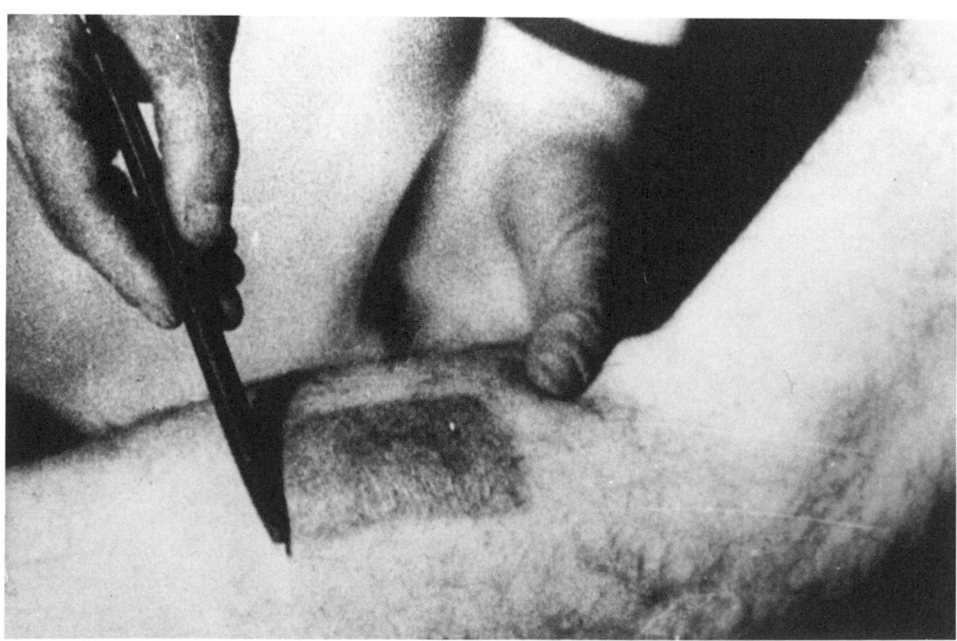

Phosphorus burn on the arm of a patient used in an experiment.

ramine, were carried out by Professor Otto Bickenbach, a member of the Strasbourg University faculty, on Karl Brandt's initiative. The NEUENGAMME camp was the place where 150 prisoners were made to drink water containing chemical-warfare substances, as part of a research project for the purification of drinking water. There were other experiments in this field, but no details concerning them have come to light.

Another area of experiment related to the immunization and treatment of infective and epidemic diseases such as malaria, infective hepatitis, and typhus. The malaria experiment was a civilian venture, carried out at Dachau by Dr. Claus Schilling, with the approval of Dr. Leonardo Conti, Reich chief of civilian medical services. The experiment involved 1,200 prisoners, most of them Catholic priests, and cost the lives of 300 to 400 persons. Of them, no more than 30 died of the disease itself; the others died from overdoses of the medicines that were being tried out on them. Infective hepatitis, which was prevalent in the Waffen-SS and the army, was the subject of experiments at Sachsenhausen, carried out by Dr. Arnold Dohmen, as well as at the Natzweiler and Buchenwald camps. In some of these experiments the death of the human subjects was a foregone conclusion, and for these Dr. Grawitz asked Himmler to put at his disposal Jewish prisoners, who were already condemned to death in any case. Following the invasion of the Soviet Union by the Germans in June 1941, typhus fever became widespread among the German army. From 1941 to the end of the war a broad program of experiments on human beings was conducted at Buchenwald and Ganzweiler to test the effectiveness of various immunization inoculations. Hundreds of prisoners were used in these experiments and hundreds died as a result.

The typhus experiments at Buchenwald were launched at the initiative of Dr. Karl Genzken, chief of the medical section of the Waffen-SS, and by Dr. Joachim Mrugowsky, chief of that formation's Institute of Hygiene. One such group of "test persons" (TPs, in SS usage) was inoculated with various serums then in general use, while a second control group was not inoculated. A third group was infected with the disease at the start of the experiment, to serve as a bank for live viruses to be used in the infecting of other victims with the disease. As a rule, typhus is transmitted by fleas, which carry the virus. When the experiments were launched, the "natural" means of transmission was tried out, but later the "test persons"—those who had been inoculated, as well as the control group, which had not been inoculated —were infected by having blood from a typhus patient injected into their bodies. Of the 729 persons used in the experiment, 154 died as a result; of the 120 persons who had served as a live-virus bank, 90 died.

Another set of typhus-immunization experiments was launched at Ganzweiler in late 1943, by Professor Eugen Haagen of Strasbourg University. Haagen asked for 300 physically fit prisoners of military age, of whom he selected 90. Using a live-virus serum that he had himself developed, Haagen infected both the non-immunized control group and the immunized group. His experiments cost the lives of 30 prisoners.

Among other experiments involving contagious and epidemic diseases was one related to yellow fever, a disease prevalent in North Africa, where German forces were fighting. In it, 485 persons were inoculated with a yellow-fever serum to test its effectiveness. Other experiments dealt with smallpox, paratyphoid A and B, cholera, diphtheria, and influenza. Tuberculosis experiments were conducted on 114 "test persons" at Dachau and on 100 men and 20 children at Neuengamme. Ganzweiler was the scene of immunization experiments on 1,700 persons relating to diseases of an unknown nature.

The above experiments were for the most part carried out on behalf of the army or civilian health authorities and at their request. In addition, however, a great many experiments were conducted that merely served the interests or the medical specialization of the doctor who devised and conducted them.

"Racial" Experiments. The second category, experiments that violated medical ethics, comprised (1) experiments designed to provide biological and physiological findings to substantiate the differentiations made by Nazi ideology between the "Aryan" race and other races; and (2) experiments to further the aims of the Third Reich's ideological policy by medical means, that is, to facilitate the destruction of the Jews.

Three types of experiments were conducted to provide biological evidence to substantiate Nazi racist ideology: experiments on dwarfs and twins; serological experiments; and a study of the skeletons of Jews.

The experiments on dwarfs and twins were carried out by Dr. Josef MENGELE at Auschwitz. The only firsthand evidence on these experiments comes from a handful of survivors and from a Jewish doctor, Miklós Nyiszli, who worked under Mengele as a pathologist. Mengele subjected his victims—twins and dwarfs aged two and above—to clinical examinations, blood tests, X rays, and anthropological measurements. In the case of the twins, he drew sketches of each twin, for comparison. He also injected his victims with various substances, dripping chemicals into their eyes (apparently in an attempt to change their color). He then killed them himself by injecting chloroform into their hearts, so as to carry out comparative pathological examinations of their internal organs. Mengele's purpose, according to Dr. Nyiszli, was to establish the genetic cause for the birth of twins, in order to facilitate the formulation of a program for the doubling of the birthrate of the "Aryan" race. The experiments on twins affected 180 persons, adults and children.

Mengele also carried out a large number of experiments in the field of contagious diseases (typhoid and tuberculosis) to find out how human beings of different races withstood these diseases. He used Gypsy twins for this purpose. Mengele's experiments combined scientific (perhaps even important) research with the racist and ideological aims of the Nazi regime, which made use of government offices, scientific institutions, and concentration camps. From the scanty information available, it appears that his research differed from the other medical experiments in that the victims' death was programmed into his experiments and formed a central element in it.

The serological experiments, conducted by Professor Werner Fischer of the Koch Institute for Contagious Diseases and Dr. Karl Georg Horneck, were intended to prove that there were serological differences among the races. The experiments were carried out on Gypsies in the Sachsenhausen camp. Similar experiments had been conducted earlier by the same doctors: in 1938, Fischer had made a comparative study of the blood serum of whites and blacks, and in 1941 Horneck had made such a study of black prisoners of war.

The project on skeletons of Jews was carried out by Dr. August Hirt at Strasbourg University. His purpose was to prove the racial inferiority of "Jewish-Bolshevik commissars" by means of an anthropological study of their skeletons. For this experiment, 115 Jews in a good state of health were selected and killed in gas chambers. Their corpses were forwarded to the anatomical institute at Strasbourg University, where Hirt hoped to prove that communism and Judaism affect the structure of the skeleton, and thus to demonstrate the inferiority of the human beings concerned.

Experiments designed to support the implementation of Nazi ideological policy included those involving methods of mass sterilization and of killing individuals as well as masses of human beings. From the very beginning of Hitler's rule, sterilization was one of the means employed in the implementation of an ideologically based health policy. As early as 1933 a program was launched in Germany for the sterilization of all genetically diseased, retarded, and alcoholic individuals, so as to ensure the well-being of the "Aryan" race. Programs of this nature were also put into effect in some of the occupied countries.

Experiments in mass sterilization, begun in 1942, were not designed as a means of installing the "Aryan" race as the future ruler of the world, but to provide an alternative to the immediate destruction of the Jews and of other people who, according to Nazi racist ideology, should not be permitted to live. Such a method would also enable the Nazis to interfere as little as possible with the MISCHLINGE (persons of "mixed blood," that is, those with at least one Jewish grandparent) and use them to meet labor requirements. The sterilization experiments were carried out on Hitler's own initiative, but by taking this step Hitler was also responding to proposals made by several doctors who had a professional interest in them. They suggested

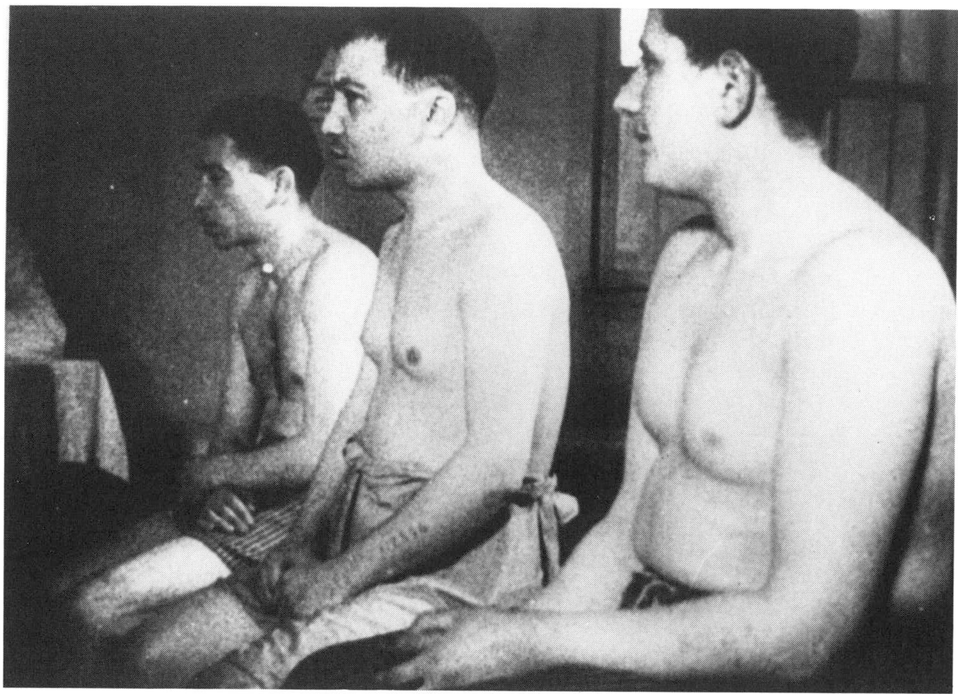

Men selected for sterilization experiments.

to Hitler that sterilization could serve as a powerful weapon in the total war against Nazi Germany's enemies.

Dr. Horst Schumann, in Auschwitz, first sterilized men, women, and children by means of radiation, exposing them to large doses of X rays, which caused severe burns. He then removed the men's testicles and transmitted them to a Breslau institute for a histopathological examination. Dozens, perhaps hundreds, of persons of different nationalities were used in these experiments. Most of them were sent to the gas chambers soon afterward, since the radiation burns from which they suffered made them unfit for work. Sterilization experiments were also conducted on women and children in Ravensbrück (many of the child victims were Gypsies). Viktor BRACK, the author of this group of experiments, proposed to Himmler that the method be used on three million Jews—out of the total of ten million earmarked for extermination—provided they were fit and could be used as forced laborers.

Other sterilization experiments were carried out at this time by Professor Carl CLAUBERG at Auschwitz and Ravensbrück; their aim was to determine the feasibility of mass sterilization by one-time injection of a chemical substance into the womb. Thousands of women were used in this experiment, most of them Jewish and the rest Gypsies. Clauberg was seeking the answer to a question put to him by Himmler regarding the time it would take to sterilize one thousand women by means of an efficient, speedy, inexpensive, and dependable method, which could then be applied in a mass sterilization program. He was soon able to inform Himmler that by using the method he had devised and tested, a team consisting of one doctor and ten assistants could sterilize up to one thousand persons a day. The procedure in Clauberg's experiment was to use a routine gynecological examination to inject a chemical into the womb that had the effect of totally destroying the lining membrane of the womb and severely damaging the ovaries. The second stage of the experiment was to surgically remove the damaged ovaries and forward them to Berlin, to be tested for the effectiveness of the method.

Clauberg's experiment resulted in the permanent sterilization of the victims and in irreversible damage to their wombs and ovaries. Clauberg had been handling the sterilization, by surgical means, of the retarded and the genetically diseased, to whom the law for the protection of the German heritage applied. He had supported this law when it was first proposed in 1933, on condition that the sterilization be carried out by specialists only, to ensure that no unnecessary damage was caused to the internal organs and hormone glands, and that the ability of the persons sterilized to continue to function, physiologically and psychologically, was not impaired.

During the war, sterilization programs were also carried out in the occupied countries. These programs were based on racist grounds rather than on the medical criteria applied to the sterilization programs in prewar Germany. In 1942, a number of doctors and political figures—including Clauberg—proposed to Himmler that nonsurgical experiments in mass sterilization, using a fast and effective method, be carried out in the concentration camps. Mass sterilization, they argued, would be the answer both to the labor requirements for the war effort (by keeping the concentration camp prisoners alive for this purpose) and to the major objective of Nazi racist policy, the rapid and total destruction of all the Jews of Europe.

Military Tribunals. On October 25, 1946, The Medical Case (the first of the twelve SUBSEQUENT NUREMBERG PROCEEDINGS tried by the Nuremberg Military Tribunals) opened, in which twenty-three doctors and other senior functionaries in the Nazi medical establishment and the army were put on trial. Of the twenty-three defendants, twenty were medical doctors, of whom nineteen had held senior posts in the administration or the army. Sixteen were found guilty under Allied Control Council Law No. 10, providing for the punishment of war crimes and crimes against peace and humanity. All the defendants were accused of crimes against humanity, and several of other crimes under that law. They were found guilty of planning and executing experiments on human beings against their will, in a cruel and brutal manner involving severe torture, and of the deliberate murder of some of the victims, in cold blood and with full awareness of the gravity of their deeds.

The Nuremberg Military Tribunals found that the medical experiments were crimes that served the ideological objectives of the Nazi regime. They also found that none of the many experiments carried out by the Nazis was of any scientific value.

Seven of the accused were sentenced to death: Karl Brandt, Rudolf Brant (Himmler's private secretary and principal secretary of the Ministry of the Interior), Karl Gebhardt, Joachim Mrugowsky, Viktor Brack, Wolfram Sievers (AHNENERBE chief), and Waldemar Hoven (Waffen-SS officer and chief medical officer at Buchenwald). All were executed on June 2, 1948. Nine of the accused were sentenced to prison terms of various lengths, and seven were acquitted.

Five persons who had played a central role in the medical experiments were not tried at Nuremberg. Ernst Grawitz committed suicide in 1945, Carl Clauberg was tried in the Soviet Union, Josef Mengele escaped to South America, and Horst Schumann disappeared and has not been traced. Siegmund Rascher was executed on Himmler's orders in February 1945 for falsely claiming that his wife gave birth to children after the age of forty-eight.

[*See also* Physicians, Nazi.]

BIBLIOGRAPHY

Friedman, P. "Crimes in the Name of Science." In *Roads to Extinction: Essays on the Holocaust*, edited by A. J. Friedman, pp. 322–332. Philadelphia, 1980.

Kudlien, F., ed. *Ärzte im Nationalsozialismus*. Cologne, 1985.

Lifton, R. J. *The Nazi Doctors: Medical Killing and the Psychology of Genocide*. New York, 1986.

Mitscherlich, A., and F. Mielke. *Doctors of Infamy: The Story of Medical Crimes*. New York, 1949.

Proctor, R. *Racial Hygiene: Medicine under the Nazis*. Cambridge, Mass., 1988.

NAVA COHEN

MEIN KAMPF ("My Struggle"). Volume 1 of Adolf HITLER's *Mein Kampf* was published in July 1925, under the title *Eine Abrechnung* (A Reckoning), and volume 2, *Die nationalsozialistische Bewegung* (The National Socialist Movement), in December 1926 (although the book gives 1927 as the year of publication). From 1930 on, further editions were published as a single volume. By 1945 some ten million copies had been put in circulation, and the book had been translated into sixteen languages. Since then it has appeared in several translations, but no new German edition has been published. There is no critical edition of the book. Over the years *Mein Kampf* underwent some corrections, mostly of style and a few of fact, but only one substantial change was made: the editions that came out in 1930 and later state that the leaders of lower rank in the Nazi party would no longer be elected but would be appointed by the next higher rank.

Volume 1 of *Mein Kampf* was meant to be Hitler's autobiography and volume 2 to show how the Nazi party came into being; the book as a whole, according to the preface, was to set forth Hitler's aims and doctrine. The autobiographical data, however, are largely untrue and have glaring omissions. They appear to have been manipulated to enable Hitler to create the impression that his political views derived from his early life, whereas in actuality these views were conceived by him only after 1919. In the same manner, in the second volume the history of the party is completely overshadowed by ideological statements.

While the book deals with all aspects of politics, German foreign policy, as envisaged by Hitler, and its basic future elements are described in particular detail in chapter 4 of volume 1 and in chapters 13 and 14 of volume 2. The goals laid down were, first, alliances with Italy and Britain, to be followed by a war with France, whereby conditions would be created that would enable Germany to capture territory in eastern Europe and Soviet Russia that would serve as LEBENSRAUM (living space) for the German people.

The book also contains Hitler's anti-Jewish program. Previously, beginning in 1919, Hitler had called for the removal of the Jews, by which he generally meant that they should emigrate or be expelled from Germany. In the book, however, his demand is for the Jews to be killed, and he ascribes global significance to this demand: "No people can remove this fist [of the international Jew] from its throat, unless it uses the sword. . . . This must necessarily be a bloody process." Hitler complains that at the beginning of World War I the German government had missed the opportunity of "mercilessly exterminating" the Jews, and that Germany would not have lost the war if it had "used poison gas" on twelve thousand to fifteen thousand Jews (chapters 14 and 15 of vol. 2).

Opinions vary on the importance of *Mein Kampf*. Some scholars believe that the book was only propaganda, while others find that it contains a clear statement of Hitler's goals, especially in the light of the policies he actually pursued when he attained power.

[*See also* Antisemitism; Racism.]

BIBLIOGRAPHY

Hammer, H. "Die deutschen Ausgaben von Hitlers 'Mein Kampf.'" *Vierteljahrshefte für Zeitgeschichte* 4 (1956): 161–178.

Jäckel, E. *Hitlers Weltanschauung.* Stuttgart, 1981.

Jäckel, E. *Hitler's Weltanschauung: A Blueprint for Power.* Middletown, Conn., 1972.

Maser, W. *Hitlers Mein Kampf: Entstehung, Aufbau, Stil, Änderungen, Quellen, Quellenwert, kommentierte Auszüge.* Munich, 1966.

EBERHARD JÄCKEL

MEISS, LÉON (1896–1966), Jewish leader in Vichy FRANCE. A distinguished lawyer, Meiss was active in communal affairs before World War II, especially in the CONSISTOIRE CENTRAL DES ISRAÉLITES DE FRANCE (Central Consistory of French Jews). With the fall of France in 1940, he joined the large exodus of Jews from the north and participated in reconstituting the Consistoire in Lyons. As vice president of the organization, Meiss took an active role in determining its policy, forcefully intervening at Vichy on various occasions to protest the regime's antisemitic policy and maintaining relations with diverse elements in the community. He was instrumental in 1943 in bringing about a rapprochement between the Consistoire and the UNION GÉNÉRALE DES ISRAÉLITES DE FRANCE. After the arrest, in October 1943, of Jacques HELBRONNER, the president of the Consistoire, Meiss succeeded in prevailing on the organization to support underground activities and align itself with political and immigrant elements of all shades in the community. These negotiations eventually led to the establishment of an umbrella organization to coordinate French-Jewish resistance activity, the CONSEIL REPRÉSENTATIF DES JUIFS DE FRANCE. After the war, Meiss played a significant role in the Jewish community's rehabilitation.

BIBLIOGRAPHY

L'activité des organisations juives en France sous l'occupation. Paris, 1947.

Cohen, R. I. "French Jewry's Dilemma on the Orientation of Its Leadership (From Polemics to Conciliation: 1942–1944)." *Yad Vashem Studies* 14 (1981): 167–204.

Cohen, R. I. " 'Religion and Fatherland': The Central Consistory in France during the Second World War." In *Israel and the Nations: Essays Presented in Honor of Shmuel Ettinger,* pp. 307–334. Jerusalem, 1987. (In Hebrew.)

Un grand Juif: Léon Meiss. Paris, 1967.

RICHARD COHEN

MELK, subcamp of MAUTHAUSEN, established on April 11, 1944, in the courtyard of a military barracks in the town of Melk, located on the banks of the Danube in Lower Austria. The camp was for forced laborers, who were to construct a system of tunnels on the slope of the hills near the village of Roggendorf, about 3 miles (5 km) east of the camp. The tunnels were to house munitions factories, which would be protected from bombing; they were dug in sandstone, hence the camp's code name, "Quartz." The first 500 prisoners were brought to Melk from Mauthausen. On January 30, 1945, the number of prisoners reached a record 10,352, and included many Russians, Yugoslavs, and Poles. After June 1944, most of the arrivals were Jews from Hungary and Poland who came to Mauthausen after *Selektionen* in AUSCHWITZ. The camp commandant was SS-Obersturmführer Anton Streitwieser until mid-May 1944, and then SS-Obersturmführer Julius Ludolf.

Only a small section of the tunnels, 3 miles (5 km) in length, was completed and prepared for the production process. Another section, 2 miles (3 km) long, remained in an advanced stage of construction. The prodigious scope of the work, which was completed in only one year, demonstrates the brutal pace of the work.

SS-Obersturmführer Julius Ludolf, commandant of the Melk camp from mid-May 1944.

The camp's regime was very harsh. The work was carried out in three shifts, with constant harassment by the SS officers and the KAPOs, most of whom were criminal offenders. Since there were no safety measures and the walls of the tunnel were not supported during the digging, daily accidents occurred in which prisoners were wounded or killed. Starvation conditions prevailed in the camp, and the prisoners were severely overcrowded, with one sleeping bunk allotted for four prisoners. These conditions resulted in a high mortality rate. In January 1945 alone more than 1,089 prisoners died; on March 12, 245 died on the same day. In the year that the camp existed, 5,000 deaths were entered in the camp records. Some prisoners were shot "while trying to escape," others were killed by phenol injections in the heart, and many were sent to the Hartheim castle, near Linz, to be killed in its gas chamber. Most of the deaths, however, were a result of the constant starvation, absolute debilitation, and disease. SS Sanitäter (medical officer) Gottlieb Muzikant was in charge of the camp hospital huts. At his trial in 1960 he confessed to having killed more than 90 sick prisoners by phenol injections in the heart, and to having strangled 100 other prisoners.

In the second week of April 1945, as the Red Army drew near, evacuation of the camp began. A small number of the prisoners was sent to Mauthausen, and the rest were taken by raft down the Danube to the city of Linz. From there they were marched to the EBENSEE camp.

At the end of the war the camp commandant, Julius Ludolf, was captured and tried by a United States Army court in Freising, Austria; he was sentenced to be hanged. The first commandant, Anton Streitwieser, was captured at the war's end, but he escaped and lived under a false identity until 1956, when he was recaptured and placed under investigation. Until his trial in 1967 he remained at liberty. The courts in Cologne found him guilty of serious crimes and sentenced him to life imprisonment. He died in jail in 1972. Gottlieb Muzikant was tried in 1960 in Fulda, Germany, and sentenced to life imprisonment with forced labor.

BIBLIOGRAPHY

Eckstein, B. *Mauthausen: Concentration and Annihilation Camp.* Jerusalem, 1984. (In Hebrew.)

Le Chêne, E. *Mauthausen: The History of a Death Camp.* London, 1971.

Marsalek, H., and K. Hacker. *Kurzgeschichte der Konzentrationslager Mauthausen und seiner drei grössten Nebenlager, Gusen, Ebensee und Melk.* Vienna, n.d.

BENYAMIN ECKSTEIN

MELNYK, ANDREI, one of the leaders of the Ukrainian nationalist movement in the interwar period. Melnyk was born in Eastern Galicia and earned a degree in agricultural engineering. In World War I be became a colonel in the Austrian army; from 1917 to 1919 he served in the army of the Ukrainian People's National Republic, first as commander of the Sichovi Striltsi (Sich Fusiliers) corps, and, from December 1918, as chief of staff. After the war he settled in Lvov and was one of the leaders of the Ukrainska Viiskova Orhanizatsyia (Ukrainian Military Organization; UVO) and later of the ORHANIZATSYIA UKRAINSKYKH NATSIONALISTIV (OUN), both nationalist Ukrainian organizations. After the death of the UVO leader, Yevheni Konovalets, in May 1938, the OUN congress held in Rome on August 27, 1939, elected Melnyk to head the movement, and he took up residence in Nazi Germany.

On February 10, 1940, the young leaders of the organization, headed by Stefan BANDERA, rebelled against Melnyk's leadership. The organization split in two, with one part remaining loyal to Melnyk and changing its name to OUN-Melnyk. It adhered to a policy of full cooperation, especially political cooperation, with Germany. In the early stage of the German attack on the Soviet Union, Melnyk published a manifesto in *Nastup,* a Ukrainian newspaper, on July 12, 1941, in which he called on Ukrainians to support the war against the Soviet Union and cooperate with the Germans. Melnyk and his faction were also instrumental in forming the Ukrainian SS division "Galicia," in the fall of 1943.

Despite Melnyk's cooperation with the Germans, they arrested him in 1943, when all the leaders of the Ukrainian nationalist movement were taken into custody, but he was released in September 1944, when the Germans made efforts to gain the support of Ukrainian nationalists. After the war Melnyk lived in Western Europe and eventually immigrated to Canada, where he died in the early 1960s.

BIBLIOGRAPHY

Kubijovyc, V., ed. *Ukraine: A Concise Encyclopaedia.* Toronto, 1963, 1971. See vol. 1, pp. 863–887; vol. 2, pp. 1073–1075.

SHMUEL SPECTOR

MEMEL (Lith., Klaipėda), port city on the Baltic; now part of the Lithuanian SSR. Founded in 1252 by the German Teutonic Order, Memel belonged to East Prussia until 1919. It was detached from Germany after World War I and annexed to LITHUANIA in 1923, with a special autonomous status for both the city and the surrounding region. Jews had been living in Memel since the seventeenth century, but an organized community was established only in the nineteenth

Hitler reviews a naval guard of honor in Memel on March 24, 1939, two days after German forces entered the city. At the extreme left is Erich Raeder, commander in chief of the navy.

century. In 1939 Memel had a Jewish population of nine thousand, 18 percent of the total population.

The political situation of the Jews in Memel was greatly influenced by the continuous friction between the Lithuanian authorities and the German population, who were in the majority. When Hitler came to power in 1933, an intensive Nazi propaganda drive was launched to have the city returned to Germany, a drive accompanied by manifestations of antisemitism, including anti-Jewish rioting. In the frequent clashes between the local Nazis and the Lithuanians, synagogue windows were often smashed.

A Jewish family leaving Memel after the German forces entered the city on March 22, 1939.

In October 1938 the local Nazis, under their leader, Dr. Ernst Neumann, demanded that the NUREMBERG LAWS be applied to Memel. Jewish concerns over the future reached a critical stage at the end of 1938, when the Nazis captured twenty-six out of the twenty-nine seats that made up the city Sejm (parliament), as a result of which Memel became a de facto part of Nazi Germany.

On March 22, 1939, German forces entered Memel. Many Lithuanians and practically all the Jews, except for a handful of the elderly or disabled, had succeeded in getting out before the German takeover. Some of the Jews moved to Kovno and others to nearby towns; following the German conquest of Lithuania in the summer of 1941, they shared the fate of the rest of Lithuanian Jewry.

Memel was liberated by the Soviet army on January 28, 1945. Not a single Jew was left in the city.

BIBLIOGRAPHY

Shulman, J. "Memel." In *Lithuanian Jewry*, edited by R. Chasman et al., pp. 281–372. Tel Aviv, 1967. (In Hebrew.)

DOV LEVIN

MEMORBUCH. *See* Yizkor Book.

MEMORIAL BOOK. *See* Yizkor Book.

MENCZER, ARON (1917–1943), YOUTH ALIYA activist. A member of the Gordonia Zionist youth movement in VIENNA, Menczer worked for Youth Aliya following the Anschluss of Austria in March 1938. In March 1939, Menczer escorted a group of Youth Aliya wards to Palestine on behalf of the organization. His sense of duty toward the Jewish youth still in Austria made him return to Vienna, where he rejected a further opportunity to emigrate.

In September 1939, Menczer was appointed head of Youth Aliya in Vienna. In 1940, when exit from the country was no longer possible, he concentrated his efforts on education through the Youth Aliya school in the city, which 400 pupils attended regularly. Under his leadership the various Zionist youth movements in Austria united into one body, with Menczer as its director. He also maintained contact with activists of the pioneer YOUTH MOVEMENTS in BĘDZIN and SOSNOWIEC in Poland, which he visited late in 1940, and helped them establish a pattern of regular activities.

After the closing down of the Youth Aliya institutions in Austria, Menczer was sent to a forced-labor camp near Linz, where he continued his educational efforts by correspondence. On September 14, 1942, he was taken back to Vienna, and on September 24 was transferred to THERESIENSTADT, where he became a youth leader and, in November, a member of the HE-HALUTS central council.

In August 1943, Menczer joined a team that cared for a group of twelve hundred children brought to Theresienstadt from BIAŁYSTOK. On October 15 of that year the children, together with Menczer and other escorts, were deported to the Birkenau camp, where they all perished.

BIBLIOGRAPHY

Rosenkrantz, H. *Verfolgung und Selbstbehauptung: Die Juden in Österreich, 1938–1945.* Vienna, 1978.

JACOB METZER

MENGELE, JOSEF (1911–1978?), doctor and SS officer. Mengele was born in Günzburg, Germany; in 1935 he was awarded a D.Phil. degree by the University of Munich, and in 1938 an M.D. degree from the University of Frankfurt. He was a member of Stahlhelm, an extreme right-wing and antisemitic organization, from 1931 to 1934; he joined the Nazi party in 1937 and the SS in 1938. From June 1940 he served in the Waffen-SS medical corps, and in August of that year he was appointed an *Untersturmführer*. In May 1943

Josef Mengele.

he was promoted to *Hauptsturmführer* and was posted to the AUSCHWITZ extermination camp, where he remained until its evacuation on January 18, 1945. Mengele spent much of his time on pseudoscientific MEDICAL EXPERIMENTS and also on the *Selektionen* of Jews who were brought to the camp. In the course of these *Selektionen*, most of the Jews were immediately sent to their death in the gas chambers; the rest were put on forced labor in concentration camps (*see* PHYSICIANS, NAZI).

Mengele's pseudoscientific experiments, in which he used human beings as guinea pigs, dealt primarily with infants and young twins, and with dwarfs. The experiments involved the maltreatment of the prisoners in various ways, such as the excision of their genital organs and a variety of harmful injections into the veins or directly into the heart.

When Auschwitz was evacuated, Mengele was transferred to the MAUTHAUSEN concentration camp; when that camp was liberated on May 5, 1945, all trace of him was lost. In mid-1949 he turned up in Argentina, where he was given asylum. Mengele's criminal actions were documented at the NUREMBERG TRIAL and in the trials of the Nazi criminals who had functioned at Auschwitz. In 1959 the West German authorities issued a warrant for his arrest, and in 1960 the West German Foreign Ministry asked Argentina for his extradition, but Mengele succeeded in escaping to Brazil and from there made his way to Paraguay. According to one version, he was drowned in December 1978, in Brazil, but this has been questioned.

In February 1985 a public trial of Mengele, *in absentia*, was held at YAD VASHEM in Jerusalem, with the participation of Auschwitz survivors on whom Mengele had carried out his experiments.

BIBLIOGRAPHY

Astor, G. *The "Last" Nazi: The Life and Times of Dr. Joseph Mengele.* New York, 1985.

Lifton, R. J. *The Nazi Doctors: Medical Killing and the Psychology of Genocide.* New York, 1986.

Nyiszli, M. *Auschwitz: A Doctor's Eyewitness Account.* New York, 1960.

SHMUEL KRAKOWSKI

MERIN, MOSHE (1906–1943), chairman of the JUDENRAT (Jewish Council) in Eastern Upper SILESIA. Before World War II, Merin was a commercial agent and an active member of the SOSNOWIEC Zionist organization. People who knew Merin have described him as an unstable and thoughtless individual who spent most of his time in coffeehouses. This did not prevent him from becoming a member of the Jewish Community Council of Sosnowiec in January 1939.

After the seizure of Sosnowiec on September 4, 1939, the Germans, at the very time that a mass attack on the Jews was in full swing, appointed Merin chairman of the local Jewish community. A German officer had demanded that the chairman of the community report to him, but the man who held that post, Lazarowicz, did not speak up, and Merin presented himself in his place as representing the community.

After the incorporation of the Zagłębie region into the Reich, as part of Eastern Upper Silesia, the Germans proceeded with the establishment of a central Judenrat for the region. In January 1940 they appointed a Central Office of the Jewish Councils of Elders in Eastern Upper Silesia (Zentrale der Jüdischen Ältestenräte in Ostoberschlesien), with Merin at its head. In the period from 1940 to 1943 this office looked after some forty-five communities, with a total population of one hundred thousand Jews.

From January 1940 to the time that the deportations from this region were launched, in May 1942, Merin carried out his task with great authority and organizational talent, and he enjoyed the confidence of his Nazi supervisors. He appointed and dismissed Jewish community leaders at will, in BĘDZIN (three times), Chrzanów, Oświęcim, and other places. He also appointed inspectors, in the name of the central Judenrat, to direct the work of the leaders of the communities under his jurisdiction and to keep watch on them. By means of the labor office and the Jewish police that he controlled, Merin vigorously enforced the German demands for Jewish forced labor.

The regional Judenrat under Merin, at the height of its activities, employed twelve hundred persons. In 1941 it consisted of an impressive number of departments: legal affairs, social work, health, supplies, education, finance, administration, statistics, and archives. From February to April of 1940, it also had an emigration department. The various local Judenräte had police forces, which at one point consisted of five hundred men. Much activity was undertaken by the department for social work, which operated twenty-eight soup kitchens and five homes for the aged, and looked after 150 Jewish orphans. Merin obtained the Germans' permission to make numerous journeys, which took him to Berlin, Prague, Slovakia, and Warsaw; wherever he went, he stressed his excellent contacts with the Nazis as the reason for his success. In the early days of the war he took a hand in the repatriation of three hundred Czech Jews who had been expelled from their country and were then staying in Sosnowiec, and of the Jews in Nisko who had been deported under the Lublin Reservation project; he claimed that it was through his efforts that these Jews were permitted to return to Czechoslovakia, (*see* NISKO AND LUBLIN PLAN). Adding to his prestige were the facts that in the Zagłębie region and Eastern Upper Silesia the Jews were not put into ghettos, that most of them were employed in the German war effort, and that, relatively speaking, they did not suffer from a starvation diet.

In the fall of 1940, when the Germans launched the draft for forced labor, Merin called upon the young Jews in his area to volunteer for the camps in order to establish kibbutzim there, under German auspices. At first Merin's domination did not encounter any opposition among the general Jewish population (except for the leaders of some communities under his authority), whose attitude toward him was a mixture of fear, respect, and ridicule. He was even called "king of the Jews." The veteran leaders of Sosnowiec and Będzin resigned or left, but some were appointed to second-rank posts in the Judenräte, one reason for such appointments being Merin's strong desire to earn legitimacy in the eyes of the Jewish population. The top posts in the Judenräte were held by a group close to Merin, made up of people between the ages of thirty-five and forty-five who, like Merin, were affiliated with Zionist parties (notable among them were Fanny Czerna, Smeitana, Chaim Molczadski, and Chaim Merin).

When the extermination process reached Upper Silesia, in May 1942, Merin adopted a policy of sacrificing one part of the community for the sake of saving another part. In taking this position he had the support of the rabbis of Będzin and Sosnowiec, and of most of the leading activists in the Judenrat. Merin did not change his stand even after the deportation of about a third of the Jews from his area to AUSCHWITZ by August 1942. He was influenced by the fact that the candidates for extermination in the area were chosen on a selective basis: Jews who were unfit to work were sent to their death; others were dispatched to forced-labor camps in Germany; and a considerable number kept on working in the "shops" that had been set up to serve the needs of the German forces. It was in this period that Merin formulated the concept of "work as a means of rescue."

In the wake of the first series of deportations, an underground was organized in the Zagłębie region, made up of members of the He-Haluts Zionist YOUTH MOVEMENTS, for the purpose of defending and rescuing Jews. It regarded Merin as a collaborator and became the core of an anti-Merin opposition. Merin, for his part, regarded underground operations as a threat to the continued existence of the Zagłębie communities, and in the spring of 1943 he handed two of its activists, Lipek Mintz and Zvi Dunski, over to the Germans. He also denounced to the Germans another underground group, suspected of Communist activities, and eight members of this group were executed in April 1943. The underground passed a death sentence on Merin. There was another clash between Merin and the youth movement activists, involving a rescue attempt by means of South American passports; Merin believed that it was dangerous to maintain contacts with Switzerland and tried to block these efforts. At that point, on June 21, 1943, without prior warning, Merin and several of his senior assistants were deported to Auschwitz. Some believed that his deportation was related to the passport affair, which involved hundreds of Zagłębie residents. About this time another mass deportation from Będzin and Sosnowiec took place, and on August 1, 1943, the Germans launched the final liquidation of the ghettos in the Zagłębie region.

BIBLIOGRAPHY

Friedman, P. *Roads to Extinction: Essays on the Holocaust*. Philadelphia, 1980. See pages 353–364.

Ranz, J. *In Nazi Claws: Bendzin, 1939–1944*. New York, 1976.

Szternfinkiel, N. E. *Zagłada Żydów Sosnowca*. Katowice, 1946.

Trunk, I. *Judenrat: The Jewish Councils in Eastern Europe under Nazi Occupation*. New York, 1972.

AVIHU RONEN

MIDDLE EAST. *See* Husseini, Hajj Amin al-; Iraq; Syria and Lebanon; Yishuv.

MIKOŁAJCZYK, STANISŁAW (1901–1966), Polish statesman. Mikołajczyk was born in Holsterhausen, in Westphalia, Germany; in his early youth he moved to Poznań, where he was active in the area's rural youth movement. From 1931 on he was one of the prominent leaders of the People's Party (Stronnictwo Ludowe) and a member of the Polish parliament, the Sejm. When the Germans invaded Poland in September 1939, Mikołajczyk left the country but remained politically active in exile. In 1940 and 1941 he was deputy chairman of the London-based Polish National Committee in Exile; from the beginning of 1942 to mid-1943 he was deputy prime minister and minister of the interior in the POLISH GOVERNMENT-IN-EXILE. In the latter post he was in charge of all ties with occupied Poland and of the efforts to alert the free world to the Nazi terror in Poland and the events of the Holocaust.

On July 14, 1943, Mikołajczyk was elected prime minister in the Polish government-in-exile. When the war ended he returned to Poland and was appointed deputy prime minister and minister of agriculture. But before long he came to reject the new Communist regime, joining the ranks of the opposition, and in October 1947 he fled the country. Mikołajczyk settled in the United States, where he was active in Polish emigré groups. He wrote *The Rape of Poland: Pattern of Soviet Aggression* (1948).

BIBLIOGRAPHY

Engel, D. *In the Shadow of Auschwitz*. Chapel Hill, 1987.

Garlinski, J. *Poland in the Second World War*. New York, 1988.

SHMUEL KRAKOWSKI

MINSK, capital of the Belorussian SSR. In 1926 the Jewish population of Minsk was 53,686; by June 1941 the number had grown to 80,000, constituting one-third of the city's population. Only a small part of the Jews managed to escape from the city in the six days between the German invasion of the Soviet Union and the conquest of Minsk on June 28, 1941. German parachutists who had been dropped east of the city intercepted thousands of Jews who were trying to flee and forced them to return. When the civil administration was set up, Minsk became the headquarters of the *Generalkommissar* for Belorussia, Wilhelm KUBE.

On July 8, 1941, the Germans killed 100 Jews, and thereafter the murder of Jews by the Germans, singly or in groups, became a daily event. On July 20, an order was issued on the establishment of the ghetto. Its area comprised thirty-four streets and alleys, as well as the Jewish cemetery. Jews from Slutsk, Dzerzhinsk, Cherven, Uzda, and other nearby places were brought into the ghetto. Married couples with one non-Jewish partner were also put into the ghetto, as were their children. Altogether, 100,000 persons were rounded up and put behind the ghetto walls.

In August, 5,000 Jews were seized and murdered. The surviving Jews were forced to pay ransom, to report every Sunday for roll call, and to wear a yellow badge (*see* BADGE, JEWISH) on their back and chest, as well as a white patch on their chest with their house number. In July 1941 a JUDENRAT (Jewish Council) was established, with Eliyahu (Ilya) MUSHKIN at its head. It had seven departments—welfare, housing, supplies, health, workshops, labor, and registration. Mushkin cooperated with the underground, and in February 1942 he was arrested and hanged. His successor, Moshe Jaffe, kept up the Judenrat's cooperation with the underground, but two Jewish collaborators, Epstein and Rosenblatt, managed to infiltrate the Judenrat and to cooperate with the Germans from within it.

On November 7, 1941, the Germans conducted an *Aktion* in several of the ghetto's streets, rounding up twelve thousand Jews and murdering them in nearby Tuchinka. The houses in which the murdered Jews had lived were now filled with Jews from Germany (called the Hamburg Jews, because that was where the first group came from), who were brought to Minsk in the wake of the November 7 *Aktion*. A second *Aktion* took place on November 20, in which the Germans murdered seven thousand Jews, also in Tuchinka. After the two *Aktionen* the ghetto underground intensified its activities, making preparations for escapes to the forests and widening its network of hiding places in the city.

On March 2, 1942, the Germans launched a third *Aktion*. They ordered the Judenrat to hand over five thousand Jews, but on orders of the underground, the Judenrat failed to comply. The Germans then fell upon the long lines of Jews who were making their way back from their places of work outside the ghetto and carried them off, killing more than five thousand, among them the children of the Shpalerna Street orphanage. When the Germans asked for the leader of the underground, Hersh Smolar, to be surrendered to them, the Judenrat chairman produced Smolar's bloodstained identity card as proof that

The hanging of two partisans in Minsk in October 1941. At the left is Masha Bruskina, a seventeen-year-old Jewish girl.

MINSK

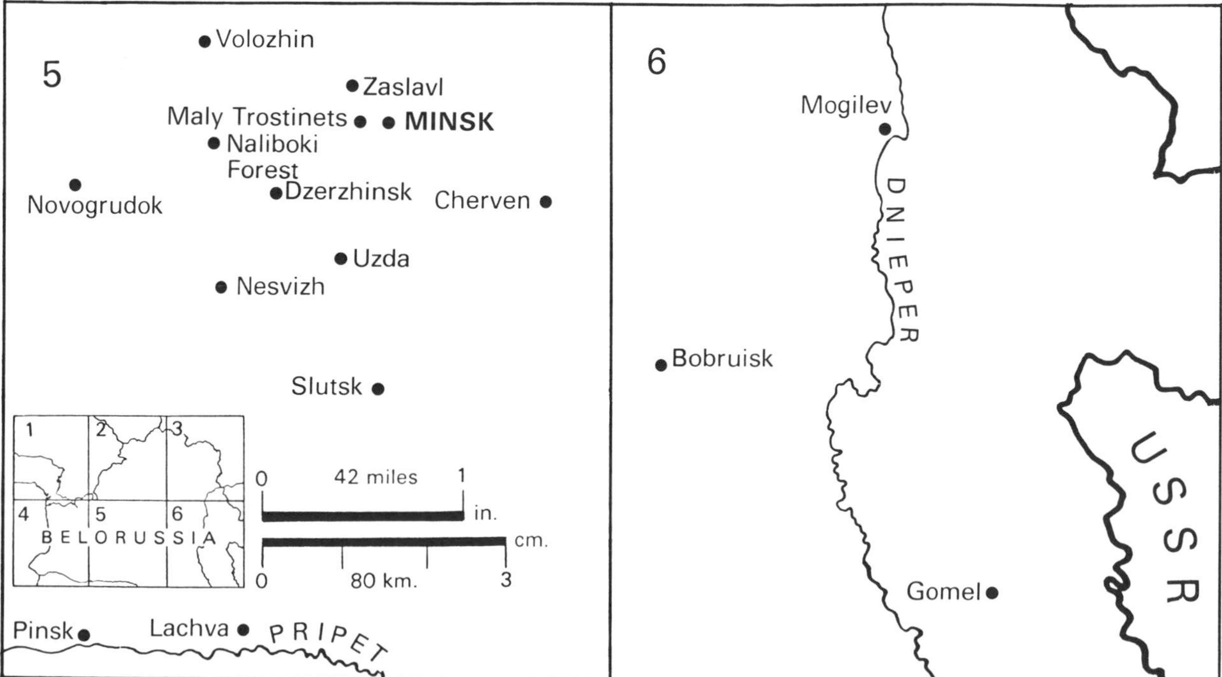

Jewish youth from Minsk.

he was dead. The Germans also instituted night *Aktionen,* resorting to them with increasing frequency in the spring of 1942. In one such night *Aktion,* on April 2, about five hundred persons were murdered.

Between July 28 and 31, 1942, the Germans killed some thirty thousand Jews, among them the German Jews who were in a separate ghetto in Minsk. The Germans forced Jaffe to speak to the Jews in terms designed to allay their fears, but when trucks with gas engines burst upon the square where they had assembled, Jaffe cried out: "Jews, the bloody murderers have deceived you—flee for your lives!" Jaffe and the ghetto police chief were among the victims of that *Aktion,* following which only nine thousand Jews were left in Minsk. The collaborators took the place of the Judenrat, which ceased to exist.

In August 1943 a transport of Minsk Jews left for the SOBIBÓR extermination camp. On September 10, two thousand Jews were sent to the labor camp at BUDZYŃ, near Lublin. During the final *Aktion,* on October 21, 1943, the last four thousand Jews were killed, at MALY TROSTINETS. When Minsk was liberated on July 3, 1944, only a few Jews of those who had gone into hiding during the final *Aktion* remained alive.

The Ghetto Underground. In August 1941 an underground was established in the ghetto, with Hersh Smolar as one of its founders. The first meeting of the founding group formulated the underground's goal, which was to escape into the forests and fight in the ranks of the partisans. Its initial activities included the formation of an underground network, the dissemination of news from the front, the setting up of a printing press, and the development of contact with the non-Jewish parts of the city (outside the ghetto no underground was yet in existence). The ghetto underground had nearly 450 members, organized into cells; about a third were young people. In this period the underground also hoarded arms. At the beginning of September 1941 an emissary of the partisans came to the ghetto and asked for money,

Elderly Jew from Minsk.

which Mushkin, head of the Judenrat, supplied. By this time an underground had also been established in the non-Jewish section of Minsk, headed by Kazinets ("Slavek"), a Jew from the Ukraine. In the wake of the first *Aktionen*, the ghetto underground made a desperate appeal to the non-Jewish underground to help Jews escape to the forests, but to no avail. In early 1942, regular contact was established with the partisans in the forests; the ghetto underground sent groups of its members out to establish its own partisan bases there. Following the third *Aktion*, in March 1942, the great flight into the forests began. The majority of the escapees made for the Kuidanov district, southeast of Minsk, and the Zaslavl district, northwest of the city, and set up partisan bases there. Most of the guides for the groups that fled the city were children from the ghetto, ranging in age from eleven to fourteen.

Minsk Jews established seven partisan units: (1) "208," in the Mogilev district; (2) "406," in Zaslavl; (3) "Budenny," also in Zaslavl; (4) "Kutuzov," between Minsk and Slutsk; (5) "Dzerzhinski," near Kuidanov; (6) "Lazo," near Kuidanov; and (7) "106," the ZORIN unit, in the Naliboki Forest. An estimated ten thousand Jews fled to the forests, the majority losing their lives on the way.

Jews from the Reich in Minsk. Between November 1941 and October 1942, a total of 35,442 Jews from Germany and the Protectorate of BOHEMIA AND MORAVIA were deported to Minsk. Most of them were taken by train directly to Maly Trostinets and murdered there. The first of these transports arrived in Minsk in November 1941; it was made up of Jews from Hamburg, Düsseldorf, Frankfurt, Berlin, Brünn (Brno), Bremen, and Vienna. They were housed in a separate ghetto, adjoining the main Minsk ghetto.

The ghetto of the Reich Jews was divided into five sections, according to the places from which they came—Hamburg, Berlin, the Rhineland, Bremen, or Vienna. There was little contact between the main Minsk ghetto and the Reich ghetto. The German Jews were killed in the major *Aktion* of July 28 to 31, 1942; on March 8, 1943; and in the fall of 1943. Some were sent to the Budzyń labor camp. Only ten Reich Jews were still alive in Minsk when the city was liberated.

BIBLIOGRAPHY

Cholawski, S. "The Judenrat in Minsk." In *Patterns of Jewish Leadership in Nazi Europe, 1933–1945.* Proceedings of the Third Yad Vashem International Historical Conference, edited by Y. Gutman and C. J. Haft, pp. 113–132. Jerusalem, 1979.

Cholawski, S. "Minsk: Its Struggle and Destruction." *Yalkut Moreshet* 18 (November 1974): 101–111. (In Hebrew.)

Even-Shoshan, S., ed. *Minsk, Jewish Mother-City: A Memorial Anthology*. Vol. 2. Jerusalem, 1985. (In Hebrew.)

Loewenstein, K. *Minsk: Im Lager der deutschen Juden*. Bonn, 1961.

Smolar, H. *Resistance in Minsk*. Oakland, Calif., 1966.

SHALOM CHOLAWSKI

MIŃSK MAZOWIECKI, town in the Warsaw district in POLAND. Before World War II, about five thousand Jews lived in Mińsk Mazowiecki, out of a population of some seventeen thousand. With the German occupation on September 13, 1939, the invading soldiers immediately began to plunder the houses and stores of Jews and to seize Jews for forced labor. Eight were taken hostage to guarantee quiet in the town. Many Jews fled east into the Soviet Union; Mińsk Mazowiecki was repopulated by the numerous Jewish refugees arriving from Warsaw and by Jews deported from territories of western Poland that had been annexed to the Reich.

In late 1939 the Germans appointed a twenty-four-member JUDENRAT (Jewish Council), and subsequently a Jewish police force was organized. On October 25, 1940, a ghetto was established. Many of the houses in the designated area had been destroyed during the September 12 shelling of the town, and living conditions were extremely difficult, with 5,242 Jews packed into the ghetto. The Judenrat established a communal kitchen where hot meals were distributed to the needy, and a hospital. In the winter of 1940–1941 the severe overcrowding and poor sanitary conditions in the ghetto led to the outbreak of a typhus epidemic.

Early on the morning of August 21, 1942, the ghetto was encircled by hundreds of SS

Jews in Mińsk Mazowiecki humiliated by being forced to ride each other and "race" in the market square.

officers, German gendarmes, Polish police, and men from Ukrainian, Lithuanian, and Latvian units. Over thirty-five hundred Jews were concentrated in the market square, where they were robbed of their money and valuables before being sent to the TREBLINKA extermination camp at dawn on August 22. About one thousand sick or old people, children, and Jews who had refused to leave their homes and offered forcible resistance were murdered on the spot. The members of the Judenrat were massacred by the Germans at the local SS headquarters.

Only 370 Jewish skilled workers remained in Mińsk Mazowiecki in the wake of the *Aktion,* employed in the Wehrmacht factories and the Rudzki steel factory; 220 of them were housed in a labor camp established by the German army in the three-story Kopernik school building on Siennicka Street. In time, hundreds of Jews who had escaped the *Aktion* stole into the camp, including women and children, and lived there secretly. In late November 1942 about 100 Jews were transferred to the nearby town of Kałuszyn, and from there to Treblinka. On December 24, 218 inmates of the Kopernik camp were massacred at the local Jewish cemetery.

On January 10, 1943, the Germans liquidated the Kopernik camp, which still contained about 300 prisoners. Thirty of the Jews in the first group taken out of the building attacked the gendarmes on the way to the cemetery, wounding three of them. In the ensuing confusion three prisoners escaped, while the rest were shot. The remaining inmates barricaded themselves within the school building, fending off the Germans with stones, firebombs, and scrap iron. In retaliation the Nazis shelled the building, burning the prisoners alive. The 104 Jews still working in the Rudzki factory were shot by the Germans on June 5, 1943.

In the second half of 1941, four resistance groups, with a total of thirty members, had formed in the ghetto, planning to leave and join the partisans in the LUBLIN district and across the Bug River. In the course of time a joint ghetto underground headquarters was established, and contact was made with the Polish GWARDIA LUDOWA (People's Army). In June and July 1942, money was raised in the ghetto for the purchase of arms; 10,000 zlotys were donated by the chairman of the Judenrat. The surviving members of the Kopernik camp underground continued their activities.

At different times, fifty to one hundred armed fighters left, in three groups. Polish peasants in the vicinity of the nearby town of Łuków informed against Józef Wiśniewski's unit, and only one Jew survived the ensuing battle, the rest dying at the hands of the Germans. The members of the two other groups reached the forest. There they joined the Gwardia Ludowa and fought under Stanisław Dąbrowski, nicknamed Brzoza ("birch"), chairman of the Siedlce district branch of the Polska Partia Robotnicza (Polish Workers' Party).

BIBLIOGRAPHY

Shedletzky, E., ed. *Minsk-Mazowiecki Memorial Book*. Jerusalem, 1977. (In Hebrew and Yiddish.)

WILA ORBACH

MIR, town in the Belorussian SSR. In the interwar period Mir belonged to Poland, as part of the Novogrudok district. Jews had lived there from the seventeenth century. Its yeshiva (rabbinical academy), founded in 1815, became one of the most famous Jewish institutions of higher learning. On the eve of World War II, the town's Jewish population of twenty-five hundred constituted about half the total. In September 1939 Mir was occupied by the Red Army and incorporated into the Soviet Union. The yeshiva, with its five hundred students, was moved to Vilna; eventually most of the students went to SHANGHAI and, after the war, made their way to the United States and Israel (*see* RESCUE OF POLISH JEWS VIA EAST ASIA).

On June 26, 1941, four days after the German invasion of the Soviet Union, German troops entered Mir. Two weeks later, 19 young Jews were executed as Communists. On November 9 of that year, the Germans organized an *Aktion* in which 1,500 Jews were murdered, among them most of the members of the JUDENRAT (Jewish Council). Following the *Aktion*, a ghetto was set up in

Students and teachers of the Mir yeshiva at study in the Beth Aharon synagogue in Shanghai, which was put at their disposal by the Baghdad Jewish community (1941). In the front row, first from the right, is Rabbi J. D. Epstein; next to him is Rabbi C. L. Szmuelowicz. On the extreme left is Rabbi C. Lewensztein. [YIVO Institute for Jewish Research]

Mir in which 850 Jews were concentrated, and a new Judenrat was established. An underground was organized in the ghetto with a membership of about 80, led by Shlomo Harhas and Berl Reznik, members of Ha-Shomer ha-Tsa'ir. It set as its goal the defense of the Jews the next time the Germans started an *Aktion*. Members of the underground acquired weapons, metal bars, and axes, and the Jewish girls among them who were working for the German gendarmerie obtained some ammunition.

A chance meeting of Harhas, Reznik, and Oswald RUFAJZEN, who had known each other since they had been in a Zionist pioneer group in Vilna, was destined to be of momentous consequence for the fate of the Jews in the Mir ghetto. Rufajzen, who had managed to be appointed district commander of the German police, smuggled weapons into the ghetto for the underground's use. On his advice, the underground dropped its original plan of resisting the Germans inside the ghetto and instead adopted another plan, which proposed escaping from the ghetto to the forest.

On August 6, 1942, the German commander informed Rufajzen that an *Aktion* against the Mir Jews was planned for August 13. Rufajzen passed the information on to the ghetto underground, adding that on the night of August 9 he would be leading the police and the Germans in the town on a "raid against the partisans." At that time the town would be empty of Germans and police, and the Jews would be free to escape to the forest. His report was transmitted to the rest of the Jews in the ghetto. Rufajzen acted as planned when the time came, and the way was clear for all the Jews to flee the ghetto. However, only 180 Jews, including the members of the underground, availed themselves of the opportunity and made their way to the forest.

Cooperation between Rufajzen—the courageous "German police chief"—and the underground was the decisive factor in the escape of Jews from the Mir ghetto. The liquidation began as planned on August 13, and all who remained in the ghetto were killed in Yablonovshchina and buried in mass graves.

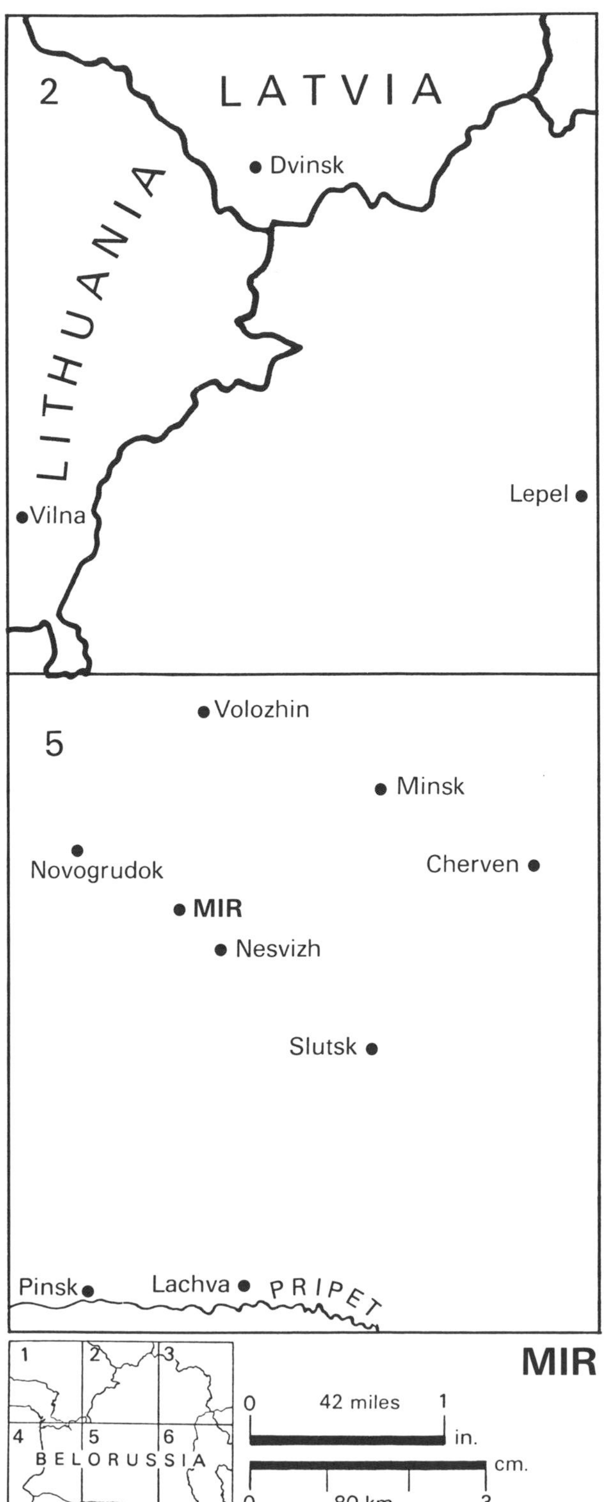

BIBLIOGRAPHY

Blumental, N. *Mir.* Jerusalem, 1962. (In Hebrew, Yiddish, and English.)

Cholawski, S. *The Jews in Belorussia (White Russia) during World War II.* Tel Aviv, 1982. (In Hebrew.)

SHALOM CHOLAWSKI

MISCHLINGE (lit., "hybrids"), part Jews. The NUREMBERG LAWS of September 1935 mentioned only Jews and Germans, but as soon as the concept of a "Jew" was defined in the first implementation ordinance of those laws, in November 1935, a third group appeared: those who were neither Jews nor Germans—the *Mischlinge.* The census of 1939 showed that seventy-two thousand *Mischlinge* of the first degree and thirty-nine thousand of the second degree were still living in Germany.

Mischlinge of the first degree, or half Jews, were those who had two Jewish grandparents, did not belong to the Jewish religion, and were not married to a Jewish person as of September 15, 1935. They had the rights of regular German citizens, although these were curtailed by a series of regulations: for example, they could marry only *Mischlinge* of the first degree. Marriage with a German or with a *Mischlinge* of the second degree required a special permit from the Ministry of the Interior and the party chancellery, which was almost never granted. As of 1940 *Mischlinge* of the first degree were excluded from military service and, as of 1942, from high schools. They were also barred from employment in the armaments industry and from taking part in Germany's trade representations abroad.

Mischlinge of the second degree, or quarter Jews, were those with one Jewish grandparent. They were subject to certain limitations in professions requiring full German origins, but were drafted into the army and were allowed to marry Germans (but not quarter, half, or full Jews). In all other matters they were treated like German "Aryans." This category also included the *Jüdischversippte* (mixed marriages). Thus, as of April 8, 1940, soldiers married to *Mischlinge* of the second degree were treated like them, and those married to *Mischlinge* of the first degree or to Jews were treated like *Mischlinge* of the first degree.

Generally, the policy was to absorb the *Mischlinge* of the second degree into the German nation, whereas those of the first degree were equated with Jews. At the end of 1941, proposals were made that all *Mischlinge* of the first degree be sterilized. The WANNSEE CONFERENCE considered a proposal of allowing those *Mischlinge* due to be deported to remain in Germany if they submitted voluntarily to sterilization. The compulsory sterilization of all *Mischlinge* was also suggested at the conference. But the question of what policy should be adopted toward the *Mischlinge* was never resolved because of the Nazis' fears of the possible repercussions among the large number of German relatives of the *Mischlinge*. The only *Mischlinge* killed were inmates of the concentration camps who had been arrested in the 1930s; these were transferred to AUSCHWITZ at the end of 1942.

A lack of uniformity in the attitude toward *Mischlinge* also characterized the policy in conquered countries. When Dutch Jews were ordered to register in January 1941, the order also included those Dutch people who had one Jewish grandparent. Such quarter Jews were not relocated to Amsterdam or deported. Dutch Jews were allowed to petition the Generalkommissariat für Verwaltung und Justiz für das Besetzte Niederländische Gebiet (General Commission for Administration and Justice for the Occupied Netherlands Territory) for exemption from the status of full Jew and half Jew. A flood of applications reached the commission, and many were handled by Dr. Hans Georg Calmeyer, who was extremely lenient and accepted 75 percent of the applications for serious consideration. He also recommended that those Jews whose applications were under consideration not be sent to a "Jewish camp" (that is, deported), because if their petitions were to be granted, all their property would have to be restored to them. Another aspect of the treatment of *Mischlinge* in the Netherlands arose in the context of marriages between Jews and "Aryans." The 8,610 registered Jewish partners in these unions were essentially given the option of deportation or undergoing sterilization to prevent them from bringing further *Mischlinge* into the world; 2,562 were sterilized, half of them men and half women. A number of those who had been sterilized were killed anyway. After the ghettoization of Polish Jewry, *Mischlinge* of all degrees were also put in the ghettos. In Slovakia, however, they were exempted from deportation to extermination camps.

For Adolf Hitler, the question of the status of Germans of partial Jewish descent was of paramount importance because of his obsession with "racial purity." Hitler's personal concern regarding the status of the *Mischlinge* in Germany rested on his racist belief that all *Mischlinge* were a menace and that the complete assimilation of foreign blood was impossible. "Families," he argued, "even if they have only a minute quantity of Jewish blood in their veins, regularly produce, generation by generation, at last one pure Jew." For this reason, applications made by Jews for a change in their status, a process known as "equalization," were handled by the Ministry of the Interior, and all potential approvals had to be referred to Hitler. His decision was then sent to the *Mischlinge*. For this reason too, on February 20, 1944, Hitler expressly ordered that all *Mischlinge* cases be dealt with by his deputy, Martin BORMANN, and submitted to himself for final approval. Hitler's intervention was also required when a number of *Mischlinge* received, according to the racial legislation, a racial classification different from that corresponding to their biological condition. In all these cases, Hitler's personal decision was needed to clarify the status of the individual concerned.

This was true also of mixed marriages involving *Mischlinge*. However, Hitler's personal intervention could still lead him at times to contradict his own principle. While saying in private conversations that he was convinced that Germany would harm itself by accepting *Mischlinge* into the army, and that exemptions from the status of full Jew or half Jew should therefore be reduced to a minimum, he exempted some 260 officers or their wives who were *Mischlinge* of the first degree. Similarly, by 1942, some 340 Jews had been equalized by him with *Mischlinge* of the first degree. By means of legal fiction, he also granted the status of half Jew to some 3,000 people considered Jews. After the attempt on his life on July 20, 1944, Hitler's obsession with Jewish influence grew so strong that he ordered that civil servants who were *Mischlinge,* or who were married to Jews or *Mischlinge,* could no longer hold high governmental office, even if their partners had previously been equalized with "Aryans." This new regulation affected a wide range of people in important posts, among them an ambassador and a high official in the Ministry of Churches.

The drafting of *Mischlinge* into the armed forces was of great concern to Hitler as well. A decree of April 8, 1940, declared that only he could grant permits to *Mischlinge* to serve in the army. The same motive underlay his order that a second-degree female *Mischling* required his permission to marry if the groom was in active service.

Hitler was obviously even stricter regarding membership in the Nazi party, which was meant to be a bastion of racial purity. The ferreting out of *Mischlinge* in the party ranks was much more thorough than demanded by state law, and expulsions from the Nazi party embraced *Mischlinge* even up to the fifth degree. However, merit prior to 1933 when there was also only a small degree of Jewish blood permitted *Mischlinge* to remain in the party. The problem was dealt with individually only in exceptional cases, as when the person involved had been unaware of his Jewish ancestry and had been active in the party for years. All applications for exemptions had to go through Hitler. Hitler also issued general instructions that the offspring of political leaders were not to marry *Mischlinge,* even if the latter had received equal status with Germans.

BIBLIOGRAPHY

Adam, U. D. *Judenpolitik im Dritten Reich.* Düsseldorf, 1972.

Hilberg, R. *The Destruction of the European Jews.* 3 vols. New York, 1985.

DAVID BANKIER

MISKOLC, city in HUNGARY, located 112 miles (180 km) northeast of Budapest, at the eastern end of the Diosgyor valley. In 1941, 10,428 Jews lived in Miskolc, constituting 13.5 percent of the population.

In August 1941, when the Hungarian authorities deported some eighteen thousand Jews to KAMENETS-PODOLSKI in the Ukraine, five hundred Jews from Miskolc were included in the transport. They were killed along with most of the other deportees. In 1942 most of the Jewish men from the city were called up for service in the MUNKASZOLGÁLAT (Hungarian Labor Service System). After the Nazi occupation of Hungary on March 19, 1944, Miskolc was assigned to the third anti-Jewish operation zone (for the purpose of deportation, Hungary had been divided into six zones). The following month most of the remaining men in the city were sent to labor service camps, and the rest of the Jews were put into a ghetto. Those taken to the labor service camps at this time were saved from deportation, and many survived. The concentration of the Jews was carried out with great cruelty under the auspices of the city prefect, Emil Borbely-Maczky; the gentile population was warned by the police not to interfere with their work. Some three thousand Jews from the surrounding area were concentrated in brickyards outside Miskolc.

The ghetto in the city was well organized. A Zsidó Tanács (Jewish Council) was set up under Mor Feldman and Elemer Banet. The local city administration handed out housing assignments, and peasants from the surrounding area brought fruit, vegetables, and chickens to the ghetto marketplace. The main synagogue was turned into a storehouse for stolen Jewish property. Most of the city's many Jewish physicians were not moved into the ghetto, because the Hungarian authorities feared their deportation might cause a health crisis. They were placed in a special Jewish medical unit.

In August 1944 the doctors were sent to the town of Pusztavam. There, a group of SS men suddenly appeared, discovered that the doctors were Jewish, took them out of the town, ordered them to dig their own graves, and then shot and killed them. In the meantime, between June 11 and June 15, almost all the

Jews of Miskolc had been deported, including 1,422 children. A few craftsmen were left behind to work in vital war industries. One hundred and five Jews from Miskolc returned from the deportations and some 300 others survived in the labor service; only 20 of the survivors were under the age of eighteen. The Jews from the surrounding area shared the fate of the Miskolc community. In 1970, a thousand Jews were living in Miskolc.

BIBLIOGRAPHY

Braham, R. L. *The Politics of Genocide.* New York, 1981.

Lavi, T., ed. *Hungary.* In *Pinkas Hakehillot; Encyclopaedia of Jewish Communities.* Jerusalem, 1976. (In Hebrew.)

Pazternak S., ed. *Miskolc és környéke mártirkönyve.* Tel Aviv, 1970. (In Hungarian, Hebrew, and English.)

ROBERT ROZETT

MITTELSTELLE FÜR JÜDISCHE ERWACHSENENBILDUNG (Jewish Center for Adult Education), Jewish educational agency in GERMANY operating from 1934 to 1938. When the Nazis came to power in 1933, the German Jewish community felt an urgent need for Jewish education, not only for children and youth but also for adults, in order to impart a sense of Jewish identity and its meaning, since many German Jews were no longer familiar with Jewish history and the sources of Jewish culture.

In May 1934 the REICHSVERTRETUNG DER DEUTSCHEN JUDEN (Reich Representation of German Jews) established the Mittelstelle für Jüdische Erwachsenenbildung as an independent agency, under its auspices. This step was taken on the initiative of Martin BUBER, who was also appointed to serve as the agency's head. His associates in the leadership of the Mittelstelle were the pedagogue Ernst (Akiva) Simon (whom Buber asked to come from Palestine for this purpose); Ernst Kantorowicz and Kurt Bondy, both of whom had previously been engaged in German youth education; and Karl Adler, who fostered community singing in the center.

In May 1934, a few weeks after the center's establishment, the sponsors held their first conference at the rural educational center of Herrlingen, near Ulm. It was attended by dozens of educators and individuals active in cultural affairs from all over the country. The conference took a close look at the needs of the community and set the goals for the new center, in the spirit of *Rüstung zum Sein* (lit., "arming for existence"), a slogan coined by Buber, meaning that the center's *raison d'être* was to provide spiritual sustenance to the persecuted Jews whose world, as they had known it, had collapsed.

The center's major instrument for promoting its aims was the *Lernzeit* (study period), a seminar based on group study that lasted several days and was usually held in isolated rural surroundings. The seminars were held in various parts of Germany; some were oriented toward specialized groups, such as teachers or youth leaders, while others were open to the general Jewish public and were attended by Jews living in the area. Some seminars were devoted to a single theme, and others covered a variety of subjects. Buber always played the dominant role in determining the theme and spirit of the meetings, finding contemporary relevance in the Hebrew Bible. The center also served as a counseling agency. In its many seminars the participants, mostly young people, were instilled with Jewish consciousness, in the humanist tradition then being persecuted in Germany. For this reason Ernst Simon regarded the center's entire operation as a form of "moral resistance."

BIBLIOGRAPHY

Colodner, S. *Jewish Education in Germany under the Nazis.* New York, 1964.

Simon, A. E. *Chapters in My Life: Building up in the Time of Destruction.* Tel Aviv, 1986. (In Hebrew.)

Simon, E. *Aufbau im Untergang: Jüdische Erwachsenenbildung im nationalsozialistischen Deutschland als geistiger Widerstand.* Tübingen, 1959.

Van de Sandt, R. *Martin Bubers bildnerische Tätigkeit zwischen den beiden Weltkriegen.* Stuttgart, 1977.

YEHOYAKIM COCHAVI

MIXED MARRIAGES. *See* Mischlinge.

MIZRAḤI. *See* American Zionist Emergency Council.

MOBILE KILLING UNITS. *See* Einsatzgruppen.

MOGILEV (Mohilev, as the Jews pronounced it), district capital in the Belorussian SSR, founded in the thirteenth century. Jews lived in Mogilev from the sixteenth century; in the nineteenth century it was a center of religious study and of Hasidism, and later on also of Zionism and Jewish socialism. Jewish life in the city declined after the Bolshevik Revolution.

On the eve of World War II, 16,200 Jews lived in Mogilev, out of a total population of 99,440. On July 26, 1941, the German invaders captured the city after a battle lasting twenty-five days. Part of the Jewish population had been evacuated or had managed to get away on their own, but the bulk, numbering some 10,000, were still there when the Germans occupied the city. After a time, Einsatzkommando 8, belonging to Einsatzgruppe B, entered Mogilev and launched *Aktionen* against the Jews, killing them by the thousands. A JUDENRAT (Jewish Council) was appointed and the Jews were ordered to wear the yellow badge (*see* BADGE, JEWISH). By mid-October a ghetto was set up and surrounded by a barbed-wire fence. The Judenrat was ordered to organize a fifteen-man Jewish police unit.

On August 19, 1941, a group of men from Einsatzkommando 8, together with German policemen from the Center Police Regiment, carried out an *Aktion* in which they murdered 3,726 Jews, the greater part of the ghetto population. Another 239 Jews were killed on October 23. By the end of that month the remaining Jews of Mogilev had been killed, and the ghetto area was reincorporated into the municipality's jurisdiction.

Mogilev was liberated on June 28, 1944, by the Red Army.

SHMUEL SPECTOR

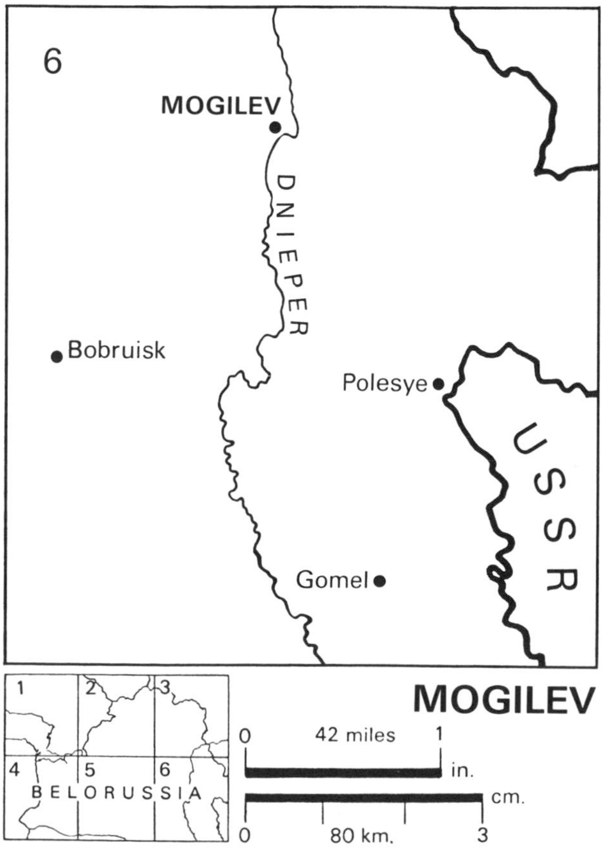

MOGILEV-PODOLSKI, town on the Dniester, in the Vinnitsa district of the UKRAINE. In 1926 it had a Jewish population of 9,622, 41.8 percent of the total. On July 19, 1941, it was occupied by German and Romanian forces. Thousands of Jews were murdered by Einsatzkommando 10b and the German and Romanian occupation troops.

Mogilev-Podolski was an assembly point for Jews expelled from BESSARABIA and BUKOVINA, and the most important among the five crossing points to TRANSNISTRIA. The Romanian town of Atachi, through which the expelled Jews had to pass, faces Mogilev-Podolski on the Romanian bank of the Dniester. During the last days of the Soviet occupation, tens of thousands of Jews tried to escape from northern Bessarabia and Bukovina to the Soviet interior. Most were caught by advancing German forces and forcibly returned to Bessarabia.

In the fall of 1941, when the first group of Jews from Romania was brought to Mogilev-Podolski, there were 25,000 Jews already in the town, including many who had been sent there after their failed escape. Half of these Jews were killed en route and the rest were pushed back by the German army. In mid-September the deportation of Jews to Mogilev-Podolski was resumed, and by November many columns of Jews from Bessarabia and Bukovina passed through the city (or stayed there). The last such column was made up of Jews from the KISHINEV ghetto and the DOROHOI district. A total of 55,913 expellees passed through Mogilev-Podolski in the period from September 15, 1941, to February 15, 1942.

The transit camp consisted of decrepit and filthy barracks in which thousands of people were packed. Conditions were so intolerable that every day many people committed suicide. The camp guards were Romanian gendarmes, and they maltreated the Jews mercilessly. Thousands of Jews who were not permitted to stay in Mogilev-Podolski were driven out and forced to walk to villages and towns in the district or to cross the Bug River, where they faced conditions even worse than in Mogilev-Podolski. Some fifteen thousand expellees stayed in Mogilev-Podolski, despite the ban imposed by the authorities, either by means of bribes or because the city's and the district's economy benefited from their presence. The Jews who managed to stay on organized themselves into groups, based on their community of origin. One of them, Shimon Jegendorf, from Rădăuţi, was an engineer by profession, and he was able to repair and reactivate the local electric power station, as well as a foundry and other factories. This led to many job openings, and two thousand to three thousand Jewish workers and their families were granted residence permits. The rest of the Jews in the city, numbering some ten thousand, had the constant threat of deportation into the interior of Transnistria hanging over their heads.

The Romanian officials in charge in the district manifested a hostile and cruel attitude to the Jews, which persisted even when Romanian official policy on the deportees took a turn for the better, after the Soviet victory at Stalingrad. There were also a German army unit and an ORGANISATION TODT detachment

stationed in Mogilev-Podolski, which supervised the Jews working on the construction of a bridge across the Dniester. These Germans mistreated the Jews and frequently executed them for minor offenses. About two thousand male Jews were sent to other parts of Transnistria on forced labor, escorted by gendarmes who also meted out harsh treatment to them. Of these Jewish men, some were transferred to areas under German control, and many perished or were shot to death.

In December 1943, 3,198 Jews who had been expelled from Dorohoi and its vicinity were returned to Romania, and the Mogilev-Podolski ghetto now held 12,836 deportees from Bukovina, 348 from Bessarabia, and 3,000 local Jewish inhabitants. In March 1944 the Jewish leadership in Bucharest obtained permission to bring 1,400 orphans back to Romania. Most of the rest of the deportees were unable to flee to Romania in time, and when the city was liberated by the Soviet army, on March 20, 1944, many of the male Jews were drafted on the spot, given several weeks of training, and sent to the front or to the coal mines in the Archangelsk basin. Of those who stayed in Mogilev-

Podolski, many lost their lives when the Germans shelled the city from across the Dniester. It was only in the spring of 1945 that most of the deportees were permitted to return to Romania; those who had survived the forced labor in the Soviet Union came back in 1947.

The number of survivors in Mogilev-Podolski was large, in relative terms, owing to the town's proximity to Romania, the Jews' own self-help organization, and the aid they received from the Jews in Romania.

BIBLIOGRAPHY

Ancel, J., and T. Lavi, eds. *Rumania,* vol. 2. In *Pinkas Hakehillot; Encyclopaedia of Jewish Communities.* Jerusalem, 1980. (In Hebrew.)

JEAN ANCEL

MOLOTOV, VIACHESLAV MIKHAILOVICH (1890–1987), Soviet leader. Molotov was born in northern Russia, in a tradesman's family. He studied at the Saint Petersburg Polytechnic Institute and joined the Bolsheviks in 1906. His wife, Polina Zhemchuzhina (Perele Karp), was Jewish. After the February revolution of 1917, Molotov was an active Bolshevik in Petrograd. From 1921 to 1930 he served as secretary of the Communist party's Central Committee and began to follow Joseph STALIN blindly, becoming his closest associate in the struggle against the opposition in the party. In 1921 he was made an alternate member of the Politburo, and in 1926 a full member.

Between 1930 and 1941, Molotov served as chairman of the Council of People's Commissars, that is, as nominal head of the Soviet government. From May 1939 he was also People's Commissar for Foreign Affairs. In August 1939 he signed in Moscow the pact with Nazi Germany (*see* NAZI-SOVIET PACT), subsequently visiting Berlin and meeting Adolf HITLER. After May 1941, when Stalin became the nominal head of government, Molotov re-

Viacheslav Molotov (left) meets Cordell Hull, United States secretary of state, as Hull arrives in Moscow in October 1943 to attend the Moscow Conference of Foreign Ministers.

mained first deputy chairman of the Council of People's Commissars, retaining the foreign affairs portfolio. For a short time his wife was a People's Commissar of Industry and a member of the central party committee, but she lost her positions in February 1941.

During World War II Molotov actively participated in negotiations with the Allies, while Stalin played a diplomatic game in which Molotov appeared as a hawk and Stalin an amiable dove. Western leaders took this pose seriously, and Stalin was regarded as a pawn of his hawkish Politburo. From 1945 to 1948 Molotov was behind the Soviet support of the Jewish state, and his wife warmly welcomed Israel's first representative in Moscow, Golda Meir.

However, in 1949 Molotov's position began to decline. When his wife was arrested, he did not protest. After Stalin's death, Molotov once again emerged as a Soviet leader, and was reinstated as People's Commissar for Foreign Affairs. His wife was immediately released.

In 1957, after participating in an abortive attempt to topple Nikita Khrushchev, Molotov was released from all his senior positions and publicly condemned as a leader of the so-called antiparty group. From 1957 to 1960 he served as ambassador to Mongolia, and from 1960 to 1962, as Soviet representative to the International Atomic Energy Agency. He retired in 1962, remaining an ardent Stalinist until his death.

BIBLIOGRAPHY

Bohlen, C. *Witness to History.* New York, 1973.

Conquest, R. *Power and Policy in the USSR.* New York, 1961.

Dallin, D. *Soviet Foreign Policy after Stalin.* Philadephia, 1961.

Khrushchev Remembers. Boston, 1970.

Medvedev, R. *All Stalin's Men.* New York, 1983.

Sontag, R. J., and J. Beddie, eds. *Nazi-Soviet Relations, 1939–1941: Documents from Archives of the German Foreign Office.* Westport, Conn., 1976.

Weinberg, G. L. *Germany and the Soviet Union, 1939–1941.* London, 1954.

MIKHAIL AGURSKY

MONOWITZ. *See* Auschwitz.

MONTELUPICH PRISON, prison in Kraków used by the Gestapo from the end of September 1939 to January 16, 1945, two days before the city was liberated. Montelupich had been a military prison under the Austrians and was retained as such by the Poles in the interwar period. It is located at No. 7 Montelupich Street, hence its name. The prison housed only male prisoners, females being detained in a former convent, on nearby Helzlow Street. The maximum number of inmates held in the prisons was one thousand males and three hundred females; a total of twenty thousand prisoners, male and female, passed through their doors. They were political prisoners, convicted SD (Sicherheitsdienst; Security Service) and SS men, Soviet and British parachutists and spies, victims seized on the streets in periodic raids, "economic offenders," Waffen-SS deserters, and ordinary criminals.

The Jewish political prisoners, both men and women, suffered more than any of the other categories; they were incarcerated under the most difficult conditions, in the cellar, and their food rations were smaller, but worst of all was the torture they had to undergo. Their stay in the prison lasted several weeks, sometimes months. From there some were taken to be killed in PŁASZÓW or were sent to AUSCHWITZ or GROSS-ROSEN.

It was within the walls of the Montelupich prison that Gusta (Dawidson) DRAENGER wrote her diary. On April 29, 1943, a group of prisoners, members of the ŻYDOWSKA ORGANIZACJA BOJOWA (Jewish Fighting Organization; ŻOB) in Kraków, who were being taken to Płaszów for execution, attacked their German guard in an attempt to escape. Most fell in the fight, but a few did get away and took part in underground operations. Only Shimshon Draenger and Gusta Draenger managed to reach the Wiśnicz forests. Montelupich is still used as a prison, but the women's wing has been turned into a home for the aged.

BIBLIOGRAPHY

Hechalutz Halochem: Journal of the Chalutz Underground Movement in Occupied Kraków, August–October, 1943. Tel Aviv, 1984. (In Hebrew.)

YAEL PELED (MARGOLIN)

MORAVIA. *See* Bohemia and Moravia, Protectorate of.

MOREALI, GIUSEPPE. *See* Beccari, Arrigo.

MORESHET. *See* Museums and Memorial Institutes: Moreshet.

MORGENTHAU, HENRY, JR. (1891–1967), American statesman. As secretary of the treasury, Morgenthau was the highest-ranking Jew in the Roosevelt administration. His importance during the period of the Holocaust stems from his eventual willingness to use his considerable influence with President Franklin D. ROOSEVELT to vitalize the American rescue effort. The creation of the WAR REFUGEE BOARD in January 1944, the zenith of the American effort to rescue the remaining Jews of Europe, is in some measure attributable to Morgenthau.

Morgenthau was born in New York City into a prominent German Jewish family. His father, Henry Morgenthau, after earning a fortune as a banker and real-estate developer, entered politics and was active in the Democratic party. He served as American ambassador to Turkey from 1913 to 1916.

Henry Morgenthau, Jr., studied agronomy at Cornell University. His family bought a large working farm in the lower Hudson valley of New York State, not far from the home of Roosevelt; a link had already been established through their common interest in the Democratic party. Later Morgenthau moved to the top of American politics as an integral

Henry Morgenthau, Jr., with President Franklin D. Roosevelt in Washington, D.C. (April 30, 1941). [Franklin D. Roosevelt Library]

part of the Roosevelt entourage, and a firm bond of friendship developed between the two men.

In 1928, after Roosevelt was elected governor of New York State, he appointed Morgenthau chairman of the agricultural advisory commission. Two years later he became conservation commissioner. Some of the innovative policies of the New Deal's agricultural program were incubated during this period. In 1933 Morgenthau was named to the Federal Farm Board and the Farm Credit Administration, and in 1934 he was appointed to the Cabinet as secretary of the treasury. It was his subordinates in the Treasury Department, John W. Pehle, Josiah E. DuBois, Jr., and Randolph Paul, who alerted him to the State Department's blocking of refugee immigration (*see* UNITED STATES DEPARTMENT OF STATE). Through the Treasury's control of export licenses, Morgenthau maintained a far-reaching influence in the foreign relations area, especially American policy toward the "New Order" in Germany. He sensed relatively early the dangers the National Socialists posed for world peace, and he advocated military preparedness. During the ambassadorship of Willian E. Dodd in Berlin, Morgenthau refused to issue a license for the sale of helium to Germany. The later conflict between the State Department and the Department of the Treasury over rescue policy is best understood in the context of Morgenthau's intrusions into the foreign-policy area, resulting in a rivalry between him and Cordell HULL, the secretary of state. Although Roosevelt shared the view on the general ineffectiveness of the State Department, he essentially agreed with the department on the low priority that should be given to the "Jewish question" during the war. In 1938, when Roosevelt requested, after the EVIAN CONFERENCE, that Morgenthau chair the PRESIDENT'S ADVISORY COMMITTEE ON POLITICAL REFUGEES, Morgenthau refused. At that time, Morgenthau still had little inkling of what Berlin had in store for European Jewry.

In the fall of 1942, as bits of news about the Nazi anti-Jewish depredations began to filter back to Washington, Morgenthau's uneasi-

Lt. Gen. Mark W. Clark, commander of the Allied Fifth Army, shows Henry Morgenthau, Jr., some of the destruction caused by Allied bombers in Caserta, Italy. [National Archives]

ness grew. His diaries show that he blamed the State Department for thwarting efforts to admit even those few who were legally entitled to enter under the immigration law. His subordinates informed him of a deliberate effort to turn off the flow of information detailing the implementation of the "Final Solution." He complained to Hull, but realized that the secretary of state was uninformed and uninterested in the issue. By mid-1943, Morgenthau, more than any other prominent Jew near Roosevelt, was showing signs that the destruction of European Jewry was having a considerable impact on him.

Morgenthau supported Roosevelt's schemes for the resettlement of Jews in "empty" territories. Unwilling to intrude on British dominance in the Middle East, and unable to bring refugees to the United States, Roosevelt and Morgenthau toyed with the idea of resettlement in Latin America and elsewhere. However, in 1943 Morgenthau overcame the State Department's foot-dragging on a purported Romanian offer to release 70,000 Jews by issuing a license to the JOINT DISTRIBUTION COMMITTEE to transfer $170,000 for that purpose. Another license to transfer $25,000 was granted to support Jewish children living in concealment in Italian-occupied France.

In January 1944, Morgenthau's assistant, Josiah Du Bois, Jr., handed him his "Report to the Secretary on the Acquiescence of This Government in the Murder of the Jews," which documented the State Department's "willful failure to act." After toning down the more dramatic phrasing of the brief, and changing its title to "A Personal Report to the President," Morgenthau convened Benjamin V. Cohen and Samuel Rosenman, two presidential advisers who were Jewish, to deliver the report together with him to the president on January 16, 1944. Following that visit Roosevelt established the War Refugee Board. Several Jewish organizations have claimed credit for mobilizing Morgenthau in the rescue cause. Whatever the case, it came too late to help the millions of Jewish victims of the Nazi death machine.

How much the revelations of the full extent of the German atrocities in 1944 and early 1945 contributed to Morgenthau's "plan" for the treatment of postwar Germany cannot be determined. He maintained that his "hard" plan for the "pastoralization" of the former Reich had no connection with the Holocaust. Morgenthau feared that a renascent Germany could bring on World War III. The policy was explained in his book *Germany Is Our Problem* (1945), published shortly before Germany's surrender. Roosevelt's successor, Harry S. Truman, soon abandoned the Morgenthau plan as impractical. The recovery of Europe could not be managed without Germany playing its customary role.

Morgenthau soon resigned his post and involved himself deeply in Jewish causes. He was recruited by Henry Montor to become general chairman of the United Jewish Appeal, in which position he served between 1946 and 1950. Morgenthau is credited with being instrumental in organizing its first $100,000,000 fund-raising campaign, a sum many were convinced could not be attained. He also drew much closer to the Zionist consensus that now held sway in the American Jewish community. In 1950 he accepted the chairmanship of the board of governors of the Hebrew University, and a year later he followed Montor to the Israel Bond Organization and the American Financial and Development Corporation for Israel. At the time of Morgenthau's death in 1967, he was fully immersed in Jewish causes.

BIBLIOGRAPHY

Blum, J. M. *Roosevelt and Morgenthau: A Revision and Condensation of "From the Morgenthau Diaries."* Boston, 1970.

Feingold, H. L. *The Politics of Rescue.* New Brunswick, N.J., 1970.

Wyman, D. S. *The Abandonment of the Jews: America and the Holocaust, 1941–1945.* New York, 1984.

Wyman, D. S. *Paper Walls; America and the Refugee Crisis, 1938–1941.* Amherst, Mass., 1968.

HENRY L. FEINGOLD

MOROCCO, Muslim kingdom in North Africa, along the Mediterranean and Atlantic coasts. From 1912 to 1956 the greater part of Morocco was a French protectorate; the rest, in the north, was a Spanish protectorate until 1958, although nominally Morocco was considered one country. Some small areas, including the towns of Ceuta and Melilla, were

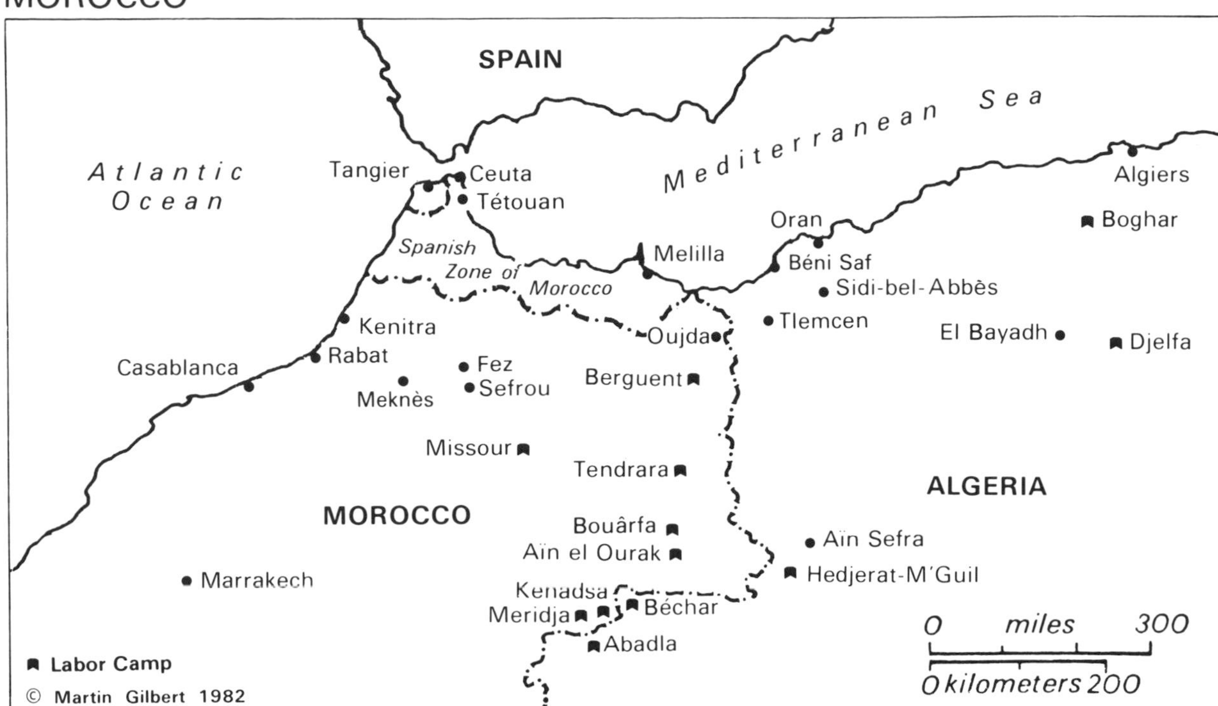

deemed to be part of Spain. Tangier was under international control from 1923; following the defeat of FRANCE in 1940, Spain annexed the city to the area under its protection, and only after the war did the city regain its previous status, retaining it until 1956.

Jews have lived in Morocco since Roman times. The Jewish community there was the largest and most important in the Atlas Mountains region. The Jews of Morocco resided in numerous cities and villages all over the country, many living in city *mellah*s (ghettos), which were often slum quarters. Their status was that of *dhimmi* (protected persons), as was the rule in Muslim countries.

On the eve of World War II Morocco's Jewish population numbered a little more than 200,000, with most of the Jews living in the French-controlled part of the country, and the smaller portion in the Spanish-controlled zone. Although the French did not change the Moroccan Jews' political status, their very presence in the country improved the situation of the Jews and provided them with greater security. As in the other North African countries, they were no longer subject to the legal inferiority suffered by Jews in other Muslim lands, and, except for a few instances of harassment, anti-Jewish riots came to an end.

On the other hand, the colonial regime dealt a heavy blow to the traditional bases of economic life in the country. For example, Jewish occupations such as moneylending, peddling, and craftsmanship suffered under the new regime. The communal organization of the Jews also underwent drastic changes under French pressure, mostly through the restrictions imposed on the internal autonomy of the Jewish communities, and the stricter supervision of the community institutions by the central authorities. The latter also affected the rabbinical courts, whose jurisdiction was now confined to matters of ritual and of the personal status of Jews.

In general, unlike the Muslim society in which they lived, the Jews were inclined to welcome the French regime, as well as the modernization process that it brought to the country. This attitude was one of the reasons for the deterioration of relations between the Jews and the Muslim majority. In the 1930s these relations took a sharp turn for the worse when—as in ALGERIA—various anti-

Jewish organizations sprang up among the European inhabitants. In Morocco, however, this phenomenon did not have the same impact as in neighboring Algeria, since Morocco was a protectorate rather than a colony, and the Jews were indigenous subjects, and not citizens of France.

Of far greater significance was the ferment among the Muslim population in the 1930s, brought on by the growing strength of Pan-Arab propaganda and the rise of nationalism in both Morocco and TUNISIA. It was the Druze leader, Emir Shekib Arslan, founder of the Syria-Palestine Committee in Geneva, who was responsible for the antisemitic propaganda being spread in Morocco. He was joined in this effort by many leaders of the Moroccan national movement, such as Abd al-Khaliq Torrés, al-Hajj Abd al-Salam Bannuna, and al-Makki al-Nasiri, who charged France with favoring the Jews over the Muslim majority and enabling the Zionist movement to operate freely in Morocco and Tunisia. This propaganda campaign had its effect on the masses of the population and even on senior officials. In October 1934, for example, the grand vizier of Morocco asked the French authorities to prohibit Jews from residing in Muslim city quarters, and in 1937 the pasha of Marrakech tried to have a regulation introduced that would outlaw the employment of Muslim house servants by Jews. The local Arabic press accused the Jews of using the money they were making in their trade with Muslims to support the Jewish struggle with Islam in Palestine; as a result of this propaganda, many Muslims in the large cities reduced their ties with the Jews.

The anti-Jewish stirrings among the Muslims were also caused, to some extent, by German propaganda. While the Third Reich did not pay too much attention to the Mediterranean basin, it did have an interest in enlisting North African nationalism against France, so that when the time was ripe, riots and other anticolonial actions would put the French colonies out of action. North African nationalists, both by direct contact and with the mufti of Jerusalem, Hajj Amin al-HUSSEINI, acting as go-between, played a significant role in German attempts at subversion in North Africa, attempts that focused on anti-Jewish and anticolonial issues. The leader of the Muslim community in Berlin was a Moroccan, and it was he who promoted ties between the Islamischer Kulturverband (Islamic Cultural Society) in Vienna and the Moroccan national movement. Following Gen. Francisco Franco's victory in the Spanish Civil War in March 1939, the Germans used Spanish Morocco as the base of their campaigns directed at Morocco, operating in Ceuta, Tétouan, and the international city of Tangier, where anti-Jewish and anti-French propaganda material was produced. Among other charges against France, German propaganda spread the rumor that France had given refuge in North Africa to hundreds of Jews from Germany.

In 1937 Italy also joined in the Germans' anti-Jewish campaign in North Africa. Radio Bari broadcasts, widely quoted in the Italian press in Tunisia (*Unione*) and in Tangier (*Vedetta* [The Sentry]), charged the Jews with being the agents of French colonialism in North Africa and the principal supporters of British imperialism in Palestine and the Middle East. Italian trading houses in Morocco were ordered to reduce their ties with Jews, and from 1938 Italian cultural centers in Tangier and Rabat no longer admitted Jews.

The Jewish community did not remain indifferent to German and Fascist propaganda. In Morocco the Jews boycotted all German products, much to the dismay of their Arab neighbors; this was also the background to the bloody clashes between Jews and Muslims that broke out in 1933, in cities such as Tétouan, Rabat, and Casablanca.

When war approached, hundreds of Moroccan Jews from all sectors of Jewish society sought to volunteer for service in the French army, but only a few were admitted, since the French authorities were apprehensive about both Muslim dissatisfaction with Jewish enlistment and the antisemitic feelings rife among the Europeans in Morocco. The Jews soon realized that their display of patriotism would not put an end to antisemitic incitement. In fact, hatred of Jews increased in 1940 as the defeat of France became certain.

Beginning in May 1940, anti-Jewish incitement intensified in all the cities of Morocco, the Jews being accused of, among other things, profiteering from a war "that had been caused by their brethren in Europe." A central role in the campaign against the Jews was played by French right-wing groups, such as the Parti Populaire Français, operating in Casablanca, Port Lyautey (present-day Kenitra), and Rabat. In several instances Muslims joined in attacks on Jews organized by the French. In September 1940, one Jew was murdered and six were injured in the *mellah* of Fez (Fès), in an attack by French and Muslim soldiers.

Quiet was restored only when the Vichy regime was constituted and the first anti-Jewish decrees were issued, among them the STATUT DES JUIFS (Jewish Law), enacted in France in October 1940. Unlike in Algeria, where the anti-Jewish laws were applied in full in their original wording, the French authorities in Morocco and Tunisia adapted the laws to the special conditions prevailing there. Thus, in these two countries, only Jews by religion were defined as Jews, in order to avoid offending the local Muslim rulers by including Jews who had converted to Islam. The restrictions barring Jews from posts in the administration, the teaching profession, the local councils, the media, and so on were fully applied.

Despite their universal application, however, the French racist laws did not have the same impact in Morocco as in Algeria. In Morocco, for example, very few Jews were affected by the *numerus clausus* (the quota of Jews allowed) in the liberal professions, simply because there were relatively few Jews in them, compared to Algeria. Most of the Jewish students in Morocco attended schools run by the French Jewish organization Alliance Israélite Universelle or other Jewish-run institutions, so that the restrictions in French educational institutions were hardly felt. Generally speaking, in contrast to Algeria, where most sectors of the Jewish population suffered from the racist laws, in Morocco (and, to a lesser degree, also in Tunisia) the Vichy period affected only the urban areas. Even there, the impact was felt only by Jews whose occupation brought them into contact with the French, and by those who wanted to be part of the French milieu. This produced one of the paradoxes of the Vichy brand of antisemitism: in complete contrast to what took place in France, in North Africa the Jews who adhered to their traditional way of life were hardly touched by antisemitism, while those who had struck roots in French culture and had become well integrated within it suffered the most.

In the months preceding the outbreak of war, as well as immediately after the fall of France, hundreds of foreign Jews arrived in Morocco—refugees from central and eastern Europe who were stranded in North Africa on their way to the United States, and foreign volunteers in the French army (including the Foreign Legion, which at the time of the French-German armistice was stationed in North Africa). In 1941 and 1942 these two groups were joined by thousands of Jewish refugees fleeing from occupied France. They soon found out that the fate in store for them in North Africa was no different from what they could have expected from the German occupation regime. Some of these Jews were given refuge by the local Jewish communities, while the others, on arrival, were put into detention camps, in which hundreds of Jewish foreign nationals had already been held since the beginning of the war (and to which British Jews were also added, after the French surrender). Dozens of local Jews, arrested on charges of subversive activities or black marketeering, were also put into these camps. Those Jews who had volunteered to serve in the French army were put on hard labor in camps on Morocco's southern border with Algeria, along the route planned for the Trans-Saharan railway that the Vichy regime had decided to construct in the desert.

The Jewish prisoners were dispersed over thirty camps, which for all practical purposes were no different from concentration camps; they had to work over ten hours a day, under unbearable climatic conditions, and were severely punished for even the slightest infringement of the rules. The camps were administered by former officers of the Foreign Legion, who went out of their way to show their disdain for the Jews and made no effort to hide their sympathy for Nazi Germany. The largest of these camps was that of Djelfa, where seven hundred to one thousand prisoners were held. It is estimated that on the eve of the American invasion of North Africa, on November 8, 1942, some four thousand Jewish prisoners were being held in camps in the south of Morocco and in Algeria. On the other hand, ten thousand refugees managed to pass through North Africa and make their way to their destinations during the course of 1941, without having to go through the experience of imprisonment in a Vichy camp. These were Jews who had *laissez-passers* in their possession when they arrived in Morocco, issued by HICEM or the JOINT DISTRIBUTION COMMITTEE in Marseilles or Lisbon. They were under the care of local committees that had been formed in Oran, Casablanca, and Tangier, who looked after them until their departure, by boat, for North or South America.

The American invasion of North Africa did not have any immediate effect on the position of Jews in Morocco and Algeria. Their situation even took a turn for the worse; behaving as though the Americans were a thousand miles away, the French right-wingers vented their spite on the Jews in various places in Morocco. In Casablanca they attacked the Jews only seconds after American troops had held their first march past in the city; the attackers invaded the Jewish quarter, desecrated the synagogue, and robbed passersby of all their belongings. The following days saw similar scenes in other cities, in which Muslim elements and the local police also took a hand. In Rabat the police surrounded the Jewish quarter on November 12 and did not move from there for several weeks; dozens of Jews were arrested in the streets for no reason and sentenced to heavy punishments on the spot. The same happened in Meknès and Fez. These events continued for a long time, even after Gen. Henri Giraud, commander in chief of the French forces, had abolished the racist laws in March 1943. In July 1944 Moroccan soldiers serving in the French army who were stationed in Sefrou launched a large-scale action against the Jewish quarter of that city, which ended in the arrest of two hundred Jews. Such violence—permitted by the French administration—was not the Jews' only problem; they were also discriminated against in the allocation of food rations, which until 1945 was based on the racist criteria laid down by the Vichy regime.

A long time elapsed before the prisoners in the labor camps were set free. This was not only because the French authorities were in no hurry to open the camps; it was also because foreign bodies, such as the Polish government-in-exile, were not willing to accept the prisoners. The situation of the prisoners from the Axis countries was even more complicated, the French being prepared to release them only on condition that they volunteer for service in a commando unit or in the Foreign Legion. The only solution for these prisoners was to work in the American and British army bases in Morocco. Officially the camps were closed down in April 1943, but until the summer of that year, seven hundred Jewish prisoners were still being held there.

BIBLIOGRAPHY

Abitbol, M. *North African Jewry during World War II*. Detroit, 1989.

Ageron, C. R. "Les populations du Maghreb face à la propagande allemande." *Revue d'Histoire de la deuxième Guerre Mondiale* 29/14 (1979): 1–39.

Hirszowicz, L. *The Third Reich and the Arab East*. London, 1966.

Judenverfolgung in Italien, den italienisch besetzen Gebiete und in Nordafrika. Frankfurt, 1962.

Szajkowski, Z. *Jews and the French Foreign Legion*. New York, 1975.

MICHEL ABITBOL

MOSLEY, SIR OSWALD (1896–1980), British fascist leader. Born into an aristocratic family (from which he inherited his title), Mosley was educated at Winchester and at the Royal Military Academy, Sandhurst, proceeding along a path well worn for his social class. When he was eighteen World War I broke out, and Mosley served in the Sixteenth Lancers in France and then in the Royal Flying Corps. His war experiences exercised a profound impact on him and his career in politics.

Between 1918 and 1931 Mosley was a Tory, then an Independent Tory, and then a member of the Labor party. In 1931 he helped to form the New party, after the cabinet of the second Labor government refused to endorse his plans for national reconstruction, a task that had been allotted to him as chancellor of the Duchy of Lancaster. With the crushing defeat of the New party in the 1931 general election, Mosley began to move toward the most decisive phase of his career. In October

Oswald Mosley, British fascist leader. [National Archives]

1932, after a visit to Benito MUSSOLINI's Italy, he formed the British Union of Fascists (BUF).

The BUF quickly developed the appearance of a major political party, but by 1934 its progress was hindered by the withdrawal of respectable support (from the Rothermere press in 1934, for example), apparently a reaction to the violence and antisemitism that had started to penetrate it. By 1936, after Mosley had failed to make further political headway, considerable energy was pumped into the local politics of the East End of London, an activity that involved Mosley and the BUF in the exploitation of antisemitism as a political weapon. That year the state, anxious about the threat to public order, passed the Public Order Act. Through its ban on political uniforms, the act placed a further brake on the activity of the BUF, whose distinguishing sign had been its black shirt. Even so, the BUF continued to function; indeed, it continued even after the outbreak of World War II. In the spring of 1940, when invasion seemed imminent, Mosley and leading members of the BUF were interned. With these detentions (Mosley was released from internment in November 1943), the BUF collapsed.

After the war Mosley reconstructed his political organization as the Union Movement, but once again the political current worked against his ambitions. Following his ignominious rejection in the 1959 general election in North Kensington, Mosley set about reconstructing the past on his own terms. For example, in his autobiography, *My Life,* which appeared in 1968, he denied that he had ever been an antisemite. Since then, sources sympathetic to Mosley have also made a systematic attempt to whitewash his reputation, as in the newsletter *Comrade,* published by "the Friends of O.M."

Mosley was a product of his times. After the trauma of World War I his aim was "to blow gusts of clean air down the corridors of power." He had the necessary degrees of arrogance and ambition to pursue his task, but he failed in his self-appointed mission.

[*See also* Great Britain: Fascism in Great Britain.]

BIBLIOGRAPHY

Holmes, C. *Anti-Semitism in British Society, 1876–1939.* London, 1979.

Lewis, D. S. *Illusions of Grandeur: Mosley, Fascism, and British Society, 1931–1981.* Manchester, England, 1987.

Lunn, K., and R. C. Thurlow, eds. *British Fascism.* London, 1980.

Mosley, N. *Beyond the Pale.* London, 1983.

Skidelsky, R. *Oswald Mosley.* London, 1975.

Thurlow, R. *Fascism in Britain: A History, 1918–1985.* Oxford, 1987.

COLIN HOLMES

MUFTI OF JERUSALEM. *See* Husseini, Hajj Amin al-.

MUKACHEVO. *See* Munkács.

MÜLLER, HEINRICH (1900–?), chief of the GESTAPO. After attending elementary school,

Müller was apprenticed to the Bavarian Aircraft Works in Munich. In 1917 he volunteered for the air force, became a fighter pilot on the western front in April 1918, and was awarded several distinguished-service medals. In June 1919 he was discharged as a noncommissioned officer. He began working at the Munich police headquarters in December 1919. In the spring of 1929 he passed with distinction the examination for the intermediate level of the police force, and became the Munich police headquarters expert in the fight against "leftist movements," especially communism. Müller was a hard and ambitious worker who on occasion disregarded the law, according to evidence given by the Nazi party district administration in 1936. Under the Weimar Republic, his political affiliation fluctuated between the German National Popular Party and the Bavarian People's Party; rumor had it that in 1933 he and some of his colleagues opposed handing over the Munich police administration to the SA (Sturmabteilung; Storm Troopers) and the SS.

Before long, however, Müller became one of the most important aides to Reinhard HEYDRICH, the new Bavarian police chief. This was a result of his intimate knowledge of the Communist party and of the German section of the Comintern (the Third Communist International), and his familiarity with Soviet police methods. Müller's reports also gained Heinrich HIMMLER's attention; this won him promotion to the rank of senior police secretary, on May 1, 1933, and, on November 16, 1933, to senior secretary of the criminal police. In 1935, he was appointed controller of the criminal police. To ensure that no problems arose in the relations between the Bavarian political police and the Gestapo and SS, Müller, who was not a party member, was in 1936 appointed a member of the SD (Sicherheitsdienst; Security Service), with the rank of *Untersturmführer*.

Soon afterward, Heydrich was appointed Gestapo chief, and he took Müller along with him, together with his former superior, Gerhard Flesch, appointing them joint directors of subsection II 1 (suppression of hostile elements). Flesch and Müller were in charge of the following subdivisions: II 1 A (communism and Marxism, including all organizations fully or partially associated with these ideologies, as well as the trade unions); II 1 B (religious organizations, Jews, Freemasons, emigrants); II 1 C (reactionaries, supporters of the opposition, Austrian affairs); II 1 D (protective-custody and concentration camps); II 1 E (economic, agricultural, and social policy; nonpolitical organizations); II 1 F (card index, good-conduct certificates, file registry); II 1 G (identification service); II 1 H (Nazi party and its affiliated organizations); II 1 W (security of weapons and explosives); and II 1 Special (special duties—surveillance and assassinations). Flesch and Müller, for their part, brought along experienced associates from Munich, such as Josef Meisinger, Franz Josef Huber, and, at a later date, Friedrich Panzinger.

Müller's phenomenal rise, however, began after the suppression of the so-called Röhm putsch on June 30, 1934, the "Night of the Long Knives" (*see* RÖHM, ERNST). Four days later Müller was promoted to SS-*Obersturmführer* and put in charge of senior officials. On January 30, 1935, Müller rose to the rank

Gestapo chief Heinrich Müller. [YIVO Institute for Jewish Research]

of SS-*Hauptsturmführer;* on April 20, 1936, to SS-*Sturmbannführer;* and on January 30, 1937, to SS-*Standartenführer.* It was only in June of that year, however, that he was given the rank of senior administrative councillor and criminal police councillor, against the recommendation of the Munich–Upper Bavaria Police District Administration, although by then he had been in charge of the Gestapo office for a year. From September 1939 to the end of the war, Müller was head of Section IV (Gestapo) of the REICHSSICHERHEITSHAUPTAMT (Reich Main Security Office; RSHA) and deputy commander of the Security Police and the SD. He was responsible to Heydrich and, after Heydrich's assassination, to his successor, Ernst KALTENBRUNNER.

Müller was one of the most powerful men in the Nazi state terror system, but he stayed out of the limelight. On April 20, 1939, he became an SS-*Oberführer;* and on December 14, 1940, an SS-*Brigadeführer;* two days later he was also promoted to *Generalmajor* of the police. On November 9, Müller, together with Arthur NEBE, was appointed an SS-*Gruppenführer* and to the equivalent rank in the police.

Müller remained loyal to Adolf HITLER to the end in the bunker where Hitler spent his last weeks. On October 15, 1944, Müller, the ex-pilot, was awarded the Knight's Cross with crossed swords (the highest German award in World War II) for excellence, in recognition of his services in the merciless pursuit of the participants in the July 20, 1944, plot against Hitler. These included some of Müller's friends, such as Count Wolf Heinrich von Helldorf, Arthur Nebe, Hans Gisevius, and Friedrich Werner von der Schulenburg.

All trace of Müller was lost on April 29, 1945. There exists no confirmation of the rumors that he defected to the Soviet secret service, or that he escaped to the Middle East or Latin America, or that he remained alive.

BIBLIOGRAPHY

Aronson, S. *Reinhard Heydrich und die Frühgeschichte der Gestapo und SD.* Stuttgart, 1971.

Delarue, J. *The Gestapo: A History of Horror.* New York, 1964.

Höhne, H. *The Order of the Death's Head: The Story of Hitler's SS.* New York, 1970.

HANS-HEINRICH WILHELM

MUNICH, capital of the German state of Bavaria. Jews were living in Munich at the beginning of the thirteenth century, but they were expelled in 1442. In 1815 a new Jewish community was formally established, and in 1910, when it was at its maximum size, it numbered 11,083, 1.9 percent of the total population. In 1933, 9,005 Jews were living in Munich (1.2 percent). The city's Jews played a prominent role in its economic, social, and cultural life, and took part in multifaceted Jewish religious and communal activities. The central offices of many Jewish national organizations were located there, and a Zionist weekly and the official organ of the Union of Jewish Communities of Bavaria were published in the city.

As World War I drew to an end, antisemitic incidents became increasingly frequent. From November 1918 to February 1919 a "Soviet"-style revolutionary government held power in Bavaria, headed by Kurt Eisner and including several other prominent Jews. As a result, an antisemitic wave set in and attacks were launched on Jews, especially those of eastern European origin. On April 23, 1920, Bavarian prime minister Gustav Ritter von Kahr issued an order for the expulsion of the Jews, and it took much effort to prevent this order from being carried out.

The Nazi party was established in Munich in 1922. In January 1923, von Kahr ordered the expulsion of 180 Jewish families of east European origin. Julius STREICHER conducted an antisemitic propaganda campaign in the Munich streets, and, at the time of the Nazi *Putsch,* in November 1923, SA (Sturmabteilung; Storm Troopers) men seized a large number of Jews and held them hostage in the cellar of their headquarters. It was in Munich, "the Nazi movement's capital," that the *Völkischer Beobachter,* the Nazi party newspaper, was published, and from 1930 on Munich was also the Nazi party's headquarters (the "Brown House") and the national head-

Reichsparteitag (Reich party day), a rally held in Munich on November 9, 1935, to commemorate Adolf Hitler's attempted Beer-Hall Putsch in 1923. [Bildarchiv Preussischer Kulturbesitz]

quarters of the SA and the SS. Jewish life in Munich, a Catholic city with a strong conservative-monarchist tradition, continued, however, and suffered no serious dislocation until the Nazi takeover of power in Bavaria, in March 1933.

On May 12, 1933, the police conducted a search for "subversive material" in the offices of all the city's Jewish organizations, fifty of which had all their property confiscated. As a result of sharp protests in Berlin, some of the confiscated property was returned to its owners. SA and SS men; members of the HITLERJUGEND, the Nazi youth movement; and employees of Streicher's newspaper, *Der Stürmer,* attacked Jewish-owned businesses and beat up Jews. Growing pressure was brought on Jews to liquidate their businesses; *Der Stürmer* published photographs and names of the customers of Jew-

Adolf Hitler at the *Reichsparteitag* in Munich, November 9, 1935.

The Ohel Yaakov synagogue of Munich in flames on November 10, 1938 (*Kristallnacht*).

ish stores. The city government too joined in the campaign against the Jews, and in 1937 ordered all non-Jewish stores to display an "Aryan Store" sign, thereby circumventing the existing legal situation, which at the time did not permit Jewish stores to be identified as such. In reaction to the growing pressure and persecution, the Jewish Community Organization intensified its activities in order to help the Jews survive. It established hospitals and social services; elementary, secondary, and vocational schools; an orchestra and a theater; clubs; an adult education institute, and so on.

In the period from March 1, 1933, to May 16, 1938, the deaths of 803 Jews were recorded in Munich, as against only 118 births; 3,574 Jews left the city, 3,130 emigrating abroad (of whom 701 went to Palestine). In the course of the official ARISIERUNG drive, from February to October 1938, the number of Jewish shopkeepers and tradesmen were reduced from 1,690 to 660. In early June of 1938 Hitler found that it was unacceptable for the Great Synagogue to be situated next door to the German Art House and ordered the synagogue to be torn down by July 8, "German Art Day." Jewish community lead-

Jewish couple in Munich wearing the Star of David badge (1941). [Bildarchiv Preussischer Kulturbesitz]

ers were informed of this order on June 8, and the work of destruction was begun the following day. During the intervening night, many members of the community joined in saving the Torah scrolls and other religious objects, by removing them from the building. The municipality paid the Jewish community 100,000 reichsmarks for the synagogue and the adjoining community building, about one-seventh of their real value.

On KRISTALLNACHT, the Orthodox Ohel Yaakov synagogue was burned down, and all its contents, including the Torah scrolls, were consumed in the flames; the Bet ha-Midrash chapel and the Jewish library suffered the same fate. About one thousand Jewish males were rounded up and taken to the DACHAU camp, among them Dr. Leo Baerwald, the community rabbi, who was subjected to physical maltreatment. A very large number of Jewish institutions, businesses, and private residences were damaged. The next day the city government accelerated the pace of the "Aryanization" of Jewish-owned property, business enterprises, houses, and apartments.

By the fall of 1941, some fifteen hundred Jewish apartments had been confiscated. The Jews who had been driven out of their homes were put on forced labor, assigned to construct a camp at Milbertshausen, a Munich suburb, for accommodating the dispossessed Munich Jews. The maximum number of prisoners in the camp was 1,376; it served as an assembly and transit camp for the Jews, prior to their deportation to extermination camps. On November 20, 1941, 980 Munich Jews were deported to RIGA, and on April 3, 1942, 343 were sent to the Piaski ghetto, near LUBLIN. Prior to its liquidation that summer, the remaining Jews, some 300 in all, were moved to the Berg-am-Leim ghetto. Of these, 113 were deported to AUSCHWITZ in March 1943, and the remaining 40 Jews were moved to the Jewish community building in Munich (which in October 1944 was destroyed in an air attack). Between May and August 1942, 1,200 Jews from Munich were sent to THERESIENSTADT in twenty-four transports, 50 persons per transport; another 135 followed in September. At this time there was an upsurge in the number of suicides. Another 105 Jews were taken to Theresienstadt between June 1943 and December 1944, and yet another 97, mostly persons of mixed blood or partners in mixed marriages, were sent there in February 1945. A total of 2,991 Jews were deported from Munich, 436 going directly to extermination camps and 1,555 to Theresienstadt. Of those who went to Theresienstadt, 297 returned after the war, most of the others having perished.

When the war was over, Munich became the center for the Jewish Agency's welfare activities in the DISPLACED PERSONS' camps and for the operations of the BERIḤA and the "illegal" immigration (*see* ALIYA BET) to Palestine. These activities were curtailed after the establishment of the state of Israel in 1948. Since then, Munich has had one of the largest Jewish communities in the Federal Republic of Germany, but it includes only a sprinkling of the Jews who had lived there before the war.

BIBLIOGRAPHY

Ophir, B. Z., et al., eds. *Germany-Bavaria.* In *Pinkas Hakehillot; Encyclopaedia of Jewish Communities.* Jerusalem, 1972. See pages 105–133. (In Hebrew.)

HENRY WASSERMAN

MUNICH CONFERENCE, conference held on September 28 and 29, 1938, in a hotel in Munich, by the government leaders of Great Britain, France, Germany, and Italy, in which agreement was reached on the transfer to Germany of certain regions of Czechoslovakia.

The Munich conference was convened following a prolonged crisis involving the political status of the German minority in Czechoslovakia and was preceded by intense negotiations, primarily between British prime minister Neville Chamberlain and German chancellor Adolf HITLER. The two other participants were French premier Edouard Daladier and Italian premier Benito MUSSOLINI, who played only minor roles. Czechoslovakia itself was not invited to the

Participants in the Munich conference. Front row, left to right: British prime minister Neville Chamberlain, French premier Edouard Daladier, Adolf Hitler, Benito Mussolini, Count Galeazzo Ciano, Italian foreign minister and Mussolini's son-in-law. [Imperial War Museum, London]

conference and did not take part in its decisions, which were presented to it as final and against which there was no appeal.

Five months later, as a direct consequence of the Munich conference, the Czechoslovak state was liquidated, when Germany seized control of it with all its economic resources and armed forces. Consequently, the balance of power in Europe shifted in favor of Germany, and Europe's rush into war gathered momentum. In economic and military terms Czechoslovakia was the strongest of the countries separating Germany from the Soviet Union. From 1925 it had had a mutual defense pact with France, and from 1935, a defense treaty with the Soviet Union; its fall signified the collapse of the international system set up in 1918.

"Munich" became a concept, a political term denoting an immoral policy: the surrender of a friendly nation to its enemies, a shameful betrayal of an ally at a decisive moment, a cowardly capitulation to an aggressive tyrant, and, above all, a short-range policy that was supposed to buy peace but in fact hastened the outbreak of war. The term "Munich" is frequently used in oratory and polemic writings, as an admonitory lesson taught by history.

Three processes were brought into focus in the Munich agreement:

1. Developments in Nazi foreign policy, which aimed, in the first instance, at seizing control of two neighboring states, Austria and Czechoslovakia, as a basis for further conquests and the expansion of the German people's LEBENSRAUM ("living space").

2. A development in British foreign policy aimed at the APPEASEMENT of Germany, on political, economic, and moral grounds, by revising the Versailles Treaty to correct the injustice that, in the eyes of many British statesmen, had been done to Germany. One instance of this injustice had been the inclusion of 3.5 million Germans, against their will, in the new Czechoslovak state, thereby violating their right of self-determination, the very principle upon which Czechoslovakia was established in the first place. This British policy of appeasement for a long time ran counter to a tenacious French policy, anchored in French security needs, that insisted on full observance of the restrictions that the 1919 peace structure had imposed on Germany, and on alliances with states bordering on Germany. From 1936, however, a tendency toward appeasement of Nazi Germany also emerged in France.

3. The evolving relations between the government of Czechoslovakia and its large German minority. At first these Germans had resisted inclusion in the new state, but in the course of the 1920s at least some of them had accepted the situation and were negotiating national minority rights with the government.

These three processes had developed independently, but in November 1937 they converged as the result of a series of significant developments. Hitler, in a secret meeting on November 5, 1937, gave specific orders to the chiefs of the armed forces and the top government ministers to conquer Austria and Czechoslovakia at an opportune moment. Neville Chamberlain, the new British prime minister, decided that Britain would no longer restrict itself to passive appeasement but would take the initiative for a comprehensive agreement with Nazi Germany, based on the revision of the Treaty of Versailles by peaceful means. On November 19 a member of the British cabinet, Lord Edward Halifax, was sent on a secret mission to Berlin to ascertain the German demands.

In Czechoslovakia, the economic depression had seriously affected the industrialized German-inhabited areas and had increased the German residents' resentment of the government, especially when they compared their own situation with that in Nazi Germany, with its achievements in the economic sphere and in foreign policy. The leader of the Nazi party in the Sudetenland (the section of BOHEMIA AND MORAVIA in which the German population of Czechoslovakia was mainly concentrated) was Konrad Henlein. Henlein had at first worked toward the attainment of power in Czechoslovakia from within, but in 1937 he changed his policy and, in a letter to Hitler dated November 19, put himself at Hitler's disposal for the conquest of Czechoslovakia. France had already adopted a policy designed to save itself at the expense of its allies in eastern Europe. Daladier, who became premier in April 1938, vacillated between toughness and appeasement, but his foreign minister, Georges Bonnet, supported the British foreign policy and sought to avoid at all costs having to go to war for the sake of Czechoslovakia, especially a war at the side of Soviet Russia. French army generals and politicians were in a defeatist state of mind and lent their support to the policy advocated by the foreign minister.

These attitudes crystallized in the course of 1938 and accelerated the Czechoslovak crisis. The ANSCHLUSS (the annexation of Austria by Germany in March 1938) had met with only a mild reaction in the West, and it paved the way for a German attack on Czechoslovakia. The British cabinet decided that it would not give Czechoslovakia any guarantees against an attack by Germany. In April 1938 the German minority in Czechoslovakia raised new and radical demands, encouraged by Hitler to ask for more than the Czechs could possibly give them and thereby to sharpen the crisis. In May, Czechoslovakia reacted to reports of troop movements in Germany by mobilizing its army, and the Western capitals issued stern warnings to Berlin. Hitler vented his rage by altering the existing operational plans against Czechoslovakia and emphasizing his determination to crush Czechoslovakia by force at an early date.

As the crisis involving Czechoslovakia intensified, the British government resolved that the changes that had to be made would not be brought about by violent means, but rather by international agreement. In August the British, with the agreement of France, sent Viscount (Walter) Runciman, a member of the government, on a mediation mission to Czechoslovakia. By early September, Runciman had gained the Czechoslovak government's consent to the demands for autonomy that the Sudeten Germans had made in April of that year. Now, however, Henlein, acting in compliance with Hitler's orders to escalate the crisis, rejected the solution that he himself had proposed earlier. Chamberlain decided to go to Germany in person to prevent the outbreak of war, and on September 15 he met with Hitler at his mountain retreat in Berchtesgaden.

The official British position was that Britain supported autonomy for the Sudeten Germans, but the truth was, as has since come to light, that Chamberlain and some of his advisers, in and outside the government, had long accepted the need for the Sudetenland to be annexed to Germany in order to appease Hitler. Both Conservative and Socialist newspapers expressed their support for annexation even before the issue came to the cabinet. Like many others, Chamberlain felt that self-determination for the Sudeten Germans—that is, Germany's annexation of the German-inhabited areas of Czechoslovakia—was a just and morally correct solution, and he knew that British public opinion would support him in this stand.

This first meeting between Chamberlain and Hitler was both pathetic and dramatic, with the British prime minister anxious to preserve peace and resolve conflicts in a decent manner, by compromise, and the German dictator scheming to conquer Europe but, for the time being, preferring to achieve his immediate end by cunning and deceit. The annexation was agreed upon in principle. Convinced that unless the Sudetenland was ceded to Germany war would break out, Chamberlain was satisfied with the result of his diplomacy and trusted the assurances Hitler had given him. His next step was to invite the French to join him in exerting pressure on the Czechs to give in and accept the truncation of their territory. A British-French plan was worked out in London and presented to the Czechs on September 19. It demanded that they hand over to Germany all areas in which the German population was over 50 percent; if Czechoslovakia refused to accept this formula it would have to face the consequences alone. Under this British-French plan, eight hundred thousand Czechs would also come under German rule. By surrendering to Germany its line of fortifications, Czechoslovakia would be exposing itself to attack and would lose its defensive capability.

Germany's military strength, and especially its air force, was highly overrated at this point; in Britain there was widespread fear that an air strike would wipe out whole cities at one fell swoop, killing hundreds of thousands. The British military chiefs recommended that the government delay any involvement in war, anticipating that Britain was about to launch a massive rearmament program. British interest in Czechoslovakia as a bulwark against Germany was also waning. Britain no longer looked upon Europe as divided into two hostile camps, as it had under the 1919 peace arrangements, but as a continent whose stability was based on cooperation between the British and the Germans, and on the settlement of all outstanding questions. The Czechs felt that they had been betrayed; they protested, but they submitted, and on September 22 Chamberlain went to Germany for a second meeting with Hitler, this time at Bad Godesberg.

In the meantime there had been more claims on Czechoslovak territory, by Poland for the Teschen area, and by Hungary for the TRANSCARPATHIAN UKRAINE. At this second meeting, Chamberlain, to his great consternation, found that Hitler was no longer content with the fulfillment of his earlier demands and was now insisting on the immediate occupation of the Sudetenland. Moreover, some humiliating conditions were added, for example, that no valuables and no livestock were to be removed from the territory before it was handed over.

Confronted by this German intransigence, the British, French, and Czechs hardened their attitude. The Czech government, under Gen. Jan Sirovy, rejected the Bad Godesberg memorandum and ordered the general mobilization of the Czech army; the French called up reserves, and the British put their navy on the alert. On September 26, Foreign Secretary Halifax sent the Germans a stern message which lent itself to the interpretation that Britain was ready to fight. For a while it seemed that a red line had been drawn which could be crossed only at the risk of war. The

Adolf Hitler and his entourage leaving the *Führerhaus* during the Munich conference. [The Philadelphia Jewish Archives Center at the Balch Institute]

Western powers also told the Czechs that they were no longer advising Czechoslovakia not to mobilize its forces.

Chamberlain's basic attitude, however, had not changed. Having agreed to annexation in principle, he could not now go to war over the modalities of the territorial transfer. In a broadcast to the British on September 27, he said: "How horrible, fantastic, incredible it is that we should be digging trenches and trying on gas masks here because of a quarrel in a faraway country between people of whom we know nothing!" This sentence, which has gone down in history, faithfully reflected British reluctance to guarantee the borders of countries in eastern Europe.

To prevent further deterioration, which might lead to war, Chamberlain wrote to Hitler and Mussolini, proposing a four-power conference. The next day, while addressing Parliament, Chamberlain was dramatically handed an invitation to a conference in Munich, to be held the following day. He did not finish his speech but left for yet another mission, with the enthusiastic blessings of the British people.

The implication of the invitation was that Hitler, having lost the element of surprise, had at the last minute decided to forgo military invasion and to accept a negotiated settlement, surprise having been an essential element in the BLITZKRIEG he had planned. Hitler also came to realize that his generals were against a war in which they might have to face the British and the French, and that public opinion in Germany was not at all eager for military action. On the face of it, therefore, the Munich conference was a victory for Chamberlain's initiative and his insistence that the partition of Czechoslovakia be implemented by means of an international agreement. The conference did not take long, and the agreement reached was essentially identical with the one offered and rejected a few days earlier at Bad Godesberg. The difference was that at Munich an international commission was set up to supervise the transfer of territory and the plebiscites that were to be held in additional areas, and that the new borders were to be guaranteed by the four powers participating in the conference. The Czechs were not invited to take part in the negotiations, and when these were concluded, they were handed a document to sign that was a fait accompli.

The Czechs, headed by President Edvard BENEŠ, played a passive role in the crisis. Czechoslovakia, by contractual ties and by virtue of its political tradition, was committed to cooperation with the Western democracies. It asked the West not to abandon it, but did not even consider trying to force France to abide by its treaty of alliance and go to war on Czechoslovakia's behalf. Such a step would have been a deviation from Czechoslovakia's traditional line in foreign affairs, and, the Czechs believed, would not have achieved its end. Czechoslovakia was even less inclined to call on its other ally, the Soviet Union, for help. That nation had not been asked to take part in the Munich conference or in any of the preceding moves. Beneš even believed that if he were to accept Soviet help against Germany, the West would side with Germany against him. As one of the architects of the French-sponsored treaty system in eastern Europe, Beneš was well aware that this system was no longer in existence and that Czechoslovakia's fate was sealed.

On his return from Munich to London, Chamberlain brandished the declaration he had signed with Hitler, claiming that it heralded "peace in our time." Britain and France sighed with relief at having been saved from the horror of war. Only a few were opposed to the Munich agreement; in the British cabinet, only Alfred Duff Cooper, first lord of the Admiralty, resigned in protest. It did not take long, however, for public opinion to become disillusioned. The Munich agreement and the completion of the conquest of Czechoslovakia, in March 1939, turned the balance of forces in Hitler's favor and made Western statesmen realize that war was now certain. Hitler had been handed the strongest line of fortifications in Europe, plus a thriving industrial complex, a center of communications, rich coal mines, and highly developed cities, as well as a sorely needed supply of gold reserves. The West had lost an ally with two thousand aircraft and a first-class army of thirty-five well-equipped divisions and one and a half million men at its disposal. Britain and France also lost their credibility in the eyes of their existing and potential allies.

Hitler's takeover of a truncated Czechoslovakia laid bare his real intentions and put an end to the era of illusions and appeasement. The new balance of power enabled Hitler to keep up his aggression, secure in the knowledge that if he had to fight for his goals he could stand his ground even against the Western forces. The old saying that "whoever rules Bohemia rules Europe" proved justified for several years.

BIBLIOGRAPHY

Loewenheim, F. L., ed. *Peace or Appeasement? Hitler, Chamberlain, and the Munich Crisis.* Boston, 1965.

Taylor, T. *Munich: The Price of Peace.* London, 1979.

Wheeler-Bennett, J. W. *Munich, Prologue to Tragedy.* New York, 1948.

HEDVA BEN-ISRAEL

MUNKÁCS (Russ., Mukachevo), town transferred to HUNGARY from Czechoslovakia in November 1938. Its Jewish population numbered 13,488, or 42.7 percent of the total, in 1941. One of the largest centers of Orthodoxy and Hasidism in Hungary, Munkács was among the first towns to be emptied of Jews in 1944. Together with the other Jews of the TRANSCARPATHIAN UKRAINE, the local Jews were ordered into a ghetto during the second half of April 1944. Munkács was the site of two ghettos: one for the local Jews, situated in the Jewish section of the town; and the other for the approximately fourteen thousand Jews brought in from the rural communities in Bereg County, including Bárdháza, Ilosva, and Szolyva. This latter ghetto was established in the so-called Sajovits brickyard. Both ghettos were under the internal administration of a JUDENRAT (Jewish Council), headed by Sándor Steiner. The deplorable conditions in the short-lived ghettos led to an outbreak of typhoid on April 23 in one of the sections. As everywhere else in Hungary, the ghettos of Munkács had their special "mints," areas in which the Jews were tortured into confessing where they had hidden their valuables. The rural Jews were the first to be deported, on May 15, 1944. Immediately thereafter, the town's Jews were transferred to the brickyard, from where they were entrained and deported by May 24. After the war, the town was transferred to the Soviet Union and incorporated into the Ukrainian SSR.

BIBLIOGRAPHY

Ha-Cohen Weingarten, S. "Munkacs." In vol. 1 of *Jewish Mother-Cities*, edited by Y. L. Ha-Cohen Fishman, pp. 345–371. Jerusalem, 1946. (In Hebrew.)

Yosefun, A., ed. *A Monument to the Community of Munkacs*. Haifa, 1968. (In Hebrew.)

RANDOLPH L. BRAHAM

MUNKASZOLGÁLAT (Hungarian Labor Service System), system of labor service in HUNGARY. After the adoption of the major anti-Jewish laws in Hungary in 1938 and 1939, the Jews of military age (twenty to forty-eight), having been classified as "unreliable" and thus deemed unfit to bear arms, were drafted into special labor service units. They were organized into military formations un-

Jewish men of Hungarian Labor Service System Brigade 101/51 who worked in a furrier's shop in the Russian town of Tatarino, near the city of Voronezh. The woman and children are Russian (December 12, 1942).

der the command of Hungarian army officers and, instead of arms, were supplied with shovels and pickaxes. These units were employed primarily in construction, mining, and fortification work for the military in Hungary proper as well as in Serbia, the Hungarian-occupied parts of Eastern Galicia, and the Ukraine. Along the front lines, they were used for constructing trenches and tank traps, maintaining roads, and clearing mine fields.

The legal basis for the labor service system was provided by Hungary's Law No. 2 of March 11, 1939, which dealt with general national defense and security issues. On the surface, the legal provisions were not necessarily discriminatory in nature, for originally persons conscripted into labor service were to receive the same pay, clothing, and rations as those in the armed forces. However, after the outbreak of World War II, and especially after Hungary declared war on the Soviet Union on June 27, 1941, the condition of the Jewish labor servicemen deteriorated. Many of the gentile officers and guards attached to the Jewish labor companies became increasingly antisemitic, and the treatment of the Jewish servicemen became more blatantly bigoted and punitive. They were gradually deprived of their uniforms and army boots, and were compelled to wear discriminatory badges—yellow armbands for Jews and white armbands for converts—that made them easy targets for abuse. Their treatment varied from unit to unit and from place to place, depending on the attitude of the officers and guards in charge.

Jewish conscripts in Hungarian Labor Service System Brigade 108/56 (September 1941). In the foreground is Karol Feher-Kassa.

The situation was particularly tragic in many of the frontline units, especially in the Ukraine. There, far from the scrutiny of the central governmental and military authorities, many officers and guards (often joined by Wehrmacht and SS elements) gave vent to their sadistic inclinations by abusing the labor servicemen under their authority. They maltreated them, withheld or stole their already meager rations, and often quartered them for long periods under the open skies. Many of the labor servicemen had to perform their duties without adequate clothing or shoes. Some were subjected to brutal "sports" such as being made to perform somersaults and to leapfrog over one another, after a long workday, for the entertainment of the troops. Others were doused with water and commanded not to move until the cold of the Ukrainian winter caused the water to freeze on them.

By 1942, 100,000 men served in these units, with over 50,000 of them outside Hungary's borders, mostly in the Ukraine. In the military disasters at Voronezh and the battle of the Don in the winter of 1942–1943, thousands of the laborers were killed, while thousands more fell to the Russians. During the chaotic retreat, the soldiers plundered and even killed many of the Jews. According to official Hungarian reports about 25,400 men fell or were captured at this time. It is estimated, however, that the service sustained over 40,000 casualties in the Ukraine by the end of 1943, with about 20,000 prisoners falling to the Red Army and the rest dying during the fighting or perishing from maltreatment, hunger, cold, and disease.

Beginning in June 1943, on the orders of ORGANISATION TODT, Jewish forced laborers were sent to work in the copper mines at Bor in Serbia; six thousand Jews, Seventh-Day Adventists, and JEHOVAH'S WITNESSES were made to work there until September 1944. Some of the laborers were brought back to Mohács in October of that year. At Crevenka, during their journey, the SS lined up over seven hundred and shot them.

Ironically, when the "FINAL SOLUTION" program was launched, soon after the German occupation of Hungary on March 19, 1944, the labor service system became a refuge for many thousands of Hungarian Jewish men threatened with deportation and almost certain liquidation. This change came about primarily for two interrelated reasons: the need for labor in Hungary itself, and pressure from figures in the Hungarian government and military establishment who supported Regent Miklós HORTHY's desire to break out of the alliance with Nazi Germany and who were able to exploit the need for labor to help some labor servicemen. As of the summer of 1940, Jewish labor servicemen worked at the Manfred Weiss Ammunition Works in Csepel, the Polgari Brewery of Kobanya, the Air Defense Works in Budapest, the Parquet and Furniture Plant in Budapest, and the Hungarian Car and Machine Works in Győr, to name a few places. After the ARROW CROSS PARTY came to power in October 1944, men from these work sites, as well as many others, were transferred into the hands of the Nazis. Many thousands were sent to Germany, supposedly on loan, for work on projects of interest to the Nazis. Many thousands more were marched to the Austrian border to build the "East Wall" for the defense of Vienna. Only relatively few of these survived. Most of the Jewish labor servicemen who fell into Soviet hands were treated as prisoners of war, and were released as Hungarian or Romanian nationals only after the peace treaties with Hungary and Romania were signed in February 1947.

BIBLIOGRAPHY

Braham, R. L. *The Hungarian Labor Service System, 1939–1945.* Boulder, 1977.

Karsai, E., ed. *Fegyvertelen álltak az aknamezőkőn . . . dokumentumok a Munkaszolgálat történetéhez Magyarországon.* Budapest, 1962.

RANDOLPH L. BRAHAM

MUSELMANN, German term, meaning "Muslim," widely in use among prisoners in CONCENTRATION CAMPS to refer to inmates who were on the verge of death from starvation, exhaustion, and despair. Numerous prisoners reached this stage soon after their arrival in a camp, owing to their inability to adapt to the conditions and their unwillingness to accept the harsh regime. Many of these had belonged to the intelligentsia or the well-to-do classes, and had come to the camps from countries that still had a measure of economic well-being and individual liberty. Others were felled by hunger, physical overexertion, and corporal punishment. Many prisoners were sick, but they sought to hide their condition, fearing that their admittance to the camp hospital would lead to their being designated for death.

Muselmänner were identified by such marks as the lack of flesh on their bodies and the tight yellow skin over their bones, a dull and expressionless look in their eyes, and the inability to stand upright for any length of time. They were indifferent to their surroundings, apathetic, and listless. The Nazis in charge of the camps regarded them as undesirables, since they were incapable of working or of standing up to the rigors of the camp regime. Most of the prisoners avoided contact with *Muselmänner,* afraid that this condition could be in store for them.

A person who had reached the *Muselmann* stage had no chance of survival, and did not remain alive for more than a few days or weeks. The origin of the term has not been

Yehuda Bacon, *Muselmann,* 1946–1947. Oil on board, 12.6 × 18.9 inches (32 × 48 cm). [Collection of the artist.]

established; some have attributed it to a certain similarity between a concentration camp *Muselmann* and the image of a Muslim prostrating himself in prayer.

BIBLIOGRAPHY

Cohen, E. A. *Human Behavior in the Concentration Camp.* New York, 1953.

Glicksman, W. "Social Differentiation in the German Concentration Camps," *YIVO Annual* 8 (1953): 123–150.

Kogon, E. *The Theory and Practice of Hell: The German Concentration Camps and the System behind Them.* New York, 1950.

ISRAEL GUTMAN

MUSEUMS AND MEMORIAL INSTITUTES. [*The seven articles in this entry deal with some of the major Holocaust museums and memorial institutes in Israel, Europe, and the United States:*

General Survey
Bet Loḥamei ha-Getta'ot
A Living Memorial to the Holocaust—
Museum of Jewish Heritage
Moreshet
Poland
Simon Wiesenthal Center
United States Holocaust Memorial Museum

For information about institutions housing archival and research materials on the Holocaust, see Documentation Centers; *for a discussion of the foremost Holocaust museum, memorial institute, and research center, see* Yad Vashem. *The Anne Frank House, preserved as a museum, is treated in* Frank, Anne.]

General Survey

In Israel, the United States, and Europe, more than one hundred museums and other memorial institutions devoted to the period of World War II and the Holocaust have been established, with dozens more planned. These memorial sites are proposed and designed at both national and local levels by survivors' groups and soldiers' organizations, by synagogues and churches, by families and individuals. In addition to drawing on traditional Jewish forms of remembrance, state museums dealing with this period inevitably make use of national and institutional traditions as well. As a result, Holocaust memorials often combine national and Jewish motifs, political and religious iconography.

In many countries, Holocaust Remembrance Day (Yom ha-Sho'ah) is observed according to the Jewish calendar, on 27 Nisan (which falls during the period when the WARSAW GHETTO UPRISING took place), with public ceremonies and gatherings of survivors. In Israel this is an official memorial day, and all public places of amusement are closed. The main ceremony takes place at YAD VASHEM, and other ceremonies and gatherings are held throughout the country. Pupils in Israeli schools also commemorate the day. In the United States the day is observed in many circles, with an officially sponsored ceremony in Washington. On April 19, the day of the uprising according to the Gregorian calendar, the Polish government sponsors a memorial ceremony.

The motives for these memorials and commemorations and the kinds of Holocaust memory they generate are varied. Some of the memorials are built in response to the Jewish injunction to remember, others to fulfill a government's need to explain a nation's past to itself. The aim of yet other memorials is to educate the next generation and inculcate in it a sense of shared experience, destiny, responsibility, and meaning for the future.

The first memorial sites were the places of destruction themselves. In October 1944, Soviet liberators made the concentration camp at MAJDANEK, near Lublin in Poland, the first memorial and museum of its kind. The only other extermination camp to be left partially standing, at AUSCHWITZ-Birkenau, was also made a state memorial. Its barracks were converted into national pavilions, and the ruins of its gas chambers were left untouched to recall their former reality. In both instances, the killing of Jews at these camps is subsumed under the Polish national remembrance of this time.

In similar ways, memorials and museums on the sites of former camps in Germany often recall collectively all the victims of the Nazis—political, military, and racial—but none is devoted exclusively to the Jews. The memorial complex at DACHAU, for example, includes a museum and archive, as well as separate memorials to Protestant, Catholic, and Jewish victims of the camp. At NEUENGAMME, near Hamburg, international youth groups are invited every summer to excavate the grounds of the former camp as part of a memorial project that now encompasses contemporary political repression, as well as that of the past.

In addition to the memorials and museums located at the sites of former camps in Poland and Germany, many other monuments dot the European landscape. Memorials ranging from elaborate statues and mausoleums to simple plaques now mark many of the sites of deportations, destroyed synagogues, and razed Jewish cemeteries. In many instances, survivors returned to their former homes in Poland and Germany only long enough to erect memorials to their lost families and communities, before moving on. In response to the dearth of official commemoration of the Holocaust in the Soviet Union, Jewish families and communities have set up unofficial monuments at the sites of mass graves and mass executions across Lithuania, Latvia, and the Ukraine.

To a great extent, the memorials and museums in Europe focus on the murder of Jews during the war and pay relatively little attention either to the millennium of Jewish life in Europe before the war or to the return to life in Israel and America afterward. In contrast, memorials in Israel and America tend to locate the Holocaust in a more extended view of Jewish history, which includes life before, during, and after the destruction, because memory of this period in Israel and America is no less shaped by the ideals and historical experiences of its people. In Israel, for example, not only are the ghetto fighters and Jewish partisans recalled alongside the more helpless victims, but representations of martyrdom and resistance in Israeli museums are often linked to the rebirth of the modern Jewish state. Projected national and state Holocaust museums and memorials in the United States similarly reflect not only current Jewish life in America, but also characteristically American ideals such as liberty and pluralism.

In view of the great diversity among Holocaust memorials, further inquiry into public memory of the Holocaust includes, in addition to the study of monuments and museums themselves, their conception and construction, their reception in the local community, and their place in national commemorative cycles.

BIBLIOGRAPHY

Berenbaum, M. "On the Politics of Public Commemoration of the Holocaust." *Shoah* (Fall–Winter 1982): 6–37.

Marcuse, H., F. Schimmelfennig, and J. Spielmann. *Steine des Anstosses: Nationalsozialismus und Zweiter Weltkrieg in Denkmalen, 1945–85.* Hamburg, 1985.

Rieth, A. *Monuments to the Victims of Tyranny.* New York, 1968.
U.S. Holocaust Memorial Council. *Directory of Holocaust Institutions.* Washington, D.C., 1988.
Young, J. E. *Writing and Rewriting the Holocaust.* Bloomington, 1988.

JAMES E. YOUNG

Bet Loḥamei ha-Getta'ot

Bet Loḥamei ha-Getta'ot (full name, Bet Loḥamei ha-Getta'ot al Shem Yitzhak Katzenelson le-Moreshet ha-Sho'ah ve-ha-Mered; The Yitzhak KATZENELSON Ghetto Fighters' House Commemorating the Holocaust and the Revolt) is a memorial institution established in 1949 at Kibbutz Loḥamei ha-Getta'ot near Naharia, western Galilee, Israel, at the time the kibbutz was settled. The museum was created on the initiative of several of the kibbutz members, survivors of the WARSAW GHETTO UPRISING, including Zivia LUBETKIN and Yitzhak ZUCKERMAN. Over the years, the institution's collection of documents developed into a full-fledged center, attracting tens of thousands of visitors annually. Bet Loḥamei ha-Getta'ot's purpose is primarily educational: to keep alive the memory of the Holocaust and the lesson of the revolt, and to transmit them from one generation to the next.

The center of its operations is the museum, which portrays in photographs and charts the fate of the Jews under the Nazi regime and the Nazi efforts to bring about the "FINAL SOLUTION," as well as the actions taken by the Jews, including their resistance. A special section is devoted to the Jewish world as it existed before the Holocaust, including the story of the pre-Holocaust Jewish YOUTH MOVEMENTS. The historical record presented by the museum is enriched by a group of artistic works.

Bet Loḥamei ha-Getta'ot's archive contains a rich collection of documents concerning Jewish fate under the Nazis, with special emphasis on the Zionist pioneering youth movements and the resistance organizations. The library contains 50,000 volumes. There is also an archive of films on the Holocaust and Jewish resistance, and the institution has produced three full-length films of its own: *The 81st Blow,* on the history of the Holocaust; *The Face of Resistance,* on Jewish resistance; and *The Last Sea,* on the drive of the Holocaust survivors to reach Palestine. The art collection contains works created in the ghettos and the camps, or after the war by artists who are Holocaust survivors. Bet Loḥamei ha-Getta'ot has also published, chiefly through the Kibbutz ha-Me'uḥad Publishing House, dozens of books containing testimonies, evidence, and Holocaust research; in addition, it plays a leading role in the international Janusz KORCZAK Society. An educational center named for Zivia Lubetkin and Yitzhak Zuckerman holds regular seminars for the study of the Holocaust and Jewish resistance, including seminars for groups of educators from abroad.

In addition to its own research, Bet Loḥamei ha-Getta'ot participates with Haifa University in the Institute for the Study of the Holocaust Period, which initiates and supports research projects and publishes annually a scholarly journal, *Dappim le-Ḥeker Tekufat ha-Sho'ah* (Research Papers on the Holocaust Period). Bet Loḥamei ha-Getta'ot also has a research and documentation bulletin of its own, *Edut* (Testimony).

YEHOYAKIM COCHAVI

A Living Memorial to the Holocaust—Museum of Jewish Heritage

The Museum of Jewish Heritage, which will be New York's principal public memorial to the six million Jewish victims of the Holocaust, is scheduled to open to the public in 1992. It is being created under the auspices of the New York Holocaust Memorial Commission, which was established in 1983 by New York City mayor Edward I. Koch. Mayor Koch was joined as Founding Chair in 1985 by New York governor Mario Cuomo.

The museum's permanent home will be on the southwestern tip of Manhattan Island, on the shoreline directly opposite the Statue of Liberty and Ellis Island. The structure, designed by the noted architectural firm James Stewart Polshek and Partners, will include some 180,000 square feet of space, with a memorial chamber, galleries for permanent and temporary exhibitions, a learning center with computer and audiovisual services, an auditorium, classrooms, archives, a reference library, and related facilities.

The name "Living Memorial" expresses two distinctive features of this institution. First, its primary purpose is to provide public education, rather than to be a major repository or research center. Given its location, the museum is expected to welcome as many as 500,000 visitors of all ages and backgrounds per year. Second, the museum will focus on a curriculum that emphasizes the nature and significance of modern Jewish civilization, and its continuity throughout the world, despite the devastation of the Holocaust. Thus, the four main themes of the institution's exhibitions and other educational programs will be The World Before (European and North African Jewish life in the late nineteenth and early twentieth centuries), The Holocaust, The Aftermath (depicting the efforts by Holocaust survivors and others to rebuild Jewish life and communities around the world), and Renewal in America (which will trace Jewish immigration to and settlement in the United States from 1654 to the present).

To create this new institution, the museum's staff began in 1986 to investigate the whereabouts and availability of objects that might be acquired for its collections of artifacts, documents, photographs, films, and artworks. By the end of 1988, more than two thousand items had been acquired from individual collectors and institutions, and the museum's reference archive of photographic images on modern Jewish history and the Holocaust contained some twenty-five thousand images, representing more than two hundred different collections around the world. At the same time, designs for the inaugural permanent exhibitions were completed by museum staff in consultation with Chermayeff and Geismar Associates, the design firm responsible for exhibitions at the Statue of Liberty and Ellis Island museums, as well as the John F. Kennedy Memorial Library in Boston.

The most innovative aspect of planning the museum was connected with creating its Learning Center, an effort that involved scholars of Jewish history and the Holocaust, designers of computer software and databases, specialists in audiovisual technologies, photograph and media researchers, and educators from varied disciplines. By the end of 1988, the museum was demonstrating a number of prototype teaching systems, including the Interactive Encyclopedia of Jewish Heritage, a computerized program that linked texts, graphics, still and moving images, and sound to document and interpret for a general audience the broad scope of the Jewish experience encapsulated by the museum's curriculum.

From its inception, the museum was governed by a board of trustees led by George Klein, a prominent real-estate developer, and Robert Morgenthau, Manhattan district attorney. David Altshuler served as the museum's founding director.

DAVID ALTSHULER

Moreshet

Moreshet ("Heritage"; full name, Moreshet, Bet Edut al Shem Mordekhai ANIELEWICZ, or Moreshet, the Mordecai Anielewicz House of Testimony) was founded in Israel in 1961. Its principal objectives are to research and document the story of the Jewish people in the Holocaust, with special emphasis on instances of active fighting resistance aimed at saving lives, in the spirit of the pioneering Zionist YOUTH MOVEMENTS; and to pass this heritage on to future generations. The institute was founded by members of the left-wing kibbutz movement Kibbutz Artsi-ha-Shomer ha-Tsa'ir. These were survivors of the Holocaust who had participated in the ghetto uprisings, had served with the partisans, or had fought in the underground in Nazi-occupied territory during World War II. They were joined by historians and researchers, leading participants in the rescue efforts, people who had served in the Soviet army and in the JEWISH BRIGADE GROUP, educators, and teachers. Among the group of sponsors were Abba KOVNER, Rozka KORCZAK-MARLA, Vitka Kempner (Kovner), Israel Gutman, Yehuda Bauer, Shalom Cholawski, and Yehuda Tubin.

To achieve the institute's ends, a number of projects were inaugurated. An archive located in Givat Haviva, an educational seminary about 4 miles (6 km) northeast of Hadera, began functioning in 1960 and has been collecting documents and testimonies of historical value. The Moreshet publishing house and the periodical *Yalkut Moreshet* (Heritage Anthology), in conjunction with Sifriat Poalim, the publishing house in Tel Aviv, were also founded in 1960. *Yalkut Moreshet* first came out in 1963 and appears twice a year. By early 1989, forty-six issues had been published; its permanent features include ideological essays, research papers, documents, and testimonies; the contributors are among the leading historians and scholars of the Holocaust. The documents and testimonies represent valuable source material for the study, understanding, and historical assessment of the course of events in the Holocaust period. In addition, about one hundred books have been published—memoirs of survivors, research studies, and philosophical writings.

A museum is situated at Kibbutz Yad Mordecai, named after Mordecai Anielewicz, the commander of the ŻYDOWSKA ORGANIZACJA BOJOWA (Jewish Fighting Organization; ŻOB) and of the WARSAW GHETTO UPRISING. It concentrates on two areas, linked chronologically and by their respective historical meaning and impact: the destruction and struggle of the Jews during the Holocaust, and the resistance offered by the YISHUV (the Jewish community of Palestine before the state of Israel was established) during Israel's War of Independence and the establishment of Israel. The design of the museum, in terms of both contents and presentation, was the work of Abba Kovner; it gives concrete expression to Jewish history in the period of the Holocaust and the renewal of Jewish nationhood.

In the second half of the 1980s, two centers were established for studying the history of the Holocaust and of Jewish resistance in that period, and for examining their implications for the future of the Jewish people. One center is at Givat Haviva, and the other at Yad Mordecai. The latter is situated close to the museum and to the site of battles fought on the grounds of the kibbutz during Israel's War of Independence. More than ten thousand students in the upper grades of secondary schools from all over the country take part each year in one-day seminars in these centers; similar seminars are attended by youth instructors and members of youth movements. An important and expanding new program, sponsored by both centers, organizes visits to Poland by youth and student groups. Such groups, after undergoing a special preparatory course in the centers, visit extermination sites, ruins of destroyed Jewish communities in Poland, and places where the underground and active resistance organizations operated and fought the Nazi enemy.

YEHUDA TUBIN

Poland

On July 2, 1947, two memorial museums were established in Poland through a resolution passed by the Polish parliament (Sejm). The resolution stated that the AUSCHWITZ-Birkenau Museum would be established on the site of the Auschwitz concentration camp, complete with all its structures and installations, as a memorial to the suffering of the Polish people and other peoples. In 1967 a monument to the victims was unveiled on the grounds of the camp. Later, at the initiative of the International Auschwitz Committee, space was allocated to the constituent member committees. The 1947 Sejm resolution also provided for the establishment of a national museum at MAJDANEK. In 1969 a memorial was built there. On this site there is an international section for modern plastic art devoted to antiwar topics. In 1962 a national museum was also established at Sztutowo (STUTTHOF), and in 1968 a memorial to the victims was built there. Research is being carried out at the three museums, which publish the scholarly journals *Zeszyty Oświęcimskie, Zeszyty Majdanka,* and *Zeszyty Museum Stutthof.*

The museum at TREBLINKA has been in existence since 1968, and a memorial and a symbolic cemetery have been built there. Monuments have also been erected at Rogoźnica, PŁASZÓW, CHEŁMNO, and SOBIBÓR. In addition, a central museum devoted to prisoner-of-war camps was established at Lambonowice-Lamsdorf.

Museums perpetuating the memory of the prisons and torture chambers are to be found in Warsaw (PAWIAK PRISON and the Gestapo

The remains of the Majdanek concentration camp site have been preserved as a Polish national memorial. This is one of the prisoner barracks (Block 15). The three-tiered wooden bunks are visible inside. [Geoffrey Wigoder]

Crematorium building with chimney at Majdanek. [Geoffrey Wigoder]

Crematoria ovens at Majdanek. [Geoffrey Wigoder]

Majdanek memorial built atop a hill of human ashes. The Polish text reads: "Our fate is a warning to you." [Geoffrey Wigoder]

Between 1959 and 1964 the Treblinka camp area was converted into a Polish national memorial in the form of a cemetery. Hundreds of stones were set in the ground, inscribed with the names of the victims' countries and places of origin. This photo shows the monument with the inscription "Never Again" in Polish, Yiddish, Russian, English, French, and German. [Geoffrey Wigoder]

In the foreground is a slag heap of human remains found on the Treblinka camp site. The cemetery memorial is in the background. [Geoffrey Wigoder]

Another Treblinka monument, representing railway ties and symbolizing the never-ending railway transports that brought 870,000 people (the vast majority of them Jews) to their death between July 1942 and April 1943. [Geoffrey Wigoder]

headquarters on Szucha Street), in Poznań (Fort VII at Zabikowo), in Lublin (the Gestapo headquarters at Pod Zegarem), and in Łódź (Radogoszcz).

BIBLIOGRAPHY

Council for the Preservation of Monuments to Resistance and Martyrdom. *Scenes of Fighting and Martyrdom Guide: War Years in Poland, 1939–1945.* Warsaw, 1966.

Novitch, M. "Memorial Monuments in the Concentration Camps of Poland and Germany." *Yad Vashem Bulletin* 13 (October 1963): 72–74.

Young, J. E. "The Biography of a Memorial Icon: Nathan Rapaport's Warsaw Ghetto Monument." *Representations* (Spring 1989): 91–121.

CZESŁAW MADAJCZYK

Simon Wiesenthal Center

The Simon Wiesenthal Center, named for the Viennese Nazi-hunter Simon WIESENTHAL, was established in Los Angeles in 1977 by its founder and dean, Rabbi Marvin Hier. As of 1989, it was supported by approximately 380,000 member families. In 1979 a museum developed by Holocaust historian Efraim Zuroff was opened. A year earlier, the center launched a national outreach project to provide educational programs for junior and senior high school students. During its initial decade of operation, the center's program reached hundreds of thousands of American teenagers.

Since its establishment, the Wiesenthal Center has focused on political issues related to the Holocaust and has specialized in the use of mass media to educate the public about the events of World War II. Among its major campaigns were the efforts to cancel the statute of limitations on war crimes in West Germany, and attempts to force South American governments such as those of Paraguay and Chile to surrender leading Nazi criminals (Dr. Josef MENGELE and Walther RAUFF). The center has also played a key role in uncovering hundreds of Nazi collaborators of eastern European origin who escaped after

World War II to Western democracies, and in convincing the governments of Great Britain, Australia, and Canada to investigate this issue and prosecute the criminals found in those countries.

In 1982, the Wiesenthal Center's documentary *Genocide* was awarded an Oscar as the best documentary film of the previous year. A year earlier the center began producing "Page One," a weekly radio program on Jewish affairs broadcast by dozens of stations and the National Public Radio Satellite throughout North America. The center also helped produce a documentary on the life and fate of Raoul WALLENBERG, and it has videotaped more than four hundred hours of testimony by Holocaust survivors and liberators.

The center has produced and published a variety of books, publications, and exhibitions that reflect its diverse agenda, among them *The Simon Wiesenthal Annual* (6 volumes since 1984), a journal of Holocaust research; the study *Egypt—Israel's Peace Partner: A Survey of Antisemitism in the Egyptian Press, 1986–1987* (Los Angeles, 1988); "Portraits of Infamy," an exhibition on the similarities between Nazi and Soviet antisemitism; and "The Courage to Remember," an exhibition on the history of the Holocaust. The latter was exhibited in Vienna in commemoration of the fiftieth anniversary of the ANSCHLUSS, and three months later it became the first Holocaust exhibition ever displayed in the Soviet Union. It was placed on permanent loan in the Solomon Mykhoels Jewish Cultural Center in Moscow.

In 1989, the Simon Wiesenthal Center had offices in Israel, France, and Canada, in addition to five regional offices in the United States.

ABRAHAM COOPER

United States Holocaust Memorial Museum

Currently under construction only 400 yards from the Washington Monument, at the heart of the National Mall in Washington, the United States Holocaust Memorial Museum will be the world's largest and most comprehensive Holocaust museum. The museum, mandated by a unanimous act of the United States Congress in 1980 to reaffirm the nation's fundamental commitment to the rights of all humankind, will be the only national Holocaust museum in the United States. It is designed to be a permanent and powerful reminder to the American people and to the world that humankind must guard forever against the danger of another Holocaust.

The museum's permanent exhibition will tell the story of Nazi terror. While it will focus on the six million Jews who were murdered, the museum will also tell the tragic story of Gypsies, Poles, Soviet prisoners of war, homosexuals, the handicapped, Jehovah's Witnesses, and other victims of Nazi persecution. In addition, it will honor the American liberators of the extermination camps and will tell another story—the failure of the free world, including the United States, to stop the Holocaust.

The museum is being built entirely through private donations, on 1.9 acres of land made available by the federal government. Construction began in 1989; the building is scheduled for completion in 1992.

In fulfilling its mission to remember and to educate, the museum will support academic research, curriculum development, and teacher training services. The archival, artifact, and library collections will provide fundamental resources for visitors, students, teachers, and scholars. The museum will be instrumental in integrating the Holocaust archival collections of institutions around the world. In addition, its theater and auditorium will offer cultural performances, lectures, symposiums, and films on the Holocaust.

The museum will overlook the Washington Monument, the Jefferson Memorial, the Tidal Basin, and, in the distance, the White House and the Lincoln Memorial. Located a half-block south of Independence Avenue, the building, adjacent to the Bureau of Engraving and Printing, will extend the entire length of the block between Fourteenth Street SW and Raoul Wallenberg Place (formerly Fifteenth Street SW).

Museum architect James I. Freed, a partner in the firm of I. M. Pei and Partners of New York, and himself a child refugee from Nazi Germany, was mandated by the U.S. HOLOCAUST MEMORIAL COUNCIL to design a museum

Model of the United States Holocaust Memorial Museum with the museum's hexagonally shaped memorial —the Hall of Remembrance. The five-story museum will extend from Raoul Wallenberg Place (formerly Fifteenth Street SW), foreground, to Fourteenth Street SW.

of "symbolic and artistic beauty, visually and emotionally moving in accordance with the solemn nature of the Holocaust." Freed, who found it "nearly impossible to deal creatively with a subject matter so heated," has designed a building filled with symbolic allusions to the Holocaust.

The building has 225,000 square feet of floor area on five levels above ground, and a below-ground concourse. The Hall of Witness serves as the museum's central gathering place, through which visitors pass to all parts of the building. This large, solemn hall, illuminated by natural light, resonates with abstract symbolic references to the Holocaust. The brick walls, exposed beams, boarded windows, metal fences, and gates will let visitors know they are in a different place. A deep crack, a symbol of the rupture of civilization during the Holocaust, runs down one wall of the hall.

The Hall of Remembrance, a hexagonally shaped skylit memorial projecting from the museum, is a spiritual space, designed as an area for contemplation and reflection as well as for public ceremonies. In the wall of the hall's ambulatory will be niches for candles —universal symbols of remembrance. The hexagon evokes the memory of the six million Jews murdered in the Holocaust.

The museum's core, its permanent exhibition, will be located on two and a half floors. Through oral testimonies, written narratives, still and moving images, and authentic objects, the story of the Holocaust will unfold as the visitor experiences evocative and unique exhibitions. The exhibition will be divided into three sections: The Assault (1933–

1939), The Holocaust (1939–1945), and Bearing Witness (1945 to the present).

Some of the people who lived the story—victims, bystanders, public officials, liberators, and rescuers—will serve as guides, thereby creating an intimate dialogue between the visitor and the devastating historical events of the Holocaust through personal narrative and memorabilia.

The visitor to the permanent exhibition will encounter the people of the Holocaust story in the fullness of their lives. He or she will confront the shattering of society, understand the vulnerability of countless victims, and discover the resilience of the human spirit even in the most extreme and inhumane circumstances.

The museum will be an educational institution dedicated to teaching children and adults and to facilitating scholarship on the Holocaust. Accordingly, the educational functions will be integrated into every aspect of the museum and its programs.

The museum's library and archive will be the central resource center for scholars and students of the Holocaust and will make available outstanding collections from Europe, Israel, and the United States. Computerized data bases, on-line catalogues, and bibliographical guides will enable visiting scholars to access source materials from around the world. The library will hold 100,000 or more volumes and is expected to be the largest Holocaust library in the world. It will enable scholars to study about other acts of genocide as well, such as the Armenian genocide.

The museum is developing plans for an innovative Learning Center that will feature the next generation in interactive learning technologies. Informal programs, including a computerized encyclopedia of the Holocaust, will offer visitors opportunities for in-depth study and learning. The Learning Center will also offer extensive data on the individuals and communities lost in the Holocaust. Retrieval programs will enable visitors to inquire about specific persons or locales and to post a record of their inquiry for later researchers.

The Learning Center is developing a library of documentaries based on film, photographs, music, and oral histories. Visitors will be able to utilize these resources easily.

In addition, school programs, public programs, and outreach activities are being planned. More than 10,000 square feet on two floors of the museum will be devoted to temporary special exhibitions on Holocaust-related subjects.

As many as a million or more people, including tens of thousands of schoolchildren, are expected to visit the museum each year, and its programs and publications should reach an even wider population.

MICHAEL BERENBAUM

MUSHKIN, ELIYAHU (d. 1942), chairman of the MINSK Judenrat (Jewish Council) and a supporter of its underground and the local partisans. A native of Minsk and an engineer by profession, Mushkin was a member of the municipality staff. The Germans occupied Minsk at the end of June 1941, and shortly afterward, Mushkin was appointed JUDENRAT chairman because of his knowledge of German or, according to one version, because he was recommended for the post by a member of the city council.

Mushkin lost little time in establishing contact with the Minsk ghetto underground. He was helpful in aiding Jews to escape from the ghetto, and supplied the partisan units in the area with money, medicines, and equipment. Through his personal authority, Mushkin exercised a decisive influence on the attitude of the other members of the Judenrat, which for all practical purposes became the executive arm of the underground, carrying out its decisions. Mushkin was able to warn the underground of impending dangers, and the Jews respected him. His close contacts with the underground, coupled with the duties that the German authorities imposed on him, put Mushkin in a precarious situation. He had to be extremely careful, and could not afford to trust even some of his own staff.

In February 1942 Mushkin was arrested. One version has it that he was charged with attempting to bribe a Gestapo officer to release a Jewish prisoner. According to another version, he was arrested when someone informed on the Judenrat to the Gestapo, revealing that the Judenrat was providing the partisans with clothing, medicines, and equipment. A third version is that Mushkin had given refuge to a German officer who sought to avoid frontline service, and that it was this officer who gave him away. Mushkin was tortured and, a month after his arrest, he was hanged. The members of his family were killed in one of the "night *Aktionen.*"

BIBLIOGRAPHY

Cohen, D. "The Holocaust and the Fighting Partisan Underground in Minsk." In vol. 2 of *Minsk, a Jewish Mother-City: A Memorial Anthology,* edited by S. Even-Shoshan, pp. 267–314. Tel Aviv, 1985. (In Hebrew.)

Smoliar, H. *The Minsk Ghetto.* Moscow, 1946. (In Yiddish.)

SHALOM CHOLAWSKI

MUSIC, THE HOLOCAUST IN. The Holocaust and the sufferings of the Jews under the Nazi regime have been extensively reflected in music and musical life. Shortly after their rise to power in 1933 the Nazis established a central office, the Reichsmusikkammer (Reich Music Office), to control all musical activities in Germany. The composer Richard Strauss was appointed its president, and the conductor Wilhelm Furtwängler as his deputy. All Jewish professional musicians in Germany were dismissed from their posts, and the works of Jewish composers were not allowed to be performed. The Jewish reaction, in July 1933, was to set up the KULTURBUND DEUTSCHER JUDEN (Cultural Society of German Jews), for promoting music and the arts among German Jews. In its eight years of existence the Kulturbund held five hundred performances of twenty-five operas, and hundreds of symphonic and chamber music concerts. Jewish musicians left Germany in large numbers, some of them going to Palestine, where they found employment with the Palestine Symphony Orchestra (later the Israeli Philharmonic Orchestra). The orchestra

Herszkowicz, a popular street singer in the Łódź ghetto who composed his own ballads based on current events. [Mendel Grossman]

was founded by the violinist Bronislaw Huberman, to rescue Jewish musicians from Nazi Germany. Huberman boycotted the works of Richard Strauss and Richard Wagner, which were of special significance for the Nazis.

During the war, there was considerable musical activity in some of the ghettos, easing a little the burdens of ghetto life. Performances were given by soloists, by street bands that Adam Furmanski (1883–1943) organized, by small orchestras, in cafés, and in the soup kitchens that were opened to help the needy. WARSAW had a Jewish symphony orchestra that gave concerts conducted by well-known conductors: Marian Neureich (1906–1943), Adam Furmanski, Shimon Fullman (1887–1942), and Israel Hamerman (1914–1943). Because of the cold, the Warsaw orchestra played under extremely harsh conditions. Sometimes the musicians had to wear overcoats and hats during the performance, and at times they had to wear gloves. On April 16, 1942, the German authorities put an end to the orchestra, punishing it for having performed works by German composers, in violation of existing orders to the contrary. In ŁÓDŹ, musical activities were centrally directed from the top, in line with the policy laid down by the JUDENRAT (Jewish Council) chairman, Mordechai Chaim RUMKOWSKI. The community center was specially adapted for musical and theatrical performances, and a symphony orchestra, the Zamir choral society, and a revue theater appeared on its stage. In the KRAKÓW ghetto, chamber music recitals and concerts of liturgical music were frequent. The VILNA ghetto had an extensive program of musical activities, with a symphony orchestra and several choirs. *The Doll,* a children's opera by L. Tropianski, was performed, and a revue theater entertained its audiences with the many popular songs composed in the ghetto. A conservatory with 100 students was established in the Vilna ghetto.

The THERESIENSTADT ghetto had a well-organized program of musical activities. The ghetto population established orchestras and choirs that gave symphonic and chamber music concerts. Operas were produced, and there were also evenings of community singing. One of the composers in the ghetto, Victor Ullman (1898–1944), composed several works there, among them the opera *Der Kaiser von Atlantis oder Der Tod dankt ab* (The Emperor of Atlantis, or Death Abdicated), with a libretto by Peter Kien. Just as the opera was about to have its premiere, in October 1944, most of the musicians of Theresienstadt were deported to the AUSCHWITZ extermination camp. Long after the war was over, the manuscript was discovered and the opera was finally staged, in Israel, Germany, and the Netherlands.

The Kovno ghetto orchestra.

Many songs were sung in the ghettos—some old, perhaps with new words, and some new. One of the first anthologies was published in 1948, under the title *Di Lider fun Getos un Lagern* (Songs of Ghettos and Camps). Edited by H. Leivick and Shmerke KACZERGINSKI, the anthology contains 236 songs. Among the best-known songs composed during the Holocaust are the "Song of the Partisans," by Hirsh GLIK; "Es Brent" (A Fire Is Raging), by Mordecai GEBIRTIG, a prophetic song written in 1938 under the impact of the pogrom in Przytyk; and "Shtiler, Shtiler" (Quiet, Quiet), with words by Kaczerginski and music by the eleven-year-old Aleksander Tamir-Wolkoviski, of the Vilna ghetto.

In the camps too, songs were composed and sung. In most of the large concentration and extermination camps, the Germans formed orchestras from among the prisoners and forced them to play when Jews arrived at the camps to be killed there; when the arrivals were on their way to the gas chambers; during the *Selektionen*; when the prisoners were

The Łódź ghetto symphony orchestra.

marched to and from their places of work; and also for the pleasure of the SS men. The Auschwitz camp had six orchestras, the largest of which, in Auschwitz I (the main camp), consisted of 100 to 120 musicians. All four of the extermination camps—TREBLINKA, MAJDANEK, BEŁŻEC, and SOBIBÓR—had orchestras.

Some of the musical works and adaptations composed in the camps have survived. One of these is the *Death Tango,* written in the JANÓWSKA camp and played there during the *Selektionen* and mass murders. In Theresienstadt many compositions were created, among them the *Theresienstadt Ghetto Anthem.* Additional works by Victor Ullman, the composer of the opera *Atlantis,* included his Piano Sonata no. 6, opus 49; his Sonata no. 7; three songs for baritone and piano; a trio for violin, viola, and cello; and a lullaby. Among the other compositions originating in Theresienstadt were three works by Gideon Klein; the children's opera *Brundibar,* by Hans Karasa (performed in Israel in 1988); and the Edelstein preludes for string quartet. Arye Abrahamson wrote a trio for voice, cello, and piano in a French camp; Percy Hayde composed his Symphonic Episodes in Yellow at Dachau; and Aldo Finzi wrote a symphonic poem while underground in northern Italy.

Musical creations on the Holocaust, many by composers who did not experience it personally, were composed while the Holocaust was still raging, and afterward. Under the impact of Herschel GRYNSZPAN's 1938 assassination of Ernst vom Rath, a staff member of the German embassy in Paris, the British composer Michael Tippett wrote the oratorio *A Child of Our Time.* Arnold Schönberg, inspired by the personal story of a Warsaw ghetto survivor, wrote *A Survivor from Warsaw* (1947), a cantata for reader, men's choir, and symphony orchestra. After a description of the *Selektion,* it ends with *Shema Israel* (Hear O Israel) being sung by the Jews marching to the gas chambers. The philosopher, sociologist, and musicologist Theodor Adorno had asserted that it was "barbaric" to write poetry after Auschwitz. But upon hearing Schönberg's cantata he changed his mind, and said that if the cantata "was written under the impact of the suffering, there may be some meaning in human suffering."

The Warsaw ghetto is the theme of Israeli composer Artur Gelbrun's *Elegies of the Warsaw Ghetto,* of Witold Rudzinski's *Warsaw Ghetto,* and of Moisei Wajnberg's *Alarm in Warsaw.* Alexander Kulisiewicz, a Polish composer living in France, wrote *Chantes de déportation* (Deportation Songs). Anne FRANK is the theme of an opera bearing her name by Grigory Fried, of a cantata by Hans Kox, and of a work by the Catalan composer Jordi Servello. Many musical works about Auschwitz have been composed: *Dies Irae,* by Krzysztof Penderecki; *Auschwitz 44,* an opera by Alexander Sinberger; *Auschwitz, Epitaph* and *Auschwitz Orchestra,* both by the Israeli composer Eddie Halpern; and *Oswiecim,* by the Czech composer Illia Zeljenka.

Dmitri Shostakovich's Thirteenth Symphony, BABI YAR, incorporates a setting of Yevgeni Yevtushenko's poem of that name. Both the poem and the symphony enraged the Soviet authorities, and for some time the symphony was banned, until changes were made in it. Charles Davidson has put to music *I Never Saw Another Butterfly,* a cycle of poems written by children in Theresienstadt, for children's choir and piano. Ben Steinberg composed *Cantata,* for reader, soloists, choir, and orchestra, setting to music poems written by children during the Holocaust. The Polish composer Stanisław Wiechowicz composed *A Letter to Marc Chagall*; Zbigniew Bujarski, *Elegies*; Zbigniew Turski, *Shadow*; and Shimon Laks, *Elegy for the Jewish Shtetlach.* In the Soviet Union, Moisei Wajnberg composed a *Requiem* as well as an opera, *The Woman Passenger,* and Henryk Wagner wrote *Life for Eternity.* The Czech Peter Kolman composed *Monumento 6,000,000,* and his countryman Pawel Haas, a suite. The Australian Wilfred Josephs also composed a *Requiem.* A group of German composers—Boris Blacher, Paul Dessau, Karl Amadeus Hartmann, Hans Werner Henze, and Rudolf Wagner-Regeney—set to music *Jüdische Chronik* (A Jewish Chronicle), by Jans Gerlach. Mikis Theodorakis, a Greek composer, set to music the *Ballad of Mauthausen,* written by Jacob Kambanelis, a Holocaust survivor. In the United States, Shalom Secunda composed *Yizkor,* and in Canada, Holocaust survivor Srol (Israel) Irving Gluck wrote his String Quartet no. 2.

In Israel, many composers have created works dealing with the Holocaust and its events. Besides those mentioned above, they include Yitzhak Edel's *Le-Zekher Kedoshei Polin* (In Memory of the Martyrs of Poland) and *Svitah Amamit le-Zekher Yahadut Polin* (Folk Suite in Memory of Polish Jewry); Oeden Partos's *Yizkor*; Yardena Alutin's *Golah Devuyah* (Diaspora in Mourning); Lev Kogan's *Tefilah le-Keren Solo* (Prayer for Horn Solo) and *Kaddish*; Leon Shidlovski's *Leil ha-Bedolah* (Night of the Broken Glass [KRISTALLNACHT]), *Tefillah* (Invocation), *Layla* (Night), and *Le-Hitorer Layla Ahar Layla* (Waking up Night after Night); Shabbetai Petroushka's *Ha-Lehavah ha-Bo'eret* (The Burning Flame); Yehuda Wohl's opera *Ha-Gader* (The Fence); Eddie Halpern's *Ha-Neder* (The Vow), *Akedah* (Sacrifice), *Li-Zekor ha-Kol* (To Remember It All), and the cantata KATYN; Eytan Avitzur and Moshe Hoch's *Yanosh Korchak vi-Yetomotav* (Janusz KORCZAK and His Orphans); Moshe Hoch's *Saloniki, Ir ve-Em be-Israel* (Salonika, a Center of Jewish Life); and Moshe Weiner's *Kantata le-Zekher Korbenot ha-Sho'ah* (Cantata in Memory of the Holocaust Victims) and *Rikud Yehudi* (A Jewish Dance), dedicated to the king of Denmark. An album of songs, *Efer ve-Avak* (Ashes and Dust), was recorded by Yehuda Poliker, the son of Holocaust survivors.

A Tel Aviv–based institution, Yad Letslilei Hashoa (The Institute for Conservation and Research of Jewish Music of the Holocaust), collects and publishes musical works and songs composed during the Holocaust.

BIBLIOGRAPHY

Bor, J. *The Terezin Requiem.* New York, 1978.

[Committee of Jews of Vilna in France.] *Dos Gezang fun Vilner Getto.* Paris, 1947.

Congress for Jewish Culture. *Lider fun Getto un Vidershtand.* New York, 1963.

Fater, I. *Yidishe Musik in Poyln: Tsvishn Bayde Velt Milkhomes.* Tel Aviv, 1970.

Feder, Z., ed. *Zamlung fun Katset un Geto Lider.* Bergen-Belsen, 1946.

Fenelon, F. *Playing for Time.* New York, 1976.

Frenkeil, Y. "Theater and Other Artistic Activities in the Lodz Ghetto, 1940–1944." *Bamah Drama Quarterly* 103 (1986): 12–42. (In Hebrew.)

Frenkeil, Y. "Theater and Other Artistic Activities in the Lodz Ghetto, 1940–1944, Part 2." *Bamah Drama Quarterly* 104 (1986): 28–60. (In Hebrew.)

Gelman, Y. "The Transformation of the Folk Song in the Ghettos and Camps." *Pirkey I'yun* (1985): 53–79. (In Hebrew.)

Kaczerginsky, S. *Lider fun di Getos un Lagern.* New York, 1948.

Kalisch, S. *Yes, We Sang!* New York, 1985.

Karas, J. *Music in Terezin.* New York, 1985.

Kohn, H. *30 Getto Lieder.* New York, 1960.

Manger, I., Y. Turkow, and M. Perenson, eds. *Yiddishe Theater tsvishen di Tsvei Velt Milkhomes, Poyl'in.* New York, 1968.

Mlotek, E., and M. Gottlieb, eds. *We Are Here.* New York, 1983.

Pups, R. *Dos Lid fun Getto.* Warsaw, 1962.
Rubin, R. *Voices of a People.* Philadelphia, 1979.
Spector, J. *Ghetto und Kazetlieder aus Lettland und Litauen.* Vienna, 1947.
Zylbercweig, Z. *Lexicon fun der Yiddishe Theater.* Vol. 5. Mexico City, 1967.

MOSHE HOCH, MARIAN FUCHS, GILA FLAM, and EDDIE HALPERN

MUSSERT, ANTON ADRIAAN (1894–1946), leader of the NATIONAAL SOCIALISTISCHE BEWEGING (National Socialist Movement) in the NETHERLANDS. Mussert was chief water engineer in the Utrecht district. He became secretary of a committee that opposed the signing of a Dutch-Belgian treaty (1925), believing that it would harm the Netherlands economically and compromise its national interest. His success in that position encouraged Mussert to enter politics. At first he supported the Liberal party, but when the fascist movements began to gain strength, he founded the National Socialist Movement, together with his friend Cornelis Van Geelkerken, on December 14, 1931.

Mussert did not fully identify with the German Nazi party, his aim being to bring about a fusion of nationalism and socialism. Although his platform contained many passages taken over from the German Nazi party, he excluded from it all the Nazi paragraphs affecting the Jews. Mussert was an able organizer, and although all the other nationalist movements in the Netherlands were very small, he succeeded in gaining the support of wide circles of the population, who saw in him a legitimate spokesman of the right wing in the country's political spectrum. Over the course of time, however, the radical wing of his party gained in strength; Mussert felt that he had to adapt to this trend and, among other things, subscribe to an increasingly extreme anti-Jewish position. After the KRISTALLNACHT pogrom in Germany (November 9–10, 1938), Mussert came up with a plan for a "Jewish national home" in the "three Guianas" (the Dutch, British, and French colonies in northern South America). The German Nazi leadership, however, did not react to his proposal.

The Nazi conquest of the Netherlands in May 1940 raised Mussert's hope that he would play a leading role in the New Europe. He submitted a proposal for the creation of a Greater Dutch State, which would incorporate Belgium and northern France, within a Union of German States. The Germans rejected his ideas and also ensured that Mussert and his movement did not have any influence in the administration of the Netherlands. They had no use for him, since he was now hated by the Dutch people; the Germans themselves did not trust him and also felt that he was not in full control of his movement. It was only in late 1942 that they permitted Mussert to claim the title of Leiter des Niederländischen Volkes (Leader of the Dutch People), which, however, was devoid of any practical content. The extremist wing of his party, which supported the incorporation of the Netherlands into Germany, sought to undermine Mussert's standing with the Germans. He disapproved of the enlistment of twenty-five thousand Dutch men into the Waffen-SS; he also did not favor the persecution of the Jews and tried to save the lives of some of his Jewish friends. He did not, however, have any power, and was forced to cooperate with the Germans.

Mussert was arrested when the war ended. He was put on trial for treason and collaboration with the enemy, sentenced to death, and executed.

BIBLIOGRAPHY

Hansen, E. "Fascism and Nazism in the Netherlands, 1929–1939." *European Studies Review* 11/3 (1981): 355–385.
Havenaar, R. *Verrader voor het vaderland: Een biografische schets van Anton Adriaan Mussert.* The Hague, 1978.
Het proces Mussert. The Hague, 1948.
Stokes, L. D. "Anton Mussert and the Nationaal-Socialistische Beweging der Nederlanden, 1931–1945." *History* 56/188 (1971): 387–407.

JOZEPH MICHMAN

MUSSOLINI, BENITO (1883–1945). Before World War I, Mussolini was a militant Socialist. During the war he was an anti-German interventionist, and after the war he founded and led the Fascist movement as Il Duce. In 1922 he became prime minister of

ITALY, and from 1943 to 1945 he headed the Italian Social Republic (Repubblica Sociale Italiana). Mussolini's attitude toward the Jews was inconsistent and mostly opportunistic, influenced by circumstances.

In 1908, Mussolini denounced rabbinical Judaism in an article on Nietzsche. However, his real target was Claudio Treves, the Jewish Socialist leader, whom Mussolini was to oust from the editorship of *Avanti*, the chief organ of the Italian Socialist party, in 1912. Among those converting the future Duce to a policy of interventionism and nationalism were the Jews Giuseppe Pontremoli, Ermanno Jarach, Elio Jona, and Cesare Sarfatti, and five Jews (Cesare Goldmann, Piero Jacchia, Riccardo Luzzatti, Eucardio Momigliano, and Enrico Rocca) were among the founders of the Fascist movement. Three other Jews, Gino Bolaffi, Bruno Mondolfo, and Duilio Sinigaglia, went down in history as "Fascist martyrs," having fallen in the Fascist cause before the March on Rome in 1922. Mussolini was also strongly influenced by two Jewish women, the Russian Angelica Balabanoff and the Italian Margherita Sarfatti.

The Fascist seizure of power on October 30, 1922, evoked a certain alarm among Italian Jews, owing partly to the enthusiasm aroused by the March on Rome among foreign antisemites. Mussolini hastened to reassure the Jews in an interview in November 1923 with the Chief Rabbi of Rome, Dr. Angelo Sacerdoti. From 1922 to 1936 the Duce's official attitude was summarily expressed in the phrase "The Jewish problem does not exist in Italy." Unofficially, however, he attacked "Jewish separatism" (with particular reference to Zionism), "Jewish Bolshevism," and "Jewish high finance." When, in 1933, the Italian Jews did not share the official enthusiasm for the triumph of "German fascism," Mussolini reacted by unleashing an antisemitic press campaign. The Ethiopian war (1935–1936) gave fresh impetus to the polemics against "international Jewry," and the rapproachement with Germany compelled Mussolini to reconsider his policy toward the Jews. At first he tried to solve the question by "Fascistizing" his Jewish subjects, but in 1938 he decided to adopt racial laws in order to oust the Jews from Italian public life. Until July 1943 the nature and extent of Fascist racial policy were determined by Mussolini; Hitler thought it wiser not to interfere. It was only after the Italian armistice (September 1943) that Heinrich HIMMLER's emissaries extended the "FINAL SOLUTION" to the German-occupied part of Italy, aided by the apparatus of Mussolini's Fascist puppet republic. At the end of the war, Mussolini attempted to flee the country but was caught and shot by Italian partisans.

BIBLIOGRAPHY

Fermi, L. *Mussolini.* Chicago, 1966.

Michaelis, M. *Mussolini and the Jews: German-Italian Relations and the Jewish Question in Italy, 1922–1945.* London, 1978.

MEIR MICHAELIS

Adolf Hitler visits Mussolini in Venice (June 14, 1934).

NAAMLOZE VENNOOTSCHAP. *See* N.V. Group.

NACHTIGALL BATTALION, Ukrainian military unit in the service of the Germans. At the end of 1940 and the beginning of 1941, the Germans, with the full support of the Ukrainian nationalist leaders, increased the numbers of Ukrainian youngsters mobilized into separate military units and paramilitary organizations. In this way the Ukrainian leaders hoped to promote their own political interests, pinning their hopes on the Germans in the anticipated war against the USSR. The Germans for their part wanted to exploit the Ukrainian nationalists to serve their own military aims in the east.

Against this background, the Germans established, at the beginning of 1941, the 700-man Ukrainian Legion. In May 1941 the legion was divided into two battalions named Nachtigall and Roland. The German military commander of Nachtigall was Albrecht Herzner, and the battalion's political control was in the hands of Professor Theodor Oberländer of the German military intelligence. The Ukrainian commander of this unit was Roman Shukhevych. After its establishment, Nachtigall was transferred to a training camp in Neuhammer, in Silesia.

When the Germans invaded the USSR on June 22, 1941, Nachtigall was sent to serve at the front in the area of Przemyśl. By June 30, Nachtigall had entered LVOV, together with some German units. The soldiers of the battalion participated, with the Germans and the Ukrainian mob in the city, in the riots and the killing of Jews that took place between June 30 and July 3. During those days, Jews were kidnapped in the streets of the city, brought to concentration centers in several prisons, and brutally killed. Four thousand of them were murdered during the four days of rioting. The pretext for carrying out this pogrom against the Jews of Lvov was the libel, maliciously spread by the Germans and the Ukrainians, that the Jews had taken part in the murder of political prisoners held by the Soviets prior to the retreat.

Many of the Ukrainian officers and soldiers of Nachtigall supported Stefan BANDERA's faction in the Ukrainian national movement (the ORHANIZATSYIA UKRAINSKYKH NATSIONALISTIV), and they were involved in the abortive attempt of the Ukrainian nationals, on July 1, 1941, to declare in Lvov the establishment of a Ukrainian state. The Germans crushed this attempt, and some believe that the involvement of members of the battalion in these events led to the unit's expulsion from Lvov on July 7 of that year and its dispatch to the eastern front. Nachtigall passed through ZOLOCHEV and TERNOPOL and reached the area of VINNITSA. On the way, members of the battalion took part in pogroms against Jews. Because soldiers of the battalion continued to be involved in activities promoting Ukrainian political objectives, in opposition to the German stand, the unit was removed from the UKRAINE. In October 1941, many of its members were attached to German military units engaged in suppressing partisans in Belorussia. On December 1 of that year, the battalion was finally disbanded. Some of its members joined Ukrainian auxiliary police units in the service of the Germans.

BIBLIOGRAPHY

Armstrong, J. A. *Ukrainian Nationalism, 1939–1945*. New York, 1955.

Szczeŝniak, A. B., and W. Z. Szota. *Droga do nikąd*. Warsaw, 1973.

AHARON WEISS

NACHT UND NEBEL ("Night and Fog"), term in a secret order, the *Nacht-und-Nebel-Erlass*, issued by Adolf Hitler on December 7, 1941. The order was signed by Wilhelm KEITEL, chief of staff of the Wehrmacht, and was also known as the *Keitel Erlass* (Keitel Order). It provided for the methods to be used in suppressing resistance movements in western European countries occupied by the Germans.

The immediate cause for issuing the order was the situation in occupied France, where, in the second half of 1941, after the German attack on the Soviet Union in June, resistance movement operations were constantly increasing. Keitel's objective was to deter the population in all of German-occupied western Europe from engaging in such underground operations, and for this purpose he ordered that actions directed at the Reich or the occupation authorities be suppressed by the severest possible terror methods. Underground activities were punishable by death, and with Keitel's order, the military courts could impose a death sentence without a unanimous decision, as had been required previously. The proceedings, including the execution of the sentence, had to be completed within eight days. If not condemned to death, the detainees, or at least the main "culprits" among them, had to be transferred to the Reich. No information whatsoever was to be given out concerning the detainees, and the prisoners themselves were not allowed to write to anyone. Prisoners arrested under this operation were to disappear in the "fog of the night" (*Nacht und Nebel*), and even their death in camps, detention barracks, or prison was not to be divulged.

Keitel gave the minister of justice, Otto THIERACK, instructions on the interpretation and implementation of the "Night and Fog" order, emphasizing that even a life sentence for anti-German activities would be regarded by Hitler as a sign of weakness. The Ministry of Justice did not raise any objection to being charged with implementing the punishments provided for in the order or to the guidelines it was given by the Wehrmacht General Staff. The order applied to France, Belgium, the Netherlands, Denmark, and Norway. In February 1942 special courts were set up to conduct the "Night and Fog" trials in the Reich: in Cologne, for persons arrested in France; in Dortmund (later Essen), for Belgium and the Netherlands; in Kiel, for Norway; and in Berlin, for all other areas to which the order applied. Up until September 1942, 262 cases were submitted to the Kiel court and 863 to Essen. The first central trial was held on September 30, 1942, the day on which the first death sentence was passed. By the end of April 1944, 2,014 cases had been registered with the military authorities, with 6,639 defendents. Of these, 807 cases were tried in courts and 1,793 defendents were sentenced to death in these trials.

In November 1943 the Allied bombing of cities in western and northern Germany forced Minister of Justice Thierack to transfer the operations of the "Night and Fog" special court in Cologne to a special court in Breslau (now Wrocław), attached to the federal courts in that city. As of the beginning of 1944, trials of persons from Belgium, the Netherlands, and northern France were transferred from Essen to Oppeln (now Opole). By April of that year the military authorities had transferred 1,273 cases, with 2,139 defendants, to Breslau; and 729 cases, with 4,048 defendants, to Oppeln. In Oppeln, 725 of the accused were sentenced to death; in Breslau, 473; and by the People's Court (*Volksgerichtshof*) in Berlin, 427. The (incomplete) data of the Ministry of Justice reveal that the largest number of "Night and Fog" death sentences—by guillotine—were carried out in Cologne, followed by Brandenburg, Dortmund, Munich, and Stadelheim. As a matter of principle the right of pardon was not applied to prisoners of Jewish origin or to Communists.

Women from France were first imprisoned in Gommern and, as of the fall of 1943, in Silesian prisons. The women's prison at Jauer (Frauenzuchthaus Jauer) also took in Belgian and Norwegian women who had been given long prison terms or death sentences by the courts in Breslau or by the People's Court in Berlin; eleven of the women who had been sentenced to death were later pardoned.

Only some of the "Night and Fog" prisoners held by the Germans were put to work in the German economy, in enterprises such as ammunition factories and sugar refineries. The death rate among the prisoners in the detention barracks and in the prisons was extremely high.

The Sicherheitspolizei (Security Police) made strenuous efforts to have the "Night and Fog" prisoners transferred to it and to take the task of implementing the "Night and Fog" order out of the hands of the military authorities and the special courts. By an order issued by the Wehrmacht General Staff in June 1943, "Night and Fog" prisoners who had been acquitted or who had served the sentences passed by the special courts in Cologne, Dortmund, Kiel, and Berlin were to be transferred to the GESTAPO. In January 1944, Minister of Justice Thierack issued his own (secret) order to hand such prisoners over to the Gestapo. Later, developments in the war situation, including the growing resistance operations in northern France after the Allied invasion, made a substantial impact on the proceedings regarding the "Night and Fog" prisoners. In September 1944 it was decided to hand over to the Gestapo all twenty-four thousand of the prisoners in this category being held at that time, irrespective of the current status of their case.

A Wehrmacht General Staff decree of September 24, 1944, brought to a "temporary" stop the trials by courts of the "Night and Fog" prisoners. In the following weeks, the prisoners were transferred from the prisons in which they were held to concentration camps, among them DACHAU, SACHSENHAUSEN, and GROSS-ROSEN. That October and November, women prisoners from Belgium and France were transferred from prisons in Silesia to the RAVENSBRÜCK concentration camp. Shortly before the Red Army crossed the borders of the Reich, the remaining "Night and Fog" prisoners were moved, under harsh winter conditions. DEATH MARCHES were now launched, taking the route from the Gross Strehlitz (now Strzelce Opolskie) prison and the Laband (now Labedy) camp to the BUCHENWALD concentration camp. This was also the route taken by the women prisoners from the Jauer (now Jawor) women's prison. The surviving "Night and Fog" prisoners were liberated in April and May 1945.

BIBLIOGRAPHY

De Martinière, J. *Le decret et la procédure Nacht und Nebel.* Orléans, 1981.

Jońca, K., and A. Konieczny. *Nuit et Brouillard: L'opération terroriste nazie 1941–1944.* Claviers, 1981.

KAROL JOŃCA

NAGYVÁRAD. *See* Oradea.

NARODOWE SIŁY ZBROJNE (National Armed Forces; NSZ), underground military organization in POLAND, nationalist and antisemitic in character. The NSZ came into being in September 1942, following splits in the right-wing nationalist Polish underground. In the summer of 1942 the Stronnictwo Narodowe (National Party), one of the four constituent political parties on which the POLISH GOVERNMENT-IN-EXILE was based, decided to place its military arm, the Narodowa Organizacja Wojskowa (National Military Organization), under the command of the ARMIA KRAJOWA (Home Army). This was ordered by the government-in-exile, in whose eyes the Armia Krajowa was the only recognized underground military formation. About half the members of the National Military Organization refused to accept the authority of the Armia Krajowa commander, and, together with the Związek Jaszczurczy (Salamander Union), the military arm of the extreme right-wing Obóz Narodowo-Radykalny (National-Radical Camp), formed the NSZ.

The first commander of the NSZ was Ignacy Oziewicz; he was followed by Tadeusz

Kurcjusz, Stanisław Nakoniecznikoff-Klukowski, and, finally, Stanisław Kasznica. The first operational order published by Oziewicz (whose code name was Czesław) stated in part: "The partisan movement can and will act with determination both to purge the area of revolutionary and criminal gangs and hostile minority formations, and to resort to counteraction, in self-defense, against punitive squads of the occupying power that are guilty of cruel oppressive measures."

That order laid down the policy of the organization, which in practice did little to fight the Nazi invader. It directed most of its efforts against the Polish leftist underground and the Soviet and Jewish partisan units, the last being the "minority formations" mentioned in the order. Hundreds of Jews who escaped from the ghettos and sought asylum among the Polish population were murdered by the NSZ.

At its maximum strength the NSZ had some seventy thousand members and was the second largest military underground organization after the Armia Krajowa. It published several underground newspapers, of which the most important were *Szaniec* (Fortress), *Agencja Narodowa* (National Agency), and *Walka* (The Struggle). These papers, especially *Szaniec*, the movement's principal organ, often published antisemitic articles, similar to those found in the Nazi press.

When Gen. Tadeusz BOR-KOMOROWSKI was appointed commander of the Armia Krajowa in the summer of 1943, he sought to induce the NSZ to join the forces under his command. He met with only partial success; in March 1944 a part of the NSZ, numbering some fifteen thousand members, accepted the authority of the Armia Krajowa command, but the majority refused to join. The NSZ commander at the time, Nakoniecznikoff-Klukowski, was assassinated by his associates for agreeing to incorporate the movement into the Armia Krajowa. In the final days of the Nazi occupation, various units of the NSZ tried to retreat from Poland into Germany. Only one, the Brygada Świętokrzyska (the largest unit, with 1,000 men), succeeded in doing so. In coordination with the German army, it withdrew from Poland to Czechoslovakia and from there to Germany. After the liberation of Poland, various NSZ groups took up an underground struggle against the new regime; they also continued the killing of Jewish survivors of the Holocaust.

BIBLIOGRAPHY

Korbonski, S. *The Polish Underground State: A Guide to the Underground, 1939–1945.* New York, 1981.

SHMUEL KRAKOWSKI

NATIONAAL SOCIALISTISCHE BEWEGING

(National Socialist Movement; NSB), Nazi movement in the NETHERLANDS, founded in 1931. Several small fascist organizations emerged in the Netherlands in the 1930s, but did not last long; many people, however, were impressed by the success achieved by fascist dictators and movements advocating dictatorship, mainly those in Italy and Germany. The NSB was established at the end of 1931 by Anton Adriaan MUSSERT, on the basis of a platform that drew upon the German Nazi party's 1931 program, with the exclusion of all paragraphs referring to Jews.

The NSB had a modest start, its adherents coming mainly from the middle class. As time went on, however, the party managed to penetrate the lower classes, especially after Hitler's rise to power in Germany in 1933, and its membership grew rapidly, from 21,000 in 1934 to 33,000 in 1935 and 52,000 in 1936. In the 1935 elections to the provincial parliaments, the NSB scored its first notable success, receiving 8 percent of the vote (300,000 votes); in some of the large cities its percentage was even higher (10 percent in Utrecht and Amsterdam and 12 percent in The Hague). The NSB success shocked the traditional political parties and also the Catholic church, the latter because it appeared that the Dutch Nazi movement had made its deepest penetration in predominantly Catholic areas. For the next elections, all the other parties joined in a common propaganda effort against the NSB, and the Catholic church also took effective measures against Catholics who had joined the Nazi party. In the 1937 elections to the Lower

House, the NSB suffered a defeat, receiving only 4.2 percent of the turnout (170,000 votes).

Its defeat in the polls did not put an end to the NSB, but rather drove it to adopt even more extreme positions, on the German National Socialist model, expressed primarily on the subject of the Jews. Previously, Mussert had not formulated any stand on the Jews, but in a pamphlet he published in 1935, "Topical Issues," he differentiated among three groups of Jews: (1) Dutch nationalists; (2) religious Jews; (3) Jews who did not share Dutch nationalism. Only the first group was entitled to full civil rights. In 1936 the NSB position on the Jews was further sharpened, owing to the influence of antisemitic circles in the party, whose leading spokesman was Meinoud Marinus Rost van Tonningen, an economist who had close contacts with the Nazi leadership in Germany. Van Tonningen was appointed editor of the NSB organ. In a pamphlet that Mussert published in 1937, he claimed that the Jews were in control in the Netherlands, a state of affairs that must be put to an end. In 1938, Jews were excluded from membership in the NSB.

When the Germans occupied the Netherlands and established a German administration there, Mussert hoped to be appointed prime minister, but this did not happen. Members of his movement had to content themselves with posts such as that of mayor, secretary-general of a government department, and the like, as well as benefits such as the award of businesses that had been confiscated from their Jewish owners. Much to Mussert's displeasure, there was a growing trend in the party in favor of annexing the Netherlands to the German Reich.

Throughout the German occupation NSB members took an active role in the German measures against the Jews, both in the posts they held in the Dutch government and police, and by keeping an eye on the Jews and informing on them to the Germans. At the beginning of 1941, NSB members launched a countrywide campaign of violence against Jews, centering on Amsterdam, and in the ensuing street fighting they also clashed with resistance groups.

When the war was over the NSB leaders were tried and given sentences of various lengths; Mussert was sentenced to death and executed.

BIBLIOGRAPHY

De Jong, L. *Het Koninkrijk der Nederlanden tijdens de Tweede Wereldoorlog*. Vols. 1–13. The Hague, 1969–1988.

De Jong, L. *Het Nationaal Socialisme in Nederland*. The Hague, 1968.

Documents of the Persecution of Dutch Jewry. Amsterdam, 1969.

Meijers, J. *Mussert: Een Politiek Leven*. Amsterdam, 1984.

Schoffer, J. *Het nationaal-socialistische beeld van de geschiedenis der Nederlanden*. Arnhem, 1956.

JOZEPH MICHMAN

NATIONAL ARMED FORCES. *See* Narodowe Siły Zbrojne.

NATIONAL SOCIALISM (Nazism; NS), German political movement led by Adolf HITLER. In combined form, the two concepts of "national" and "social" had become fashionable among Christian Socialist and *völkisch*-antisemitic movements before 1914, in Germany (Adolf Stoecker) and Austria (Karl Lueger, Georg von Schönerer). This was taken up by the Deutsche Arbeiterpartei (German Workers' Party), founded in Munich in 1919. A year later it added *Nationalsozialistische* to its name and thus became the Nationalsozialistische Deutsche Arbeiterpartei (NSDAP), the party that, under Hitler's leadership, was to pave the way for a "German dictatorship" and play a role of fateful consequence in world history (*see* NAZI PARTY).

Manifestations of *völkisch* antisemitism and pan-Germanism—two basic elements of the ideology that the NSDAP proclaimed at its inception—had appeared in Germany long before World War I. The works of Paul de Lagarde, for example, already contained, in unmistakable and blatant form, all the ingredients of future Nazi ideology: the myth of blood and soil, the "master race" idea, and the utopian vision of Germany conquering LEBENSRAUM ("living space") in the east and "Germanizing" the conquered area. In Lagarde's writings, moreover, these ideas are anchored in an antiliberal, anti-Marxist, and pseudoreligious chauvinistic nationalism. Many things had to happen, however, before such precursors of Nazism could gain a broad response in Germany and a dynamic, aggressive, and defiant German nationalism could emerge: World War I, which shattered the belief in the orderly progress of civilization and shook to its foundations the traditional law-and-order-based bourgeois society; the defeat in the war; and the humiliating "dictate" of Versailles. The returning war veterans in particular responded to the call, and were ready to take to the streets and resort to extralegal acts—indeed, to violence—to defend national interests in the east (in the Freikorps) and to "save" the country from Marxist coups. This trend was given further impetus by the emerging DOLCHSTOSSLEGENDE ("stab-in-the-back" myth) and the abortive attempt in Munich to set up a leftist socialist Soviet republic, an attempt in which several Jewish intellectuals played a prominent role. A climate was created that called for revenge against the "November criminals" and other, reputedly Jewish, "wire-pullers," who were blamed for the tragedy that had overtaken Germany.

In 1921 Hitler, after a brief career as party propagandist, became the undisputed Führer (leader) of the NSDAP and rapidly transformed the party into the instrument of his political will and spectacular demagogic gifts. Before 1923, the NSDAP was largely restricted to Bavaria. Within a short period, by the use of sensational forms of political agitation—the deliberate provocation of clashes by the party's SA (Sturmabteilung; Storm Troopers) and a variety of methods patterned after the Communists and the Fascists (such as street marches, mass rallics, and punitive expeditions)—the NSDAP acquired the nimbus of an extraordinarily aggressive nationalist movement. At this time the NSDAP had an especially profound effect on the very large number of *völkisch* and patriotic organizations in Bavaria, which in the early 1920s had coalesced into the counterrevolutionary Ordnungszelle (Order Unit). An immediate result was that Hitler became the political leader of an abortive attempt to overthrow the Weimar Republic (the *Hitler-Putsch,* also known as the Munich Beer-Hall Putsch, of November 8 and 9, 1923). The NSDAP was outlawed—for a while—and Hitler was incarcerated for nine months, in Landsberg. Shortly after his release, the NSDAP was revived (February 1925) and spread from Bavaria to western and northern Germany. Under the influence of the brothers Gregor and Otto Strasser, as well as of the young Joseph GOEBBELS, the party took on the character of a pronounced antibourgeois, national revolutionary, and social revolutionary movement. This "social" side, however, was of short duration: Hitler opposed socialism, "national" or otherwise, and his declared belief in it was no more than rhetoric. His basic position was that of Social Darwinism, which projects into human society Darwin's theory of the survival of the fittest.

In the short period in which the Weimar Republic managed to achieve a degree of relative normalcy (1925 to 1928), the NSDAP did not gain more than marginal significance as an extremist splinter party, despite its efforts to obtain influence and power by legal means and participation in elections. In the 1928 Reichstag elections it received less than 3 percent of the vote. It was in this period that the National Socialist "bible," Hitler's MEIN KAMPF (My Struggle), was published. This was essentially a waiting period, which the NSDAP used to consolidate its organizational strength, absorbing into its ranks other *völkisch* groups and raising a core of fanatical *"alte Kämpfer"* ("old fighters") who would always be on call. The "old fighters" remained the kernel of the NSDAP even when it became a mass movement in the wake of the economic depression of 1929 and 1930. By 1932 it had 800,000 members and 14 million voters, and had attracted to its ranks very many ideologically more moderate elements, including Young Conservatives and Christian Socialists.

Another precondition for the rise of the NSDAP was the discrepancy that had developed, ever since the unification of the country by Otto von Bismarck in 1871, between its technical and material progress—which had made Germany into a highly industrialized society—and the backwardness of its political institutions. The model for these institutions had been the Prussian military monarchy, and they had been perpetuated by the ruling classes, which were largely antiliberal, especially in the Protestant areas. These classes retained strong positions under the Weimar Republic, especially in the Reichswehr (the armed forces), the large landholders' lobby, and the circle of Paul von HINDENBURG, the former imperial general field marshal, who in 1925 had been elected president of the republic. These were the forces that persuaded Hindenburg to use his emergency powers to replace the democratically elected parliament-based cabinet by appointing "presidential" cabinets (under Heinrich Brüning, Franz von PAPEN, and Kurt von Schleicher), all of whom belonged to the right wing of the political spectrum. Hindenburg's action had resulted from the inability of the democratic cabinets to take the decisions necessitated by the economic crisis, but the real objective was to replace the democratic form of government, based on political parties, with an authoritarian regime, and ultimately, if at all possible, to reinstate the monarchy. A de facto constitutional move to the right and the unpopular austerity measures that Brüning was forced to impose upon the country enabled the NSDAP, in a series of spectacular election campaigns from 1930 to 1933, to become the largest political party in the country (37 percent in the July 1932 elections). Facilitating the Nazis' rise were the conservative elite groups, which lent their support to the NSDAP while underestimating its real nature and potential. For many Germans, one has to assume, Hitler's leadership seemed to hold out greater promise in the crisis than either the democratic-party state or the authoritarian-style regime as practiced by Brüning and von Papen.

From the sociological and socio-psychological aspect, the attraction that National Socialism exercised had its primary source in the national and social frustrations experienced by broad sectors of the German middle class, especially the younger generation. The 1848 bourgeois revolution had failed, and even the Weimar Republic was unable to meet the still outstanding need for greater political and social participation, because of inflation and the global economic crisis. Instead, under the impact of the merciless exploitation of Germany by the victorious powers (through reparation payments) and the particularly harsh effect that the economic crisis had on Germany, the various national and social depressions fed on one another, creating the ideal breeding ground for Nazi agitation and attracting large numbers of the jobless young to the militant NSDAP fighting organizations. Hitler, by disseminating stereotypical enemy images ("Jew-Republic," "Jewish Marxism," "Culture-Bolshevism," and so on), by holding out the promise of a "people's community" (*Volksgemeinschaft*), and with the help of the Nazi movement's appeal of freshness and power, was able to gain the allegiance of the same young bourgeois generation that had withheld it from the "dreary" Weimar Republic, and to enlist it as a dedicated and dynamic force in Nazism.

Additional peculiarly German prerequisites for the triumph of Nazism were the comparatively strong religious and social contrasts, the parochial divisions, and the great regional differences in social structure and political and cultural traditions. This lack of national homogeneity had prevented a truly national society from emerging in Germany even when the country was united into a single Reich. As a result, the practically permanent crisis of the Weimar period created an exaggerated demand for national integration, a demand to which only Hitler, with his beguiling rhetoric, could address himself adequately. It was this socio-psychological pathology that, to the astonishment of the outside world, persuaded large parts of the educated German bourgeoisie, at a critical point in the nation's history (which turned out to be the end of the Weimar Republic), to commit themselves to an irrational, almost religious belief in the Führer. After the Nazi takeover, this blind belief, superbly molded by Goebbels's propaganda, was to become the Nazis' major instrument for rallying the country under its banner.

It should be borne in mind, however, that the support the Nazis achieved was never large enough to enable them to gain an absolute majority in the elections, so long as these were free and democratic. The Nazis owed their rise to power on January 30, 1933, to the intrigues of the conservative "kingmakers," primarily von Papen, who, in order to obtain Nazi participation in an authoritarian regime, were now ready to pay for it the price of making Hitler chancellor, and had finally succeeded in overcoming Hindenburg's objections to the "Bohemian corporal." In the coalition cabinet that was now formed, Hitler and the handful of other Nazis, who became cabinet ministers, easily asserted themselves over their conservative partners and took power into their own hands. The major role in this process was played by Hermann GÖRING and Wilhelm FRICK, Prussian minister of the interior and Reich minister of the interior, respectively. The Reichstag fire of February 27, 1933, which the Nazis claimed was the signal for a planned Communist uprising, served them as a pretext for suspending the existing constitutional guarantees. The next step was to outlaw the Communists and some of the Social Democrats. Next, concentration camps were established, as permanent institutions for the internment of political opponents. Through combined pressure from below (by its paramilitary organizations) and above (by the police), the Nazis within a few months succeeded in forcing the remaining non-Nazi political parties out of existence and bringing the state governments and major organizations into line, in a process of *Gleichschaltung* (coordination under Nazism). By means of new Nazi-directed mass organizations, such as the Deutsche Arbeitsfront (German Labor Front), the Reichsnährstand (Reich Food Estate, encompassing agricultural production, marketing, and processing), and the Reichskulturkammer (Reich Cultural Affairs Office), as well as the many party divisions and Nazi professional societies, a close-meshed system of totalitarian control and mobilization came into being.

In the spring of 1934 Hitler became concerned about his own position, during a difficult phase both in foreign relations and on the local scene, marked by internal party quarrels. His remedy was to stage a mass purge on June 30 with the support of the Reichswehr, Himmler's SS, and Göring's Prussian police, in which the SA chief, Ernst RÖHM, several regional SA commanders, and a whole range of other rivals and conservative adversaries of Hitler, including Gregor Strasser and General von Schleicher, were murdered. This action was a clear demonstration of the criminal energy that drove Hitler and the criminal nature of the Nazi regime. It was followed by yet another action designed to reinforce Hitler's position as the undisputed leader, when, upon Hindenburg's death on August 2, 1934, Hitler also assumed the functions of head of state.

That initial revolutionary phase of 1933 and 1934 was succeeded by a quiet period, marked by Nazi consolidation of power and a steady flow of achievements, at home and abroad, that also raised the regime's prestige in the world. The economic crisis and unemployment were brought to an end, Germany was no longer isolated, and it unilaterally restored its sovereignty with regard to the country's military affairs. In this period, the conservative partners of the regime still retained some influence and were able to preserve a degree of legality and moderation in the Nazi use of force. But this moderate phase came to an end in 1938, at the latest, following the sensational foreign-policy successes of that year—the annexation of Austria and of the Sudetenland. Hitler could now call himself Führer of the "Greater German Reich," and there was no restraining his hubris. A new Nazi activism was set in motion, accompanied by the removal of any remaining conservative influences, in the economy (Hjalmar SCHACHT), foreign affairs (Konstantin von NEURATH), and the armed forces (generals Werner von BLOMBERG and Werner von Fritsch); and by the ascendancy of individuals and organizations under Hitler's immediate control. This development was directly linked to increasingly urgent demands to achieve more of the goals of Nazi ideology, and to renew anti-Jewish manifestations and other forms of hatred. The orgy of violence on KRISTALLNACHT (November 8–9, 1938) was an unmistakable sign of this new radicalization of the Nazi system. Embodying that system in its more radical form were the SS—the "Blackshirt" order built by Heinrich HIMMLER—and the Sicherheitspolizei (Security Police) and SD (Sicherheitsdienst; Security Service). It was in the SS, in particular, that men were bred to carry out even the most inhuman orders without hesitation and with utter callousness, and were taught that such behavior was an expression of courage and heroism. In 1939 all the state and party police, as well as the intelligence organizations, were amalgamated into a single body, the REICHSSICHERHEITSHAUPTAMT (Reich Security Main Office; RSHA), headed by Reinhard HEYDRICH.

For Hitler, the war that he unleashed in 1939 was not only a means of realizing the Nazi dream of the German master race's empire in eastern Europe. The legal vacuum created by the war and the opportunity the war provided for mass killing were used by the Nazi leaders to rid themselves of any inhibitions they might still have had left in the pursuit of their racist, Social Darwinist, and *völkisch*-political aims. This was evidenced by the EUTHANASIA PROGRAM (the killing of mental patients), the destruction of the Polish intelligentsia, the liquidation of Soviet commissars, and, above all, the deportation of the Jews, ending in their extermination. The extraordinary powers wielded by the Nazis and the Nazi police in the occupied eastern territories made it possible to put into operation in these territories, especially in Poland, the secluded extermination camps where the "FINAL SOLUTION" of the "Jewish question" was carried out: AUSCHWITZ, TREBLINKA, BEŁŻEC, SOBIBÓR, and others—placenames that have been burned for all time into the moral memory of mankind.

A tremendous capability for effort and accomplishment on the one hand, and on the other (especially as personified by Hitler) a destructive and finally self-destructive drive—these are the two sides of National Socialism, contradicting each other and yet belonging together. It was only when the fortunes of war took a sharp turn in 1943 (after STALINGRAD) that the Nazi regime began to crumble and Hitler's nimbus, too, began to dim. The suggestive power that National Socialism exercised over large parts of the German population was linked to Hitler as a person, far more than to the content of Nazi ideology, as was demonstrated by the reaction to the abortive attempt on Hitler's life on July 20, 1944. When Hitler took his own life on April 30, 1945, he also, for all practical purposes, extinguished the existence of National Socialism. Without Hitler, and in the face of the total fiasco of his policies, National Socialism disappeared from the public scene in Germany almost overnight, much to the astonishment of contemporary observers in other parts of the world.

BIBLIOGRAPHY

Bracher, K. D. *The Age of Ideologies: A History of Political Thought in the Twentieth Century.* London, 1984.

Bracher, K. D. *The German Dictatorship: The Origins, Structure, and Effects of National Socialism.* New York, 1970.

Broszat, M. *German National Socialism, 1919–1945.* Santa Barbara, Calif., 1966.

Hitler, A. *Mein Kampf.* London, 1979.

Jäckel, E. *Hitler's Weltanschauung: A Blueprint for Power.* Middletown, Conn., 1972.

Mosse, G. L. *The Crisis of German Ideology.* New York, 1964.

Mosse, G. L. *Nazism: A Historical and Comparative Analysis of National Socialism.* Oxford, 1978.

Neumann, F. *Behemoth: The Structure and Practice of National Socialism.* New York, 1961.

Nolte, E. *Three Faces of Fascism: Action Française, Italian Fascism, and National Socialism.* New York, 1969.

MARTIN BROSZAT

NATIONAL SOCIALIST MOVEMENT IN THE NETHERLANDS. *See* Nationaal Socialistische Beweging.

NATZWEILER-STRUTHOF, a concentration camp near the town of Natzweiler, 31 miles (50 km) south of Strasbourg, on a hill in the Vosges Mountains. One of the smallest concentration camps, it was apparently set up after Albert SPEER had been on an inspection tour of recently occupied FRANCE and had noted the presence of granite deposits in the Natzweiler area. The Deutsche Erd- und Steinwerke GmbH (German Earth and Stone Works Ltd.) promptly reacted to Speer's observations, and by the fall of 1940 had launched a project to quarry the granite, with the work to be done by prisoners. The first batch of prisoners, 300 German nationals, arrived on the site in May 1941. At that

A view of the Natzweiler-Struthof camp through the barbed wire after it was disbanded in September 1944. [CICR Archives]

time, construction of the camp had not been completed, and the prisoners were assigned temporary housing in the former Hotel Struthof (hence the second part of the camp's name). The number of prisoners increased at a slow pace, compared to the situation in other concentration camps, and it was only on August 15, 1942, that Natzweiler became available for routine REICHSSICHERHEITSHAUPTAMT (Reich Security Main Office; RSHA) postings of prisoners.

By the end of 1943, the prisoners in the main camp numbered two thousand. Most were employed in arms production, and at no time were more than five hundred prisoners put to work in the quarries, a project that turned out to be costly. In the summer of that year several sheds were erected in the quarry area, serving as workshops in which prisoners were assigned to overhaul Junkers aircraft engines. In the same area, deep tunnels were made underground to provide space for subterranean factories that would be safe from air attacks.

The Natzweiler camp was expanded in 1944, as part of the efforts made by Nazi leaders in charge of economic affairs to relocate vital armaments plants to subterranean facilities. Natzweiler also had attached to it new satellite camps on Reich soil, mainly in Baden-Württemberg. One of these camps was in Neckarelz, where an existing gypsum mine was converted to an intricate tunnel system into which Daimler-Benz Aircraft moved its engine plant from the Berlin area, in a joint project undertaken by Daimler-Benz, the Natzweiler camp, and the Ministry of Armaments. Another satellite was Leonberg, near Stuttgart, where a disused autobahn tunnel was put at the disposal of the Messerschmitt Aircraft Company. When it went into operation in the spring of 1944, Leonberg started out with fifteen hundred prisoners, their number rising to three thousand within a year.

Yet another satellite was the Schörzingen camp, established in February 1944 for extracting crude oil from oil shale, one of the Nazi regime's desperate last-minute efforts to recoup the losses of raw materials caused by the ongoing retreat from the east and by bombing from the air. At the end of 1944, more than one thousand prisoners were working in Schörzingen, and the plan was to bring in another four thousand.

The total number of prisoners in the Natzweiler satellites in October 1944 was nineteen thousand. In Natzweiler itself the number had risen to between seven thousand and eight thousand. During the course of 1944, members of the French Résistance were among the prisoners brought to Natzweiler; most of them were killed on arrival. In a special category were the so-called NN (NACHT UND NEBEL) prisoners, selected by the SS for road construction and work in the quarries, where conditions were at their worst. An RSHA order of September 24, 1944, had decreed that "all Germanic NN prisoners" were to be transferred to Natzweiler. The mortality rate was exceptionally high, owing to the harsh working conditions and the harassment of these prisoners. Statistical data, however, are not available.

In August 1943 a gas chamber was constructed in Natzweiler, in one of the buildings that had formed part of the hotel compound. The contractors for the project, Waffen-SS Natzweiler, left behind a rare document in which, contrary to the coded terminology generally employed by the Nazis, specific mention was made of "the construction of a gas chamber at Struthof." This clear language appears in an invoice that the SS sent to the Strasbourg University Institute of Anatomy, charging it 236.08 reichsmarks for the job. It was for the skeleton collection of the director of that institute, Professor August Hirt, that at least one hundred and thirty prisoners were transferred from AUSCHWITZ to be killed in the Natzweiler gas chamber (*see* AHNENERBE). Most of these prisoners were Jews. Another member of the Strasbourg University faculty, Professor Otto Bickenbach, also availed himself of the Natzweiler gas chamber, to conduct experiments on prisoners with antidotes of phosgene, a poisonous gas. The victims were GYPSIES who had been transferred from Auschwitz the previous year to serve as human guinea pigs for SS doctors experimenting with antityphus injections.

The main camp was disbanded in August and September of 1944, but most of the satellites were evacuated only in March 1945. The prisoners were sent on DEATH MARCHES, in the general direction of DACHAU.

In 1989 a memorial plaque was placed on the wall of the Natzweiler-Struthof crematorium in memory of the Jews who were put to death at the camp.

[*See also* Appendix, Volume 4.]

BIBLIOGRAPHY

Webb, A. M., ed. *The Natzweiler Trial.* London, 1949.

FALK PINGEL

NAZI ANTISEMITIC FILMS. *See* Films, Nazi Antisemitic.

NAZI-DEUTSCH. *See* Sprachregelung.

NAZI DOCTORS. *See* Physicians, Nazi.

NAZI PARTY (Nationalsozialistische Deutsche Arbeiterpartei, or National Socialist German Workers' Party; NSDAP). Founded on January 5, 1919, the Nazi party had its origins in the Politischer Arbeiterzirkel (Political Workers' Circle), a small right-wing group that met beginning in November 1918 under the leadership of Anton Drexler, a locksmith at the locomotive works in Munich, and Karl Harrer, a racist reporter and member of the *völkisch*-mystical Thule Society. A rabid antisemitism characterized its meetings. In 1919, under Drexler, this circle became the Deutsche Arbeiterpartei (German Workers' Party), and its foundation by Drexler marked the beginning of the development of politically organized NATIONAL SOCIALISM. In early 1920 it was renamed the Nationalsozialistische Deutsche Arbeiterpartei. Adolf HITLER joined the party on September 12, 1919, becoming its leader in 1921. As a result of his failed putsch in Munich on November 9, 1923, the party was banned, with the ban lasting until February 27, 1925. Refounded on that day, it remained in existence until after Germany's defeat in World War II, when it was declared illegal by the Allies on September 20, 1945.

The Nazi party was characterized by a centralist and authoritarian structure based on the FÜHRERPRINZIP (leadership principle). At its head stood the Führer (leader), Hitler, beneath him the Führer's deputy. Organizationally, the party was run by eighteen *Reichsleiter* (the highest-ranking party officials, most of whom also held ministerial and administrative posts), and territorially by thirty-two *Gauleiter* (the highest-ranking NSDAP officials below the *Reichsleiter*). Its affiliated formations (*Gliederungen*) included the SA (Sturmabteilung; Storm Troopers), the SS, and the HITLERJUGEND, and its unions (*Verbände*) included the Deutsche Arbeitsfront (German Labor Front), and the NS Lehrerbund (National Socialist Teachers' Association). The diffuse organization intensified the harsh rivalry among the Nazi functionaries that was characteristic of the regime, while enabling Hitler to reserve all the main decisions to himself.

In the elections of 1924 the Nazi party obtained only 3 percent of the votes. Its dramatic expansion began in the 1930s, when its parliamentary power grew steadily from 18.3 percent in 1930 to 37.4 percent in 1932 and 43.9 percent in the elections of March 5, 1933. Its membership increased from some 6,000 in 1922 to 8.5 million in 1945. Much of the party's popularity during the *Kampfzeit* (the period of struggle) was based on mass mobilization: rallies, demonstrations, and other forms of political expression; under Nazi rule during the 1930s, the yearly Nuremberg party rallies became the public center of Germany's political life.

The party's platform of twenty-five objectives, published in 1920, was formulated by Hitler and Drexler and included militaristic, nationalistic, social, economic, and antisemitic clauses. Point 4 of the party program declared that only a member of the *Volk* could be a citizen of the state. Only a person of German blood, regardless of religious affiliation, could be a member of the *Volk*. Consequently, no Jew could be a *Volksgenosse* (member of the nation). Other points stated that Jews should be treated as foreigners; that persons who were not German "by race" should be prohibited from publishing German newspapers; that Jews should not hold public office and should be expelled from the Reich if it proved impossible to sustain and create employment for the entire population of the state; that non-Germans (that is, Jews) should be denied any further immigration into Germany; and that those who had entered after August 2, 1914, should be expelled.

[*See also* Auslandsorganisation der NSDAP.]

BIBLIOGRAPHY

Deuerlein, E., ed. *Der Aufstieg der NSDAP in Augenzeugenberichten.* Munich, 1974.

Orlow, D. *The History of the Nazi Party.* 2 vols. Pittsburgh, 1969, 1973.

Phelps, R. H. "Hitler and the Deutsche Arbeiterpartei." *American Historical Review* 68 (1963): 974–986.

DAVID BANKIER

NAZI PROPAGANDA. *See* Propaganda, Nazi.

NAZISM. *See* National Socialism.

NAZI-SOVIET PACT, an agreement between the Soviet Union and Nazi Germany that was signed on the eve of World War II. On August 14, 1939, German Foreign Minister Joachim von RIBBENTROP informed the Soviet government that Germany was prepared to improve its relations with the Soviet Union and that he was willing to go to Moscow. Speedy negotiations took place, in which the Soviet side was represented by the Soviet foreign minister, Viacheslav MOLOTOV. The two countries signed two agreements: one dealing with economic relations, and the other a nonaggression pact that also divided eastern Europe into two spheres of interest, of Germany and the Soviet Union, respectively.

The economic agreement, signed on August 19, 1939, provided for an exchange of goods in the value of 200 million reichsmarks, with Germany committing itself to sell equipment, machinery, and manufactured goods, especially chemical and electrical supplies and items for oil production and transportation. For its part, the Soviet Union undertook to make available to Germany cereals and other food products, as well as raw materials.

Four days later, on August 23, Ribbentrop went to Moscow, and the nonaggression pact was signed that same day. Both sides undertook to refrain from attacking the other and from helping another side to attack either party; they also agreed that any differences between them would be settled in an amicable manner. The pact was to be in force for ten years. Ribbentrop signed on behalf of Germany, and Molotov on behalf of the Soviet Union; thus, the agreement is often called the Ribbentrop-Molotov Pact.

The pact had a secret protocal attached to it, dealing with the delineation of respective spheres of interest. The Baltic states (Estonia, Latvia, and Lithuania) were recognized as part of the Soviet sphere, with Lithuania's claim to Vilna acknowledged by the Germans; Bessarabia too was declared to be in the Soviet sphere. Poland was to be divided between the two countries, by a line consisting

NAZI-SOVIET PACT Partition of Poland September 28, 1939

of the Narew, Vistula, and San rivers. Both sides agreed that Poland should remain independent, but its borders were to be determined at a later stage.

The Nazi-Soviet Pact and its secret protocol were signed a week before the outbreak of the German-Polish war (September 1, 1939), and as a result Poland came to be divided between the two signatories, with the eastern part (consisting of Belorussia and the western Ukraine) annexed to the Soviet Union and the other parts retained by Germany. In 1940 the Soviet Union also annexed the Baltic states, as well as Bessarabia and northern Bukovina. The pact was in force until the Germans invaded Soviet territory, on June 22, 1941.

BIBLIOGRAPHY

Carr, E. H. *German-Soviet Relations between the Two World Wars.* Baltimore, 1951.

Documents on German Foreign Policy. Series D, vol. 7. London, 1956. See pages 142–147 and 245–247.

Gay, G. *Molotov: Author of the Soviet-Nazi Pact.* London, 1940.

Viacheslav Molotov, Soviet foreign minister (seated), signing the Nazi-Soviet Pact in Moscow on August 13, 1939. Joseph Stalin (second from right) and German foreign minister Joachim von Ribbentrop (third from right) look on.

Read, A., and D. Fisher. *The Deadly Embrace: Hitler, Stalin, and the Nazi-Soviet Pact, 1939–1941*. New York, 1988.

Weinberg, G. L. *Germany and the Soviet Union, 1939–1941*. Leiden, 1954.

SHMUEL SPECTOR

NAZI WAR CRIMINALS. *See* Trials of War Criminals; *see also under* War Criminals.

NEBE, ARTHUR (1894–1945), officer in the Reich criminal police. Nebe's father was a teacher in Berlin, and his mother was of Huguenot origin. Wishing to be a theologian, Nebe learned Hebrew. In World War I he volunteered for the army; he was promoted to the rank of second lieutenant in 1916, and in March 1920 he was discharged from the army as a regimental adjutant in the engineering corps, with the rank of lieutenant. Nebe then studied law and legal medicine at Berlin University, and in April 1920 his candidacy to the criminal police was accepted. On July 1, 1923, despite initially failing the examination, he was appointed commander of the criminal police, thanks to the intervention of two officers, one of whom was Dr. Bernhard Weiss, deputy commandant of the Berlin police.

After World War I the criminal police in Prussia were not highly regarded, and the Nazi press, led by Joseph GOEBBELS, began to mock Weiss, who was of Jewish origin. Nebe, now dealing mainly with murder and drug cases, also made fun of Weiss behind his back. In June 1931 Nebe joined the SS, in July the Nazi party, and in November the SA (Sturmabteilung; Storm Troopers); in 1932 he formed Nazi party groups among the Berlin criminal-police officers. A racist and nationalist career officer who joined the Nazis only after their impressive victories in the elections, Nebe tried to create the impression that he had always been an antisemite, and he took advantage of the political situation in order to advance to the top of the operative branch of the state police.

On April 1, 1933, Nebe, who was the SS liaison man in the eastern zone under the command of Kurt DALUEGE, was taken to serve in the Gestapo, with the rank of *Kriminalrat* (criminal-police commissar). About six months later, on October 1, he was promoted to the rank of *Regierungsrat* (government adviser), and two months later to the rank of *Oberregierungsrat* (chief government adviser). In 1936 Nebe rose to the rank of SS-*Sturmbannführer*, and on June 30, 1937, to *Reichskriminaldirektor* (director of the Reich criminal police), thus becoming head of the united police (Kripo) of all Germany. In 1938 he rose to the rank of SS-*Obersturmbannführer*, and then to that of SS-*Standartenführer*. On Hitler's fiftieth birthday (April 20, 1939), he was made an SS-*Oberführer*.

Nebe was in contact with members of the German opposition movement, including Ludwig Beck and, later, Hans Oster. After the Blomberg-Fritsch crisis in January and February 1938 (which resulted in the dismissal of Minister of War Werner von BLOMBERG and Chief of the General Staff Werner von Fritsch, and the assuming of these offices by Hitler), Nebe became one of the most important informers for the opposition movement. He retained this contact through his friend Hans Bernd Gisevius, who served in the Gestapo, the Ministry of the Interior, and the consular service in Switzerland, and who in 1943 and 1944 was an informer for the Americans. On December 14, 1940, Nebe rose to the rank of *Generalmajor der Polizei*, and about two weeks later, to that of *Brigadeführer* in the SS.

Nebe volunteered for the campaign against the Soviet Union as a participant in the EINSATZGRUPPEN, and in August 1941 he commanded Einsatzgruppe B on the central front. The units under his command, according to their calculations, killed 45,467 people, mostly Jews, up until late October of that year. Nebe had been associated with the EUTHANASIA PROGRAM from its outset: he personally transmitted Viktor BRACK's instructions to Dr. Albert Widmann that the latter should help the Führer's Chancellery find a suitable killing method. In September 1941 Nebe again summoned Widmann, instructing him to find out whether explosives could be used as effectively as firearms in the mass killing of Jews in the Minsk vicinity, and whether this could be accomplished without attracting attention. Nebe also cooperated closely with Adolf EICHMANN in the fall of 1939, during the deportation of GYPSIES from Berlin to the east.

After the failed attempt on the life of Hitler in July 1944, Nebe took part in the arrests of the conspirators, but after three days, on July 23, 1944, he disappeared. On January 16, 1945, after a simulated suicide attempt, he himself was arrested. He had already been expelled from the Nazi party on a charge of "treason" and demoted to the rank of private in the SS; finally, he was expelled from the SS. The People's Court (*Volksgerichtshof*) sentenced him to death by hanging. Before the sentence was carried out (on April 3, 1945), Nebe managed to leave perplexing "confessions" that implicated many acquaintances and associates in serious crimes.

BIBLIOGRAPHY

Gisevius, H. *To the Bitter End.* London, 1948.

Gisevius, H. *Wo ist Nebe? Erinnerungen an Hitlers Reichskriminaldirektor.* Zurich, 1966.

Hohne, H. *Order of the Death's Head: The Story of Hitler's SS.* London, 1969.

Krausnick, H., and H.-H. Wilhelm. *Die Truppe des Weltanschauungskrieges: Die Einsatzgruppen der Sicherheitspolizei und des SD, 1938–1942.* Stuttgart, 1981.

HANS-HEINRICH WILHELM

NEBENREGIERUNG. *See* Pracovná Skupina.

NEO-NAZISM. *See* Holocaust, Denial of the.

NESVIZH (Pol., Nieśwież), town in the Belorussian SSR, southeast of Novogrudok. In the interwar period Nesvizh was in independent Poland; in September 1939 it was occupied, as part of eastern Poland, by the Red Army and incorporated into the Soviet Union.

On the eve of the German invasion, Nesvizh had a Jewish population of approximately 4,500. The Germans occupied the town on June 27, 1941, and lost little time in establishing a JUDENRAT (Jewish Council) and killing Jews. The first to be killed was Aharon Levin, a prominent figure in the community, whose "crime" was that he had gone to a neighboring community to perform the circumcision of a newborn boy. On October 30, 4,000 of the town's Jews were murdered and the remainder, numbering 585, were confined to a ghetto. Before this *Aktion* took place, an underground headed by Shalom Cholawski had become active (this group had operated as a Zionist underground under the Soviet regime). It collected weapons, with the help of young Jews who worked in German storehouses and smuggled arms into the ghetto, where explosive devices were manufactured. The underground established a school for the ghetto children and was also active within the trade unions' executive committee.

The underground's plan was to establish contact with the local partisans and organize an escape into the forest; it also prepared for an uprising in the ghetto if an *Aktion* was launched to liquidate the ghetto. On July 17, 1942, it was learned that all the Jews in the neighboring ghetto of Gorodishche had been murdered. At a memorial meeting for the destroyed community in the Nesvizh synagogue, the underground representative called upon Jews of the ghetto to prepare to defend themselves. The underground now intensified its activities, preparing weapons such as knives and digging bunkers. On July 19, forty-six youngsters who were physically fit were divided into fighting teams. The plan for the uprising was for the Jews to set fire to a pile of straw in the ghetto and to the houses, and then to fight their way out to the forest.

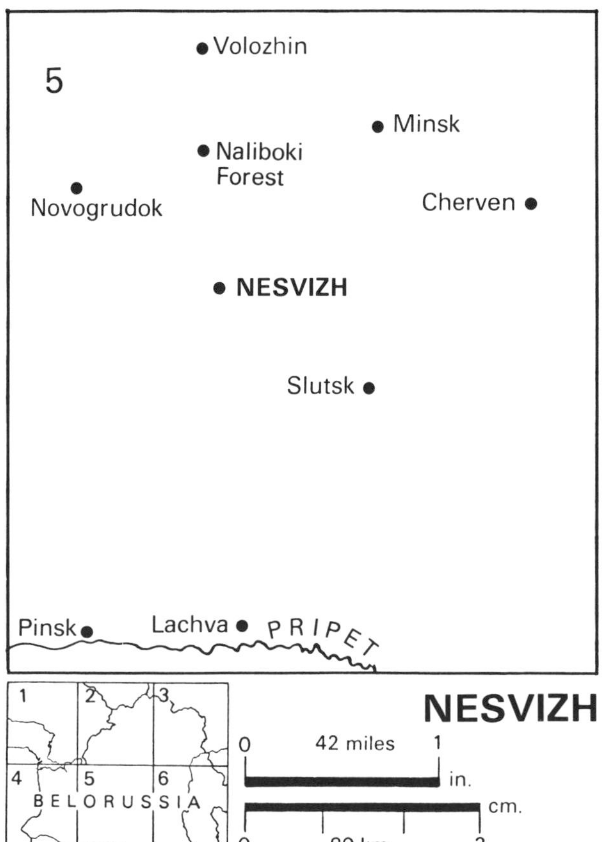

Thc following day, July 20, Belorussian policemen surrounded the ghetto. During the night a machine gun was placed on the roof of the synagogue, facing the ghetto gate. When the German commander announced that a *Selektion* would take place in the ghetto that would leave thirty essential skilled persons alive, the Jews responded that either all in the ghetto would stay alive or they would take up arms to defend themselves. The Germans opened fire, which the fighting team in the synagogue returned. The Jews set fire to their houses and fighting broke out, with the Jews defending themselves against the Germans and the policemen, mostly with knives and similar weapons. The fire spread to the town outside the ghetto and some of the Jews fled to the forest. Many were killed on the way or were handed over to the Germans by the local population.

One group, led by Shalom Cholawski, reached the Kopil Forest and united with Jews from other ghettos to found the "Zhukov" Jewish partisan unit. Another group, led by Moshe Damesek, escaped into the Naliboki Forest and joined partisan units there. The revolt at Nesvizh was one of the first instances of a ghetto uprising.

BIBLIOGRAPHY

Cholawski, S. *Beleaguered in Town and Forest.* Tel Aviv, 1973. (In Hebrew.)

Cholawski, S. *Soldiers from the Ghetto.* New York, 1980.

Lachovitsky, M. *The Destruction of Nieszwiez: From an Eyewitness.* Tel Aviv, 1948. (In Yiddish.)
Stockfish, D., ed. *Nieswiez Book.* Tel Aviv, 1976.

SHALOM CHOLAWSKI

NETHERLANDS STATE INSTITUTE FOR WAR DOCUMENTATION. *See* Documentation Centers: Rijksinstituut voor Oorlogsdocumentatie.

NETHERLANDS, THE. The Jewish community that had existed in the Netherlands in the Middle Ages was expelled or destroyed. In the late sixteenth century, Portuguese Marranos (Jews forcibly converted to Christianity who remained secret Jews) and the descendants of Portuguese Marranos living in Antwerp, Brussels, and Italy began to settle in the Netherlands and to practice their Judaism openly. They were followed by Ashkenazic Jews, especially after the 1648 and 1649 massacres of Jews by the Cossacks in Poland and the Swedish invasion of Lithuania in 1655. In the Netherlands the Jews enjoyed tolerance and security of life and property; following the establishment of the Batavian Republic in 1795, they were granted full civil rights. The Jews took part in cultural life and also held political posts; there was a large Jewish proletariat, many of whom joined the trade unions, and Jews were prominent in the workers' movement. At the time of its occupation by the Germans in 1940, the Netherlands had a Jewish population of 140,000, representing 1.6 percent of the total population of 8.9 million; this figure includes refugees from Germany, Austria, and the Protectorate of BOHEMIA AND MORAVIA (see below).

Amsterdam was the foremost and largest Jewish community in the Netherlands. In many respects Amsterdam, and particularly its Sephardic ("Portuguese") community, was the pioneer of modernity among the Jews. It was renowned for its organization, its educational institutions, and its personalities, and it maintained its unique character until the twentieth century. On the eve of the Holocaust, Amsterdam had a rabbinical seminary, Jewish periodicals, and a number of

NETHERLANDS

synagogues, two of which, one Sephardic and one Ashkenazic, were of outstanding beauty. In 1940 Amsterdam had a Jewish population of 75,000, 53 percent of the total Jewish population in the country. The Nazi treatment of the Amsterdam Jews and the status given to the Amsterdam JOODSE RAAD (Jewish Council) affected all the Jews of the Netherlands.

The Period from 1933 to 1940. When Adolf Hitler came to power in Germany, many Jews (and non-Jews) from Germany moved to the Netherlands. Dutch Jews detested the Nazis and wanted to express their feelings with deeds. In order to forestall spontaneous acts and to find a solution for the refugee problem, the Comité voor Bijzondere Joodse Belangen (Committee for Special Jewish Affairs) was established, with Abraham ASSCHER serving as its chairman. Before long care of the refugees became the committee's principal activity, and, in accordance with government policy, it looked for ways and means to enable the refugees to emigrate to other countries. Those among the refugees who had entered the country illegally were detained in camps, and in 1939 a central camp was put up for this purpose, in the village of WESTERBORK. The Committee for Special Jewish Affairs was made responsible

Jewish wedding in The Hague, 1941 or 1942; note the yellow stars. [Collection of Mala Wassner, photograph courtesy A Living Memorial to the Holocaust—Museum of Jewish Heritage, New York]

for maintaining the camp. From 1939 to 1940 a total of 34,000 refugees entered the Netherlands, and of these, 15,174 were still there when the Germans invaded the country in May 1940. The refugees from Germany had a beneficial impact on the economy, especially the textile, fashion, and film industries.

The growth of NATIONAL SOCIALISM in Germany and of similar movements in other European countries also had an effect on the Netherlands, and there were manifestations of antisemitism, which hitherto had not been known in the country. Most important among the radical right-wing movements was the NATIONAAL SOCIALISTISCHE BEWEGING (NSB).

May 1940 to Mid-1941. On the night of May 9–10 the Germans invaded the Netherlands, and four days later, on May 14, the Dutch army capitulated. Great panic seized the Jews; many tried to flee to Britain or to the south, and several dozen Jews committed suicide rather than face the persecution they expected would take place. In the first few months the Germans behaved in a restrained manner, trying first to gain popularity among the Dutch population, who were stunned by the course of events. At Hitler's express order, a civil administration was installed in the Netherlands, under SS auspices. Arthur SEYSS-INQUART was appointed *Reichskommissar* (Reich Commissioner), with five commissioners-general serving under him: Dr. Friedrich Wimmer (administration and justice), Dr. Hans Fischböck (finance and economy), Otto Bene (Foreign Office representative), Fritz Schmidt (representative of the Nazi party), and Hans Albin Rauter (commissioner-general for public safety and Heinrich HIMMLER's representative, as higher SS and police leader). The police apparatus was under Rauter's control; for most of the time it was headed by Dr. Wilhelm Harster, and attached to it was a branch office of IV B 4, Adolf EICHMANN's section in the REICHSSICHERHEITSHAUPTAMT (Reich Security Main Office; RSHA). On Seyss-Inquart's instructions, Dr. Hans Böhmcker, his representative in Amsterdam, was also in charge of Jewish affairs in the city.

A Dutch administration existed side by side with the German administration. Since

Queen Wilhelmina and the Dutch government had fled to Britain and set up a government-in-exile there, the principal secretaries of the government ministries constituted the highest Dutch authority in the country. They held regular meetings, acting as though they were a kind of cabinet. While the German administration did not recognize them as a representative body, it did at first permit them to continue functioning. As time went on, however, the Germans replaced most of the principal secretaries.

In August 1940 rumors were rife of a comprehensive anti-Jewish policy that had been worked out by the German administration. In September the Jewish newspapers were banned, with the exception of one weekly, *Het Joodse Weekblad* (The Jewish Weekly Newspaper). At the same time the Germans also banned the appointment of Jews to the Dutch administration, and ordered all civil servants to fill out a form in which they had to declare whether they were Jews or married to a Jewish woman. This order caused a stir among the Dutch population, but only a few civil servants failed to comply with it.

On November 4, an order was given for all Jewish civil servants to be "suspended." For a while they continued to draw a salary, but this was replaced by a kind of retirement pay. Among the suspended civil servants was Lodewijk Ernst VISSER, the president of the supreme court. The reaction to the German order was much stronger in academic circles, particularly among the students; they protested the dismissal of Jewish professors, and in the universities of Leiden and Delft they went on strike, as a result of which these universities were closed.

A decree was then issued ordering the registration of Jewish enterprises or those in which Jews had a measure of control (October 22, 1940). This registration—a first step toward "Aryanization"—was carried out by Fischböck's Commissariat General for Finance and the Economy, which by this act put itself in charge of dealing with Jewish property. A total of 20,690 enterprises were registered. The registration showed that the Jewish share in the economy was modest, and that most of the Jewish enterprises were small. On January 10, 1941, a further decree was issued under which all Jews, and any person with a Jewish grandfather or grandmother, had to report for registration. A total of 159,806 persons registered: 140,245 were Jews, and 19,561 the offspring of mixed marriages (*see* MISCHLINGE).

These measures, and others that followed, convinced the Jews that an authoritative body ought to be established whose composition, of persons of standing and prestige, would enable it to serve as the leadership of Dutch Jewry, with its three communities, the Ashkenazic, Sephardic, and Liberal. With the consent of the large Jewish organizations, such a body was set up in December 1940, the Joodse Coördinatiecommissie (Jewish Coordinating Committee), chaired by Visser. One of its members was Professor David CO-

Jewish books and ritual objects hidden behind a plastered niche in the Meijerplein synagogue in Amsterdam, uncovered by the Germans.

HEN, who served as liaison officer between the committee and the Committee for Special Affairs; the staff of the latter now also worked for the Coordinating Committee. The new committee undertook to guide the Jews on political issues and to advise and aid Jews who had suffered economically; it also developed a program of cultural activities, in conjunction with other organizations.

The German occupation of the Netherlands led to a decline in the economic situation and threw many people out of work. The Dutch administration's decision, as agreed upon with the Germans, was to compel the unemployed to take up work in Germany. This caused much resentment among their families, and the clandestine Communist party sought to exploit this mood among the population by strikes and public demonstrations. These had the effect of persuading the authorities to retreat, to some degree, from their original plans. Among the Dutch Nazi party members there was dissatisfaction of a different sort: they had hoped that the Germans would entrust the power in the Netherlands to them, thereby enabling them to purge the country, and especially "Jewish" (*verjudet*) Amsterdam. The German authorities, however, restrained the Dutch Nazis and did not permit them to run riot. In early 1941 the Dutch Nazis decided to take matters into their own hands, launching an anti-Jewish campaign of their own.

In the Jewish quarter, Jews and non-Jews organized to resist the Nazi attacks. During a march organized by the Dutch Nazis, a clash took place that cost the life of one of their Storm Troopers (February 11). The Germans reacted by sealing off the Jewish quarter. Böhmcker, Seyss-Inquart's representative in Amsterdam, called in Abraham Asscher and two rabbis and ordered them to set up a Jewish council; he also demanded that they ask the Jews to surrender to the police any weapons in their possession. Asscher agreed to these demands. The Joodse Raad was set up by Asscher and Cohen within a day, and it held its first meeting on February 13, 1941.

On February 19, a troop of German ORDNUNGSPOLIZEI (regular police) entered a Jewish café. The owner, who mistook the police for Dutch Nazis, put into motion a prearranged scenario, in which ammonium gas was sprayed on them. In the wake of that incident, Rauter decided to teach the Jews a lesson. On Saturday, February 22, the Jewish quarter was blockaded and young Jewish men were hunted down; 389 persons were arrested and taken to BUCHENWALD. Fifty of them died within three months, and the others were deported to MAUTHAUSEN. Of the whole group only one person survived the ordeal. The same fate overtook Jews who were seized in September 1941 and sent straight to Mauthausen. The arrests and the brutal treatment of the prisoners by the German police shocked the Amsterdam population. Communist activists used the resulting ferment as an occasion to call for yet another strike. The strike soon encompassed all sectors of the population, and the entire transportation system, the large factories, and the public services came to a standstill. The strike of February 25 spread to other cities in the Amsterdam region and continued into the next day. The Germans were taken by surprise and put large forces into the field to suppress it, which they succeeded in doing by the third day. This strike had far-reaching consequences. The Dutch realized that it had not led to any tangible results, since the Germans refused to make any concession regarding their treatment of the Jews. The German administration no longer had any doubts about the total failure of their plan to gain support for the Nazi ideology among the Dutch population. In his first public appearance after the strike (March 12), Seyss-Inquart vehemently denounced the Jews and called on the Dutch people to choose between sympathy for the Jews and collaboration with the Germans.

The events of February 1941 prompted Seyss-Inquart and his aides to harden their anti-Jewish policy. At this point, Reinhard HEYDRICH decided that Hans Rauter should set up a Central Office for Jewish Emigration in the Netherlands, similar to those already in existence in Vienna, Prague, and Berlin (*see* ZENTRALSTELLE FÜR JÜDISCHE AUSWANDERUNG), which would serve as a model for other European countries. Officially the office was headed by Willy Lages, but its day-to-day administration was in the hands of Ferdinand aus der Fünten. The original proposal also included the establishment of a Jewish

Joodse Raad staff sorting clothing in a storeroom. The box on the shelf reads "Men's socks"; on the table it reads "Children's socks." [Joh. de Haas]

emigration fund to be run by the SS. Seyss-Inquart, however, was not prepared to relinquish control of the Jews. In the course of the preparations that were put into motion to implement the "Final Solution" program throughout Europe, it was the police that became the operational arm of all the measures undertaken against the Jews, which followed one upon the other in the second half of 1941.

Separation. The first goal of the Germans toward the implementation of the "Final Solution" was the separation of the Jews from the general population to the greatest possible extent. In the summer of 1941 Jews were barred from public places. A night curfew was imposed on Jews only, from 8:00 p.m. to 6:00 a.m., and Jews could shop only from 3:00 p.m. to 5:00 p.m. Jews were allowed to use public transportation by special permit only, and then only if space was available. On September 15, Rauter issued an order barring Jews from public assemblies, museums, libraries, public markets, the stock exchange, and so on. On the other hand, certain halls, stores, and boardinghouses were designated for Jews only, and placed out of bounds to non-Jews. Jews could remain as members only in societies of an economic character, and were excluded from the compulsory new trade unions set up for journalists, actors, musicians, and so on.

The Germans did not interfere with religious life, except for outlawing ritual slaughter; fowl could be ritually slaughtered in the privacy of the home. In 1940 and 1941 the Germans permitted the import of *etrogim* (citrons) from Italy for ritual use on the Festival of Tabernacles. When an order was put into effect prohibiting gatherings of more than twenty people, the Germans still permitted religious services to be held.

In August 1941, Wimmer ordered that all Jewish students be removed from public schools and be put into special Jewish schools to be set up for this purpose. As for the universities, no new Jewish students had been admitted since early 1941; in 1942 the exclusion of Jews was extended to apply to those already enrolled.

Organized Plunder. The first German

agency to embark upon the confiscation of Jewish property was EINSATZSTAB ROSENBERG (Rosenberg Special Operations Staff), which had been authorized by Hitler to confiscate any item it required in order to promote the National Socialist cause. Alfred ROSENBERG's men were interested mainly in acquiring public and private Jewish libraries. Following his appointment as Reich Minister for the Occupied Eastern Territories in November 1941, Rosenberg also received Hitler's permission to seize the household furniture left behind by the Jews who were deported (see below) and to distribute it among the German population in the eastern territories. This operation, called Aktion M (for *Möbel*, furniture), was of enormous dimensions. From the Netherlands alone, in a single year, 17,235 apartments (9,981 in Amsterdam) were emptied of their contents, and loads totaling 16,941,249 cubic feet (479,725 cu m) were sent to eastern Europe.

Einsatzstab Rosenberg was an independent operation and was not part of the plunder program carried out by the German administration in the Netherlands, a program that Seyss-Inquart's commissioner-general for finance and economy, Hans Fischböck, had drawn up on the basis of the data obtained from the forced registration of Jewish enterprises. On March 12, 1942, the first of four decrees was issued concerning the confiscation of Jewish property. Under the decree, trustees (*Treuhänder*) were appointed for every Jewish enterprise, most of which were earmarked for liquidation and the rest for transfer to "Aryan" hands. The purchase price was to be paid to the Jewish owner of the enterprise in twenty-five yearly installments, but in fact no such payment was ever made.

The "Aryanization" process was handled by a special agency created for this purpose, the Vermögensverwaltungs- und Rentenanstalt (Property Administration and Annuities Institute)—that is, an office for the administration of the seized property—which invested the proceeds of its operations in German government bonds. During the course of the "Aryanization" program, some nine thousand to ten thousand Jewish enterprises were designated for liquidation, of which about two thousand were transferred to "Aryan" hands. Jewish influence was eliminated from some ten thousand other enterprises. By the end of the war, some one thousand Jewish enterprises had not been dealt with.

In the first two years of the occupation the Germans hardly touched the diamond trade; they hoped to develop it and were aware that in the early stage they would need the help of the experienced Jewish owners and workers in the industry. They lost no time, however, in ousting Jews from the textile industry, a branch of great importance in the economic life of the Jews, second only to the diamond branch. Within a few months hundreds of merchants, shopkeepers, and itinerant salesmen in the textile industry found themselves in the street and deprived of their livelihood.

In May 1941 a decree was issued ordering the registration of agricultural land in Jewish ownership. There was not much of it, only 22,500 acres, no more than 0.9 percent of all agricultural land in the Netherlands. Of greater impact was the forced registration of real estate and mortgages: the value of the 19,000 Jewish-owned buildings was 200 million gulden, and of the 5,600 mortgages, approximately 26 million gulden.

In mid-August, Fischböck's confiscation program reached its climax in a decree on the liquid assets owned by Jews. The Jews now had to deposit, in one bank, all the cash and checks in their possession worth over 1,000 gulden, as well as all their deposits and accounts, including their stocks, bonds, and saving accounts. Fischböck selected for this purpose a Jewish bank, Lippmann, Rosenthal and Company, which had been placed in the hands of a trustee. A special section was set up for the Jewish accounts, under Fischböck's direct supervision, over which the bank had no control whatsoever. The Jews could not draw freely on their accounts and had to submit applications, which were subject to a commission and were carefully scrutinized. Their approval was regarded by the Germans as a privilege rather than a right. By the end of 1942, 7,458 accounts belonging to 6,540 private individuals and totaling 25 million gulden had been opened with LIRO (the Jewish section of Lippmann-Rosenthal), as well as stocks and bonds to the nominal amount of 213 million gulden.

The Germans had no intention of maintaining the private accounts for long. On January 1, 1943, all the private accounts were abolished and all the money belonging to Jews was put into one general account. Henceforth the Jews received their salaries and other payments only from the Joodse Raad. Once LIRO was set up, the Raad was stripped of its financial independence, which had been based on contributions from Jews; the contributions were discontinued and LIRO, in the first year, remitted 400,000 gulden to the Joodse Raad. The Raad's monthly requirement, however, was 45,000 to 60,000 gulden, and it therefore had to take loans from LIRO, at the high interest rate of 5 percent. From the time the general account was established, the Joodse Raad had to present budget estimates and financial reports to the German authorities, on a monthly basis. The Germans determined the monthly allocation, which was usually late in arriving. Until its dissolution in September 1943, the Joodse Raad received a total of 4.9 million gulden. On Seyss-Inquart's orders the securities were sold; because of the large quantities that were put on the market, they were sold at a price below their real value, which in turn led to a buying spree on the Amsterdam stock exchange. Insurance policies of Jews deposited with LIRO had to be paid out by the insurance companies as though LIRO were the legal heir, and as of April 1943 LIRO was also authorized to cash in the mortgages it held. In addition to these liquid assets, the Germans appropriated valuables such as jewelry, paintings, and stamp collections. Some of these items found their way into private possession, but on the whole, Fischböck succeeded in transmitting to the German treasury most of the Jewish money and other assets.

Deportation. In late 1941 the Germans told the Joodse Raad that labor camps were being opened to which "unemployed" Jews would be sent, to be put to work. In reality, this was a camouflage for the preparatory steps that the Germans were taking toward eventual deportation. Ostensibly, the Jews sent to the camps were to be employed in Dutch factories and for Dutch institutions, but in fact the camps were German forced-labor camps, and the Jews held there lived and worked under much poorer conditions than those of Dutch workers. Not only unemployed Jews were sent to the camps; those with gainful employment were also affected, when the Germans canceled their work permits and thereby turned them into "unemployed" persons. Strong pressure was put on the Joodse Raad to fill the constantly increasing quota for workers. At first it refused to submit, but later it cooperated. In April 1942, conditions in the camps deteriorated and many Jews deserted. Officially there were 7,500 laborers in the camps, but the actual average number was no higher than 5,000. Together with the forced laborers' dependents, the camp population numbered some 15,000.

The deportation plan also provided for the removal of the Jews from all the provinces and their concentration in Amsterdam. This phase was launched on January 14, 1942, beginning with the town of Zaandam; the Dutch nationals among the Jews were ordered to move to Amsterdam, while those who were stateless were sent to the Westerbork camp. In the initial six months it was mainly the Jews from the coastal strip who were forced to leave. The evacuation of the provinces followed, coinciding with the start of the deportations. Not all the Jews were permitted to move to Amsterdam; a new camp was set up, near VUGHT, as an alternative to Amsterdam or Westerbork. In April 1943 Jewish residence throughout the Netherlands (with the exception of Amsterdam) was forbidden, and those still in the provinces were ordered to report to Vught.

Another step designed to ensure that no Jew escaped the German net was the introduction of the yellow badge (*see* BADGE, JEWISH). On April 29, 1942, Asscher and Cohen were advised that as of May 3 every Jew aged six and over would have to wear such a badge. The yellow badges—570,000 of them—had been prepared in advance (apparently in the ŁÓDŹ ghetto) and the Joodse Raad was ordered to distribute them to all the Jews, with the Germans threatening that any person caught without the badge after the appointed day would be deported to Mauthausen. Asscher and Cohen, after strong protests, agreed to carry out what appeared to be an impossible task: to hand out the badges, in the space of two days, to Jews all over the country. The Dutch population was

Jews in Amsterdam on their way to the collection point for deportation (1943).

highly critical of this humiliation of the Jews, and some of them expressed their feelings by wearing, in public, a yellow badge of their own. This particular protest movement, however, did not last for long. The yellow badge was soon overshadowed by far more ominous developments.

On June 26, 1942, Willy Lages and Ferdinand aus der Fünten informed David Cohen that "the Jews of the Netherlands will be employed by the police in labor camps in Germany—men, women, and entire families." From that point on it was the Zentralstelle, the Central Office for Jewish Emigration, that had the decisive say on Jewish policy, with only economic and financial affairs remaining under Fischböck's control. Cohen was also told that at first, young Jews, for the most part of German origin, would be sent to the labor camps; each would receive an individual notification and would have to register with the Joodse Raad. The Amsterdam Jews panicked and only a small number did in fact register. In order to frighten the Jews into registering, Rauter ordered a large manhunt to be conducted when the date for the first transport drew near; 540 Jews were arrested and held as hostages. Nevertheless, the quota that had been fixed for the first three transports was not filled. When the trains arrived at Westerbork and the camp commandant realized that he was 400 Jews short of the 2,000 he was to move to the AUSCHWITZ extermination camp, he made up the shortage with prisoners from the camp. The removal of entire families, including the old and the very young, left no doubt that the term "employed by the police" was no more than an effort to camouflage what was really the deportation of Dutch Jewry.

Large sectors of the population reacted with fury to this development. The country's churches took the unprecedented step of protesting in a body to Seyss-Inquart, and also instructed all the clergymen to read out the text of their protest at the following Sunday's services. The German administration exerted heavy pressure on the churches to call off the public protest, and the Protestant churches gave in. The Catholic archbishop, Johannes de Jong, insisted that the protest telegram to Seyss-Inquart be read out. The Germans retaliated by arresting all Jewish converts to Catholicism—201 persons, some of them monks and nuns—and deporting them to Auschwitz.

The public protests had no effect on the Germans, who continued to send Jews to Westerbork and from there to Auschwitz and SOBIBÓR, as planned. In large measure, the Germans' design was facilitated by the Dutch agencies' readiness to cooperate: the municipal administration, the railway workers, and the Dutch police, with few exceptions, all contributed to the roundup of the Jews and their expulsion from the country.

On October 2, 1942, a countrywide operation was launched to speed up the deportation of the victims. All the Jewish men in labor camps in the Netherlands were transferred to Westerbork, where they were joined by their families from Amsterdam, a total of 12,296 persons. The Westerbork camp could not possibly accommodate such a large number, and overnight, conditions there became utterly unbearable. The Germans raised the quota for the trains taking Jews to the east, and in a single month sent 7,463 Jews to their death, thereby relieving some of the congestion at Westerbork. At this point the method used for assembling the Jews in Amsterdam was also changed; as of October 14, the Jews who had been detained were held in the Jewish theater building pending their dispatch to Westerbork. In May 1943 the rate of deportations was accelerated. Lages, the German police chief (and chief of the Zentralstelle), told the Joodse Raad that 7,000 of its employees, who until then had been protected, would have to assemble in an Amsterdam city square and then go to Germany for "employment" there. Despite the strong objections of many of their associates, the Joodse Raad leadership decided to comply with the German demand. Those who were notified by the Raad to report for "employment in Germany" were warned that severe action would be taken against them if they failed to comply. Nevertheless, only 500 persons showed up, of the 7,000 who had received the summons. The Germans reacted at once: the Jewish quarter was sealed off the following day, and a manhunt was launched in which 3,435 Jews were caught. The Joodse Raad was not dismissed, but the Germans no longer relied on it for the roundup of Jews.

When the reservoir of Jews for deportation ran dry, another wide-ranging manhunt was carried out, on June 20, 1943, and 5,524 Jews were arrested. By that summer, only a small remnant of Jews was left, and they too were doomed. On the eve of the Jewish New Year, September 29, 1943, the last roundup took place, and 2,000 Jews, including the Joodse Raad leaders and senior staff, were taken to Westerbork. On arrival there, Asscher and Cohen were informed that the Joodse Raad had ceased to exist. One section was still functioning in Amsterdam to take care of the remaining Jews, most of them the Jewish partners of mixed marriages. Food parcels were still being sent to Westerbork, with German permission.

The deportations were based on a systematic method and proceeded gradually, enabling groups or individuals to have their deportation postponed, held up, or speeded up. In the best position, in relative terms, were the nationals of enemy or neutral countries, to whom all of the anti-Jewish laws did not apply. The fate of nationals of the satellite states, on the other hand, depended on the position taken by these states; some of them (for example, Italy, Finland, and at a later stage Hungary and Romania) protected their Jewish citizens, while others (such as Slovakia and Croatia) abandoned them to their fate. As time went on it transpired that Germany was interested in the Exchange of Jews and Germans (*see* EXCHANGE: JEWS AND GERMANS). In July 1944 an arrangement was made under which German residents of Palestine were exchanged for 220 Dutch Jews. In addition, thousands of Jews were being held in the BERGEN-BELSEN camp for exchange, for whom the Jewish Agency had applied for immigration permits to Palestine. Another category of Jews who were released from Bergen-Belsen had passports purchased for them from one of the Latin American countries. Two secretaries-general of the Dutch administration succeeded in having 654 prominent Jews exempted from deportation to the extermination camps, but that group was eventually taken to Westerbork, and from there to THERESIENSTADT, contrary to assurances given by Seyss-Inquart. They were eventually set free when Theresienstadt was liberated by the Soviet army.

A few Jews with substantial financial assets

were permitted to emigrate, and some Jews bought themselves off from deportation. For the most part, however, exemption from deportation was only temporary; this was the case with thousands of Jews who had taken part in Germany's war effort, as laborers (*Rüstungsjuden*). Rauter exerted great pressure on the military industrial plants, and they gradually reduced the number of Jews working for them; in June 1943 the last such group was released and sent to their death.

One special group of persons who had been registered as Jews lodged an appeal against this designation, claiming that they were of pure or partial "Aryan" descent. Those whose appeal was allowed were released from the strictures of the discriminatory laws, depending on the category to which they were finally found to belong. The number of these cases would have been small had it not been for Dr. Hans Georg Calmeyer, a German lawyer who headed the relevant section and who regarded it as his moral duty to save as many Jews as he could. In his struggle with Rauter's men, Dr. Calmeyer was supported by Wimmer (himself an antisemite), and this made it possible for Calmeyer to continue his activities. His accomplishments are reflected in the figures for January 1944: 4,767 applications were submitted; of these, 1,868 (fewer than 40 percent) were turned down. In 2,026 cases the applicants were reclassified as "half" Jewish, and in 873 cases, as one-quarter Jewish or "Aryan." Many of these findings were based on false evidence, of which Calmeyer was fully aware.

The mixed marriages represented a vexing problem for the Germans, and their policy on this issue was not consistent. Some of the Jewish partners in such marriages ended up in Westerbork and remained there; others were deported to the extermination camps. At one stage an effort was made to solve the problem by giving these Jews the choice between deportation to the extermination camps and sterilization, and in this the Germans went further in the Netherlands than in Germany itself. Only a few were actually sterilized, but many were confirmed, after cursory examination, as being infertile, thanks to a German physician, Dr. Eduard Meyer.

Some people in the Netherlands sought to profit from the situation by extorting money from Jews, in exchange for a promise to delay their deportation. The largest fraud was perpetrated by Friedrich Weinreb, a Jewish economist who promised that for a small fee he could arrange for people to go to Portugal with the help of a highly placed German with whom he had contact. Many Jews were taken in, and for a while Weinreb managed to fool even the Germans. When it turned out that it was all a fabrication, he became an informant, causing the arrest of 118 Jews, of whom 70 perished. Weinreb and his family went into hiding, where they stayed to the end of the war.

Beginning in May 1943, the number of deportees from Westerbork increased. That month, 8,056 Jews were deported to the extermination camps; in June, 8,420; and in July, 6,614. Thereafter the figures declined: in August, 2,005; in September, 1,984; in October, 1,007; and in November, 2,044. Subsequently, one train a month left Westerbork for Auschwitz, each with about 1,000 Jews. From March 1944 the number of deportees per month ranged from 240 to 600. On September 3, 1944, when it looked as though the Allied armies were about to conquer all of the Netherlands, one more fully loaded train was dispatched to Auschwitz, with 1,019 Jews aboard.

Very few Jews deported from the Netherlands survived, as shown in Table 1. After deducting the number of Jews who survived in Auschwitz and in labor camps because of special circumstances (women in the MEDICAL EXPERIMENTS block, and the Philips groups in the Vught camp), it transpires that only a very small proportion of those deported survived, far fewer than among eastern European Jews.

Approximately three thousand Jews from the Netherlands, many of them refugees from Germany, were deported from Theresienstadt to Auschwitz. Living conditions in Theresienstadt were poor, and toward the end of the war epidemics of contagious diseases broke out there. However, the mortality rate was relatively low, and for those in Theresienstadt who were not sent on to Auschwitz, this was the least difficult camp to be in.

Hiding Out and Escaping. By the summer of 1942, Jews who had not responded to sum-

TABLE 1. *Deported Netherlands Jews Who Survived the Holocaust*

DESTINATION	NUMBER OF DEPORTEES	NUMBER OF SURVIVORS	PERCENTAGE OF SURVIVORS
Auschwitz	60,026	1,052	1.75
Sobibór	34,313	19	
Theresienstadt	4,894	1,980	40.4
Bergen-Belsen	3,751	2,050	54.6
Mauthausen	c. 1,750	1	
Other camps	200	(?)	
Dutch Jews deported to Auschwitz from Belgium and France	c. 2,000	100 (?)	5
Total	c. 107,000	5,200	4.8

monses for deportation had to go into hiding, and the number of such Jews grew, especially in 1943. In the early stages, they used their personal contacts with non-Jews to find hiding places. Later, groups and organizations were formed that made it their job to find hiding places for Jews and for threatened non-Jews. Many of those taking part did so without any recompense, or asked only for modest sums to cover their expenses. Some, however, used the situation as an opportunity to make a profit. It was also accepted practice that Jews paid double the fee paid by non-Jews, because of the higher risk involved in saving Jews. A large number of men and women acted as liaison officers, providing ration coupons and forged papers and, in many instances, also helping Jews to move from one hideout to another.

As time went on, those in hiding found it increasingly difficult to pay for their maintenance costs, and in early 1944 the national underground organization that had come into being to financially assist people being persecuted set up a special Jewish section to aid the Jews in hiding. That section, with the help of other underground organizations, paid out a total of 400,000 gulden for this purpose. At a rough estimate, twenty-five thousand Jews went into hiding, of whom about a third fell into German hands. Among these was the family of Anne FRANK. Non-Jews who were caught giving refuge to Jews in their homes were not executed, but they were sent to concentration camps, where many perished. Frequently the Germans also destroyed the property of the non-Jews in whose homes Jews had been hidden.

A special chapter was the rescue of children, for whom it was easier to find refuge. As early as July 1942 a group of students had organized for this purpose, and later on there were three more such groups; together, they placed about one thousand children in hiding. In many instances the children were whisked away from the Jewish theater building to the children's home across the street, and from there to hideouts. In all, about forty-five hundred children were hidden, and only a very few were discovered by the Germans.

Escape from the Netherlands to other countries was very difficult. Nearly all the attempts to cross to Britain ended in failure. The journeys through Belgium and France were long and extremely risky, but some Jews did succeed in reaching the Swiss border and, unless turned back by the Swiss police, were able to stay there until the end of the war. The outcome of such escape attempts depended on contacts in various places. The largest group that smuggled young people out of the country was the Westerweel group (*see* WESTERWEEL, JOOP), which cooperated with the Haluts (Zionist pioneering) organizations. Dozens of members of these groups succeeded in moving the young Jews from their hideouts in the Netherlands to France, and from there to Spain, from where most made their way to Palestine.

The role of the Jews in the Dutch underground was not insignificant, but no data are available on the subject. Jews helped to found major underground newspapers, and they transmitted intelligence reports to Britain. There were also instances of spontaneous resistance to the Germans, and a number of Jews joined armed groups of the Dutch underground who launched attacks on Dutch Nazi leaders, only to be caught by the Germans and put to death.

After the Holocaust. The reintegration of the Jews into Dutch society after the war was a protracted and painful process. The Netherlands had suffered more from the German occupation than any other country outside eastern Europe, and its economic rehabilitation necessitated a strict policy. There was also an antisemitic streak in government circles and an inclination not to permit the Jews to regain the position they had had before the war. A determined struggle had to be waged by the Jews to gain recognition of their claims to the property that had been stolen from them. A government proposal to reimburse the holders of LIRO accounts with only 70 percent of the balance was vehemently denounced by the country's leading jurists, and in the end the government retracted and paid close to 100 percent. The banks that had sold the Jewish-owned securities also had to recognize the Jewish owners' rights, and the insurance companies, after long litigation, had to acknowledge the validity of the policies they had sold to the Germans without the knowledge of the policyholders.

A bitter struggle was waged over the war orphans. The groups that had specialized in hiding the children felt that they should be the ones to take care of them even now, when the war was over. They succeeded in having a royal decision passed and then a law, authorizing a committee (made up largely of Christians) to determine which orphans should stay with the families that had saved them and which should be put under Jewish guardianship. Of the 3,481 children registered with the committee, 1,540 were restored to their parents, or one of them. The Jews established the "Help the Children" guardianship committee and fought—first with the committee and then in the courts—for the children to be put under Jewish guardians. In the end, 360 children (17.5 percent of the orphans) remained with non-Jewish families. In two widely publicized cases, the Christian families refused to abide by the courts' decision to give up the children, and smuggled them out of the country. One of the children was found, but the other, who came from a religious Jewish family, went into hiding in the south of France, and when she came of legal age declared herself a Catholic.

As soon as the war was over, a bitter feud erupted between the Jewish repatriates and the Joodse Raad, the repatriates' fury focusing on its two leaders, Asscher and Cohen. A Jewish court of honor found the two men guilty of collaboration with the Germans and barred them from holding office in Jewish institutions. Several trials were held of Jews who had collaborated with the Germans, the best known among them that in which Weinreb was accused. In 1947 he was twice found guilty, but he was pardoned on the occasion of Queen Juliana's coronation in 1948. In a 1965 book on the Holocaust of Dutch Jewry, the historian Jacob Presser suggested that Weinreb's trial was a miscarriage of justice. At the same time, Weinreb himself published his memoirs, and the two events raised a storm of protests against the alleged wrong done to him. An official commission of inquiry was appointed, whose findings, published in 1976, proved that Weinreb had been driven by a craving for power, by greed, and by sexual lust, and that his work for the Gestapo had cost many lives. These findings and a supplementary report published in 1981 silenced any further demands for the revision of Weinreb's trial.

The resistance organizations and the Dutch government-in-exile had planned to conduct trials against Germans who had committed crimes in the Netherlands and against Dutch collaborators. The huge number of suspects (130,000) and the conciliatory policy adopted by the postwar Dutch government, whose primary goal was to rehabilitate the economy, soon had the effect of reducing to a fraction the number of cases that reached the courts. A total of 242 Germans were tried, of whom 203 were sentenced, including 18 sentenced to death. Only 5 were actually executed, one of them Rauter. The death sentences of 3 defendants who had been tried for their crimes against the Jews were commuted to life imprisonment, but when the government wanted to release them in 1972, the storm of protest raised by the public made it reverse the decision. In January 1989 the last 2 remaining prisoners, Ferdinand aus der Fünten, who oversaw mass roundups of Jews, and Franz Fischer, who had headed a local branch of the SD (Sicherheitsdienst; Security Service) and was responsible for the deportation to extermination camps of 13,000 Dutch Jews, were granted amnesty by the Dutch government, a decision causing angry demonstrations in many parts of the country. Of the Dutch collaborators, many of whom had tortured their victims, only 4 were executed. The collaborators who were sentenced to prison, including those sentenced to life terms, were pardoned after a relatively short time and released.

[*See also* N.V. Group; Trials of War Criminals: The Netherlands.]

BIBLIOGRAPHY

De Jong, L. *Het Koninkrijk der Nederlanden tijdens de Tweede Wereldoorlog*. Vols. 1–13. The Hague, 1969–1988.

Documents of the Persecution of Dutch Jewry. Amsterdam, 1969.

Herzberg, A. J. *Kroniek der Jodenvervolging*. Amsterdam, 1978.

Hirschfeld, G. *Nazi Rule and Dutch Collaboration*. New York, 1988.

Michman, J. "The Controversial Stand of the Joodse Raad in the Netherlands: Lodewijk E. Visser's Struggle." *Yad Vashem Studies* 10 (1974): 9–68.

Michman, J., et al. *The Netherlands*. In *Pinkas Hakehillot; Encyclopaedia of Jewish Communities*. Jerusalem, 1985. (In Hebrew.)

Presser, J. *The Destruction of the Dutch Jews* (1965). New York, 1969.

Sijes, B. A. *Studies over Jodenvervolging*. Assen, 1974.

JOZEPH MICHMAN

NEUENGAMME, concentration camp situated in the outskirts of Hamburg, Germany. Initially, Neuengamme was an annex of the SACHSENHAUSEN concentration camp. The first group of prisoners arrived at Neuengamme on December 13, 1938, for the task of constructing the camp. They were housed in a disused brick factory. The factory's existence was the reason for the establishment of a concentration camp in Hamburg, which at the time had only temporary, small camps (Wittmoor and Fuhlsbüttel); the SS wanted to reactivate the brick factory and use its products primarily in the huge public structures that were being planned for the city.

In April 1940 the Deutsche Erd- und Steinwerke GmbH (German Earth and Stone Works Ltd.), an SS economic enterprise, signed an agreement with the city of Hamburg that provided for a substantial expansion of the brick factory, the digging of a canal to connect the factory with a tributary of the Elbe River, and a siding linking it to the railway network. The work was to be done by prisoners. Barracks were put up and more prisoners were brought in, the total reaching about 1,000. As of June 1940, Neuengamme became an independent concentration camp. Beginning in the fall of 1941, thousands of Soviet prisoners of war were brought there as well. Soviet nationals eventually became the largest national group in the camp, numbering 34,500, including 5,900 women.

In 1942, private firms such as the well-known Walther weapons factory established branches at Neuengamme. Numerous annexes to the camp were set up at various centers of the armament industry, especially the Bremen and Hamburg shipbuilding and machine works. They were also established in Hannover and in the industrial area of Brunswick, which adjoined the Volkswagen Company (the present site of Wolfsburg) and the Hermann Göring Works (today the location of the town of Salzgitter). By 1945 the total number of annexes to Neuengamme reached seventy. Most of the new prisoners were put into these satellites. In 1944 the main camp had a prisoner population of twelve thousand; about twice that number were in the satellites. Beginning in the summer of 1944 large transports of Jewish prisoners were brought in, mainly from Hungary and Poland. Some thirteen thousand Jewish prisoners passed through the main camp and its annexes (among them three thousand women) in 1944 and 1945.

It is estimated that the total number of prisoners sent to Neuengamme was one hundred and six thousand. The mortality rate was high, compared to that of other concentration camps situated in the Reich, especially in the early years when the brick factory was being reactivated. It is assumed that at least fifty-five thousand prisoners perished

Christmas celebration of SS guards in Neuengamme (1943). [Bildarchiv Preussischer Kulturbesitz, Berlin]

in Neuengamme and its annexes. The main camp was evacuated in the second half of April 1945, following the evacuation of most of the annexes.

BIBLIOGRAPHY

Bauche, U., et al., eds. *Arbeit und Vernichtung: Das Konzentrationslager Neuengamme 1938–1945.* Hamburg, 1986.

Bringmann, F. *KZ Neuengamme: Berichte, Erinnerungen, Dokumente.* Frankfurt, 1981.

Johe, W. *Neuengamme: Zur Geschichte der Konzentrationslager in Hamburg.* Hamburg, 1981.

FALK PINGEL

NEURATH, KONSTANTIN FREIHERR VON (1873–1956), foreign minister of Germany from 1932 to 1938 and Reich Protector of BOHEMIA AND MORAVIA from 1939 to 1941. Born in Württemberg, Neurath entered the diplomatic service in 1901 and served as ambassador to Denmark, Italy, and Great Britain in the 1920s. In June 1932 he was appointed foreign minister in Franz von PAPEN's "nonpolitical" cabinet of experts, a position he continued to hold under Kurt von Schleicher and then (at Paul von HINDENBURG's insistence) under Hitler. He provided a useful facade of respectability while Hitler still moved cautiously in foreign policy, but was replaced by Joachim von RIBBENTROP in February 1938, when the Führer was ready for a more aggressive course of action.

Hitler again used Neurath for appearance' sake when he made the ex-minister the Reich Protector of Bohemia and Moravia following the destruction of Czechoslovakia in March 1939. In that capacity Neurath presided over, even if he did not initiate, the crushing of all autonomous political and cultural life and the implementation of anti-Jewish measures identical to those already in force in Germany. He was once again brushed aside, this

Konstantin von Neurath in his prison cell at Nuremberg during his trial before the International Military Tribunal. [United States Army]

time by Reinhard HEYDRICH, when even more draconian measures were desired in September 1941.

Accused by many of indolence and apathy, Neurath was characterized by his biographer as an intensely private man who felt a strong sense of duty but never conceived of political life in moral terms. Joseph GOEBBELS complained of him, "This man has nothing in common with us." In fact, Neurath was all too typical of the many nationalist-conservative fellow travelers whom the Nazis so effectively duped and exploited. A defendant before the International Military Tribunal at Nuremberg, he was sentenced to fifteen years' imprisonment for war crimes, crimes against peace, and crimes against humanity (*see* NUREMBERG TRIAL). He was released in 1954 after eight years in the Spandau prison.

BIBLIOGRAPHY

Heinemann, J. L. *Hitler's First Foreign Minister: Constantin Freiherr von Neurath.* Berkeley, 1979.

CHRISTOPHER R. BROWNING

NÈVEJEAN, YVONNE (d. 1987), Belgian rescuer of Jewish children during the Holocaust. Yvonne Nèvejean headed the Oeuvre Nationale de l'Enfance (National Agency for Children; ONE), a Belgian government-subsidized agency supervising children's homes throughout the country. When the deportations of Jews began in the summer of 1942, she was contacted by heads of the Comité de Défense des Juifs en Belgique (Committee for the Protection of Jews in Belgium; CDJ), the principal Jewish clandestine organization at the time. She was asked whether she was prepared to help rescue Jewish children separated from their parents (who had been deported or were hiding) by placing the children, through the ONE network, in religious and lay institutions and with private families. Without even consulting the ONE board of directors, Nèvejean committed the ONE to a vast rescue operation that eventually saved up to four thousand Jewish children (nicknamed "Yvonne's children"). They were referred to her by trusted CDJ personnel, and were then fetched by ONE nurses and social workers and provided with the necessary new identities and ration cards. After a brief stay in ONE-sponsored children's homes, they were sent off for permanent refuge in institutions and with private families. The financing for this wide-ranging operation came initially from CDJ sources. When these proved insufficient, Yvonne Nèvejean obtained funds from banks and from the London-based government-in-exile, which were then parachuted into Belgium.

Yvonne Nèvejean.

An operation of such magnitude, with the participation of untold numbers of lay and religious persons, could not go on without denunciations. Some rescuers and rescued persons were arrested, but on the whole the Gestapo failed to disrupt the ONE network. On one occasion, Nèvejean was made to accompany a suspicious German official to a children's home in Tervueren at which a third of the 250 children were Jewish. But by directing the German's attention to a non-Jewish mulatto child, she was able to avoid his scrutiny of the other children. In another instance, when the Gestapo broke into the Wezembeek children's home and transported its staff and the Jewish children to the MECHELEN camp, Nèvejean interceded with Queen Mother Elisabeth, who, with the help of Léon Platteau of the Belgian Ministry of Justice (both later recognized as "RIGHTEOUS AMONG THE NATIONS"), succeeded in securing the release of the children and their supervisors.

In 1965, Yvonne Nèvejean, now known as Yvonne Feyerick-Nèvejean, was awarded the YAD VASHEM title of "Righteous among the Nations."

BIBLIOGRAPHY

Garfinkels, B. *Les Belges face à la persécution raciale, 1940–1944.* Brussels, 1965.

Steinberg, L. *Le Comité de défense des Juifs en Belgique, 1942–1944.* Brussels, 1973.

MORDECAI PALDIEL

NICACCI, RUFINO. *See* Nicolini, Giuseppe.

NICOLINI, GIUSEPPE, rescuer of Jews in Assisi, in central Italy. Soon after the German invasion of Italy in September 1943, Giuseppe Nicolini, bishop of Assisi, summoned Rufino Nicacci, father guardian of the San Damiano monastery in Assisi. He charged Nicacci with finding temporary shelter for a group of fleeing Jews, mostly from the Trieste area in northern Italy, who had unexpectedly appeared in town. Nicacci arranged for some two hundred Jews to be supplied with false identities and hidden in parishioners' homes, moved out of the area, or given sanctuary in monasteries and convents. To provide for the religious needs of the Jews staying in the convent, the sisters operated a kitchen where dietary kosher laws were observed.

Also involved in this extensive rescue operation (several thousand Jews passed through the town at one point or another) was Aldo Brunacci, a professor canon at the San Rufino Cathedral of Assisi. The person formally in charge of the operation, he insisted that Jews could be hidden in cloisters as well, such as the Convent of the Stigmata. Father Brunacci was also in charge of a clandestine school for Jewish children, in which they received instruction in Judaism from their own mentors. In May 1944, Brunacci was arrested and tried by a Perugia court. He was spared only through the Vatican's intercession, on condition that he be banished from Assisi for the duration of the war.

Not a single Jew was ever betrayed in Assisi, nor was there any attempt to induce the many fleeing Jews passing through the town to convert. Father Brunacci remarked after the war: "In all, about two hundred Jews were entrusted to us by Divine Providence; with God's help, and through the intercession of Saint Francis, not one of them fell into the hands of their persecutors."

After the war, Giuseppe Nicolini, Rufino Nicacci, and Aldo Brunacci were recognized by YAD VASHEM as "RIGHTEOUS AMONG THE NATIONS."

BIBLIOGRAPHY

Ramati, A. *The Assisi Underground: The Priest Who Rescued Jews, as Told by Padre Rufino Nicacci.* New York, 1978.

MORDECAI PALDIEL

NIEBUHR, REINHOLD (1892–1971), American theologian. Niebuhr was a pioneer in the recovery of the biblical foundations of Christian theology. His pastorate in Detroit and his subsequent professorship at Union Theological Seminary in New York were marked by his use of the moral and ethical teachings of the Hebrew prophets. He was a popular speaker on the college circuit and in university pulpits, and a leader in the World Student Christian Federation and other early ecumenical developments. Niebuhr wrote and preached more widely on the issues of the German church struggle than any other American churchman; he was the most vocal on the plight of the Jews in Hitler's Reich, attacking antisemitism and pleading for the abandonment of Christian triumphalism. He was also the first prominent theologian to repudiate Christian missionary activity directed toward converting Jews. Niebuhr's 1943 articles in *The Nation* calling for the postwar creation of a Jewish state in the British Mandate of Palestine and his leadership in the American Christian Palestine Committee gave political expression to his realistic theology.

BIBLIOGRAPHY

Brown, R. M., ed. *The Essential Reinhold Niebuhr.* New Haven, 1986.

Fox, R. W. *Reinhold Niebuhr: A Biography.* New York, 1986.

Harries, R., ed. *Reinhold Niebuhr and the Issues of Our Time.* London, 1986.

Kegley, C. W., and R. W. Bretall, eds. *Reinhold Niebuhr: His Religious, Social, and Political Thought.* New York, 1956.

FRANKLIN H. LITTELL

NIEMÖLLER, MARTIN (1892–1984), Protestant pastor and leader of the anti-Nazi Confessing Church (Bekennende Kirche). Born in Westphalia, the son of a pastor, Niemöller entered the German navy in 1910 and in World War I served as a U-boat commander, with great distinction. He was ordained in 1924, and in 1931 became pastor of the influential Berlin parish of Dahlem, where his naval fame and his preaching attracted large congregations.

Niemöller was unsympathetic to the Weimar Republic and welcomed the Nazis initially, but he soon saw the dangers of the regime. In 1934 he formed the Pfarrernotbund (Pastors' Emergency League), and in 1937 he assumed leadership of the Confessing Church. He was arrested for "malicious attacks against the state," given a token sentence, and fined the modest sum of 2,000 reichsmarks. Upon his release, Niemöller was re-arrested on Hitler's order and spent the next seven years in the concentration camps of SACHSENHAUSEN and DACHAU, usually in solitary confinement. At the outbreak of World War II, moved by patriotism, he offered his services to the navy, but his offer was rejected. He was released in 1945 by Allied forces and helped to issue the "Stuttgart Confession of Guilt" (1945), which confessed the collective war guilt of the Germans.

Niemöller himself shared the guilt: "First they came for the Jews. I was silent. I was not a Jew. Then they came for the Communists. I was silent. I was not a Communist. Then they came for the trade unionists. I was silent. I was not a trade unionist. Then they came for me. There was no one left to speak for me." After the war Niemöller became a convinced pacifist, denounced nuclear weapons, and advocated a neutral, disarmed, and reunited Germany.

BIBLIOGRAPHY

Bentley, J. *Martin Niemöller.* New York, 1984.

Davidson, C. S. *God's Man: The Story of Pastor Niemöller.* New York, 1959.

Helmreich, E. C. *The German Churches under Hitler: Background, Struggle, and Epilogue.* Detroit, 1979.

Littell, F., and H. G. Locke, eds. *The German Church Struggle and the Holocaust.* Detroit, 1974.

Niemöller, W. *Neu Anfang, 1945: Zur Biographie Martin Niemöllers.* Frankfurt, 1967.

Schmidt, J. *Martin Niemöller im Kirchenkampf.* Hamburg, 1971.

LIONEL KOCHAN

NIEŚZWIEŻ. *See* Nesvizh.

"NIGHT AND FOG." *See* Nacht und Nebel.

"NIGHT OF THE BROKEN GLASS." *See* Kristallnacht.

NINTH FORT, site in KOVNO, Lithuania, of mass slaughter of Jews. The Ninth Fort was one of a chain of forts constructed around Kovno in the nineteenth century; its distance from the city center was about 4 miles

(6 km). Under independent Lithuania, between the two wars, the Ninth Fort was used as a prison.

During the German occupation of Kovno in World War II, from June 1941 to the summer of 1944, over 50,000 people—men, women, and children—were killed in the Ninth Fort and buried there. Most of the victims were Jews from Kovno and deportees from Germany. In the fall of 1943 an operation was launched by the Germans to burn the corpses of the victims in order to obliterate the traces of the mass murder. The operation, carried out in utmost secrecy, was in the hands of a Sonderkommando 1005 (*see* AKTION 1005). Thirty-four prisoners from the Kovno ghetto, some of whom had been caught while trying to make their way to the forests, were forced to take part in the operation, as were twenty-six Jewish prisoners of war from the Red Army and four non-Jews. The prisoners were kept under strict guard and after work were put in chains. Despite these precautions, sixty-four prisoners managed to escape from the fort, in an organized attempt, on December 24, 1943. Some succeeded in reaching the Kovno ghetto, from which Jewish partisans took them to the Rudninkai Forest to join partisan units. As a result, the German atrocities in the Ninth Fort became known a year before the war ended. Today the site is an official museum.

BIBLIOGRAPHY

Brown, Z. A., and D. Levin. *The Story of an Underground: The Resistance of the Jews of Kovno (Lithuania) in the Second World War.* Jerusalem, 1962. (In Hebrew.)

DOV LEVIN

NISKO AND LUBLIN — January 1940

NISKO AND LUBLIN PLAN, attempted territorial solution to the "Jewish question" through expelling the Jews of the expanding Third Reich to the Lublin area in the eastern extremity of German-occupied Poland; the idea of such a solution prevailed in SS circles between September 1939 and March 1940.

The Nazi victory over Poland in September 1939 brought nearly two million Polish Jews under German control, including over one-half million in the "incorporated territories" that were annexed to Germany in early October, including Danzig, West Prussia, Poznań, and Eastern Upper Silesia. At the same time, the war constricted even further the already fast-shrinking possibilities of Jewish emigration. The temptation to use Polish territory as a "dumping ground" for Jews of the Third Reich (now including Austria, the Protectorate of BOHEMIA AND MORAVIA, and the "incorporated territories," as well as Germany itself) proved too great to be resisted.

In the spring of 1939 Adolf EICHMANN had been transferred to Prague, where, in July, he set up an agency charged with effecting the emigration of the Jews of the newly acquired Protectorate of Bohemia and Moravia as he had done earlier in VIENNA. According to Eichmann, he and the *Höherer SS- und Polizeiführer* (Higher SS and Police Leader), Franz STAHLECKER, conceived of the idea of "resettling" Jews in Poland in September 1939. Stahlecker proposed the idea to Reinhard HEYDRICH, who gave his approval.

It is likely that Stahlecker and Eichmann were not the only people thinking along these lines in September 1939, and that their initiative simply dovetailed with similar plans originating among their superiors. On September 14, Heydrich reported to the division chiefs of the SD (Sicherheitsdienst; Security Service) and Sicherheitspolizei (Security Police), in reference to racial policy in Poland, that Heinrich HIMMLER had submitted proposals to Adolf Hitler about which only the Führer could decide.

When Heydrich met with Eichmann and the EINSATZGRUPPEN commanders on September 21, he revealed to them Hitler's approval of a plan to concentrate Polish Jews in the cities as a short-term goal, and, as a secret, long-term goal, apparently to deport them eastward into territory not intended for Germanization and even to expel some of them over the demarcation line into the Soviet sphere. Initially the only region exempt from concentration was the Galician territory east of Kraków and north of the Slovak border, which was to become, in Heydrich's words, "a Jewish state under German administration" that would also contain "Gypsies and other undesirables."

On September 28, 1939, a new agreement between Nazi Germany and the Soviet Union placed the Lublin region between the Bug and Vistula rivers in the German zone, while yielding Lithuania to the Soviets. Immediately, this new extremity of the German empire was substituted for Western Galicia, and the concept of the "Lublin Reservation" emerged. On September 29, Heydrich referred to a "Reichs-Ghetto" around Lublin, and on the same day Hitler told Alfred ROSENBERG of his plans for placing in the region "between the Vistula and Bug all Jews (also from the Reich) as well as all so-called unreliable elements."

The plans for a Lublin Reservation were part of a wider scheme for the racial restructuring of eastern Europe. The Nazis intended to extend the ethnic boundary of "Germandom" eastward by expelling not only Jews and Gypsies but also Poles from the incorporated territories, and resettling these regions with ethnic Germans (VOLKSDEUTSCHE) repatriated from the Soviet sphere. Himmler was named *Reichskommissar für die Festigung des Deutschen Volkstums* (Reich Commissar for the Strengthening of German Nationhood) on October 7, 1939, and charged with both repatriating the ethnic Germans and eliminating the "harmful influence" of alien populations in the Reich. He was thus responsible for a vast program of demographic engineering, of which expulsions of Jews to Lublin formed only one facet.

On October 6, Gestapo chief Heinrich MÜLLER instructed Eichmann to make contact with Joseph Wagner, the *Gauleiter* of Eastern Upper Silesia, concerning the expulsion of seventy thousand to eighty thousand Jews over the Vistula, to "gather experience" for the evacuation "of much greater numbers." However, Eichmann went first to Vienna and Mährisch Ostrau, (today called Ostrava), a town in the Protectorate near the Polish border, before reaching Katowice (Ger., Kattowitz) in Eastern Upper Silesia on October 9, and he arranged for deportations from all three places.

In Mährisch Ostrau the Gestapo summoned all the Jewish engineers, carpenters, and artisans, who were to bring their tools with them. Jewish firms were to supply food and building materials. Great effort was taken to give a voluntary character to what Eichmann called his "model transport." Thus, the evacuees were forced to sign a statement to the effect that they had volunteered for a "retraining camp." In Vienna the Jewish leaders were also informed that they were to prepare a list of one thousand to twelve hundred working men for deportation. To Rabbi Josef LÖWENHERZ, head of the Vienna Jewish community, Eichmann cynically painted rosy pictures of the Jews creating for themselves a new existence in Poland, free of the legal restrictions imposed upon them in the Third Reich.

Eichmann still had to establish what he called a "transit camp" in the Lublin region to receive the deportees. On October 12, he and Stahlecker flew to Poland. They explored for several days before deciding on Zarzecze, a village near Nisko on the San River. On October 18, the first transport of 901 Jews left Mährisch Ostrau. The Jewish deportees were marched from the train station at Nisko to a swampy meadow near Zarzecze and put to work setting up barracks. The meaning of the term "transit camp" then became clear, for on the following morning the best workers were selected from the group, and the rest were marched eastward and dispersed all over the area of the Lublin district. Transports of 875 Jews from Katowice and 912 Jews from Vienna departed on October 20 and were treated similarly upon arrival.

Eichmann was clearly operating under the assumption that his experimental transports to the transit camp at Nisko were the prelude to a general deportation of all Reich Jews. By mid-October he was referring to "continuous" transports that within three to four weeks would leave Germany itself as well. This expectation was short-lived, however. On October 19, Müller cabled that all deportations to Poland required central direction and thus explicit approval from Berlin. When Eichmann's deputy, Rolf Günther, inquired if this included a second transport from Mährisch Ostrau that had already been agreed upon between Müller and Eichmann, he was informed that "every transport of Jews had to be stopped."

Eichmann hurried off to Berlin to salvage what he could of his ambitious dreams, with very limited success. He did secure approval for a second transport of 672 Jews from Vienna that departed on October 26, and a combined transport of 400 Jews from Mährisch Ostrau and 1,000 from Katowice that left on October 27, but that was all. A small transport from Prague was turned back when a bridge over the San was washed away. Attempts to schedule another transport from Vienna failed owing to military claims on railway transport on that day. No further transports to Nisko were attempted thereafter. The camp at Nisko remained in existence, however, and its inmates suffered through a difficult winter of hard labor and harsh weather. In April 1940, the camp was finally dissolved on the order of the higher SS and police leader in the GENERALGOUVERNEMENT, Friedrich Wilhelm KRÜGER. The remaining 501 Jews who had not been expelled throughout the Lublin area were returned to Austria and the Protectorate.

Eichmann blamed the abrupt halting of the Nisko experiment on the opposition of Hans FRANK, the governor-general of Poland, but this is not persuasive. Müller's stop order was issued on October 19, and Frank's deputy, Arthur SEYSS-INQUART, did not even learn of these deportations until early November, when the *Gauleiter* of Vienna, Josef Bürckel, angrily accused him of being responsible for their cancellation. Frank himself was deeply embroiled in the imminent transfer of the Generalgouvernement from army jurisdiction to that of his own administration. His opposition to Jewish deportations came only much later, in early 1940. Local protest in the Lublin region against the influx of Jews was vehement, but likewise too late to explain a decision taken in Berlin even as the first transport from Nisko was just arriving. Himmler later claimed that the decision to halt the Nisko transports was his own and had been made on the basis of "technical difficulties."

These "technical difficulties" were probably related to problems Himmler faced in finding jobs and housing for the ethnic Germans from the Baltic. The first contingent arrived in Danzig in mid-October 1939, and thereafter the focal point of German resettlement activity shifted from Eastern Upper Silesia, the Protectorate, and Vienna to the north. At the end of October 1939 Himmler ordered that all 550,000 Jews from the annexed territories of West Prussia and the WARTHEGAU region, together with 450,000 Poles, be deported within four months in order to make room for the incoming Baltic Germans. In a swift and brutal operation that December, 87,000 Poles and Jews were deported from the Warthegau in eighty trainloads. However, this deluge of penniless refugees quickly aroused the opposition of Hans Frank, leading to a temporary postponement of further Jewish deportations, as well as a curtailment of Polish deportations..

At a meeting on February 12, 1940, with Hermann GÖRING, Frank, and Arthur GREISER, the Nazi *Gauleiter* of the Warthegau, Himmler still spoke of the Lublin region as "destined to become the *Judenreservat*" (reservation for the Jews), and deportations were subsequently scheduled for August. But by March 1940 Hitler was expressing doubt about such a solution, since he noted that the "Jewish question" really was a space question that was difficult to solve, particularly for him, since he had no space at his disposal. Neither would the establishment of a Jewish state around Lublin ever constitute a solution. Hitler's change of heart about the Lublin Reservation had quick repercussions. When German authorities in Warsaw suggested deporting the Jews there to Lublin in April 1940, they were informed that the idea of a Jewish reservation in Lublin had been dropped. German attention thereafter shifted to the possibility of expelling the European Jews to a distant territory overseas, with particular focus on the island of Madagascar (*see* MADAGASCAR PLAN).

Thus, the Nisko scheme never got beyond

the experimental stage, and the Lublin Reservation was a plan that the Nazis never really implemented. Nonetheless, they represented the first Nazi thinking about a solution to the "Jewish question" under the impact of victory in Poland and in the west and the resultant vast increase in the number of Jews within the German sphere.

BIBLIOGRAPHY

Browning, C. R. *The Final Solution and the German Foreign Office*. New York, 1978.

Browning, C. R. "Nazi Resettlement Policy and the Search for a Solution to the Jewish Question, 1939–1941." *German Studies Review* 9/3 (1986): 492–519.

Friedman, P. "The Lublin Reservation and the Madagascar Plan: Two Aspects of Nazi Jewish Policy during the Second World War." In *Roads to Extinction: Essays on the Holocaust*, edited by A. J. Friedman, pp. 34–58. Philadelphia, 1980.

Hilberg, R. *The Destruction of the European Jews*. 3 vols. New York, 1985.

Moser, J. "Nisko: The First Experiment in Deportation." *Simon Wiesenthal Center Annual* 2 (1985): 1–30.

Poliakov, L. *Harvest of Hate*. New York, 1979. See pages 33–37.

CHRISTOPHER R. BROWNING

NONSECTARIAN REFUGEE ORGANIZATIONS IN THE UNITED STATES. In addition to Jewish and Christian refugee agencies, a number of nonsectarian organizations devoted to solving the refugee problem functioned in the United States between 1933 and 1945. They included the American Committee for the Relief of Victimized German Children; the American Council of Voluntary Agencies for Foreign Service; the Emergency Committee in Aid of Displaced Foreign Physicians; the Emergency Committee in Aid of Displaced German Scholars; the National Committee for Resettlement of Foreign Physicians; the National Coordinating Committee for Aid to Refugees and Emigrants from Germany; the National Refugee Service; the Non-Sectarian Committee for German Refugee Children; the Non-Sectarian Foundation for Refugee Children; the Placement Committee for German and Austrian Musicians; the President's Advisory Committee on Political Refugees; the Self-Help of Emigrés from Central Europe; and the United States Committee for the Care of European Children.

The establishment of nonsectarian committees was the result of Jewish efforts to co-opt well-known Christian personalities in order to make the American public aware of Christian interest in the refugee cause. Because of the antisemitic feelings that were encountered in academic and professional institutions, including universities, hospitals, and the American Medical Association, nonsectarian activities were considered the best way to ensure the greatest public support. The creation of nonsectarian agencies also stemmed from the need to care for groups with specific problems. Physicians, scientists, musicians, psychologists, lawyers, and children required special care, which only professional committees could provide.

Some organizations, such as the National Coordinating Committee, the National Refugee Service, and the committees for physicians, musicians, lawyers, and social workers, with annual budgets of tens of thousands of dollars, were funded largely by Jewish sources. They were nonsectarian only in the sense that they provided relief to persons of all faiths without distinction, although most of their clients were Jews. There were some Christians on the executive board, who used their influence when necessary, but those who did the actual work, as executive secretary, chariman, and treasurer, were Jews. It is, therefore, doubtful whether most of these committees can truly be considered nonsectarian organizations.

Because of a serious shortage of funds, clearly reflecting the apathetic (if not hostile) mood of the American people toward REFUGEES, the help offered by nonsectarian committees was far from sufficient. The Emergency Committee in Aid of Displaced Foreign Physicians granted only 125 scholarships between 1934 and 1942, amounting to a total of $294,075. The Emergency Committee in Aid of Displaced German Scholars allocated grants to 335 individuals out of 6,000 scholars listed in its files. Up to May 1943, the United States Committee for the Care of European Children brought into the United States 1,193 children from England, France, and Spain. Yet, in spite of their limited achievements, nonsectarian committees increased interfaith cooperation and paved the way for better understanding after the war.

BIBLIOGRAPHY

Close, K. *Transplanted Children: A History.* New York, 1953.

Davie, M. R. *Refugees in America: Report of the Committee for the Study of Recent Immigration from Europe.* New York, 1947.

Duggan, S., and B. Drury. *The Rescue of Science and Learning: The Story of the Emergency Committee in Aid of Displaced Foreign Scholars.* New York, 1948.

Genizi, H. "American Non-Sectarian Refugee Relief Organizations (1933–1945)." *Yad Vashem Studies* 11 (1976): 164–220.

HAIM GENIZI

NORTH AFRICA. *See* Algeria; Libya; Morocco; Tunisia.

NORWAY. [*The two articles in this entry are an overview of Norwegian history during the German occupation in World War II, and an account of the fate of Norwegian Jewry in that period.*]

General Survey

Upon the dissolution of Norway's union with SWEDEN in 1905, neutrality formed the basis of Norwegian foreign policy. During World War I Norway maintained an effective neutrality, and after the war it strongly supported the League of Nations and its concept of collective security. In 1939, on the eve of World War II, Norway joined the other Scandinavian countries in a proclamation of strict neutrality in the event of war.

In May 1933 Vidkun QUISLING had founded the Nasjonal Samling (National Unity; NS) party, a fascist organization that modeled itself after Adolf Hitler's NAZI PARTY. After the outbreak of the war, Quisling offered to the Germans the party's cooperation in putting bases at the disposal of German forces.

The German assault in Norway began on the night of April 8–9, 1940, and caught the Norwegians completely unprepared. At most of the landing points the armed resistance to the German forces was totally inadequate. The battle for Norway was fought by German, Norwegian, British, French, and Polish forces. By April 26, less than one week after the British troops had gone into battle, the British military coordination committee made a decision to withdraw. German military strength, together with effective use of airpower and the services of Norwegian collaborators who disrupted transportation and communications and seized power plants, forced the Norwegian armies to surrender on June 9.

King Haakon VII and the government leaders escaped to London, where they set up a government-in-exile. During the war they maintained continuous radio contact with loyal elements in Norway and managed to divert practically the entire Norwegian merchant fleet to the service of the Allies.

Within six hours of the invasion Quisling proclaimed himself prime minister, but the Germans speedily became disillusioned with him, and his ministry lasted only six days. On April 24, Hitler appointed Josef Terboven as *Reichskommissar* (Reich Commissioner) in occupied Norway, representing not only the German state but the Nazi party. Generaloberst Nikolaus von Falkenhorst was the commander of the German troops in Norway. He maintained the level of German military strength at twelve infantry divisions, one armored division, and two hundred and fifty coastal batteries.

On February 1, 1942, a national government was formed in which Quisling assumed office as *Ministerpresident,* but no real redistribution of power took place. Terboven planned to organize a government in Norway that would be responsive to German pressure and capable of controlling the Norwegian population. Internal control was consolidated by abolishing the parliament, banning all political parties except the NS, and taking over the court system. In February 1943 a national labor law was instituted whose purpose was the conscription of all labor to serve the government.

Nazi ideology failed to take root in Norway, and an underground soon arose. Two military resistance organizations evolved from the early resistance attempts. One was a military intelligence organization called

NORWAY

XU, which conveyed information to the Norwegian government-in-exile in London. The second, Milorg, was the Norwegian underground army. In 1943 the civilian and military resistance drew closer together, and in 1944 they formed the joint Hjemmefrontens Ledelse (Home Front Command). The small but well-organized Communist resistance movement advocated a policy of force against the Germans. Despite Norwegian antipathy to communism, the Communists' call for active resistance gained support as the war progressed. Distrust between Milorg and the Communists, however, continued to the end of the war. The combined forces of the Norwegian underground and the British effected one of the most damaging sabotage operations of the war—the destruction of the Norsk Hydroelectric Company plant, which produced heavy water, a key element in the German effort to produce an atomic bomb. Other forms of resistance activities included strikes, boycotts, an illegal press, and the establishment of escape routes.

On May 7, 1945, the German forces capitulated, and the following day the surrender was signed. A few days later, Crown Prince Olav returned to Norway as commander in chief of the armed forces. On June 7, exactly five years after he had gone into exile, King Haakon returned.

[*See also* Trials of War Criminals: Norway.]

BIBLIOGRAPHY

Hayes, P. M. *Quisling: The Career and Political Ideas of Vidkun Quisling.* London, 1971.

Höye, B., and T. M. Agev. *The Fight of the Norwegian Church against Nazism.* New York, 1943.

Petrow, R. *The Bitter Years: The Invasion and Occupation of Denmark and Norway, April 1940–May 1945.* New York, 1974.

Riste, O., and B. Nokleby. *Norway, 1940–1945: The Resistance Movement.* Oslo, 1970.

JACQUELINE ROKHSAR

Norwegian Jewry in the Holocaust

At the beginning of the Nazi invasion of Norway (April 1940) there were about 1,700 Jews living there, including some 200 Jewish refugees from other countries. A total of 763 Jews were deported, of whom 739 perished, mainly at AUSCHWITZ and other camps. Twenty-four of those deported (3.15 percent) returned at the end of the war. In Norway itself, 23 Jews died as a result of war-related actions and Nazi persecutions. Of the Jewish refugees, 101 were deported, and 13 of them were among the returning survivors. About 900 Jews escaped to SWEDEN with the help of the Norwegian underground. Altogether, 762 Jews (45 percent) perished, some families being wiped out entirely. Among the non-Jewish Norwegians, 5,431 were deported to concentration camps in Germany, and 649 of them (12 percent) perished there. Most were rescued through the Red Cross operation of Count Folke BERNADOTTE. About 50,000 Norwegians escaped to Sweden.

In the early days of the German occupation of Norway, restrictions on Jews were sporadic. However, with the German invasion of the Soviet Union on June 22, 1941, numerous Jews in northern Norway were arrested and sent to various camps and prisons. Thus, on June 23, 60 Jews were incarcerated in the camp of Grini, where they were singled out for beatings and hard forced labor. In the northernmost Jewish community in Norway, that of Trondheim, with about 150 members, the synagogue was confiscated by the Germans as early as April 1941 and completely vandalized. Four Trondheim Jews, after being arrested in January 1942 on trumped-up charges, were shot on March 7 of that year. The Jewish community of Oslo, numbering 800, was less molested. However, in August 1942 nine of its Jews were arrested, including Rabbi Julius Isak Samual, who had served the congregation since 1930. He was released but had to report to the Gestapo every day. Rabbi Samual refused suggestions to escape to Sweden, not wishing to abandon his community in the hour of danger. He was rearrested on September 2, deported, and eventually perished in Auschwitz on December 16, 1942.

The main persecution of Norway's Jews followed, in the fall of 1942. Its initiators were Vidkun QUISLING, at that time prime minister of a puppet government, and the German authorities, under the guidance of Reichskommissar Josef Terboven and with the cooperation of the Norwegian police. At the beginning of October, all the male Jews in Trondheim over the age of fourteen were arrested. Mass arrests began on October 26. They were organized by the Norwegian chief of state police, Generalmajor Karl A. Marthinsen, Sturmbannführer Helmuth Reinhard, head of the SD (Sicherheitsdienst; Security Service), and Hauptsturmführer Wilhelm Wagner, head of the Gestapo office for Jewish affairs. Lists of Jews to be arrested had been prepared on the basis of questionnaires that the Jews had had to fill out the previous spring. They were now distributed to 62 squads, made up of 124 policemen.

On October 26 and 27, 260 male Jews were arrested in Oslo. The main onslaught followed, during the night of November 25–26. The Norwegian police, together with the Norwegian Nazi formations and SS units, rounded up all the remaining Jews of Oslo —women, elderly people, children, the sick, and the mentally ill and retarded. However, as before, acting on warnings received from policemen and the underground, some went into hiding and escaped. Those who had been arrested at the end of October and had been held in a camp were sent together with the newly arrested Jews on the specially requisitioned *Donau* via Stettin to Auschwitz. The deportation was organized mainly by the Quisling bureaucracy in cooperation with the Nazi authorities in Oslo, leaving Adolf EICHMANN's office at the REICHSSICHERHEITSHAUPTAMT (Reich Security Main Office; RSHA) the opportunity to intervene only at the last moment. Preparations for the *Aktion* included the official confiscation of all Jewish property in October.

The deportation was carried out despite the protests of the Norwegian populace, guided by the Norwegian church leaders. On November 11, 1942, after the *Aktion* of October, the bishops of Norway, together with other Protestant congregations, sent a letter of protest to Quisling. Denouncing the illegal acts, the letter stated: "God does not differentiate between people." On December 6 and 13 the letter was read from church pulpits while the congregations rose to their feet. It was also quoted in the church's 1943 New Year message. Nevertheless, on February 25, 1943, an additional 158 Jews from the Norwegian provinces were sent on the *Gotenland* to Stettin, from where they were transported via Berlin to Auschwitz. Out of the 739 deported, 410 were men, 268 were women, and 61 were children under fifteen years old. The oldest was a man of 82 and the youngest a baby eight weeks of age. Fifty persons with family connections in Sweden were interned on the initiative of the Swedish consul, Claes Adolf Hjalmar Westring, and were released to Sweden that month.

BIBLIOGRAPHY

Friedman, T. *Dokumentensammlung über "Die Deportierung der Juden aus Norwegen nach Auschwitz."* Ramat Gan, Israel, 1963.

Johansen, P. O. *Oss selv naermest: Norge og jødene 1914–1943.* Oslo, 1984.

Ulstein, R. *Svensketrafikken: Flyktinger till Sverige 1940–1943.* Oslo, 1974.

SAMUEL ABRAHAMSEN

NOSSIG, ALFRED (1864–1943), writer, sculptor, and Zionist theoretician whose interest in Jewish emigration made him a collaborator with the German authorities. Nossig was born in Lvov and attended several universities, studying natural sciences, medicine, law, and philosophy. In his youth he favored assimilation into Polish culture, but later he became a Zionist. Nossig was active as an artist, intellectual, and founder of Jewish public projects and institutions. He made a name for himself with his many talents and his efforts to increase the self-confidence of Jews and improve their self-image. His career was also marked by abrupt shifts and sharp changes of direction; he proved to be unstable and inconsistent in his views as well as in his politics. In 1892 he moved to Vienna and in 1894 to Paris; in 1900 he took up residence in Berlin.

As early as 1887, while still living in Lvov, Nossig wrote a pamphlet dealing with the "Jewish question," in which he advocated the establishment of a Jewish state in Palestine. In the early 1900s he was one of a group who proposed the creation of a Jewish institution of higher learning, and in 1904 he became head of the Jewish Bureau of Statistics, which he had founded in Berlin together with Arthur Ruppin and Jacob Thon. Nossig became close to the Democratic Faction in the Zionist movement, in which Chaim WEIZMANN played a leading role and which represented an opposition to Theodor Herzl.

Alfred Nossig. [Schwadron Collection, Jewish National and University Library, Jerusalem]

In 1908 Nossig left the Zionist movement and founded the Jewish Settlement Association (Allgemeine Jüdische Kolonisations-Organisation), engaging in political lobbying on behalf of Jewish emigration to parts of the world other than Palestine. During World War I he pursued this goal in Germany, and went so far as to seek a declaration from Turkey and the Central Powers recognizing the right of Jews to enter the Ottoman empire. These efforts, which had no success, were regarded by the Zionists as subversive to their cause; but they seem to have reinforced Nossig's pro-German attitude, which he retained to the end of his life.

In the early 1920s Nossig, responding to an invitation by the Polish authorities, went to Poland in order to mediate between the leadership of the Jewish organizations and the newly established Polish republic. The Jews, however, regarded him as a representative of foreign interests; before long this appraisal was also shared by the Poles, and Nossig's involvement in the Polish-Jewish relationship had no tangible results.

Soon after World War II broke out, Nossig arrived in Warsaw, apparently after a short stay in Prague. Despite his age—he was now seventy-five—he began to deal with emigration from occupied Poland, presumably at the suggestion of the German authorities. As early as October 17, 1939, Adam CZERNIAKÓW, the WARSAW ghetto Jewish leader, wrote in his diary about the *Tausendkünstler* ("man of a thousand parts") Alfred Nossig visiting him. On December 9 of that year, Czerniaków noted that the Germans had ordered him "to take Dr. Nossig onto the Jewish community staff," apparently to deal with emigration affairs. Later, Nossig became director of the department of culture and the arts in the JUDENRAT (Jewish Council). On April 11, 1940, Czerniaków's diary has an entry noting that Nossig was "addressing letters to the authorities for which there is no need." Subsequent entries imply that Nossig was representing German security services, apparently the Gestapo. On May 17, 1941, Czerniaków noted: "Yesterday Nossig was thrown out of the German *Transferstelle* [place of transfer] by the German official Josef Steyert. Nossig complained at the proper quarters—and today there was a response."

Nossig was executed by the ŻYDOWSKA ORGANIZACJA BOJOWA (Jewish Fighting Organization; ŻOB), at the end of January or in February 1943 (the precise date is unknown). Many unsubstantiated reports have been written about this affair and about how the ŻOB came to condemn Nossig to death and carry out the sentence; Nossig's character and his deeds have aroused a great deal of interest. A neighbor in the building where the Judenrat employees lived during the final phase of the ghetto's existence testified that the door of Nossig's apartment bore a sign stating that the occupant was under the Gestapo's protection. A report found in the ONEG SHABBAT Archive, listing thirteen Jews who were shot to death by the ŻOB, describes Nossig as an "active collaborator with the Germans (the Gestapo) who provided them with information on the life of the Jews. When he was executed a report was found on him that he had drawn up for the Gestapo, dealing with the January 1943 *Aktion.*"

BIBLIOGRAPHY

Almog, S. "Alfred Nossig: A Reappraisal." *Studies in Zionism* 7 (Spring 1983): 1–29.

Friedman, I. *"The Austro-Hungarian Government and Zionism, 1897–1918." Jewish Social Studies* 27 (1965): 147–167, 236–249.

Mendelsohn, E. "Wilhelm Feldman and Alfred Nossig: Assimilation and Zionism in Lvov." *Galed: On the History of the Jews in Poland* 2 (1975): 89–111. (In Hebrew.)

ISRAEL GUTMAN

Franz Novak.

NOVAK, FRANZ (b. 1913), one of Adolf EICHMANN's assistants in the deportation of Jews to their death. A native of Wolfsberg, in Austria, Novak joined the HITLERJUGEND (Hitler Youth) in 1929 and became a Nazi party member in 1933. In July 1934 Novak was involved in the Nazi-staged putsch in which Chancellor Engelbert Dollfuss of Austria was assassinated; he had to flee the country, taking refuge in Germany, and the Austrian government deprived him of his citizenship.

Following the annexation of Austria by Germany in 1938, Novak returned to Vienna, where he was assigned to the SD (Sicherheitsdienst; Security Service) and became a senior staff member of the ZENTRALSTELLE FÜR JÜDISCHE AUSWANDERUNG (Central Office for Jewish Emigration)—headed by Eichmann—which at the time had the task of forcing Jews to emigrate. Novak joined Eichmann in setting up the same kind of office in BERLIN and, later, in PRAGUE.

When Eichmann was appointed head of Section IV B 4 (Evacuation and Jews) of the REICHSSICHERHEITSHAUPTAMT (Reich Security Main Office; RSHA) and launched the extermination of the Jews, Novak was put in charge of the transportation subsection. Here he helped requisition the trains that took Jews from the ghettos and from western Europe to extermination camps and concentration camps. In 1944 he played a very active role in the Eichmann Sonderkommando, which had the task of deporting the Jews of HUNGARY to their death.

After the war, Novak went into hiding in Austria under an assumed name. In 1957 he reverted to his real name, but the Austrian police took no action, even though his name was on the list of wanted war criminals. It was only under the impact of the EICHMANN TRIAL, in which Novak's share in the "FINAL SOLUTION" was revealed, that he was arrested, in 1961. In 1964 he was sentenced to eight years' imprisonment; following an appeal, the Austrian Supreme Court ordered a retrial, which took place in 1966. Novak was acquitted and set free.

SHMUEL SPECTOR

A workshop in the Nováky camp.

NOVÁKY, forced-labor and concentration camp in SLOVAKIA, near the town of that name in the central part of the country. Jews were brought to the site in the autumn of 1941, but the camp began functioning fully only in the spring of 1942, at the time of the mass deportation of Slovak Jews. The Slovak Jewish Center (ÚSTREDŇA ŽIDOV) had conducted a campaign with the Ministry of the Interior for the creation of forced-labor camps, where the inmates would be safe from deportation; Nováky was one such camp, but this did not save some of its inmates from deportation.

Nováky was situated in a military compound where Jews were being assembled for deportation to Poland. The prisoners were mostly skilled craftsmen, and they began working even before the workshops were completed. The camp commandant, a HLINKA GUARD officer named Polhora, was an unstable and moody drunkard whom the Jewish leaders in the camp were able to manipulate. He was assisted by a Jewish council made up of a chairman, an administrative officer, a camp police chief, and various other functionaries, as well as representatives of the workers themselves. The chairman of the council, an engineer by the name of Otto Mandler, was a first-rate administrator with great influence, both with the Jews in the camp and with their guards. The products manufactured in the camp met the requirements of the "clients"—government agencies, the army, the police, and the Hlinka Guard.

Nováky was the largest forced-labor camp in Slovakia, holding sixteen hundred prisoners. The income that it earned represented 38.5 percent of the total income of the labor camps in Slovakia, and in economic terms the camp was a success. In 1943 conditions in the camp improved and the food rations be-

The Jewish police in the Nováky camp.

came satisfactory. The camp ran its own institutions—a kindergarten and elementary school, medical clinics, and welfare agencies. Of great importance were the camp's cultural activities, which included dramatic performances, and religious studies. The youth in the camp also took up sports, and a swimming pool was constructed in the camp. The unusual conditions prevailing in Nováky—situated as it was in the midst of a population that had no sympathy for the clerical-fascist regime, in a heavily wooded mountainous area at the foot of Mount Vtacnik—made possible the formation of an active underground movement, which emerged from the Communists and the Zionist YOUTH MOVEMENTS.

When the SLOVAK NATIONAL UPRISING took place in August 1944, Nováky was liberated, and a fighting unit, made up of 205 prisoners from the camp, joined the rebel forces. The unit was posted to the front near the town of Batovany, where it fought with tenacity against the German forces charged with suppressing the uprising. Thirty-five members of this Jewish unit fell in the fighting.

BIBLIOGRAPHY

Jelinek, Y. "The Role of the Jews in Slovakian Resistance." *Jahrbuch für Geschichte Osteuropas* 15/3 (September 1967): 415–422.

AKIVA NIR

NOVOGRUDOK (Pol., Nowogródek), town in the Belorussian SSR that belonged to Poland in the interwar period. In September 1939, Novogrudok was occupied by the Red Army and incorporated into the Soviet Union. Jews had been living there from the sixteenth century, and in the nineteenth century it was the seat of a well-known yeshiva (rabbinical academy). On the eve of World War II the town's Jewish population numbered approximately seven thousand.

Novogrudok was occupied by the Germans on July 3, 1941, and three days later 150 Jewish intellectuals were put to death. Another 50 Jews were murdered on July 11. In an *Aktion* that took place on December 8 of that year, the Germans murdered 4,000 Jews, including members of the JUDENRAT (Jewish Council) that had been set up in the town. A Wehrmacht unit participated in this *Aktion*, after which thousands of Jews from nearby towns—Ivenets, Naliboki, Rubezhevichi, Korelichi, and Lubach—were brought to Novogrudok. The ghetto that had been established earlier was divided into three sections: Section A, the courthouses, where skilled craftsmen were concentrated; Section B, the Pereselka area; and Section C, Nazaratanek, where the school buildings were located.

On August 8, 1942, the Germans carried out another *Aktion*, in which 2,500 Jews from Section C were murdered; in a third *Aktion*, on February 4, 1943, all the Jews from Section B were murdered. Section A, which contained the skilled craftsmen, was made into a labor camp. A fourth *Aktion* was launched on May 7 of that year in which the inhabitants of Section A were killed, except for 230 who were spared. These survivors had learned of partisan operations in the region in letters they received from Tuvia BIELSKI and his

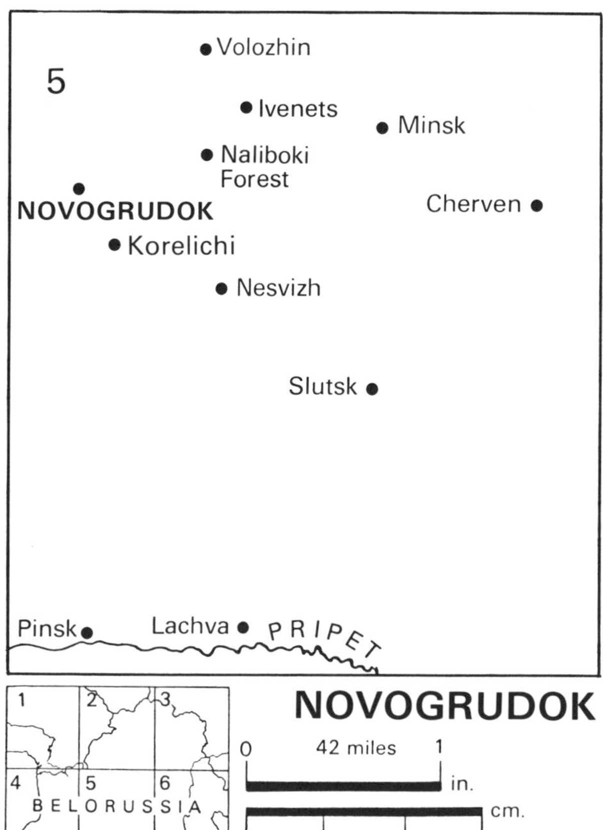

brothers, urging them to try to make their way into the forest. In the summer of 1942 the number of Jews escaping to the forest increased. The underground groups in Novogrudok were in touch with the ARMIA KRAJOWA (Home Army), the Polish underground organization.

In September 1942, Dr. Jakov Kagan, a member of Po'alei Zion Right who before the war had lived in Baranovichi, had called a meeting of youth movement members and unaffiliated Jews, and proposed that they stage an uprising and then escape into the forest. His proposal was accepted, and he was appointed commander of the uprising. A detailed plan was worked out, weapons were acquired, and a date was set for the uprising; April 15, 1943. When that day came, however, the authors of the plan backed away, mainly because of the opposition of many Jews in the ghetto. Instead, a group that included Kagan, Berl Joselovits, and Nathan Sucharski took the lead in digging an escape tunnel, which was in fact completed. It measured 31 inches (80 cm) in height, 23.5 inches (60 cm) in width, and 820 feet (250 m) in length, and was dug 4.9 feet (1.5 m) under the ground. On September 26, 1943, 233 Jews broke out through the tunnel, but in the darkness they lost their way and walked straight into the camp's barbed-wire fence. The German guard opened fire and killed 120 of them, including the group who had taken the initiative in digging the tunnel. About 100 Jews reached the partisans and joined the Bielski and other partisan units.

BIBLIOGRAPHY

Belsky, T. "Jews of the Forest." In *The Fighting Ghettos,* edited by M. Barkai, pp. 170–183. Philadelphia, 1962.

Belsky, T., and Z. Belsky. *Jews of the Forest: From the Stories of Jewish Partisans in the Forests of Belorussia.* Tel Aviv, 1946. (In Hebrew.)

Novogrudok Record. Tel Aviv, 1963. (In Hebrew.)

Yaffe, Y. *Partisans: The History of Jewish Partisan Units in Belorussia.* Tel Aviv, 1951. (In Hebrew.)

SHALOM CHOLAWSKI

NOWAK, FRANZ. *See* Novak, Franz.

NSB. *See* Nationaal Socialistische Beweging.

NSDAP. *See* Nazi Party.

NSZ. *See* Narodowy Siły Zbrojne.

NUREMBERG. Jews lived in Nuremberg from the twelfth century; the Jewish community knew periods of prosperity and growth, as well as of riots and expulsions. In 1922 the community, numbering 9,280, was the second largest in Bavaria.

Many of Nuremberg's Jews were affluent merchants, industrialists, bankers, and professionals. Their situation took a turn for the worse after the founding in Nuremberg of *Der* STÜRMER, the notorious Nazi weekly, by Julius STREICHER in 1923. This was also the year of Hitler's putsch attempt in Munich; and it was in that year that young Nazis in uniform attacked hundreds of Jews in Nuremberg on the streets and in cafés and broke into the Jewish cemetery. One Jew died of wounds received at the Nazis' hands. The Reich Union of Jewish Frontline Soldiers (REICHSBUND JÜDISCHER FRONTSOLDATEN) reacted by posting armed guards at community institutions. Riots against the Jews and the damaging of Jewish-owned property were renewed after the Nazi success in the 1930 elections.

In Nuremberg, assaults on Jews after the Nazi rise to power were worse than in other places. On July 20, 1933, SA (Sturmabteilung; Storm Troopers) men broke into four hundred Jewish houses and confiscated cash and savings accounts; some three hundred Jews, most of them members of the fraternal order B'NAI B'RITH (including some who were over seventy), were arrested by the SA, herded into empty lots in the suburbs, and beaten up.

From the beginning of the Nazi regime in January 1933 until March 31, 1934, 1,476 Jews left Nuremberg. The rate decreased sharply thereafter, and in the year beginning April 1937, only 298 Jews left the city. The Nazis' efforts to rid the city of its Jews were countered by the Jews' radical reorganization of their religious, educational, cultural, and

SS troops evacuated forced-labor camps as Allied troops were closing in. The inmates were driven on death marches, and those who survived them were often killed. This photo shows the bodies of slave laborers killed by SS troops in a forest outside Nuremberg.

social life, with the object of making themselves independent of their hostile environment. At the same time, the Jewish community organization's revenue and expenditures increased, unlike those of other Jewish communities in the country. This was made possible by the Jews' generally strong economic condition, with 728 Jewish enterprises still in existence at the end of 1936.

On August 10, 1938, on Streicher's orders, the Great Synagogue and the adjacent Jewish community building were torn down, the pretext being that they were "spoiling the look of the city." The synagogue's "Jewish stone," a remnant of a medieval synagogue that served as the base for the Holy Ark, was saved by a non-Jewish architect.

On KRISTALLNACHT (November 9–10, 1938), at 2:00 a.m., SA men armed with sticks gathered in the main city square and set fire to the Adas Israel synagogue and the Ahiezer prayer hall. Gangs of hoodlums went on a rampage through the streets of Nuremberg, attacking Jews and wounding hundreds of them: sixteen Jews were murdered and ten committed suicide. These twenty-six victims constituted a substantial proportion of the total loss of life among German Jewry on *Kristallnacht*. One hundred and sixty Nuremberg Jews were arrested and beaten up in the city jail, and most were later sent to the DACHAU concentration camp. Hundreds of Jewish apartments and businesses were ransacked by the rioters, often joined by passersby.

At that point the Jews of Nuremberg began to flee the city. City officials, led by Nazi party leaders, bought up Jewish-owned property at a fraction of its value. The corrupt practices at this time were so outrageous that the authorities had to set up a commission of inquiry, which denounced the events that had taken place and called for the punishment of those responsible.

On November 29, 1941, 535 Jews from Nuremberg were deported to RIGA; on March 24, 1942, 650 were sent to Izbica, near Lublin; and on September 10 of that year, 686 went to THERESIENSTADT. From these three deportations, only a handful of Jews survived. Another 139 Jews were deported in four different groups, and 67 more were deported on an individual basis. In the fall of 1942, after several dozen Jews had been transferred to the nearby city of Fürth, the only Jews left in the city were those married to non-Jews. The Nazi newspapers boasted that Nuremberg had become *judenrein* ("cleansed of Jews").

When the war was over, sixty-five Jews returned to Nuremberg; of these, some eventu-

When United States Third Army troops entered the Nuremberg area, they found the bodies of those slain by the SS and ordered the citizens of Nuremberg to place the bodies in wooden coffins. Here, the Germans carry the coffins of the slain camp inmates through the city.

The bodies of the camp inmates killed by the SS were brought to a local cemetery, where the Nurembergers, the soldiers, and camp inmate survivors attended a memorial service held by United States Army chaplains.

ally emigrated from Germany. Only a few of the persons who had committed crimes against the Jews were put on trial, and most of those tried were acquitted or given light sentences. A new Jewish community organization was formed, one of its tasks being to look after the two Jewish cemeteries. Both cemeteries, however, have been desecrated on several occasions.

BIBLIOGRAPHY

Ophir, B. Z. *Germany—Bavaria.* In *Pinkas Hakehillot; Encyclopaedia of Jewish Communities.* Jerusalem, 1972. (In Hebrew, with English summary.)

HENRY WASSERMAN

NUREMBERG LAWS, two constitutional laws issued on September 15, 1935, that became the basis for the further legal exclusion of Jews from German life and the ensuing anti-Jewish policy. The Nuremberg Laws were proclaimed at a special session of the Reichstag summoned to Nuremberg during the annual Nazi party rally in that city.

The first of the two Nuremberg Laws, the Reich Citizenship Law, stated that only Germans or people with related blood could be citizens of the Reich. German Jews lost their political rights through this law, which made them *Staatsangehörige* (state subjects), whereas the "Aryan" Germans were declared *Reichsbürger* (citizens of the Reich). The Reich Citizenship Law was complemented by thirteen implementation ordinances issued from November 1935 to July 1943 that systematically excluded the Jews from German life. The second of the two laws, the Law for the Protection of German Blood and Honor, prohibited marriages and extramarital intercourse between Jews and Germans, the employment of German maids under the age of forty-five in Jewish households, and the raising by Jews of the German flag.

With the promulgation of the Nuremberg Laws, the exceptions made in earlier ANTI-JEWISH LEGISLATION for World War I veterans and state officials who had held their posts before 1914 were no longer valid. The new racial laws not only had a symbolic function, dramatizing the exclusion of Jews from German society; they also provided a rationalization and legitimization for the campaign of antisemitic riots and arrests of Jews that had taken place during the previous months, while putting an end to the political instability created by these riots.

The Nuremberg laws have been depicted by some scholars as the result of a hasty and last-minute decision on the eve of the Reichstag convention. According to a number of historians (Raul Hilberg, Karl Schleunes, and Hans Mommsen), Hitler had meant to deliver an address on foreign policy in the presence of the diplomatic corps. However, because of an unexpected change, this proved impracticable, and Hitler, needing to fill the vacuum created on the festive occasion, decided instead to devote his speech to the Jewish question. He ordered the laws to be drafted quickly; Nazi experts on the Jewish question were brought to Nuremberg and told to formulate a law regulating marriages between Jews and Germans. Hitler chose one out of four drafts. This account of the genesis of the Nuremberg Laws relies chiefly on testimony given at the postwar Nuremberg trials by Bernard LÖSENER, the expert on Jewish affairs in the Ministry of the Interior. However, it seems more likely that the laws were not some sort of improvisation but the implementation of a policy, with the party congress providing the suitable occasion. The laws related directly to the party platform and the principles outlined in Hitler's writings.

The need to clarify and define the status of the Jews in Germany had become urgent, since state and party antisemitic policy lacked unity. Regional governmental officials and the Gestapo had repeatedly asked for an official authoritative decision and an unequivocal stand on the policy toward the Jews because the absence of a clear-cut policy had resulted in clashes between party activists and state officials. The turbulence of the spring and summer of 1935 aroused expectations of antisemitic legislation within the party, and the situation became particularly pressing when anti-Jewish rioting erupted in the summer of that year. The party and the public were demanding that the Jewish question be explicitly clarified, defined, and made public. Three main issues dominated the discussion: the exclusion of Jews from German citizenship; *Rassenschande* (race defilement), that is, mixed marriages and sexual relations between "Aryans" and Jews; and the boycotting of Jewish enterprises. By the beginning of 1935 several leading Nazi officials, including Wilhelm FRICK, the Reich minister of the interior, had announced that the state meant to revoke the citizenship of the Jews of Germany; and Hjalmar SCHACHT, the minister of economics, hinted that various anti-Jewish laws and decrees were being prepared in order to coordinate all governmental antisemitic measures. On September 12, before Hitler made the alleged change, the head of the Reich Medical Association, Gerhard Wagner, announced the intention of promulgating a law for the protection of German blood. Anti-Jewish measures were now taken from the party and were "legalized." This led to a certain frustration among the more extreme antisemites, whose resentments were to break out in 1938 with the renewed anti-Jewish riots on KRISTALLNACHT.

BIBLIOGRAPHY

Bankier, D. "The 'Jewish Question' as a Focus of Conflict between Trends of Institutionalization and Radicalization in the Third Reich, 1934–1935." *In Nation and History: Studies in the History of the Jewish People; Based on Papers Delivered at the Eighth World Congress of Jewish Studies,* vol. 2, edited by S. Ettinger, pp. 357–371. Jerusalem, 1984. (In Hebrew.)

Gruchmann, L. "'Blutschutzgesetz' und Justiz: Zur Entstehung und Auswirkung des Nürnberger Gesetzes vom 15 September 1935." *Vierteljahrshefte fur Zeitgeschichte* 31 (1983): 418–442.

Kulka, O. D. "Die Nürnberger Rassengesetze und die deutsche Bevölkerung um Lichte geheimer NS-Lage und Stimmungsberichte." *Vierteljahrshefte für Zeitgeschichte* 32 (1984): 582–624.

Margaliot, A. "The Reaction of the Jewish Public in Germany to the Nuremberg Laws." *Yad Vashem Studies* 12 (1977): 193–229.

Schleunes, K. A. *The Twisted Road to Auschwitz: Nazi Policy toward German Jews, 1933–1939.* Urbana, Ill., 1970.

DAVID BANKIER

NUREMBERG MILITARY TRIBUNALS. *See* Trials of War Criminals: Subsequent Nuremberg Proceedings.

NUREMBERG TRIAL. *See* Trials of War Criminals: Nuremberg Trial.

N.V. GROUP (Naamloze Vennootschap, or "Anonymous Company"; also known as the Limited Group), a Dutch underground cell responsible for the rescue of some two hundred and fifty Jewish children. The N.V. Group transferred the children from Amsterdam to safe hiding places in many different locations, mostly in the Limburg province in the south of the NETHERLANDS. The group also provided false credentials and ration coupons for the children in hiding, and it succeeded in obtaining gifts of clothes and other necessities from Dutch firms.

Among its active members, who numbered more than a dozen, were John Theo Woortman (formerly an owner of a taxicab company), who was eventually arrested and deported to the BERGEN-BELSEN camp, where he perished; and Jaap Musch (a laboratory worker), considered the most dominant figure within the group. He too was arrested, in September 1944, and was tortured to death in the Ommen camp a few days later.

Most of the children were spirited out of the Hollandsche Schouwburg (Dutch Theater) in Amsterdam, which served as an assembly point for the deportation of Jews to the WESTERBORK camp, and taken by different routes to distant locations. Baroness Anne Marie van Verschuer, a member of the group, is said to have accompanied fifty such children. The N.V. Group restricted itself to rescuing Jewish children. Sixteen members of the group were recognized by YAD VASHEM as "RIGHTEOUS AMONG THE NATIONS."

MORDECAI PALDIEL

NYILASKERESZTES PÁRT. *See* Arrow Cross Party.

O

OBERG, CARL ALBRECHT (1897–1965), SS officer. Born in Hamburg, Oberg served in World War I and earned several military decorations. In 1920 he took part in the nationalist attempt at a coup d'état (the "Kapp putsch"). In the early 1920s he was the liaison man in Schleswig between the nationalist organizations and the German army (the Reichswehr). He worked for several months in 1926 at a tropical-fruit trading company and was then unemployed until 1930, when he acquired a tobacco stand in Hamburg.

In 1932 Reinhard HEYDRICH took Oberg along with him to Munich and then to Berlin. Oberg became Heydrich's right-hand man in the SD (Sicherheitsdienst; Security Service). He rose in rank at a rapid pace and by 1935 was a *Standartenführer.* In 1938 he was the commanding officer of an SS battalion in Mecklenburg, and in January 1939 he became chief of police in Zwickau. In September 1941 he was appointed *SS- und Polizeiführer* (SS and Police Leader) in the Radom district of the GENERALGOUVERNEMENT, where he was responsible for the massacring of Jews and the drafting of Poles for forced labor. He was promoted in March 1942 to SS-*Brigadeführer,* and on May 12 of that year he was posted to Paris as *Höherer SS- und Polizeiführer* (Higher SS and Police Leader) in occupied FRANCE.

Oberg was responsible for putting into effect the order for wearing the yellow Jewish badge (*see* BADGE, JEWISH), for severe measures against the French Résistance, and, above all, for applying the "FINAL SOLUTION" to the Jews of France. On Oberg's orders some seventy-five thousand Jews from France were deported to the extermination camps in Poland; only a few thousand of them survived. In August 1944 he was promoted to SS-*Obergruppenführer* and police general. In December of that year, Oberg was posted to

Carl Oberg. [National Archives]

the command of a military unit that was part of an army formation commanded by Heinrich HIMMLER.

In June 1945, Oberg was arrested by the Americans and sentenced to death. On October 10, 1946, he was extradited to France, and on October 9, 1954, was again sentenced to death, but this was reduced to life imprisonment on April 10, 1958. Under a presidential amnesty his sentence was further reduced, on October 31, 1959, to twenty years' imprisonment with hard labor. In 1965 Oberg was granted a pardon by President Charles de GAULLE and was repatriated to Germany, where he died the same year.

BIBLIOGRAPHY

Marrus, M. R., and R. D. Paxton. *Vichy France and the Jews.* New York, 1981.

HANS-HEINRICH WILHELM
and SHMUEL SPECTOR

OBSHCHESTVO ZDRAVOOKHRANENIYA EVREYEV. *See* Oeuvre de Secours aux Enfants.

ODESSA, port city in the Ukrainian SSR, on the shore of the Black Sea. The rapid development of Odessa began after the Russian conquest (1789). Its Jewish population also grew quickly, and in the late nineteenth and early twentieth centuries it was the most important Jewish literary and Zionist center in tsarist Russia, with the country's largest Jewish community after Warsaw. In 1926 there were 153,194 Jews in Odessa (36.4 percent of the total population), and by 1939 their numbers reached 180,000.

On August 5, 1941, the Romanians and Germans laid siege to Odessa; it fell on October 16. When the siege began, at least half the city's Jews had already managed to leave, and on the day of occupation, the Jewish population was between eighty thousand and ninety thousand. Immediately, Einsatzkommando 11b, together with an operational division of the Romanian intelligence service, slaughtered over eight thousand residents, mainly Jews.

Odessa was established as the capital of the TRANSNISTRIA region, which was handed over to Romanian rule. On October 22, the Romanian general military headquarters (formerly the headquarters of the Soviet secret police, the NKVD) was blown up and sixty-six officers and soldiers were killed, including the military governor of the city. In reprisal, the Romanian ruler, Ion ANTONESCU, ordered that two hundred Communists be executed for each officer who had been killed, and one hundred for each soldier. He also ordered the arrest of every Communist and the taking of one member of every Jewish family as hostage. On the next day, October 23, nineteen thousand Jews were taken to the square at the harbor, where gasoline was poured over them and they were burned to death. That same afternoon, the Romanians assembled another twenty thousand Jews at the local jail; they were taken the next day to the village of Dalnik, where some were shot and others shut in warehouses that were set on fire. Following this massacre, many Jews were sent from Odessa to their death in the camps of BOGDANOVKA, DOMANEVKA, and Akhmetchetka in the Golta region.

Between October 25 and November 3, 1941, the remaining 35,000 to 40,000 Jews of Odessa were assembled in the ghetto of Slobodka, near the city, where they were left in the open for about ten days. Many old people, women, and children froze to death. On November 7, the Jewish men were concentrated in the local jail before being deported to various camps in Transnistria, and their valuables were confiscated. Many who attempted to hide in the homes of non-Jewish residents were handed over. On January 12, 1942, the deportations began; by February 23, 19,582 Jews had been deported. In the meantime most of the remainder were killed by German settlers in the area; others died of starvation, disease, and the bitter cold. Some Jews (several thousand, it is estimated) were saved by local Russians and Ukrainians. After the deportations, 54 Jewish artisans, mostly from Romania, were brought to Odessa and concentrated in one building, called the "skilled-labor ghetto."

On April 10, 1944, Odessa was liberated by the Red Army. According to the report of the authorities, about 99,000 Jews had been killed in the city. After the war it again became an

important Jewish center, and according to the 1959 census, 102,000 Jews were living there.

BIBLIOGRAPHY

Ehrenburg, I., and V. Grossman, eds. *The Black Book of Soviet Jewry*. New York, 1981. See pages 72-92.

Litani, D. "The Destruction of the Jews of Odessa in the Light of Rumanian Documents." *Yad Vashem Studies* 6 (1967): 135-154.

JEAN ANCEL

OEUVRE DE SECOURS AUX ENFANTS (Children's Aid Society; OSE), worldwide Jewish organization for health care and children's welfare. The OSE was founded in Russia in 1912 as the Obshchestvo Zdravookhraneniya Evreyev (Society for the Protection of the Health of Jews; OZE). After the organization had expanded to several European countries, the OSE Union was created in Berlin in 1923, and after 1933 it transferred its headquarters to Paris. In 1938, 80 percent of its work was devoted to children, and it received and cared for several hundred refugee children from Germany in four homes near Paris.

After the German invasion of FRANCE in May 1940, the administration of the OSE in France split in two, along the lines of France's new boundaries. The Paris section, managed by Dr. Eugène Minkowski, concerned itself with the northern zone under German control, in conditions that from the start were very difficult. The overall administration, which withdrew to Montpellier in the Vichy south, was able to operate legally, even after its incorporation in March 1942 into the UNION GÉNÉRALE DES ISRAÉLITES DE FRANCE (UGIF) as the Troisième Direction (Third Department, that is, the Health Section).

The OSE engaged in diverse medical and social aid activities, as follows:

1. Medical and social assistance to children and adults in centers established in about fifteen towns.
2. Medical and social assistance in the internment camps in the southern zone, especially in GURS and Rivesaltes, through the initiative of Joseph WEILL and Andrée Salomon, assisted by teams of doctors and volunteer internee social workers.

3. The reception in fourteen homes of about thirteen hundred children who were orphaned or placed there by their families, or who were officially removed from the internment camps. The OSE was able to organize, in conjunction with HIAS (the Hebrew Immigrant Aid Society; *see* HICEM) and the JOINT DISTRIBUTION COMMITTEE, three departures by ship for the United States from May 1941 to May 1942 for some three hundred and fifty of these children.
4. Medical assistance for non-French Jewish doctors.

The situation in France deteriorated considerably after the mass roundup of Jews in the summer of 1942 and, subsequently, the total occupation of France that November. In the northern zone, the OSE went completely underground and succeeded in sheltering seven hundred children. In the southern zone, after the "Night of Venissieux" (August 20, 1942), during which OSE workers succeeded in removing children from the Venissieux children's home near Lyons and dispersing them among Christian institutions and homes, the OSE created an underground network, the Circuit Garel, named after its leader, Georges Garel. This branch of OSE became responsible for hiding children hunted by the Nazis. Later, after the Germans invaded the Italian zone of France in September 1943, an autonomous network was created by Moussa Abadie that worked in collaboration with Garel. Their combined efforts proved to be relatively successful. With the assistance of Jewish and non-Jewish associations and the support of the Catholic and Protestant religious hierarchy, several thousand children were hidden and a thousand transferred to Switzerland under the care of Jacques Salon, Georges Loinger, and others. These transfers were made in liaison with the OSE Union, whose headquarters had moved to Geneva.

The OSE continued to function legally within the UGIF, and at the beginning of 1943 it moved its headquarters from Montpellier to Chambéry. The children's homes continued their operation and began to disband only after the seizure of the La Verdière children's home near Marseilles, in October 1943. The organization's headquarters and centers were ordered to go completely underground only after the arrest of seven OSE workers at the Chambéry headquarters, on February 8, 1944. Even then, the self-dissolution was not complete. On April 6, 1944, the Gestapo, under the direction of Klaus Barbie, arrested and deported the children and staff of the home at Izieux (*see* BARBIE TRIAL).

In the final months preceding the liberation, the OSE continued its work of rescue. After September 1944 it reopened its homes to receive children whose parents had disappeared, and those who had survived the concentration camps. Several dozen employees of OSE and a hundred supporters who cooperated in its work paid with their lives for a heroic venture that made possible the rescue of more than five thousand children.

BIBLIOGRAPHY

L'activité des organisations juives en France. Paris, 1947.

Cohen, R. I. *The Burden of Conscience: French Jewish Leadership during the Holocaust.* Bloomington, 1987.

Kieval, H. "Legality and Resistance in Vichy France: The Rescue of Jewish Children." *Proceedings of the American Philosophical Society* 124 (1980): 339–366.

Lazare, L. *La résistance juive en France.* Paris, 1987.

Zeitoun, S. *L'OSE du légalisme à la résistance (1940–1944).* Paris, 1988.

ALAIN MICHEL

OFFICE FOR JEWISH AFFAIRS. *See* Commissariat Général aux Questions Juives.

OFFICE OF SPECIAL INVESTIGATIONS (OSI), an agency established in the United States Department of Justice to investigate and take legal action against Nazi war criminals living in the United States. A "Nazi war criminal" was defined for this purpose as an individual who "in collaboration with the Nazi regimes of Europe from 1933–1945, assisted, incited, or took part in persecution of any person based on race, religion, or political beliefs."

The OSI was established in 1979 following revelations that hundreds of Nazi war criminals had emigrated to the United States after World War II. (Its first director was Walter Rockler, who was succeeded in 1980 by Allan Ryan, Jr. In 1983, Neal Sher was appointed director.) Congresswoman Elizabeth Holtzman of New York and Congressman Joshua Eilberg of Pennsylvania played an instrumental role in the office's establishment. According to American law, United States courts do not have jurisdiction to try individuals for crimes committed outside the United States unless they were committed against American citizens. Therefore the OSI prosecuted Nazi war criminals for violating United States immigration and naturalization laws, which forbade the entry into the United States and the subsequent naturalization of anyone who had participated in the persecution of civilians during World War II. Such criminals obtained entry into the United States by concealing and misrepresenting their wartime activities, violations of United States law that are grounds for denaturalization and deportation from the United States.

During the initial nine years of its existence, the OSI investigated hundreds of cases and filed complaints against seventy-three Nazi war criminals. The overwhelming majority of the cases investigated involved Lithuanian, Latvian, Ukrainian, or VOLKSDEUTSCHE collaborators who emigrated to the United States shortly after the war from displaced persons' camps in Germany. The criminals can be classified, in accordance with their crimes, into the following categories:

1. Top-level decision makers, initiators of persecution;
2. Individuals who directed the apparatus of mass annihilation, implementers of large-scale murder;
3. Members of mass-murder squads whose primary function was to annihilate civilians and which operated in a wide geographic area over a considerable period of time;
4. Members of local police involved in persecution in a limited geographical area during a limited time period;
5. Members of the local administration established by the Nazis who assisted in the implementation of the "Final Solution";
6. Persons involved in propaganda and incitement to kill Jews;
7. German scientists who employed concentration camp inmates as slave labor in special projects related to the war effort.

In addition, the OSI conducted two special investigations at the request of the United States government. The first concerned Klaus Barbie (*see* BARBIE TRIAL), head of the Gestapo in Lyons, France, who was employed by the United States as an agent after the war and was subsequently assisted by the United States to escape to South America. The second related to Dr. Josef MENGELE, a physician at AUSCHWITZ who made many *Selektionen* and performed pseudoscientific genetic experiments that resulted in the death of numerous inmates; he was reported to have been arrested and released by United States authorities late in 1946. As a result of the OSI investigation in the Barbie case, the United States issued a formal apology to the French government. The OSI investigation in the Mengele case did not reveal any deliberate wrongdoing by United States authorities.

In the course of its work, the OSI has conducted extensive research on the fascist movements in eastern Europe and the extensive role played by local collaborators in the murder of the Jews of Lithuania, Latvia, Estonia, the Ukraine, Belorussia, and elsewhere. The findings of OSI historians in this area of Holocaust research constitute an important contribution to the historiography of the destruction of European Jewry. Also of note is the part that the OSI played in obtaining the cooperation of Soviet authorities, who in several cases provided documentation from Soviet archives. In addition, they permitted OSI and defense attorneys to come to the Soviet Union and to take testimony from and cross-examine Soviet witnesses. These proceedings were videotaped and accepted as evidence in American courts.

The OSI has been severely attacked by eastern European emigré groups in the United States who objected to the use of evidence from Soviet archives and claimed that the individuals under investigation were framed by the KGB because they were anti-Communist. These protests have also taken the form of attempts to rewrite history and to expunge all mention of the active role played by eastern European collaborators in the murder of Jews during the Holocaust.

By December 1986, sixteen Nazi war criminals investigated by the OSI had been forced (by means of extradition, deportation, or escape) to leave the United States. Among the most important cases are the following:

1. Andrije Artuković, minister of the interior of Croatia; extradited to Yugoslavia in 1986; tried and sentenced to death; implementation of sentence postponed owing to ill health; died in Zagreb in 1988.
2. Feodor Federenko, Ukrainian guard at the TREBLINKA extermination camp; deported to the Soviet Union; tried and sentenced to death; executed in 1987.
3. John Iwan Demjanjuk, Ukrainian; operated the gas chambers at Treblinka; extradited to Israel in 1986; tried in 1987–1988; found guilty and sentenced to death in 1988.
4. Valerian Trifa, leader of Iron Guard (Romanian fascist) students; escaped to Portugal (to avoid deportation to Romania), where he died in 1987.
5. Arthur Rudolph, Nazi rocket scientist; involved in use of inmates at the DORA-MITTELBAU camp; returned to Germany after a resolution stripping him of United States citizenship.

In two additional cases, those of Alfred Deutscher and Michael Popczuk, both participants in persecutions in the Ukraine, the criminals committed suicide immediately after the OSI filed charges.

In July 1988, 28 cases were in litigation and a total of 578 suspects were under investigation. The files of 663 additional suspects have been closed by the office. The OSI's success played an important role in convincing other Western governments (of Canada, Australia, and England) to investigate and/or prosecute the Nazi war criminals living in those countries.

BIBLIOGRAPHY

Ryan, A. A., Jr. "Attitudes towards the Prosecution of Nazi War Criminals in the United States." In *Contemporary Views of the Holocaust*, edited by R. L. Braham, pp. 201–226. Boston, 1983.

Ryan, A. A., Jr. *Quiet Neighbors: Prosecuting Nazi War Criminals in America.* San Diego, Calif., 1984.

Zuroff, E. *Occupation: Nazi-Hunter.* Southampton, England, 1988.

EFRAIM ZUROFF

OHLENDORF, OTTO (1907–1951), one of the Nazi administrators responsible for the extermination policy against the Jews. Ohlendorf was born in the Hannover district, studied law and economics, and joined the Nazi party and the SS in 1925 and 1926, respectively. In the early 1930s he was a lecturer at several economics institutions, and was active in party organizational affairs and propaganda. He joined the SD (Sicherheitsdienst; Security Service) in May 1936 with the rank of SS-*Sturmbannführer*, and took up a senior post. In September 1939 he became chief of the SD Inland (Interior) section in the REICHSSICHERHEITSHAUPTAMT (Reich Security Main Office; RSHA), with the rank of *Standartenführer*.

Ohlendorf was appointed commander of Einsatzgruppe D in June 1941. On numerous occasions he was cited as a model young man who had dedicated himself and his abilities to the party and to Nazi ideology, and who had become head of an Einsatzgruppe (that had murdered at least ninety thousand people). By June 1942 the unit under Ohlendorf's command had moved along the Black Sea coast and through the Crimea and Ciscaucasia (Northern Caucasia), killing masses of Jews and other Soviet citizens as it went from place to place. For his service in the Soviet Union, the Oberkommando der Wehrmacht (Armed Forces High Command) awarded him the Military Service Cross, Class 1, with swords.

In November 1943 Ohlendorf was appointed deputy director general and chief of the foreign-trade section in the Reich Ministry of Economic Affairs, in addition to his SD post. A year later he was promoted to the rank of *Gruppenführer* in the SS and to lieutenant general in the police. After the war, Ohlendorf was the chief defendant in the Nuremberg Military Tribunals' Case No. 9, the *Einsatzgruppen* Case. In January 1946 he appeared as a witness in the NUREMBERG TRIAL of major war criminals, tried by the International Military Tribunal at Nuremberg. In reply to the prosecutor's question as to what order the Einsatzgruppen had been given, Ohlendorf replied, "The order was to liquidate the Jews and the Soviet political commissars in the Einsatzgruppen area of operations and on Russian territory." Asked whether "to liquidate" meant "to kill," Ohlendorf answered: "Yes, I mean to kill." In his own trial, Ohlendorf explained why the Jews had to be murdered. Asked whether Jewish children also had to be murdered, Ohlendorf's answer was that this was unavoidable "because the children were people who would grow up, and surely, being the children of parents who had been killed, they could constitute a danger no smaller than that of the parents."

Ohlendorf was sentenced to death, and on June 8, 1951, he was hanged in the Landsberg prison.

BIBLIOGRAPHY

Krausnick, H., and H.-H. Wilhelm. *Die Truppe des Weltanschauungskrieges: Die Einsatzgruppen der Sicherheitspolizei und des SD, 1938–1942.* Stuttgart, 1981.

SHMUEL SPECTOR

ONEG SHABBAT (Heb.; "Sabbath delight," a term applied to a Sabbath afternoon gathering), code name for a secret archive in the WARSAW ghetto under the German occupation. Founded and administered by the historian Emanuel RINGELBLUM, Oneg Shabbat is also known as the Ringelblum Archive. The name "Oneg Shabbat" was given to it because the group that kept the archive held its clandestine meetings on the Sabbath.

Ringelblum took the first steps to establish Oneg Shabbat as early as October 1939. He felt, and indeed foresaw, that unprecedented historical experiences were in store for the Jews and that as a historian it was his task to document the unfolding events for future generations. At first Ringelblum confined himself to collecting information on developments that came to his knowledge in his capacity as the organizer of the Jewish welfare system, then in its nascent stage. In the evenings he recorded such information in his diary, which gradually took on the form of a chronicle, and he kept up this practice until the mass deportation from the Warsaw ghetto in July 1942. In May 1940 Ringelblum, who until then had one senior assistant (Rabbi Shimon Huberband, a young historian), engaged several other dedicated helpers and embarked upon the project of making the archive a more complex undertaking.

The decisive development in the work of Oneg Shabbat came in November 1940, when the Warsaw ghetto was closed off. At that time, Ringelblum and his associates decided to transform the archive into an organized underground operation with several dozen participants, including writers, teachers, and others who had studied history. Most of the financing was provided by the American Jewish JOINT DISTRIBUTION COMMITTEE.

The management of the archive was made up of persons representing the different political and social groupings active in the ghetto underground; in early 1941 it consisted of Ringelblum, Hirsch Wasser (the secretary), Menahem Kahn (the treasurer), Eliahu Gutkowski, Rabbi Huberband, Abraham Lewin, Shakhne ZAGAN, Yitzhak GITTERMAN, Alexander Landau, David Guzik, and Shmuel Breslaw. Their main objectives were (1) to document, by means of an ongoing record, the events taking place in the Warsaw ghetto and all over occupied Poland; (2) to collect relevant items of historical value (including underground newspapers published by the political parties and the youth movements, letters received in the ghetto whose contents were of public interest, minutes of meetings, and reports and data on the operations of Jewish public organizations functioning in the ghetto on a clandestine basis); and (3) to record the testimony of Jewish refugees from Polish ghettos who happened to come to Warsaw and of Jews who had been released from prisoner-of-war and labor camps.

A new phase was inaugurated when the archive staff began collecting materials reflecting the many aspects of the suffering that the Jews were experiencing. Among these were descriptions of the profound changes taking place in the life of the individual, the family unit, and various social frameworks, and detailed analyses of the manifestations of these changes. To provide a comprehensive record of these processes and a faithful description of the stubborn fight that the ghetto population was putting up for its physical survival, the archive sponsored papers to be written on different ghettos and specific subjects. The categories of papers initiated covered a very wide range of topics, such as the Jewish woman in the war; children and youth in the ghetto; problems of health; welfare and self-help; humor and folklore; relations between Poles and Jews; relations between Germans and Jews; education; cultural activities; religious affairs; the theater in the ghetto; the activities of the political organizations and movements in the underground and its branches; the smuggling of food into the ghetto; and the secret economy. The archive staff recruited authors from among persons who were active in these fields and familiar with their inner workings. Ringelblum himself drafted detailed guidelines for the papers commissioned, and he read and edited most of the papers submitted.

In a final report on Oneg Shabbat that Ringelblum wrote, apparently in January 1943, he stated: "So much material of great value has been accumulated to make us all feel that the time is ripe to draw up a synthesis, or at least a summary, of the various problems and manifestations in the life of the Jews under the occupation." It was decided that the archive would embark upon a project, to be called "Two and a Half Years," that would provide a multifaceted summary of the experience gained and the material accumulated. This project did not come to fruition, for before its details could be worked out and a start made on collating the relevant material, reports reached Warsaw of the mass murder that had been taking place in the territories occupied in the east since the end of June 1941. This was a turning point in the archive's operations, and its work now addressed itself to different concerns.

The archive staff sought to obtain as many German documents as possible relating to the deportation of Jews and the process of their annihilation. These efforts also extended to the provincial towns, and Oneg Shabbat put out a regular bulletin on the details of the deportations that were taking place in different localities.

A tremendous effort was made to transmit to the free world reports of the developments in Poland. In early 1943, Oneg Shabbat activists took down the testimony of a Jew who had escaped from the CHEŁMNO extermination camp and transmitted it to London, by way of the Polish underground. The same method was used to transmit to London a detailed report on the mass deportation from the Warsaw ghetto in the summer of 1942, to which were attached a collection of documents relating to that period. Oneg Shabbat archivists also took down the testimony of persons who had escaped from TREBLINKA at the time when the deportations from Warsaw were at their height. In the final phase, Ringelblum tried to persuade Jews who had kept diaries in the ghetto to hand them over to Oneg Shabbat for safekeeping. In this he had only partial success; many of the diarists apparently could not let go of the written record they had kept, which they cherished above everything else, once their families had been broken up and destroyed. Ringelblum also attached great importance to the collecting of data and documents on the operations of the resistance organizations and on the fighting in the ghetto during the period from September 1942 until the WARSAW GHETTO UPRISING in April 1943.

The deposits held by the archive were sealed inside metal containers and milk jugs and concealed in various hiding places in the ghetto on three occasions, in August 1942 and in March and April 1943. The young people who carried out the job did not survive; those in charge of the operation in August 1942 left a note, written by one of the youths, which says in part: "I wish I would be present at the moment when the treasures which we have concealed here are discovered and the world finds out the truth of what happened. Blessed be those whom fate saved from suffering."

On September 18, 1946, the first part of the Oneg Shabbat archive was discovered in the ruins of a house at 68 Nowolipki Street. The second part was found four years later, on December 1, 1950, at a nearby location. The third part, which apparently contained a great deal of material on the resistance and the fighting, has not been recovered, despite the many searches that have been made. The first part, all of which is kept in the ŻYDOWSKI INSTYTUT HISTORYCZNY in Warsaw, consists of 1,209 items, according to a classification made after the war, and the second part consists of 484 items.

The Oneg Shabbat archive contains, among other materials, a collection of underground newspapers; the diaries and notes of Ringelblum, Abraham Lewin, Peretz Opoczynski, Shimon Huberband, and others; and thousands of other original documents. It is the most important single source for the history of Polish Jewry during the war and the Holocaust. Selected parts of the archive have appeared in print in various languages, but the archive as a whole has yet to be published in a complete, scholarly edition.

[*See also* Łódź Ghetto, Chronicles of the.]

BIBLIOGRAPHY

A Commemorative Symposium in Honor of Dr. Emanuel Ringelblum and His Oneg Shabbat Underground Activities. Jerusalem, 1983.

Kermish, J., ed. *To Live with Honor and Die with Honor: Selected Documents from the Warsaw Ghetto Underground Archives "O.S." (Oneg Shabbath).* Jerusalem, 1986.

Sakowska, R. *Archiwum Ringelbluma getto warszawskie, lipiec 1942–styczeń 1943.* Warsaw, 1980.

ISRAEL GUTMAN

OPERATIONAL STAFF ROSENBERG. *See* Einsatzstab Rosenberg.

OPERATION "ERNTEFEST." *See* "Erntefest."

OPERATION 1005. *See* Aktion 1005.

OPERATION REINHARD. *See* Aktion Reinhard.

OPOLE LUBELSKIE, town in Poland in the Puławy subdistrict, in the western part of the Lublin district. On the eve of World War II,

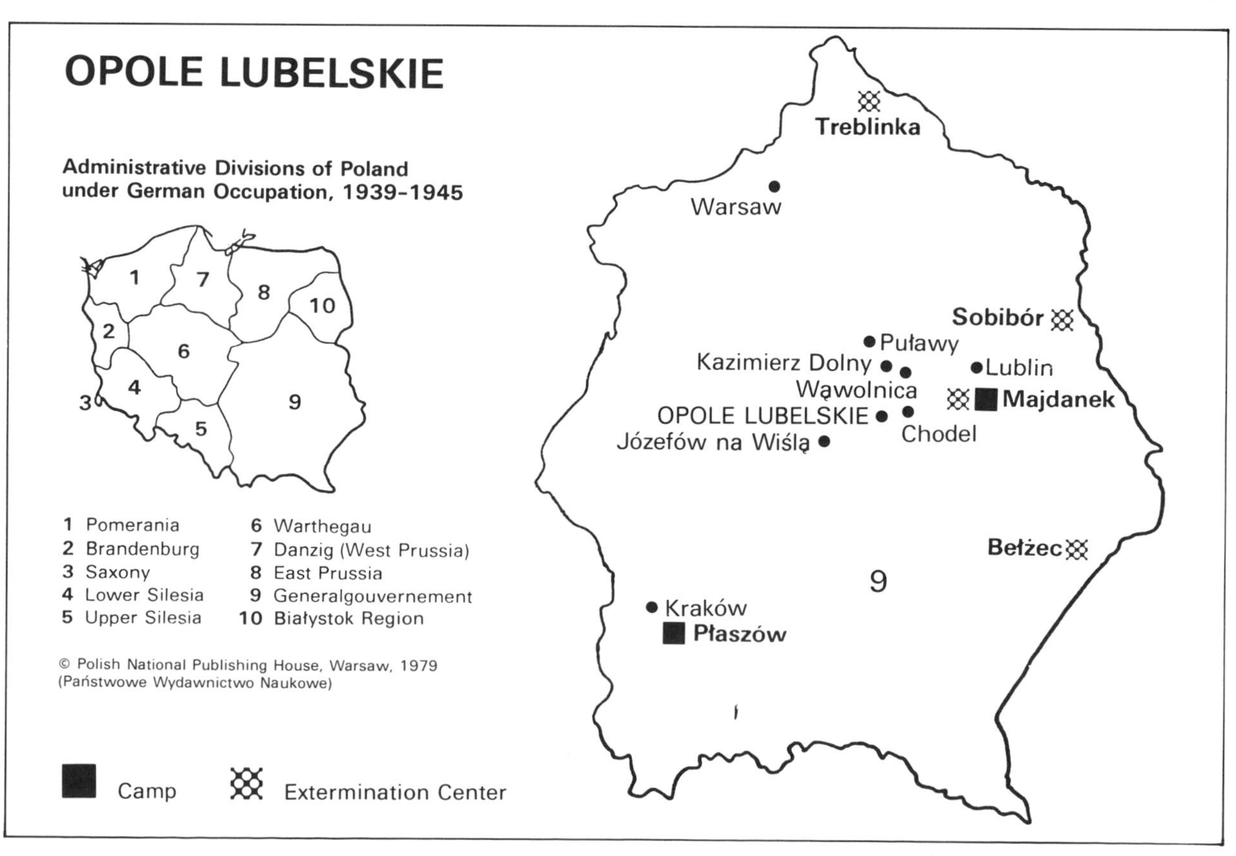

A Jewish family from Vienna, deported in February 1941 to Opole Lubelskie.

Opole had a Jewish population of 4,325, two-thirds of the total.

Opole was occupied by the Germans in September 1939, and a month later, after the establishment of the German administration, a ten-member JUDENRAT (Jewish Council) was appointed and a Jewish police force (JÜDISCHER ORDNUNGSDIENST) formed. The Jews in the town were put on forced labor—on road repairs, on the nearby farms, and in the local sugar factory. In early December, fifty Jewish families from Józefów na Wiśle were brought to Opole, followed, on December 29, by twenty-five hundred Jews who were driven out of their homes in the town of Puławy and forced into Opole.

In the summer of 1940 work was begun on making the old section of the town into a ghetto. Two transports of Jews from Vienna, totaling two thousand persons, were brought to the ghetto on February 15 and 26, 1941. By March eight thousand Jews were assembled in Opole, their number being further augmented by the end of the month with Jews brought from Kazimierz Dolny, Chodel, and Wąwolnica. The extreme overcrowding in the ghetto led to the outbreak of typhus and typhoid epidemics, in which fifteen hundred persons died.

On March 31, 1942, the Jews from Kazimierz Dolny and Wąwolnica were deported to BEŁŻEC, and their place in the ghetto was taken by Jews from the nearby villages and from Slovakia. Late that May, nearly all the Jews imprisoned in the Opole ghetto were deported to SOBIBÓR; some five hundred were murdered on the spot. Only members of the Judenrat and the Jewish police, and a small number of skilled artisans and their families, were left. In late October 1942, they too were killed.

SHMUEL SPECTOR

OPPOSITION, GERMAN. *See* Bonhoeffer, Dietrich; Christian Churches; Dibelius, Otto; Galen, Clemens August Graf von; Lichtenberg, Bernhard; Niemöller, Martin; Stülpnagel, Karl Heinrich von; Wurm, Theophil.

ORADEA (Oradea Mare; Hung., Nagyvárad; Ger., Grosswardein), city in northern TRANSYLVANIA, now in Romania; before 1918 and between 1940 and 1944 it was in Hungary. The earliest recognized Jewish settlement in

Oradea dates from the mid-eighteenth century. By 1835, 100 Jewish families lived there, and Jews played a central role in the city's commerce. They became cultural and intellectual leaders, and many among them were devoutly patriotic Hungarians. Between December 4 and 6, 1927, during a gathering of the National Union of Romanian Students in Oradea, Jews were attacked in a vicious pogrom. In 1941, 21,337 Jews lived in Oradea, constituting 22.9 percent of the population and making the city the second largest Jewish center in Hungary.

Like the rest of Hungarian Jewry before the German occupation on March 19, 1944, the Oradea community was affected primarily by the drafting of men into the MUNKASZOLGÁLAT (forced-labor battalions) and by the economic restrictions that followed the two anti-Jewish laws passed in 1938 and 1939 (*see* HUNGARY: JEWS DURING THE HOLOCAUST). In the summer of 1941 a number of Jews who had never held Hungarian citizenship were deported to KAMENETS-PODOLSKI, where they were massacred along with some sixteen thousand other Hungarian Jews. The draft into the Munkaszolgálat was intensified after 1942, and of the approximately six thousand draftees, more than 80 percent died during their term of service.

Soon after the Germans occupied Hungary, they made their presence felt in Oradea. On March 31, 1944, the SS commandeered the Jewish hospital and began demanding that the Jewish community turn over various materials to supply it. The head of the Jewish community at the time, Alexander (Sándor) Leitner, was charged with directing the collection. On April 6 the Germans forcibly took over a number of Jewish homes, arresting the men and evicting the women and children into the street. This process of violent confiscation of Jewish apartments was interrupted, however, because it interfered with the drive to outfit the hospital. On April 18, the Honvéd (the Hungarian army) began to expropriate Jewish property in Oradea. But these activities became obsolete with the promulgation of the order that established a ghetto for the city's Jews.

On May 1, Adolf EICHMANN's representative, Theodor DANNECKER, arrived to supervise the concentration of the Jews of Oradea into a ghetto near the city center, and of the Jews from the vicinity of Oradea into an additional ghetto near the Mezey lumberyard on the city's outskirts. Most of the actual task of herding Jews into the ghettos was carried out by Hungarian gendarmes. The commander of the gendarmerie for the Oradea region (Gendarmerie District IX) was Lt. Col. Jenő Peterffy, and the immediate commander responsible for the concentration of the Jews of Oradea itself was the city's deputy mayor, László Gyapay. On May 2, posters announcing the formation of a ghetto for the Jewish residents of the city were posted, bearing Gyapay's signature. The ghetto was commanded by police captain Imre Nemeth, who was assisted by another police officer, István Kovacs-Nagy. Teams of regular policemen and gendarmes herded the first few thousand Jews into the ghetto area that same day. They were forcibly removed from their homes and made to stand in front of them until there were enough people to fill a wagon, which was then driven to the ghetto. The ghetto itself was surrounded by gendarmes and policemen to prevent Jews from escaping. By May 6, more than ten thousand Jews had been placed in the ghetto, and when it was declared full on May 9, nearly twenty thousand Jews lived in it. Their over-

ORADEA

0 160 miles 1 in.
0 300 km. 3 cm.

Annexations from June to September 1940: (1) Bessarabia and (2) N. Bukovina to USSR; (3) N. Transylvania to Hungary; (4) S. Dobruja to Bulgaria.

all rations were set by the authorities at 400 loaves of bread and 106 quarts (100 liters) of milk each day. On the day the concentration began, a Zsidó Tanács (Jewish Council) under Leitner was officially convened by the authorities. Some twenty-five hundred Jewish men were assembled for forced-labor service on May 9.

The following day, Peterffy himself took command of the ghetto and with his gendarmes instituted a reign of terror. In particular, they interrogated and cruelly tortured Jews in the Dreher brewery in an attempt to learn where Jewish valuables might still be hidden. According to Péter Hain, the chief of the Hungarian secret police, a great deal of money was uncovered, and proceedings were begun against more than two thousand gentiles for having concealed Jewish property. In the meantime, the ghetto near the Mezey lumberyard was established, and about eight thousand Jews from many small Jewish communities in Bihor county were concentrated there.

The first transport bound for AUSCHWITZ left the Mezey lumberyard on May 24, containing mostly Jews from that ghetto, but also about 300 Jews from the ghetto in the city itself. Three days later, the deportation from the city ghetto began in earnest. Nearly every day until June 3, some 3,000 Jews were sent to Auschwitz, until the Oradea ghettos were virtually emptied. On June 16 and 17, 2,819 Jews from several small Jewish communities southeast of DEBRECEN were brought to Oradea, where they were concentrated for a short time and then deported to Auschwitz.

Rescue was attempted by the Zsidó Tanács and by individual Jews. A handful of Oradea Jews escaped from the ghetto, and about forty families tried to hide in bunkers they had hastily created in the ghetto itself. Most were discovered by the authorities, but twenty-eight Jews successfully hid in the Rothbert soap factory, with the help of a Hungarian military officer named Appan and his wife. Six others succeeded in fleeing from the ghetto. When the deportations began, the Zsidó Tanács tried to thwart them by simulating a typhus epidemic in the city ghetto. The idea was put forth by a Dr. Sebastian, who was aided by a gentile physician outside the ghetto, Dr. Konrad Bathy. Their success, however, was small; they only managed to receive permission for eighteen patients and staff members to remain in Oradea. Another attempt to rescue a handful of Jews was made by the head of the welfare branch of the Zsidó Tanács, Yaakov Mittleman, and an associate, named Kasztenbaum, who received certificates for immigration to Palestine. With the backing of the Zsidó Tanács, they approached the authorities, seeking exemptions for themselves and their families as potential British citizens. Their request was denied, and they were deported. Six Jews of the Leitner family, including the head of the Zsidó Tanács, Alexander Leitner, were included in the "Kasztner train" (*see* KASZTNER, REZSŐ) and were thus saved from the deportations. They were brought to Budapest, and eventually reached a haven in Switzerland.

During October 1944, Hungarian and Soviet troops fought in the Oradea area. The city itself changed hands several times until it was finally taken by the Soviets, on October 17. After the war Oradea became a crossroads for returning Hungarian and Romanian Jews. Many Jewish children who had survived in Budapest were also brought to Oradea, where shortages were less of a problem; most of them were later taken to Palestine. As of 1947, about 8,000 Jews had settled in Oradea, of whom perhaps 2,000 were former residents who had survived the war. Jewish community life was reestablished. After the creation of the state of Israel most of the Jews emigrated there, and in 1976 only 820 Jews lived in Oradea.

BIBLIOGRAPHY

Ancel, J., and T. Lavi, eds. *Rumania,* vol. 1. In *Pinkas Hakehillot; Encyclopaedia of Jewish Communities.* Jerusalem, 1980. (In Hebrew.)

Braham, R. L. *The Politics of Genocide: The Holocaust in Hungary.* New York, 1981.

Braham, R. L., ed. *Genocide and Retribution: The Holocaust in Hungarian-ruled Northern Transylvania.* Boston, 1983.

Grossman, O., ed. *A Tegnap Varsosa: A nagyvaradi zsidósag emlekkonyve.* Tel Aviv, 1981.

ROBERT ROZETT

These burned and blackened ruins were all that was left of Oradour-sur-Glane after the Nazis killed the inhabitants and set fire to their houses.

ORADOUR-SUR-GLANE, French village in the Limoges area, the entire population of which was killed by SS men. After the Allied landings in Normandy on June 6, 1944, there was an upsurge in partisan operations all over FRANCE, and German army convoys traveling on French roads had to contend with extensive interference. The Germans resorted to deterrent and revenge operations. In one of these operations, on June 10, 1944, an SS unit fell upon Oradour, rounded up all the residents—634 men, women, and children—and forced them into the village church. Then they set the church afire, and all the people inside were burned to death. There were no survivors. After the war, Oradour was rebuilt and resettled. Its name became a symbol of the brutality that marked the German occupation of France.

BIBLIOGRAPHY

Amoroux, H. *La vie des Français sous l'occupation.* Paris, 1961.

LUCIEN LAZARE

ORANIENBURG, concentration camp near Berlin; one of the earliest camps founded by the Nazis. The first transport of prisoners arrived at Oranienburg on March 31, 1933; it consisted of forty "Marxists" (in Nazi terminology this meant primarily Communists and Social Democrats). On its own initiative, SS-Standarte (Regiment) 208 had converted an abandoned brewery into a temporary prison, although allegedly the SA (Sturmabteilung; Storm Troopers) had originally planned to use it for housing unemployed SA men who had no place of their own. Located in the Potsdam district of Germany, Oranienburg soon gained districtwide importance.

A few weeks after the Oranienburg camp had been established, the Potsdam police chief, Count Wolf Heinrich Helldorf, assumed responsibility for the camp's current expenses, and the camp commandant, SA-Sturmbannführer Werner Schäfer, officially recognized Helldorf as his superior. The number of prisoners increased rapidly and by August 1933 it reached 900, which was probably close to its maximum. This made Oranienburg one of

Prisoners guarded by SA men line up in the yard of the Oranienburg concentration camp (April 6, 1933).

the three largest concentration camps in the Reich in 1933, the other two being DACHAU and Esterwegen.

Even at an early stage, Oranienburg earned a reputation of being a place where prisoners were maltreated. This fact and the camp's limited capacity induced Hermann GÖRING, who at the time was acting Prussian minister of the interior, to gradually disband the camp. In the summer of 1933, Göring and Rudolf Diels (the first chief of the Gestapo) decided that the existing prison facilities for political prisoners, which had come into being in an uncontrolled and haphazard fashion, should be replaced by a few large camps and that these should be put under state control. In November of that year, 300 prisoners from Oranienburg were transferred to Sonnenberg, Brandenburg, Moringen, and other camps. At that time only opposition by the SA could have assured the camp's continued existence. The fact was that in the wake of the Christmas amnesty of 1933 the number of prisoners was further reduced, and now stood at no more than several hundred.

Schäfer left his post in Oranienburg in March of 1934 to assume the administration of the penal prisons in the Ems area. When the SA was stripped of its power, on June 30, 1934, the Oranienburg administration was taken over by the SS. At this point the Prussian Ministry of the Interior increased its efforts to abolish the camp; the final date of its dissolution, however, is not known. That September, Göring issued an order according to which Oranienburg was to function as a reserve camp only. The last eyewitness report about the camp is dated March 1935.

BIBLIOGRAPHY

Gutman, Y., and A. Saf, eds. *The Nazi Concentration Camps: Structure and Aims; The Image of the Prisoner; The Jews in the Camps.* Proceedings of the Fourth Yad Vashem International Historical Conference. Jerusalem, 1984.

Seyer, G. *A Nation Terrorized.* Chicago, 1935.

FALK PINGEL

ORDER POLICE. *See* Ordnungspolizei.

ORDNUNGSDIENST. *See* Jüdischer Ordnungsdienst.

ORDNUNGSPOLIZEI (Order Police; Orpo), the reorganized German police, in which the Schutzpolizei (conventional police) and the Gendarmerie were merged into a single force in 1936, on Heinrich HIMMLER's orders. The new organization was headed by the Orpo main office. In the urban areas it was the Schutzpolizei that functioned as the national police, while in the rural areas this was the job of the Gendarmerie. Both formations, however, were organized along the same lines, wore the same uniform, and were equipped with the same arms. In 1938 the professional fire-fighting services were unified and became the Fire-fighting Police, joining the other two police forces as part of the Orpo. Similarly, in 1942 the civil-defense police and the urban and rural Hilfspolizei (auxiliary police) were also put under the Orpo.

Beginning in 1938, a large number of police units (police battalions, police regiments, and Schutzpolizei regiments) were formed that were also subordinated to the Orpo main office in matters of organization and discipline. In the occupied countries these units were supposed to perform police duties, but their main role was to fight against the partisans and, in rare instances, also to support combat troops. In addition, Schutzpolizei units made up of Ukrainians, Lithuanians, Latvians, and Estonians were formed under German command, and in France, the Netherlands, Italy, and the Balkan countries there were volunteer police units. The total amounted to forty police battalions (also known as police rifle battalions, which in 1943 were renamed SS and police battalions), some three hundred police regiments, and two hundred Orpo regiments. In 1944 the number of men serving in the Orpo, including its auxiliary forces, was estimated at three and a half million.

Many of the Orpo units and officers deployed in Poland, the Soviet Union, and the Balkan countries joined the Sicherheitspolizei (Security Police) in the deadly measures taken against the Jews (evacuation of ghettos, deportation to extermination camps, and mass shootings), and were conspicuous for their cruelty and brutality.

BIBLIOGRAPHY

Buchheim, H. "The SS: Instrument of Domination." In *Anatomy of the SS State*, edited by H. Krausnick et al., pp. 125–301. London, 1968.

Neufeld, H. J., J. Huck, and G. Tessin. *Zur Geschichte der Ordnungspolizei, 1936–1945*. Koblenz, 1957.

ADALBERT RÜCKERL

ORGANISATION SCHMELT, name commonly used to refer to a system of FORCED LABOR for the Jewish population of Eastern Upper SILESIA. It operated from 1940 to 1944 in the ghettos and labor camps and was set up and administered by Heinrich HIMMLER's *Sonderbeauftragter des Reichsführers-SS für Fremdvölkischen Arbeitseinsatz in Oberschlesien* (Special Representative of the *Reichsführer-SS* for the Employment of Foreign Labor in Upper Silesia). SS-Oberführer Albrecht Schmelt, chief of police in Breslau (Pol., Wrocław), was appointed Special Representative, with his headquarters first in SOSNOWIEC and later in Annaberg. Schmelt was in charge of coordinating all programs designed to exploit Jewish labor, and local authorities were under orders to support his efforts by all means at their disposal. By the end of 1940 Schmelt had forced certain Judenräte (Jewish councils) to draw up lists of all Jews who were fit to work, making the JUDENRAT members personally responsible for the lists, under the threat of disbanding the Judenrat and dispatching its members to labor camps.

As early as 1940, Organisation Schmelt began setting up forced-labor camps for Jews. These were located in the vicinity of important war-essential German enterprises in Upper Silesia and Zagłębie Dąbrowskie, or on their premises. Before long, Organisation Schmelt extended its operations beyond the borders of the region designated by Himmler, and organized labor camps in Lower Silesia and the Sudetenland as well. The allocation of Jewish workers to the German plants was based on an agreement between Schmelt and each German plant; these agreements specified conditions of employment, wages, and the internal organization of the labor camps. For example, an agreement with the Luranil Company (an I.G. FARBEN subsidiary), drawn up in 1942, states that 180 Jews would be employed in the construction of a plant for war gas production at Dyhernfurth. The company would pay to Organisation Schmelt 6 reichsmarks per twelve-hour day for each skilled worker and 4.5 reichsmarks per twelve-hour day for each unskilled worker. The subsistence cost per day was fixed at 90 pfennigs. Responsibility for drawing up the lists of workers for the labor camps was placed on the central Judenrat in Sosnowiec. The Jews chosen for these assignments had to report to a local transit camp and were threatened with arrest and withdrawal of ration cards from their families if they failed to comply.

In March 1941 Himmler decided to use labor from the Organisation Schmelt camps for constructing the plants that were under Albert SPEER's administration. This decision led to the employment of large numbers of Jews in the construction of the hydrogenation plant at BLECHHAMMER. The number of workers rose from fifteen hundred to four thousand. Additional forced-labor camps were established at Gleiwitz (Gliwice) for the construction of a soot-processing plant, at Miechowitz (Miechowice) and Ober Lazisk (Laziska Górne) for electronics factories, at Ratibor (Racibórz) for a light-metals plant, and at Fünfteichen (Miloszyce), near Breslau, for the construction of the Krupp Ordnance Factory (Bertha-Werk Fünfteichen).

A number of camps were built at important railway junctions where new lines were being constructed to serve military requirements: Bobrek, Löwenstadt (Brzeziny Śląskie), Golonog, Kochanowice, Lagischa (Łagisza), Lazy, Schoppinitz (Szopienice Miejskie), and Kunzendorf (Trzebinia). At least seventeen camps were established in the Opole district, along the projected course of the Breslau-Gleiwitz highway that was under construction. The better known among these camps were Annaberg, Brande, Eichtal, Gross Sarne, Klein-Mangersdorf, and Geppersdorf.

By April 1942, forty forced-labor camps for Jewish prisoners were in existence and six more were being set up; the total number of prisoners in the camps was sixty-five hundred. While it existed, Organisation Schmelt established ninety-three forced-labor camps in Upper Silesia. Of these, forty-eight contained a fairly small women's section. Thirty-six camps were exclusively male, and six were exclusively female; for three camps the available information does not specify the composition of the inhabitants. Fifty camps were built in Lower Silesia and seventeen in the Sudetenland.

The grand total of Organisation Schmelt camps known to have existed was 160. In early 1943, 50,570 Jewish prisoners were employed in the enterprises of Organisation Schmelt. At first, only Jews from Zagłębie Dąbrowskie were sent to the camps, but when the Organisation Schmelt plants gained in importance for the military, Jews from the GENERALGOUVERNEMENT as well were dispatched to the Organisation's camps. In the summer of 1942, Speer obtained Himmler's consent to choose 10,000 Jews from the transports of Jews being deported from western Europe (from DRANCY, MECHELEN (Malines), and WESTERBORK) to AUSCHWITZ-Birkenau. These *Selektionen* took place in Cosel, in the presence of a representative of the manpower section of the SS WIRTSCHAFTS-VERWALTUNGSHAUPTAMT (Economic-Administrative Main Office; WVHA).

Later, the Organisation Schmelt officials stopped such transports on their own initiative, to exchange Jews unfit for work—and, at times, dead Jews—for Jews in good physical condition. The Auschwitz camp commandant lodged repeated protests against such interference, and Schmelt finally put a stop to it.

The Jewish prisoners in the Organisation Schmelt camps, for the most part, shared the fate of all the other concentration camp inmates. The Organisation Schmelt camps had from the beginning been devised as a temporary measure. Late in 1941, in light of the order that had been issued to kill all Jews, it was expected that the camps, as well as the workshops employing Jews, would be designated for liquidation and the Jewish prisoners would be sent to Auschwitz. It was only when the military authorities intervened with the REICHSSICHERHEITSHAUPTAMT (Reich Security Main Office; RSHA) and with Himmler that the liquidation of the camps was postponed to a later date.

In 1943 Himmler made the final decision to liquidate the plants and forced-labor camps and to deport the Jews working there to Auschwitz. An exception was made for those camps whose prisoners were working for the most essential armament and ammunition factories, but these camps were now supervised by the administration of the concentration camps in Auschwitz or GROSS-ROSEN. The entire process of liquidating the camps was to be carried out under the supervision of Adolf EICHMANN, and it lasted up to mid-1944. Twenty-eight camps in Lower Silesia and the Sudetenland were attached to Gross-Rosen; of these, twenty became Gross-Rosen satellite camps (but not before *Selektionen* had taken place in them), and from the other camps the Jewish prisoners were moved to other satellite camps. In Upper Silesia the prisoners of at least fifteen camps were put at the disposal of the Auschwitz camp authority; prisoners from five of them became Aussenkommandos (working detachments of prisoners billeted outside the concentration camp). The five were Łagisza, Fürstengrube (near the Wesoła mine), Blechhammer, Laurahütte (in Siemianowice Śląskie), and Gleiwitz (as Gleiwitz Aussenkommando II). Jewish prisoners were transferred to Blechhammer from the camps at Reigersfeld (Birawa), Grabowce, Mała Panwia, and Brawde (Prady).

BIBLIOGRAPHY

Rapaport, J., ed. *Pinkas Zaglembie Memorial Book.* Tel Aviv, 1972. (In Hebrew, Yiddish, and English.)

ALFRED KONIECZNY

ORGANISATION TODT, organization in Nazi Germany for large-scale construction work, particularly in the military and armaments field; it was named after its founder, the engineer Dr. Fritz Todt (1891–1942). In June 1933 Todt was appointed inspector general of road construction in Germany, and in December 1938, plenipotentiary general for coordination of the building sector, as part of the FOUR-YEAR PLAN. He was also responsible for the construction of the *Westwall,* the system of fortifications along the western border of Germany. After the defeat of France in June 1940, Todt worked on the expansion of the western coastal defense, from Norway to the Bay of Biscay. From March 1940 he was also minister for armaments and munitions. On February 8, 1942, Todt was killed in a mysterious plane crash. All his offices were taken over by Albert SPEER, who gave extensive powers to Xaver Dorsch to run Organisation Todt as he saw fit.

The organization expanded steadily and was divided into task force (Einsatzkommando) units, subordinated to the different army groups. In 1944 the number of Organisation Todt employees reached 1,360,000, including about a million foreign workers and prisoners of war, and 20,000 concentration

Fritz Todt.

camp prisoners. Among its best-known enterprises between 1942 and 1945 was the construction of Mittelwerk, near Nordhausen, with its scores of tunnels, for the production of missiles and plane engines. Ten thousand concentration camp laborers and criminals worked in this largest underground factory in the world. The organization also constructed fortifications for the air force, and at least six underground Jäger factories (*Jägerfabriken*) with takeoff and landing strips. After tens of thousands of Jews were brought from Hungary, it also built the *Südostwall* (Southeast Wall). In April 1944, Hitler promised Organisation Todt that he would personally instruct Heinrich HIMMLER to provide it with the 100,000 men it required from Hungary. After the SS brought Jews to Germany from Hungary to work in the different programs, Speer complained to the commander in chief, Wilhelm KEITEL, that only 50,000 to 60,000 of them were fit for work; the rest were children, sick people, and the elderly and were not able to do the work, which consisted principally of the construction of large bunkers.

[*See also* Forced Labor.]

BIBLIOGRAPHY

Boelcke, W. A. *Deutschlands Rüstung im Zweiten Weltkrieg: Hitlers Konferenzen mit Albert Speer, 1942–1945*. Frankfurt, 1969.

Milward, A. S. *Die deutsche Kriegswirtschaft, 1939–1945*. Stuttgart, 1966.

Pingel, F. *Häftlinge unter SS-Herrschaft: Widerstand, Selbstbehauptung und Vernichtung im Konzentrationslager*. Hamburg, 1978.

Speer, A. *Technik und Macht*. Esslingen, 1979.

HANS-HEINRICH WILHELM

ORGANIZACJA BOJOWA ŻYDOWSKIEJ MŁODZIEŻY CHALUCOWEJ. *See* He-Haluts ha-Lohem.

ORHANIZATSYIA UKRAINSKYKH NATSIONALISTIV (Organization of Ukrainian Nationalists; OUN), a nationalist Ukrainian organization with an antisemitic ideology. When the Civil War in Russia came to an end and the 1920 peace treaty with Poland was signed, the Ukrainians had to give up their hopes for independence. The greater part of the UKRAINE became a Soviet socialist republic, and its western part was incorporated into the Polish republic. On August 30, 1920, a group of Ukrainian exiles, former officers and men of the defeated Ukrainian National Army, met in Prague and established a new organization, under the leadership of Col. Yevheni Konovalets, which they named the Ukrainska Viiskova Orhanizatsyia (Ukrainian Military Organization; UVO).

The UVO, with the help of German intelligence, founded its own underground cells in Poland, and tried to form similar cells in the Soviet Union. In February 1929 representatives of the UVO and of other Ukrainian nationalist groups formed a new body, which they called the Organization of Ukrainian Nationalists. This movement, one of whose leading ideologists was Dmitri Dontsov, sought to follow in the footsteps of Italian Fascism and German National Socialism. It expressed support for the application of totalitarian principles in public life and government and adopted the FÜHRERPRINZIP (leadership principle), which obligated every member of the movement to obey its leader unconditionally. The OUN saw in communism and the Soviet Union the principal enemies of the Ukrainian people; as time went on, the organization, under the influence of Nazi ideology and traditional Ukrainian hatred of Jews, also adopted antisemitism in its Hitlerite version. This identity of ideology and political aims between the OUN and Nazi Germany led to close contacts. The OUN moved its headquarters to Berlin, where it was given financial and other kinds of support. At the same time, in the Soviet Ukraine, millions of people died as a result of the collectivization drive. In Poland, the Ukrainian people were discriminated against in national and economic terms under the policy of the Polish government, with the legal Ukrainian political parties unable to make any headway in their efforts to advance the lot of their people. Under the impact of these developments, the younger generation of Ukrainians adopted extremist political views, and many of them joined the OUN underground cells. On May 23, 1938, the head of the movement, Konovalets, was assassinated; another colonel, Andrei Melnyk, took his place as *providnik* (leader).

After the German invasion of Poland in September 1939, the OUN made a successful bid for the creation of a Ukrainian military unit. A 600-man unit was formed, with Roman Sushko as its commander, and it was given the task of assisting the Germans in their contacts with the Ukrainian population. As it turned out, the German army did not enter the western Ukraine at this time, and the unit was disbanded; its personnel joined the police in the GENERALGOUVERNEMENT.

Following the division of Poland between Germany and the Soviet Union prior to the German invasion (*see* NAZI-SOVIET PACT), Ukrainian political parties in both areas of occupation were outlawed. The OUN kept up its underground activities in the Soviet-occupied western Ukraine, while in German-occupied Poland the organization was permitted to operate in the open, as a trusted ally of Nazi Germany. At a 1940 congress of the movement in Kraków, the OUN split into two. The activist majority, headed by Stefan BANDERA, called for the expansion of underground operations and for preparatory steps to be taken for an uprising in the Soviet-occupied area; this faction was called OUN "B" (Bandera). The other faction, headed by Melnyk and accordingly called OUN "M," felt that it was preferable to preserve whatever strength the movement had for the moment, and in the meantime to cooperate unconditionally with the Germans.

During the preparations for the German invasion of the Soviet Union, the OUN took part in the formation of two Ukrainian battalions within the German army, the NACHTIGALL BATTALION and the Roland Battalion. The battalions' commissioned and noncommissioned officers were chosen from among OUN members. Another group of Ukrainian units was the Pokhidni Grupy (Mobile Units), which were attached to the combat units of the Wehrmacht and provided them with interpreters. The mobile units were also given the task of setting up the Ukrainian administration and police in all the towns and villages, to be made up of loyal members of the movement.

In the initial stage of the German invasion of the Soviet Union, at the end of June 1941, the armed underground cells of the OUN were activated and attacked the retreating Soviet forces from the rear. Once the Soviet local government had withdrawn, OUN activists and teams from the mobile units established the Ukrainian civil administration and police force in the German-occupied territories.

On June 30, after the conquest of LVOV, the Bandera faction of the movement announced the establishment of a national Ukrainian government, headed by Yaroslav Stetsko, with the blessing of the head of the Greek Catholic (Uniate) church, Metropolitan Andrei SHEPTYTSKY. This step, however, conflicted with the Germans' plans for the Ukraine; the SD (Sicherheitsdienst; Security Service) promptly arrested the members of the "government," as well as Stefan Bandera, and sent them to Germany, where they were kept under house arrest. The OUN leadership had to go underground, but its members continued to cooperate with the Germans in the administration and the police.

The split between the two factions of the OUN became increasingly pronounced; from time to time there were armed clashes and mutual assassinations. When the SS-Schützendivision Galizien (SS Rifle Division Galicia) was formed in the spring of 1943, it had the support of the Melnyk faction of the OUN and of other Ukrainian groups, while the Bandera faction did not want Ukrainians to join the division.

The Third Congress of the OUN underground movement, held on February 21, 1943, came up with the following political and military analysis of the situation at the time: both sides would be greatly exhausted by the war, at which point a new war would break out between the Western powers and the Soviet Union. That would be the moment for the rise of an independent Ukrainian state. In order to achieve this goal, the congress resolved to establish a Ukrainian Liberation Army (Ukrainska Vyzvolna Armyia). Before long its name changed to UKRAINSKA POVSTANSKA ARMYIA (Ukrainian Insurgent Army; UPA), although its popular name was Banderovtsi. As this new force gained in strength, the OUN became its political arm. At a meeting held from July 11 to 15, 1944, it was decided to broaden the scope of the OUN's national base by establishing a Ukrainian Supreme Liberation Council (Ukrainska Holovna Vyzvolna Rada).

After the UPA was liquidated by Soviet security forces in the 1950s, the OUN suffered a similar fate. Those of its leaders who were not killed escaped to the West.

BIBLIOGRAPHY

Alexander, J. *Ukrainian Nationalism, 1939–1945.* New York, 1955.

Kubijoviyc, V., ed. *Ukraine: A Concise Encyclopedia.* 2 vols. Toronto, 1963, 1971.

Torzecki, R. *Kwestia ukrainska w polityce III Rzeszy (1933–1945).* Warsaw, 1972.

SHMUEL SPECTOR

ORPO. *See* Ordnungspolizei.

OSE. *See* Oeuvre de Secours aux Enfants.

OSI. *See* Office of Special Investigations.

OSTBATAILLONE (Eastern Battalions; also called Osttruppen or Ostverbände), armed units in the German army, made up of Soviet prisoners of war and Soviet civilians serving in the German-occupied Soviet territories. The Germans' need to recruit Soviet personnel arose out of the heavy losses incurred by the German army in the early months of the war against the USSR and in the early stage of the partisan fighting, especially on the northern and central fronts. In a letter dated October 6, 1941, Gen. Eduard Wagner, *Generalquartiermeister* (Quartermaster General) of the army, proposed to the army group commanders that they recruit Cossack, Ukrainian, and Belorussian prisoners and form them into cavalry troops (*Hundertschaft Sotnia*) for fighting Soviet partisans. At a later stage, prisoners hailing from the Caucasus and Central Asia were added to these categories. In the course of 1942 the troops grew in numbers and formed battalions, which were attached to German divisions serving the command of the rearguard military administration of the army groups. On October 1, 1942, the formation of a large number of such Ostbataillone was launched, including also Ostlegionen (Eastern Legions), a designation applied to units composed of Tatars and nationalities from the Caucasus and Central Asia.

The establishment and training of the units took place for the most part on GENERALGOUVERNEMENT territory. By May 1943, nine brigades, sixty independent battalions, and eight Cossack battalions were in existence (the last eventually forming a corps), as well as six antiaircraft batteries, seventy-eight independent companies, and dozens of battalions serving with the engineering and supply corps. Battalion strength was often over one thousand. The commanding officers were mostly German, but in some units—such as those of Kaminski and Gil-Rodionov—the officers were all Soviet citizens (*see* RUSSKAYA OSVOBODITELNAYA ARMIYA).

In early 1943 a special headquarters was set up for these units, headed by a *General der Osttruppen* (Commander of the Eastern Troops), but its task was confined to the troops' pay, welfare, and related matters. In fact, the conditions of service in the Ostbataillone—such as clothing, pay, and food—were comparable to those of German soldiers.

In June 1943, on Hitler's orders, most of the Ostbataillone were transferred to the western front, from Norway to Italy. The largest contingent went to France, to protect the "Atlantic Wall"; the Cossack corps was sent to Yugoslavia to fight the Yugoslav partisans under Josip TITO. Several German commanders, on their own initiative, began referring to those Ostbataillone whose ethnic composition was uniform as though they were part of a national army, such as the Russkaya Osvoboditelnaya Armiya (Russian Liberation Army) or Ukrainske Vyzvolne Viisko (Ukrainian Liberation Army). This practice was soon stopped, because of opposition from the commanders of the rearguard divisions to which the Ostbataillone belonged, as well as from the Nazi leadership itself. Instructions issued by the Army High Command on May 29, 1944, to identify the Ostbataillone by their national origin did not take hold either. It was not until February or March of 1945 that these national armies were officially established. The accepted estimate is that about one million Soviet nationals served in the German army. Most of them were handed over to the Soviet authorities after the war, as provided for at the February 1945 Yalta Conference.

[*See also* Hilfswillige.]

BIBLIOGRAPHY

Hoffmann, J. *Die Ostlegionen, 1941–1943: Terkotataren, Kaukisier und Wolgafinnen im deutschen Heer.* Freiburg im Breisgau, 1981.

Tessin, G. *Verbände und Truppen der deutschen Wehrmacht und Waffen-SS im II Weltkrieg, 1939–45.* Vol. 1. Osnabrück, 1975.

SHMUEL SPECTOR

OSTINDUSTRIE GMBH (East Industry, Inc.; Osti), enterprise founded by the SS on March 13, 1943, to exploit Jewish labor in the GENERALGOUVERNEMENT for as long as an appreciable number of Jews continued to live there. Under the program presented at the WANNSEE CONFERENCE, the Jews of the Generalgouvernement were to be concentrated in ghettos pending their deportation to the EXTERMINATION CAMPS, and those among them who were fit were to be put to work. Accordingly, the SS set up labor camps that came under the jurisdiction of the *Höherer SS- und Polizeiführer* (Higher SS and Police Leaders; HSSPF). As in the CONCENTRATION CAMPS, the SS sought to be the direct beneficiary of the work performed by the Jews, by establishing its own economic enterprise, the Osti.

Osti's main office was in LUBLIN, since most of the surviving Jews were concentrated in the Lublin district at the time (officially, Osti was based in Berlin). The close connection between Osti's purposes and the extermination measures was also expressed in the person of its chief executive officer, Odilo GLOBOCNIK, who was the HSSPF in the Lublin district. Globocnik was Heinrich HIMMLER's representative for the implementation of AKTION REINHARD, the code name for the extermination of the Jews in the Generalgouvernement. Osti assumed control of several economic enterprises in Lublin and its vicinity, including ironworks, brush factories, peat works, and a fur-manufacturing plant. Up until November 1943, Osti employed some sixteen thousand Jews and one thousand Poles.

Osti's economic operations, however, were subordinate to the real purpose of the labor camps: they were to serve as assembly points for the transports being sent to the extermination camps. The German army was the recipient of considerable quantities of goods produced by Osti, and individual military commanders lodged protests against the cessation of such supplies, but to no avail. By the fall of 1943, SS Kommandos had killed most of the Jews in the Generalgouvernement, and the BEŁŻEC, SOBIBÓR, and TREBLINKA extermination camps had been dissolved or destroyed; in November 1943 the SS killed the Jewish inmates of the MAJDANEK concentration camp. Globocnik could now report that Aktion Reinhard had been completed.

The liquidation of the Jews of the Generalgouvernement also meant the end of Osti, which had no more working hands at its disposal. In his final report on Osti, Globocnik—who had personally become a wealthy man by expropriating the property of the murdered Jews—expressed his regrets that he had just been promised new orders from the Wehrmacht, and that Osti had outstanding orders in the amount of 31 million zlotys. Yet it was Globocnik himself who had disposed of the people who could have fulfilled these orders.

[*See also* Forced Labor.]

BIBLIOGRAPHY

Georg, E. *Die wirtschaftlichen Unternehmungen der SS.* Stuttgart, 1963.

Luczak, C. *Polityka ludnosciowa i ekonomiczna hitlerowskich Niemiec w okupowanej Polsce.* Poznań, 1979.

FALK PINGEL

OSTLAND. *See* Reichskommissariat Ostland.

OSTLEGIONEN. *See* Ostbataillone.

OSTTRUPPEN. *See* Ostbataillone.

OSTVERBÄNDE. *See* Ostbataillone.

OSWEGO FREE PORT. *See* Fort Ontario.

OŚWIĘCIM. *See* Auschwitz.

OUN. *See* Orhanizatsyia Ukrainskykh Natsionalistiv.

OVERDUIJN, LEENDERT (1901–1976), Dutch pastor who rescued Jews during World War II. Reverend Overduijn headed a close-knit organization of more than forty persons in Enschede, in the eastern part of the Netherlands. It helped Jews find hiding places in various parts of the country, but mostly in towns and villages in the northern province of Friesland, where the German occupation was not as ubiquitous and pervasive as in the more populous industrialized regions in the south. The division of labor was such that Overduijn stayed at home most of the time while his daughter and other helpers traveled in different localities to seek suitable places of hiding.

Nevertheless, Overduijn frequently visited Jews in hiding, bringing ration cards, cigarettes, and, most important of all, news from friends and relatives. His comings and goings were noticed by the authorities, and Overduijn was eventually taken in for questioning and imprisoned for an extended period. After the war, he refused to accept any honors or commendations for his work.

At least 461 persons owe their lives largely to Overduijn's wide-ranging activities and his network of friends and trusted colleagues. YAD VASHEM added his name, in 1973, to the list of the "RIGHTEOUS AMONG THE NATIONS."

BIBLIOGRAPHY

Van Zuylen, F. *De joodse gemeenschap te Enschede 1930–1945*. Hengelo, Netherlands, 1983. See pages 58–62.

MORDECAI PALDIEL

OZE. *See* Oeuvre de Secours aux Enfants.

PAC. *See* President's Advisory Committee on Political Refugees.

PALESTINE. *See* Aliya Bet; Beriḥa; White Paper of 1939; Yishuv; Youth Aliya.

PAPEN, FRANZ VON (1879–1969), German statesman and diplomat, born in Werl (in Westphalia) to an ancient Westphalian Catholic family of nobles. In 1897 von Papen was an officer in the Prussian army, and from 1913 to 1915 a military attaché, first in Mexico and then in Washington. Accused of espionage and sabotage, he was expelled from Washington at the request of the United States government. Until the end of World War I, von Papen served in Turkey, attaining the rank of lieutenant colonel, and on the Palestinian front, where he was chief of staff of the Ottoman Fourth Army and advised the German commander of the front, Gen. Erich von Falkenhayn, to retreat from Jerusalem without fighting. During the war von Papen made the acquaintance of many Turkish public figures, and in particular he became friendly with Mustafa Ismet (later Ismet Inönü), who was to become prime minister, and later president, of Turkey.

At the end of the war von Papen joined the extreme right-wing branch of the Zentrum (center) party, and sat in the Prussian parliament from 1920 to 1928 and again from 1930 to 1932. For many years he was chairman of the board of directors of *Germania*, the journal of the Zentrum party in Berlin, and held most of its shares. Through his marriage to the daughter of a leading Saar industrialist, he formed close ties with industrial circles in the Saar area. He was a leader of the Herrenklub (Club of Nobles), a social organization for political aspirants who included industrialists, owners of large estates, contractors, senior civil servants, military officers, scientists, and members of the conservative-

Franz von Papen in his cell at Nuremberg during his trial by the International Military Tribunal (November 23, 1945). [United States Army]

extremist press. The Herrenklub was opposed to democracy, advocating plenipotentiary rule by an elitist, aristocratic hierarchy—a Prussian tradition of an authoritarian state with a "northern, Christian nature" and "superior German people." Accordingly, he dissociated himself from any kind of "rule of the masses," and in particular the Soviet model.

Von Papen played a decisive role in the fall of Chancellor Heinrich Brüning's Zentrum government. After withdrawing from the party, he was prime minister (from June 1 to November 17, 1932) of a right-wing government without party affiliation that depended solely on the authority of President Paul von HINDENBURG and on the initiative of army officer and statesman Kurt von Schleicher. Von Papen forcibly removed the minority government in Prussia headed by Social Democrat Otto Braun, and appointed himself *Reichskommissar* for Prussia. His leanings toward openly authoritarian direction of the state were revealed principally in his antidemocratic emergency regulations, published on June 14 and September 4 and 5, 1932. They reached a climax with the dissolution of the Reichstag (the German parliament) on September 12, after this elected institution rejected his latest emergency regulation by an overwhelming majority. The "new state" that von Papen was attempting to create would have changed the Weimar Constitution completely, abolished parties and trade unions, and introduced a system of two houses of representatives with a plural right of vote for family heads.

The Nazis gained from von Papen's decision to repeal the June 15 ban on the SA (Sturmabteilung; Storm Troopers), introduced by Brüning two months previously, and from the appointment of Wilhelm von Gayl as minister of the interior. Gayl had been prominent as an adviser to the Supreme Command on the eastern front in World War I, when he had proposed the expulsion of the Jews, Lithuanians, and Russians from Lithuania. As minister of the interior, Gayl wished to make the citizenship of people of an "inferior culture" dependent on a minimum permanent residence of twenty years in Germany. One of his officials, Hans GLOBKE, ordered the police under his command not to allow Jews to change their names in cases when it was clear that the purpose was to "mask the Jewish origin" of the petitioner.

After the fall of von Papen's government, Kurt von Schleicher, who had initially helped him come to power and then played a decisive role in his fall, became chancellor. The embittered von Papen opposed Schleicher's attrition tactics against the Nazis, and on January 4, 1933, he met with Adolf Hitler for a decisive talk, reaching a general agreement with him and thereby paving the way for Hitler's rise to power. On January 30 Hitler became chancellor, with von Papen as his deputy. It rapidly became clear that von Papen's hope of becoming actual ruler was unrealistic, but as Hitler's deputy he bore much of the responsibility for the "political cleanup" that was immediately instituted; certainly he approved of its direction.

Von Papen was soon pushed aside. In a speech in Marburg on June 17, 1934, he carefully dissociated himself from certain aspects of the regime. Two weeks later, in the purge connected with the RÖHM affair (June 30, 1934), he lost his position in the government, and the man who had written the Marburg speech was put to death.

From 1934 to 1938 von Papen was ambassador to Austria and paved the way for its annexation (ANSCHLUSS). Between 1939 and 1944 he was ambassador in Ankara, failing in his efforts to persuade Turkey to join the war on the side of Germany, but managing to influence his World War I comrades in arms to maintain neutrality almost until the end of World War II.

In April 1945, von Papen was arrested by the Allies. He was one of the accused at the NUREMBURG TRIAL, but was acquitted since his participation in sponsoring the war of aggression could not be proved; in 1949 a DENAZIFICATION court sentenced him to twelve years in a labor camp. However, since he had already spent some years in prison, he was released immediately after an appeal. Von Papen wrote *Memoirs* (New York, 1953) and *Vom Scheitern einer Demokratie, 1930–1933* (The Failure of a Democracy, 1930–1933; 1968).

BIBLIOGRAPHY

Bracher, K. D. *Die Auflösung der Weimarer Repu-*

blik: Eine Studie zum Problem des Machtverfalls in der Demokratie. Stuttgart, 1955.
Bracher, K. D. *The German Dictatorship: The Origins, Structure, and Effects of National Socialism.* New York, 1970. See chapter 4.
Schotte, W. *Das Kabinett Papen-Schleicher-Gayl.* Leipzig, 1932.

HANS-HEINRICH WILHELM

PARACHUTISTS, JEWISH, a group of Jewish volunteers from Palestine who were sent on missions to several countries in Nazi-occupied Europe between 1943 and 1945. The idea of sending emissaries from the YISHUV (the Jewish community in Palestine) to encourage the Jews in the Nazi-dominated countries, to organize their RESISTANCE, and to try and rescue them had developed after the change in the Yishuv's attitude toward the news from Europe in the fall of 1942. This change had resulted from the testimonies of sixty-nine Jewish civilians, holders of Palestinian passports, who had been brought to Palestine from Poland in mid-November in exchange for German civilians. In the absence of independent means for transporting the emissaries, the Jewish Agency for Palestine had to apply to the British and resort to secret cooperation with the British Special Operations Executive (SOE) and several branches of the British intelligence service that had been created at the beginning of World War II for clandestine operations in the Balkans and the Middle East.

In early 1943 the British rejected the more ambitious proposals of the Jewish Agency to send hundreds of volunteers into Nazi-occupied territory. Recognizing, however, the special motivation of the volunteers, their linguistic skills, and their knowledge of the terrain in the target countries, the British were prepared to drop individual parachutist agents. The SOE intended to employ them as wireless operators and instructors with its liaison missions to the PARTISANS. The MI 9 —the military intelligence branch in charge of prisoners of war—assigned to the volunteers the task of rescuing prisoners of war, escapees, and evaders (men who had evaded captivity). Both the SOE and the MI 9 knew of and consented to the volunteers' double role as British agents and Jewish emissaries.

Zvi Ben-Yaakov.

The candidates were selected from members of the German and Balkan sections of the Palmah (the strike force of the Hagana, the Yishuv's underground army), Jewish volunteers serving in the British army, and activists of pioneering YOUTH MOVEMENTS who had recently immigrated to Palestine from the target countries. Most of them enlisted with the assistance of a special committee formed by the Jewish Agency; the Mosad le-Aliya Bet (the Jewish immigration authority in Palestine); and the Hagana. Few were recruited directly by British organizations. About 250 men and women volunteered; 110 underwent training, but owing to operational and technical difficulties only 32 were actually dropped and 5 infiltrated into the target countries. Of the 37, 12 were captured and 7 executed by the Germans. Zvi Ben-Yaakov, Rafael Reiss, and Haviva REIK were captured in October 1944 during the SLOVAK NATIONAL UPRISING, imprisoned in Banská Bystrica, and taken to Kremnica, where they were exe-

Center: Yona Rosen; in back, from right to left: Peretz Goldstein, Yoel Palgi, and an unidentified man. [Yona Rosen; Beth Hatefutsoth]

cuted. Abba Berdiczew was captured in Slovakia in October 1944 and taken to Bratislava, where he was tried by a military court and executed.

Peretz Goldstein and Hannah SZENES were captured in Hungary. Szenes was executed by a firing squad in Budapest on November 7, 1944, and Goldstein was apparently sent to the ORANIENBURG concentration camp, where he was killed. Enzo SERENI was captured in Italy, sent to Dachau, and executed there.

The first parachutist, Peretz Rosenberg, was dropped in Yugoslavia in May 1943. The last one, Chaim Waldner, was dropped in southern Austria on the last day of the war, to assist the inmates of a remote prisoner-of-war camp. Several parachutists—Dan Laner, Chaim Hermesh, Berdiczew, Rechavam Amir, and Reuven Dafni—set out on more than one mission.

Three parachutists were infiltrated into Hungary (Szenes, Goldstein, and Yoel Palgi), five participated in the Slovak National Uprising (Reik, Ben-Yaakov, Rafael Reiss, Berdiczew, and Hermesh), and six operated in northern Italy (Sereni, Efraim Dafni, Yaakov Shapira, Binyamin Gefner, Yechiel Kassap, and Refaeli). Waldner was dropped in Austria, Adolph Rabinowicz jumped seven times in France before he was captured and executed, and Aaron Ben-Yosef and Yosef Varon were infiltrated into Bulgaria after its liberation by the Soviet army. Nine parachutists operated in Romania, where they succeeded in aiding Allied prisoners of war during the interim period after the Romanian capitulation and in organizing immigration to Palestine: Liowa (Yehuda) Gukowsky, Arye Fichman, Riko Lupesku, Arye Makaresku, Dov Harari, Baruch Kamin, Itzhak Ben-Efraim, Uriel Kaner, and Yeshayahu Dan. Ten served with the British liaison missions to the Yugoslav partisans: Rosenberg, Amir, Reuven Dafni, Yona Rosen, Nissim Testa, Zadok Dorogoyer-Doron, Sara Braverman, Eli Zohar, Shalom Finzi, and Laner.

The Jewish parachutists were meant to be only a spearhead of larger groups following them. But the missions of the latter did not materialize, because of British political reservations, insurmountable operational obstacles, or the liberation of the target country.

BIBLIOGRAPHY

Bauer, Y. "The Defense Plan." *Yalkut Moreshet* 1 (November–December 1963): 86–94. (In Hebrew.)

Gelber, Y. "The Mission of the Jewish Parachutists from Palestine in Europe in World War II." *Studies in Zionism* 7/1 (Spring 1986): 51–76.

Gilad, Z. *Defense under Cover: From the Operations of the Palestine Underground during World War II*. Jerusalem, 1962. (In Hebrew.)

YOAV GELBER

PARIS. On the eve of World War II, Paris was the home of about 200,000 Jews. Only a quarter were French-born, and the CONSISTOIRE CENTRAL DES ISRAÉLITES DE FRANCE (Central Consistory of French Jews) was the recognized representative of this minority. The majority were eastern European Jews who had immigrated to FRANCE before and especially after World War I and had created a vast network of institutions and a vibrant Yiddish cultural and political atmosphere. Several thousand refugees from Germany, Austria, and Czechoslovakia augmented the Jewish community after Adolf Hitler's rise to power and his annexations. A heterogeneous community with diverse political and cultural orientations, Parisian Jewry lacked unity as it entered World War II.

The German offensive that began on May 10, 1940, was followed by a massive exodus from northern France. Within six weeks France was defeated and an armistice agreement was quickly reached, leaving the country divided: the north under German occupation, and a free zone in the south, with a new French government at the spa town of Vichy. The reestablishment of a French government under the authoritarian leadership of Marshal Philippe PÉTAIN, with the promise of stability and normality, encouraged hundreds of thousands of Frenchmen who had fled to the south to return to the occupied zone.

Some 20,000 to 30,000 Jews joined the migration back, among them community leaders and activists. Jewish organizations were slowly reestablished. Immigrant community activists, Zionists, and Bundists gathered around the FÉDÉRATION DES SOCIETÉS JUIVES DE FRANCE and established the AMELOT committee. The Communists formed a special underground organization known as Solidarité. The Consistoire reopened its synagogues; the Comité de Bienfaisance, the OEUVRE DE SECOURS AUX ENFANTS , and the ORT vocational schools followed. By October 1940 the Vichy government had adopted a xenophobic antisemitic policy and began issuing wide-ranging anti-Jewish laws. The first German measure, begun in late September, was a census, which showed that there were 150,000 Jews in Paris. It was followed by the

The Vélodrome d'Hiver arena, which was used as an internment area for the Jews of Paris.

"Aryanization" of Jewish enterprises (*see* ARISIERUNG).

From September 1940 the Consistoire was under pressure from Theodor DANNECKER, the Germans' "Jewish expert," to centralize all the Jewish organizations. Prompted by awareness of the community's material needs and assured by Dannecker that he would not interfere, in January 1941 the Consistoire and Amelot established the Comité de Coordination des Oeuvres Israélites de Bienfaisance (Coordinating Committee [CC] of Jewish Welfare Societies). All the organizations accepted centralization on this basis except for the Communists, who chose to close their canteen service for the needy shortly thereafter. In March, Dannecker brought in two men from Vienna to run the Jewish organization, causing a split within the CC. Whereas Amelot resigned, the Consistoire decided to remain rather than have the community led by Dannecker's designees. In May 1941 Dannecker ordered, on the basis of a Vichy law, the first internments: 3,700 Jewish men were rounded up and sent to Pithiviers and Beaune-La-Rolande (Loiret). To the sixty thousand monthly meals distributed by the CC's various agencies was now added the need to help these men and their families. Further tension ensued when in August the CC refused to accede to Dannecker's demand to supply 6,000 men for work in the Ardennes. In reprisal, Dannecker ordered the internment of 4,300 French and immigrant Jewish men in the newly established camp at DRANCY, northeast of Paris.

These measures exacerbated the deteriorating economic situation of the community, faced with the continuous "Aryanization" of thousands of Jewish enterprises, which also brought a deterioration in the employment situation. The order to surrender radios, bicycles, and telephones, and the bombing of seven synagogues in October, heralded worse to come. The activities of the French Résistance led the Germans to take repressive measures against the Jews in December 1941: a fine of a billion francs was imposed and 750 French Jews were interned, constituting part of a group of 1,000 men held as hostages to be deported. The UNION GÉNÉRALE DES ISRAÉLITES DE FRANCE (UGIF), established by Vichy on November 29, 1941, on German orders, was held responsible for payment of the fine. The year ended with further measures: Jews were no longer allowed to leave Paris or to change their address. By then some 9,000 Jewish men had been interned and 10,000 had fled to the Vichy zone.

The year 1942 began with an ordinance forbidding Jews to leave their homes between 9:00 p.m. and 6:00 a.m. In March the first deportation took place, consisting of the 1,000 hostages; it was followed in June with those previously interned. The Berlin decision of June 1942, ordering preparations for mass deportations, led to new measures: the wearing of the yellow star (*see* BADGE, JEWISH), which provoked widespread public resentment among the French, and the prohibition of access by Jews to all public places. After detailed planning among German and French officials, the stage was set for a major Nazi operation in Paris. Mass arrests of foreign Jews, regardless of sex, age, or physical condition, began on July 16. Rounded up by thousands of French police and interned in the Vélodrome d'Hiver sports arena, almost 13,000 Jews were seized, soon to be taken to Drancy before being deported to AUSCHWITZ. Out of the 28,000 envisaged by Dannecker, 15,000 had evaded arrest. Apart from escaping to the Vichy zone or hiding, the only means of survival was to obtain an *Ausweis* (an identity card that served as a protective pass), either by working for German industry or through employment with the UGIF.

By early 1943 there were only 60,000 "legal" Jews left in Paris: 30,000 had been deported, thousands had fled or gone into hiding, and some 3,000 from Turkey, Hungary, Italy, and neutral countries had been repatriated. The diminishing numbers available for deportation led the Germans to order arrests in children's homes, homes for the aged, and the Rothschild Hospital. Mid-1943 was a critical period: the *Ausweis* no longer provided protection, the UGIF was forced to release most of its foreign employees, and even Jews of mixed marriages were interned. Solidarité, committed to the armed struggle, had been decimated by the Gestapo. Amelot, dedicated to helping those in hiding, saving children, and distributing forged papers, at that time lost its dominant figure, David Rapoport, and was seriously shaken. Nevertheless, a reconstituted leadership under Abraham Alpérine carried on until the liberation. In June 1943, SS-Obersturmbannführer Alois BRUNNER arrived to increase the tempo of deportation, and he took over Drancy from the French administration. The UGIF's refusal to carry out Brunner's order to participate in arrests led to the deportation of its vice president, André BAUR, and of many of its stalwarts.

Early in 1944, when only 7,000 immigrant Jews and at least that many French Jews still resided openly in Paris, even French Jews who had never been the object of definite deportation orders filled convoys. Within the Jewish organizations, realignments ensued: Solidarité, reconstituted as the UNION DES JUIFS POUR LA RÉSISTANCE ET L'ENTR'AIDE (UJRE), joined together with Amelot and Zionist representatives to form the Comité Général de Defense des Juifs. The UGIF nevertheless refused to terminate certain services or to disperse its children's homes.

The Allied armies' landing in June 1944 held out hope for those remaining, but deportations continued until the liberation. On July 31, Brunner ordered the deportation of almost 300 children seized a week earlier from UGIF homes. Paris was freed on August 25, 1944, and the remaining 1,400 Jews at Drancy were saved. Estimates of the number still left in Paris vary between 20,000 and 50,000. Of the 150,000 present at the October 1940 census, a third were no longer alive to celebrate the liberation.

Parisian Jewry had shown a very diverse response to the cataclysm of Nazi occupation and Vichy collaboration. Hundreds had fought in the August 1944 insurrection, and hundreds had been executed or had died after being deported for engaging in Résistance activities. Amelot and the UJRE had saved 3,000 children and countless adults, while the UGIF continued to distribute aid until the very end. Among the efforts to aid and protect the doomed community, the responses of some of the organizations were later viewed with pride; others, like those of the UGIF, were sharply criticized. With the liberation, Parisian Jewry began to rebuild the shattered community and its organizational structure, without denying the internal tensions that had marked its past history.

BIBLIOGRAPHY

Adler, J. *The Jews of Paris and the Final Solution: Communal Response and Internal Conflicts, 1940–1944.* New York, 1987.

Marrus, M. R., and R. O. Paxton. *Vichy France and the Jews.* New York, 1981.

Wellers, G. *De Drancy à Auschwitz.* Paris, 1946.

JACQUES ADLER

PARKES, JAMES WILLIAM (1896–1981), English Protestant minister and pioneer in Jewish-Christian relations. After studying at Oxford, Parkes traveled a number of years for the Student Christian Movement and International Student Service. For the latter he initiated the study of antisemitism, which led him to return to doctoral studies and to enter a lifetime of publication and practical work in the field.

Representing the International Student Service in eastern Europe, Parkes became aware of the antisemitism rampant in Germany, Austria, Poland, and elsewhere. From his headquarters in Geneva he began to work with refugee groups helping Jews to escape from Nazi Germany. His work came to the attention of the Nazis, who in 1933 made an abortive attempt on his life. Parkes returned to England, where he continued to work with refugee groups. He also opposed missionary groups in England who were trying to exploit the plight of Jewish refugee children, and he sought to force these groups to return the children to the Jewish community.

Parkes's initial work, *The Conflict of the Church and the Synagogue* (1934), was a pathbreaking study of the roots of Christian antisemitism. He wrote on antisemitism, Jewish-Christian relations, Zionism, and the correction of the traditional Christian theology of alienation and rejection of Judaism and the Jewish people. Even before the advent of Nazism, Parkes had identified many of the key issues that are still central to the post-Holocaust interfaith dialogue. His writings include *Antisemitism* (1963), *The Jew in the Medieval Community* (1938), and *Judaism and Christianity* (1948).

BIBLIOGRAPHY

Everett, R. "Christian Theology after the Holocaust." *Christian Attitudes on Jews and Judaism* 51 (December 1976): 11–12, 17.

ROBERT A. EVERETT

PARTEITAGE ("party days"; sg., *Parteitag*), national rallies of the NAZI PARTY, held in the city of NUREMBERG. The Reichstag had frequently met in Nuremberg, which was a "royal city" in the Middle Ages, and its selection as the venue of the *Parteitage* aimed at maintaining the city's ancient tradition. The ceremonies and festivities of the *Parteitage* were marked by considerable exhibitionism. Many Nazi organizations took a prominent part in them, including the SS, the SA (Sturmabteilung; Storm Troopers), the Nazi women's organization, and the Nazi trade unions. Modern mass-staging effects aimed at stigmatizing perceived enemies and glorifying the concept of the *Volksgemeinschaft* ("community of the *Volk*"), which culminated in the Führer cult.

The first general gatherings of the members of the Nazi party, in 1920, 1921, and 1922, and the first *Parteitag*, which took place from January 27 to 29, 1923, were held in Munich. The second *Parteitag* was held in August 1926 in Weimar, with 12,000 members participating. The third rally, in which about 30,000 took part, was held in Nuremberg in August 1927. At that meeting, Alfred ROSENBERG delivered a wildly antisemitic speech, and Dr. Artur Dinter, a nationalist ideologue, then put forward a "five-point plan for the solution of the Jewish problem." The plan anticipated the 1935 NUREMBERG LAWS: Jews would be denied civil rights, the right to occupy public offices, the right to own immovable property, and the right to enter Germany; all Jews who had come to Germany after 1914 would be expelled; and Jews would be banned from marrying "Aryans." In 1929, the last *Parteitag* prior to the Nazi seizure of power was held in Nuremberg; this time, the number of participants exceeded 100,000. From 1933 through 1938, *Parteitage* were held yearly in Nuremberg. The 1938 *Parteitag* was the last. For 1939 a "party day for peace" was prepared, but at the last moment it was canceled because of the outbreak of the war.

Party rallies came to be known outside the borders of the Reich through the screening of Leni Riefenstahl's film *Triumph des Willens* (Triumph of the Will), which depicted the 1934 *Parteitag*. On average, about half a million people participated in the *Parteitage* between 1933 and 1938. Some of the speeches at the rallies were printed in special pamphlets, and from 1934 annual anthologies of the *Parteitage* were published. These were extensively reviewed in the world press, with sometimes surprisingly positive reviews.

The fixed agenda in Nuremberg included speeches on topics such as anti-Bolshevism, antiliberalism, and antisemitism. In the "*Parteitag* of Unity and Might" in 1934, Dr. Gerhard Wagner, chief medical officer of the Nazi party, delivered a speech titled "Race and National Health." It was this speech that created the ideological infrastructure for the EUTHANASIA PROGRAM. The "Freedom *Parteitag*," held from September 10 to 16, 1935, was accorded the status of a Reichstag session, and it enacted the antisemitic Nuremberg Laws.

BIBLIOGRAPHY

Burden, H. T. *Die programmierte Nation: Die Nürnberger Reichsparteitage.* Gütersloh, 1967.
Espe, W. M. *Das Buch der NSDAP: Werden, Kampf, und Ziel der NSDAP.* Berlin, 1934.
Speer, A. *Inside the Third Reich.* New York, 1970.

HANS-HEINRICH WILHELM

PARTISANS, irregular forces operating in enemy-occupied territory, for the most part using guerrilla tactics. In World War II, partisans in Nazi-occupied Europe operated primarily in eastern Europe and in the Balkan states.

The resistance that emerged in the war had its origin in the tension between having to obey and cooperate with the occupier, and the reluctance to do so. Cooperation with the Nazis, for the individual, meant obeying the orders of the Germans, working for them, and surrendering to them property or the fruit of one's labors. Such cooperation was a general and unavoidable phenomenon in occupied Europe. It took some time before the individual citizens of an occupied country came to feel the urge to upset the enemy's plans and interfere with them. When they reached that state, they acted by evading orders, committing sabotage, failing to fulfill production quotas, and avoiding or refusing to go to GERMANY for FORCED LABOR. Such steps inevitably led to outright resistance. Many of those who offered resistance were undoubtedly motivated by an abhorrence of racism, violence, Nazi ideology, and the methods used by the Nazis.

Organized resistance—on partisan political, national, or religious grounds—also passed through several phases. It began with efforts to continue group existence under the occupation, but since sooner or later such existence was outlawed and led to arrests and executions, the organized groups resorted to clandestine, underground operations. Certain political parties (especially the

PARTISANS

Communists, who adopted a sharp and uncompromising anti-Nazi line after the German invasion of the Soviet Union in mid-1941) had at first been confused and hesitant about the war and had spoken of it as a confrontation between two "imperialisms"; in that early period, one of these "two imperialisms," the Nazi camp, was tied to the Soviets by a pact.

The political parties in the resistance movement embarked upon propaganda operations, circulation of underground newspapers, organized strikes, and sabotage acts. Even at this early stage, fragmentation, lack of cooperation, and outright differences could be discerned among the different political movements taking part in one and the same national resistance movement. In the final stage of resistance—the stage of guerrilla warfare and armed struggle—these differences, at least in some places, led to confrontations and clashes and even took on the aspect of a civil war.

Armed struggle in realistic dimensions began when the war reached a turning point in late 1942 and early 1943, following the decisive Nazi defeat at STALINGRAD and the success of the Allies in North Africa. In this new stage the various national political movements began to jockey for position in the postwar era, with their mind on the relationship they wanted with the Allies when peace came, and on the sociopolitical form they wished for the future regime of their country. These considerations induced the movements to intensify armed resistance against the occupier, and also led to internal confrontation between rival movements. Such confrontations took place in YUGOSLAVIA, GREECE, and POLAND.

In Poland, an underground military organization was created at the very beginning of the occupation, headed by officers of the regular Polish army. On more than one occasion the leaders of that organization refrained from putting its main force into action, preferring to save it for a decisive test at the end of the war. This major Polish organization, the ARMIA KRAJOWA (Home Army), was in sharp conflict with the Polish Communists when the latter set up their own underground organization, in early 1942. For the non-Communist Poles, there was no difference between the Germans and the Soviets; both were enemies who had occupied their land.

Controversies of a similar nature also arose in other occupied countries. In some, resistance to the Nazis was confined to sporadic attacks against top Nazi officials who stood out in their brutality and were hated for it; or to one-time special operations involving a sensitive security target (such as the sabotage of the heavy-water plant in NORWAY). In these countries no attempt was made to train combat units and put guerrilla forces into the field on an ongoing basis, to take up street fighting, or to engage the enemy in some other form. In many countries, such as the Protectorate of BOHEMIA AND MORAVIA, the resistance refrained from guerrilla warfare because of the great risk of retaliatory action, which would take many lives. In the satellite states, little military resistance was offered.

There were also differences in what the great powers—Britain and the United States on the one hand and the Soviet Union on the other—expected of the Nazi-occupied countries. Britain and the United States (after the latter entered the war) primarily wanted the occupied countries to provide them with intelligence, to aid prisoners of war who were trying to escape (especially air force pilots whose planes had been hit and who had parachuted into German-occupied territory), and to carry out one-time attacks of particular military importance. The Soviet Union had different expectations: it asked its supporters to engage in fighting the enemy in the rear, to attack lines of communication and industrial plants, and to impair mobility.

Guerrilla warfare is war of the weak against superior forces that have heavy and sophisticated arms at their disposal. On the other hand, guerrilla forces usually have the advantages of familiarity with the area, the sympathy of the population, and the ability to employ hit-and-run tactics. Polish partisans frequently operated in units that were called out for a specific mission or for a period of training. When the mission was accomplished or the training period was over, they returned to their homes and civilian pursuits. They used the same methods to vanish from the scene when the Germans combed the forests in their search for partisans.

It has been asked why the Jews did not

organize a guerrilla movement of their own, independent of the Allies and of other national partisan organizations. Various answers to this question have been suggested. The Jew who went into the forest was not a fighter who left parents and relatives behind in a safe home, having made a personal decision involving only himself. Such a Jew was leaving behind his immediate family and his community with fear in his heart, certain that he would never see them again. Non-Jewish partisans went forth to do their patriotic duty in the knowledge that they had the support of the Allies, a supporting country, or a government-in-exile on whose behalf they were acting. Such partisans could approach a farmer and request food and intelligence as fellow citizens; if they were handed over or betrayed, they would be avenged. Not so the Jew; he was a stranger, he was persecuted, and he had a chance of surviving in the forest only as part of a broad framework, as a fighter in a large general unit or in a Jewish unit integrated into a larger formation. Moreover, the individual Jew or group of Jews who sought to join up with an existing partisan formation had special obstacles to overcome. They had first to escape from a ghetto and locate a partisan base in the forest, and even when they finally joined a partisan unit they were not put on an equal footing with the other fighters.

In countries outside eastern Europe, the Jew who wanted to join the partisan forces faced a different situation. In the Balkan states (Yugoslavia, BULGARIA, and Greece), Jews were accepted as equals into fighting organizations and into units operating in the area. In western Europe, including FRANCE and ITALY, many Jews joined the underground fighters' ranks not as Jews, but either as citizens of the country fulfilling their duty, or out of loyalty to a particular political and ideological movement—although it stands to reason that their Jewishness also played a significant role in their decision to join. On the other hand, many Jews in western Europe, deeply perturbed as they were by the suffering of their fellow Jews, instead of joining a partisan unit devoted themselves to the rescue of Jews, which they believed was as important a challenge, and which appealed to them as Jews. When the stage of the "FINAL SOLUTION" was reached, Jewish participation in partisan operations became part of a hopeless struggle and a determination for revenge.

In the Baltic states and the VILNA area, in BELORUSSIA and the western UKRAINE (which in the interwar period had been part of Poland), partisan activities by Jews reached considerable dimensions. It is estimated that twenty thousand to thirty thousand Jews were in the partisan units in the forests. A combination of factors, both objective and subjective, made this possible:

1. The nature of the territory, with its thick forests and many swamps, which made it suitable for the partisans to establish bases there;
2. The fact that at a later stage of the war most partisan units in that area were under Soviet command and for various reasons accepted Jews into their ranks (except for Polish and Ukrainian units, which on occasion were hostile to Jews);
3. The fact that many of the Jews in that area had lived in its towns and villages, were familiar with the layout, and were willing and able to adapt to life in the forests.

The growth of the partisan movement passed through three stages, as follows.

1. In a broadcast to the nation on July 3, 1941—twelve days after the German attack—Joseph STALIN called for the establishment of an underground movement in the occupied territories, to fight the enemy. Communist party committees in the Ukraine and Belorussia trained special combat teams and sent them into the occupied territories, where they tried to form partisan units together with Soviet army soldiers who were stranded in the thick forests. These efforts were not very successful. In the areas further east, special units were formed and partisan bases established even before the Germans arrived, and when that happened, these units became partisan units. From mid-1942 they grew into what became well-known partisan formations, such as the Kovpak, Fyodorov, Saburov, Kapustin, Korzh, and other brigades.

2. The second stage began in late June 1942, when a central headquarters was established for the entire partisan movement. This headquarters assumed direct command, su-

The French Résistance had many Jews in its ranks. In this Résistance unit, the man sixth from the left in the front row is a Jew, Michael Banda. [Yvonne Banda and Beth Hatefutsoth]

pervision, and direction of partisan fighting and became the channel through which means of communication, arms, equipment, and other supplies were provided to the partisans. The numerical strength of the partisan movement grew rapidly and their operations were now coordinated and mutually supportive. The partisans eventually reached a high standard of organization and discipline, were well equipped, maintained lines of communication with the operational centers, took part in many combat operations, and effectively eluded the enemy's efforts to cut them off. The partisan units tormented the enemy by interfering with communications, attacking groups of soldiers, meting out punishment to collaborators, and, above all, instilling fear into the German soldiers, giving them the sense of being surrounded by hostility.

3. In 1944 the partisans in the east acted as auxiliary or integrated forces in military operations on the front, or made efforts to liberate areas in anticipation of the advancing Soviet army.

Despite the generally hostile attitude that the Jews encountered among the partisans, they penetrated into the forests in groups beginning in the spring of 1942 and created nuclei of partisan units. In one such example, the Jews of SLONIM in April 1942 set up a base for a partisan battalion in the forest. That summer, growing numbers of groups of Jewish insurgents were to be found in the forests. Some had escaped from the small towns that were then being systematically liquidated; others, larger in size, were composed of members of fighting organizations (from Vilna, KOVNO, and BIAŁYSTOK) who wanted to organize into Jewish units and turn their fight into a Jewish struggle.

In the countries of western Europe, except for France and Italy, there were no partisan operations of large dimensions. Jews were very prominent in the partisan movement in Italy, and in the French Résistance. The Organisation Juive de Combat (Jewish Fighting Organization) in France took part in combat operations. The failure of a large-scale guerrilla movement to develop in western Europe was the result of topographical conditions, which precluded the rise of such a movement, and was also due to the structure of the respective RESISTANCE movements.

ISRAEL GUTMAN

Belorussia. Belorussia had the largest concentration of partisans in eastern Europe. Partisans began to operate there as early as the summer of 1941, most of them Soviet army troops whom the Germans had cut off and who were roaming the villages and forests; a few were Communist party activists who had fled their homes when the Germans entered the area. The conditions in Belorussia, with its wide expanses of forest and swamp, were ideal for large-scale partisan operations. As early as July 1941, just a few weeks after the German invasion of the Soviet Union, activists who had been assigned to this mission crossed the front line and reached the Starobin, Slutsk, and Kopyl areas, south of MINSK, where they organized small partisan units. Two of these early partisan leaders were Kozlov and Varvashenya. By late August 1941, according to Soviet sources, some 230 partisan units were in existence. Commanding these first units were Bumazhkov, Pavlovski, Smyriev, Zaslonov, and Korzh. Partisan units were also formed in the Vileyka and Kurenets areas.

In the spring of 1942 thousands of automatic rifles and artillery pieces were supplied to the partisans in Belorussia from inside the Soviet Union. That summer the partisan units formed into brigades and landing fields were constructed, at Luban, Klichev, Mogilev, and other places; a Belorussian partisan headquarters was set up in September. The partisan units provided a safe haven for some of the Belorussian population who were threatened with deportation or death by the Germans for the aid they were giving the partisans and their ties with them. The scope of partisan activities expanded, and in 1943 some 60 percent of Belorussia was an area of partisan actions.

The Germans formed Belorussian and Lithuanian auxiliary units to help them, and embarked upon extensive operations against the partisans. The latter, seeking to gain and hold the civilian population's loyalty, conducted a broadly based propaganda campaign, by word of mouth and through underground newspapers.

Three Jewish partisans from Belorussia. Center: Shalom Cholawski.

At an early stage, the partisans' operations were coordinated with the Soviet army. The cooperation between the two was particularly close in the summer of 1944, during the German retreat from Belorussia. At that stage the partisans carried out large joint operations, blowing up railway tracks in the German rear and harassing enemy units during their withdrawal. In late 1941, according to Soviet data, Belorussia had some 5,000 partisans; by 1942 their number had grown to 73,000; by 1943, 243,000; and by 1944, 374,000 (of whom 91,000 were in FAMILY CAMPS IN THE FORESTS). Belorussian partisans were organized into 1,108 units, most of them part of brigades, of which there were 199. The partisan movement in Belorussia included Belorussians, Russians, Jews, Poles, Georgians, Slovaks, and other groups.

The Jewish partisans in Belorussia came

from the ghettos and the Nazi-run camps—some in groups made up of members of the underground organizations that had been formed in many ghettos, and some as individuals who had managed to escape. In the forests the Jewish partisans had their own Jewish units, operating as part of the general Belorussian partisan movement. Some of these Jewish units eventually lost their distinctive Jewish character. Individual Jews were also to be found in non-Jewish units. Jews who sought to join the partisans had a long and arduous road to travel before reaching their goal, and even when they had joined a unit they still had more than the "normal" difficulties to contend with. The situation of the Jews in the partisan units depended in large measure on the timing of their joining up, that is, during which of the three phases of the partisan movement's growth they joined it.

In the early spring of 1942 a group of seventeen Jews made their way to the NOVOGRUDOK forests, led by Tuvia BIELSKI and his brothers Asael, Zusya, and Aharon. This was the core of what eventually became a large camp (known as the Bielski camp) of Jewish partisans in the Naliboki Forest. This solid block of forest land (*puszcza*) covers 1,158 square miles (3,000 sq km) in the Novogrudok region, on the right (northern) bank of the Neman River, in western Belorussia, northeast of the town of Novogrudok. North of the Naliboki Forest lie the towns of Volozhin and Vishnevo; to their east, Ivenets and Rubezhevichi; to their south, Yeremichi; and to the west, Deliatichi and Ivie. In the north, the *puszcza* borders on the Lida-Molodechno railway line. The town of Naliboki, after which the forest land is named, is situated in its southeastern part. A network of Neman tributaries runs through the forests, including the Berezina and Svisloch rivers. The area between one tributary and the next is often covered by swamps, and in between there are "islands" that serve as natural shelters. The Naliboki block of forests lies within a close network of Jewish towns, whose inhabitants, especially the timber experts and dealers, knew their way around in the maze of forests.

The partisan units operating in the Naliboki Forest between the spring of 1942 and the summer of 1944 included the Aleksandr Nevski, Sokolov, Chkalov, Bolshevik, First of May, Iskra, Ponomarenko, Voroshilov, Strelkov, and Svoboda units. This was also the base of the interregional partisan headquarters, headed by major generals Platon, Dubov, and Sokolov. Polish partisan units too operated in the area, one of them the Kościuszko unit. Next to be founded after the Bielski unit, comprised of twelve hundred Jews who had escaped from the Novogrudok area and beyond, was the Zorin unit, made up of Jews who had escaped to the Naliboki Forest from the Minsk ghetto and other ghettos. The Zorin camp eventually contained eight hundred Jews. Dr. Yeheskel ATLAS's unit was formed in the DERECHIN area, and the "Schorr's 51" unit in the Slonim area. The Zhukov unit (made up of Jews who had fled from the NESVIZH, Stolbtsy, and Sverzhna ghettos) and the company commanded by Hirsch KAPLINSKI (made up of Jews from the DIATLOVO [Zhetl] area) set themselves up in the Kopyl area, south of Minsk. In July and August 1943 the Germans raided Naliboki, burned the town and dozens of nearby villages, and transported hundreds of local peasants to labor camps in Germany. It is estimated that twenty thousand partisans operated in the Naliboki Forest, of whom about three thousand were Jews.

In the Lipiczany *puszcza*, Jewish partisan groups operated in the Borba (Struggle) battalion and the Lenin unit. A partisan company made up of Jews from MIR joined the "For Soviet Belorussia" unit of the Chkalov brigade, as well as the Yozhik group. The Chkalov brigade was also joined by Jews from the Gorodok and Volozhin areas. In Kurenets, members of the Ha-Shomer ha-Tsa'ir Zionist youth movement had made contact with an anti-Nazi Russian underground group while still in the ghetto. When they came to the forests they joined partisan units in western Belorussia and in the Pleshchenitsy and VITEBSK areas of eastern Belorussia. In the Vileyka area, Jews fought in the Frunze, Zhukov, Budenny, Fourth Belorussian, and Gastello brigades, among others.

The Białystok fighters and Jewish underground members from the nearby towns, including Supraśl and Slonim, set up the

Vperyod Jewish partisan unit and the small Krinki, Baumats, and Briansk units. Jewish girls served as couriers between the JEWISH ANTIFASCIST COMMITTEE in Białystok and partisan units in the forest. Jews who had fled from ghettos in northern Volhynia and the southern part of the Novogrudok area, including those of BARANOVICHI, Stolbtsy, and Nesvizh, concentrated in the Polesye area and set up Jewish partisan groups there, such as the Baranovichi group.

Jews from Lenin, Pogost-Zagorodski, and Lachva joined the Komarov fighting brigade (made up of former residents of PINSK), the Kaganovich Jewish unit, and the Bumazhkov, Bolotnikov, Pavlovski, Mikhalovski, Shveiko, and Gulyayev units. The Soviet No. 123 brigade had Jews from eastern Belorussia in its ranks (from Glusk, Starobin, Luban, and other places), and also Jews who had escaped from Lachva and Lenin in western Belorussia.

The Minsk ghetto underground was active in helping Jews to escape from the ghetto to partisan units, and it is estimated that thousands of Jews from the Minsk ghetto fled to the forests. Minsk Jews were among the founding members of seven partisan units, the No. 406, Kutuzov (the second Minsk brigade), Budenny, Dzerzhinski, Sergei Laso, Parkhomenko, and No. 106 (Zorin) units. Later, however, the Jews were in the minority in most of these units. Jewish partisans also joined partisan units in other parts of eastern Belorussia, in Vitebsk, GOMEL, and Mogilev.

In their units, the Jewish partisans carried out daring operations, and many were awarded medals for their exploits. In addition to the military actions, they engaged in rescue operations and helped Jews from ghettos to escape into the forests. Many of the Jewish escapees from the ghettos were not accepted into the Soviet partisan units because they did not have any weapons. Some of them organized into separate Jewish units, managed to acquire arms, and carried out attacks. A number of the Jewish escapees—the adults among them and those with families—organized into family camps. In some cases these were under the protection of Jewish partisans in the Soviet units, who provided them with food and other needs. Many thousands of Jews were eventually taken into the family camps. Jewish partisans had to operate in the midst of a hostile civilian population and often had to contend with hostility in the partisan units as well. As the Soviet army drew near, hostile acts against Jewish partisans decreased. The number of Jewish partisans in the area ranged from twelve thousand to fifteen thousand—the largest concentration in the Jewish partisan movement.

Lithuania. In Lithuania the partisan movement came into existence long after that in Belorussia, to which it was linked geographically and, to some degree, organizationally. This relatively late development of a partisan movement in Lithuania resulted from the deep animosity that most of the Lithuanian population had toward the Soviet Union, and because Lithuania, in the early part of the war, was a considerable distance from the fighting front in the east. Belorussia's western areas were also suitable as halfway bases for armed Soviet groups who were infiltrated from across the front in order to reinforce partisan operations in Lithuania. Up to mid-1943 the forests of Belorussia were the only place where Jews who had fled from ghettos and labor camps in eastern Lithuania could hide out. Hundreds of Jews took refuge in the Nacha Forest, 45 miles (80 km) south of Vilna, and in the lake and swamp area in the Kazian and Naroch forests, 93 miles (150 km) east of Vilna.

It was from Lithuania, however, that the call rang out for the Jews to rise up against the Nazis in the ghettos and to create a Jewish partisan movement. This call was contained in the manifesto that Abba KOVNER published in the Vilna ghetto on the night of December 31, 1941–January 1, 1942. Three weeks later, on January 21, the FAREYNEGTE PARTIZANER ORGANIZATSYE (United Partisan Organization; FPO) was created in Vilna.

Toward the end of 1941 the first Jews from Lithuanian towns made their way into the Nacha Forest, mostly as individuals or in small groups. They were soon joined by refugees from the Vilna ghetto. Some of these Jews formed family groups, and others joined the Leninski Komsomol battalion. Youngsters who fled to the Naroch Forest were incorporated into the Voroshilov brigade, commanded by Fyodor Markov. In the spring of 1943, ten young Jews who had escaped from the Švenčionys ghetto joined the Chapayev battalion of that brigade, and some were sent back to the ghetto to bring more Jewish reinforcements for the battalion.

In August 1943 a group of fighters from the Vilna FPO, headed by Josef GLAZMAN, reached the Naroch Forest. A Jewish battalion named Nekamah (Revenge) was formed, with two hundred fighters. The parachutist Z. Ragauskas-Butenas (his former name was Zerakh Ragovski) was appointed its commander, and Glazman became the battalion chief of staff.

About two months after its establishment the Nekamah battalion was disbanded without prior warning, and some of its fighters were transferred to the Komsomolski battalion. Many of the latter's fighters perished in the fierce siege that powerful German forces laid to the area in November 1943. When the siege was over, the Voroshilov brigade headquarters abandoned many Jews to their fate, apparently with the knowledge of the commanding officer, Markov. A change for the better came early in 1944. A considerable number of Jewish remnant groups, including those who were unarmed, were taken on by the partisan battalions. Many of these were Jews from Lithuania; a total of 450 Lithuanian Jewish fighters joined the ranks of the Belorussian partisans.

The partisan headquarters in the Soviet Union had groups of political and military instructors parachuted into German-occupied territory in order to intensify partisan operations there. One such group was dropped into northern Lithuania on March 7, 1942. It consisted of ten men, four of whom were Jews, and it was led by the secretary of the Lithuanian Communist party's Central Committee, Isaac Meskop, whose code name was Adonas. The group was discovered after a short while and all its members perished. A similar fate lay in store for many of the other groups dropped behind the lines.

In the summer of 1943 a forty-member group was dropped over an improvised landing strip in Belorussia, leading to a real change in the fortunes of the entire Lithuanian partisan movement. Heading the group were two senior members of the Communist party, Motiejas Sumaukas (Kazimieras) and Henrik ZIMAN (Jurgis), the latter a Jewish teacher from Kovno. Sumaukas established himself with some of the men in the Naroch Forest near the Lithuanian Zalgiris battalion, and from there commanded partisan operations and political activities in northern Lithuania. Ziman and some of the other men reached Lithuanian soil in October 1943, and they set themselves up in the Rudninkai Forest. The area of which Ziman was in charge comprised all of southern Lithuania, including Kovno and Vilna, which still had twenty thousand Jews. By then, dozens of Jewish partisans were already serving in the Pro Patria battalion of the Troki brigade. Later, when the Free Lithuania and Liberator battalions were formed, they absorbed many of the Jews who fled from the Kaišiadorys and Palemonas labor camps in the Kovno area. In the final stage, about one hundred of the Troki brigade's total complement of six hundred were Jewish.

The largest concentration of Jewish fighters from Lithuania came into existence in the Rudninkai Forest. The Rudninkai *puszcza,* 25 miles (40 km) south of Vilna, covered an area of 965 square miles (2,500 sq km); the highway from Vilna to Grodno and Białystok crossed the area, and its population consisted of Poles and Lithuanians. Partisan operations in the Rudninkai Forest started in the summer of 1943, when a group of Soviet paratroopers under the command of Captain Alko established its base there. In early September the first group of Lithuanian Soviet partisans from the Naroch Forest arrived in the Rudninkai Forest. That same month the first group of Jewish partisans entered the Rudninkai Forest; they were seventy members of "Yechiel's combat group" who had escaped from the Vilna ghetto a few days after the September 1 *Aktion* there. Their leaders were Elhanan Magid, Shlomo Brand, and Nathan Ring. They did not all have their own weapons, and when they tried to gain acceptance into Alko's partisan group, Alko agreed to accept only twenty members of the group who were in possession of arms. In late September and early October, two groups of FPO members arrived at Rudninkai; numbering some seventy to eighty members, they were led by Abba Kovner and Heena Borovska. This group joined "Yechiel's combat group," bringing its total membership up to one hundred and fifty.

The Jewish partisans put themselves under the authority of the Soviet Lithuanian partisan movement. They sent couriers to the labor camps in Vilna to bring in more Jews from there, and by the end of October there were two hundred and fifty persons at the Jewish partisans' base. They undertook sabotage actions against roads, bridges, and electricity and telephone poles; Jewish partisans also penetrated into Vilna and sabotaged the city's power station and water supplies. Some of their operations were designed to obtain arms and food supplies.

Vilna Jews established four battalions, with a total of four hundred fighters: Ha-Nokem (The Avenger), commanded by Abba Kovner, with Isser Schmidt as commissar; To Victory, with Shmuel Kaplinski as commander and Heena Borovska as commissar; Death to Fascism, commanded by Yankel Prenner; and Ha-Ma'avak (The Struggle), commanded by Aharon Aharonovits. Berl Shershenevski was political commissar both for the Death to Fascism and the Ha-Ma'avak battalion; these two battalions also took in Jews from towns that were close to Vilna. In early 1944 non-Jewish fighters were assigned to the Vilna battalions; most of the commanders of the battalions were replaced, and their Jewish character was eroded. The official explanation was that the Soviet partisan movement was based on the republics that made up the Soviet Union, and since no Jewish republic existed, there was no room for Jewish battalions. Even so, Jews retained a decisive majority in these battalions.

In November 1943 a group of fighters belonging to the General Jewish Fighting Organization in the Kovno ghetto converged on Rudninkai. By May 1944 their number reached two hundred, most of them belonging to one of three battalions making up the Kovno brigade: Death to the Occupiers, Kadima (Forward), and Vladas Baronas. About fifty of these fighters fell in battle. Most of the commanders of these battalions were Soviet officers who had escaped from German imprisonment. About ten Jews were appointed deputy commanders, mostly squad leaders.

In the spring of 1944, Polish partisans of the Armia Krajowa made their appearance in Rudninkai. They tried to eject the Soviet partisans from the area; this led to fighting between the Polish and Soviet partisans, in which some Jews lost their lives. Antisemitic elements who regarded the Jews as pro-Soviet murdered dozens of Jews who had been hiding out in villages in the area. Two other concentrations of dozens of Jewish fighters existed among the Lithuanian partisan units in central Lithuania, in the Kazlu Rūda and Kaidan forests. Individual Jews were to be found in other partisan units, such as the Kestutis battalion in western Lithuania. Another 250 Jews were in the groups composed of armed families living in family camps in the forests. That spring, when arms shipments dropped by air reached the partisans, their operations were intensified. In early July the Soviet army advanced into the Rudninkai area, and the partisans took part in the liberation of Vilna on July 13.

The Lithuanian partisan movement contained some 850 Jews, representing 10 percent of its total strength. Together with the 450 Lithuanian Jewish fighters in the Belorussian partisan movement and 350 Lithuanian Jews in other territorial formations, a total of 1,650 Lithuanian Jews fought in the partisan movement. Most of them fought in the ranks of twenty-two battalions (out of the ninety-two that made up the Lithuanian partisan movement) that were outstanding in battle. They were credited with 461 train derailments (79 percent of the total of 577), 288 out of 400 (72 percent) locomotives destroyed, 3,663 (22.9 percent) out of 16,000 Nazi soldiers who were hit, and so forth. The Avenger battalion had to its credit 5 train derailments, 2 miles (3 km) of railway embankments destroyed, railway tracks blown up in 350 places, five bridges and three power stations destroyed, 2 miles (3 km) of telephone and telegraph lines disconnected, and so forth. Two hundred and fifty Jewish fighters fell in battle, and many Jews were awarded medals for distinguished service. Nevertheless, even in some of the mixed partisan units, Jewish fighters suffered from discrimination. The partisan movement was the only fighting formation available to Jews under the Nazi occupation, but their admission to its ranks was restricted for political and military reasons, and because of anti-Jewish prejudice. Thousands of Jews from Lithuania served in the regular units of the Soviet army.

SHALOM CHOLAWSKI and DOV LEVIN

The Ukraine. In the northern part of the Ukraine, with its wide expanses of forests and swamps, a large Soviet partisan movement arose. From the very first days of the occupation, these forest areas provided refuge to Jews who had fled the extermination, and to Jewish prisoners of war (officers and other ranks), who were also designated for murder. Both of these categories of Jews joined the partisan units that began to organize as early as July 1941. Specific information on the role played by the Jews is scarce; many Jews did not identify themselves as such and therefore only a part of the story is known. Among those who made a name for themselves in the Kovpak partisan formation were Dina Mayevskaya, a medical doctor; Misha Tartakovski, an interpreter; Grigori Lubienski, a platoon commander; and scouts Mudril Kulka and Moshe Rubinov. Notable in Melnyk's formation in the Sumi district were Dr. Joseph Bulak; the radio operator, Joseph Malyi; and the reconnaissance officer and sapper, Yevgeni Volianski. Fifty Jews served in the Naumov cavalry unit and took part in its drive into the central and western Ukraine. Jews in large numbers served in the units commanded by Maj. Gen. Aleksandr Saburov and Maj. Gen. Aleksei Fyodorov, among them company commander Levin, platoon commander Aleksandr Margalit, and sapper Samuel Gotsban. In the Chernigov district, Salai's brigade had Jewish company commanders Elijah Shklovski and Aleksandr Kaminski, and sapper officer Nakhumi fighting in its ranks. Jews fought with the Schorr's company in the Kiev area, among them platoon commander Boris Pinchasovich; the units in the Vinnitsa area had Yaakov Talit as deputy commander of the Lenin division; and company commander Benjamin Shakhnovich fell in battle among the units in the DNEPROPETROVSK area. The same area had Leonid Bernstein as battalion commander; he was later transferred to Kiev and dropped into Slovakia. Jews also fought in the catacombs of Odessa, among them the officers Forman and Jacob Vasin.

The fight put up by the Jews in the western Ukraine forms a special chapter. During the extermination and murder that went on in the summer of 1942, many groups of armed Jews organized and escaped into the forests and mountains. In Volhynia some one thousand Jewish fighters, in thirty-five to forty groups, kept on fighting on their own before joining up with the Soviet partisan movement, which did not make its appearance there until late that year. Some of them fell in heavy fighting and others joined the Soviet units. These included Moshe GILDENMAN's unit, which became a Jewish company in the Saburov division; the Sofiyevka and Kolki groups, which joined the Kovpak division; the Dombrovich and Sernik groups, which formed the Maksim Misyura unit; and the Manyevich, Leshnyovka, and Povurski groups, which formed the Mikula Konishchuk and Joseph Sobiesiak units. The last later joined the Rovno division, commanded by Maj. Gen. Vasily Begma.

Jewish partisans fought in the Polish battalions belonging to the Soviet partisan movement (the Poland Is Still Alive, Wanda Wasilewska, Traugut, and other battalions), in the independent self-defense units of the Polish villages, and even in the Armia Krajowa's Twenty-seventh Division. Approximately nineteen hundred Jews fought with the partisans in Volhynia.

In Eastern Galicia, owing to the difficult terrain and the operations of the UKRAINSKA POVSTANSKA ARMYIA (Ukrainian Insurgent Army), the Jewish fighters had a very hard time and most of their groups were wiped out, leaving no trace. Jewish groups are known to have been active in the Ternopol, Borshchev, Chortkov, Stanislav, Bolekhov, Skalat, Przemyśl, Tlumach, Olnik, and Bukachevtsy areas; Jews from camps in Skalat and Stanislav joined the Kovpak division during its drive into the Carpathian Mountains in the late summer of 1943 and formed a Jewish platoon, which was commanded by Jews from the Sofiyevka and Kolki groups.

Jewish fighters were to be found in every kind of position. Many Jews held command appointments and some were brigade commanders, such as Stefan Kaplun and Robert Satanovski. Alek Abugov commanded a reconnaissance unit in the Rovno divisions, Moshe Gildenman commanded a company, and Joseph Karpus was the quartermaster of the Pinsk division. The medical service contained a large number of Jewish doctors, such as Dr. Erlikh from Dombrovich, who was chief medical officer of the Rovno divisions, and Dr. Benjamin Tsezarski, chief medical officer of the Medvedev brigade.

Russian Soviet Federated Socialist Republic (RSFSR). Jews also fought among the partisans in the part of the RSFSR that was occupied by the Germans. Boyevoi, the partisan unit operating in the northernmost sector reached by the German forces, in the Leningrad district, had many Jews in its ranks, including the unit commander, Dmitri Novakovski.

Jews who escaped from ghettos fought in the Schorr's battalion (a second unit, different from the one mentioned above), which operated in Briansk, southwest of Moscow. Lazar Bliakhman was commanding officer of the Furmanov company, and surgeon Arkady Eidlin, Dr. Tiomkin, and Dr. Unkovska served in the partisans' medical service. Hungarian Jews who had escaped from the MUNKASZOLGÁLAT (Hungarian Labor Service) served in the Dzerzhinski company (a second unit bearing that name).

SHMUEL SPECTOR

The Generalgouvernement. A large-scale underground movement functioned within the Jewish communities and ghettos of Poland. While this movement exhibited initiative and daring in many areas, it did not have great success in guerrilla warfare or in the partisan struggle outside the cities.

The reasons why the Jewish partisan struggle in Poland failed to reach large dimensions are complex. First, central Poland is thinly wooded in comparison with the great forests of the east. Second, the strong military resistance (the Armia Krajowa, or AK) under the sponsorship of the Polish government-in-exile did not make use of guerrilla tactics at the start and saved most of its strength for military operations during the final stages of the war. In 1942, there was very little AK partisan activity in the forests. The AK did not encourage Jews to escape into the forests, and in most cases the unit commanders were not willing to accept Jews into their ranks. The fascist faction NARODOWE SIŁY ZBROJNE (National Armed Forces), which remained, for most of the period, outside the AK, was extremely antisemitic and even murdered Jews who escaped to the forests. Some AK men were sincerely concerned about the fate of the Jews and tried to defend them in the forests, but their numbers were small and their power limited.

The Polish Communists were more friendly to the Jews, for two reasons. First, unlike the AK, the Communists wanted to begin an immediate struggle with the Nazis, and the Jews were a natural ally in this aspiration. Second, the Communists and the political Left in general were somewhat more sensitive to the fate of the Jews.

In the period between the two world wars, there were many Jewish activists in the Polish Communist party. Communist partisan activity did not begin, however, until mid-1942, and was not fully organized until 1943. The Communists, who had been rejected by the great majority of the Polish people, invested much effort in winning the sympathy of their countrymen. Even though they were willing to accept Jews into their ranks, they made sure that the percentage of Jews was not too high, so that they would not be accused of being a Jewish organization. The Armia Ludowa (AL) was a Communist partisan unit that did not become a force to be reckoned with until the end of 1943. By that time, most of the ghettos had been destroyed and their inhabitants deported. Only those few Jews who had managed to enter the forests and survive in them before that time were able to benefit from this change.

This illustrates the importance of the third factor—timing. While the extermination campaign was at its height (from the spring of 1942 to the spring of 1943), the partisan movement in the Generalgouvernement was still weak. By the time it gained in size and strength and included elements friendly to

Jewish partisans from the Yehiel Grynszpan unit in the Parczew Forest area (1943).

the Jews, very few Jews were left; those still alive were imprisoned in labor and concentration camps.

According to data published by the Poles, about twenty-five thousand people took part in the partisan movement in the Generalgouvernement, both in the Communist-associated AL and in the AK. The number of Jews who succeeded in escaping and finding shelter in villages, forests, and mountains was apparently in the tens of thousands. Of them, only two thousand ended up as armed fighters in the forests, and three thousand wandered the forests and villages. The rest were caught and killed, or died in the wild.

Jews played a major role in the crystallization of the partisan force organized by the Communists. Among the Communist partisan commanders were many Jews, though most of them hid their origin. There were some Jews among the paratroopers who came from the Soviet Union to organize partisan warfare in Poland.

The years 1942 to 1944 saw the organization of twenty-seven Jewish partisan units. The most notable was the unit commanded by Yehiel Grynszpan, which recruited its members among the many Jews from towns in the northeastern part of the Lublin district who escaped from the deportations to SOBIBÓR in the summer and fall of 1942. In January 1943 the Grynszpan unit numbered 50 men, operating in the nearby Parczew Forest and functioning as the protective force of the family camps that had been set up there by the fleeing Jews. On Christmas of 1942, Easter of 1943, and in May 1944 the Germans launched large-scale manhunts in the Parczew Forest, during which they murdered most of the Jewish refugees—over 4,000 persons. However, the family camp was not completely destroyed, and the Grynszpan unit held out. In the spring of 1943 the unit was given help by the AL and also joined that organization officially. This aid given by the Polish resistance, followed by Soviet airdrops and paratroops, enabled the Grynszpan unit to attack German police positions and German army lines of communication. When the area was liberated, on July 23, 1944, about 200 persons had survived in the family camp, and Grynszpan's unit had 120 men in its ranks.

The Jewish partisan units in Poland included the unit commanded by Shmuel Jegier, composed of Jewish prisoners of war who had escaped from a Lublin camp; and the unit commanded by Abraham Amsterdam, which numbered forty-seven men and operated in the Dolcza Forest east of Kraków. Surrounded by the Germans, this unit succeeded in breaking through and linking up with the Soviet army, at a heavy cost in lives. There were also the unit commanded by Shmuel Gruber, with thirty men; and the unit named after Mordecai ANIELEWICZ, which fought in the vicinity of Warsaw and was made up partly of fighters from the Warsaw ghetto who had survived the uprising.

Nine Jewish units eventually joined the AL. According to Shmuel Krakowski (1984), most of the fighters of these units fell in various actions and operations, and the few who survived joined Polish partisan units. It may be assumed that hundreds of Jews also fought in the AK without revealing their Jewish identity. There were also Jews who did not hide their Jewish origins, and some of these achieved high ranks in their units. Many Jews fought in the AL, in both its Polish and international units. The Jewish units, for the most part, operated in the Lublin, Kielce, and Radom areas. About one thousand Jews, some of them surviving fighters of the WARSAW GHETTO UPRISING, took part in the Warsaw Polish uprising in the summer of 1944.

Slovakia. In Slovakia, the Zionist YOUTH MOVEMENTS, as well as members of the Communist party, played a key role in organizing resistance cells to go into action in the event of the resumption of deportations. Such cells existed in all the labor camps—in NOVÁKY, SERED, and VYHNE. In early 1944 contact was established between these cells and the Slovak National Council. When the SLOVAK NATIONAL UPRISING broke out in late August of that year the members of these cells joined it, along with other Jews who had not previously belonged to resistance cells. Twenty-five hundred Jews participated in the Slovak uprising, of whom 1,566 were partisans, representing 10 percent of the total number of partisans in Slovakia. Five hundred Jews fell in the uprising; of these, 269 were partisans, that is, one out of every six Jewish partisans who took part. The Nováky cell, consisting of 200 men, fought as a unit of its own, first in the regular Slovak army. Later, after the uprising was suppressed in October 1944, most of the unit's survivors joined partisan groups. During the uprising, five PARACHUTISTS from Palestine reached Slovakia. Four of them—Haviva REIK, Zvi Ben-Yaakov, Rafael Reiss, and Abba Berdiczew—were killed. The one survivor, Chaim Hermesh, fought on with the Slovak partisans until the war was over.

Yugoslavia, Bulgaria, and Greece. In Yugoslavia, Bulgaria, and Greece, Jews were accepted into the ranks of the partisans as equals, but no separate Jewish units, or any units of a Jewish character, existed in these countries. The number of Jewish partisans there was relatively large, especially in Yugoslavia, whose partisan movement was the most important among all the Nazi-occupied countries. The number of Jews who joined Josip TITO's partisans is all the more impressive in view of the great difficulties they had to overcome to make their way to the remote areas where the fighting took place, and in view of the fact that by the time the Yugoslav partisans launched their struggle (in the fall of 1941 and, with greater strength, in the second half of 1942), the majority of the country's Jews had already been killed. The nominal list of Jews who served in the resistance movement contains 4,572 names, and of this number some 3,000 served in combat units. A total of 1,318 Jews fell in battle; 150 were awarded the First of the Fighters medal, and ten Jews received the National Hero award, the highest decoration that Yugoslavia had to offer. Among Jews who achieved high command ranks were Gen. Voja Todorović, who after the war became the commander of the land forces, and Dr. Rosa Papo, the first woman to achieve the rank of general in the Yugoslav army. Jews played a key role in the creation of the medical corps, which was headed by Dr. Herbert Kraus.

ISRAEL GUTMAN

BIBLIOGRAPHY

Ainsztein, R. *Jewish Resistance in Nazi-occupied Eastern Europe.* London, 1974.

Armstrong, J., ed. *Soviet Partisans in World War II.* Madison, Wis., 1964.

Bielski, T., and Z. Bielski. *Jews of the Forests.* Tel Aviv, 1946. (In Hebrew.)
Cholawski, S. *The Jews in Belorussia (White Russia) during World War II.* Tel Aviv, 1982. (In Hebrew.)
Gefen, M., et al., eds. *The Jewish Partisans.* 2 vols. Tel Aviv, 1958. (In Hebrew.)
Jelinek, Y. "The Jewish Unit in Novaky Camp." *Yalkut Moreshet* 1 (November–December 1963): 47–62.
The Jewish Partisans. Merhavia, Israel, 1958. (In Hebrew.)
Kabeli, I. "The Resistance of the Greek Jews." *Yivo Annual* 8 (1953): 281–288.
Kahanovich, M. *The Fighting of the Jewish Partisans in Eastern Europe.* Tel Aviv, 1954. (In Hebrew.)
Kowalski, I. *Anthology on Jewish Resistance, 1939–1945.* 3 vols. New York, 1986.
Krakowski, S. *The War of the Doomed: Jewish Armed Resistance in Poland, 1942–1944.* New York, 1984.
Levin, B. *In the Forests of Vengeance.* Tel Aviv, 1968. (In Hebrew.)
Levin, D. *Fighting Back: Lithuanian Jewry's Armed Resistance to the Nazis.* New York, 1984.
Porter, J. N., ed. *The Jewish Partisans: A Documentary of Jewish Resistance in the Soviet Union during World War II.* Lanham, Md., 1982.
Staras, P. *Partizaninus Judejimas Lietuvoje.* Vilna, 1966.
Yaffe, Y. *The History of the Jewish Partisan Units in the Forests of Belorussia.* Tel Aviv, 1952. (In Hebrew.)

PART JEWS. *See* Mischlinge.

PAVELIĆ, ANTE (1889–1959), Croatian fascist leader. By profession a lawyer, Pavelić entered politics as a member of the Croatian Justice Party (Stranka Prava), and in 1929 was elected one of its representatives on the Zagreb City Council and the Belgrade parliament. When King Alexander established a dictatorial regime in Yugoslavia in 1929, Pavelić formed the terrorist organization, the USTAŠA, which advocated CROATIA's secession from Yugoslavia. From his exile in Italy, Pavelić directed the terrorist acts committed by his followers in Croatia. He introduced fascist concepts into his movement, and when Adolf Hitler came to power in Germany, Pavelić added rabid antisemitism to the Ustaša's ideology.

Ante Pavelić (left), Nazi leader of Croatia, with Benito Mussolini. [National Archives]

After the conquest of Yugoslavia in 1941, the Germans and Italians appointed Pavelić head of the puppet government of "Independent Croatia," with the title of *poglavnik* (leader). He introduced a reign of terror, and in the four years that it lasted, hundreds of thousands of Serbs and tens of thousands of Jews were killed.

After Germany's defeat Pavelić fled to Argentina, where he established an Ustaša exile organization. In 1957 he was injured in an assassination attempt in Madrid, and two years later he died of his wounds.

BIBLIOGRAPHY

Krizman, B. *Pavelić i Njemci.* Zagreb, 1984.
Krizman, B. *Pavelić i Ustaše.* Zagreb, 1978.
Krizman, B. *Pavelić izmedju Hitlera i Musolinija.* Zagreb, 1980.

Paris, E. *Genocide in Satellite Croatia, 1941–1945: A Record of Racial and Religious Persecutions and Massacres.* Chicago, 1961.

MENACHEM SHELAH

PAWIAK PRISON, the main prison used by the German Sicherheitspolizei (Security Police) and SD (Sicherheitsdienst; Security Service) in the Warsaw district, serving this purpose from October 2, 1939, to August 21, 1944. Pawiak was located in the Jewish quarter of WARSAW, at the juncture of Dzielna and Pawia streets (hence its name). It was primarily a prison for men, with a women's section called "Serbia." Established in 1835, Pawiak had served as a prison both under tsarist rule and in the period between the two world wars. The Germans made it into the main Warsaw prison. Its personnel consisted, for the most part, of SS men and Ukrainian auxiliary police.

During World War II, some of the Poles employed in the prison service, many of them on the Pawiak staff, were dismissed, and others were imprisoned. A total of some sixty-five thousand persons passed through Pawiak and "Serbia," most of them Poles from Warsaw. No figures are available for the number of Jews who passed through Pawiak. The Jewish prisoners were mainly persons who had been caught on the "Aryan" side of the city. There was also a group of Soviet prisoners of war; both the Jews and the Soviet prisoners were shot to death shortly after being imprisoned. About thirty-two thousand prisoners were shot to death, some of them in public executions, and twenty-three thousand were deported to concentration camps, in ninety-five transports. Several thousand prisoners were set free.

Conditions in the prison were extremely harsh, despite the efforts made by Polish welfare organizations and the Polish staff of the prison hospital to ease the prisoners' lot. In a few instances prisoners succeeded in escaping from Pawiak, but an attempt to stage an uprising in July 1944 failed.

The last transports from Pawiak left the prison on July 30, 1944. Thereafter some prisoners were released and the rest were shot to death. On August 21 the Germans blew up Pawiak, as well as "Serbia." Throughout the period of its existence as a German prison, Pawiak had an active underground organization that maintained contact with the outside world.

BIBLIOGRAPHY

Czuperska-Sliwicka, A. *Cztery lata ostrego dyżura: Wspomnienia z Pawiaka 1940–1944.* Warsaw, 1965.

Polska Akademia Nauk. Instytut Historii, Zakład Historii Polski w II Wojnie Światowej. *Wspomnienia więźniów Pawiaka.* Warsaw, 1964.

KRZYSZTOF DUNIN-WASOWICZ

PECHERSKY, ALEKSANDR (Sasha; b. 1909), leader of the SOBIBÓR uprising. Pechersky was born in Kremenchug, in the Ukraine, and as a child moved to Rostov-on-Don, where he graduated from a music conservatory. He became a bookkeeper, but was also active in drama and music circles. He served in the Red Army, holding the rank of second lieutenant.

When the Germans attacked the Soviet Union, Pechersky was called up and posted to the front. In September 1941 he was promoted to lieutenant. He was taken prisoner the following month and contracted typhoid fever; he managed, however, to conceal his illness and turn up for the prisoners' parades, since the Germans shot all Soviet prisoners of war who fell ill. In May 1942 Pechersky escaped, together with four other prisoners, but they were all caught. Contrary to the usual German procedure, they were not shot but were sent to a penal camp, in Borisov. It was there, when Pechersky had to undress, that he was identified as a Jew, a fact he had previously managed to hide from the Germans. On August 20 of that year, Pechersky was transferred to an SS camp on Sheroka Street, in Minsk, in which some one hundred Soviet Jewish prisoners of war were held, together with several hundred Jewish civilians from the Minsk ghetto. He stayed there for over a year.

On September 18, 1943, the Minsk ghetto

Aleksandr Pechersky (left), the leader of the Sobibór uprising, with Aleksei Weizen, a survivor of Sobibór.

was liquidated and Pechersky was sent to the Sobibór extermination camp, together with two thousand Jews from the ghetto and the camp on Sheroka Street. They reached Sobibór on September 23. Pechersky was one of eighty Jewish prisoners of war who, on arrival in the camp, were selected for construction work; the rest of the transport was sent to the gas chambers to be killed.

Shortly after Pechersky's arrival in Sobibór, he was contacted by the camp underground; as an officer, he agreed to take over the command of the underground and to lead it in an uprising. During the next three weeks Pechersky reorganized the underground, making the prisoners of war its core and planning the uprising. It took place on October 14, 1943, under Pechersky's command; in its course most of the SS men in the camp were killed and a mass escape from the camp took place. Together with a group of prisoners of war, Pechersky succeeded in crossing the Bug River, and on October 22, he made contact with Soviet PARTISANS in the Brest area. He joined the partisans and fought in their ranks until the summer of 1944, when the Soviet army advanced into the area and the partisans joined up with the regular army units. Pechersky, now fighting in the Soviet army, was badly wounded in August 1944, and was hospitalized for four months. On recovering, he was discharged and returned to his hometown, Rostov, where he settled.

Pechersky was the chief witness for the prosecution in the trial, held in Kiev in the spring of 1963, of eleven Ukrainians who had served as guards in the Sobibór camp. His account of the Sobibór uprising was published in Yuri Suhl's *They Fought Back* (New York, 1957) and in *The Fighting Ghettos*, edited by Meyer Barkai (Philadelphia, 1967).

BIBLIOGRAPHY

Arad, Y. *Belzec, Sobibor, Treblinka: Operation Reinhard Death Camps.* Bloomington, 1987.

YITZHAK ARAD

PEOPLE'S GUARD. *See* Gwardia Ludowa.

PÉTAIN, PHILIPPE (1856–1951), French military leader and head of state of the Vichy regime. A distinguished and popularly acclaimed soldier best known for his defense of Verdun during World War I, Pétain rose to commander in chief of the French armies under Marshal Ferdinand Foch in 1917, and became a marshal in 1918. Pétain argued for ending hostilities against the enemy in June 1940 when the French defenses crumbled before the German BLITZKRIEG. He formed a new government on June 16, and negotiated an armistice that set the terms of the occupation years. Enjoying immense prestige, Pétain then obtained from the National Assembly full authority to re-order the French government, and became head of a new regime, organized at Vichy.

Exercising determined if not always vigorous leadership, the octogenarian Pétain was the principal spokesman for the "National Revolution"—an extensive program to transform France into an authoritarian, corporate society within the framework of the Nazis' New Order in Europe. One important aspect of this policy was the elimination of "Jewish influence" in France. Pétain thus presided over the French-sponsored persecution of Jews that continued throughout the occupation period and greatly facilitated the Nazis'

Trial of Marshal Philippe Pétain. Pétain was tried on charges of high treason and betrayal of his country. [National Archives]

"FINAL SOLUTION" in France. His reputation for probity and solicitude toward those he led helped legitimize the machinery of repression. He does not seem to have been inspired by antisemitism; but he was certainly indifferent to the fate of the Jews who suffered grievously from French policies.

Pétain was convicted of treason by a French court in 1945, but his death sentence was commuted by Gen. Charles de GAULLE. He was exiled to the island of Yeu, where he died at the age of ninety-six.

BIBLIOGRAPHY

Kupferman, F. *Le procès de Vichy: Pucheu, Pétain, Laval.* Brussels, 1981.

Lottman, H. R. *Pétain—Hero or Traitor: The Untold Story.* New York, 1985.

Marrus, M. R., and R. O. Paxton. *Vichy France and the Jews.* New York, 1981.

MICHAEL R. MARRUS

PETLIURA DAYS, a pogrom that took place in LVOV on July 25 through 27, 1941. Organized by Ukrainian nationalists and encouraged by the German occupiers, the pogrom was presented as a revenge action, to commemorate the "anniversary" of the death of Simon (Semyon) Petliura. Petliura, the last premier of independent UKRAINE, was responsible for large-scale pogroms against Jews in 1919. He was shot to death in Paris (by Shalom Schwarzbard) on May 25, 1926, but the organizers of the 1941 Lvov pogrom transferred the date to July, so as to exploit it to awaken in the Ukrainian population the anti-Jewish feelings associated with Petliura's death.

In July 1941 rumors circulated among the Lvov Jews of a pogrom being planned by the Ukrainians, who had already staged one, lasting for four days, immediately after the German conquest of Lvov at the end of June and early in July. As the planned day, July 25,

The second pogrom in Lvov, on July 25 and 26, 1941, known as the Petliura Days, was perpetrated by the Ukrainian police and Ukrainians in the city.

drew near, unusual commotion was noticed among the Ukrainian police and population. The Jews stayed inside their houses, leaving them only when they had to, mainly in order to report for forced labor.

In the early hours of July 25 groups of peasants from the neighboring villages began converging upon the city. They assembled in the courtyards of the Ukrainian police stations and then, joined by the Ukrainian police and armed with sticks, knives, and axes, set out on their rampage. They attacked every Jew they found in the streets; they stopped streetcars to take off the Jewish passengers, beating them and killing many of them; and they took Jews, in groups, to the Jewish cemetery to murder them there. In the afternoon they went after the Jews who were in their houses. Any Jew found was beaten up, and many were killed. Acts of robbery went hand in hand with the attacks. The next day, July 26, the participation of the Ukrainian policemen was especially prominent. In groups of five, they raided Jewish houses and took the Jews they found inside to the warehouses of the Axelbrod bakery on Zulkeyewska Street or to the Lunecki prison. There all the Jews were severely beaten. Some were released after paying a ransom, some were killed on the spot, and most of the others were killed the following day.

Among the Jewish intelligentsia, the Petliura Days took a particularly heavy toll, the Ukrainian police having searched for them by name according to lists prepared in advance. More than two thousand Jews were killed in the pogrom.

BIBLIOGRAPHY

Kahana, D. *Lvov Ghetto Diary*. Jerusalem, 1978. (In Hebrew.)

Maltiel, Y. *That Which Cannot Be Avenged*. Tel Aviv, 1947. (In Hebrew.)

Zadereczki, T. *When the Swastika Ruled in Lvov: The Destruction of the Jewish Community as Seen by a Polish Author*. Jerusalem, 1982. (In Hebrew.)

AHARON WEISS

PHYSICIANS, NAZI. Nazi genocide and the murderous apparatus that effected it was a command decision of the National Socialist leaders, not of medical doctors. Nonetheless, direct medical killing—within medical channels, by means of medical decisions, and carried out by doctors and their assistants—was central to the working of AUSCHWITZ and reflected a general connection between German physicians and the concentration and extermination camps. The Nazis developed a "biomedical vision" of healing a sick Nordic race by means of destroying "bad genes"—those of the weak and sick, and those of the cause of "racial infection," the Jews. A message held out by the Nazis to physicians was that "National Socialism is nothing but applied biology."

Prior to their service in the camps, German physicians participated in two preliminary programs aimed at creating a German people worthy of National Socialism: coercive sterilization and the killing of "impaired" children and then adults. The EUTHANASIA PROGRAM, carried out in centers equipped with carbon monoxide gas chambers, shared both personnel and technology with the extermination camps.

Medical killing required the Nazification of the medical profession. As in other instances of *Gleichschaltung,* or coordination, a combination of ideological enthusiasm and systematic terror accomplished this end. Pre-Nazi medical societies were either disbanded or "coordinated" into a Reich Physicians' Chamber (Reichsärztekammer), to which all practicing physicians had to belong. The first chamber leaders came from among ardent early-Nazi doctors who in 1929 had formed a Nazi physicians' league. Gerhard Wagner served as first head of the Chamber. At his death in 1939, Wagner's role as chief Reich physician was briefly assumed by the more bureaucratic Leonardo Conti. Eventually, Karl Brandt emerged from more distinguished university connections to become the dominant figure in Nazi medicine.

Physicians had one of the highest ratios of party members of any profession: 45 percent. Their ratio of membership in the SA (Sturmabteilung; Storm Troopers) and SS was, respectively, two and seven times that of teachers. This related both to the authoritarian and nationalistic tendencies among physicians and to the Nazi stress on a biomedical vision of national cure.

Nazification of medicine also required the elimination of Jewish physicians from practice. Within two months of Hitler's chancellorship, Jewish doctors were being boycotted and terrorized. They were gradually excluded from national health insurance programs and ultimately officially barred from medical practice altogether. An amendment to the NUREMBERG LAWS nullified in 1939 the medical licenses of all Jewish doctors. Academic medicine was coordinated through such means as a medical school curriculum that stressed Nazi genetic theories, the ousting of Jewish professors, and the organized enthusiasm of Nazi medical students.

In June 1933, Interior Minister Wilhelm FRICK introduced a sterilization law. The threat of *Volkstod* ("racial death") required the sterilization of such categories as the congenitally feebleminded, schizophrenics, manic depressives, epileptics, and victims of various hereditary or congenital physical afflictions. An "asocial" category was subsequently developed. Two of the three members on the "Hereditary Health Courts" that decided on cases were physicians. Some of the regime's most recognized medical leaders served in the appeals process. All physicians were legally required to report candidates for eventual sterilization to public-health officers. Physicians performed the surgical procedures. Although it cloaked considerable chaos and arbitrariness, the principle of legality was important, and the secrecy of court deliberations lent power and mystery to this medicalized expression of authority. Reliable estimates for the number of sterilizations fall between 200,000 and 350,000.

As a further expression of racial policy, a national card index of people with hereditary taints was begun. Research institutes for hereditary biology and racial hygiene were established at universities, notably those of Otmar von Verschuer in Frankfurt and Ernst Rüdin in Munich. A Swiss-born psychiatrist, Rüdin had helped found the Deutsche Gesellschaft für Rassenhygiene (German Society for Racial Hygiene). A party member from

1937, he became director of the prestigious Kaiser-Wilhelm-Institut für Psychiatrie. Himself not a participant in medical killing, Rüdin was representative of many scientists who provided legitimacy to Nazi racial policies.

The Nazis based their justification for medical killing on the concept of "life unworthy of life" (*lebensunwertes Leben*). This concept can be traced particularly to a crucial book that preceded National Socialism, *The Permission to Destroy Life Unworthy of Life*, published in 1920 by two distinguished German professors, jurist Karl Binding and psychiatrist Alfred Hoche. The authors identified as "unworthy" the incurably ill, as well as large segments of mentally ill, retarded or feebleminded, and deformed adults and children. They professionalized and medicalized the concept and stressed the therapeutic goal. It was left to the Nazis to invest "unworthy life" with their own ideology and to carry it to its ultimate biological, racial, and "therapeutic" extreme.

Mental hospitals became an important focus for the development of a "euthanasia" consciousness. In 1934 they were encouraged to neglect their patients, as funds and inspections declined. Hospitals held "courses" for leading government officials and functionaries, SS members, party leaders, the press, healing professionals, and ultimately the general public. These efforts often featured grotesque "demonstrations" with the most repulsive and debilitated cases. Films, both theatrical and documentary, were produced to spread the eugenic message. It was not, then, surprising that the regime sometimes received requests for mercy killings from relatives of newborns or young infants with severe deformities or brain damage.

In late 1938 or early 1939, Hitler ordered Karl Brandt, his personal physician and confidant, to investigate one such case. If it warranted, Brandt was to empower—as Hitler's deputy—the carrying out of "euthanasia." Upon a positive finding, Hitler authorized Brandt to formalize a program with the help of Chancellery chief Philip Bouhler.

The children's program was run secretly from the Chancellery with the aid of the Interior Ministry's health division. Midwives and physicians were to report likely names and cases to the new Reich Committee for the Scientific Registration of Serious Hereditary and Congenital Diseases. Three central medical experts then made either–or decisions based on questionnaire forms. A death verdict required unanimity, which was facilitated by mandate and procedure. Questionable cases were sent to special committee units for observation and presumably treatment by the most up-to-date methods. The committee set up its first children's center in a state institution at Görden; some thirty sites in Germany, Austria, and Poland formed the ultimate network. These "observation" centers were predominantly killing centers, with Luminal injections as the usual method, although some facilities—notably Eglfing-Haar under Dr. Hermann Pfannmüller—employed starvation and neglect.

A *Führerbefehl* ("Führer decree") of October 1939 extended the project to adults, and thus rendered medical killing an official overall policy. It expanded the authority of physicians by allowing them to grant a "mercy death" (*Gnadentod*) to patients deemed "incurable." Backdating the decree to September 1, the outbreak of World War II, reflected Hitler's conviction that a wartime atmosphere would make Germans more amenable. Perhaps more importantly, the war itself was subsumed to a larger, heroic biomedical vision of which "euthanasia" was a part.

Hitler soon turned responsibility for the secret program over to Brandt and Bouhler. Aided by top physicians from the Health Ministry and the SS, they chose a leadership corps of physicians, some from the children's program and some psychiatrists with prominent academic credentials, such as Werner Heyde of Würzburg, Carl Schneider of Heidelberg, and Max de Crinis of Berlin. Others, such as Friedrich Mennecke, were Nazified psychiatrists. Heyde came to direct the program, aided and ultimately replaced by Dr. Paul Nitsche of the Sonnenstein state institution.

Bureaucratically the program was known as T4, after the Berlin Chancellery office at Tiergarten 4, from whence a camouflage Reich Work Group of Sanatoriums and Nursing Homes (Reichsarbeitsgemeinschaft Heil- und Pflegeanstalten) operated. T4 came to depend on virtually the entire German psychiatric

Trial 1, The Medical Case, tried by the Nuremberg Military Tribunals in 1946 and 1947. Standing in the foreground is Dr. Robert Servatius, a member of the defense counsel and later (in 1961 and 1962) head of the defense team at the Eichmann Trial in Jerusalem. [United States Army]

community and the related general medical community. Questionnaires went to all institutions that might house appropriate patients as defined by the conjunction of inability to perform useful work with such criteria as specific illnesses or syndromes, long-term institutionalization, criminal insanity, and non-"German" ethnicity. T4 combined efficiency with mystification; diagnosis and "treatment" were prompt; pseudomedical justification elaborate. SS personnel manned the buses transporting patients to a facility, where they were usually killed within twenty-four hours. The six main killing centers were Hartheim, Sonnenstein, Grafeneck, Bernburg, Brandenburg, and Hademar; most were converted mental hospitals or nursing homes. It was T4 policy that a doctor did the killing, in line with the motto of T4 bureaucrat Viktor BRACK: "The syringe belongs in the hand of a physician." Despite the metaphor, the centers pioneered in the use of carbon monoxide gas, first tried in early 1940 at the Brandenburg facility under Heyde's medical advice. The gas chamber, marked "Shower Room," was constructed with the help of Christian WIRTH of the SS KRIMINALPOLIZEI. Senior physicians served as T4 "experts" and policymakers, while younger doctors, chosen for both their inexperience and political enthusiasm, did much of the actual killing. Irmfried Eberl headed Brandenburg at the age of twenty-nine, and was assisted by twenty-six-year-old Aquilin

Ullrich. The medical mystification was carried out by such means as fake death certificates, concocted according to guides for plausible causes of death.

T4 procedures excused Jewish inmates from the usual criteria for inclusion. Their systematic treatment began in April 1940 with a proclamation by the Reich Interior Ministry that within three weeks all Jewish patients were to be inventoried. The first gassings of Jews followed in June. Meanwhile, Jewish patients were concentrated in German facilities, and in the fall of 1940 were transported to Nazi-occupied Poland as part of a larger policy of Jewish removal. They were typically sent first to Lublin, then to various extermination camps. T4 set up an elaborate camouflage, the "Cholm Insane Asylum," as part of this operation.

As German troops pushed eastward, the SS shot inmates in order to empty mental hospitals for military uses. Once Germany invaded Russia, in June 1941, the EINSATZGRUPPEN liquidated hospital patients, among other groups. Psychiatric extermination facilities similar to the T4 establishments were also set up in the east. Shooting came to be relied on less, partly out of concern for psychological damage to troops, and GAS VANS using exhaust (carbon monoxide) gas became increasingly popular. In October 1941, the bureaucrat Brack and Adolf EICHMANN decided to use these vans for Jews in general who were "incapable of working." Three were installed at the first pure extermination camp at CHEŁMNO (Kulmhof). In replica of T4 procedure, the victims were told that they would shower while their clothing was disinfected, and the SS personnel wore white coats and carried stethoscopes. Chełmno was followed by the extermination centers of BEŁŻEC, SOBIBÓR, and TREBLINKA in the GENERALGOUVERNEMENT area of Poland, which resembled "euthanasia" killing centers more closely in using stationary gas chambers and T4 personnel.

In August 1941, Hitler gave Brandt a verbal order to end or at least bring to a stop the T4 operation. This was one instance in which public protest—especially from the clergy—affected Nazi policy. Yet the killing of mental patients did not stop, and mass murder was just beginning.

In the phase known as "wild euthanasia," large-scale gassing gave way to killing by starvation and drugs. Encouraged by the regime, physicians acted increasingly on their own initiative, with even fewer controls from above. Children had not been included in T4; indeed, their killing had all along approximated that of the adult "wild" phase, nor had there been public and clerical protests against what apparently seemed a eugenically more acceptable program.

Before it came to an end, T4 was extended to the concentration camps under a program bearing the code name 14f13. Early in 1943, T4 leader Bouhler loaned Heinrich HIMMLER personnel and facilities to rid the camps of "excess" prisoners, especially the most seriously ill. That spring, T4 psychiatrists began touring the camps. Questionnaires, briefer than T4's, were used; criteria were looser, often based on the inmate's ostensible crime or political deviation. Indeed, the focus soon shifted from the mentally ill to political prisoners. The 14f13 program provided an ideological and institutional bridge from "euthanasia" to Auschwitz. It also increased the initiative of individual doctors, moving further toward a "medicalized killing" removed from any even remote medical consideration.

SS doctors did no direct medical work at Auschwitz, apart from treating German personnel. Their principal function was to carry out Auschwitz's institutional program of medicalized genocide. They performed the initial large-scale *Selektionen* of Jewish prisoners arriving at the Birkenau camp, usually according to formulas that permitted only young and healthy adults at least temporary survival. Physicians also had supervisory responsibility for carrying out gassing, though a medical technician, trained in the handling of the ZYKLON B material, which had been largely developed at Auschwitz, usually installed the gas pellets. If only by looking through a peephole, doctors declared that the gassed were dead. Beyond the initial *Selektionen,* SS doctors carried out two additional forms of selection: thinning out Jewish inmates to allow room for presumably healthier new arrivals; and the caricature of triage that took place in the medical blocks as the most ill and debilitated, or those whose convalescence would tax the facilities, were sent to the gas chambers.

SS doctors also practiced a murderous "epidemiology," sending prisoners with a contagious disease, especially typhus and scarlet fever, to the gas chambers, sometimes with their fellow patients, contagious or not, so that the entire block could be "disinfected." In the medical blocks, SS doctors ordered and supervised, and sometimes themselves killed debilitated prisoners with phenol injections. (This became less frequent as the gas chambers were fully developed.) They had similar responsibility for "hidden executions" of such people as Polish political prisoners or the occasional member of the German military personnel condemned to death; here they acted for the Auschwitz Gestapo. Doctors attended shooting executions to declare the victim dead. Arriving Jews selected for the gas chambers without entering the camp required no death certificates, but for the many victims who died within the camp, Nazi doctors signed death certificates that falsely invoked a specific illness and the claim of medical treatment.

SS doctors served as experts in determining the amount of corporal punishment an inmate could absorb, and were present for the administering of such punishment. They consulted on determining how best to keep *Selektionen* running smoothly, and on how to balance the costs and benefits of keeping prisoners alive. Their technical knowledge also contributed to the efficient burning of bodies.

Finally, and apart from the strict requirements of the camp and its operations, physicians exploited the large number of "guinea pigs" in camps such as Auschwitz by engaging in a variety of experiments, some related to the larger Nazi ideological mission, and others reflecting their own particular scientific or pseudoscientific interests. Nazi doctors became particularly infamous for their MEDICAL EXPERIMENTS through the SUBSEQUENT NUREMBURG PROCEEDINGS (Trial 1, The Medical Case, October 25, 1946–August 20, 1947), although these activities formed a small part of the medicalized killing in Nazi Germany. As noted, such experimentation fell into two categories. The sterilization and castration experiments of Carl CLAUBERG and Horst Schumann were officially encouraged as an expression of racial theory and policy. Similarly, typhus injections were connected with concern about epidemics among German troops. The high-altitude experiments of Dr. Sigmund Rascher at DACHAU reflected problems of German flyers. On the other hand, Dr. Eduard Wirths's studies of precancerous cervical conditions arose from his own scientific interests, but that did not prevent the work from becoming, under Auschwitz conditions, corrupted scientifically and sometimes fatal in the infections and the complications it caused. Sometimes categories overlapped, as in the research on twins by Dr. Josef MENGELE, containing strong and distorting ideological elements as well as reflecting earlier scientific interests.

The center for experimentation at Auschwitz was Block 10, which, although it contained mostly women, was located in the men's camp. The Block 10 inmates, though temporarily safe from the gas chambers, were totally vulnerable to SS doctors. A male experimental block was created from part of Block 28 in the medical area of the main camp. Auschwitz also served as a source of human guinea pigs for research done elsewhere, for example, the anthropological skeleton collection of Professor August Hirt in Strasbourg and the Jewish children shipped to NEUENGAMME in Hamburg for tuberculosis experiments.

SS doctors also took occasional advantage of the presence on medical blocks of renowned Jewish physicians to bolster their own medical skills and knowledge, especially important for younger doctors whose medical training during the Nazi era and wartime had been compromised. This sometimes took the form of totally unwarranted surgery.

Actual professional requirements did not require that doctors conduct *Selektionen* or participate in several of the other murderous activities. Yet once Nazi ideologues had defined Auschwitz as a public-health venture, the involvement of doctors became impertive. They were thereby plunged into a "healing-killing paradox," with killing some a prerequisite for others' survival, and mass killing a prerequisite for racial healing. On the level of camp ecology, overstraining of facilities had to be avoided, and on the level of ideology, Germany had to be rid of its "Jewish infection."

The policy of selecting doctors was apparently set by chief SS doctor (*Reichsarzt*) Ernst Robert GRAWITZ. Camp physicians (*Lager-*

ärzte) operated under the authority of the Auschwitz chief doctor (*Standortarzt*), who for most of the period of peak operation was Eduard Wirths. He was subordinate to the chief concentration camp physician of the Berlin SS WIRTSCHAFTS-VERWALTUNGSHAUPTAMT (Economic-Administrative Main Office; WVHA), Enno Lolling. Wirths was also subject to the authority of the camp commandant, with whom he dealt on a day-to-day basis.

Other doctors had different duties and different chains of command. For example, troop physicians (*Truppenärzte*) took care of SS personnel. Other doctors, such as Carl Clauberg and Horst Schumann, were sent to Auschwitz to experiment on inmates. Some doctors belonged to the local camp Hygiene Institute, located outside the main camp, which was part of a separate chain of command. Concerned with genuine questions of epidemiology and bacteriology and sheltering many prisoner physicians, it was by no means free of various forms of medical corruption.

Crucial to the activities of the Nazi doctors was the psychological mechanism of "doubling," that is, the formation of a second self, for instance an Auschwitz self, which could function in relative autonomy from the prior self and enable a doctor to adapt to, and participate actively in, the Auschwitz environment. The doubling was furthered by the attraction of doctors to various elements of Nazi ideology. To invoke this or other psychological mechanisms, however, is in no way to replace moral judgment with insight, but rather to attempt to probe the psychological and historical conditions conducive to evil.

BIBLIOGRAPHY

Kater, M. *Doctors under Hitler.* Chapel Hill, 1989.

Klee, E. *"Euthanasie" im NS-Staat: Die "Vernichtung lebensunwertes Lebens."* Frankfurt, 1985.

Langbein, H. *Menschen in Auschwitz.* Vienna, 1972.

Lifton, R. J. *The Nazi Doctors: Medical Killing and the Psychology of Genocide.* New York, 1986.

Mitscherlich, A., and F. Mielke. *Doctors of Infamy: The Story of the Nazi Medical Crimes.* New York, 1949.

Müller-Hill, B. *Murderous Science.* New York, 1988.

Naumann, B. *Auschwitz: A Report on the Proceedings against Robert Karl Ludwig Mulka and Others before the Court at Frankfurt.* New York, 1966.

Nuremberg Military Tribunals. *United States of America v. Karl Brandt et al., Case I ("The Medical Case").* 2 vols. Washington, D.C., 1947.

Proctor, R. *Racial Hygiene: Medicine under the Nazis.* Cambridge, Mass., 1988.

ROBERT JAY LIFTON and AMY HACKETT

PINSK, city in the Polesye district of Poland, now belonging to the Belorussian SSR. Jews lived in Pinsk from the early sixteenth century; it was a center of Hasidism (the Karlin dynasty), Enlightenment, and Zionism. In 1941 the Jewish population of Pinsk was thirty thousand, amounting to 70 percent of the total.

On July 4, 1941, Pinsk was taken by the Germans. The following day, sixteen Jews were seized and killed. In the second half of July a JUDENRAT (Jewish Council) was set up, consisting of twenty-eight members and headed by David Alper, a former principal of the local Tarbut (Zionist-oriented) secondary school. On August 5, eight thousand Jewish men were rounded up, on the pretext that they were needed for repair work on the railway line, among them twenty members of the Judenrat and its chairman. All were taken out of town and murdered. Two days later, another twenty-five hundred to three thousand men were rounded up, including old men and children; they too were taken to burial pits and killed.

Pinsk was included in the REICHSKOMMISSARIAT UKRAINE. At the beginning of September 1941, a newly appointed *Gebietskommissar* (district commissioner) assumed his post in the city and, as a first step, imposed a collective fine on the Jews of twenty kilograms of gold. From time to time the Judenrat was ordered to supply substantial quantities of goods and commodities.

The Judenrat had a Jewish police force consisting of twelve men and their commander. When the ghetto was set up, their number grew to fifty. On April 30, 1942, an order was announced giving the Jews one day to move into the ghetto—by 4:00 p.m. on May 1. The ghetto area, located in a poor quarter, was quite small, and had twenty thousand people packed into it. The Judenrat maintained various public institutions in the ghetto: a hospital, an orphanage, a soup kitchen, a law court, and a prison, as well as several shops where the rationed food was sold.

There was an underground in the Pinsk ghetto, with some fifty members. Twenty of these fled to the forest, but they returned under pressure from the Judenrat, which feared that if the Germans found out about the flight, they would impose a collective punishment on the Jews. The underground planned to set the ghetto on fire on the eve of its projected liquidation, and made the necessary preparations. On October 28, however, when rumors of an impending liquidation were rampant, the Judenrat publicized statements by the *Gebietskommissar* dismissing the rumors, and the underground abandoned its plan.

Between October 29 and November 1, 1942, almost all the inhabitants of the ghetto were rounded up and murdered. Many dozens of Jews managed to escape or went into hiding. Meanwhile, 143 skilled artisans were kept alive and put into a "mini-ghetto"; that number grew as people came out of their hiding places to join the "mini-ghetto." On December 23, the last remnant of that ghetto as well was liquidated and all its inhabitants killed.

Pinsk was liberated on July 14, 1944, by the Red Army.

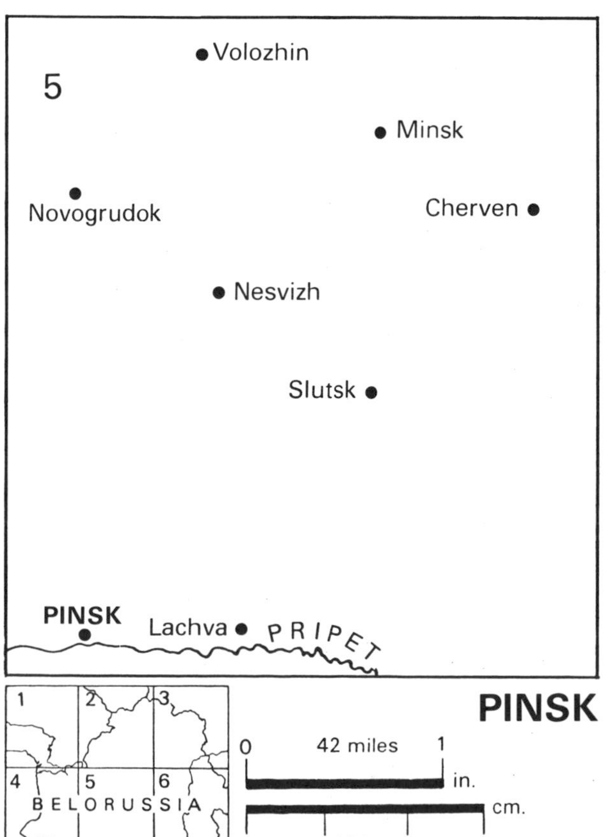

BIBLIOGRAPHY

Rabinowitsch, W. Z., ed. *The Story of the Jews of Pinsk, 1506–1942.* Vol. 1. Tel Aviv, 1977. (In Hebrew and English.)

SHMUEL SPECTOR

PIOTRKÓW TRYBUNALSKI, town in central Poland, about 16 miles (26 km) south of Łódź. In 1939 there were some eighteen thousand Jews in Piotrków, about one-third of the total population, with a vibrant community life.

Piotrków was occupied by the Germans on September 5, 1939, four days after the outbreak of World War II. Anti-Jewish excesses took place at once: brutal beatings, kidnappings for forced labor, and killings. Jewish valuables and household effects were plundered in large quantities. The Germans broke into the main synagogue, famed for its beauty, robbed it of all its sacred objects, and beat and seized twenty-nine worshipers. When the Day of Atonement came, ten days later, nothing remained of the synagogue except the four walls. Some two thousand Jews of Piotrków managed to escape during the initial days of the occupation, but the number of Jews in the town swelled as refugees from neighboring towns poured in.

On October 8, Hans Drexel, commander of the city, issued a decree establishing a ghetto, the first in occupied Poland. All Jews from outside the designated ghetto area were ordered to leave everything behind and move into the ghetto, taking only their bedding. The Jewish BADGE had to be worn by all Jews, under penalty of death. The series of decrees issued in Piotrków soon became standard for all Poland: Jews were not to possess

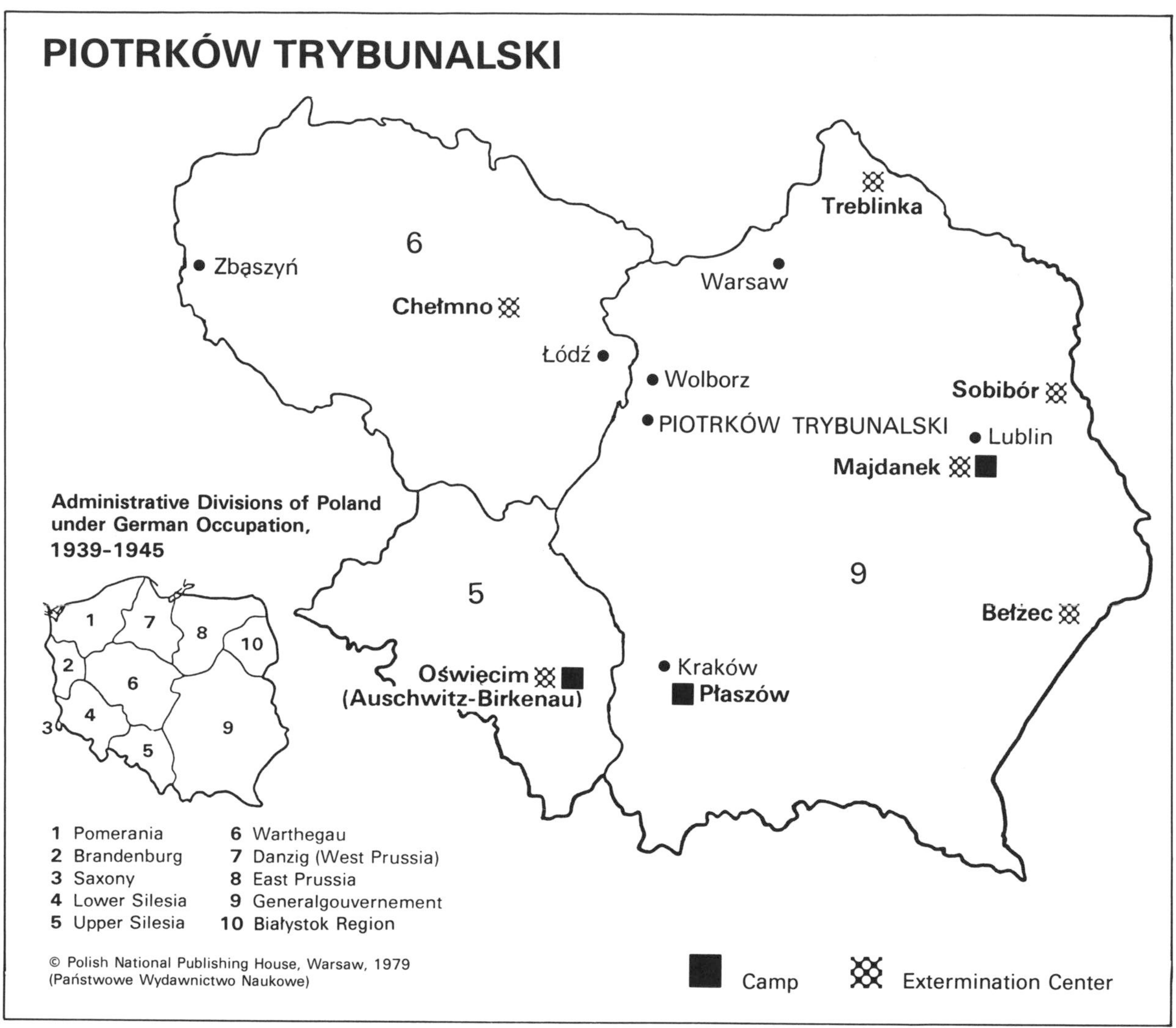

more than 2,000 zlotys; all gold and jewelry was to be surrendered to the Germans; Jews were not allowed to work in any public institutions or in industry; Jews were not permitted to trade with non-Jews; Jewish doctors were not to treat "Aryans," nor were "Aryan" doctors to treat Jewish patients; and no Jew was allowed to leave town without a permit.

A JUDENRAT (Jewish Council) was formed to represent the community vis-à-vis the Germans. One of its tasks was to deliver daily contingents of workers; another was to build barracks for Jews (some four thousand) from neighboring townships, especially Wolborz.

The liquidation of the Jewish community of Piotrków Trybunalski lasted from October 13 to 21, 1942. The *Aktion* began at dawn: Ukrainian SS men aided by Polish police surrounded the ghetto, while German SS troopers entered the area and drove the Jews to the assembly point in town. Two columns of Jews were formed: those with work cards (numbering some two thousand) were allowed to stay, and those without (some twenty thousand) were deported to TREBLINKA. Five hundred Jews managed to escape into the forests. About two thousand other Jews remained in hideouts, only to be rounded up later on and murdered in the nearby Rakow Forest. On March 21, 1943, the day of the Jewish feast of Purim, ten Jewish doctors were murdered by drunken Nazis in the cemetery "to avenge the ten sons of Haman."

Three labor camps remained: the significantly reduced ghetto, the Dietrich und Fi-

Jewish youths from Piotrków Trybunalski.

scher wood-processing plant, and the Kara glassworks. However, by July 1943 a sign was put up at the railway station, "Petrikau ist judenrein" ("Piotrków is cleansed of Jews"), the surviving workers having been transferred to other labor camps or to AUSCHWITZ.

After the war, attempts to form a new Jewish community were halted when several Jews trying to reclaim their former homes were murdered by the Poles. Some fourteen hundred Piotrków Jews who survived in the forests (as remnants of partisan groups) or in the camps, or who returned from the USSR, joined the BERIḤA (the exodus from eastern Europe) and eventually reached Palestine.

BIBLIOGRAPHY

Granatstein, Y. *Splendor and Heroism, Hod u Gvurah. Rabbi Itzchak Finkler of Radoshitz-Piotrkow: His Life and Events in the Ghetto and Camps.* Jerusalem, 1987. (In Hebrew.)

Kermish, J. "The Destruction of the Jewish Community of Piotrkow by the Nazis during World War II." In *Piotrkow Trybunalski and Vicinity,* edited by Y. Meltz and N. Lau, pp. 6–63. Tel Aviv, n.d.

SINAI LEICHTER

PIUS XII (Eugenio Pacelli, 1876–1958), pope (1939–1958). Born in Rome, Pacelli studied philosophy at the Gregorian University and theology at Sant' Apollinare, both in Rome. After his ordination in 1899 he entered the Secretariat of State in 1901 and began a long career in papal diplomacy. He became assistant secretary of state in 1911, pro-secretary of state in 1912, and secretary of the Congregation for Extraordinary Ecclesiastical Affairs in 1914.

On May 13, 1917, Pacelli was consecrated titular archbishop of Sardes and appointed nuncio to Bavaria. He became nuncio to Germany in June 1920 and signed the concordats with Bavaria in 1924 and Prussia in 1929. Pacelli was made a cardinal in 1929, and a year later he was appointed secretary of state. He concluded the concordat with Baden in 1932. From the time of Adolf Hitler's accession to power (January 30, 1933), the acts of Cardinal Pacelli have been a matter of controversy.

According to official Catholic sources, Pacelli did not in any way influence the German bishops who, on March 28, 1933, lifted previous prohibitions against the Nazi party so that any Catholic could now "be loyal to the lawful authorities."

On April 10 of that year, Franz von PAPEN and Hermann GÖRING were received by Pope Pius XI, who, according to von Papen, "remarked how pleased he was that the German government now had at its head a man uncompromisingly opposed to communism and Russian nihilism in all its forms." The strong anticommunism of the Holy See played a major role in the stand of Pacelli. On July 20, a concordat was signed at the Vatican by Pacelli and von Papen that represented a great diplomatic victory for Hitler.

Hitler, however, never intended to implement the concordat. With religious liberty at stake, Pope Pius XI on March 21, 1937, issued the encyclical *Mit brennender Sorge* (With Burning Concern), in which he questioned the errors of Nazi ideology: "Whoever detaches the race, the nation, the state, the form of government . . . from the earthly frame of reference and makes them into the highest norm of all, higher than religious values, and worships them with idolatry, perverts and distorts the order of things provided and commended by God." The encyclical condemned neo-pagan theories such as the "idolatric doctrine of the race," but not the constitutional form of the Nazi regime.

Cardinal Pacelli was elected pope on March 2, 1939, and took the name Pius XII. Regarding his attitude to Jews, his pontificate is the subject of disagreement among scholars, some praising his aid to individual Jews in distress, others criticizing his silence and his failure to publicly condemn the Nazi persecutions. Even Catholic authors who base themselves only on the official documents published by the Holy See have deplored some aspects of the conduct of the papacy in general and of Pius XII in particular.

From the very beginning of the Nazi regime, the church tried to alleviate the fate of Jews who had converted to Catholicism. This is illustrated by the remonstration of the Holy See against those aspects of the Italian racial laws of 1938 that dealt with mixed marriages and the children of such marriages. As a general rule it can be said that the Holy See relied exclusively on diplomacy, while human suffering and moral principles were ignored.

Nevertheless, when it became urgent to find a haven for thousands of Jewish refugees after the KRISTALLNACHT pogrom, the Holy See intervened in March 1939, in Catholic Brazil. It obtained 3,000 visas for baptized Jews, of which 2,000, however, were not granted because of alleged "improper conduct," in Cardinal Luigi Maglione's words. This was probably a reference to the returning of Jews to Judaism once they reached Brazil. Some historians believe that in its policies toward refugees, the church manifested antisemitism, indifference to the plight of the non-Christian Jews, and excessive neutralism.

In the spring of 1940, the Chief Rabbi of Palestine, Isaac Herzog, asked the papal secretary of state, Cardinal Maglione, to intervene in Spain to keep Jews there from being sent back to Germany, and he later wrote again about a similar situation in Lithuania. But the Holy See did not intervene.

Some historians claim that the pope had only partial knowledge of the Nazi program of extermination of the Jews, but this seems not to have been the fact. The papal Secretariat of State was among the first bodies in the

Signing of the concordat between the German Reich and the Holy See in the chancellery of the Vatican on July 20, 1933. Second from the left is Franz von Papen, vice-chancellor of the Reich. At the head of the table is Eugenio Pacelli, cardinal and Vatican secretary of state (Pius XII, 1939–1958), chief architect of the concordat.

world to receive information about the massacre of the Jews. At the beginning of 1941, Cardinal Theodor Innitzer of Vienna told Pius XII about the deportation of Jews that was taking place. The chargé d'affaires in Slovakia, Giuseppe Burzio, as early as October 27, 1941, sent a report to his superiors at the Holy See in Rome, according to which Jews were being systematically destroyed. On March 31, 1942, Burzio forwarded a new report and wrote that the deportation of eighty thousand Slovak Jews to Poland was equivalent to sending a large number of them to certain death.

That September, a common diplomatic move was made by the diplomatic corps accredited to the Holy See. The British government was most anxious to secure a public papal condemnation of the Nazi treatment of inhabitants of occupied territories and of the persecutions of the Jews. Osborne Francis d'Arcy, the British representative, wrote to the secretary of state: "A policy of silence in regard to such offenses against the conscience of the world must necessarily involve a renunciation of moral leadership and a consequent atrophy of the influence and authority of the Vatican."

On September 18, Monsignor Giovanni Battista Montini, the future Pope Paul VI, noted: "The massacres of the Jews reach frightening proportions and forms." But when the United States representative to the Vatican, Myron Taylor, forwarded a note to Cardinal Maglione that month, stating that the Jews were being sent to the east to be killed, the secretary of state replied that it was not possible to verify the accuracy of such rumors.

On October 7, 1942, the chaplain of a hospital train in Poland wrote: "The elimination of the Jews, through mass assassination, is almost total . . . they say that two million Jews have been murdered." That December, prior to Christmas Eve, many telegrams, including one from Chief Rabbi Herzog, brought urgent appeals to the pope to save the Jews of eastern Europe. Pius XII decided to break his reserve, and in his message broadcast by the Vatican radio on December 24, he spoke about the "hundreds of thousands who through no fault of their own, and solely because of their nation or race, have been condemned to death or progressive extinction." The reference to Jews was clear but not explicit. In March 1943, Burzio wrote again: "Jews in Poland are [being] killed by gas or machine guns."

In Slovakia, where a Catholic priest, Monsignor Jozef TISO, was head of state, "therefore the scandal is greater, and greater the danger that responsibility can be shifted to the Catholic church itself," according to the historian John Morley (p. 101). Morley comments that the Vatican perhaps did not act because of indifference to the deportation of the Jews, because of German influence, or because it cared only for Catholic interests.

In France, following the German invasion and the establishment of the Vichy government, Marshal Philippe PÉTAIN wrote in August 1941 to his ambassador in the Holy See, Léon Bérard, asking him to verify whether the Vatican would object to anti-Jewish laws. Bérard made an inquiry at the Secretariat of State and answered that even if the church condemned racism, it did not repudiate every measure against Jews. Morley writes that the Vatican's role was ambivalent; there was little opposition to anti-Jewish laws, and only a quiet protest against the deportations of 1942. The papal nuncio in France, Valerio Valeri, considered the reaction of the French bishops to be "a platonic protest." Monsignor Jules-Gérard SALIÈGE, the archbishop of Toulouse, made public a pastoral letter against the persecution of the Jews, but the Holy See itself did not react in France.

In Germany, the Jews could not find a champion who would try to stop the killing through an appeal to the public. The papal nuncio in Berlin, Cesare Orsenigo, was so weak in his remonstrations to the Nazi government that even the bishop of Berlin, Konrad von Preysing, asked the pope, in January 1943, whether he should be represented at all at the German government. Pius XII apparently wished to avoid the reprisals that might have been provoked by publicly condemning the persecution of the Jews, and he therefore left the responsibility for such decisions to local clergy.

Italy, after the armistice of September 8, 1943, was also occupied by the Nazis. At the end of that month the Nazis demanded 50 kilograms of gold from the Jewish community. The Vatican is said to have offered 15 kilos, but this was not taken up. On October 16 of that year, the Nazis arrested more than a thousand Jews in ROME and sent them to their death in AUSCHWITZ. No intervention stopped the action, taken almost under the papal windows. Baron Ernst von WEIZSÄCKER, the German ambassador to the Holy See, sent a report on October 28 to the German Foreign Office in which he wrote:

> Although under pressure from all sides, the pope has not let himself be drawn into any demonstrative censure of the deportation of Jews from Rome. Although he must expect that his attitude will be criticized by our enemies and exploited by the Protestant and Anglo-Saxon countries in their propaganda against Catholicism, he has done everything he could in this delicate matter not to strain relations with the German government and German circles in Rome.

Catholic authors explain that Weizsäcker wanted only to avoid Nazi reprisals against the pope. The fact remains, however, that no public protest was made on that occasion. At the same time, in many monasteries, churches, and ecclesiastical buildings in Italy, Jews were saved during the Nazi occupation, and the simultaneous opening of so many Catholic institutions could have taken place only under clear instructions by Pius XII. Moreover, the pope protested officially, if only privately, against the persecution of the Jews in those countries where he felt that he might have some influence.

In Bulgaria, the Holy See was asked to help save 6,000 Jewish children by transferring them to Palestine. On this occasion the secretary of state, Cardinal Maglione, wrote to the apostolic delegate, Amleto Cicognani, in Washington and expressed his reserve concerning Zionism.

Throughout the period of the German occupation of Hungary, which began on March 19, 1944, the papal nuncio in BUDAPEST, Angelo Rotta, as well as the pope himself, took measures to help Hungarian Jews. As early as March 24, Rotta advised the Hungarian government to be moderate in its plans concerning the Jews. When this admonition was not heeded, he continued throughout April to approach the Hungarians about their treatment of the Jews. Speaking in the name of the pope, Rotta protested against the planned deportation of the Jews—as it happened, on the very day that they began (May 15, 1944)—but again to no avail. On June 25, the pope himself cabled the Hungarian regent, Miklós HORTHY, asking him to reverse Hungarian policy on the Jews. The cable read:

> We have been requested from several sides to do everything possible to ensure that the sufferings which have had to be borne for so long by numerous unfortunate people in the bosom of this noble and chivalrous nation because of their nationality or racial origin shall not be prolonged and made worse. Our fatherly heart, in the service of a solicitous charity which embraces all mankind, cannot remain insensitive to these urgent wishes. Therefore I am turning personally to Your Excellency and I appeal to your noble feelings, in full confidence that Your Excellency will do everything in your power to spare so many unfortunate people further suffering.

On July 1, the regent replied to the pope's message:

> I received your Holiness's telegraphic message with the deepest understanding and with thankfulness, and I beg you to be convinced that I am doing all in my power to see that the demands of Christian and humane principles are respected. May I be permitted to ask that in the hour of grievous trial Your Holiness may continue to look with favor on the Hungarian people.

Shortly thereafter, on July 7, Horthy ended the first wave of deportations from Hungary. Undoubtedly, the papal protest, along with those of King Gustaf V of Sweden, Anthony EDEN, and President Franklin D. ROOSEVELT, contributed to his decision to stop the transports.

After the ARROW CROSS PARTY seized power in Hungary on October 15, Rotta again registered numerous protests on behalf of the Jews. Many of his actions were taken jointly with the representatives of several neutral states. Like them, Rotta issued letters of protection (*Schutzpässe*) in the name of the Vatican to Jews. These letters helped safeguard some twenty-five hundred Jews from the Arrow Cross reign of terror. All of these acts were significant contributions toward the rescue of the remaining Hungarian Jews.

During the war, criticism was heard from within the Catholic church itself. Cardinal Eugène Tisserant told Cardinal Emmanuel Suhard on June 1, 1940, of his fears that history would prove critical of the Holy See for having adopted an accommodating political line "for its own exclusive advantage." Cardinal August Hlond of Poland reported in August 1941 to the secretary of state that the Polish people believed the Pope had abandoned them. This was said in light of the Nazi persecution of the Polish church and clergy.

The attitude of the pope toward Nazi officials "dramatically changed" after September 1942, when Myron Taylor told him that the Allies were determined to achieve total victory. This would suggest that for Pius XII considerations of *Realpolitik* were more important than moral principles.

The major question that arises is why Pius XII did not raise his voice in public forcefully against the Nazi cruelty. Here are some possible answers to this question, given by Catholic writers:

- No successful results could be expected, public condemnation would have had little influence on the Nazi authorities, and it could endanger other activities that were still possible;
- Speaking publicly would harm the Jews, whom the pope in fact wanted to help;
- Some of the victims could still be saved, but only through discreet private interventions;
- A public intervention against the German government could provoke a schism among German Catholics, as well as measures against the Vatican and the head of the church;
- Pius XII's hope of acting as a mediator in the war was incompatible with the condemnation of any one of the belligerents; he could forfeit any claim to the role of peacemaker if he once modified his position of neutrality;
- The international character of the Catholic church, its freedom from politics, and its impartiality toward all belligerents;
- The fear that the Gestapo might seize the pope and the Vatican;
- The alarm caused by the increasing threat of communism to eastern Europe.

The controversy about Pius XII and the Holocaust is still open. At the end of his visit to Israel in 1964, Pope Paul VI came to Pius's defense in Jerusalem. On March 12, 1979, Pope John Paul II met with Jewish leaders in Rome and said: "I am happy to evoke in your presence today the dedicated and effective work of my predecessor Pius XII on behalf of the Jewish people." In a meeting with American Jewish leaders in September 1987 in Miami, John Paul II again recalled the positive attitude of Pius XII. However, his passivity in the face of the Holocaust remains a controversial subject.

BIBLIOGRAPHY

Chadwick, O. *Britain and the Vatican during the Second World War*. Cambridge, 1986.

Falconi, C. *The Silence of Pius XII*. Boston, 1970.

Friedlander, S. *Pius XII and the Third Reich*. New York, 1966.

Kulka, O. D., and P. R. Mendes-Flohr, eds. *Judaism and Christianity under the Impact of National Socialism*. Jerusalem, 1987.

Levai, J. *Hungarian Jewry and the Papacy: Pope Pius Did Not Remain Silent*. London, 1968.

Lewy, G. *The Catholic Church and Nazi Germany*. New York, 1964.

Morley, J. *Vatican Diplomacy and the Jews during the Holocaust*. New York, 1980.

SERGIO I. MINERBI

PŁASZÓW, forced-labor camp that became a concentration camp. The Płaszów camp was established in 1942 in a KRAKÓW suburb; its official designation was *Zwangsarbeitslager Plaszow des SS- und Polizeiführers im Distrikt Krakau* (Płaszów Forced-Labor Camp of the SS and Police Leader in the Kraków District). In January 1944 Płaszów was made a concentration camp.

The construction of the camp was launched in the summer of 1942, within the Kraków city limits, on a site comprising two Jewish cemeteries, other Jewish community property, and the private property of Polish resi-

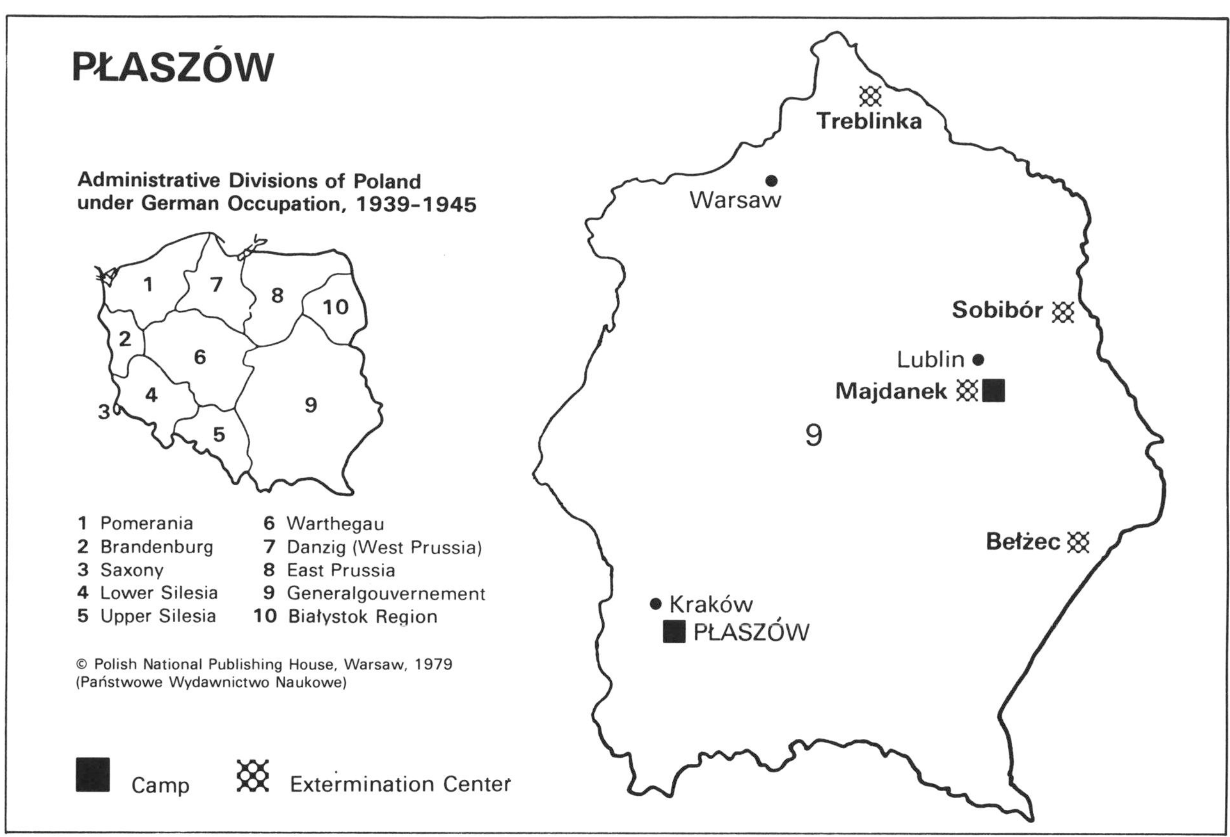

dents who had been evicted. From time to time the camp was enlarged, its maximum size in 1944 being 200 acres (81 hectares). It was encircled by an electric double-apron barbed-wired fence 2.5 miles (4 km) in length. The camp was divided into several sections—the German quarters, the factories, and the camp itself, which was divided into men's and women's sections, with separate subsections in each for Poles and Jews.

During the liquidation of the Kraków ghetto, on March 13 and 14, 1943, most of its Jewish inhabitants were deported to BEŁŻEC, about two thousand Jews were murdered in the Kraków streets (and buried in a mass grave in Płaszów), and the rest, some eight thousand persons, were put into Płaszów. In early July of that year a separate camp for "retraining by work" was established in the camp, for Polish prisoners charged with disciplinary infractions or political offenses. The former were held there for several months, and the latter were given unlimited terms of "retraining." The Polish camp also contained several dozen Gypsy families, including small children (*see* GYPSIES).

The number of prisoners held in Płaszów varied from time to time; prior to the liquidation of the Kraków ghetto, it contained 2,000 persons, while in the latter half of 1943 its population was 12,000 persons. In May and June of 1944 the number of prisoners was at its height—22,000 to 24,000, including 6,000 to 8,000 Jews from Hungary. The number of Polish prisoners in the early stage was 1,000, jumping to 10,000 after the WARSAW POLISH UPRISING.

Płaszów also contained German criminal prisoners, who were employed on various camp duties. The number of "permanent prisoners" (that is, prisoners who were given personal numbers) is estimated to have been twenty-five thousand, and in addition there was an unknown number of "temporary" prisoners and hostages. Amon GOETH, the camp commandant from February 1943 to September 1944 (one of five men to hold the post), was the person responsible for most

The Płaszów camp.

of the heinous crimes committed in the camp—mass murder, *Selektionen*, death from overwork, and personal participation in murder.

Until 1944 most of the camp guards were Ukrainians in Nazi service; when Płaszów became a concentration camp, 600 SS men from the SS TOTENKOPFVERBÄNDE (Death's-Head Units) took over. While still functioning as a forced-labor camp, Płaszów was the scene of mass killing of Jews. When the SS took over, Poles who had been sentenced in summary police trials for patriotic activities were brought there and shot to death. Some eight thousand persons, individually and in groups, are estimated to have been murdered in Płaszów. In the summer of 1944, as the Red Army was drawing near, work was begun on the breakup of the camp, and prisoners were transferred to other camps or deported to extermination camps. The latter was the fate of two thousand Jewish prisoners who in late May 1944 were deported to AUSCHWITZ and gassed to death there.

In September 1944 the Polish section was also liquidated, and efforts were made to obliterate the traces of the crimes that had been perpetrated in the camp by opening the mass graves, exhuming the bodies, and burning them in heaps. On January 14, 1945, the last prisoners were evacuated from Płaszów and sent to Auschwitz.

BIBLIOGRAPHY

Federber-Salz, B. *And the Sun Kept Shining.* New York, 1980.

Gutman, Y., and A. Saf, eds. *The Nazi Concentration Camps: Structure and Aims; The Image of the Prisoner; The Jews in the Camps.* Proceedings of the Fourth Yad Vashem International Historical Conference. Jerusalem, 1984.

Standig, Y. *Plaszow: The Last Station for Cracow Jewry.* Tel Aviv, 1970. (In Hebrew.)

JOZEF BUSZKO
and RYSZARD KOTARBA

PLOTNICKA, FRUMKA (1914–1943), a leader of the He-Haluts underground in Poland. Born in Plotnicka, near Pinsk, she was a member of the Freiheit (Dror) movement from her youth. Late in 1938 she worked at the Dror main office in Warsaw.

When World War II broke out, Plotnicka, together with most of the people in the *hakh-*

sharot (Zionist training farms), moved to Kovel, in Soviet-occupied eastern Poland, in the hope that there they would find a way of reaching Palestine. In 1940 she was one of a group of Dror headquarters members who were asked to return to the German-occupied area in order to reorganize Dror as an underground movement. Basing herself in Warsaw, Plotnicka endeavored from the beginning of the invasion of the Soviet Union (in June 1941) to consolidate and strengthen the Haluts underground movements throughout occupied Poland, even visiting near-inaccessible ghettos. In September 1942 she went to BĘDZIN on a mission for the ŻYDOWSKA ORGANIZACJA BOJOWA (Jewish Fighting Organization; ŻOB), to assist in setting up a self-defense organization there. She was in contact with several people and organizations in Switzerland and Slovakia and with the RESCUE COMMITEE OF THE JEWISH AGENCY IN TURKEY, to which she passed on information about the situation in occupied Poland. Plotnicka rejected opportunities to save her life and move to Slovakia, and to obtain documents as a foreign national. She fell in battle on August 3, 1943, together with the last group of fighters in Będzin.

BIBLIOGRAPHY

Ashkenazi, S. *Heroines in Israel.* Tel Aviv, 1961. (In Hebrew.)

Gottesfurcht, D., H. Hadar, and A. Reichmann, eds. *The Dror Book.* Ein Harod, Israel, 1947. (In Hebrew.)

Hantsia and Frumka: Letters and Memoirs. Tel Aviv, 1945.

BRONIA KLIBANSKI

POGROMS. *See* Kielce; Kristallnacht; Petliura Days.

POHL, OSWALD (1892–1951), head of the WIRTSCHAFTS-VERWALTUNGSHAUPTAMT (Economic-Administrative Main Office; WVHA) during World War II. Pohl joined the Nazi party in 1926 and the SS in 1929, reaching the rank of *Standartenführer* in 1934. His organizational gifts caught the attention of

Oswald Pohl, former head of the Wirtschafts-Verwaltungshauptamt (Economic-Administrative Main Office; WVHA), at the witness stand in his own defense.

Heinrich HIMMLER, who brought Pohl to prominence in 1935 as chief of administration in the SS-Hauptamt (SS Main Office).

In 1939 Pohl was promoted to the rank of ministerial director of the Ministry of the Interior, where he rapidly developed SS economic enterprises with the help of sympathetic specialists from German industry. These activities were grouped together in 1942 as the WVHA, and Pohl's position made him one of the most powerful members of the SS structure. He had at his disposal a work force of more than half a million concentration camp prisoners, some of whom were also "leased out" to industry. Pohl's authority covered all works projects for camp inmates and also the camp inspectorate.

In effect, it was Pohl who masterminded the "economic" aspect of the program to exterminate the Jews, as part of Himmler's emphasis on the efficacy and financial independence of the SS. Pohl ensured that all the personal possessions of the gassed Jews—hair, clothing, gold tooth fillings, wedding rings, jewelry, and so on—were sent back to Germany and turned into cash or otherwise utilized commercially.

At the end of the war Pohl went into hiding, but he was found and arrested in May 1946. In 1947 he was condemned to death for crimes against humanity, war crimes, and membership in a criminal organization. After a number of appeals he was executed in 1951.

BIBLIOGRAPHY

Speer, A. *Infiltration.* New York, 1981.

Wormser-Migot, O. *Le système concentrationnaire nazi (1933–1945).* Paris, 1968.

LIONEL KOCHAN

POLAND. [*The first of the two articles in this entry is an overview of Polish history that focuses on the period from 1930 to the end of World War II. The second article chronicles the destruction of Poland's thousand-year-old Jewish community.*]

General Survey

Between the two world wars, Poland bordered in the west on Germany, in the south on Czechoslovakia and Romania, in the east on the Soviet Union, and in the north on Latvia and Lithuania. The Poles are a Western Slavic people who created a unified state in the tenth century and accepted Roman Catholicism. In the course of Poland's thousand-year existence, its area has alternately expanded and contracted, covering 424,710 square miles (1,100,000 sq km) at its greatest size and only 38,610 square miles (100,000 sq km) at its smallest. In the first few centuries of its existence, Poland's domain in the west included areas along the Oder River and the shores of the Baltic Sea. By the fourteenth century, however, Poland lost, de jure or de facto, the territories of Silesia, Pomerania, and areas along the Baltic Sea, which took on a German character. The cities of Poland also contained a strong German element.

Poland began to expand in the east mainly when it established links with Lithuania at the end of the fourteenth century; the two countries united in 1569. This unified state included all of Belorussia, most of the Ukraine, and large parts of western Russia. Polish influence, rather than that of Lithuania, prevailed in it, and most of the nobility assimilated with the Poles. However, beginning in the seventeenth century Poland was a country of many contradictions, without a strong central regime of its own and prey to its neighbors, who were gaining in strength and who in the eighteenth century intervened in Poland's internal affairs. Poland's three large neighbors—Russia, Prussia, and Austria—divided the country among them in 1772, 1793, and 1795, and except for a short period (1807–1813) when Poland was under French protection, this situation prevailed until the end of World War I. Polish uprisings against Russia in 1830–1831 and 1863–1864, and against the Austrians and Prussians in 1846 and 1850, were suppressed. This aggravated the condition of the Polish people, except in Austrian-ruled Galicia, which was governed by a moderate regime and which in 1846 also annexed KRAKÓW, the last remnant of independent Polish rule.

At the end of World War I, owing to the downfall of its enemies and the struggle waged by the Poles, Poland regained its independence, and the Second Polish Republic was created. Its borders were the cause of discussions among the victorious powers at the Paris Peace Conference, of military encounters, and of numerous political crises. Poland's aim was to restore its historical borders, but neither Germany nor the Soviet Union was prepared to give up areas close to its own national borders. This led to compromises, such as the special status devised for DANZIG. In the eastern territories an acute problem of ethnic Slavic and Baltic minorities was created, which was not resolved by the League of Nations Treaty on Minorities. Poland's situation forced it to maneuver among the powers in the complex and weak European political alignment. In early 1934 Poland signed a treaty with Germany, indicating a Polish rapprochement with that country and a cooling of relations with its traditional ally, France. Poland's policy, designed to protect its independent status, did not take into account the fact that Hitler was ready at best to accept the existence of Poland as a satellite state, that the revision of Poland's border was only a question of time, and that a clash between the two countries was inevitable.

Poland also had pressing internal problems. In its first years the newly independent country suffered from galloping inflation, and in the late 1920s it was struck by the world economic depression. During the 1930s, a fifth of all its workers were unemployed. In addition, in the early years its

Administrative Divisions of Poland under German Occupation, 1939 to 1945

parliamentary regime lacked stability, one short-lived coalition cabinet following another, and corruption in the regime becoming widespread. On May 12, 1926, Józef Piłsudski staged a military coup, with the slogan "Sanacja" ("Recuperation"). He established an authoritarian military regime, and ruled the country as minister of defense until his death in 1935. Power in the country was then taken over by a troika, consisting of President Ignacy Mościcki; the army commander, Gen. Edward Rydz-Śmigły; and Foreign Minister Józef Beck. In the ensuing period antisemitic tendencies gained strength in government circles, as did radical rightist movements in the country. On September 1, 1939, Germany attacked Poland and WORLD WAR II began.

The Attack. Germany's advantage over Poland was not confined to superiority in numbers. In the west, north, and south, Poland was surrounded by German forces, and Germany had a commanding advantage in modern military equipment. On September 3, Britain and France declared war on Germany, but they failed to take any military measures that could have led to fighting on a second front and a reduction of the pressure on Poland. Romania, an ally of Poland, on September 6 declared itself neutral in the conflict. As a result, Poland stood alone in the face of German aggression and, despite its heroic resistance, was vanquished. On September 28 WARSAW surrendered, and the last battle was fought in the early days of October. However, the heads of the Polish government and army did not officially surrender. A total of 66,000 Polish troops fell in the battles, and 133,000 were wounded. German losses were 16,000 dead and missing and 30,000 wounded. Sixteen thousand Polish and Jewish civilians and prisoners of war were killed in more than seven hundred mass executions carried out by the Wehrmacht and the EINSATZGRUPPEN.

Until October 26, 1939, occupied Poland was in the hands of a military administration. Thereafter, Germany annexed parts of western and northern Poland (the so-called *eingegliederten Ostgebiete*, or eastern territories incorporated into the Reich). These consisted of Greater Poland, Pomerania, Upper Silesia, part of Mazovia, and parts of the ŁÓDŹ, Kraków, and KIELCE districts. In the remaining areas of Poland held by the Germans, a civil administration, the GENERALGOUVERNEMENT, was formed. Over 22 million inhabitants of Poland were now under German occupation. More than 10 million of them lived in the territories annexed by the Reich, including 600,000 to 1 million Germans and 600,000 Jews. The rest, some 12 million people, including 1.5 million Jews, lived in the Generalgouvernement.

The Soviet forces that entered eastern Poland (which the Soviets regarded as constituting parts of Belorussia and the Ukraine) on September 17—when it was clear that the war had been decided in favor of the Germans—met with little spontaneous resistance from Polish units. The Polish High Command had ordered the Polish army to desist from fighting the Soviet army, except when Polish units were being attacked. An agreement between the Soviet Union and Germany, signed on September 28, fixed the final border between the two countries. The Soviets seized an area of 75,675 square miles (196,000 sq km), with a population of 4 million to 5 million Poles and 1.2 million Jews. The non-Polish population, including the Jews, gave the Soviet units a warm welcome.

The Polish Leadership. On September 17, in view of the new situation that had arisen in the country, the top Polish leaders decided to leave and cross into Romania. There they were interned, as a result of German pressure. President Mościcki resigned from his post and his place was taken by Władisław Raczkiewicz, a moderate activist of the Sanacja group, who was then in France. Raczkiewicz in turn appointed Gen. Władisław SIKORSKI as prime minister. A national council-in-exile was also formed, to take the place of the Sejm (parliament), as well as a military force, commanded by Sikorski.

When France fell, in June 1940, the Polish government moved to Britain, on which it pinned its hopes for a favorable postwar political settlement in Europe. Most of the Polish army in France, however, did not escape in time, either falling into German hands or crossing the border into Switzerland, where its soldiers were interned.

Legal Status of Occupation. In September 1939 the central Polish government institutions dissolved. As time went on they were reestablished as underground organizations, by the POLISH GOVERNMENT-IN-EXILE and the Polish underground authorities in Poland: the DELEGATURA (the Polish government's representation on Polish soil) and the Krajowa Rada Narodowa (National Council). To the Germans, the Polish state had ceased to exist both legally and politically; the occupying power could thus rule at will, without taking into account the fact that the Polish government was continuing the war abroad. In the areas incorporated into the Reich, the Polish administration, the local government, and all existing Polish organizations were liquidated, and new administrative units were set up. These consisted of Wartheland (the WARTHEGAU), with Arthur GREISER as governor; the administrative district (*Regierungsbezirk*) of Upper Silesia (previously a part of Lower Silesia), with Fritz Bracht as local governor; and Danzig–West Prussia (including Pomerania, the city of Danzig, and a small part of East Prussia), with Albert FORSTER as governor. The northern part of Mazovia was incorporated into the territory of East Prussia.

Hitler expected the men he had appointed as governors to "Germanize" the areas under their control with all speed, by expelling

Poles, placing a part of the population on the *Volksliste* and accepting them as ethnic Germans (VOLKSDEUTSCHE), and settling Germans there. Before 1939 had come to an end, 90,000 Jews and Poles were expelled from the annexed areas into the Generalgouvernement. During the entire German occupation a total of 900,000 persons were expelled, not counting the Jews who were deported for extermination. In their place, 600,000 Germans from other parts of Poland and from other countries of eastern Europe were settled in these areas, together with 400,000 Germans from the Reich. The Poles who were temporarily permitted to stay were treated as subhumans, especially in the Warthegau; they were not allowed to live in the same place as Germans or to associate with them (except in their place of work), and they were robbed of all their property and personal belongings. In December 1941 a special penal code for Poles and Jews was introduced in all areas that were officially part of the Reich.

A German plan for the creation of a Polish state in the remaining part of Poland (the *Reststaat*) was based on the expectation that once Poland had been defeated, Britain and France would not remain in the war. When this did not happen, the Germans created the Generalgouvernement, in which a Polish administration was permitted to function, within the limits set by Generalgouverneur (Governor-General) Hans FRANK. Following the June 1941 attack on the Soviet Union and the German occupation of the formerly Soviet-held parts of Poland, the district of Galicia was formed, and in August 1941 was incorporated into the Generalgouvernement. This step meant that the Germans were rejecting the Ukrainian nationalists' hopes and aspirations for the establishment of a Greater Ukraine.

In May 1941 plans were drawn up for the Germanization of these areas. Frank's staff proposed a *Bodenordnung im Generalgouvernement* (land settlement in the Generalgouvernement), a program for the gradual transfer of agricultural areas to German hands. In March 1942 Heinrich HIMMLER told the governor-general of his plans for Germanization and repopulation, over the next few years, in the Lublin district and the mountain region. Himmler ordered the SS and police in those areas to begin preparations for the resettlement plans, and in November 1942 the operation itself was launched, in the ZAMOŚĆ province. For an entire year, from mid-1942 to mid-1943, a sharp dispute went on over the proper division of authority, against the background of the rivalry between Hans Frank and Himmler, who was chief of the SS and police and *Reichskommissar für die Festigung des Deutschen Volkstums* (Reich Commissioner for the Strengthening of German Nationhood). Himmler also sought to restrict the operations of various central departments of the Reich. Thereafter, Frank's position was strengthened, and it was he who was responsible for the terror campaign launched in September 1943, consisting of public executions and indiscriminate murderous raids on villages.

In March 1944 the Generalgouvernement became an active operational area of the eastern front, but no change took place in its administration. After the liberation of the area between the Bug and Vistula rivers by Soviet and Polish forces, the territory comprising the Generalgouvernement shrank in size, and for two months, during the Warsaw Polish uprising, Warsaw itself was not under the Generalgouvernement's control. At this point the Germans came up with a plan for a Polish puppet government, but they could not find any Poles who were prepared to take part in such a government. In the Soviet offensive of January to March 1945, the rest of the Generalgouvernement and all the areas that had been incorporated into the Reich were liberated.

Nazi occupation policy was implemented by the administrations of the occupied areas; the SS, police, and Waffen-SS; and the Wehrmacht units stationed there, which in 1942 numbered some 500,000 troops and in 1944 varied between 600,000 and 1.1 million. Neither side was prepared to cooperate with the other. The conquerors had no interest in such a relationship, since their plan was to transform Poland into German LEBENSRAUM ("living space"), and the vanquished felt sheer hatred for the conquerors. The basic goal of Nazi policy was to destroy Polish society so that Poland would cease to exist as a nation.

The means used to achieve this goal were the destruction of the Polish leadership; the murder of persons regarded as present or potential enemies of the Reich; the murder and extermination of "undesirable" racial and other groups (Jews, GYPSIES, and sick persons, the last by means of the EUTHANASIA PROGRAM); indiscriminate retaliatory measures against the population of areas where the Nazis encountered resistance; provision of food in quantities just large enough to enable the Poles to perform hard labor; efforts to reduce the natural increase of the population; and the allotment of an appropriate role for the Poles in GENERALPLAN OST (General Plan East). The expulsion of Poles from certain areas was designed to break up the territorial ethnic concentration of the Polish population.

The German intention of destroying Poland as a nation from the inside was also demonstrated by the creation of special groups among the population, such as the Poles on the *Volksliste*, the *Goralenvolk* (Poles from the Carpathian Mountains whom the Germans planned to categorize as an ethnic minority), and groups of *Leistungspolen* ("meritorious" Poles).

The Jews were at first separated from the Polish population and imprisoned in ghettos and camps, and later nearly all killed in the "FINAL SOLUTION." According to official estimates, the loss of life in Poland as a result of the fighting and of actions taken by the occupying authorities was 6 million, half of this number Jews. The expulsions affected 1.2 million persons; 500,000 persons were expelled after the WARSAW POLISH UPRISING; 2.5 million were sent to work in Germany; and more than 2 million Poles were included in the *Volksliste*, which meant that the military draft was applied to them. The loss of life among the civilian population was ten times that suffered by the fighting formations. However, the biological extermination practiced by the Nazis did not meet Hitler's expectations.

Only with the liberation was the threat removed from the Polish people. Six months before the Reich's surrender, Warsaw was almost totally destroyed, and the nation's economic assets had been reduced by 40 percent.

The Church under the Occupation. The attitude of the occupation authorities toward the Polish church organizations, the Polish clergy, and religious life in general had its basis in national and political considerations. The attempt to destroy the Polish nation as such also included the religious sphere of Polish life. Clashes between German authorities and the Catholic church in Poland had taken place as early as the nineteenth century. In the eyes of the Reich authorities, the Catholic church in Poland was an integral element of the Polish people and the Polish state. For this reason, in the areas incorporated into the Reich, the Polish elements in the church were liquidated, so that the church became a German institution. Many churches were turned into warehouses or stripped of their contents. The most radical policy in this respect was followed in the Wartheland, where segregation between Germans and Poles was also introduced in the churches. In the Generalgouvernement, Frank tried to exploit the church for his own purposes—to help keep the peace, fill manpower quotas, and promote an anti-Communist atmosphere—but he had little success. Archbishop Adam Sapieha was the unofficial head of the Polish church, the head of the church being absent from the country. Some of the clergy cooperated with the underground movement and helped the persecuted, including Jews, giving them refuge in convents and monasteries. Various circles in Poland expressed their dismay over the lack of a clear-cut condemnation by Pope PIUS XII of the persecution of Polish Catholics by the Nazis. During the war, close to 3,000 Christian clerics were killed or fell in battle, 900 were shot to death, and 1,345 perished in concentration camps.

The Evangelical church, in the areas annexed by the Reich, was well disposed toward the Nazi authorities. Churchmen of German origin who were known for their loyalty to Poland, however, suffered harsh treatment. In the Generalgouvernement the policy toward the Augsburg Evangelical church was extremely hostile; indeed, that church was to be liquidated, because of its allegiance to Poland. Excellent relations prevailed between the Greek Orthodox church, with a membership of 300,000, and the Nazi authorities.

Organized Terror. During the September 1939 fighting, terror was practiced on an organized basis, but it was not uniform in character. While the fighting was going on, the terror's main purpose was to serve as a deterrent. Differences in its application depended on its purpose—short-range or long-range—and on the organization of the different occupation agencies. In the areas incorporated into the Reich, the terror practiced against the Polish population between 1940 and 1945 was more or less uniform, with slight variations in its intensity. In the Generalgouvernement there were marked differences in the degree of violence used and also in the methods applied, depending on the military and political situations and the effectiveness or noneffectiveness of the methods used. The Generalgouvernement authorities employed terror on a large scale. When they could not control or suppress the population, the terror frequently took the form of indiscriminate mass beatings and manhunts. The Wehrmacht's retreat from occupied Poland was also accompanied by the murder and massacre of prisoners. Worst among the crimes committed by the Third Reich in occupied Poland was the murder of the Jews. The 150,000 civilians killed in the Warsaw Polish uprising, and the tens of thousands imprisoned in concentration camps in its wake, were also the victims of terror, whose object it was to break resistance, instill fear, and wreak destruction.

The largest Nazi camp system was set up on the soil of Poland. Four extermination centers—CHEŁMNO, TREBLINKA, SOBIBÓR, and BEŁŻEC—were constructed there for the immediate extermination of Jews, in addition to the three concentration camps of AUSCHWITZ, MAJDANEK, and PŁASZÓW. A fourth concentration camp, STUTTHOF, was located near Danzig. Besides these there were 1,798 labor camps and 136 refugee camps. Transit camps for deportees were also used as killing sites, as were several prisons and ghettos. Poles were to be found in nearly every concentration camp, where they underwent the harrowing experience of the highly efficient Nazi camp system. This system affected every aspect of the prisoners' lives, achieving its purposes by exposing the prisoners to intolerable living conditions, forcing them to work to the very limit of their strength, meting out cruel punishments, holding lengthy roll calls in freezing cold, and generally seeking to humiliate the prisoners in every possible way. Even under these circumstances, however, there were always some who continued to offer resistance.

Polish Areas Annexed to the Soviet Union, Lithuania, and Slovakia. The areas occupied by the Soviet Union after September 17, 1939, were incorporated into western Belorussia and the western Ukraine. In October elections were held to the national assemblies, and in November, the areas officially became part of the Ukrainian SSR and the Belorussian SSR. The land was confiscated, industry and banks were nationalized, and from mid-1940 agriculture was collectivized.

Soviet policy toward the various ethnic sectors was designed to win the support of the non-Polish population. Most of the Jews also rapidly adjusted to the new situation and to the revolutionary changes that had been brought about, and they took part in the new administrative apparatus, on both the local and central levels. The Poles, as a result, became distrustful of the Jews. This attitude was exploited by Nazi anti-Jewish propaganda after the Nazi attack on the Soviet Union. Especially up to mid-1940, Soviet policy in Poland toward the different nationalities in the region lacked a constructive approach, and its basic principles were frequently violated.

The forced evacuation of population groups from the newly occupied area into the Soviet interior was designed to remove class elements that were regarded as posing a threat because of their anti-Soviet tendencies. About a million people, 60 percent of them Poles, were transferred in this operation to remote places in other parts of the Soviet Union. This policy was revised in the middle of 1940, when the Polish school system, the Polish theater, and Polish newspapers were again permitted to function.

VILNA and the surrounding district, with a predominantly Polish population of over half a million, was incorporated into LITHUANIA according to the provisions of the Soviet-Lithuanian Treaty of October 10, 1939. In the summer of 1940 Vilna became part of the Soviet Union, together with the rest of Lithuania.

The areas that the Soviet Union had occupied in September 1939 were captured by the Germans during their attack on the Soviet Union in June 1941. A new territorial district, BIAŁYSTOK, was created, with a population of 1.7 million, and it received a status similar to that of the Polish areas incorporated earlier into the Reich. Erich KOCH was put in control of the district. Other areas became part of REICHSKOMMISSARIAT UKRAINE and REICHSKOMMISSARIAT OSTLAND. German control of these territories lasted from the summer of 1940 until the first half of 1944.

On July 30, 1941, Poland and the Soviet Union signed a treaty in which they agreed to cooperate in the war against the Germans and in which the Soviet government acknowledged that the provisions affecting Polish territory that it had negotiated with Germany in 1939 were no longer valid. Agreement was also reached on the creation of a Polish army on Soviet soil. However, the expectations raised by this agreement were not fulfilled. Owing to British influence and to the Polish command's own desire, the Polish army that had been formed in the Soviet Union (the Anders army) was moved from there into Iran. This act lent itself to the interpretation that the idea of the Poles fighting shoulder to shoulder with the Soviets against the Germans had been abandoned. Another issue causing tension between the two governments was the citizenship status of the population of the areas incorporated by the Soviets in 1939.

In April 1943 the Soviet Union and the Polish government-in-exile severed relations as a result of the KATYN affair. At the Tehran Conference (November 28–December 1, 1943), the Soviet Union, the United States, and Great Britain reached agreement that the Curzon Line (named after the British statesman Lord Curzon, who had proposed that boundary in 1919) would constitute the border between Poland and the Soviet Union. On a bilateral basis, the Polski Komitet Wyzwolenia Narodowego (Polish Committee of National Liberation) reached agreement on Poland's eastern border with the Soviet Union, on July 26, 1944. The definitive agreement on the border between the two countries was signed by Poland and the Soviet Union on August 16, 1945.

From 1942 to 1945, clashes took place in Volhynia and Galicia between Ukrainian nationalists (primarily of the UKRAINSKA POVSTANSKA ARMYIA, or Ukrainian Insurgent Army) and the local Polish population, whom the former sought to destroy. A Polish area in the Tatra Mountains, containing several dozen localities with a total population of forty thousand, had been annexed by SLOVAKIA under an agreement with the Reich. It continued to be held by Slovakia until the end of the war.

The Resistance Movement in Poland. More than in any other country (except for the Soviet Union), the Germans in Poland suppressed the population that was under their occupation with the utmost severity and consistency. Nevertheless, resistance to the Germans was widespread. Over three hundred underground political and military groups were formed. Resistance took the form of individual and public self-defense, and of opposition to orders issued by the occupation authorities. Economic sabotage, both spontaneous and organized, served to reinforce patriotic convictions. Other kinds of resistance were active sabotage, especially on lines of communication; a well-organized military intelligence apparatus; partisan units; uprisings (such as the Warsaw Polish uprising); an underground press with fifteen hundred correspondents; and an underground educational network.

Two major political movements predominated in the underground. One consisted of the ARMIA KRAJOWA (Home Army), together with the Delegatura, which was linked to the Polish government-in-exile and its political platform (having been formed by a coalition of four political parties) and which operated in all parts of prewar Poland. The other included the GWARDIA LUDOWA (People's Guard) and its successor, the Armia Ludowa (People's Army), together with the Krajowa Rada Narodowa (National Council). The council was set up by the Communists, who as of 1942 were members of the Polska Partia Robotnicza (Polish Workers' Party; PPR). In 1943 the PPR became opposed to the Armia Krajowa. Other groups were close to the political camp that had governed Poland before the war, and there were also radical nationalist organizations, prominent among them the NARODOWE SIŁY ZBROJNE (National Armed Forces), which had antisemitic leanings.

At its inception the Polish resistance movement was the expression of opposition to the occupying power—a phenomenon that was not new in Polish history. When the Jews were being exterminated and Poles were being expelled from the Zamość region (between November 1942 and August 1943), the underground movements (especially the leftist camp) began to suspect that the Poles might be next in line for extermination, and resistance became a struggle for sheer survival. As the occupation neared its end, the resistance movement linked to the Polish government-in-exile sought to have its underground institutions recognized as representing the official regime, and its underground military forces recognized as representing the country's regular military force.

Resistance movements were widespread in the German-occupied countries of Europe. In Poland the resistance took the form of an underground state, which to a degree did in fact coordinate the actions of the population. The movement suffered heavy losses in its daily struggle, and among those who fell in the fighting were Stefan ROWECKI, commander of the Armia Krajowa, and Jan Piekalkiewicz, the delegate of the Polish government-in-exile.

At times the resistance movements were unable to extend help to the endangered population, and, in the case of the Armia Krajowa, they sometimes deliberately refrained from doing so, maintaining that it was better to abstain from a premature uprising and concentrate on the decisive struggle that would come when the occupation was approaching its end.

Prospects of Liberation. By 1943 no analysis had been made of the policy to be followed during the final phases of the war. This, together with the absence of diplomatic relations with the Soviet Union (which the Polish resistance viewed as either a friend of the Allies or an enemy second only to Nazi Germany), inevitably led to a policy of creating *faits accomplis*. It found its expression in Operation "Storm," in which the Armia Krajowa was to pave the way for Soviet forces, and in the Warsaw Polish uprising of August 1 to October 2, 1944. The aim of the uprising was to accelerate the expulsion of the Nazi occupier from Polish soil and to present the advancing Soviet armies with an accomplished fact: the existence of underground administrative institutions that were now functioning as the Polish government.

On July 22, 1944, the Polish Committee of National Liberation was formed in Lublin. Headed by Edward Osobka-Morawski, it was composed of political forces that maintained ties with the Związek Patriotów Polskich (League of Polish Patriots) in the Soviet Union and with the Krajowa Rada Narodowa. These elements supported an agreement with the Soviet Union and the settlement of all outstanding issues between the two countries, and they advocated economic and political changes that were to take place when Poland was liberated. When liberation came, the "Lublin Poles" were clearly in a minority in the country.

Winston CHURCHILL strongly urged the Polish government-in-exile in London to reach agreement with the Soviet Union. It was his hope that Stanisław MIKOŁAJCZYK would become prime minister in the new Polish government and that the members of the government-in-exile would have a majority in the cabinet. Two visits made by Mikołajczyk to Moscow, in August and October 1944, were not promising. Nevertheless, Mikołajczyk supported the establishment of a coalition with the leftist forces. In this, however, he was opposed by the members of his cabinet, and he was forced to resign. A short while later the Polish Committee of National Liberation in Poland became the provisional government. This was followed by lengthy negotiations designed to implement the decisions taken at the Yalta Conference, and led, on June 28, 1945, to the formation of a government of national unity, with the participation of the liberal-bourgeois wing of the government-in-exile, and with Mikołajczyk as deputy prime minister.

Role of the Polish Forces Fighting with the Allies. Polish armies were formed in western Europe and in the Soviet Union. Those in western Europe fought in Norway, France, North Africa, and Italy. They took part in the landings in Normandy and then fought in northern Germany, while the Polish air force took part in the Battle of Britain. In the Soviet Union the First Polish Division joined the fighting in 1943. By 1945 two Polish armies had been formed, which fought side by side with the Soviet army and took part in the battle for Berlin. In 1945 the Popular Polish Army (Ludowe Wojsko Polskie) numbered 400,000 men, and another 200,000 Poles fought on the western and northern fronts.

End of the War. In Poland the end of the war had complicated and in some cases even tragic effects. This was the result of revolutionary forces appearing on the scene that were ready to seize power in the country, as well as of the geographical situation, which called for a solution that would safeguard the east from another German *Drang nach Osten* ("drive to the east") in the future.

The loss of territory to the Soviet Union reduced the prewar area of Poland by 71,042 square miles (184,000 sq km). However, because of the decisions taken at the Potsdam Conference (July and August 1945) on the Oder-Niesse border—decisions that were to be confirmed by a peace conference—40,540 square miles (105,000 sq km) were added to Polish territory in the west. Poland now had a total area of 120,849 square miles (313,000 sq km), that is, 30,501 square miles (79,000 sq km) less than it had had before the war. Demographically, owing to the German extermination of the Jews, the expulsion of Germans from the newly Polish territory added by the Potsdam decisions, and the "exchange of population" with the Soviet Union (repatriation), Poland became an ethnically homogeneous country, very different from what it had been before the war.

Poland was one of eleven countries occupied by the Germans, but in terms of the economic and social impact of the occupation it suffered more than all others, and the loss of life can only be compared with that of the Soviet Union and Yugoslavia.

BIBLIOGRAPHY

Bor-Komorowski, T. *The Secret Army*. New York, 1951.

Davies, N. *God's Playground: A History of Poland*. Vol. 2. Oxford, 1981.

Gora, W., ed. *Wojna i okupacja na ziemiach polskich, 1939–1945*. Warsaw, 1984.

Gross, J. T. *Polish Society under German Occupation: The Generalgouvernement, 1939–1944*. Princeton, 1979.

Korbonski, S. *The Polish Underground State*. New York, 1978.

Landau, L. *Kronika lat wojny i okupacji*. Warsaw, 1963.

Luczak, C. *Polityka ludnościowa i ekonomiczna hitlerowskich Niemiec w okupowanej Polsce*. Poznań, 1979.

Madajczyk, C. *Polityka III Rzeszy w okupowanej Polsce*. Warsaw, 1970.

CZESŁAW MADAJCZYK

The Jews in Poland

Jews lived in Poland from about the tenth century, coming from three directions: the west (Germany and Bohemia), the south (the Byzantine Empire), and the area east of Romania. The persecution of Jews in Germany in the thirteenth and fourteenth centuries brought more Jews from that region to Poland, and it was they who introduced into Poland the dialect that was to become the Yiddish language. Reports on the permanent settlement of Jews in the western part of Poland date from the thirteenth century.

The legal base for the status of the Jews in Poland was the *privilegium* (charter) granted to them by Prince Bolesław the Pious of Kalisz, in 1264. This document put the Jews in the category of *servi camerae* (servants belonging to the king's treasury) who were under the sovereign's protection and had a wide range of permitted economic activities and the right to practice their religion. The statute was adopted, with changes, by the kings of Poland. From the late fifteenth century, owing to the decline of the kings' power and the growing strength of the nobility, other elements had their effect on the situation of the Jews—the leaders of the nobility, the church, and the burghers. The church prohibited the residence of Jews in towns under its control, and demanded in public that they be restricted to an inferior and humble social status. The Jews were often victims of libels and riots based on religious prejudice. The Christian townsmen, many of German origin, imposed restrictions on the Jews, barring them from the guilds and various economic activities. Many of the royal cities obtained the special right of prohibiting the settling of Jews (*de non tolerandis Judaeis*). In the "private" cities, the Jews were usually tolerated and protected by noblemen.

In the early stages, the Jews of Poland engaged in moneylending, leasing property, and trade, and some engaged in agriculture. Jews also ran taverns and inns, and worked as merchants and tradesmen. For the most part they were an urban element, but many lived in the villages, where they served as middlemen, leaseholders appointed by noblemen, and innkeepers. The Jews played an important role in Poland's international and internal trade. Many poor Jews turned from commercial activities and peddling to various kinds of handicrafts.

At the end of the fifteenth century, approximately 20,000 to 30,000 Jews were living in Poland and Lithuania, and by the end of the sixteenth century their number had risen to 200,000, spread over 190 communities. By 1648 the Jewish population is estimated to have reached 300,000. This growth was the result of a high birthrate, and of immigration from Germany, Austria, and Bohemia. The Jews in these countries were attracted by the tolerance (in relative terms) that prevailed in Poland, and by the large number of economic activities to which Jews had access.

The Kehillah, the organized Jewish community, was the basis of Jewish life. The leadership of the communities in the large cities also served the small communities in their respective areas. These regional leaderships consolidated into the Council of the Four Lands (Great Poland, Lesser Poland, Ruthenia, and Lithuania), an autonomous institution that came to direct Jewish life in Poland. The authorities supported this united institution, established in 1580, which they were able to use to collect on their behalf the taxes imposed on the Jews of the country. The council, which generally met at the Lublin and Jarosław fairs, represented the Jews' internal leadership, and dealt with their problems and vital issues. In the sixteenth century Poland gained its preeminent status as a center of Jewish learning.

The massacres of 1648 and 1649, the Cossack revolt led by Bohdan Khmelnytsky, and the subsequent invasion of Poland and the wars in which it became involved, constituted a turning point in the history of Poland and its Jews. The Jews suffered from the Ukrainian population's hatred of its Polish masters, since in Ukrainian eyes the Jews were the lackeys of the Polish rulers. In addition, in periods of turmoil the Jews were persecuted by the Poles (especially during the Swedish invasion), and were subjected to increasing hostility on the part of the various Christian denominations. Tens of thousands of Jews perished in Poland or fled the country during the pogroms and wars.

From the end of the seventeenth century the situation of the Jews deteriorated further, owing to the destruction that Poland had endured, the ensuing economic depression, and the ineffectiveness of government authority. The participation of Jews in the country's economic life was sharply reduced and their overall situation grew worse, as a result of religious fanaticism, blood libels (accusations that they killed gentiles to obtain their blood for Jewish rituals), and the spread of antisemitism among the Poles. In 1764 the Council of the Four Lands was abolished and the authorities introduced more stringent methods of exacting taxes from the Jews. Nevertheless, the Jewish population increased in size in the private cities and in the newly acquired eastern territories. In 1775 Poland-Lithuania had a Jewish population of 750,000. Prior to the third partition of Poland (1795), the leader of the Polish revolt, Tadeusz Kościuszko, invited the Jews to take part in the uprising against Russia and Prussia, which some Jews did. A Jewish regiment was formed, under the command of Berek Joselewicz.

In the Russian-dominated kingdom of Poland, set up by the Congress of Vienna in 1815, the leading nationalist circles in Polish society were not prepared to introduce the emancipation measures for the Jews that were being adopted in the West, and this situation continued until the 1863 uprising against Russia. Jews participated in the patriotic insurrection, and the Poles showed a readiness to undertake genuine changes. But the rebellion was put down and so was the hope of liberating the country by the force of arms. The Jews obtained a measure of equality, but it was the conquerors who gave it to them: first the Austrians, in Galicia, and eventually also the Russians, in "Congress" Poland.

A reformist tendency in Poland was willing to confer benefits on the Jews, but as in other places, they were asked to give up their cultural traditions and their distinctiveness as a separate entity, and instead to adopt the culture and way of life of the society among which they lived. These ideas found a ready response among a limited sector of wealthy and educated Jews, but the results were negligible. This group of prominent Jews played a role in the development of a capitalist economy in Poland, and some Jews distinguished themselves in science, culture, and the arts, clearing a path for modern culture to penetrate into Jewish society. But they themselves were lost to the Jewish people within a generation or two, whereas the Jewish masses remained faithful to their heritage.

Outside their own society, the Jews had to face a new situation. The capitalist economy that was taking hold in Poland, the entry of the declining Polish aristocracy into urban life and industrial and commercial enterprises, and the growing intelligentsia—all this created a structure in which the Jew figured as a competitor. The new class divisions led to the formation of new political movements, leftist movements of various shades on the one hand, and nationalistically inclined groups on the other. The new nationalism coincided with the growth in western and central Europe of modern political antisemitism, with which it had many ideological affinities. Early in the twentieth century, the outstanding leader of this movement, Roman Dmowski, declared that he opposed the trend for the assimilation of masses of Jews, who represented a different and foreign body; the penetration of Jews in large numbers into the Polish community might corrupt its original Polish character. A political confrontation between the Jews and the Polish nationalist movement during the elections to the Fourth Duma (the Russian parliament), on the eve of World War I, prompted Dmowski to call for an economic boycott of the Jews and to embark on an all-out antisemitic campaign. The prevalent objections raised against the Jews were their large number in the country, their separateness, and the growing influx of Jews from Russia who were seeking to escape the hostile antisemitic policy of the Russians in the Pale of Settlement. These Jews, the Poles claimed, were furthering the cultural "Russification" of Poland and introducing Jewish nationalist political ideologies among the Polish Jews.

The Jewish population continued to grow in size, notwithstanding the large-scale emigration of Jews from different parts of Poland to the West, mainly to the United States, beginning in the early 1880s. At the same time that the Polish population was undergoing a transformation, far-reaching changes were also taking place among the Jews. The Haskalah (the modern Jewish Enlightenment), Yiddish culture, and modern Hebrew all flourished. A Jewish national identity, anchored in Zionism, was firmly established, as was the concept of Jewish cultural autonomy, propagated by the BUND as part of its socialist ideology.

Between the Wars. A new chapter in the life of the Jews of Poland and their relationship with the Poles was recorded in independent Poland in the interwar years. The Polish struggle for independence from 1918 to 1920 was accompanied by anti-Jewish riots in hundreds of cities and towns. Even at this early stage of Poland's political rebirth, contentious issues concerning the Jews came to the fore. Most significant was the treaty for the protection of the ethnic and religious rights of minorities, which Poland and other countries in eastern and southeastern Europe had to sign after World War I, at the insistence of the Allied leaders. Two basic elements determined the Polish attitude toward the Jews in the interwar period. One was the size of the Jewish population, which in the new Poland constituted 10 percent of the total, rising as high as 30 percent in the major cities. The other issue, which the Poles stressed, was the key role allegedly played by the Jews in Poland's economy, which, many Poles believed, necessitated a drive for the "Polonization" of economic life in the country's cities and towns. In the first few years of independent Poland's existence, the National Democrats (Endeks) and their partners were in the majority or were very influential in the successive governments. The cabinets that

POLAND'S LARGEST JEWISH COMMUNITIES ON THE EVE OF WW II

served in this period restricted Jewish participation in various sectors of the economy and in the professions, and, in effect, barred Jews from the civil service. Jewish political organizations (especially the Zionists, led by Itzhak GRUENBAUM) tried to protect Jewish interests by combining with other minority groups in parliament, such as Ukrainians and Germans, into minority blocs. Many Poles regarded this as indicating disloyalty to the country.

In 1926 Marshal Józef Piłsudski seized power, with the help of the army. He had no anti-Jewish tendencies and refrained from using antisemitism as an instrument for furthering political and socioeconomic policies. At first, the Piłsudski regime promised to take steps to improve the situation of the Jews, but little was accomplished in practice, although the general atmosphere with regard to the Jews showed signs of improvement. However, the worldwide economic depression, which hit Poland very hard, the authoritarian methods that replaced any democracy in the country, and, above all, Piłsudski's death in 1935, led to a radical change in the Jewish situation.

Piłsudski's successors placed their maintenance of power above any other consideration. The new political movement that they established—operating, at times, with political blindness—tightened relations with Nazi Germany and adopted a clear anti-Jewish policy as a means of strengthening Poland's internal cohesion. In this new situation the government, while denouncing brutal acts of violence against the Jewish minority, gave its blessing to an anti-Jewish economic boycott, and declared that accelerated emigration of Jews and reduction in the size of the country's Jewish population were high-priority targets in its policy. For the nationalist and pro-fascist elements in the country this was not enough, and the more extreme factions tried using violent methods to force the Jews to emigrate, such as deliberately instigating anti-Jewish riots in the towns and cities. In general, the idea of depriving the Jews, or at least a large proportion of them, of the right to live in Poland had wide support among the population in the second half of the 1930s. This pressure, together with the policy of dislodging the Jews from their positions in the country, and accompanied by such abortive schemes as the government's proposal that the Jews emigrate to Madagascar, came at a time when the Jews had no realistic prospects of emigration and the gates of possible countries of immigration were closed to them. Anti-Jewish political movements and policies, however, did not totally dominate the scene. Broad political circles, composed of socialists and liberals, publicly attacked antisemitism and joined the Jews in the struggle for their rights and in their self-defense actions.

The Jewish population of Poland was experiencing a process of pauperization and losing the tenuous economic hold that it still had. It was not only, and perhaps not even primarily, anti-Jewish policy that caused the Jews' economic downfall, but rather the general depression and poverty that afflicted the country. In educational, cultural, and political communal activities, the Jews enjoyed a large measure of freedom, and sometimes even obtained renewed state support and encouragement. In the wake of the suppression of Jewish life in the Soviet Union and the isolation of Soviet Jewry from the rest of the Jewish world, Polish Jewry became the world center of Jewish national, social, and political activities. Despite their precarious economic situation, the Jews of Poland excelled, in their devotion to traditional values, on the

Execution by firing squad of Jews from the Polish town of Bochnia, 20 miles (32 km) east of Kraków, probably soon after the Germans occupied the town on September 3, 1939.

one hand, and in energetic dedication to national and ideological aims, on the other. Their multifaceted activities included efforts to protect Jewish life in Poland, and determined Zionist organizational advocacy of emigration to Palestine, especially among the YOUTH MOVEMENTS. The tragic aspect in the situation of the Jews of Poland on the eve of World War II was that all these initiatives were doomed to failure, in light of the fragmentation and conflicts existing in Europe, which in large measure were characterized by radical anti-Jewish tendencies.

World War II. Immediately after the Germans overwhelmed Poland in September 1939, a wave of riots and murders followed, perpetrated by the EINSATZGRUPPEN that accompanied the German forces and that continued their murder operations under the military administration that existed for about two months. The *Aktionen* of the Einsatzgruppen struck Poles too, but even in their first blows, the Jews were singled out.

The German-held part of Poland was divided between the area incorporated into the German Reich and the GENERALGOUVERNEMENT. On the eve of the war Poland had a Jewish population of 3.3 million. After the division of Polish territory between the Germans and the Soviets in September 1939, the area annexed to the Reich and that constituting the Generalgouvernement contained 2.1 million Jews, whereas the Soviet part had 1.2 million. From early September 1939 to February and March 1940 there was an ongoing flow of refugees from the German-controlled part to the eastern, Soviet-held part. Several sources estimate that 300,000 Jews, mostly young males, took this route. Some of the refugees, however, returned from the east to their homes in the west after a short stay, either because they were tired of living as refugees, or because they wanted to be reunited with the families they had left behind. The migration of Jews from one place to another within German-held territory was caused in September 1939 by the flight from the advancing German forces, and later, by the persecution to which they were exposed and their expulsion from the northwestern parts of Poland that were annexed to the Reich. After this phase, and until the German attack on the Soviet Union in June 1941, the German-occupied part of Poland had a Jewish population of 1.8 million to 2 million, of whom 1.5 million were in the Generalgouvernement.

During the prewar German-Polish confrontation, which lasted from March to the end of August 1939, Hitler had missed no opportunity to threaten Poland, stating that the Poles would not be spared. After his January 1939 speech in which he predicted the liquidation of European Jewry if a war were to break out, Hitler did not concern himself with the Jews of Poland and did not threaten a special line of action against them. It was not clear whether the anti-Jewish policy that was being pursued against the entire Jewish community in the Reich, aimed at eliminating the Jews from the different spheres of German life and forcing them to emigrate, would also be applied in occupied Poland. At any rate, the Jews of Poland did not experience the interval that the Jews of Germany, Austria, and Czechoslovakia had had before the outbreak of the war to emigrate to free countries. The few possible exit routes that did exist were blocked when the war began, and in the summer of 1940 Jews were forbidden to emigrate from Poland—a ban that was introduced inside Germany only in October 1941. One of the reasons given for the earlier application of the ban on emigration in Poland was to save whatever few emigration prospects that were available for the Jews of the Reich. No more than two thousand to three thousand Jews were able to leave Poland legally, most of them persons of means or with good connections.

The first instructions on the policy to be applied to the Jews in Poland were issued by Reinhard HEYDRICH, in a special letter addressed to the Einsatzgruppen chiefs dated September 21, 1939, when the fighting in Poland was drawing to a close. These instructions were based on talks in which Hitler apparently took part, and were worked out in discussions between Heydrich and his aides. The directive makes it clear that the policy on the Jews was to be implemented in two stages: an immediate operational stage, and a long-range stage defined as a "final aim" (*Endziel*). The latter was not elaborated, except for a warning to the Einsatzgruppen chiefs that the very existence of such a "final aim" must be kept strictly secret, and that they were to bear in mind that the measures being taken in the immediate operational stage were a preparation for that "final aim."

There were three immediate measures, as follows:

1. The expulsion of the Jews from the northwestern districts to the area that was designated to form the Generalgouvernement, and their concentration in the large cities, near major rail junctions;
2. The establishment of Ältestenräte (councils of elders) or Judenräte (Jewish councils) in the Jewish communities, to consist, insofar as possible, of "influential personalities and rabbis," where such people were still to be found. The councils were to be made "fully responsible . . . for the exact and punctual execution of all directives issued or yet to be issued," to prepare censuses of the Jewish population in their jurisdiction, and to make arrangements for housing Jews expelled from their homes and for evacuating Jews from the countryside to larger towns;
3. The taking into consideration of German economic interests, especially the requirements of the army, by the German officials in charge of the expulsions and evacuations. Jews whose continued presence was economically essential were to be left in place until further notice.

Heydrich's instructions to the Einsatzgruppen chiefs were not fully honored by the civil administration that took the place of the Einsatzgruppen in the occupied territories. A large part of the Jewish population in the northwestern districts (Danzig, West Prussia, and the Warthegau), who were first in line for expulsion, were indeed deported to the Generalgouvernement. But only a part of the Jews of ŁÓDŹ and the Łódź district were included in these deportations, while the Jewish population of Zagłębie and Eastern Upper SILESIA, numbering some 100,000, stayed where they were, and for a time their living conditions were far superior to those of the Jews in the rest of the occupied territories.

On November 25, 1939, Hitler officially announced the end of the military administration and the establishment of the Generalgouvernement, with Hans FRANK as its head. Its administration was subject to instructions from Berlin, while on-the-spot decisions were to be made by German officials. Frank began his term of office by issuing a series of anti-Jewish orders. In the late autumn, decrees were published that, among other things, ordered all Jews aged ten and above to wear a white armband with a blue Star of David on the right sleeve of their inner and outer garments as of December 1; prohibited Jews from changing their place of residence without express permission from the local German administration; and introduced forced labor for the Jews. Even while the fighting was still raging in Poland, Jewish stores and Jewish-owned enterprises had to be marked with a Star of David. In January 1940 Jews were barred from traveling by train except by special permit. These decrees had the object of humiliating the Jews, restricting their freedom of movement in the Generalgouvernement, and isolating them from the rest of the population. They were the marks of a regime far more oppressive than that operating in the Reich and in the Protectorate of BOHEMIA AND MORAVIA.

From its very inception, the anti-Jewish campaign was not confined to official decrees and bans. There was a variety of other manifestations that were no less severe and sometimes far worse, such as roundups of Jews on the streets by Germans in uniform for various temporary jobs, assaults on Jews, especially bearded Jews wearing traditional garb, taking goods from Jewish homes and the shelves of Jewish stores without paying for them, and confiscating Jewish apartments.

The Judenrat. On November 28, 1939, Frank issued his own version of the establishment of Judenräte in the Generalgouvernement. According to his order, each JUDENRAT was to be elected by the members of the respective Jewish community, a practice that hardly existed anywhere. Within a short time, Judenräte were established in all parts of German-occupied Poland.

The Judenrat served as the German authorities' main instrument for implementing their policy on the Jews. Most of the Judenrat members (some of whom had been forced to accept the appointment), as well as the Judenrat chairmen, believed that they would be able to serve the interests of their community and protect it as best they could under the existing circumstances. This was not the first time in Jewish history that Jews had had to represent their co-religionists before hostile authorities. In the past, Jewish representatives in such difficult assignments had often been able to mitigate the decrees issued by their oppressors, and evidently they hoped that this time too they would be able to play such a role. The Judenrat was the only institution permitted to appear on behalf of individual Jews and the Jewish community, and the only channel of communication between the Jews and the authorities in a situation in which the Jews had lost all traces of their civil and legal status.

Each Judenrat operated on its own, in its respective community, and without any umbrella organization or other type of coordinating body. It was only in the urban region of Zagłębie; in Silesia; and, to a lesser extent, in RADOM, that a regional Judenrat existed which supervised the local community or local ghetto Judenräte. The Judenrat chairmen and members, to some extent, had previously been public figures and members of Jewish community boards in Poland. The Judenrat chairmen, who had a great deal of power, generally belonged to one of two categories. In some ghettos, such as those of WARSAW (Adam CZERNIAKÓW), KRAKÓW (Marek BIBERSTEIN), and LVOV (Dr. Joseph Parnes), they tried to deal with the affairs of their community in the same way as this had been done in the past. They were unable to do so because of the nature of the demands put upon them and the orders given to them by the Germans, and because of the enormous range of the tasks for which they were responsible. These tasks, especially after a ghetto had been established, also included responsibilities that ordinarily had been in the hands of the municipal government authorities (as for housing, employment, and sanitation) and had never been the concern of the traditional Jewish community boards. The Judenräte also had to establish a Jewish police, a function in which they had had no experience and that was alien to Jews. In most places this police force had a grim role to play during the deportations.

In contrast to the Judenrat chairmen who did their best to maintain a traditional pattern of internal Jewish life and to implement German orders only to the extent that they could not be evaded, there was a second category of Judenrat chairmen. Those in this group believed that they had to take the initiative and seek ways to alleviate the situation, and, at a later stage, to try and save the Jews, or at least some of them, by coming to an understanding with the Germans. These chairmen generally sought to make the Germans believe that Jewish labor was indispensable. This category included Mordechai Chaim RUMKOWSKI in Łódź, Moshe MERIN in Zagłębie, and, in the east, Jacob GENS in VILNA and Efraim BARASZ in BIAŁYSTOK. The Germans gradually disposed of those Judenrat chairmen who refused to carry out decrees designed to inflict grave harm upon the Jews. The role of some of the Judenräte chairmen in the *Selektion* process and the final liquidation of the ghettos remains an issue of serious debate and even condemnation. These men took it on themselves to decide who would live and who would die, hoping that by sacrificing some the rest would be saved.

Forced Labor and Pauperization. Chronologically, the history of the Jews of Poland under German occupation is divided into two distinct periods. The first was from the outbreak of war to the middle of 1941, at which point the Germans launched their mass murder campaign, after their attack on the Soviet Union and the conquest of territories in the east. In the Generalgouvernement and the areas incorporated into the Reich, the first phase lasted until early 1942, and in parts of Zagłębie and Silesia, until the second half of that year. Once the German administration was installed in the respective occupied areas, the Jews there were inundated with decrees and regulations. These had the purpose either of humiliating them and isolating them from the rest of the population, or of robbing them of their belongings and making them into a population group that would be confined to hard labor only. For this work they received no remuneration at all or, at best, nominal pay that was completely inadequate for the necessities of life.

In the earliest days of the occupation, Jews were rounded up in city streets for casual jobs such as carrying loads, performing tasks in military barracks, and cleaning the streets of the rubble piled up during the air raids. The random seizures and the assaults on Jews brought Jewish life outside the home to a virtual standstill. As a result, the Judenräte in the large cities offered to supply the Germans with a fixed quota of workers, on condition that the random roundups in the streets be discontinued. This was the beginning of the Jewish labor gangs, who were not paid for their work by the Germans but by the Jewish community.

The confiscation and liquidation of Jewish and Polish factories and businesses in the areas annexed to the Reich began as early as September 1939, when the administration was still in the hands of the military. Most of the property that was seized was taken over by HAUPTTREUHANDSTELLE OST (Main Trustee Office East), operating on behalf of Hermann GÖRING'S FOUR-YEAR PLAN. In January a regulation was published in the Generalgouvernement ordering every business enterprise whose owners were absent or which was not run efficiently to be handed over to German trusteeship. The "inefficiency" provision served as a pretext for confiscating even the largest Jewish industrial plants and businesses. From 1939 to 1942, some 112,000 Jewish-owned businesses and shops and 115,000 workshops were confiscated. Only retail shops were left in Jewish hands, mostly small groceries and small workshops. Jews were permitted to withdraw no more than 250 zlotys a week from their bank accounts, and to possess no more than 2,000 zlotys in cash (in January 1940 the black-market rate for the United States dollar was 100 zlotys). These regulations made it impossible for Jews to engage in economic activities. Later, the regulations on the possession of cash were relaxed, but the Jews remained wary of being caught with sizable sums.

In January 1940 the Jews were ordered to register their property with the local authorities. In addition to factories, business enterprises, workshops, and houses, goods and valuables found in homes and in warehouses were also confiscated. Jews who had goods secreted away ran the risk of being betrayed or being robbed of their property. Taking part in the plunder drive were Germans in and out of uniform, and with or without formal authorization. Jews who did not possess the kind of property that was officially subject to confiscation were not safe from being robbed; in some cities, furniture, pianos, books, valuables, and artworks were removed from Jewish apartments, and the apartments themselves were requisitioned.

Most of the Jewish breadwinners in Poland who were salaried workers—laborers, business employees, clerks, teachers, and most of the professionals—were left without work or any alternative source of income. They had a hard time surviving on their savings and the proceeds from the sale of valuables they owned. From the very beginning of the occupation, refugees and the very poor suffered from hunger. On October 26, 1939, Frank issued a decree according to which every Jewish male of working age was subject to forced labor, as directed by the SS and police chief in the Generalgouvernement, Friedrich Wilhelm KRÜGER, who was put in charge of implementing the decree. This became the basis for sending Jews to labor camps. At first many volunteered for the camps, assuming that persons engaged in physical work would receive the food they needed and a minimum standard of living conditions. When the true—and dreadful—situation in the camps became known, volunteering came to an abrupt end and forced recruitment took its place. By early 1941 some two hundred Jewish labor camps were in operation, with tens of thousands of Jews forced to work there. The work consisted of flood control, road construction, and construction of defense works and buildings, as well as agriculture. Because of the intolerable working conditions, in terms of food, housing, sanitary facilities, and medical care, the workers in the camps were sapped of their strength, epidemics broke out, and a high mortality rate was recorded.

Olkusz, a town in southern Poland, 19 miles (30 km) east of Sosnowiec. On July 31, 1940, the Germans conducted a mass execution of Jews in the town square. In the photograph, German soldiers humiliate a Jew who is forced to stand by the rows of bodies wearing his *tallit* (prayer shawl) and *tefillin* (phylacteries). The phylactery on his head has been split open and desecrated.

Ghettoization. Unlike the Judenräte, which were established under a central directive and on short notice, the process of confining the Jews to ghettos (*see* GHETTO) was drawn out, depending largely on decisions taken by authorities on the spot. Sealed-off (closed) ghettos with an internal Jewish government of sorts, an economic life, and essential services were introduced only in eastern Europe, the Baltic states, and the Soviet Union. The first ghetto was established in October 1939, in PIOTRKÓW TRYBUNALSKI, but for most of the time it was an open ghetto. The first large ghetto, in Łódź, was sealed off in May 1940. In the Generalgouvernement the ghettos were set up in 1940 and 1941 (the Warsaw ghetto in November 1940, Lublin and Kraków in March 1941), and in Zagłębie, as late as 1942 and 1943, that is, when the mass extermination was already in full swing. In the Soviet territories occupied in 1941, the ghettos were generally set up soon after the occupation.

The process of sealing the ghetto off from its environment and guarding it also differed from one place to another. The Łódź ghetto was hermetically sealed (by fences and barbed wire), was completely cut off from the outside, and had its own currency, which was totally worthless outside the ghetto. The Warsaw ghetto was enclosed by a wall, but it was possible (though dangerous) to get in and out, especially for the smuggling of food and manufactured goods. In many cases, however, especially in small places, the ghetto was open, with only a sign to indicate its boundaries; or the Jews were permitted to leave it at certain hours of the day in order to buy food. The sites selected for the ghettos were usually the most crowded and neglected sections in the cities. In some cities, such as Radom and Tomaszów Mazowiecki, the ghetto consisted of two or three separate parts. The Warsaw ghetto was surrounded by a wall 11 miles (18 km) long; other ghettos had wooden or barbed-wire fences.

The way the ghetto was guarded also differed from place to place. German, Polish, and Jewish policemen were posted at the Warsaw ghetto gates. In Łódź, German police guarded the ghetto from the outside, and Jewish policemen patrolled inside the fence. The ghetto guard in small places consisted of one German policeman or several local policemen, who were all that kept the ghetto apart from the outside.

Attempts to leave some closed ghettos were punishable by death. In Łódź any person in-

Street scene in the Lublin ghetto, as photographed by Germans from their car.

side the ghetto approaching the fence and suspected of trying to cross to the "Aryan" side was shot; in Warsaw, as of the autumn of 1941, Jews (including women and children) found in the Polish part of the city were executed. On October 15, 1941, Frank ordered that all persons leaving the ghetto without permission were to be shot. The governor of the Radom district, Ernst Kundt, in November 1941 also introduced the death penalty for Jews who left the ghetto without permission, as well as for Poles who gave them shelter.

The Germans used various pretexts to explain the need for the establishment of the ghettos: they were needed to keep the Jews away from black-market activities and prevent them from spreading defeatist rumors among the population; the Jews were the bearers of contagious diseases and the source of epidemics; and so on. Of these pretexts, it was only the fear of contagious diseases and epidemics that the Germans took seriously and against which they took certain measures. The real reason for creating the ghettos was to implement a radical method of isolating the Jews, separating the Jewish communities from one another, and keeping the Jews apart from the rest of the population. Disease and epidemics were undoubtedly a genuine threat, considering the conditions in which the Jews had to live. But the overcrowding, starvation, general shortages, and absence of proper sanitary facilities in the neglected sections where the ghettos were put up could only serve to increase the risk of epidemics, and it was unlikely that their further spread would be avoided by quarantining the Jews.

The ghettos were primarily a further stage in the dynamics of the anti-Jewish policy, which was steadily escalating from bad to worse. The first ghettos served as a model, a radical new step that the German authorities in various places wanted to adopt. The Łódź ghetto was originally intended as a provisional measure for the concentration of Jews, and was to be evacuated after a few months, but in fact it remained in existence for longer than any other ghetto in Poland. Moreover, the way it was established and structured served as a model for subsequent ghettos. Until the advent of the "FINAL SOLUTION"

Jewish women, wearing the Star of David, from Włocławek, a city in Poland on the Vistula River, 87 miles (140 km) northwest of Warsaw. The city had a Jewish population of about 13,500 when the German army occupied it on September 14, 1939. The ghetto was liquidated on April 27, 1942.

—the physical destruction of all the Jews and persons defined as Jews under the Nazi racist principles—Jews were imprisoned in ghettos. During that process, Jewish rural and small urban communities were liquidated and their residents moved elsewhere.

Conditions in the ghettos, and the situation of their inhabitants, were largely determined by the degree to which the ghettos were segregated and sealed off, and by the size of their population. The worst off were the two most populated ghettos, Warsaw and Łódź, which in 1940 and 1941 had 600,000 Jews imprisoned in them. Joseph GOEBBELS in his diary called the ghettos *Todeskisten* ("death boxes"). At its highest point, the number of Warsaw ghetto inhabitants who were employed did not exceed 60,000. Those who were employed worked in industrial plants, workshops, and home industries. The pittance they were paid was not enough to cover minimum food costs and did not spare them from hunger, but it helped keep the recipients alive, considering the prevailing intolerable conditions.

The ghetto population was divided into three strata. At the top was a small group, consisting of no more than 3 percent to 5 percent of the population, who either conducted enterprises in the ghetto, such as the smuggling of food, or had managed to hold on to all or part of their prewar assets. These people did not go hungry. Each of the other two strata contained about half of the remaining ghetto inhabitants. One of these groups, although suffering from hunger, was able to exist for the time being. The other group, in the lowest stratum, was starving, lacking even the minimum to stay alive; those in it were in the throes of death. This situation was not static; it was a process of deterioration, with thousands of persons belonging to the lowest level dying every month, and thousands of others becoming reduced to that level. Among the tens of thousands whose suffering was the worst, and for whom there was no hope, were people who had been hired workers, or had belonged to the intelligentsia and had drawn a monthly salary, who had no property, and no qualifications that were useful in the ghetto. In the Łódź ghetto, during the last eighteen months of its existence, 90 percent of its inhabitants had jobs, but their work in German plants did not stave off starvation. The pay they received and the food rations supplied to the ghetto (in quantity and quality) were not enough to satisfy even the barest needs. According to a Polish source, in 1941 the official daily food rations (distributed on the basis of ration cards) were allocated on the basis of the following ethnic division: Germans were allotted 2,613 calories; Poles, 669; and Jews, 184. In the Warsaw ghetto, 80 percent of the food consumed was smuggled in.

In some of the small towns the mortality rate was extremely high, owing to the ghetto's complete isolation and the resultant food shortage. But in the rest of the small places, where the Jews were not completely cut off from their environment, they were able to work and trade with their non-Jewish neighbors. Outbreaks of contagious diseases and epidemics also caused the death of many of the starving and exhausted inhabitants, or speeded it up. In Warsaw the killer disease was typhus, and in Łódź it was tuberculosis. In these two large ghettos a total of 54,616 deaths were recorded in 1941—43,238 in Warsaw and 11,378 in Łódź—a mortality rate of 90 per 1,000 and 76 per 1,000, respectively. For the following year, 1942, the rate for Warsaw was 140 per 1,000 and for Łódź 160 per 1,000. This raises the question of whether the German authorities intended to destroy the Jewish population within a given period of time and achieve the biological liquidation of the Jews by means of the ghettos. Some researchers have voiced the view that the ghettos served the Germans as a means of destroying Jews in a "bloodless extermination," without having to kill them in cold blood. The available German data do not make it possible to give a definitive answer to that question.

A memorandum drawn up by Erhard Wetzel and Gerhard Hecht, two experts in the Nazi party's Racial Policies Office (Rassenpolitisches Amt), in November 1939, contains a proposal to intensify the existing discord between Poles and Jews and turn it into a policy, without relating it to the physical destruction of the Jews. In March 1940, Frank, in discussing the Jews, said: "We have no interest in introducing [in the Generalgouvernement] racist legislation to benefit the Poles. It is not in our interest to put a stop to mixed marriages or sexual relations between Jews and Poles." Only in July of that year was the NUREMBERG LAWS' definition of the term "Jew" introduced in the Generalgouvernement. In August 1942, Frank declared: "Nothing much has to be said about the fact that we are starving 1,200,000 Jews to death; that is self-evident, and if the Jews do not die from hunger, anti-Jewish decrees will have to be speeded up, and let us hope that this is what will happen." By the time this was said, though, the "Final Solution" was already in full swing. Earlier, in November 1941, in a lecture at Berlin University, Frank still spoke about the qualified Jewish workers he had discovered in the Generalgouvernement, who could be useful for German industry; these Jews should be permitted to work, whereas for the rest, "appropriate arrangements should be made." On several occasions, Germans in senior positions even proposed that the food rations for working Jews be increased.

In Łódź the German officials and their superiors, including even Arthur GREISER, governor of the Warthegau (who in the early stage of the occupation had sought the rapid and complete expulsion of the Jews from Łódź), gradually became interested in the ghetto as a source of labor and goods, and did not want to hand the benefits they were deriving over to the SS. This makes it difficult to state that there was a consistent policy for liquidating the Jews by means of their ghettoization. The local German authorities were not at all troubled by the huge mortality rate among the Jews (especially among Jews who were not working for them), but there is no evidence of a full-fledged specific plan to bring about the physical disappearance of the Jews during the ghetto stage, that is, in 1940 and 1941. In any case, the definitive decisions on the fate of the Jews were made on the top level, in Berlin.

Internal Jewish Life. Most of those who had belonged to the leadership group in Polish Jewry on different levels—in the parliament, the municipal government, and Jewish communal life—left Poland during the fighting in September 1939, or in the first few months of the occupation. They included leaders of the political parties and the central Jewish organizations. The Jews who left believed that they were endangered by their past activities, since the Nazi regime would first of all seek out those who had given public expression to their anti-Nazi views. As a group, the Jews were well aware that the German Nazi regime was extremely anti-Jewish, but many sought to convince themselves that the Germans were a nation with a civilized Western tradition, and, moreover, a people who had exercised tolerance in their treatment of the Jews during their occupation of Poland in World War I. The first few months of the new occupation and the first encounter with the Germans in their new image soon disabused the Jews of their illusions. Still, it was impossible to foresee where Nazi policy on the Jews would lead. In a way, the Jews of Poland were better prepared for adversity than the Jewish communities in western Europe; for generations they had experienced material shortages and civil discrimination, and had developed an inner strength of resistance and a talent for circumventing anti-Jewish legislation.

Common to all the Jews of Poland, irrespective of their attitudes and political views, was the stubborn determination to survive (*iberlebn*), to see the war through. The term that has been handed down to describe this determination to survive physically is KIDDUSH HA-HAYYIM ("Sanctifying Life"). Few Jews expected that the Germans might win the war and that it was necessary to prepare for a situation in which they and their regime would predominate the world over. Such a possibility did not enter most minds, since the Jews would not believe that extreme evil in its Nazi incarnation could last for long. Perhaps they also realized that they had no chance of surviving under a prolonged Nazi regime, and therefore tried to ignore it or repress the very thought.

At the beginning of the occupation, Jewish political, social, and cultural organizational networks ceased to exist. Although no specific announcement to this effect was made, anything not expressly permitted had to be regarded as prohibited. The first effort to reorganize was made in the sphere of mutual help and social welfare. In many cities and towns the Jews were called upon to take in refugees, to repair war damage, and to lend aid to the thousands of persons affected by the war. As early as October 1939, a self-help organization and a coordinating committee for welfare institutions were founded in Warsaw, and soon had branches in all parts of the Generalgouvernement. As related by the historian Emanuel RINGELBLUM, the chronicler of the Warsaw ghetto and a leader of the Jewish population's underground movement in Warsaw, social workers had not joined the exodus of public figures, and most of the leaders of the American Jewish JOINT DISTRIBUTION COMMITTEE (known as the Joint) had also stayed behind. Since the Joint enjoyed a certain immunity as an American organization, it had relatively large sums at its disposal. Its officials began to set up aid centers, beginning with soup kitchens where a bowl of soup and a piece of bread were dispensed to the hungry. Welfare institutions for children and for the sick were also reactivated, and an aid network for refugees established. Special soup kitchens for children also kept them busy with games and some instruction. The aid center in Warsaw recruited many unemployed members of the intelligentsia to its ranks of employees. Heading the center during the war were Yitzhak GITTERMAN, David Guzik, Leon Neustadt, David Bornstein, and Emanuel Ringelblum, who had had experience in social work and were deeply rooted in the life of Polish Jewry.

Emissaries of the self-help organization sponsored by the Joint went out from Warsaw to the provincial cities, and representatives of remote Jewish communities came to Warsaw to seek help. In the first few months the self-help effort was of considerable importance, but it declined rapidly when its funds ran out. The funds received up to late 1941—as long as the United States was neutral and money from American sources could be transmitted legally—did not even cover minimum welfare needs. Until the spring of 1940 the aid provided by the Żydowskie Towarzystwo Opieki Społecznej (Jewish Mutual Aid Society; ŻTOS, later the Żydowska Samopomoc Społeczna, or ŻSS) was relatively substantial, and many who were going hungry benefited from it. However, as of that summer, its resources and the financial means at its disposal declined. The financial assistance rendered by the Joint in 1940 was higher than in the following year, 1941—the year of distress, hunger, and mass starvation. The Joint leaders, however, did not give up in the face of growing difficulties, and appealed to Jews in the ghettos who had money hidden away to lend some of it to ŻTOS, with the assurance that the loan would be repaid when the war was over. This method, risky for both the parties involved, provided additional financial resources for the self-help organization, but it could not meet the growing needs. Ringelblum expressed the dilemma facing ŻTOS, writing in May 1942: "What to do? To give a spoonful to everybody, in which case nobody will stay alive, or to hand it out in generous portions—in which case only a few could benefit?"

ŻTOS operated on two levels. It functioned first on the legal and officially recognized level—and, as of the summer of 1940, as a Jewish component of a welfare organization sponsored by the Generalgouvernement administration, the Naczelna Rada Opiekuńcza (Main Welfare Council), a body in which Poles took part, and eventually also Ukrainians. On the second, clandestine, level ŻTOS worked with the self-help organization and the Joint-supported soup kitchens, which also served as meeting places of underground political parties. In addition, ŻTOS provided financial assistance to the underground Warsaw ghetto archive and to operations organized by the underground, and it officially recognized the fighting organizations.

Illegal cultural activities in the ghettos of Poland took many forms. In Warsaw, Kraków, and elsewhere the authorities did not permit schools for Jewish children to be kept open. Only in the 1941–1942 school year were elementary-school classes permitted to open in the Warsaw ghetto. In place of legal schools a network of secret study cells operated on the elementary and secondary level; Warsaw also had clandestine secondary schools. Lectures on forbidden subjects were given in the ghettos, orchestras and choirs played and sang, and theaters performed plays from the classical Jewish repertoire and sketches dealing with current life. Writers and poets in Warsaw, Łódź, Vilna, and Kraków created new works—works that reflected the horror they were witnessing. In Warsaw, on Ringelblum's initiative, the ONEG SHABBAT Archive was founded to collect documentary material and accounts of life in the Warsaw ghetto and other ghettos. An archive on similar lines was created in the Białystok ghetto, by the underground Dror–He-Haluts movement. Many DIARIES were kept in the ghettos; the diarists included writers, public figures, Jews who had never before tried their hand at writing, and even children, who confided their experiences and anxieties, in their childish handwriting, to exercise books. Only some of the diaries, written in different languages and styles, have been preserved, but what has remained constitutes highly impressive original material, documenting the life of the Jews in the ghettos.

The Jews also refused to abide by the antireligious decrees issued by the occupiers. In the Warsaw ghetto public prayer services were prohibited, and in Kraków the synagogues were closed down when the ghetto was established. Nevertheless, the Jews continued to pray in prayer quorums (*minyanim*; the minimum of ten male adults required for a prayer service), and to observe the dietary laws. The formulators of Jewish law were not, however, generally able to cope with the extraordinary situation posed by the Holocaust.

Leadership functions were carried out, on different levels, by underground political organizations. One of these, comprising representatives of underground political parties, served the board of the Joint in Warsaw as an advisory council. Political party representatives met together and were active in two spheres, those of political information and mutual help. Party activists maintained contact by means of postal services, which, with certain limitations, functioned in the ghettos, and they even set up controlled contact with foreign countries. The underground political parties published clandestine newspapers, to take the place of the newspapers and other media that had existed previously. In Warsaw, the underground papers openly published the views of the different political movements that were active in the underground. Nor did they hesitate to criticize the policy of the Judenräte and to point out flaws and blemishes in public life and individual behavior among the ghetto population. Some of the political parties, including the BUND, managed to smuggle copies of their newspapers into other ghettos.

More intensive and more important were the activities carried on by the youth movements and the younger age groups of the political parties. Among them, the Zionist pioneering youth movement, in its various forms, distinguished itself by its efforts to train and educate the young generation for the challenges that lay ahead for them when the war was over.

Initially, underground activities did not lead to loss of life or to confrontation with the Nazi authorities; the Germans apparently took little interest in the political underground functioning among the Jews. Only when they discovered that the Jews were maintaining contact with the Poles did the Nazis become furious. The Germans were not interested in what the Jews were thinking and in their political divisions; from statements made by top Nazis in the occupation administration, the Nazis evidently did not imagine that Jews were capable of forming an underground that could disturb the status quo and the Jews' passive acceptance of it, or that they could inflict damage which would harm the occupation authorities. In any case, during the initial stage the Nazi authorities' murder drives were directed at persons who violated Nazi decrees and the economic order that had been set up. Nazi attacks on the underground, except for a few sporadic incidents, were not as yet too severe and injurious.

Jews and Poles. At this stage, contacts between the Jewish resistance and the main Polish underground were loose and noncommittal. The central organs of the Polish underground—the DELEGATURA, the political arm of the Polish government-in-exile on Polish soil; and the ARMIA KRAJOWA, the underground's main military arm—had no contact with the Jews and were not active among them. Jewish citizens of Poland were not asked to participate in any way whatsoever in the Polish underground's institutions, and the situation of the Jews and their distress did not move them to any action in behalf of the Jews, even though the Polish underground was a widespread movement active in many fields all over the country and had at its disposal considerable human and financial resources. Individual Poles, in some cases, did maintain contact with their Jewish friends and helped them. Some Polish groups that had had contacts with Jewish organizations in the past, such as a Catholic scouting group of activists, continued to meet with their Jewish associates and to help them in the wartime and underground conditions. Some members of the Polish nobility who administered the Supreme Welfare Committee manifested understanding for the Jews and sympathy for their plight and their requirements.

Until the stage of total physical extermination, most of the Poles were indifferent to the fate of the Jews. This was undoubtedly due in part to the war conditions, the suffering, and the terror, which were also the lot of the Poles. But it is also true, as stated by many writers and scholars at the time (including Ringelblum), that the spirit of antisemitism, which affected the masses of the Polish population in the 1930s and was widespread in the country, also had an impact on the behavior of the Polish population during the occupation. Yet the attitude of the Poles was not uniform. Besides those who were apathetic, some were eager to take over Jewish property and businesses. But there were also instances when former antisemites changed their attitude toward the suffering Jews and supported them.

Some of the anti-Jewish sentiments held by Poles were based on the charge that the Jews had joyfully welcomed the Soviet forces when they entered the eastern parts of Poland; this was proof that the Jews were not loyal to Poland and to Poles in general. The claim had some foundation; but for the Poles, there was no difference between the Germans and the Soviets, who had divided their country among them; both were enemy conquerors. The Jews, on the other hand, distinguished between the Nazis—who persecuted them because they were Jews—and the Soviets, under whose occupation they would suffer like everybody else, but would not be discriminated against on account of being Jewish. Some historians do ascribe Polish hostility toward the Jews to the warm and joyful welcome the latter accorded the Soviet army when it entered eastern Poland, but the truth is that at most, this reinforced the existing hatred of Jews, long a widespread phenomenon among the Polish people.

Preparations for the "Final Solution." In late 1939 and early 1940, when Jewish emigration from Nazi-held territory was still permitted, an attempt was made to concentrate Jews in one area, the Lublin Reservation (*see* NISKO AND LUBLIN PLAN). In the summer of 1940 the German Foreign Office and the Gestapo produced the MADAGASCAR PLAN, which Hitler himself was ready to consider. Under this plan, the Jews of Europe were to be deported to that distant island in the Indian Ocean, to be held there under German control. But any prospects for implementing the plan were precluded by the situation in the war zones and on the high seas. According to some sources, the Germans also considered a plan to deport the Jews into the remote expanses of the Soviet Union, but this plan too had to be abandoned, when the German advance was brought to a halt within the confines of European Russia. An examination of the measures taken by the Nazis in the occupied countries also fails to reveal the existence of a clear-cut resolve on their part in the first years to undertake the physical destruction of the Jews. There were even German officials, here and there, who tried to improve the food rations and general living conditions of the Jews in the ghettos, especially of those Jews who were working for the Germans.

It is clear, though, that for the Nazi authorities the anti-Jewish measures and regulations that they were implementing at the time—the separation of the Jews from the general population, the elimination of Jews from economic life, the drafting of Jews for forced labor, and their imprisonment in ghettos—did not represent the limit of their planned actions against the Jews and their ultimate goal. Even the ghettos, where the Jews were almost completely isolated and forced to live under intolerable conditions and strict control, represented no more than an intermediate station. More radical measures were being considered that, when implemented, could only mean the total elimination of the Jews. Generalgouverneur Frank (whose statements on the fate in store for the Jews were always inspired by the opinions prevailing among the top officials in Berlin and the orders Hitler issued) remarked at a meeting of the Generalgouvernement in December 1941: "To be quite honest, the Jews have to be disposed of, one way or another." He made it clear that the plans for such final disposition had been worked out in Berlin and confided to him there. There can be no doubt that the "Final Solution" that was carried out in Poland was the result of a decision that originated in Berlin.

With regard to the views of the local German authorities in Poland and the actions taken by them, it was the Nazi doctors who warned of dangers emanating from the existing conditions of the Jews as a breeding ground for diseases, and it was they who at times came up with the most radical recommendations for action against the Jews. On the other hand, the German officials who were responsible for production and economic affairs gradually came to appreciate the contribution the Jews were making with their work, and wanted to have that contribution kept up and even enlarged. Frank's statement of August 1942—that the fate of the Jews was sealed—was made when the "Final Solution" was already in full swing. But only a month earlier, when the deportations were launched (in the course of which 90 percent of the Warsaw ghetto Jews were deported to their death), the governor of the Warsaw district, Ludwig FISCHER, was still saying that "a considerable number of Jews are employed . . . and this work force must

SS roundup of Polish Jews in 1942.

certainly be given better food."

Extermination Operations. The attack on the Soviet Union in June 1941 with the accompanying anti-Bolshevik (or "Judeo-Bolshevik") campaign was for Hitler the right moment to intensify the policy against the Jews, by deploying the Einsatzgruppen for their mass murder by shooting. In the very first stage of this intensified policy hundreds of thousands of Jews were killed by the Einsatzgruppen. This marked the beginning of the campaign that had as its aim the destruction of European Jewry; from the Russian front, that campaign was extended to Poland and the other German-occupied areas of Europe. The German authorities in each country took part in the campaign, under a special task force responsible for planning and execution. At the WANNSEE CONFERENCE (January 20, 1942), the Generalgouvernement state secretary, Dr. Josef Bühler, requested that the implementation of the "Final Solution" begin in the Generalgouvernement.

On December 7, 1941, the first camp in which gas was used for killing was put in operation, at CHEŁMNO, northwest of Łódź, in a Polish area that had been incorporated into the Reich. The first victims of that camp were Jews from the small towns of Dąbie, Sompolno, and Koło, killed on December 8. On December 15 the first Jews were deported from the Łódź ghetto to Chełmo, marking the beginning of a process that was maintained, with intervals, until May 15, 1942. In the course of this phase of deportations, a total of 55,000 Jews were taken to Chełmno, in sixty-six transports. The figure included 10,500 Jews who had been brought to Łódź from Germany, Austria, and the Protectorate of Bohemia and Moravia. In October and November 1941, preparations began for the murder of the Jews in the Generalgouvernement, including the Jews of Lvov and Eastern Galicia—a total Jewish population of 2 million. Responsible for this operation, later named AKTION REINHARD, was Odilo GLOBOCNIK, *Höherer SS- und Polizeiführer* (Higher SS and Police Leader) in the Lublin district, a confidant of Heinrich Himmler and one of the most brutal SS officers. A total of 450 men were assigned to Globocnik, of whom 92 had previously taken part in the EUTHANASIA PROGRAM and were regarded as experts in killing by gassing.

In the first half of 1942, three more extermination camps were established as part of Aktion Reinhard: BEŁŻEC, SOBIBÓR, and TREBLINKA. The Jews of Eastern and Western Galicia were taken to Bełżec, the Jews of the Lublin district to Sobibór, and the Jews of the Warsaw and Radom districts and the Białystok district, for the most part, to Treblinka, which was 50 miles (80 km) from Warsaw. Bełżec was the first of these extermination camps and was put into operation on March 17, 1942. According to a report submitted by SS-Brigadeführer Fritz KATZMANN, Higher SS and Police Leader in the Lvov district, by November 10, 1942, about 50 percent of the Jews of that district, a total of 252,989 persons, had been deported. In March 1942, 15,000 Jews from Lvov were deported, followed by another 50,000 Jews from that district in the second large-scale *Aktion* to take place there, in August 1942. During March and April 1942, Jews from a number of towns and cities in Galicia were deported, from such places as STANISŁAWÓW, DROGOBYCH, and KOLOMYIA. The second wave included tens of thousands of Jews from PRZEMYŚL, TERNOPOL, and elsewhere. Between mid-March and mid-April, the Jews of Lublin were deported and that ancient Jewish community was liquidated. Some 2,500 to 3,000 persons were murdered on the spot, 30,000 were deported, mostly to Bełżec, and 4,000 were left in the *Restgetto* (residual ghetto), situated in the suburb of Majdan-Tatarski. In an *Aktion* against the Radom Jewish community on August 16, 18,000 Jews were deported from there.

In Kraków the Jews were first expelled to other places, following a complaint by Hans Frank that Jews were still living and could still be encountered in a city serving as the Generalgouvernement's capital and housing many German officials. Accordingly, in May 1942, the mayor of Kraków announced that only 15,000 Jews, whose presence was essential for the economy, would be permitted to stay there, and that the rest, some 40,000 Jews, would have to get out of the city within the following three months. During May and June of 1942 an *Aktion* took place in Kraków, in the course of which 6,000 Jews were dispatched to Bełżec. In a second *Aktion*, in October, another 7,000 Kraków Jews were sent to Bełżec, and 600 were murdered on the spot. In the fall of 1942 a number of *Aktionen* and deportations took place in the Białystok district, and the first deportation from the city of Białystok was carried out in February 1943. The largest and most dreadful deportation to take place on the soil of occupied Poland was that from the Warsaw ghetto, which began on July 22, 1942, and lasted until mid-September, an operation that cost the lives of 300,000 persons, with most of the victims sent to Treblinka.

The Aktion Reinhard task force planned the *Aktionen*, organized the roundup of Jews in the streets and the deportations (in which it used SS and police forces, Ukrainian and Latvian auxiliaries, and Jewish police), and administered the extermination camps. In addition, it robbed Jewish property and, at a later stage, employed some of the Jews in the SS labor camps of the Lublin district, in workshops equipped with machinery and work tools that had been the property of the victims.

The *Aktionen* were conducted in a more or less uniform pattern. They came as a surprise, and various forms of deception and camouflage were employed to mislead the prospective victims. In the large ghettos, where the *Aktionen* were carried out in stages, the story used was that the persons being expelled were "unproductive elements," whereas the Jews who had an occupation and were working would remain untouched. The deportees were not informed of their destination, but were told only that they were being taken to a new place where jobs and a decent living were awaiting them. On July 19, 1942, Himmler issued an order according to which the expulsion of the Jews from the Generalgouvernement was to be completed by December 31, 1942. By that date no more Jews were to be left there, except for those who were being held in *Sammellager* (assembly camps) in Warsaw, Kraków, CZĘSTOCHOWA, Radom, and Lublin. "These measures," stated the decree, "in the spirit of the 'New Order of Europe' [*Neuordnung Europas*], are needed to ensure the ethnic separation of races and nations from one another, and for the safeguarding of the security and purity of the German Reich and the general area of German influence, and must lead to the complete purification [*totale Bereinigung*] of that area."

In the towns and cities of Zagłębie the fortunes of the Jews reflected the form of administration introduced in that area, which was similar to that of the Reich. The Jews here were subject to the operations of ORGANISATION SCHMELT. From late 1940, SS-Oberführer Albrecht Schmelt was in charge of the exploitation of the Jewish labor force on behalf of the SS. As chief of the organization that bore his name, Schmelt presided over a network of labor camps in Upper and Lower Silesia and the Sudetenland, in which tens of thousands of Jews were working. Organisation Schmelt also had at its disposal factories that had been put up in the cities and ghettos, in which Jews were working for the German war effort. Conditions in these camps and factories were very harsh, and the pay received by the Jews did not cover their minimum needs, but working for the organization protected the Jews for a relatively long time from deportation. In May 1942 the extermination of the Jews of Zagłębie was launched; the method used by the "Schmelt men" was to purge the "unproductive elements" and deport them. At first this new drive affected only small localities, but by August 1942 it was greatly expanded. This was a turning point for the Jews of Zagłębie; a general *Selektion* was made among the Jews of BĘDZIN, SOSNOWIEC, and Dąbrowa Gornicza, and 11,000 of them were deported to the extermination camps. After this, most of the remaining Jews worked for Organisation Schmelt. The deportations were resumed in early 1943, and thereafter the Zagłębie Jewish communities were gradually liquidated and the Jews deported to AUSCHWITZ. In August 1943 the last mass deportation took place. The few survivors who were left were also eventually sent to Auschwitz, the liquidation coming to an end by January 1944.

From April to September 1942 the Łódź ghetto was relatively quiet. This was the period when the ghettos in the Warthegau were being emptied of their Jews and liquidated, and some people from those ghettos, who were fit to work, were moved to the Łódź ghetto. In September 1942 the so-called Sperre Aktion was carried out in Łódź, which in its brutality and severity exceeded anything that had been experienced in other ghettos. The target figure for the deportation was 20,000, to consist of children under ten and elderly people over sixty-five. Babies were taken out of their mothers' arms, and when the *Aktion* was over, 16,000 persons had been deported. After "Sperre," the Łódź ghetto became a labor camp in which the entire population worked for the Germans. The German authorities in Łódź, and in the entire Warthegau, who initially had set their sights on a swift liquidation of the ghetto, were now deriving benefit from it. Not only were they in no hurry to evacuate or destroy it, but they even resisted attempts by the SS to absorb the Łódź ghetto into its concentration camp system. As a result the Łódź ghetto, which originally had been one of the first designated for liquidation, remained in existence longer than any other ghetto in eastern Europe.

The fate of the Łódź ghetto was sealed when the war front drew near, and between June and late August of 1944 it was gradually evacuated. Its inhabitants were moved to the SKARŻYSKO-KAMIENNA camp and to Auschwitz, and in the end small groups of skilled workers were transferred to Germany. Several hundred Jews stayed in the Łódź ghetto and were there when the city was liberated in January 1945. When its liquidation was launched, it had a population of 76,000, and some people believe that these Jews could have been saved if the Soviet army, in August 1944, had not halted its attack on the Vistula line. However, the validity of this theory is doubtful, since the Germans had demonstrated that they were quite capable of murdering tens of thousands of Jews on the spot, as they had done in the Lublin camps in November 1943, or of driving out Jews in similar numbers at a few days' notice, as they were to do in the evacuation of the Auschwitz complex of camps during January 1945.

Throughout 1943 the liquidation of ghettos or parts of them in the Generalgouvernement continued, and by the beginning of 1944 none of the ghettos were left. Under a special order issued by Frank on June 3, 1943, the Jews and Jewish affairs were handed over to the Sicherheitspolizei (Security Police), putting an end to the friction between the civil administration on the one hand and SS and police on the other over the control of the Jewish sector. By issuing this order, Frank acknowledged that now that the "Final Solution" was being executed, the SS and police were the sole authority for Jewish affairs. The only differences that still existed among the German authorities concerned the disposal of Jewish property—that is, which authority had the right to claim ownership of the possessions stolen from the Jews or left behind by them.

Appeals against the removal of the Jews, and sometimes outright resistance, came from other quarters. German factory owners, for one, were not happy about being deprived of the Jews who were working for them and whom they were shamelessly exploiting. They objected as best they could, but not much attention was paid to these objections. Himmler cleverly managed to keep the complainants quiet by pointing out the enormous profits they had already accumulated by this time through their exploitation of the Jews. Another sector, which could not be disposed of so easily, was the Wehrmacht, various installations of which benefited from the work that Jews were doing for them, mainly the manufacture of items of equipment required by the military. The complaint lodged by the quartermaster's branch was that the Jews working in war-essential factories were being removed without prior notice, whereas the Poles who were supposed to take the Jews' place were being transferred to the Reich for forced labor. In September 1942 Gen. Kurt Freiherr von Gienanth, the Wehrmacht commander in the Generalgouvernement, lodged a sharp complaint in a memorandum on this issue that he submitted to the High Command. By this act, von Gienanth challenged Himmler and his men in the Generalgouvernement, and he was soon relieved of his post.

That same month, however, the subject of Jewish manpower came up at a meeting held in Hitler's headquarters. On that occasion, at which the gravity of the manpower problem was stressed, Hitler was inclined to permit Jewish manpower to be retained in the Generalgouvernement on a temporary basis. Himmler, who could force his will on Field Marshal Wilhelm KEITEL and had easily disposed of General von Gienanth, could not ignore Hitler's opinion, especially since the shortage of manpower led to pressure from various sides; even the local SS chiefs in the Generalgouvernement requested that the Jews engaged in manufacturing work not be deported. The result was that in late 1942 and early 1943 the SS heads were forced to desist from the killing of Jews regarded as essential or fit for work. The condition was, however, that the Jewish workers had to be held in SS-supervised camps and that their wages would go to the SS. It was also laid down, as Himmler stressed more than once, that this was a temporary arrangement and that these Jews too would have to be eliminated in the near future.

A number of camps now came into existence in which Jews were put to work —PONIATOWA and TRAWNIKI in the Lublin district; camps in the cities of Radom and Częstochowa; PŁASZÓW, near Kraków; and the JANÓWSKA camp, near Lvov. In addition, in the concentration and extermination camps of Auschwitz-Birkenau and MAJDANEK, not all Jews were murdered on arrival; some of those who were fit for work, after going through a *Selektion* process, were assigned to concentration camps as manpower reinforcements. In early 1943, some 250,000 Jews of the Generalgouvernement were still being kept in camps (including 55,000 to 60,000 Jews in the Warsaw ghetto). The temporary exploitation of Jews as manpower, however, did not hold up the extermination process. In practice, once the Jews who were not needed as workers had been murdered, the remaining Jews, who were still working for the Germans, were also gradually liquidated—as a result of the brutal regime to which they were exposed, through physical exhaustion, by the murder of some who had become inessential, and by the disbandment of some camps and the transfer of the inmates of other camps (such as Płaszów) to Auschwitz.

On November 3, 1943, for security and other reasons, all camps for Jews in the Lublin district were liquidated, including Poniatowa and Trawniki, in Aktion "ERNTEFEST"; according to official records, 42,000 Jews were murdered on the spot. The massacres were halted only in November 1944, when the hopeless situation of the Germans on the front induced Himmler to order a stop to the murders in Birkenau, and to try to use the surviving Jews as a bargaining counter in negotiations with the West. At that point all he had left to bargain with were some tens of thousands of Jews.

It is sometimes argued that the Germans deliberately selected Poland as the place to set up the extermination camps and implement the "Final Solution" because the antisemitism that was rife among the Poles held out the promise of local support for such deeds. There is no firm foundation for this argument, and other factors appear to have determined the choice. Poland had a total occupation regime, with no autonomous Polish authorities permitted to function; the Germans did not have to ask the Poles or any Polish authorities whether they accepted the establishment of such camps on their soil, and in fact the Germans did not address any such question to the Poles. Moreover, the Poles, except for auxiliary forces of the Polish police, did not take an active part in carrying out the "Final Solution." It may also be assumed that the Nazis chose Poland as the site for most of the extermination camps because Poland, and the rest of eastern Europe, was where millions of Jews were concentrated, and because in this geographical region it was easier to keep atrocities secret from the knowledge of the general population than in the occupied countries western Europe.

Another question relates to the Poles' attitudes and reaction to the murder, on Polish territory, of millions of Jews who were Polish citizens. The Polish underground did not undertake any military action to help the Jews or to sabotage the Nazi deportation and murder operations; but neither did it take such action to liberate non-Jewish Poles from any of the many camps in which they were imprisoned. Tens of thousands of Jews escaped from the ghettos and sought refuge or some means of existence in Polish cities and villages; in Warsaw and its environs alone, twenty thousand Jews looked for a safe haven. For Poles, saving Jews was much more difficult and dangerous than in any of the occupied countries of western Europe. Tens of thousands of Jews also escaped to the forests. But because there was no organized Polish partisan movement, and because of the prevailing hostility toward Jews in the rural areas, most of the escapees could not save themselves.

Before October and November 1942, no clandestine public organization existed in Poland to extend help to the Jews. Whatever help was given was on a personal basis, resulted from individual political ties, or was in exchange for large sums of money. It was only in late 1942 and early 1943 that a provisional council for aid to the Jews was set up, which later became the permanent Council for Aid to Jews (Rada Pomocy Żydom, known as ZEGOTA). This organization was recognized by the Polish underground institutions and had their support. Several thousand Jews were taken care of and protected by Zegota, which was made up of Poles belonging to the Polish political Center and Left, some of whom were totally dedicated to their task. Thousands of Poles risked their lives to help Jews, and later they were officially recognized as "RIGHTEOUS AMONG THE NATIONS" by YAD VASHEM in Jerusalem. Many Poles paid with their lives for saving Jews; persons who helped Jews also jeopardized the members of their households, and in quite a few instances the Germans executed family members of Poles who had saved Jews or had tried to do so.

There also existed various gangs of Poles, some of them underworld types, who methodically, almost professionally, engaged in uncovering Jews who were in hiding or were posing as non-Jews, extorting money and possessions from them and handing them over to the Germans. No figures are available for the number of Jews victimized by these gangs (or by individual Polish Jew-hunters, the so-called *szmalcowniki*). But to judge by the memoirs of survivors who had been in hiding, hardly a single Jew in that situation avoided falling into the hands of extortionists at one point or another. Obviously, the existence of such blackmailers and informers deterred many Jews from trying to seek refuge among the Polish population—especially Jews whose appearance and pronunciation of Polish easily identified them as Jews, which was true of the greater part of Polish Jewry.

Yet another question still being discussed is that of awareness: to what extent did the Jews of Poland know what was in store for them, what were their reactions to events, and what resistance did they or could they offer? In the deportation stage, a considerable proportion of the victims had not heard the rumors about the wholesale murder that was going on in the camps, or, if such rumors had reached their ears, they did not trust them. Even those who had received reports on what was in store for the deportees and on the existence of the extermination camps found it hard to believe that there were more than local and sporadic killings, and that there existed an elaborate program for the total destruction of the Jews of Europe.

Resistance. Definite information on developments was undoubtedly an important element in motivating Jews to fight and offer resistance, but for many, such knowledge was not enough to persuade them to react. Experience in modern times has shown that people are unlikely to rise up in rebellion against a totalitarian regime of unrestrained terror, under which there is no chance of achieving any concrete result, such as the rescue of many lives, or even only a few. This kind of passive submission is not a peculiarly Jewish phenomenon. It was widespread in the Third Reich, in the Soviet Union under STALIN, and generally in concentration camps, as, for example, among the Soviet prisoners of war who were killed, perishing in large numbers in Germany and during slave labor there. In addition, pious Jews were traditionally reluctant to resort to the use of force, and this too was a factor contrib-

A Carmelite convent at Auschwitz was established in a building (left) that was used during the operation of the camp to store the Zyklon B gas. The building was given to the Carmelites by the mayor of Oświęcim (Auschwitz) on October 14, 1984. A broad spectrum of worldwide Jewish organizations have protested to the Vatican and to members of the Catholic hierarchy, declaring that the location of so Christian a symbol on a site that claimed the lives of some 1.5 million Jewish men, women, and children is a desecration of their memory. Negotations between the Jewish organizations and the Catholic hierarchy about the removal of the convent to another site have been going on for several years and have yet to be resolved.

uting to the limited extent of Jewish resistance to the Nazis.

The idea of offering armed resistance without counting the costs, and of being prepared to fall in a last hopeless battle against the murderous enemy, was conceived by the Jewish youth movements, and particularly by the pioneering Zionist movements. This idea was first conceived in Vilna, and from there it spread. In Warsaw it led to the emergence of a strong resistance organization, with the participation of young people of different shades of political opinion, whose activity culminated in the WARSAW GHETTO UPRISING. It also had its effect on resistance organizations in the ghettos of Białystok, Częstochowa, Kraków, and Sosnowiec, and on the struggle they decided to wage, varying in form according to local conditions. These Jewish groups suffered from a severe shortage of arms and training facilities. They received no aid from the Armia Krajowa except in Warsaw, where the ŻYDOWSKA ORGANIZACJA BOJOWA (Jewish Fighting Organization; ŻOB) gained the Armia Krajowa's recognition and received limited assistance from it. The Polish Left, which was under Communist control, was more inclined to help the Jewish resistance bodies, but in practice its ability to do so was disappointing and ineffectual.

The fighting organizations in the ghettos also had to engage in a difficult internal debate. Their assumption was that if the Jewish masses knew the truth, they would spontaneously flock to the fighting organizations and join their struggle when the test came and they were facing the final deportation. However, the appeals of these organizations, in a number of places, had to contend with the opposition of the Judenräte and other Jewish circles, which maintained that the only way to save the Jews, or at least some of them, was by engaging in productive work for the Germans. Most Judenrat chairmen believed that the Germans were deliberately starving the Jews and were ready to kill them, viewing them as an unnecessary burden; the only chance the Jews had to save themselves was to prove themselves useful to the Germans by making a contribution to their requirements. But the Jews who held this view, unlike the leaders of the youth movements and the fighting organizations, failed to detect the Nazis' real intent and to grasp the fact that the "Final Solution" was rooted in the fanatical Nazi ideology. Nevertheless, the view that German treatment of the Jews could be affected by demonstrating the Jews' usefulness to them was not entirely without foundation, and in the final stages of the war certain German circles tried to influence the course of events, with a view to ameliorating the critical shortage of manpower.

Except in the Warsaw ghetto, the majority of the Jews, despite their admiration for the fighters' heroism and their longing for revenge, were inclined in practice to share the views of the Judenräte, or, alternatively, felt that their overriding task was to keep the family cell intact as long as possible. The great achievement of the ghetto fighters lay less in the military effect of their struggle (although the Warsaw ghetto uprising and other ghetto revolts did have an impact that was far from negligible) than in the fact that under conditions of the most extreme oppression and the disintegration of all public and social structures, the Jews were able to produce forces that were motivated and guided by national and idealistic human imperatives.

Another way of fighting the Nazis, chosen by many Jews, was to join the PARTISANS or the FAMILY CAMPS IN THE FORESTS. This method of continuing the struggle was also adopted by forces that had fought in the ghettos and had survived the final struggle there, and by large groups of Jews living in communities and ghettos situated close to extensive tracts of forests and swamp areas in eastern Poland.

Even the Jews who sought to gain a foothold in the forests and from there to embark upon partisan fighting had to overcome special difficulties. The conduct of partisan warfare presupposes the existence of a supportive or sympathetic rural hinterland, an intelligence network, and a line of communication with a country that supports and aids the partisans. The Jews did not have such support, and generally had to contend with hostility on the part of the population. It was only at a comparatively late stage, from the middle of 1942—by which time most of the Jews had been uprooted and killed—that a partisan movement was consolidated in the eastern areas, under Soviet supervision, that accepted young Jews into its ranks. In the central part of Poland topographical conditions were not conducive to the creation of a large partisan movement, and the Armia Krajowa did not encourage the concentration of Jewish partisans in the forests.

Despite these difficulties, groups and camps of Jewish partisans also established themselves in central Poland. Large partisan forces were concentrated in the Vilna area and in Belorussia; it was in the Naliboki Forest in that area that Tuvia BIELSKI and his brothers had their large camp, consisting of more than one thousand persons. In the Naroch and Naliboki forests and in the Lublin area, Jewish partisan movements operated that included fighters who had escaped from the Vilna ghetto. The camp commanded by Yehiel Grynszpan maintained itself in the Parczew Forest, despite the difficulties with which it had to contend. Groups of Jews were concentrated in partisan units in the Białystok area, and partisan units commanded by Yeheskel ATLAS and Hirsch KAPLINSKI operated in the Lipiczany Forest near SLONIM. Small groups of partisans were also to be found in the Lublin and Kraków districts, and a unit bearing the name of Mordecai ANIELEWICZ, which eventually also included survivors of the Warsaw ghetto uprising in its ranks, was based in the Wyszków Forest. No data are available that would permit an estimate to be made of the number of Jews who penetrated into the forests and sought to join partisan forces but who never reached the stage in which they could join the fighting.

Another form of struggle waged by Jews was the uprisings in the camps. Only Jews carried out such revolts according to preconceived plans and succeeded in escaping from the camps in large groups. Revolts were made by SONDERKOMMANDO units—Jewish prisoners who were forced to work in auxiliary services in the extermination camps or in the killing installations at Treblinka, Sobibór, and Birkenau. In Treblinka and Sobibór some members of groups who after careful planning rebelled and broke out of the camps survived to tell the tale; the Birkenau rebels who operated in the vast Auschwitz camp complex were caught and all were shot to death.

No emissaries from the free world reached the Jews of Poland during the war, and only loose contact could be maintained with it. A few attempts were made to smuggle foreign citizenship papers (mainly South American passports granting citizenship) to Jews in the Nazi-occupied areas and thereby to help save them. Some of the bearers of such documents were killed in Auschwitz, and only a few were saved by this method. With some help from agents sent to Poland by the Slovakia-based PRACOVNÁ SKUPINA (Working Group) and the Hungary-based RELIEF AND RESCUE COMMITTEE OF BUDAPEST, some two thousand to three thousand Jews crossed the border into Slovakia, and many of them made their way to Hungary.

After the War. At the end of the war, 380,000 Jews of Poland had survived. By June 1945, 55,509 Jews had registered with the Jewish committees set up in the areas of liberated Poland. This figure included Jews who had returned from the concentration camps, who had been in hiding among Poles or had been saved by them, and who had served in partisan units in the forests of Poland, as well as some of the repatriates from the Soviet Union. Approximately 165,000 Jews were repatriated to Poland under the Polish-Soviet Repatriation Agreement of July 1945, and under a subsequent agreement a few years later, another 20,000 went back. Some Polish Jews survived in the camps in Germany and Austria, and about 13,000 Jews who had served in the Polish army that was formed in the Soviet Union and liberated Poland survived, in addition to a further 6,000 Jews who left the Soviet Union with the Anders army. The total figure of 380,000 survivors also includes Jews who managed to leave Poland at the beginning of the war for the West or for neighboring countries (excluding the Soviet Union), as well as several thousand Jews who served in the Soviet army. This figure encompasses all the survivors among the Jews who were living on the soil of Poland when the war broke out; it represents fewer than 12 percent of the Jews of Poland, including the 7 percent who were saved within the Soviet Union.

The maximum number of Jews registered in Poland in the postwar period was 240,489, in June 1946. Many of them had no intention of staying in Poland and planned to rehabilitate themselves in other countries, mainly in Palestine. Poland after the war was the scene of sharp confrontations concerning the regime that the Soviets had forced upon the country, and the rivalry between the opposing camps—some factions of which included a strong antisemitic element of the extreme radical right—assumed the dimensions of a civil war. The violent campaign against Jews reached its most serious point in a pogrom that took place in KIELCE in July 1946 in which 42 Jews were murdered, including pregnant women and children. For the Jews the Kielce pogrom was a traumatic event, and it greatly accelerated the departure of Jews from Poland to the West, as part of the BERIḤA movement; by the end of 1947, only 80,000 Jews were left in the country.

The Communist regime in the postwar People's Republic of Poland generally treated the Jews with restraint and understanding, and the Jewish population that was left in the country enjoyed a relatively large degree of freedom with regard to its social and cultural activities. Jewish institutions were created, among them the ŻYDOWSKI INSTYTUT HISTORYCZNY (*see* DOCUMENTATION CENTERS) and the Towarzystwo Społeczno Kulturalne Żydów (Social and Cultural Association of Jews).

A memorial to the Jews of Lublin who were killed by the Germans during the Holocaust. It is located in one of the main squares of the city. [Geoffrey Wigoder]

Despite the small number of Jews in Poland, tensions involving them continued to make themselves felt in the country. Many persons among the Polish population regarded the Jews as a prop of the new regime, and claimed that they were occupying numerous central positions in its administration and top echelons. Certain government circles that had previously stayed clear of antisemitic manifestations began blaming the Jews for the regime's wrongdoings, and in particular for the aberrations committed by the secret police. Only a small, yet visible, proportion of Jews were to be found in the top ranks of the administration, as against a large number of Jewish workers and members of the intelligentsia and the creative professions—scientists, academics, writers, and artists. Still, the predominant fact was that many of the Polish Jews were Communists or Communist sympathizers who had no intention of living as Jews; many of them had non-Jewish spouses and nearly all expected to be fully assimilated within the foreseeable future.

Between 1967 and 1969, however, a sharp anti-Jewish campaign shook the country, inspired by certain circles in the ruling Communist party. In that campaign the Jews were charged with loyalty to Zionism—a movement depicted as a subversive international agency that constituted a threat to Poland—and with being largely responsible for the strong mood of political opposition that was making itself felt in the country, especially among the young people. Denounced as a disloyal element, Jews were summarily dismissed from party membership and their places of work, and evicted from their apartments. The result was that most of the Jews then in Poland left the country, with only a few thousand choosing to stay.

Subsequently the small Jewish community remaining in Poland declined, in spite of its freedom to organize its social and cultural life and engage in artistic creativity. Beginning in the mid-1980s there has been a remarkable rise of interest in the past history of the Jews and of sympathy for them among the general population and in church circles. This new spirit addresses itself primarily to the past and to a moral stocktaking. The basic situation, however, is that in Poland, a country where Jews had been dwelling for a thousand years, only two Jews are left out of every thousand who lived there before the war broke out in 1939.

[*See also* Aid to Jews by Poles; Literature on the Holocaust: Poland; Museums and Memorial Institutes: Poland; Polnische Polizei; Rada Główna Opiekuńcza; Trials of War Criminals: Poland; Umwandererzentralstelle.]

BIBLIOGRAPHY

Dabrowska, D., and A. Wein, eds. *Poland*, vol. 1. In *Pinkas Hakehillot; Encyclopaedia of Jewish Communities*. Jerusalem, 1976. (In Hebrew.)

Dabrowska, D., A. Wein, and A. Weiss, eds. *Poland*, vol. 2. In *Pinkas Hakehillot; Encyclopaedia of Jewish Communities*. Jerusalem, 1980. (In Hebrew.)

Eisenbach, A. *Hitlerowska polityka eksterminacji: Żydów w latach 1939–1945 jako jeden z przejawów imperializmu niemieckiego*. Warsaw, 1953.

Frank, H. *Hans Frank's Diary*. Warsaw, 1961.

Friedman, P. *Roads to Extinction: Essays on the Holocaust*. New York, 1980.

Gutman, Y., and S. Krakowski. *Unequal Victims: Poles and Jews during World War Two*. New York, 1986.

Ringelblum, E. *Notes from the Warsaw Ghetto: The Journal of Emmanuel Ringelblum*. New York, 1958.

Trunk, I. *Judenrat: The Jewish Councils in Eastern Europe under Nazi Occupation*. New York, 1972.

Wein, A., and A. Weiss, eds. *Poland*, vol. 3. In *Pinkas Hakehillot; Encyclopaedia of Jewish Communities*. Jerusalem, 1984. (In Hebrew.)

ISRAEL GUTMAN

POLICE, GERMAN. *See* Gestapo; Kriminalpolizei; Ordnungspolizei.

POLICE IN OCCUPIED COUNTRIES. *See* French Police; Gendarmerie, Hungarian; Policiniai Batalionai; Polnische Polizei; Ukrainische Hilfspolizei. *See also entry on the Jewish ghetto police,* Jüdischer Ordnungsdienst.

POLICINIAI BATALIONAI (Lithuanian Police Battalions), paramilitary formation composed of Lithuanians who collaborated with the Germans. Shortly after the German occupation of LITHUANIA in the summer of 1941 a reorganization was launched of local Lithuanian units, made up of police, ex-soldiers and ex-officers, and nationalist elements of all sectors (among whom high school and university students predominated), who had been attacking the retreating Soviet forces from behind and had been brutally harassing and murdering Lithuanian Jews. That July, many of the units in Kovno and elsewhere were incorporated into a paramilitary organization, the Tauto Darbo Apsauga (National Labor Guard). In Vilna and other places the corresponding military organization was named the Lietuvia Savisaugos Dalys (Lithuanian Self-Defense).

At the end of 1941 these formations were absorbed into a new framework based on battalions, and were renamed Policiniai Batalionai. By August 1942, twenty such battalions were in existence, with a complement of 8,388 men, of whom 341 were officers, 1,772 noncommissioned officers, and the rest privates. The command of these battalions was, for the most part, in the hands of former officers and men of other ranks who had served in the army of independent Lithuania. On the higher level these officers had German liaison officers assigned to them, and on the top level the Lithuanian commanders were directly subordinated to the district SS and police leader (*SS- und Polizeiführer*) in Lithuania.

The battalions' police operations, especially those of Battalion 1 (later 13) and Battalion 2 (later 12), also included the mass murder of Jews in Lithuania, as well as in the adjacent territories of Poland and Belorussia. Several of the battalions' veterans were identified in postwar investigations and trials held in Lithuania, the United States, and elsewhere. Some of them were tried and found guilty of killing civilians and prisoners of war.

BIBLIOGRAPHY

Baranauskas, B., et al., eds. *Masines Zudynes Lietuvoje.* Vilna, 1965.

Hilberg, R. *The Destruction of the European Jews.* 3 vols. New York, 1985.

Zeimantas, V. *Teisingumas Reikalauja.* Vilna, 1986.

DOV LEVIN

POLISH COUNCIL FOR AID TO JEWS. *See* Zegota.

POLISH GOVERNMENT-IN-EXILE, government formed after POLAND was occupied in September 1939 by Germany and the Soviet Union. The cabinet was sworn in on October 1, 1939, by the new president, Władysław Raczkiewicz, with Gen. Władysław SIKORSKI as prime minister. After Sikorski's tragic death on July 4, 1943, his place was taken by Stanisław MIKOŁAJCZYK. The latter resigned on November 24, 1944, and Tomasz Arciszewski, of the Polska Partia Socjalistyczna (Polish Socialist Party), was appointed to his place on November 29.

The Polish government-in-exile was composed of representatives of political groups that before the war had been opposed to the policies of the Polish government. Centered first in Paris and then in Anger, in western France, it moved to London following the fall of France. In January 1940 a national council was formed as a substitute for a representative political body, its function being to advise the government-in-exile and express its views. The first chairman of the council, appointed in June 1941, was Ignacy Paderewski. After a reshuffling of the council in February 1942, Paderewski was replaced by Stanisław Grabski. The council consisted of thirty-one members, two of whom, Ignacy Isaac SCHWARZBART and Samuel Artur ZYGELBOJM, were its Jewish representatives.

The government-in-exile was recognized by all the Allied powers and, from July 1941 to April 1943, by the Soviet Union as well, until diplomatic relations were severed over the KATYN massacre. It also gained the recognition of most countries that were not taking part in the war. Determined to maintain the struggle for the independence, sovereignty, liberty, and territorial integrity of the Polish republic, it believed that a total victory over the Third Reich, to be achieved by alliance with the Western democracies, was a prerequisite for the achievement of these goals.

The Polish government-in-exile sought to form European alliances of states in the form of federations, but after July 1942, no other government-in-exile was prepared to negotiate such proposals with Poland. Moreover, in the spring of 1943, after the Soviets broke off diplomatic relations with it, the government-in-exile's major concern became the settlement of its differences with the Soviet Union. It was not, however, prepared to accept the formula agreed upon by Roosevelt, Churchill, and Stalin in Tehran, and in 1944 opposed conciliation with the Polish Committee of National Liberation (Polski Komitet Wyzwolenia) that had just been formed under Soviet auspices in Lublin. The government-in-exile invested great effort in the creation of land, air, and naval armed forces; it had 100,000 men serving in these forces by the end of 1942, and more than double that number by May 1945. The Polish air force distinguished itself in the Battle of Britain in 1940, and Polish land forces made significant contributions to the liberation of Italy, France, Belgium, and the Netherlands.

From the fall of 1939, the demand for the postwar punishment of Nazi criminals figured as an important item in Poland's war aims. When the first reports of the mass murder of Jews reached London, the government-in-exile, its president, and the national council issued a series of declarations. In June 1942 it submitted a memorandum to the Allied powers, dealing exclusively with the destruction of Polish Jewry and stating, in part, that the Jews in Poland "are experiencing the worst persecution they have suffered in their history; the criminals that are perpetrating these foul deeds will have to account for them, and this has to be a principle of supreme importance in the policy of the Allied powers."

On November 27, 1942, the national council was summoned to an extraordinary meeting in which the fate of the Jews under the Nazi occupation was the sole item on the agenda. On a motion by Zygelbojm, the council voted unanimously to ask the government-in-exile to demand that the Allied powers draw up, without delay, a retaliation plan against the Germans, "to force them to stop the mass murder of the civilian population and the planned destruction of the entire Jewish people." The government-in-exile issued a memorandum in this vein on December 10, 1942. On January 3, 1943, President Raczkiewicz made an appeal to Pope PIUS XII, asking him to denounce the German actions against the Jews.

Much too late, in April 1944, the Polish government-in-exile appointed a Council for the Rescue of the Jewish Population of Poland. Headed by Adam Ciolkosz, with national council member Dr. Emanuel Scherer of the BUND as its secretary, this council functioned until the summer of 1945.

[*See also* Armia Krajowa; Delegatura.]

BIBLIOGRAPHY

Avital, Z. "The Polish Government in Exile and the Jewish Question." *Wiener Library Bulletin* 28/1 (1975): 43–51.

Engle, D. *In the Shadow of Auschwitz: The Polish Government-in-Exile and the Jews, 1939–1942.* Chapel Hill, 1987.

Gutman, Y., and S. Krakowski. *Unequal Victims: Poles and Jews during World War II.* New York, 1986.

Kacewisz, G. V. *Great Britain, the Soviet Union, and the Polish Government in Exile (1939–1945).* The Hague, 1979.

Lewin, I. "Attempts at Rescuing European Jews with the Help of Polish Diplomatic Missions during World War II." *Polish Review* 22/4 (December 1977): 3–27; 24/1 (March 1979): 46–61; 27/1–2 (March–June 1982): 99–111.

Rozek, E. J. *Allied Diplomacy: A Pattern in Poland.* New York, 1958.

EUGENIUSZ DURACZYNSKI

POLISH HOME ARMY. *See* Armia Krajowa.

POLISH NATIONAL ARMED FORCES. *See* Narodowe Siły Zbrojne.

POLISH PEOPLE'S ARMY. *See* Gwardia Ludowa.

POLNISCHE POLIZEI, Polish police subordinate to the German occupation authorities in the GENERALGOUVERNEMENT; among the Polish population they were known as the Granatowa Policja (Blue Police) because of the color of their uniforms.

In the wake of Poland's surrender after the September 1939 campaign, the German occupation authorities called on the policemen of the Policja Państwowa (State Police) to report for continued service. Most reported for service in the police stations. After several weeks, the Polish police units were dispersed throughout the areas annexed to the Reich. Some policemen who were not considered worthy of serving on the force were arrested and others were transferred by the Germans to the Generalgouvernement area.

After the creation of the Generalgouvernement, the German authorities formed the Polnische Polizei there from policemen of the former Polish State Police. This force operated in the prewar police stations of the cities and subdistricts, but no general or regional headquarters was created; the individual headquarters were all subordinate to the respective local headquarters of the ORDNUNGSPOLIZEI (German regular police).

Polish police manpower rose from 8,700 in February 1940 to 11,000 in April 1941 and 12,000 in November 1942, reaching a peak of 16,000 in 1943. In October 1941 a school for Polish policemen was established in the town of Nowy Sącz, with the aim of strengthening the Polish police. The new recruits, and the policemen from the former Polish State Police, were issued revolvers and other guns and wore their prewar uniforms (except for the Polish insignia, which were removed).

The German authorities gave the Polish police the duty of dealing primarily with criminal activities, but they were also used widely in combating smuggling and in measures taken against the Jewish population. The Polish police patrolled the Generalgouvernement ghettos and searched for Jews who had escaped from the ghettos and camps and had sought refuge among the Polish population or in the forests. In carrying out these tasks, the Polish police demonstrated their complete devotion to the Nazi authorities, apart from the few policemen who gave assistance to the Jews.

The Polish police played a particularly important role in WARSAW, the center of the opposition movements in occupied Poland; 3,150 policemen were stationed there in June 1942, including 60 officers. The Polish police commanders in Warsaw were Marian Kozielewski (October 1939 to May 1941), Aleksander Reszczynski (May 1941 to March 1943), and Franciszek Przymusinski (March 1943 until the Warsaw Polish uprising in August 1944), all with the rank of lieutenant colonel.

The Polish police were used to guard the gates of the Warsaw ghetto, and a force of 400 policemen was designated to patrol the ghetto. In the suppression of the WARSAW GHETTO UPRISING, 367 Polish policemen were used within the German force under Gen. Jürgen STROOP. The Polish police also sought out Jews who had escaped from the ghetto to the "Aryan" side of the city, and assisted the Germans in seizing Poles on the streets of Warsaw for forced labor in Germany.

From 1942 the Polish police were employed in the struggle against the PARTISANS. Their losses in that year were eighty-four dead and ninety wounded. In June 1942 a special Polish police regiment, Regiment 202, was formed to fight against the partisans, initially against partisan units of Jews and former Soviet prisoners of war in the forests of the Kolbuszowa area. In late 1943 the regiment was transferred to combat partisans in the Ukraine, where it disintegrated and was destroyed in battle. All the streams of the Polish underground violently censured the behavior of the Polish police—for the scope of its collaboration with the German occupier, its practice of extortion, the moral degradation it demonstrated, and its large-scale participation in the persecution and massacres of the Jews. Several policemen were executed by the underground for collaborating with the Nazis, including the Warsaw police commander Reszczynski and the police officer Roman Swiecicki.

On July 27, 1944, after the liberation of the Lublin district, the Polski Komitet Wyzwolenia Narodowego (Polish Committee for National Liberation) issued an edict disbanding the Polish police and terminating its service, as a body that had served the Nazi occupier. In its place a new police force was created, the Milicja Obywatelska (Civil Militia).

BIBLIOGRAPHY

Gutman, I. *The Jews of Warsaw, 1939–1943.* Bloomington, 1983.

Ringelblum, E. *Polish-Jewish Relations during the Second World War.* Jerusalem, 1974.

SHMUEL KRAKOWSKI

POLONSKI, ABRAHAM (b. 1903), founder of the Jewish underground in FRANCE. Born in Russia, Polonski was an electrical engineer in Toulouse, France. After the fall of the French army in June 1940, Polonski, who was a follower of the Zionist activist Vladimir JABOTINSKY, reacted by creating a secret military organization, La Main Forte (The Strong Hand), the aim of which was to recruit a fighting force throughout the world to conquer Palestine from the British. Polonski was the first French Jew who worked to create a Jewish military underground under the Nazi occupation. With the participation of Labor Movement Zionist activists, the ARMÉE JUIVE was founded in January 1942, uniting the best of the forces of Zionist youth. Its command, headed by Polonski and by Lucien LUBLIN, trained Jewish partisans, and in 1943 and 1944 smuggled about three hundred of them into Spain, from where they continued on to Palestine. Armée Juive groups were active in the cities of Toulouse, Nice, Lyons, and Paris; they took revenge on informers who helped the Gestapo, and they fought in liberation battles of the summer of 1944. After the war, Polonski participated in the "illegal" immigration from France to Palestine.

BIBLIOGRAPHY

Kapel, S. R. *Un rabbin dans la tourmente (1940–1944)*. Paris, 1986.

Knout, D. *Contribution à l'histoire de la résistance juive en France*. Paris, 1947.

Latour, A. *Jewish Resistance in France, 1940–1944*. New York, 1981.

Lazare, L. *La résistance juive en France*. Paris, 1987.

LUCIEN LAZARE

POLTAVA, city and capital of Poltava Oblast (district), in the Ukrainian SSR. Jews first settled in Poltava in the seventeenth century. On the eve of World War II, 20,000 Jews lived there, out of a total population of 130,305. The Germans captured the city on September 18, 1941, by which time most of the Jews either had been evacuated or had left on their own. On November 23, 1,531 Jews were rounded up, taken to an antitank ditch outside the city, and shot to death by men of Sonderkommando 4a of Einsatzgruppe C, as well as by German and Ukrainian police.

Poltava was liberated by the Soviets on September 23, 1943.

SHMUEL SPECTOR

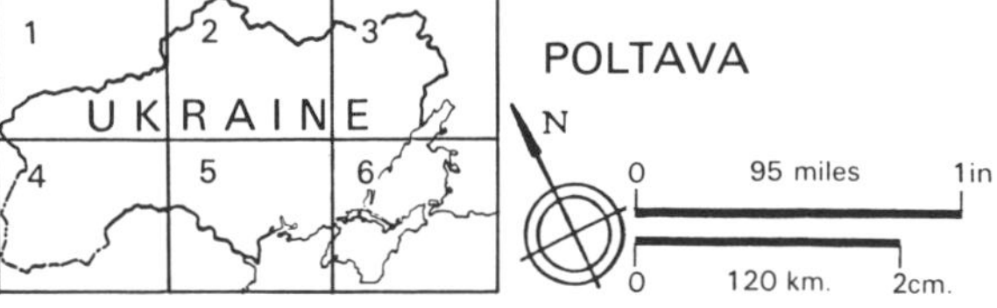

PONARY, mass extermination site near VILNA, in LITHUANIA. Originally a resort, Ponary was situated in a wooded area 6.2 miles (10 km) from Vilna, on the highway to GRODNO. In 1940 and 1941 the Soviet authorities excavated large pits at Ponary in which they planned to install fuel storage tanks, but they left the area before the project was completed. During the German occupation, the pits were used for the massacre of tens of thousands of Jews from Vilna and the surrounding area, as well as of Soviet prisoners

Photographs taken during the killing operation at Ponary. The victims were herded into a narrow circular passage between the construction planks of an unfinished fuel-tank site. They were guarded by civilian Lithuanian collaborators.

The victims emerged from the passage and were guided to the area where they would be shot.

of war and other inhabitants who were suspected of opposition to the Nazis.

The victims were brought to Ponary on foot, by road, and by rail, in groups of hundreds or even thousands, and were shot to death in the pits by SS men and German police, assisted by Lithuanian collaborators. The mass murder of Jews at Ponary was launched at the end of June or the beginning of July of 1941, and continued until the beginning of July 1944. During the early stages the victims were buried on the spot, in the existing pits. In September 1943 the Nazis began opening the pits and burning the corpses, in an effort to destroy the evidence of their crime. Some eighty Jewish prisoners were put on this gruesome job. On April 15, 1944, these prisoners made a daring escape attempt; most of them were killed, but fifteen got away and joined the partisans in the Rudninkai Forest. Estimates of the number of persons who were murdered at Ponary range from seventy thousand to one hundred thousand; the great majority of the victims were Jews.

BIBLIOGRAPHY

Arad, Y. *Ghetto in Flames.* New York, 1982.

YITZHAK ARAD

PONIATOWA, a prisoner-of-war and forced-labor camp situated in the town of that name in POLAND, 22 miles (36 km) west of Lublin. In September 1941 a prisoner-of-war camp for captured Soviet soldiers, Stalag 359, was set up at the site; twenty-four thousand Soviet prisoners were put into the camp, most of them in November and December of 1941. As a result of the terror regime imposed by

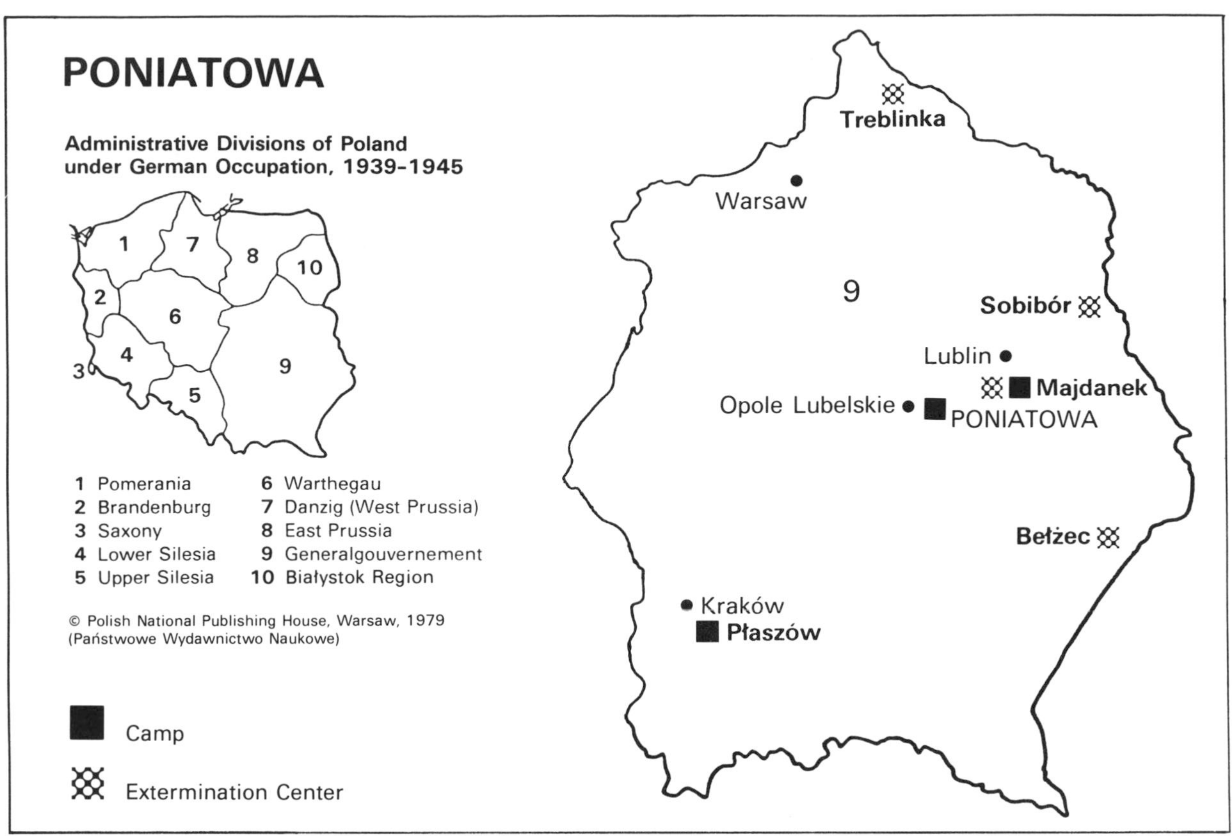

the German camp staff, the unspeakable sanitary conditions, the hard labor, and the starvation diet, hundreds of prisoners died every day. By the early spring of 1942, no fewer than twenty-two thousand had died or been murdered; they were buried in the camp grounds in thirty-two mass graves. Of the survivors, five hundred were prepared to enlist in auxiliary units attached to the German army and the Nazi police. The military handed over control of the camp to the SS, and the camp was used to house Jewish prisoners on forced labor.

The first consignment of Jews arrived at the camp in October 1942 from the OPOLE LUBELSKIE ghetto. By January 1943 there were fifteen hundred Jewish prisoners in the camp. In the wake of the WARSAW GHETTO UPRISING, sixteen thousand to eighteen thousand Jews were moved into Poniatowa in May 1943. Ten thousand prisoners were employed in the textile works owned by a German industrialist, Walther Többens, which had been transferred from the Warsaw ghetto to Poniatowa. The remaining prisoners were put on various outdoor jobs, in and outside the camp.

The first commandant of the Poniatowa camp was Obersturmführer Gottlieb Hering, who was succeeded by Otto Hantke. The camp command had a German staff of forty SS men. A unit of six hundred Nazi collaborators, mostly Ukrainians, guarded the camp, which was run by a regime of terror. Hundreds of prisoners were executed or tortured to death. The Jewish Fighting Organization (ŻYDOWSKA ORGANIZACJA BOJOWA) was active in the camp and aimed to prepare for an uprising, in case it was decided to liquidate the camp. Commanding the organization was Melech Feinkind, who had been a Po'alei Zion Left activist in Warsaw. In September 1943 the Germans discovered some weapons that the underground had acquired and hidden, and as a result the regime became harsher.

On the night of November 3–4, 1943, substantial SS forces from East Prussia and Katowice arrived in the camp, together with a special unit of Auschwitz guards. Their assignment was to carry out the mass murder operation known by the code name "ERNTEFEST" ("Harvest Festival"). The prisoners were driven out of the barracks and, group by group, were forced to run to pits dug in the ground near the camp, where they were all killed by machine-gun fire. Some of the prisoners resisted, refusing to leave their barracks; the Germans reacted by setting fire to the barracks, with the prisoners inside. Members of the underground managed to burn several of the factory warehouses. Fifteen thousand prisoners were murdered on November 4, 1943. The Germans tried to make about two hundred prisoners burn the bodies of the victims, but they refused and were also killed. A few survivors managed to escape from the camp before it was liquidated.

BIBLIOGRAPHY

Gicewicz, R. "Oboz pracy w Poniatowej 1941–1943." *Zeszyty Majdanka* 10 (1980): 88–104.

SHMUEL KRAKOWSKI

PORTUGAL. *See* Sousa Mendes, Aristide de.

POZSONY. *See* Bratislava.

PRACOVNÁ SKUPINA (Working Group; Ger., Nebenregierung), Slovak Jewish semi-underground group devoted to fostering the rescue of Slovak and other European Jews, and to gathering and disseminating information concerning the fate of Jews who had been deported to POLAND. In many ways a cross section of Slovak Jewry, the Working Group was comprised primarily of members of the ÚSTREDŇA ŽIDOV (Jewish Center; ÚŽ). The group was led by Gisi FLEISCHMANN, the head of the Slovak branch of the Women's International Zionist Organization and the Emigration Department of the ÚŽ, and Rabbi Michael Dov WEISSMANDEL, the son-in-law of the rabbi of Nitra, Samuel David Ungar. The other prominent members were Rabbi Armin Frieder (1911–1946), the founder of Ohel David, which aided Jewish refugees who reached SLOVAKIA; the engineer Andrej Steiner (b. 1908), head of the ÚŽ Department of Labor and Construction; Dr. Tibor Kovacs (d. 1958), head of the ÚŽ Secretariat and a leading Zionist; Dr. Oskar (Yirmiyahu) Neumann (1894–1981), president of the Zionist Histadrut in Slovakia, head of the ÚŽ Department of Vocational Training, and the last head of the ÚŽ; Dr. Vojtech (Eugene) Winterstein (1903–1970), a Zionist leader; Wilhelm Furst (d. 1944), director of the ÚŽ Finance Department and an ardent assimilationist; and Ernst Ables, a Zionist leader. Various other Slovak Jewish public figures collaborated with the Working Group in different fields of rescue.

The precursor to the Working Group was the Committee of Six, which was convened ad hoc on February 25, 1942, following the arrival of information in the ÚŽ about impending deportations. The Committee of Six, under the leadership of Fleischmann, sought to avert the catastrophe by appealing to prominent people in the Slovak government and the Catholic church, as well as representatives of various organizations and governments who, they hoped, could influence events in Slovakia. Among those contacted were the Vatican chargé d'affaires in Bratislava, Monsignor Giuseppe Burzio; Slovak bishops; the cardinal primate of Hungary, Jusztinian Seredi; various Vatican representatives throughout the world; Dr. Josef Sivak, the Slovak education minister; and Dr. Stefan Tiso, the cousin of the Slovak prime minister, Jozef TISO. Despite these appeals, the first wave of deportations began on March 26, 1942, and continued until October of that year.

While the transports laden with Slovak Jews rolled toward Poland, the Committee of Six expanded into the Working Group. Until the final deportation of Slovak Jewry in the aftermath of the failed SLOVAK NATIONAL UPRISING in the autumn of 1944, the group considered and exercised virtually every possible means to rescue the Jews of Slovakia.

The best known of their deeds were the rescue negotiations they conducted with the representative of Adolf EICHMANN's office in Slovakia, SS-Sturmbannführer Dieter WISLICENY. At first directed toward stopping the deportations from Slovakia in 1942, the negotiations developed into the EUROPA PLAN for the rescue of a large segment of European Jewry, and in 1944 resurfaced in Hungary as part of the rescue activities of the RELIEF AND RESCUE COMMITTEE OF BUDAPEST. For most of the period between the summer of 1942 and the autumn of 1943, these negotiations were the focal point of the Working Group's rescue measures. Concerning this line of rescue, the Working Group (primarily Gisi Fleischmann) maintained a significant correspondence with the American Jewish JOINT DISTRIBUTION COMMITTEE representative in Switzerland, Saly MAYER, and the He-Haluts representative, Nathan Schwalb.

Among the other, more limited, rescue methods employed by the Working Group was the establishment and expansion of Jewish labor camps in Slovakia itself, managed in part by Jews. Steiner and Neumann were the originators of this scheme, which began at the height of the deportations in 1942. They managed to convince Slovak government officials that instead of sending Slovak Jews abroad to work, as was the official reason given for the deportations, it was more beneficial to the nation to employ Jews within its borders. The pressure that had been brought to bear on Slovak officials by the Committee of Six earlier in the year, as well as some well-placed bribes, helped bring about the establishment of three camps—NOVÁKY, SERED, and VYHNE—as havens for Jews. Although not all the inmates were safe during the deportations, most were spared, and from October 1942 until September 1944, some four thousand Jews lived in these camps. The Working Group maintained contact with them and gave assistance whenever possible.

Running parallel to this line of rescue was the fostering of escape from Slovakia to Hungary, where until the German occupation of that country in March 1944, Jews lived in relative security. Initially this operation, called Tiyyul ("Excursion"), was the province of members of the Zionist youth movement and various Orthodox Jews, mostly associated with Rabbi Weissmandel. Late in 1942 the Working Group began financing escape to Hungary. Early in 1943, along with Tiyyul activists in Slovakia, the Relief and Rescue Committee, and Zionist youth in Hungary, they helped smuggle Polish Jews to Hungary, mostly by way of Slovakia. This rescue operation is known as the Tiyyul from Poland. Through these efforts, between six thousand and eight thousand Slovak Jews reached Hungary, as did at least twelve hundred Polish Jews. As the number of escapees suggests, this means of rescue could be effective, but could not provide a solution for all Slovak Jews.

The Working Group also played an important role in the foundation of armed Jewish resistance in Slovakia and, later on, in the establishment of contact with the organizers of the Slovak national uprising. Like the idea of rescue through negotiations, rescue through a successful national uprising could potentially lead to the safeguarding of masses of Jews. In each of the three work camps, armed cells organized on their own during the first wave of deportations. When the Working Group became aware of their existence it began helping them, mostly by providing funds. Oskar Neumann and his liaison with the camps, Zvi Feher, were the channels through which aid was rendered. With the outbreak of the rebellion, the Working Group's other methods of rescue became impracticable. The failure of the uprising led to the execution or deportation of most of the remaining Jews of Slovakia. Both Gisi Fleischmann and Rabbi Weissmandel were sent to AUSCHWITZ. Rabbi Weissmandel escaped en route without his family; Gisi Fleischmann was killed by an explicit order in the extermination camp.

As important as the rescue work, and indeed a prerequisite for much of it, was the gathering and dissemination of information about the fate of Jews who had been deported to Poland. One of the first acts of the Working Group was to send messengers to follow the deported Jews and divulge their fate. At the end of July 1942, they brought back information about a high death rate among the deportees, stressing the role of starvation. The Working Group forwarded this information to their contacts in the West. In October, news reached them of the disappearance of deported Jews, and more messengers were dispatched to confirm the information. They returned early in November with news about the murders in BEŁŻEC and TREBLINKA. From then on, especially in the negotiations and the pleas sent abroad for the rescue of Jews, the Working Group passed on information about the murders. The best known of their messsages sent abroad was a summary of the AUSCHWITZ PROTOCOLS and a request to bomb the camp and the railways leading to it, which Rabbi Weissmandel succeeded in cabling to Isaac Sternbuch in Switzerland on May 16, 1944.

The death of some seventy thousand of the ninety thousand Jews who were in Slovakia on the eve of the deportations attests to the virtual powerlessness of Jews at the time. The Working Group's efforts, however, illustrate the heroism, dedication, concern, and moral sensibility of this unique group of Jewish leaders.

BIBLIOGRAPHY

Bauer, Y. *American Jewry and the Holocaust: The American Jewish Joint Distribution Committee, 1939–1945.* Detroit, 1981.

Fuchs, A. *The Unheeded Cry.* New York, 1984.

Rothkirchen, L. *The Destruction of Slovak Jewry: A Documentary History.* Jerusalem, 1961.

Rothkirchen, L. "The Dual Role of the Jewish Center in Slovakia." In *Patterns of Jewish Leadership in Nazi Europe, 1933–1945.* Proceedings of the Third Yad Vashem International Historical Conference, edited by Y. Gutman and C. Haft, pp. 219–227. Jerusalem, 1979.

ROBERT ROZETT

Signs in German and Czech at a children's park in Prague (1939). The uppermost sign reads: "No Entry for Jews." [Bildarchiv Preussischer Kulturbesitz]

PRAGUE, home of one of the oldest and most revered Jewish communities in Europe (the earliest documentary evidence dates back to 1091). During the Middle Ages and later, Prague was known as a major center of Jewish learning. Jews formed a considerable part of the Germanized minority at the beginning of the twentieth century and became an element in the conflict between the Czech and German nationalities. At the same time, the Czech Jewish movement and Zionism struck root, growing in importance during the interwar period. Jews contributed greatly to the economic progress of the city and played a key role in its cultural life.

After Hitler's seizure of power in Germany on January 30, 1933, waves of refugees arrived in Prague, followed in 1938 by refugees from Austria and the Sudetenland. As a result, the city's Jewish population grew from forty-five thousand to about fifty-six thousand. After the occupation of Prague by the German army (March 15, 1939), Reichsprotektor Konstantin Freiherr von NEURATH ordered (July 21, 1939) the establishment of the ZENTRALSTELLE FÜR JÜDISCHE AUSWANDERUNG

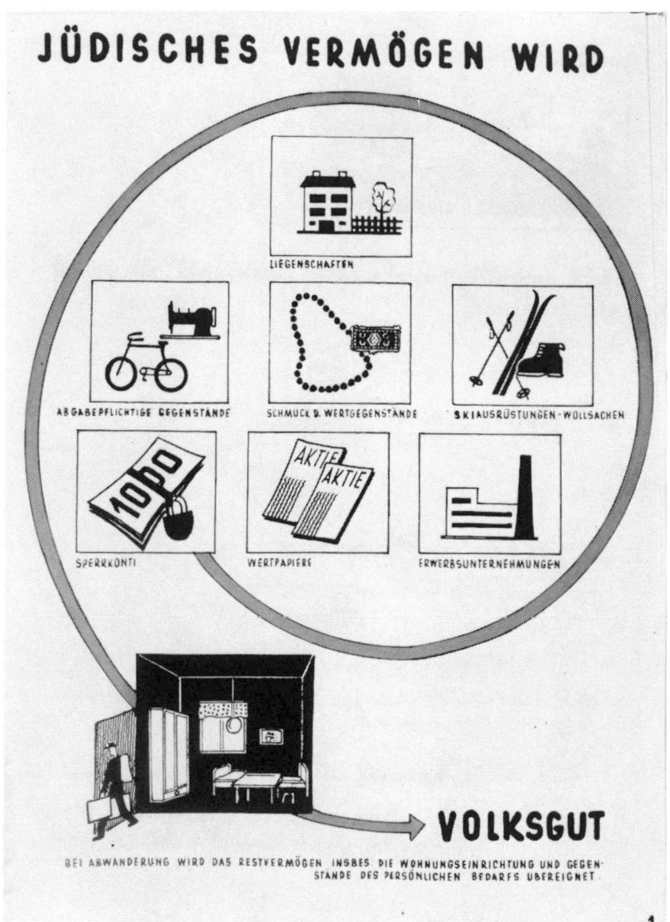

A report on the activities of the Treuhandstelle (Trustee Office) in Prague for the period from January to June 1944 included colored graphic charts and statistical tables. This chart states: "Jewish wealth passes into the hands of the people."

in Böhmen und Mähren (Central Office for Jewish Emigration in BOHEMIA AND MORAVIA), headed by Adolf EICHMANN.

At the outbreak of World War II (September 1, 1939), the prominent persons arrested in Prague as hostages included Marie Schmolka and Hanna Steiner, both active in the field of refugee and rescue work. Jewish organizations clandestinely continued to provide social welfare, educating the youth and training in languages and new vocations in preparation for emigration. The Palestine Office in Prague, directed by Jacob EDELSTEIN, was instrumental in enabling about nineteen thousand Jews to emigrate (legally or otherwise) by the end of 1939. The leadership of the Prague Jewish Religious Congregation was forced to provide the Nazis with lists of candidates for deportation. As of February 1943, the Council of Jewish Elders (Ältestenrat der Juden) in Prague was made responsible for the affairs of Prague's Jewish community. The Germans appointed as Jewish elders Dr. František Weidmann, Salo Krämer, and Dr. František Friedmann.

Between October 6, 1941 and March 16, 1945, 46,067 Jews were deported from Prague to "the east" (ŁÓDŹ and MINSK), and to the THERESIENSTADT (Terezín) camp. The Nazis set up a Treuhandstelle (Trustee Office) in charge of evacuated Jewish apartments, furniture, and other possessions; fifty-four warehouses, including eleven synagogues, were used to store the confiscated Jewish property. Jewish religious articles from 153 provincial communities were brought to Prague, including 5,400 religious objects, 24,500 prayer

The Treuhandstelle report also contained artistically designed photographic displays of Jewish possessions confiscated by and stored at the Treuhandstelle. Here, a display shows works of art taken from Jews.

Another display from the Treuhandstelle report, of china confiscated from Jewish homes.

books, and 6,070 artifacts of historical value that were catalogued by a team of devoted Jewish scholars in an effort to save the materials for posterity. The Nazis meant to use this collection after the war in a projected "Central Museum of the Extinguished Jewish Race"; instead, it became the core of the Jewish Museum of Prague, reopened after the end of the war. Today, on the walls of the Pinkas Synagogue, which is part of the museum complex, the names of 77,297 Jewish victims of the Nazi extermination process in Bohemia and Moravia are inscribed. In April 1945 the Prague Jewish community was reconstituted, and a Council of Jewish Communities in Czechoslovakia established. Ernst Frischer, a former member of the State Council of the CZECHOSLOVAK GOVERNMENT-IN-EXILE in London, became its head.

The Jewish population of Prague numbered around eleven thousand after the war. Chief Rabbi Gustav Sicher, who had returned from Palestine, led the community. Many of the survivors emigrated overseas after the war and settled in Israel in 1948 and 1949.

BIBLIOGRAPHY

Dagan, A., ed. *The Jews of Czechoslovakia: Historical Studies and Surveys.* 3 vols. Philadelphia, 1968, 1971, 1984.

LIVIA ROTHKIRCHEN

PRESIDENT'S ADVISORY COMMITTEE ON POLITICAL REFUGEES (PACPR), quasi-governmental group of eleven prominent Americans appointed by President Franklin D. ROOSEVELT in April 1938 to coordinate the work of private refugee agencies in the United States and to advise the Roosevelt administration on developing refugee policies for European Jews. Among the committee's members were Hamilton Fish Armstrong, editor of *Foreign Affairs;* Samuel M. Cavert of the Federal Council of Churches; Most Reverend Joseph F. Rummel, Archbishop of New Orleans; Rabbi Stephen S. WISE, one of the country's foremost Jewish leaders; and Professor Joseph P. Chamberlain of Columbia University. Throughout the committee's existence, James G. MCDONALD, former League of Nations High Commissioner for Refugees, served as its chairman, and George L. Warren as its executive secretary. For the most part, the PACPR worked cautiously behind the scenes. Functioning almost without access to Roosevelt, it dealt mainly with the State Department (*see* UNITED STATES DEPARTMENT OF STATE).

The PACPR was most active during the period before Pearl Harbor (December 7, 1941). It was involved in the effort to settle Jewish refugees at Sosua in the Dominican Republic, and it played an important part in a Roosevelt administration program that bypassed the regular immigration system to bring 2,000 endangered political and intellectual refugees to safety in the United States (*see* REFUGEES, 1933–1945). These people were granted temporary visitors' visas that, by a clear stretching of the law, they were allowed to renew indefinitely. The PACPR took responsibility for screening the lists of political and intellectual refugees submitted by the private refugee-aid agencies. Approved names were then sent to the State Department with positive recommendations for visas to the United States.

In two instances, both before Pearl Harbor, the PACPR took sharp exception to State Department steps to obstruct immigration. In September 1940, only two months after it had begun, the State Department, led by Assistant Secretary Breckinridge Long, moved to terminate the special program to provide visitors' visas for political and intellectual refugees. Long claimed that Nazi spies and saboteurs were attempting to enter the United States in the guise of refugees. The PACPR was able to confer with President Roosevelt on this issue, but the president was noncommittal. With help from the Justice Department, the PACPR managed to obtain a compromise that extended the program until mid-1941, though only on a very limited basis.

A second showdown with Long and the State Department took place in July 1941, when the latter sharply cut immigration coming under the regular quota system. Visa issuance was reduced to about 25 percent of the legally available quotas. Again, the claim was that subversive elements might penetrate the United States. Once more the PACPR went to Roosevelt, and once more the president sidestepped the issue. The only modification that the PACPR could extract from the State Department was the establishment of a complex system for appealing rejected visa applications. This arrangement provided a small amount of relief.

After Pearl Harbor, the PACPR fell into near dormancy. In September 1942, it was instrumental in persuading the Roosevelt administration to make visas available for 5,000 Jewish children in France whose parents had been sent to Poland in the mass deportations of that summer. (The Nazis never permitted the children to leave, however.) After that, the committee was virtually inoperative, although from time to time it did apply tempered pressure on the State Department for modification of its stringent immigration policies. The last recorded meeting of the PACPR was held in December 1943. Of the sixty-one times the committee met, only ten took place after Pearl Harbor.

One reason for the PACPR's weakness was its uncertain financing. It was a presidential committee, yet it received no government funds. The American Jewish JOINT DISTRIBUTION COMMITTEE provided most of its tiny budget of about $15,000 a year. For a time, Zionist organizations paid half the costs, but they stopped contributing in 1941, partly because changes in immigration regulations meant that the PACPR could no longer help refugee Zionist leaders as it had done in the past, and partly because of the shortage of Zionist funds. The American Catholic and Protestant refugee-aid committees each provided a total of only $500 during the PACPR's seven years.

BIBLIOGRAPHY

Feingold, H. L. *The Politics of Rescue: The Roosevelt Administration and the Holocaust, 1938–1945.* New Brunswick, N.J., 1970.

Wyman, D. S. *The Abandonment of the Jews: America and the Holocaust, 1941–1945.* New York, 1984.

Wyman, D. S. *Paper Walls: America and the Refugee Crisis.* Amherst, Mass., 1978.

DAVID S. WYMAN

PRESIDENT'S COMMISSION ON THE HOLOCAUST. *See* U.S. Holocaust Memorial Council.

PRESSBURG. *See* Bratislava.

PRISONERS OF WAR. [*The two articles in this entry focus on aspects of the treatment accorded by the Nazis to captured Jewish and Soviet soldiers, the prisoners of war who suffered most from the Nazi racist policies.*]

Jewish Prisoners of War

During World War II approximately two hundred thousand Jewish soldiers belonging to the various Allied armies fell into German

hands. The treatment by Nazi Germany of these Jewish prisoners of war (POWs) depended on which army they were serving in. Jewish soldiers from the armies of Western countries (the United States, Britain—including the Jewish units from Palestine—France, Canada, and Australia) were treated no differently than other POWs from those countries, except for some attempts that were made to separate them from the rest. Quite different was the German policy on Jewish POWs from the Polish army who were captured in the September 1939 fighting, and on Jews serving in the Red Army; the former were systematically killed in stages and almost totally annihilated, whereas the policy on the latter was immediate and total annihilation, with no delay.

Jewish POWs from the Polish Army. Some sixty thousand to sixty-five thousand Jewish soldiers were taken prisoner by the Germans in September 1939. As soon as they were captured and wherever they were gathered—mostly in the open but also in transit camps set up in abandoned factories, churches, jails, and schools—the policy of severe terror was applied. Generally, the separation of the Jews from the rest of the prisoners began while they were still in the assembly points and transit camps, and was continued in the permanent camps. The separation was based on the manual of instructions for POW-camp commandants, which the chief of staff of the German army, Wilhelm KEITEL, had approved on February 16, 1939. One of the provisions of the manual, which had been drafted during the preparations for the invasion of Poland, stated: "Prisoners will be segregated on the basis of their national and racial affiliation." From the assembly points and transit camps the enlisted men among the prisoners were taken to *Stammlager* (stalags), POW camps for enlisted men. Most of the Jewish prisoners were taken to one of the following stalags: Stablack, Hohenstein, Neubrandenburg, Hammerstein, Stargard, Luckenwalde, Hammer, Rathorn, Dortmund, Moosburg, Lamsdorf, Altengrabow, Limburg, Frankenthal, Nuremberg, Kaisersteinbruch, Pernau/Wels, and Markt Pongau.

In all of these camps, the Jews were separated from the other POWs. They were placed in a separate section where accommodation and food rations were greatly inferior to those in the rest of the camp; in fact, with regard to nourishment, terrorization, and hard labor, the lot of the Jewish POWs was no different from that of concentration camp prisoners. In the winter of 1939–1940 most of the Jewish prisoners were housed in unheated and overcrowded tents without sanitary facilities. The food rations they received were extremely meager and left them hungry at all times, with thousands dying from starvation. The Jewish POWs also experienced brutal treatment at the hands of the German camp guards. There was no end to the harassment, especially at the roll calls that took place several times a day, and at work. A great many prisoners perished from cold and from torture. Of the 400 Jewish prisoners in the Insterburg camp in East Prussia, no more than 70 were still alive in 1940. A total of 25,000 Jewish prisoners died or were killed by the spring of 1940. In late 1939 the Germans began releasing prisoners who came from the German-occupied territories of Poland (whereas those whose homes were in the Soviet-annexed parts were not released). The Jewish prisoners were taken to the ghettos then being established in occupied Poland, where they all perished together with the rest of the ghetto population when the ghettos were liquidated.

In 1940 and 1941, Jewish POWs who hailed from the Soviet-annexed part of Poland were transferred to camps in the Lublin district: Biała Podlaska, Końska Wola, and Lublin. The Biała Podlaska and Końska Wola camps were liquidated shortly thereafter, while the LUBLIN-LIPOWA camp fell victim to Aktion "ERNTEFEST" (Operation "Harvest Festival") on November 3, 1943. Of the sixty thousand Jewish enlisted men who were taken prisoner in the September 1939 battles, no more than a few hundred survived the war.

One thousand Jewish officers were taken prisoner in September 1939, and most of them were saved from extermination. Although they too were separated from their Polish fellow officers, they did not suffer the same fate as the enlisted men. The Jewish officers were put into *Offlager* (POW camps for officers) in Woldenberg, Dorsten, and Dossel, where "ghettos" were created for them; that is, they were put into separate barracks or into a separate section of a barrack. Their situation was worse than that of the Polish officers, but the mortality rate in these camps was not high and no mass murders took place in them.

The conditions in which the Jewish officers lived deteriorated in the last few months of the war, and the advance of the Allied armies led the Germans to transfer the officer camps into the German interior. The evacuation of the camps proceeded along lines similar to the DEATH MARCHES from the concentration camps: the prisoners were hurried along for hundreds of miles, they were starved and harassed, and the feeble and weak among them, who could not keep up with the rest, were shot to death. No figures are available for the number of officers shot to death on these death marches.

Jewish POWs from the Red Army. Some eighty-five thousand Jewish soldiers serving in the Red Army were taken prisoner. Once they were identified as Jews, they were all killed without exception, irrespective of rank or the branch of service to which they belonged. The official order for the murder of all the Jewish prisoners was in the *Richtlinien* (guidelines) for the treatment of Soviet prisoners of war issued by Reinhard HEYDRICH on July 17, 1941.

The killing of the Jewish POWs took place in various ways. Generally, as soon as a large number of prisoners had been taken, an identification roll call was held at the assembly point or at the time when the prisoners were about to be admitted to a camp. All those identified as Jews were killed on the spot, before the rest of the prisoners were taken in. Thousands of non-Jewish prisoners, mainly Georgians and Asiatics, were also murdered, because the Germans suspected them of being Jewish. When small groups of prisoners were captured, the German captors would select those they suspected of being Jewish and hand them over to EINSATZGRUPPEN men or other SS units to be killed by them. Thousands of Jewish prisoners of war were also murdered by camp guards, made up mostly of the personnel of auxiliary units (Landesschützenbataillone).

Jews who had succeeded in concealing

their identity during the identification roll call and had been put into a POW camp with the other prisoners were still in constant danger of being found out. A systematic search for Jews trying to conceal their identity was conducted in every camp for Soviet POWs. Two methods were employed for this purpose—checking and rechecking (*Überprüfung*) and one selection after the other (*Aussonderung*).

The search for Jewish POWs was carried on by four different authorities or groups: the ABWEHR; the counterintelligence section of the SD (Sicherheitsdienst; Security Service); the camp police (Lagerpolizei), made up of POWs—for the most part Ukrainians—who agreed to collaborate with the camp administration; and teams of informers (*Vertrauensmänner*) who were themselves prisoners. Soviet soldiers who were identified as being Jewish were executed on the spot, or were put into a special barrack and killed in groups. Only a few Jewish prisoners managed to hide their true identity throughout their imprisonment and were still alive when the war ended.

Palestinian Jewish POWs. More than fifteen hundred Jews from Palestine who volunteered to serve with the British army were captured by Axis forces during World War II. The majority were captured during the fighting in Greece and Crete in the spring of 1941, and most of them eventually reached POW camps and labor detachments in Germany. A small contingent were taken prisoner in the Western Desert campaigns in North Africa and interned in POW camps in Libya or Italy. The Germans were initially uncertain how to treat captive Jewish soldiers in British uniform. Eventually, with the support of their British comrades in the camps, they were given the same treatment as all captured British soldiers.

Several thousand British troops, among them hundreds of Jews and 400 Arabs from Palestine, were captured on April 29, 1941, at the Kalamata shore in the southern Peloponnesian peninsula. During the last days of May 1941, another several thousand British soldiers, among them 120 Jews from Palestine, were captured in the fighting near Sphakia, Crete. Most of the prisoners from both campaigns were interned in Corinth, where, according to the German report, there were 1,907 POWs from Palestine, including both Jews and Arabs. The POWs from the Corinth camp were sent to Salonika at the end of June 1941, from where they were shipped by rail to Germany. The trip was made in cattle cars holding 50 men each, and the prisoners suffered from overcrowding and lack of food, water, and basic sanitation.

On July 3, 1941, they reached the Austrian-Yugoslav border, where the Jews from Palestine were divided into two groups and placed in transit camps in Marburg and Wolfsberg. In Wolfsberg the Jews were separated from the other POWs, and those of German and Austrian origin were not allowed to leave the camp on work details. The Jewish POWs in Marburg were also segregated. At the end of July the POWs were taken to Lamsdorf in Silesia (Stalag VIII B, later renamed Stalag 344), where 1,160 Palestinian Jews were interned together with 12,000 British prisoners and 7,000 of other nationalities—French, Belgian, Polish, and Yugoslav. In this camp the Jews were treated like the rest of the prisoners. Keeping to themselves, they developed support groups and even organized classes in Hebrew and other subjects.

In the summer of 1942, German POWs were interned in a camp in Latrun, Palestine. There they complained of mistreatment, and in retaliation eighty-two Palestinian noncommissioned officers and sixty-eight British noncommissioned officers were transferred to a special punishment camp in Chełm, near Lublin (Stalag 319). At the end of May 1943, with the improvement of conditions in the Latrun camp, the noncommissioned officers were transferred from Chełm to a camp near Nuremberg with much better conditions.

During the winter of 1942–1943, several hundred Palestinian Jewish POWs were transferred from Lamsdorf to labor detachments in Gliwice (Gleiwitz) and Blechhammer. Here they met Jewish forced laborers who told them of the atrocities perpetrated by the Nazis. For their part, the Jewish POWs tried to ameliorate the conditions of the Jewish laborers by smuggling food for them. Early in 1944 most of the forced-labor camps in Silesia were dismantled, and the POWs lost contact with the Jewish laborers.

In the summer of 1944 hundreds of POWs, including the Jews, were removed from Stalag 344 in preparation for an exchange with the Allies; 540 Jewish POWs remained in Lamsdorf. Some of the exchange programs did not take place, and most of these Jewish POWs, along with those who had remained in the camp, were marched back to Germany as the Soviet army advanced. During this chaotic time, the POWs from Palestine were dispersed throughout Germany along with other POWs.

About one hundred Palestinian Jewish POWs escaped during the war, and many more were caught trying. Of the escapees, some joined partisan units in Greece and Yugoslavia, and a few even reached Palestine. Four also escaped from Italy and reached Switzerland.

Unlike their counterparts from the Soviet army, the Polish army, and the armies of most of the nations defeated by the Germans, Jewish POWs in British uniform were not singled out to be killed. They were not even treated differently from other British POWs once the Germans determined a policy regarding them, probably because the Germans feared reprisals against their own captured servicemen. This allowed the vast majority to survive their imprisonment, and most were liberated when Germany surrendered.

BIBLIOGRAPHY

Gelber, Y. *Jewish Palestinian Volunteers in the British Army during the Second World War.* Vol. 4. Jerusalem, 1981. See pages 131–206. (In Hebrew.)

Gelber, Y. "Palestinian POWs in German Captivity." *Yad Vashem Studies* 14 (1981): 89–137.

Krakowski, S. "The Fate of Jewish Prisoners of War in the September 1939 Campaign." *Yad Vashem Studies* 12 (1977): 297–333.

SHMUEL KRAKOWSKI and
YOAV GELBER

Soviet Prisoners of War

Second only to the Jews, Soviet prisoners of war (POWs) were the largest group of victims of Nazi extermination policy. There are no precise data available on the fate of Soviet troops who were taken prisoner by the Germans. Existing sources provide the following rough picture. Some 5.7 million Red Army personnel fell into German hands between June 22, 1941, and the end of World War II. In January 1945, 930,000 were still in German camps. Approximately 1 million had been released from the camps, most of them HILFSWILLIGE (volunteer helpers; Hiwis), who served as auxiliaries in the German forces. Another 500,000, according to estimates made by the Oberkommando der Wehrmacht (Armed Forces High Command; OKW), had escaped or been liberated by the Red Army. The remaining 3.3 million (57.5 percent of the total) had perished.

Comparable figures for Anglo-American POWs are 8,348 dead by the end of the war, out of 235,000 (3.6 percent). Of the 3,155,000 German POWs taken prisoner by the Soviets, 1,185,000, or 37.5 percent, died in captivity, according to the findings of a Federal German commission of historians.

Five causes account for the extraordinarily high mortality rate among Soviet POWs: starvation; totally inadequate accommodation; the methods used in their transportation; the treatment they had to undergo; and the murder, by design, of certain categories of POWs.

German policy on the Soviet POWs was made easier by the lack of clarity in the reciprocal obligations of the two countries in war, under international law. The Soviet Union had not ratified the 1929 Geneva Convention on Prisoners of War, nor had it specifically declared its commitment to the 1907 Hague Convention on the Rules of War. Both nations, therefore, were bound only by the general international law of war, as it had developed in modern times. But under that law, too, prisoners of war had to have their lives protected, and they had to be treated humanely and to receive nourishment, clothing, and housing that were on a par with those accorded to its own reseve troops by the country in which they were held.

The Reich government exploited this ambiguous situation by claiming that it was under no obligation to the Soviet Union under international law; and it had no intention of restricting itself in any way with respect to the conduct of the war, the policy it pursued in occupied territories, and its treatment of prisoners of war. It also rejected an offer made by the Soviet Union in July 1941 for mutual recognition of the Hague Convention on the Rules of War, since it was convinced that a German victory was imminent.

The exploitation of potential Soviet resources of agricultural production was one of Germany's major war aims in the east. As early as May 1941, the German planners of the economic exploitation of Soviet territory were well aware that such exploitation by Germany would "inevitably" result "in millions of people starving to death." Soviet POWs were destined to be the first victims of this policy. Even before the invasion was launched, the OKW agreed that the Soviet prisoners would be given "no more than the bare essentials," as far as their food rations were concerned. In August 1941 a ration scale of 2,200 calories per day for working prisoners was fixed by the OKW, less than the minimum required for existence. Generally, the rations actually provided were even below that insufficient official scale. For example, Soviet POWs who were marched through Belorussia in the summer of 1941 en route to POW camps are reported to have had a daily ration of "20 grams of millet and 100 grams of bread, with no meat" or "100 grams of millet, with no bread"—in other words, daily rations that were less than a quarter of the required minimum. Numerous reports from the late summer and fall of 1941 show that in many camps the desperate POWs tried to assuage their hunger by eating grass and leaves.

Tens of thousands lost their lives while still en route to the POW camps. Most of the prisoners captured in 1941 had to march to the rear across hundreds of miles, and those who were too exhausted to continue were shot to death on the spot, by the thousands. There are reports of such incidents taking place even in the center of large cities, such as Smolensk and Minsk. Some of the German military commanders were outraged and tried to put a stop to the shooting by issuing appropriate orders; others, like Field Marshal Walter von REICHENAU, commander of the Sixth Army, ordered that "any prisoner who collapses is to be shot."

When Soviet POWs were transported by train, the OKW permitted only open freight cars to be used. This meant not only a reduction of available space but also an enormous loss of life when the winter came. According to a report dated early in December of 1941, from 25 percent to 70 percent of the prisoners on these transports in the REICHSKOMMISSARIAT OSTLAND (German-occupied Soviet territory) died en route; an additional cause was that sometimes days went by without the prisoners receiving any rations.

Hardly any preparations were made for housing of the POWs. There were plans for enormous compounds to be set up, in the Reich and in occupied Poland, for thirty thousand to fifty thousand POWs each, on German army training grounds. In practice, all that was done was to put up a barbed-wire fence around the designated camp site. The POWs were expected to construct their own housing, with the most primitive means. In many camps, even those in the Reich (such as Senne-Stukenbrock, Fallingbostel, and BERGEN-BELSEN), the prisoners were forced to eke out their existence in holes that they had dug in the ground or in huts made of foliage, right into the winter.

The effects of this policy were apparent as early as August 1941. According to reports received by the OKW at the time, in many cases only 20 percent of the prisoners on a transport survived the journey, and in some camps epidemics had already broken out, caused by the lack of basic necessities. In October of that year there was a sudden steep rise in the mortality rate. Totally exhausted by hunger and the strain of the march, the prisoners, existing on a starvation diet, had no strength left to resist the cold, the contagious diseases, and the epidemics. As one report states, "they dropped dead like flies."

By February 1942, some 2 million of the 3.5 million prisoners captured in 1941 were dead. The mass deaths had reached their climax in the period from October to December of 1941. Thus, for example, in December 1941 the death rate among the POWs in the GENERALGOUVERNEMENT and the Reichskommissariat Ostland was 46 percent. By April 1942 it had fallen, to between 6 percent and 8 percent.

This decrease was due, above all, to the realization on the part of the German leadership that the German war economy urgently needed the POWs to supplement the manpower at its disposal. The important change introduced was to provide the Soviet POWs with slightly better rations—though these were still far short of the rations allotted to other POWs and to the German civilian population. As a result, the enormous death rate among the Soviet POWs was contained, but until the end of the war it was still much higher than that among the other POWs. The death rate again began to climb at the end of 1943, by which time the long years of deprivation were taking their toll, in the form of internal diseases among the prisoners. The poor nutrition that they received also accounted for the low rate of productivity of Soviet POWs, which was far below what had been expected. The number of Soviet POWs put to work in the German economy was also relatively small, the top figure (in August 1944) being 631,000.

German troops in 1941 must have had the impression that the lives of Soviet POWs were worth very little. This was the result not only of Nazi propaganda—in which the Soviet population was portrayed as consisting of subhumans—but also of the basic orders issued by the military leadership, in letter and spirit. The "Barbarossa" decree called on the German troops to react to any type of resistance, even when passive, with shooting. In retribution for partisan attacks, entire villages could be put to the torch and whole sections of the rural population shot to death. On the other hand, crimes committed by German soldiers were not to be punished if they were claimed to have ideological considerations as their motive. The KOMMISSARBEFEHL (Commissar Order) issued by the OKW ordered that all political commissars of the Red Army who were taken prisoner were to be shot. In the summer of 1941 this order was complied with almost fully (contrary to earlier claims). The order was rescinded in May 1942 at the urging of field commanders, who had come up against much stronger Soviet resistance when the regular shooting of Soviet army political commissars became general knowledge.

From the very beginning, the orders on the treatment of Soviet prisoners were determined by Nazi ideology. The "Bolshevik soldier" was described as being extremely dangerous and, quite often, devious; he had "lost any claim he had to be treated as an honorable soldier." Time and again German troops were called upon to take "energetic and ruthless action" and "use their arms" unhesitatingly "to wipe out any trace of resistance." Prisoners trying to escape were to be shot without warning. Moreover, a decree issued on September 8, 1941, stated that the use of arms against Soviet POWs was, "as a rule, to be regarded as legal"—a clear invitation to murder. Six months later this clause was rescinded when it was found that too many arbitrary shootings had taken place.

Evidence exists of a number of instances in which German soldiers and civilians tried to improve the treatment of the Soviet prisoners, but they were unable to prevail against the hard-core Nazis. The improvements that did take place in the spring of 1942, in the prisoners' rations, their housing, and even their general treatment, were based exclusively on pragmatic considerations.

One of the most significant efforts made to bring about a complete reversal in the treatment of Soviet POWs was undertaken by Adm. Wilhelm CANARIS, chief of Ausland/Abwehr in the OKW (the armed forces' espionage, counterespionage, sabotage, and foreign information office), at the urging of Helmuth James Graf von Moltke. Canaris asked Field Marshal Wilhelm KEITEL, chief of the OKW, to repeal the basic decree of September 8, 1941. He not only attacked the decree as a violation of international law, but also brought up weighty reservations about the policy on Soviet prisoners from the political and military points of view. Keitel's reply was unambiguous: "These reservations correspond to a soldier's concept of a chivalrous war! What we are dealing with here is the destruction of a political philosophy [*Weltanschauung*]. This is why I approve these measures and stand by them."

Canaris's protest and Keitel's reply also referred to the systematic mass murders that were taking place. In the middle of July 1941, Gen. Hermann Reinecke, who was the officer in charge of prisoner-of-war affairs in the OKW, and Reinhard HEYDRICH, as chief of the REICHSSICHERHEITSHAUPTAMT (Reich Security Main Office; RSHA), came to an agreement under which the Einsatzkommandos of the Sicherheitspolizei (Security Police) and SD

(Sicherheitsdienst; Security Service) would seek out the "politically and racially intolerable elements" among the Soviet prisoners, and kill them. This amounted to an enormous rise in the number of victims, since not only were "all important state and party functionaries" regarded as "intolerable," but so were "intellectuals," "all fanatic Communists," and "all Jews." Estimates of the number of victims of this operation (whose list of categories to be murdered was somewhat pared down as of March 1942) range from at least 140,000 to 500,000. The Einsatzkommandos, under the Reinecke-Heydrich agreement, carried out the total murder of all Jews among the Soviet POWs.

The AUSCHWITZ-Birkenau and MAJDANEK extermination camps had originally been constructed for the Soviet POWs that Himmler had claimed for himself; they were to be put to work in the huge industrial conglomerates that the SS was planning to set up, together with firms such as I.G. FARBEN. But in January 1942, only a few hundred of the Soviet prisoners who had originally been brought to Auschwitz—out of a total of 10,000—were still alive, and no further influx was expected. For this reason Himmler decided, in the week following the WANNSEE CONFERENCE, to fill the camps with 150,000 Jews. In this manner the SS camps for POWs became part of the infrastructure for the murder of the Jews.

In September 1941 the deputy commander of Auschwitz, Karl Fritzsch, took approximately six hundred Soviet POWs (who had been brought to Auschwitz by the Einsatzkommandos as "intolerable" elements to undergo "special treatment" there) and experimented on them with ZYKLON B pesticide. The method was thus found that would kill millions of people with minimal effort.

BIBLIOGRAPHY

Boog, H., J. Förster, et al. *Der Angriff auf die Sowjetunion.* Stuttgart, 1983. See especially the articles by Förster and R. D. Müller.

Hirschfeld, G., ed. *The Policies of Genocide: The Jews and Soviet Prisoners of War in Nazi Germany.* London, 1986.

Jacobsen, H. A. "The Kommissarbefehl and Mass Executions of Soviet Russian Prisoners of War." In *Anatomy of the SS State,* edited by H. Krausnick et al., pp. 505–535. London, 1968.

Krausnick, H., and H.-H. Wilhelm. *Die Truppe des Weltanschauungskrieges: Die Einsatzgruppen der Sicherheitspolizei und des SD 1938–1942.* Stuttgart, 1981.

Streim, A. *Die Behandlung sowjetischer Kriegsgefangner im "Fall Barbarossa."* Heidelberg, 1981.

Streit, C. *Keine Kameraden: Die Wehrmacht und die sowjetischen Kriegsgefangenen 1941–1945.* Stuttgart, 1978.

CHRISTIAN STREIT

PRISONS. *See* Montelupich Prison; Pawiak Prison.

PROPAGANDA, NAZI. The Nazis used propaganda in many different ways, and in their efforts to gain support and influence they introduced new methods in the field. In addition to ideological indoctrination, they employed mass meetings, visual aids, mass pageants, radio, and film. Prior to the Nazi seizure of power in January 1933, the purpose of these methods was to attract public attention and media coverage; once they were in control, their aim was to entrench the totalitarian regime and strengthen its hold on the population. By means of false claims, deception, and outright lies the Nazis concocted pseudo-justifications for their political and military aggression, engendered enthusiasm and a strong identification with Nazi aims, and, often, succeeded in intimidating and misleading their victims. Adolf Hitler, in MEIN KAMPF, described the essence and force of verbal propaganda and its objectives in the following terms:

> To whom should propaganda be addressed? To the scientifically trained intelligentsia or to the less educated masses?
>
> It must be addressed always and solely to the masses.
>
> What the intelligentsia . . . need is not propaganda but scientific instruction. The content of propaganda is as far from being science as the object depicted in a poster is from being art. A poster's art lies in the designer's ability to capture the attention of the masses by form and color.
>
> The function of propaganda does not lie in the

> scientific training of the individual, but rather in directing the attention of the masses toward certain facts. . . . It must be directed toward the emotions, and only to a very limited extent toward the so-called intellect.
>
> The receptive ability of the masses is very limited, their intelligence is small, their forgetfulness enormous. Therefore, all propaganda has to limit itself to a very few points and repeat them like slogans until even the very last man is able to understand what you want him to understand.

These were the principles on which Hitler based Nazi propaganda. It had to convey a message aimed at the masses, so that they would accept it as a dictate; it had to appeal to the emotions and should not address itself to the intellect. Propaganda had to be popular, adapted to the limitations of the simplest individual; its purpose was not to spread the objective truth but to disseminate the particular truth that the politician or leader wanted to be spread. Propaganda was used in the Nazi system to instill the main elements of the ideology and to change the patterns of traditional behavior; it was directed toward establishing the Nazi way of thinking and acting in everyday life, in and outside of the family circle. According to Hitler, the masses must not have two or more enemies put before them, to avoid the "dissipation of their fighting strength." Their full attention had to focus on a major enemy—that enemy being primarily the Jew. Nazi propaganda superimposed its racist ideology on traditional antisemitism by asserting that the Jew was the enemy of the German people. These two elements, racism and Jew-hatred, were joined into a single propaganda message which proclaimed that Germany must be rid of the parasitic Jew. To Hitler, antisemitism was an important propaganda weapon; he claimed that in all countries in which antisemitic propaganda was used it had a devastating effect, and that it could not be ignored as a tool in political warfare.

To achieve their purpose, the Nazis made use of all means at their disposal. In the cinemas, for example, they showed films with strong antisemitic overtones, such as *Jud Süss*. They sought to evoke revulsion for Jews among the population, and the repugnant scenes in the Polish ghettos had the effect of predisposing a great many people to accept the killing of the "Jew pests" and their liquidation. When, on the other hand, the Nazis wanted to silence the protests that were being voiced all over the world, they put on a show of the "decent" conditions of life in the concentration camps; the most notorious of these attempts was the masquerade put on in the THERESIENSTADT camp.

Because of the significant role played by propaganda in the Nazi system, the Reich Ministry of Public Enlightenment and Propaganda (Reichsministerium für Volksaufklärung und Propaganda) was created on March 5, 1933, with Joseph GOEBBELS at its head. Goebbels manipulated the propaganda apparatus that controlled the radio, press, theater, cinema, and the arts. The ministry's administrative structure was set up that same year, with seven sections: (1) administration and organization; (2) propaganda; (3) radio; (4) the press; (5) films; (6) theater; and (7) adult education (including literature). Goebbels attached the highest importance to propaganda, which in his view was a tool for directly attracting the masses of the population. He declared that propaganda was no more than a means to an end, and if the end was not achieved, this meant that the wrong means were being used. It has rightly been said of Nazi propaganda that it was not a substitute for violence, but part of it.

[*See also* Films, Nazi Antisemitic; Stürmer, Der.]

BIBLIOGRAPHY

Baird, J. W. *The Mythical World of Nazi War Propaganda, 1939–1945*. Minneapolis, 1974.

Welch, D., ed. *Nazi Propaganda: The Power and the Limitations*. London, 1983.

Zeman, Z. A. *Nazi Propaganda*. London, 1973.

ZVI BACHARACH

PROSKAUER, JOSEPH MEYER (1877–1971), American jurist and Jewish community leader. From 1923 to 1930 Proskauer served as judge in the Appellate Division of the New York Supreme Court. He was president of the AMERICAN JEWISH COMMITTEE from 1943 to 1950. Until after the end of World War II he was a determined opponent of political Zionism and believed that the establishment of a Jewish state would be a "Jewish disaster."

In the 1930s Proskauer was opposed to the boycott of Nazi Germany (*see* BOYCOTTS, ANTI-NAZI), regarding it as the "emotional response of a noisy minority." Anti-Nazi demonstrations sponsored by Jews embarrassed him; he wanted gentiles to take the lead in the opposition to Hitler in the United States. His argument was that American Jews did not have the right to interfere with the smooth conduct of economic and diplomatic relations between the United States and a country with which it was at peace. It was only after long hesitation that Proskauer agreed to the American Jewish Committee's participation in the AMERICAN JEWISH CONFERENCE, which the Zionists initiated in 1943 to discuss the situation of the Jews in the war and the postwar era.

When the full dimensions of the Holocaust became known after the war, Proskauer was deeply shocked and began to take part in the efforts to find a solution to the problem of the Holocaust survivors. At first, until the fall of 1946, he favored the repatriation of the DISPLACED PERSONS to their former homes, or, alternatively, their immigration to other countries. He also believed that the adoption of the Human Rights Declaration by the United Nations would have a beneficial effect on the situation of the Jews in countries in which they were in distress. When he realized the impracticality of these programs and his hopes, he changed his position to support the establishment of a Jewish state in Palestine, provided that this accorded with United States policy. During the special session of the United Nations General Assembly on the partition of Palestine, in the fall of 1947, Proskauer helped in the effort to gain votes in favor of partition, having reached the conclusion that only a Jewish state could provide a haven for the Jewish refugees.

In March 1948, when the United States retreated from the partition plan, Proskauer was not prepared to accept the switch in American policy, but he tried to persuade the Jewish Agency leaders to postpone the declaration of the Jewish state so as to bring the fighting in Palestine to an end. When President Harry S. Truman immediately recognized the new state of Israel, Proskauer gave it his support, and made a point of emphasizing his own contribution to its establishment during the 1947 United Nations special session.

BIBLIOGRAPHY

Cohen, N. W. *Not Free to Desist: The American Jewish Committee, 1906–1966.* Philadelphia, 1972.

Hacker, L. M., and M. D. Hirsch. *Proskauer: His Life and Times.* Tuscaloosa, Ala., 1978.

Halperin, S. *The Political World of American Zionism.* Detroit, 1961.

Proskauer, J. M. *A Segment of My Time.* New York, 1950.

MENAHEM KAUFMAN

PROTECTORATE OF BOHEMIA AND MORAVIA. *See* Bohemia and Moravia, Protectorate of.

PROTEKTORAT BÖHMEN UND MÄHREN. *See* Bohemia and Moravia, Protectorate of.

PROTESTANT CHURCHES. *See* Christian Churches.

PROTOCOLS OF THE ELDERS OF ZION, a forged document that purports to reveal Jewish machinations to take over the world. First widely disseminated in Russia, it was adapted from a satire by Maurice Joly against Napoleon III, the *Dialogue aux Enfers entre Montesquieu et Machiavel* (Dialogue in Hell between Montesquieu and Machiavelli), published in Brussels in 1864.

According to the *Protocols* and the different introductions and commentaries to them, the Jews were going to use various weapons to achieve their domination. They would undermine European society by invoking the French Revolution, liberalism, socialism, communism, and anarchy. At the same time, they would manipulate the price of gold and foment financial crisis, gain control of the media, foster religious and tribal prejudices, and, in case of opposition, construct railways

"The Jewish Peril." Cover of a French edition of the *Protocols of the Elders of Zion* (c. 1934).

and underground passages from which cities could be blown up. Once in power, they would demand unswaying obedience to a Jewish king. In these schemes, the Jews would be aided by the FREEMASONS.

The seeds of the *Protocols* can be seen in reactionary attempts to explain the French Revolution as a Freemason conspiracy and in a forged letter of 1806 by J. B. Simonini which said that the Freemasons were a Jewish tool in a plot to become the rulers of the world. By midcentury such claims appeared in the German press as well. A prototype of the *Protocols* appeared in the novel *Biarritz* (1868), written by Hermann Goedsche and published in Berlin under the pseudonym Sir John Retcliffe (later changed to Readclif). In the chapter "In the Jewish Cemetery in Prague," the representatives of the twelve tribes of Israel are depicted at their convocation, held once every hundred years, where they report on the progress of their plot to take over the world. At the end of the session a speech is made by the presiding Levite, who expresses the hope that at the next convocation, one hundred years hence, the Jews will be the "princes of the world." This speech, eventually known as the "Rabbi's Speech," constituted a basic element of the *Protocols* and was published widely both before and after their emergence. Similar ideas were publicized in Russia at the end of the nineteenth century, especially in the books of Osman Bey.

The *Protocols* themselves were apparently forged at the time of the Dreyfus affair (1894) by Pyotr Ivanovich Rachkovski, head of the foreign branch of the Russian secret police (Okhrana), based in Paris. The French Right wanted a document that would implicate Alfred Dreyfus in the supposed conspiracy, whereas the Russians would use it to support their antisemitic policies.

In 1903 a tsarist agent, Pavolaki Krushevan, published an abridged version of the "document" in a pamphlet, *Program for World Conquest by the Jews.* In 1905, together with Krushevan, G. V. Butmi (a founder of the antisemitic Black Hundreds organization) published an unabridged version of the *Protocols,* entitled *The Root of Our Troubles.* But the version that was to make the greatest impact was the one published (also in 1905) by Sergei Nilus in the third edition of his popular book *The Great in the Small: The Antichrist Considered as an Imminent Political Possibility.* Nilus was probably supplied with the "document" by Rachkovsky, one of his associates.

When opponents of the Russian Revolution fled to the West, they brought the *Protocols* with them. Among those who reached Germany were Pyotr Nikolayevich Shabelsk-Bork and Fyodor Viktorovich Vinberg, who published the full text of the *Protocols* in the third edition of their yearbook, *Luch sveta* (A Ray of Light; Berlin, 1920). One year earlier, a German-language edition of the *Protocols, Die Geheimnisse der Weisen von Zion* (The Secrets of the Elders of Zion), had been published by Ludwig Müller (alias Müller von Hausen) under the pseudonym Gottfried zur Beck. Soon the Nazis began to make use of the *Protocols.* Between 1919 and 1923 their ideologist, Alfred ROSENBERG, also a Russian emigré, wrote five pamphlets about the conspiracy. Until the collapse of the Third Reich, Julius STREICHER's newspaper, *Der* STÜRMER, and the Nazi party newspaper, the *Völkischer Beobachter,* often cited the *Protocols;* a Nazi party edition was published in 1933.

In the 1920s the *Protocols* made their first appearance in the United States, where a number of newspapers publicized their essence, linking the Jewish conspiracy to Bolshevism. Among them was Henry Ford's paper, *The Dearborn Independent,* which published a series of articles based on the *Protocols* in the summer of 1920 and then issued them in book form as *The International Jews: The World's Foremost Problem,* in 500,000 copies. In June 1927 Ford disclaimed responsibility for the articles and tried to take the book out of circulation, but in the meantime it had been translated into six languages.

In Britain, the *Protocols* were published by most of the major newspapers in 1920; even the London *Times* treated them seriously, publicizing them in their edition of May 8, 1920. But when their own correspondent showed the document to be a forgery, the *Times* declared it to be so in a large headline on August 18, 1921. From then on the *Protocols* were discredited in Great Britain.

Between the world wars, numerous editions of the *Protocols* were published throughout the world in Polish, Romanian, Hungarian, Czech, Serbo-Croatian, Greek, Italian, Spanish, Portuguese, Flemish, Swedish, Latvian, and Arabic. During World War II, editions also came out in Norwegian and Dutch. Two trials were held before World War II in which the *Protocols* were declared to be a forgery: in Port Elizabeth, South Africa, in 1934; and in Bern, Switzerland, during 1934 and 1935.

The *Protocols* and the ideas contained in them were not only widespread at this time, but quickly became deeply rooted as well. It is clear that many leading Nazis, including Adolf HITLER, Heinrich HIMMLER, and Rosenberg, believed them. For Hitler, with his convoluted logic, the fact that Jews claimed the *Protocols* were a forgery was proof that they were genuine. In conversation with Hermann RAUSCHNING (*Conversations with Hitler,* 1940), Hitler boasted that he had learned much from the *Protocols:* "political intrigue, techniques, conspiracy, revolutionary disruption, camouflage, diversion, and methods of organization." Alfred Rosenberg's philosophy, as set out in his book the *Myth of the Twentieth Century,* is also firmly rooted in his acceptance of the "truth" of the *Protocols.* Undoubtedly, such ideas brought many Germans and other Europeans into the Nazi fold, and, as Norman Cohn has written, the *Protocols of the Elders of Zion* provided a kind of "warrant" for the attempted annihilation of the Jewish people.

After World War II, the *Protocols* continued to be published throughout the world and to foster hatred of Jews, most notably in the Middle East and the Communist-bloc countries. But they have not been confined to these two areas. In many South American countries, as well as in Spain, Italy, and Japan, new editions have been published, and the ideas put forth by the *Protocols* have been the staple of those who have sought to deny the Holocaust.

BIBLIOGRAPHY

Bernstein, H. *The Truth about the Protocols of Zion.* Introduction by N. Cohn. New York, 1971.

Cohn, N. *Warrant for Genocide: The Myth of the Jewish World-Conspiracy and the Protocols of the Elders of Zion.* London, 1967.

Mosse, G. L. *Towards the Final Solution: A History of European Racism.* New York, 1978.

Wistrich, R. *Hitler's Apocalypse: Jews and the Nazi Legacy.* New York, 1985.

ROBERT ROZETT

PRÜTZMANN, HANS-ADOLF (1901–1945), SS officer. Born in Tolkemit, in the Elbing district of East Prussia, Prützmann joined the Nazi party in 1929 and, a year later, the SS. He advanced rapidly in the police and in 1934 was promoted to the rank of SS-*Gruppenführer.* In 1938 he became a senator in Hamburg, and he was subsequently appointed the *Höherer SS- und Polizeiführer* (Higher SS and Police Leader; HSSPF) in the Nordsee district. In April 1941 he was advanced to the rank of lieutenant-general of the police.

On the day of the German invasion of the Soviet Union (June 22, 1941), Prützmann was appointed HSSPF for the Heeresgruppe (Army Group) North; on October 31 of that year, he was transferred to the Southern Command (Ukraine). Two years later, on October 22, 1943, he also became HSSPF for the REICHSKOMMISSARIAT UKRAINE.

When the war was drawing to an end, in the last quarter of 1944, Prützmann was given various special assignments, such as organizing the WERWOLF bands and supervising the special intelligence service; he was also appointed commander in chief of Croatia. At the end of the war he committed suicide after falling into British hands.

SHMUEL SPECTOR

PRUZHANY (Pol., Prużana), town in the southwest of the Belorussian SSR. In 1931 Pruzhany had a Jewish population of 4,208, more than half of the total of 7,626.

Pruzhany was occupied by the Germans on June 23, 1941. On July 10, eighteen Jews were arrested on the charge of being Communists and were killed. On July 20 a twenty-four-member JUDENRAT (Jewish Council) was set up, consisting mostly of veteran public figures. The first order given to the Judenrat, as soon as it had come into being, was to collect a ransom from the town's Jews of 176 ounces (5 kg) of gold, 110 pounds (50 kg) of silver, and 500,000 rubles ($95,000, according to the 1940 value of the ruble). At the end of July, Pruzhany was annexed to the Białystok district, which was incorporated into the Reich as part of East Prussia, under the governorship of Erich KOCH. In early September of 1941 a ghetto was formed in Pruzhany, and on September 18 thousands of Jews from Białystok and nearby towns were brought to the new ghetto. Although many of the new arrivals managed to make their way back to their homes clandestinely, the ghetto was fully packed, the average space per person being 21.5 square feet (2 sq m). There was hunger in the ghetto, but the mortality rate was not very high, since the Judenrat smuggled in food and ran welfare institutions for the needy, as well as a hospital. On January 3, 1942, all the furs and warm clothing owned by the Jews were confiscated and a second ransom payment, of 750,000 reichsmarks ($300,000) was imposed. In March 1942 more Jews were brought in, from Ivanovichi, Stolbtsy, and other places.

In the spring of 1942, several underground groups were organized in the Pruzhany ghetto. One of these, the Antifascist Organization, led by Yitzhak Shereshevski, established contact with a Belorussian underground group. On January 2, 1943, an armed group of the organization's members, consisting of twelve Jewish fighters, left the ghetto and made its way into the forest. Another group, led by Yitzhak Friedberg, armed itself with weapons taken by its members from the German troop barracks and made contact with Soviet partisans, and in December 1942 eighteen armed fighters left for the forest. Some members of the Judenrat helped these groups by financing the purchase of arms and equipment. The groups kept in communication with the ghetto and helped more fighters leave the ghetto for the forest, providing them with arms and food.

On November 1, 1942, the ghetto was put under a blockade. In the belief that the ghetto was about to be liquidated, 47 Jews committed suicide, but as it turned out, there was only a roll call; 9,976 persons were counted and registered, and then permitted to return to their homes. A second blockade was imposed on January 28, 1943. This time the Jews of Pruzhany were taken to the railway station at Linova, and from there were transported by train to AUSCHWITZ-Birkenau in three transports, the last leaving Linova on January 31. In Auschwitz, 2,000 Jews (1,200 men and 800 women) were separated out; the rest were sent to the gas chambers. Of the 2,000, no more than 200 were still alive when the camp was liberated. In the course of the liquidation *Aktion,* 2,700 Pruzhany Jews tried to flee and go into hiding; the greater part were caught and killed, and only 20 survived. Most of the fighters who had gone into the forest fought in the ranks of the Kirov Soviet Partisan Brigade, belonging to the Ponomarenko Division.

Pruzhany was liberated by the Soviet army on July 20, 1944.

BIBLIOGRAPHY

Cholawski, S. *The Jews in Belorussia (White Russia) during World War II.* Tel Aviv, 1982. (In Hebrew.)

Friedlaender, J. ed. *Pinkas Pruzany and Its Vicinity (Bereze, Malch, Shershav, Seltz and Linive).* Tel Aviv, 1983. (In Hebrew.)

SHMUEL SPECTOR

PRZEMYŚL, city in POLAND, situated on the San River in the Lvov district, Eastern Galicia. Before World War II, about twenty-four thousand Jews lived in Przemyśl. On September 14, 1939, the Germans occupied the city for the first time. Before they handed over Przemyśl to the Soviets, as part of the division of territories agreed to in the NAZI-SOVIET PACT, the Nazis killed six hundred Jews. At least half of the victims were refugees who had reached Przemyśl from western Poland. On September 28 the Soviets took possession of the city. As in other places that came into Soviet hands in 1939, the lives of the Jews changed greatly. Jewish cultural and political activity, especially religious and Zionist, came to an end. Private industries and businesses were made into cooperatives, and in April and May of 1940 about seven thousand Jews were deported to the Soviet interior.

When the Germans reoccupied Przemyśl on June 28, 1941, some seventeen thousand Jews were living there. The Nazis immediately began rounding up Jews for forced labor. On their own initiative, the Jews established a committee to represent themselves, headed by Dr. Ignatz Duldig. Within a few days the Gestapo arrived and enforced anti-Jewish measures, such as the wearing of the Jewish BADGE, the registration of all Jews in the labor office, and the establishment of a JUDENRAT (Jewish Council) under Duldig. During the following year, Jews were forced to hand over their valuables and various household goods. Those who did not comply with the Nazi decrees were beaten and imprisoned. On December 26, 1941, Schutzpolizei, along with VOLKSDEUTSCHE (ethnic Germans) and Polish policemen, entered Jewish homes and seized furs and other clothing. By the summer of 1942 some five thousand Jews from neighboring villages had been brought to Przemyśl.

In June 1942 rumors of Nazi savagery began to reach the city, such as the murder of forty-five women who had been imprisoned in nearby Zasanie. The violence soon reached Przemyśl. On June 18, one thousand Jewish men from the city were sent to the JANÓWSKA camp near Lvov. On the day of the deportation, the Gestapo guard shot many of the deportees' relatives as they parted from one another. They also shot men who tried to evade the deportation. The establishment of a sealed ghetto was announced on July 14, and all Jews had to be within its boundaries by the following day. On July 23, the Judenrat was told that in three days some Jews would be taken away for forced labor and others would be given work permits. In the end the Gestapo gave Duldig only 5,000 work permits.

The ensuing *Aktion* was carried out on three separate days, July 27 and 31, and August 3, 1942. On the first day the ghetto was surrounded by Schutzpolizei and Gestapo units. They deported 6,500 Jews to the BEŁŻEC extermination camp and shot Duldig and his deputy. On the second day, 3,000 Jews were deported to Bełżec, and on the last day another 3,000. At the end of the *Aktion* the Jews were forced to turn over a sum of money to the Gestapo, ostensibly to defray transportation costs. By the end of August, the Gestapo had murdered 100 more Jews in Przemyśl.

During the first day of the *Aktion* an extraordinary rescue took place. The military governor of the town, Lt. Dr. Alfred Battel, requested of the Gestapo that the Jews who worked for the Wehrmacht, whether they had work permits or not, be spared. When his request was not granted, Wehrmacht forces took control of the bridges that connected the two parts of the city and threatened that they would not let any transports leave. After calling their commander in Kraków, Julien Scherner, the Gestapo acceded to his request. For this, Battel was named a "RIGHTEOUS AMONG THE NATIONS" by YAD VASHEM.

Toward the middle of November, the Jews started to fear that another *Aktion* was brewing and began to build bunkers. When the second *Aktion* came, on November 18, 1942, more than 8,000 Jews without work permits were slated for deportation and about 1,500 workers were to be exempted. Only 3,500, however, showed up at the concentration point; the rest of the Jews were hiding in bunkers. During the day some 500 were found and added to the transport bound for Bełżec.

After the second *Aktion* the ghetto was divided into two sections. Section A, with 800 and later about 1,300 Jews, was reserved primarily for workers; Section B was for the remaining Jews, primarily nonworkers. In February 1943, Unterscharführer Joseph Schwamburger took over Section A, which was officially declared a labor camp.

There was no massive armed resistance in Przemyśl. In mid-April of 1943, twelve young men escaped from the ghetto and tried to join the partisans. They were intercepted by Ukrainians not far from the city and all but one were murdered. The survivor, known only by his surname, Green, was hanged in public shortly thereafter, along with Meir Krebs, who had stabbed a Gestapo man, Karl Friedrich Reisner, on May 10.

The liquidation of Section B began on September 2–3, 1943. During the *Aktion,* 3,500 Jews, most of whom were hiding in bunkers, were rounded up and sent to AUSCHWITZ. An additional 600 Jews were selected from the labor camp and sent to the Szebnie camp. From there they were sent to Auschwitz several weeks later. On September 11, 1,000 other Jews who had been enticed to leave their bunkers, or had been discovered in them, were killed by the Nazis at the edge of the city. On October 28, 100 more Jews were brought to Szebnie from the Przemyśl work camp. They too were sent to Auschwitz. At the end of February 1944 the final 150 inmates were sent to Stalowa Wola, and from there to Auschwitz. From October 1943 to April 1944, the Nazis continued to search for Jews in hiding, finding and killing about 1,000. Only 300 Jews of those living in the Przemyśl area in June 1941 survived the war.

BIBLIOGRAPHY

Dabrowska, D., A. Wein, and A. Weiss, eds. *Poland,* vol. 2. In *Pinkas Hakehillot; Encyclopaedia of Jewish Communities.* Jerusalem, 1980. (In Hebrew.)

Menczer, A., ed. *Przemysl Memorial Book.* Tel Aviv, 1964. (In Hebrew.)

ROBERT ROZETT

PSYCHOLOGY OF SURVIVORS. *See* Survivors, Psychology of.

Q

QUAKERS. *See* American Friends Service Committee.

QUISLING, VIDKUN (1887–1945), head of the Nazi-controlled puppet government of NORWAY from 1942 to 1945. Quisling, who in December 1939 had invited German troops to take over his country, openly met the invading Nazis in April 1940. His actions inspired the London *Times* to use his name as the symbol for all collaborators and traitors; thus a new word was introduced into the English language. Quisling was born in rural Fyresdal in southern Norway, the son of an erudite village pastor. He enrolled as a cadet in the Norwegian military academy, and in 1911 joined the Norwegian General Staff.

In 1918 he was appointed military attaché in Petrograd, and served there until relations with the Soviet Union were severed in early 1919. From 1922 until 1930, Quisling was assistant to the League of Nations High Commissioner for Refugees, Fridtjof Nansen. He worked on relief for starving Russian peasants in the Ukraine and on similar projects in Bulgaria, the Balkans, and Armenia. By the time he left the Soviet Union, in 1929, he had come to view the Bolshevik regime as a danger and a threat to Norwegian security.

Quisling was a co-founder, in 1931, of the Nordisk Folkereisning (Nordic Folk Awakening) movement, which reflected Nazi ideology. In 1931 Quisling, who was also a supporter of the Agrarian party, was appointed minister of defense in the Agrarian government, which was in control until February 1933. That May, he founded a fascist-inspired political party called Nasjonal Samling (National Unity; NS). The following year, he organized the young party activists into a group called the Hird, to act as bodyguards.

As early as 1930, Quisling had sought contact with the German Nazis. His political

Vidkun Quisling saluting a visiting German officer. [National Archives]

ideas were similar to those of Alfred ROSENBERG. Quisling believed that a strong leadership elite was essential to protect individual rights; the Hird was to be the spearhead of this new elite. The Jews, in his view, were impure, and their existence was a threat to the fulfillment of the ideal society. However, Quisling's movement failed to gain popularity.

Determined to save Norway in spite of itself, Quisling began negotiating with the Germans. In December 1939 he met with Rosenberg, Erich Raeder, and Hitler. During his meeting with Hitler, Quisling asked for and was assured of German financial and moral support. The plan devised during his talks in Berlin called for the occupation of Norway "by peaceful means," that is, via German forces called in by Norway.

The German assault on Norway began on the night of April 8–9, 1940, and once the German troops were in Oslo, Quisling broadcast a speech proclaiming a new government, with himself as prime minister. The German army very soon became disillusioned with him, and he was removed from office on April 15. The new government was staffed by Quisling supporters but without Quisling. He remained leader of the NS, however, and for two years worked behind the scenes.

On February 1, 1942, a national government was formed in which Quisling was *Ministerpresident*, but with limited power. Quisling hoped for a treaty with Germany that would give his regime formal status, making it independent of the German occupation power.

After the war, Quisling was arrested and tried. On September 10, 1945, he was found guilty and sentenced to death. He was executed on October 24 of that year.

BIBLIOGRAPHY

Andenaes, J., O. Riste, and M. Skodvin. *Norway and the Second World War.* Lillehammer, Norway, 1983.

Hayes, P. M. *Quisling: The Career and Political Ideas of Vidkun Quisling, 1887–1945.* Devon, England, 1971.

Hoidal, O. K. *Quisling: A Study in Treason.* New York, 1989.

Petrow, R. *The Bitter Years.* New York, 1974.

JACQUELINE ROKHSAR

RAB (Ital., Arbe), Italian internment camp on the Yugoslav island of Rab, in the northern Adriatic. The camp was established in July 1942, initially for the internment of opponents of the Italian occupation regime and supporters of the Yugoslav opposition movement from the Slovenia region. Living conditions and the regime prevailing in the camp for the Slovenians were very harsh. Of the approximately fifteen thousand prisoners who passed through the camp, some four thousand died.

Early in 1943 it was decided to set up a camp for all the Jews in Italian-occupied Yugoslavia alongside the Slovenian camp, in accordance with Italy's Jewish policy in the areas it occupied in Greece, Yugoslavia, and the south of France. The Italian authorities were totally opposed to the "FINAL SOLUTION" policy of their German ally, and categorically rejected the German request to hand over all the Jews in the Italian-occupied areas. In early 1943 the confrontation between Italy and Germany over this matter reached its peak; the Italians, however, stood firm. Fearing drastic steps by the Germans and anticipating that their own army was about to retreat from most of the area that they occupied in Yugoslavia, the Italians decided that the Jews, for their own good, should be concentrated in one place, as close as possible to the Italian border. The Rab camp seemed the most suitable. Preparations began in April 1943, and on May 20 the concentration of the Jews (who until then had been dispersed in several places along the Dalmatian coast in comparatively acceptable conditions of arrest) began; it terminated on July 10 of that year.

According to the incomplete reports of the Italians, 2,700 Jews were brought to Rab; the actual number, however, was 3,577, of whom about 500 were children under the age of fifteen.

The Italian command in the locality, in accordance with central government instructions, made great efforts to maintain decent living conditions in the camp. The diet was adequate, the living accommodations suitable, and the detainees directed all the affairs of the camp. A school was established and youth movements were very active, as were cultural institutions such as a choir, a drama circle, and study circles. An underground was established in the camp that prepared for the possibility of an Italian retreat and made contact with the Communist underground in the Slovenian camp. The day after Italy's capitulation to the Allies, on September 8, 1943, the Rab camp was liberated by the Jewish and Slovenian prisoners. Contact was quickly made with the partisan units in the area. After a few days, most of the camp inmates were taken to the liberated areas. Those who could bear arms joined the partisans, and the old people, the women, and the children found refuge among the partisans, most of them in the town of Topusko. The attempt of the Jewish youth in Rab to join the partisans' army as a separate Jewish fighting unit (to be called the Rab Jewish Battalion) failed, principally because of the ideologically inspired opposition of the partisan Communist leadership.

For various reasons, several hundred of the Jewish inmates of the camp refused to leave for the liberated areas, or to join the partisans, with the rest of the inmates. Later, on their own, some reached liberated southern Italy. About two hundred, who were captured by the Germans after their conquest of the island in March 1944, were deported to AUSCHWITZ, where they were killed.

BIBLIOGRAPHY

Carpi, D. "The Rescue of Jews in the Italian Zone of Occupied Croatia." In *Rescue Attempts during the Holocaust.* Proceedings of the Second Yad Vashem International Historical Conference, edited by Y. Gutman and E. Zuroff, pp. 465–526. Jerusalem, 1977.

Romano, J. "Jevreji u logoru na Rabu, u njihovo ukljucivanhe u narodnooslobodilacki rat." *Zbornik* 2 (1973): 1–72.

Shelah, M. *Blood Account: The Rescue of Croatian Jews by the Italians, 1941–1943.* Tel Aviv, 1986. (In Hebrew.)

Shelah, M. "The Fate of the Jewish Refugees on the Island of Rab." *Yalkut Moreshet* 35 (April 1983): 203–211. (In Hebrew.)

MENACHEM SHELAH

RACE AND RESETTLEMENT MAIN OFFICE. *See* Rasse- und Siedlungshauptamt.

RACISM, doctrine that regards the racial origin of an individual or a community as the decisive factor determining ability, inclinations, state of mind, appearance, and behavior, and that classifies humanity into "superior" and "inferior" races. The term "racism" is derived from "race," a word having different connotations to different people; it has been in use since the Renaissance to denote groups that have common traits, both humans and animals. The influence achieved by racism in modern times is the result of its becoming a sort of secular religion, based on science and history. Racism is a complete view of society and politics that is based on aesthetics and morality, as well as on science and history.

The evolution of racism can be traced through separate stages of development. Its theoretical foundations were laid during the course of the eighteenth and the first half of the nineteenth century. In the next phase, the period from the mid-nineteenth century to the end of World War I, racism gained in strength and acquired a clearer and better-defined direction. In the interwar period, it went on to penetrate the policies of political mass movements in Europe, above all, those of National Socialism in Germany, and racist theories were successfully translated into the popular political vocabulary used in large parts of the European continent. Racism continued into the years following World War II, but its protagonists were subdued by the general reactions to the crimes that had been committed in its name.

Early Concepts. The reawakening of the romantic idea of history in the eighteenth century was of supreme importance for the development of the concept of race. It was then that the principles of "organic" development were formulated, later to be introduced also into anthropology and philology—two disciplines that were to play a decisive role in the evolution of the theory of racism.

Scholars and philosophers of the Enlightenment such as Georges-Louis Buffon and Charles de Montesquieu held that historical development was conditioned by environmental factors, for example climate and geography, and they therefore regarded the differences between various peoples as purely accidental. This view was contested by the "organic" theory, which taught that an unlimited gap existed among individuals and among peoples, a gap that was not the result of sociohistorical developments but had been ordained by nature and "providence." This idea, propounded by Johann Gottfried von Herder (1744–1803), was to arouse tremendous interest in Europe. Herder believed that the roots of a people represent an unspoiled genuineness of feeling, spontaneity, and force, and it is in these roots that a people's attributes and "character" are permanently anchored. A people's national language, songs, and mythology are the authentic expressions of its spirit; the individual is no more than a part of the *Volk* (people in the ethnic sense, as conceived by Herder). In Herder's philosophy, the nation was endowed with aesthetic, historical, and linguistic dimensions, by virtue of which it became a separate entity, distinct from any passing political organization. The elevation of the "organic *Volk*" to a status that made it superior to the state was evident in every phase of the evolution of the theory of racism that followed Herder. Herder himself, however, as a product of the Age of Enlightenment, did not believe in the superiority of one people over another, and his love for his *Volk* did not entail a lack of respect for other peoples.

The emphasis on language as the expression of a shared past was common to a whole generation of philologists at the end of the eighteenth and the beginning of the nineteenth century. Most of them, however, did not share Herder's interest in the humanist aspects and concentrated on scholarly research into the genetic affinity among various languages. This research seemed to confirm that Sanskrit, ancient Persian, and languages descended from them were related to many European languages, and that therefore there must have been an original "proto"-language that had been imported from Asia into Europe by the migration of "Aryan" peoples—a language named by the philologists "Indo-European" or "Aryo-European." It was in this context that the ominous term "Aryan" made its first appearance. From here it was only a short step for research to venture into the field of value judgments and to link up with the organic view of history.

On the premise that a people's language is the expression of its accumulated experience over the ages, these scholars claimed that the "Aryan" past reflected the superiority of contemporary Europe. And so, with the help of philology, they were able to establish a link with the "Aryan" prehistory of the Germanic peoples. The philologists described the "Aryans" as courageous and virile "tillers of the soil" who led a solid family life. A historical myth was created that gave legitimacy to pretensions of moral and national superiority—an element destined to be a part of the theory of racism throughout its development.

Joseph-Arthur de Gobineau (1816–1882) was only repeating a belief accepted by the philologists of his time when he argued that the "pure" language of the "Aryans" was evidence of their ability to rise above the materialistic dimensions of life. Those opposed to the Jewish Emancipation asserted that the Jews were by nature incapable of speaking the language of their host nation, a trait that had historical roots and reflected the Jews' materialistic character. The German-born British Orientalist Friedrich Max Müller, who taught at Oxford from 1850 to 1875, claimed that the "Aryans," following an "irresistible impulse," had swept into northwestern Europe (Germany and England), and that their migration had reinforced their independence and self-reliance.

Philology, in combination with the historical myth of "Aryan" strength of character and spirituality, led to various conclusions. One such conclusion was that fate had ordained that it would be the Anglo-Saxons who would put into practice the principle of maintaining liberty by means of free institutions of government. Another was the theory that the organization of Germanic tribes (the Comitatus) had been a model of democracy in action. What these and similar conclusions meant was that the races who had not shared that common past lacked the qualities required for self-government. Tacitus's book *Germania* provided evidence of the special qualities and unique institutions of the ancient Germanic tribes.

Both the Germans and the French dug into the past for their national roots. In this the French were encouraged by Fustel de Coulanges, a nineteenth-century French historian who asserted that French love of liberty had its origin in the Roman and Celtic heritage of the French, rather than in the Comitatus. Whether ancient Germans or Celts, the characteristics ascribed to them were precisely those that the middle class all over Europe valued most: self-reliance, morality, hard work, a thirst for culture, and a wholesome family life.

The Anglo-Saxon myth was strong in the United States. It was an American, J. E. Homer, who in the late nineteenth and the beginning of the twentieth century claimed that the progress made by the European nations and by Japan was merely an imitation of the notions of true freedom as conceived by the Anglo-Saxons. Theodore Roosevelt, in his popular work *The Winning of the West,* extolled the vitality of the Germans, who "went forth from their marshy forests" to conquer the American continent. One feature of that myth was "manifest destiny"—the claim that it was the Anglo-Saxons' mission to spread their influence to all parts of the globe. This claim became part of British imperialism as well. Yet imperialism and racism were never identical; their interrelationship was dependent on time and place. During the eighteenth century, for example, Europeans could entertain enlightened and even utopian views of some non-Europeans; the image of "darkest Africa," on the other hand, was a nineteenth-century construct.

The term "race" properly belongs to anthropology rather than to history or philology. At the very time that the study of history and philology was flourishing, anthropology came up with a more accurate definition of "race," making its own contribution to the rise of racism. The classification of mankind into races was introduced by anthropology in the eighteenth century. Buffon and Carl Linnaeus (1707–1778) classified nations according to the color of their inhabitants' skin and the shape and size of their bodies; it followed that those people who shared similar characteristics of color, size, and shape made up a "race." Even this "pure" scientific definition, however, involved the character of human beings, and led to the assumption that a person's outward appearance and physical measurements reflected his spiritual qualities. Peter Camper, a Dutch anatomist, made a study of racial typology (1792–1793) based on a comparison of the facial and cranial measurements of blacks, apes, and Europeans. These showed an orderly progress from monkeys through blacks to average Europeans, and from them to the ideal Greek type.

The close connection between anthropology—which claimed to be a scientific discipline—and aesthetic criteria was to be of supreme significance for the rise of racism, which from the beginning of the nineteenth century sought to establish a model for the "ideal type" of human being. Franz Joseph Gall, writing in 1796, based the "science" of phrenology on the principle that the formation of the cranium is the key to a person's mental faculties and moral qualities. Skull measurements became of great importance for "racial biology" in its effort to establish the "ideal type." The Nazis, as well as other racists, were to make ample use of such "racial biology" (*see* ANTHROPOLOGY AND NATIONAL SOCIALISM).

Anthropology combined scientific observation with aesthetic and moral judgments. In the eighteenth century, environmental factors took pride of place. Yet Immanuel Kant (1724–1804) employed the term "race" in its anthropological meaning only in order to separate it from the influence of climate or geography. Racial purity was a basic element and had to be preserved despite external conditions. Kant believed that blacks and whites had remained separate races because they had never commingled in the course of history. Kant, however, like Herder, was a man of the Enlightenment, and never asserted that one race was superior to another.

Once the importance of environmental factors had been questioned in the name of racial purity, anthropologists increasingly began to turn their attention to the origin of the races. In the nineteenth century, efforts were made to differentiate between one "pure" race and all other races. Like the historians and the philologists, the anthropologists assumed the existence of an inherited substance that appears in one specific form and is characteristic of all persons belonging to the same race. The substance of a race, based on shared language and history, was always expressed through bodily structure and outward appearance. Racism was a visual ideology based on stereotypes. This was one of its main strengths: stereotyping made the abstract concrete, giving racism a clarity and simplicity essential to its success.

Racial concepts were spread by various learned societies, such as the Ethnological Society of Paris, which in 1839 declared that races differed from one another by their "physical organization, their moral and mental faculties, and their historical tradition." The idea that race was identical with culture, for example, was part of the program of the Ethnographical Society of London (founded in 1843) and the American Ethnological Society (1842).

Racism, however, was not yet fully accepted; the Ethnographical Society of London, concerned about the native races in the far reaches of the British Empire, believed that primitive man can be "improved," and for the same reason also rejected slavery. By then the anthropologists and the philologists had already paved the way for a school of thought which held that all "foreign" races were to be placed in between the human race and the apes. Beginning in the mid-nineteenth century, many learned societies, such as the Anthropological Society of London (1863), adopted a clearly racist attitude to the peoples that were the subject of their studies. The results of these "studies" were acclaimed in the United States, while in England itself they gained only limited popularity. In France, the studies of colonial peoples by anthropologists, historians, and philologists were also suffused with racism, even though racism was not yet deeply entrenched in the country. Altogether, racism gathered momentum and came to be accepted in some intellectual and scholarly circles.

Growth and Spread of Racist Ideology to World War I. Gobineau's *Essai sur l'inegalité des races humaines* (Essay on the Inequality of Human Races; 1853–1855) was based on anthropology and philology as they had developed by the middle of the nineteenth century. Gobineau added a distinct political and cultural dimension to the scientists' findings. His theory of racism had the purpose of explaining contemporary politics; the depravity of the modern age was the result of racial corruption. This assertion was a portent of the political exploitation of racism in days to come. Gobineau feared the emergence of a centralist government in which the masses would have too much influence. It was this combination, in Gobineau's view, that had destroyed true nobility, as well as freedom itself; and the key to this development was to be found in the existence in the world of superior and inferior races.

Gobineau classified the races—black, yellow, and white—on the basis of the kind of social structure they had created. The yellow race had proved itself in commerce and trade, but was incapable of looking beyond these materialistic achievements. The blacks were incapable of establishing any form of stable society and had to be under permanent external control. Only the white race embodied all that was noble in Gobineau's eyes: a high degree of spirituality, love of freedom, and a code of personal conduct based on honor.

This, no doubt, was a utopian vision; Gobineau himself believed that the Aryan race, having failed to stay pure, was gradually losing its age-old superiority and degenerating to the level of the other, inferior races; bourgeois regimes, the modern state, and the rise of democracy confirmed the truth of this conclusion. This pessimistic thesis was excised from later editions of the *Essai,* Gobineau's basic work. The importance of that work was not in the influence it had at the time, which was limited, but in the fact that it demonstrated the direction that racism would take in subsequent periods.

Carl Gustav Carus, a contemporary of Gobineau and a leading romantic, took the racist theory a step further, toward the creation of a racist mystique. Like Peter Camper before him, Carus concentrated on the search for ideal races and believed that such races were created by the mystical power of the sun. The ideal man, so Carus thought, was of light color and had blond hair and blue eyes, reflecting the vital force represented by the sky and the sun. In this definition of the ideal type the emphasis is on the aesthetic elements of racism, elements that developed side by side with scientific observation. The notion of "Aryan" beauty, based in part on the Greek model and in part on the symbolism of nature, gained particular significance in Germany.

From the second half of the nineteenth century, it was not so much the existence of so-called black or yellow races but antisemitism that served as the breeding ground for racist views. The reason was simple: Jews were looked upon as the representatives of a foreign culture in the heart of Europe; they dressed differently, prayed differently, and spoke a different language (Yiddish). As long as they lived in ghettos they had not aroused much interest, but this attitude changed in the wake of their emancipation, at the beginning of the nineteenth century.

Emancipation had been granted to the Jews on the assumption that they would divest themselves of their "peculiarities." But when the Jews were given full civil rights and were able to compete with their Christian neighbors in the economic and social spheres, their enemies accused them of remaining distinct, despite the Emancipation. For the people who disapproved of Emancipation and resented the Jews' success in a Christian environment, the continued existence of ghettos in eastern Europe was proof that the differences between the Jews and other peoples could never be overcome. The ghetto Jews, who were urban types with a standard of living often no higher than the bare minimum, appeared to be the antithesis of the "Aryan" ideal. Furthermore, many Jews, both those who lived in the ghetto and those who had migrated to western Europe, were still wearing their traditional clothes, their beards and *peyot* (sidelocks), and made a strange and mysterious impression on the peoples of central and western Europe.

Assimilated Jews, however, were also looked upon as a subversive element in the Christian world. In fact, the charge that the Jews were "a state within a state" was first raised in the period of Emancipation and almost inexorably led to the demand to bar the Jews from taking part in European life. Moreover, they were successful in the field of finance capitalism—which played a central role in the industrialization of Europe—because this was a field that was open to them and, being new, was not tied to old traditions that barred the Jews in most professions. Thus, Jewish families such as the Rothschilds and the Pereiras were able to accumulate great wealth. Those classes, however, who felt threatened by finance capitalism regarded such success on the part of the Jews as proof of the existence of a criminal Jewish conspiracy.

Hatred of Jews found an outlet in the 1819 uprisings in Germany, with the participation of all the social classes who most feared industrialization. In the 1848 revolution it was the artisan class—again a victim of industrialization, and indeed its first victim—that called for the exclusion of the Jews from all walks of life. But the artisans did not monopolize resistance to Jewish Emancipation. Members of the middle class and the nobility—all those who looked for economic and social stability—were inclined to blame the Jews for the crisis of industrialization. Early socialists such as Charles Fourier (1772–1837) and Pierre-Joseph Proudhon (1809–1865), bitterly antisemitic, regarded the Jews as exploiters of the working class.

Anti-Jewish feelings did not necessarily lead to racism, since most people still believed that the "good Jew" was able to rid himself of his "Jewish" qualities. Those circles, however, who believed in racial differences and in the existence of a Jewish conspiracy tended to give their support to the idea of race war. It was Darwinism that, in the second half of the nineteenth century, provided an apparently scientific basis for the inexorability of war and struggle. The principle of the "survival of the fittest" incited the races against one another and encouraged race war. The works of the zoologist Ernst Heinrich Haeckel, widely read at the end of the nineteenth and the beginning of the twentieth century, served to propagate the thesis that the biological history of an individual must in abbreviated form reflect the biological development of his ancestors (the so-called biogenetic law). And so the mythical continuity of the *Volk* coalesced with the Darwinist view of the world.

The title that the German journalist Wilhelm Marr gave to his 1867 book *Der Sieg des Judenthums über das Germanenthum* (The Victory of Judaism over Germanism) was symptomatic of this attitude. In his book Marr claimed that the Jews had declared war against the Germans and were about to achieve final victory in that war by seizing control of the German economy; this was a war between two races, which did not allow for any compromise. Influential writings such as Ludwig Woltmann's book *Politische Anthropologie* (Political Anthropology; 1903) expressed support for aggressive wars of conquest that had the purpose of ensuring the survival of the race. Here again the "proof" of "Aryan" superiority is linked to aesthetics, for Woltmann claims that only the "Aryans" were able to revive "the absolute proportions of architectural beauty" according to the Greek model.

This was also the central theme of Houston Stewart CHAMBERLAIN's book *Die Grundlagen des 19. Jahrhunderts* (Foundations of the Nineteenth Century; 1899). The Germans are the saviors of mankind and the bearers of Western culture; all cultural achievements of the modern age are evidence of their indomitable soul, steeled in an unending struggle. The "Aryans" had preserved their purity in the "chaos of the races," but a bastard race, the Jews, had entered history at the same time as the Aryans and now face them in a fight to the finish. The Jews are the antithesis of the "Aryan." They are incapable of rising to superior levels of thought and culture. They have a lust for power that is devoid of all metaphysical depth. The struggle for survival between the races can end only in victory or extinction; what the "Aryans" need to overcome the Jews is a leader. Toward the end of his life, Chamberlain believed that such a leader had indeed been found, in the person of Adolf Hitler. Chamberlain's book is one of the classics of racism. It had a wide circulation and was a compendium of nineteenth-century racism.

Another popular book that helped propagate the doctrine of racism was Julius Langbehn's *Rembrandt als Erzieher* (Rembrandt as Educator; 1890). It asserts that the Germans must become creative once again, accepting an Aryan mystique that incorporates theosophist and Swedenborgian elements. According to Langbehn, a life force flows from the cosmos to the soul of the *Volk*. Racism, in this form, became a mystique, based on movements dedicated to the supernatural and the occult. Langbehn was not alone in this approach; at the beginning of the twentieth century a circle of "cosmic" philosophers, among them Ludwig Klages, emerged in Munich that held similar views. According to these "cosmic" philosophers, "Aryan" blood had a unique capability to fathom the extrasensory world and reflect the cosmos. Through this circle Hitler himself, who believed in secret sciences, became imbued with the mystery rather than the science of race.

This form of racism met with greater success in Protestant than in Catholic areas. Catholic theology presented to its faithful a well-defined view of the world, and its authoritative hierarchy made sure that its doctrine remained intact. Protestantism, on the other hand, was often unclear and divided in its theological systems and was, moreover, linked to the secular state. But this was a difference in degree only; in the end the great majority of both Catholics and Protestants accepted the racist policy of National Socialism, although a few leading theologians in both camps opposed that policy.

Science continued to make its contribution. The French philosopher Vacher de Lapouge, in his book *L'Aryen, son rôle sociale* (The Aryan's Social Role; 1890), connected eugenics with Gobineau's ideal of "Aryan" superiority. It was in Germany, however, that eugenics as racial eugenics became popular, and that many ideas were put forward as to how the superior race might procreate itself under ideal conditions. This development reached a climax in Nazi Germany with the SS-sponsored Lebensborn (Fountain of Life) experiment to ensure racial purity by pairing carefully selected males and females who were found to possess authentic "Aryan" qualities. Programs of this sort also considered the use of "mercy killings," and this idea too was put into practice by the Nazis (*see* EUTHANASIA PROGRAM). Euthanasia—the killing of the congenitally ill, the mentally ill, and the physically deformed—was justified because such individuals represented the degeneration of the "superior race." The term "degeneration" had been coined by physicians such as Jean-Baptiste Morrel and Cesare Lombroso, who thought that certain physical defects and weakness of nerves indicated a process of human degeneration. The racists adopted the term "degeneration" and used it for their own purposes. Through the use of eugenics, the "Aryan" stereotype would become a self-fulfilling prophecy; if the race did not reflect that stereotype, the race's ranks had to be purified to make sure that the ideal type would prevail.

Even apart from eugenics, medical theory made important contributions to racism during the nineteenth century. The medical vocabulary of health and sickness was applied to the so-called inferior race, stereotyped through its lack of the strength, vigor, and manliness thought essential for progress. Medicine supported society's ideal of respectability, and anyone who differed from the norm was morally and medically suspect. Above all, so-called sexual normality and restraint became a symbol of society's health, and those who did not conform were thought to be deformed, suffering from shattered nerves, and close to death. Jews as real or potential outsiders were also medicalized toward the end of the century. Thus, the famous psychiatrist Jean-Martin Charcot thought Jews especially subject to nervous diseases and hysteria. Yet such physicians were not necessarily racist—Charcot, for example, believed that some Jews might be cured. Yet the subjectivity of medicine, and its moral judgments as part of its medical ones, were easily annexed by racism. Indeed, racism made good use of the fears of the respectable classes confronted by the "vibrations of modernity."

The association between racism and sexuality was direct: playing the protector of middle-class respectability, racism endowed so-called inferior races with dangerous sexual passions that seemed to threaten the stability and cohesion of the existing order. First blacks and then Jews were accused of knowing no love but only lust, directed against the women of the superior race. Undue or illicit passion was associated, in turn, with an inborn tendency toward nervousness and instability on the part of Jews, homosexuals, and the insane—precisely those whom the Nazis later intended to kill, with some doctors playing an important part in the killing process (*see* PHYSICIANS, NAZI). The race war was directed principally against the Jews, but racism also wanted to eliminate all those who seemed to menace the health of the superior race. Such health was demonstrated through outward appearance as well as by conformity to the manners and morals of the existing order.

The developments in racism during the latter half of the nineteenth century were also imported into America. At the end of the century, America witnessed the immigration of huge numbers of people from central and southern Europe, and the racist theories that were already being applied to blacks were now extended to include all peoples who were not of Anglo-Saxon descent. Typical of this trend was Madison Grant's *Passing of the Great Race* (1916), which was intended as a warning to the American nation that it was about to lose its Nordic character. The principles of racism were used, to some degree, to justify the imposition of restrictions on immigration from areas other than northern Europe.

Meanwhile, the American South enforced strict segregation of the black and white races. The physical segregation of the whites from the blacks was the most far-reaching measure introduced in the Reconstruction period (1865–1877) that followed the Civil War. In the South, segregation was meticulously observed, but it also existed in the North, where blacks were restricted to certain parts of the cities. Hopes for full emancipation were shattered, with the color bar retaining its hold on the consciousness of both races. The same charges that in Europe were leveled against the "inferior" Jewish race were raised in America against the blacks as well: claims about external appearance, cranial measurements, and moral inferiority. Even supposed differences in odor and in the texture of hair, which antisemites had used to stress racial differences, were applied to the blacks. Accusations of uncontrolled sexuality were especially important here. The fear of miscegenation—of whites interbreeding with blacks—led to lynchings of blacks suspected of having raped white women, just as the racists in Europe were to accuse the Jews of raping "Aryan" women.

In France, Catholicism presented an obstacle to the full development of racial doctrines, particularly among the middle and upper classes. In its early stage antisemitism in France was a phenomenon of the Left rather than the Right. The Jew was the symbol of the exploitation of the workers. Jewish control of finance capitalism dominated the imagination of early French socialists such as Alphonse Toussenel, whose *Les Juifs, rois de l'époque* (The Jews, Kings of the Age; 1845) coined a slogan used in Germany as well as in France. Edouard-Adolf Drumont, whose book *La France juive* (Jewish France; 1886) played a leading role in the rise of French antisemitism, emphasized such a Jewish conspiracy, which, he alleged, was aiming to seize control of France. This was the time of the Panama Canal scandal, in which Jews were involved, and of the collapse of the Union Générale, a Catholic bank. "Anti-Dreyfusards," like Drumont and Auguste-Maurice Barrès, while contrasting the French with the Jewish race, were careful to pay lip service to the Jewish religion; they disclaimed any intention of attacking the Jewish faith, despite their stated belief that "contemporary Jews are materialist." Such men were populists and national socialists who wanted to use the state to abolish finance capitalism, even while maintaining the social hierarchy. The workers must be guaranteed the right to work and encouraged to become small-scale proprietors. These aims could be accomplished by driving out the Jews and confiscating their apparently enormous wealth for the benefit of the nation. Similar views were expressed in Germany by Eugen Dühring, who, even while championing the workers' right to strike and to form unions, unleashed a tirade of hate against the Jews as the inferior race in his book *Die Judenfrage* (The Jewish Question; 1880).

Racism gathered strength everywhere before World War I, perhaps most significantly in France, with its national socialist movements inspired by Drumont and others, which gathered an important following among the lower classes. ACTION FRANÇAISE was not, properly speaking, a racist movement; its spiritual father, Charles Maurras, hated the Jews, the Germans, and the English, but his views were not based on racial premises. In Maurras's concept, France should be Catholic and monarchist, and there would be no room for any kind of secular religion.

France's major contribution to racism in the second half of the nineteenth century, apart from national socialism, was the PROTOCOLS OF THE ELDERS OF ZION, a forgery concocted during the Dreyfus affair. The *Protocols* purported to be minutes of a secret meeting attended by the leaders of international Jewry in which a plan was drawn up for world domination, to be achieved "by cunning and by force." They had in fact been created in Paris in collaboration with the Okhrana, the tsarist secret police, and the text itself was made up by Frenchmen. The purpose of the forgery was to provide "evidence" of the many allegations of the existence of a Jewish conspiracy, a theory that had become an important element in racist thought and was to be adopted by all racists after World War I. In the United States, for example, Henry Ford gave the *Protocols* a wide circulation. Refugees from Bolshevik Russia introduced the *Protocols* into Germany, where they soon became a staple of the political Right. Hitler, for example, believed them to be true.

In Italy, racist philosophy did not make a great impact. Both the Catholic church and Giuseppe Mazzini's humanist nationalism served as effective brakes on the development of racism. Virulent Catholic antisemitism existed in Italy, as in France, but it could not support racism. Racism by its very nature denied the validity of Christian baptism; moreover, as a full-fledged ideology it threatened to create a rival religion. It was in central and eastern Europe that racism and nationalism formed the most effective alliance. In a number of these countries—Romania, Hungary, and Poland—the Jews were the "most visible" element of the commercial middle class. Furthermore, the presence of an urban ghetto civilization encouraged the belief in difference based on race. Here, too, the strong Catholic church put some restraint on the spread of racism; however, the view in these countries that nationalism was under siege by internal and external forces encouraged racism. Nationalism of this kind always wanted to revoke the Jews' Emancipation.

In the last two decades of the nineteenth century, a large number of groups and political parties with antisemitic leanings were founded. Some of these, like the Christian-Socialist party in Germany (1887–1894), established by Adolf Stoecker, were conservative and based their ANTISEMITISM on conventional Protestantism. Others adopted a National Socialist and racist orientation, such as Bauernverein (Peasant Association; 1887–1894) in Hessen, founded by Otto Böckel, and various antisemitic societies. These organizations reached their peak in 1893, when all the German antisemitic groups united under one banner and ran in that year's elections, obtaining 116,000 votes; thereafter they entered a rapid decline and spent their time bickering with one another.

Of greater importance was the alliance between the German Conservative party and the antisemitic forces in 1892 (the Tivoli Program). The Conservatives advocated disfranchisement of the Jews, on the ground that Germany was a Christian country; one influential faction in the party adopted racist views in the course of its contacts with the Bund der Landwirte (Farmers' Union), an organization of large landowners with a long record of promoting racism. Before World War I, conservative political groups and parties did not resort to violence against the Jews, and except for tsarist Russia, where the government encouraged pogroms from time to time, the use of outright violence before that war was restricted to marginal groups.

From Ideology to Mass Movement: Racism and Politics. Prior to 1918, the ideas of racism found fertile ground among small sects that were competing with one another. These sects maintained the mystical, rather than the "scientific," tradition of racism; they focused on "Aryan" man as a product of the sun who was in touch with the cosmos, and based their ideal on this type of image, instead of on anthropological or philological findings. In Austria, Lanz von Liebenfels published a small racist periodical and sold it on the streets of Vienna; it was named *Ostara,* after the German goddess of spring, and its subtitle was *Zeitschrift für Blonde* (Journal for Blond People). Hitler, whose racism was inspired by similar sources, may well have been one of *Ostara*'s readers.

In MEIN KAMPF Hitler relates that he became antisemitic after seeing in the streets of Vienna Jews from eastern Europe, dressed in their strange black garb. His reaction was no different from that of many other persons in the second half of the nineteenth century, who, when faced by what seemed a strange-looking people, felt that they had to embark upon a racist war on behalf of the German spirit. Thus, Hans Friedrich Karl Günther, a leading Nazi racist theoretician, placed emphasis on the physical differences between the "Aryan" and the Jewish race, and even drew up a list of typical "Jewish" bodily movements and physical traits. His adversary, the psychologist Ludwig Ferdinand Clauss, in his book *Die nordische Seele* (The Nordic Soul; 1932), deprecated the significance of outward appearance and claimed that it was the "internal qualities" of race that were decisive. This was Clauss's way of getting around the problem that most so-called Aryans were not blond, slim, and well formed.

The doctrine of racism did not undergo any substantive change in the post–World War I period, but new factors were adduced in its support. Psychology, or some forms of it (not Freudian psychology), now emphasized the differences between the races. One was the school of psychology that in Europe was linked to Carl Gustav Jung and in the United States to William McDougall. McDougall found that the herd instinct was weak among the northern peoples and strong among the Mediterranean peoples. An American school of psychology used IQ tests to prove its racist theories. Jungian psychology tended to slip into the realm of mystical symbolism; it placed an emphasis on immutable archetypes and found it easy to accept racist overtones. Jung himself for several years edited a leading journal of psychology published under the Nazi regime. Many scientists tried to differentiate between their work in the laboratory, where they adhered to the scientific method, and in the outside world, where they treated with respect all sorts of irrational ideas. Such differentiation, however, proved to be untenable, and before long the scientists' irrational attitudes on political and social issues brought forth "Aryan" physics, "Aryan" medicine, and "Aryan" biology.

The success of the Bolshevik revolution in Russia and the revolutions in Germany and eastern Europe added yet another dimension to the dynamics of racism. Russian refugees took pains to circulate the *Protocols of the Elders of Zion* all over Europe, and Bolshevism was depicted as an achievement of the Jewish conspiracy. Jews had always been charged with trying to undermine the stability of the Christian world, and now the Jewish-Communist conspiracy was added to the arsenal of the racist doctrine, encouraged by the presence of many Jews in the leadership of the revolution.

After World War I, the ideas that Madison Grant had propounded in an academic setting were widely circulated in the United States. The Ku Klux Klan grew by leaps and bounds, and in 1923 estimates of its size ranged from 3 million to 6 million. Contrary to what happened in Europe, however, no mass political movement based on racist principles was formed in the United States. In large part, racism was absorbed into the existing two-party political system, with opponents of racism found in both parties; there was no room left in which a separate, anti-establishment racist policy could operate. This was not so in Europe, where racism permeated mass politics after the war.

Following World War I, an attempt was made to put theory into practice. Political movements used racism as a dynamic in order to wage war against their enemies. In that respect there was no difference between NATIONAL SOCIALISM in Germany, the IRON GUARD in Romania, and the USTAŠA in Croatia. In the nineteenth century the racists had confined themselves to theory, but in the period after World War I, the leaders of racist movements took part in the political action of the time, resorting to violence, which most of the "respectable" racists of earlier generations had sought to avoid. Leaders of racist movements were no longer content with removing the Jews from economic or social life but called for their destruction. The renewal of pogroms in Romania during the short period that the Iron Guard was in power (1940–1941), and similar atrocities committed by the racist political movements in Hungary and Croatia, were clear evidence that wherever there was racism, violence was taking hold.

The increased role and strength of violence also helped to dehumanize the enemy. It was Dietrich Eckart, Hitler's adviser in the early stage of his entry into politics, who said that no people would have left the Jews alive if they had known what the Jews' true nature was and what goals they had set themselves. In Eckart's case this was rhetoric, but Hitler believed it, and declared that an inferior human specimen was closer to the apes than to the superior races of mankind. Heinrich HIMMLER, in order to reinforce his men's motivation for their part in the Holocaust, compared the Jews to fleas and mice—obnoxious forms of life that had to be destroyed. Visual "documentation" for these theories (*see* FILMS, NAZI ANTISEMITIC) was a crucial part of the propaganda addressed to the masses.

The call for violence emanated in large part from National Socialist movements. Corneliu Codreanu's Legion of the Archangel Michael (the forerunner of the Iron Guard) in Romania was a peasant movement that also attracted industrial workers. Like most movements of its kind in the underdeveloped countries of eastern Europe, Codreanu's Legion placed emphasis on a national and mystical Christianity, to which it added belief in the existence of a Jewish-Communist conspiracy. In Hungary, Ferenc SZÁLASI's ARROW CROSS PARTY rivaled the Iron Guard in its brutality; 43 percent of its membership consisted of industrial workers. During the short period that the Croatian state was in existence (1941–1944), its national movement, the Ustaša, slaughtered half a million Serbs and Jews by the most primitive and cruel methods. In Slovakia, Andrej HLINKA's party introduced brutal anti-Jewish racial legislation that met with little resistance in the party, even though many of its members were devout Catholics, including clerics. In these countries, racist movements succeeded in attracting the lower classes to their ranks at the precise moment when the latter were becoming a force in political life. In central Europe, which had strong Socialist and Communist parties, racism after the war mobilized mainly the middle classes. But in Austria and Bohemia, the first large groups to join Hitler's National Socialism came from the working class; in that region the decisive factor was not fear of Bolshevism but rivalry with Slavic workers, such as the Czechs.

In Germany, where "respectability" was a very important consideration, the Nazi platform called only for the elimination of Jews from the nation's social and political life. In practice, however, the Germans' "respectability" did not keep the youth of the lower classes from joining the SA (Sturmabteilung; Storm Troopers) in a civil war against the enemies of the movement. The combination worked well, and the momentum was maintained. Yet youthful violence was no longer needed once the movement had attained power; the SA was disciplined in 1934 and lost its power.

For the policy of race war to succeed in a country suffused with bourgeois values, it had to be in the hands of a "respectable" movement. Such a movement could not present itself as advocating a policy of pogroms, as did the Iron Guard, or of lynchings of the kind that took place from time to time in the United States. Fanatic actions of this sort against individuals were by now out of date. Instead, National Socialism set in motion a process of dehumanizing the racial enemy, so that when the attacks were launched the designated targets no longer appeared as human beings but as the embodiment of evil.

Racism fully achieved its goal of genocide not through open violence but by means of a systematic, bureaucratic process. The tactics that Hitler employed consisted of the gradual removal of obstacles, and of propaganda and indoctrination. The principal measures taken by the Nazis to erect the first racist state in Europe can be easily identified. Of decisive importance for the evolution of racism were the NUREMBERG LAWS (1935), which not only provided the legal basis for separating the Jews from the Christians, but also gave a precise definition of who was a Jew—something that the racist doctrine had failed to do up to that time. Under these laws a Jew was someone with four, or at least three, Jewish grandparents; a person who had two Jewish grandparents was defined as a *Mischling* (a person of mixed blood; *see* MISCHLINGE). This category was doomed to extinction for lack of progeny, since *Mischlinge* were not allowed to have sexual relations with either Jews or "Aryans." The same laws also for the first time defined with legal precision who was an "Aryan": a person whose paternal and maternal grandparents all belonged to the "Aryan" race. In order to become a member of the elite SS corps, however, a person had to provide evidence of pure "Aryan" ancestry dating back to the period before the greater emancipation of the Jews (that is, before 1850). Racism had become an integral part of the legal system of a major European state.

The Nazi conquests during World War II tested the strength of racism in Europe as Germany sought cooperation from its satellite states in implementing the "FINAL SOLUTION" of the "Jewish question." The conservative-minded dictators in some of those states, however, resisted, or tried to resist, the Nazi demands to hand over their Jews. In Romania, Marshal Ion ANTONESCU at first issued orders for the deportation and extermination of Jews, but under the impact of the changing war situation he reversed himself and tried to mitigate the outcome of his earlier decisions. In Hungary, Adm. Miklós HORTHY held out against Nazi pressure until the German occupation of his country. In the West, Marshal Philippe PÉTAIN surrendered to the Germans the foreign Jews who had taken refuge in France, but tried to save the native French Jews from deportation.

Even before World War II, there was a clear difference between reactionary dictatorships and racism. Such men as Engelbert Dollfuss in Austria and Francisco Franco in SPAIN may not have been overly fond of the Jews, but in their eyes, and in the eyes of similar autocrats who came to power during the war, racism was not a policy that they could accept. It was incompatible with the Catholic religion on which their regimes were based, and, more importantly, racism as a dynamic mass movement represented a threat to their own conservative regimes.

In the West, resistance to racism was stronger, because Nazi influence on the fascist movements there had never struck deep roots. Such fascist movements as the Rexists in Belgium, or even the NATIONAAL SOCIALISTISCHE BEWEGING (National Socialist Movement) in the Netherlands, were not at first antisemitic, and became racist only as they collaborated with the Nazi occupiers. In France, racism after World War I was a marginal political movement. The Parti Populaire Français, France's largest fascist movement, did not proclaim a racist policy before World War II, and prior to the German victory over France regarded resistance to Bolshevism as the most important issue. FASCISM in western Europe followed the example of Italy, which had no racist policy before 1938. In the end, when Benito MUSSOLINI did adopt such a policy, he did so in order to reinvigorate his tired regime and cement the alliance with Germany. The Italian Fascists found it difficult to discover any traces of an indigenous racist tradition. The most that Italian writers such as Giovanni Preziosi could do was to transpose foreign-made racist elements onto Italy's Roman past. Mussolini rediscovered Gobineau, whose racism, however, was not directed against the Jews. He was also impressed by Julius Evola, who tried to graft the qualities of the northern "Aryan" on a "Mediterranean Aryan race" and stressed the difference between biological racism and a "spiritual" racism resembling that espoused by Clauss. Evola also regarded race as an "idea" in the Platonic sense, which should lead to the aristocratic behavior extolled by Gobineau. "Spiritual racism" had the advantage of flexibility, adding a fresh dimension to the "new type of man" that Fascism had promised to produce.

The racism of the Italian Fascist leaders was no more than opportunism, and even the veteran antisemite Roberto Farinacci did not really believe in the racist doctrine he was propagating. When racism became the official policy of the Italian regime, Mussolini coined the slogan "Rather discrimination than persecution." The fact is that while Italian Jewry went through difficult times and suffered many humiliations, the policy of genocide was carried out only under the German occupation. Italian public opinion never accepted racist ideas.

The nations that fought National Socialism in World War II were overtly united in their rejection of racism. Britain's racist inclination had traditionally found its expression in contacts with the empire's colonial population. At home in Britain, Oswald MOSLEY's fascist movement had never received widespread support, even when it adopted racism in the hope of galvanizing the movement. In Russia, antisemitism in the old style appeared here and there during the war, but it was opposed by official Soviet policy. In the United States, where Nazi racism was strongly opposed, racism against blacks nonetheless persisted.

Racism after World War II. After the war, racism as an element of government policy ceased to be acceptable in most countries where it had previously existed. One exception was South Africa, where racism became the official policy of the state. The National party had been established there in 1914 for the avowed purpose of restoring the Afrikaner tradition. In the 1920s a policy that discriminated against blacks was adopted in all parts of the country, the Afrikaners liquidating the liberal tradition of the English-speaking province of Cape Town. During World War II the Dutch Protestant church of South Africa gave all-out support to the strict separation of the races; like many German Protestants under the Nazis, it believed that the difference between the races was ordained by divine law. In 1948 the National party succeeded in having a series of laws enacted that formalized its policy of apartheid. All forms of racial integration were prohibited, and the country's black population was restricted to certain designated areas.

The war did not end racial segregation in the United States. It took the civil rights struggle in the 1960s to obtain full voting rights and greater equality for blacks. Anti-Jewish discrimination in employment and in hotels and vacation resorts ended earlier, as a reaction against the Nazi crimes. There were sporadic outbursts of anti-Jewish racism in France during the Algerian war, and racism itself revived in both France and England as a result of black, colored, and North African immigration from the former colonies. Some Arab nations, and especially Egypt before the peace agreement with Israel, made use of racism as a weapon directed against the Jewish state.

Racism continues to exist, if not overtly, then beneath the surface. Stereotypes continue to mold the attitudes of many people when faced with those who are foreign or different from the accepted norm. Legendary historical roots still play a vital role in modern nationalism. People still view with suspicion and fear the differences they perceive between their own community and the outside world.

[*See also* Genocide.]

BIBLIOGRAPHY

Mosse, G. L. *The Crisis of German Ideology.* New York, 1964.

Mosse, G. L. *Toward the Final Solution: A History of European Racism.* New York, 1980.

Poliakov, L. *The Aryan Myth: A History of Racist and Nationalist Ideas in Europe.* London, 1974.

GEORGE L. MOSSE

RADA GŁÓWNA OPIEKUŃCZA (Central Welfare Council; RGO), organization of Polish volunteers active from 1940 to 1945 in the GENERALGOUVERNEMENT, with the permission of and under the supervision of the German occupation authorities. The first chairman of the council was Adam Ronikier, followed in October 1943 by Konstanty Tchorznicki. The council's center was in KRAKÓW. In the districts, Polskie Komitety Opiekuńcze (Polish Welfare Committees) functioned under the direction of the council, and in the local communities, under the direction of the committees' representatives. Many social welfare stations were operated by the committees and representatives. The number of persons receiving aid from the council varied according to the circumstances: in 1941, 1 million persons; in the summer of 1944, 550,000; and in the fall of 1944, 1.2 million.

The council supplied food, clothing, fuel, health services, money, and other forms of aid. It operated welfare institutions and organized special care services for children, exiles, and prisoners. The council received its financial support through contributions from the public and from Polish institutions, allocations from the occupation authorities, independent income, and one-time donations from the Polish underground. Articles of clothing and equipment were received from overseas; as gifts from different government offices; through purchase on the free market; and as donations from Poles and Polish institutions.

The RGO had extensive connections with the leaders of the underground and its branches, and with groups within the Polish community. It was influenced by them and cooperated with them. Since it was under the supervision of the occupation authorities and had to function within the restrictions imposed by the latter, the council tried to influence the authorities to improve the situation of the population within the Generalgouvernement, negotiating courageously and bypassing bans and restrictions. It did not submit to the attempts the Germans made to induce it to cooperate with them.

Other welfare organizations active during this period were the Żydowska Samopomoc Społeczna (Jewish Self-Help Society; ŻSS) and the Ukrainska Rada Główna (Ukrainian Central Council), which constituted part of the Naczelna Rada Opiekuńcza (Main Welfare Council).

The RGO attempted to provide assistance to Jews, and Poles and Jews worked together within it. Ronikier supported the interests of the ŻSS and the Jewish population. On a number of occasions the council came to the defense of Jews before the occupation authorities.

After the ŻSS was closed down in the fall of 1942, Ronikier continued to distribute to the Jews contributions received from overseas, and the council also gave financial support to the Jüdische Unterstützungsstelle (Jewish Welfare Bureau). In Kraków the council cooperated with the ZEGOTA organization in rescuing Jews.

BIBLIOGRAPHY

Friedman, P. *Their Brothers' Keepers.* New York, 1978.

Kroll, B. *Rada Główna Opiekuńcza, 1939–1945.* Warsaw, 1984.

BOGDAN KROLL

RADA POMOCY ŻYDOM. *See* Zegota.

RADEMACHER, FRANZ (1906–1973), Nazi Foreign Office official. Rademacher was the head of D III, the so-called Jewish desk (Judenreferat) of the German Foreign Office, from May 1940 until April 1943. The son of a locomotive engineer, Rademacher studied law, entered the civil service, and, like many government employees, joined the Nazi party in March 1933. He was called to the Foreign Office in 1937 and served several years abroad before being appointed head of D III.

As the new Foreign Office "Jewish expert," Rademacher sought immediately to transcend the rather mundane tasks of his predecessor and claim for the Foreign Office a major role in realizing a "final solution to the Jewish question" within the framework of Germany's war aims and anticipated victory. Among the possibilities he suggested in this regard was the expulsion of the European Jews to the island of Madagascar, a French colony in the Indian Ocean. When this notion met with approval from above, Rademacher devoted himself to preparing the MADAGASCAR PLAN (simultaneously developed by Adolf EICHMANN), until German failure to defeat Great Britain made clear that it could not soon be realized.

In the fall of 1941 Rademacher became directly involved for the first time in the mass murder of Jews when he was sent to Serbia to help occupation authorities there find a "local solution" (in this case firing-squad executions) to the Jewish question. Most of the time, however, he did his work behind a desk in Berlin. As the "FINAL SOLUTION" was implemented throughout Europe, Rademacher's Judenreferat was responsible for minimizing foreign-policy complications that might jeopardize or delay the deportations, and in this regard he was all too successful. His desk also served as the liaison between Eichmann's office in charge of coordinating the deportations, the German embassies, and special "advisers for Jewish affairs" in the Axis and satellite countries.

As part of a reorganization of the German Foreign Office in the spring of 1943, Rademacher was released for military service in the navy. After the war he was tried in the German state court in Nuremberg-Fürth and convicted. However, he jumped bail while the case was being appealed and fled to Syria in 1953. Penniless and in ill health, he returned to Germany in 1966 and faced a further trial, conviction, and appeal before his death in 1973.

BIBLIOGRAPHY

Browning, C. R. *The Final Solution and the German Foreign Office: A Study of Referat D3 of Abteilung Deutschland, 1940–1943*. New York, 1978.

CHRISTOPHER R. BROWNING

RADOM, city in central POLAND, about 62 miles (100 km) south of Warsaw. Jews began settling in Radom only in the second quarter of the nineteenth century. In 1827 there were 230 Jews in the city, about 23 percent of the total population. The Jewish community grew to approximately 23,500 in 1921 and 30,000 on the eve of World War II, amounting to 33 percent of the population.

The German army seized Radom on September 8, 1939, and immediately subjected the Jewish population to severe persecutions. During the first months of the occupation, several thousand Jews from the Poznań and Łódź provinces were expelled to Radom. In turn, 1,840 Jews from Radom were expelled to the smaller towns in the vicinity. The anti-Jewish persecutions were intensified with the creation of the GENERALGOUVERNEMENT in October 1939. Radom became the capital of one of the four original districts of the Generalgouvernement.

In December 1939 a JUDENRAT (Jewish Council) was appointed by the German authorities, with Josef Diament as its chairman, as well as a JÜDISCHER ORDNUNGSDIENST (Jewish police), headed by Joachim Geiger. Beginning in August 1940, in a wave of deportations, about two thousand young Jewish men and women were deported to forced-labor camps in the Lublin district, where almost all of them perished owing to the reign of terror and the inhuman conditions. Hundreds of others were deported to a number of small forced-labor camps set up in the vicinity of Radom, notably Kruszyna, Jedlinsk, Lesiow, Dąbrowa Kozłowska, and Wolanow.

In March 1941 a decree was issued ordering the establishment of a ghetto, and by April 7 the entire Jewish population was concentrated in two separate ghettos: a large ghetto in the center of the city, and a small ghetto in the Glinice suburb. The Jews enclosed in the two ghettos suffered from hunger—the Germans had allotted a ration of 100 grams (3.5 oz) of bread daily per person and 200 grams (7 oz) of sugar a month—and from poor sanitary conditions, a consequence of the overcrowding in the limited area of the ghettos. Ghetto inmates tried to save themselves and their families from hunger by smuggling in food from outside. A few hundred of them (including a high percentage of women) were shot by German guards either when attempting to leave the ghetto or upon being discovered outside its borders.

At the beginning of 1942 the local Gestapo conducted a number of terror *Aktionen* within the ghettos, which were aimed first of all against members of the intelligentsia. One of the first such *Aktionen* was the so-called Bloody Thursday, on February 19, when 40 to 50 men in the large ghetto were seized by the Gestapo according to a prepared list and shot on the spot; about 100 others were deported to AUSCHWITZ. On April 18 another 21 men were shot in the large ghetto, and 60 deported to Auschwitz. On the night of April 27–28 there were terror *Aktionen* in both the large and the small ghettos. About 70 persons were shot and another hundred arrested and

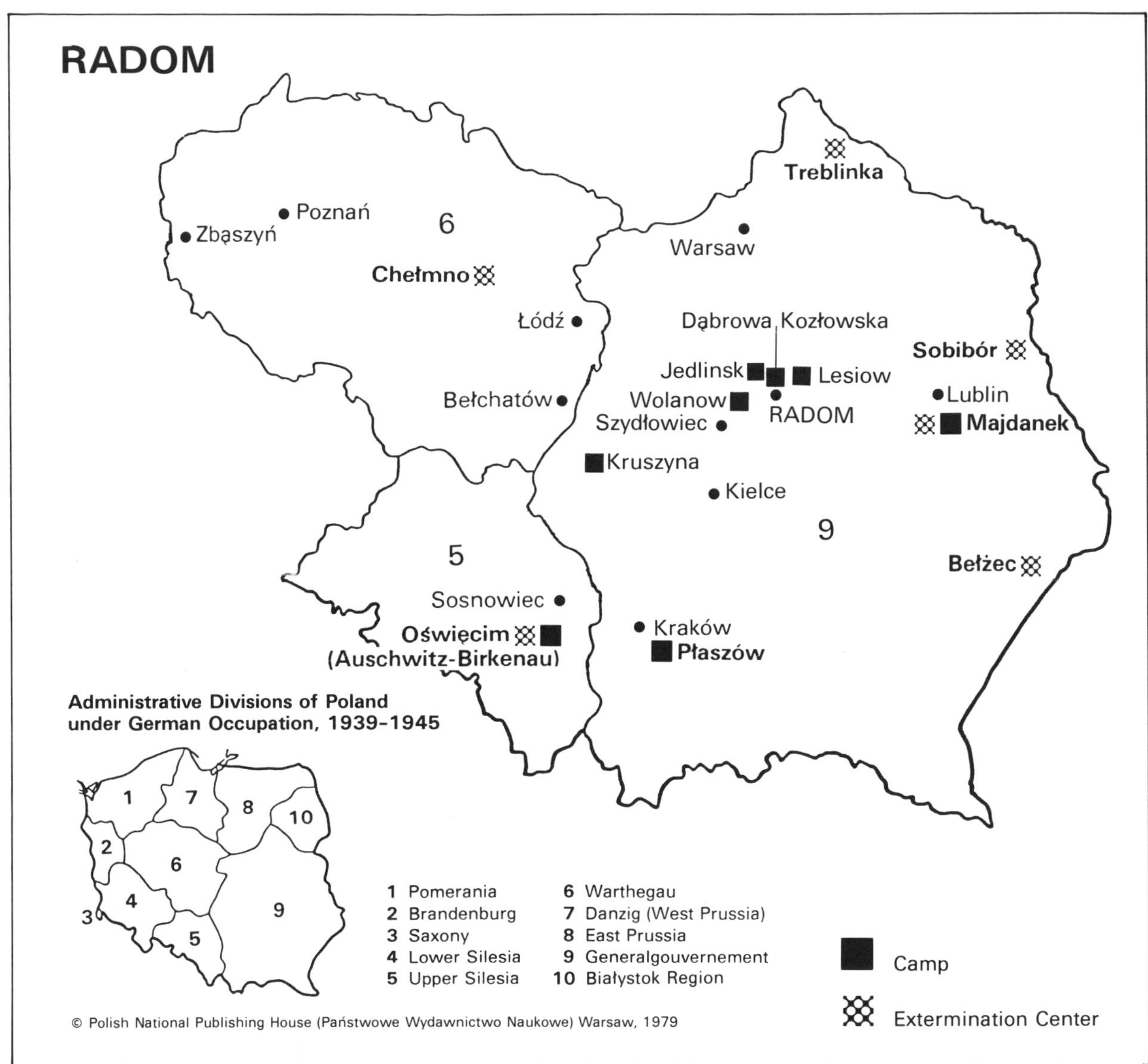

deported to Auschwitz, among them the chairman of the Judenrat, Diament, and the head of the Jewish police, Geiger.

On August 5, 1942, the Nazis liquidated the small ghetto. For this purpose a special unit of the Sicherheitspolizei (Security Police) was organized, called Sonderkommando Feucht, under the command of Hauptsturmführer Adolf Feucht. It was reinforced by a company of Ukrainian collaborators commanded by Un tersturmführer Erich Kapke. The ghetto was sealed off by the local German police (the Ordnungspolizei), and its inmates were ordered to appear at a concentration point near a railway siding. The Germans and Ukrainians searched house after house, and hundreds who tried to hide were shot on the spot. About 600 older people and children were shot at the concentration point. Some 800 men and 20 women were chosen for forced labor, and all the others, more than 6,000 men and women, were deported to the TREBLINKA extermination camp. In addition, on that day 2,000 persons from the large ghetto were deported to Treblinka, together with the inmates of the small ghetto.

From August 16 to 18 the same German and Ukrainian units liquidated the large ghetto, applying the same terror methods. On the first day the southern part of the ghetto was liquidated, and on the next, the northern part; one thousand to fifteen hundred Jews who tried to resist or hide were shot on the spot. A group of children were driven into a local slaughterhouse and killed there by the Gestapo men led by Hauptscharführer Erich Schildt, who threw grenades into the building. About four thousand persons were selected for forced labor, and the remaining eighteen thousand were deported to Treblinka. On the site of each liquidated ghetto, a forced-labor camp was established—at Szwarlikowska Street in the large ghetto, and Szkolna Street in the small ghetto.

On December 4, 1942, about eight hundred inmates of the Szwarlikowska camp were deported to Szydlowiec, in the Kielce district, and afterward murdered. Another fifteen hundred prisoners from that camp were deported to Treblinka on January 13, 1943. The Szwarlikowska camp was liquidated on November 8 of that year; about one hundred prisoners were shot and the others were transferred to the Szkolna Street camp. On July 26, 1944, the prisoners of that camp (who had in the meantime been joined by about a thousand prisoners evacuated from the MAJDANEK extermination camp) were deported to Auschwitz. Only a handful of them survived.

Attempts to establish a united resistance organization did not succeed in the Radom ghetto, but several underground groups were formed that aimed to break out of the ghetto to engage in resistance activities in the vicinity. The largest of these groups was headed by the Borenstein brothers (Zalman, Leib, and Yona), and another group was led by Noach Szlaperman. At the time of the deportations, hundreds of Jews from these groups succeeded in fleeing to the forest. Several partisan units were organized, but almost all of their members soon fell in battles with German police units. A few dozen of those who escaped from the Radom ghetto reached Warsaw and took part in the WARSAW POLISH UPRISING of August and September 1944.

A few hundred Jewish survivors tried to settle in Radom after the war, but they soon left the city.

BIBLIOGRAPHY

Habas, B. "How the Jewish Community of Radom Was Exterminated." *Jewish Frontier* 10/5 (May 1943): 7–12.

Rutkowski, A. "Martyrologia, walkai zagłada ludności żydowskiej w dystrykcie radomskim podczas okupacji hitlerowskiej." *Biuletyn* 15–16 (1955): 75–182.

Stein, A. S., ed. *Radom: A Memorial to the Jewish Community of Radom (Poland)*. Tel Aviv, 1961. (In Hebrew.)

SHMUEL KRAKOWSKI

RAILWAYS, GERMAN (Deutsche Reichsbahn; German State Railways). A crucial role in carrying out the "FINAL SOLUTION" was played by the German railway system. (The material presented here is based primarily on Raul Hilberg's monumental work *The Destruction of the European Jews,* published in 1985.) In 1942 the Reichsbahn, a large administrative department under the German Ministry of Transportation, employed half a million clerks and 900,000 other staff and serviced both the military and the civilian population. Albert GANZENMÜLLER, an energetic young technocrat who was close to Albert SPEER, was appointed head of the Reichsbahn in May of that year. Among the Reichsbahn sections under Ganzenmüller's direct control were the civilian traffic and tariff section, the operations section (which determined the train routes), and Section L, which was responsible for dealing with the requirements of the army.

In terms of territorial coverage, the railway system consisted of two major branches: the Reich branch, which included Austria and other territories annexed to Germany; and the branch for the occupied countries. In the latter, three different railway organizations operated: one under the direct control of the Reichsbahn; an autonomous agency; and a railway agency run by the military. Inside the Reich, the Reichsbahn was split into three subdivisions (*Generalbetriebsleitungen*), each with its own center: East, West, and South. It was from Generalbetriebsleitung Ost (East), centered in Berlin, that most of the trains moved to the eastern front—and to the extermination camps.

For the Jews who were being deported to the camps, freight cars were used, but the

Reichsbahn charged for the trip according to the tariff for third-class passenger train tickets. The charge for children in the four-to-ten age bracket was half of the full fare, while those aged under four were transported "free." A half fare was also granted to "organized" groups of four hundred and above.

Under the prevailing conditions of war, organizational arrangements and an established system of payment—however complicated—did not in themselves ensure that the train transports of Jews would indeed proceed as scheduled. Priority of rail transport was reserved for the requirements of the armed forces. In the jumble of military priorities on the one hand, and the traffic jams and breakdowns on the other (the latter often caused by sabotage acts of resistance movements), the transportation of Jews to the camps had a place of its own. The movement and coordination of these transports were handled by SS-Hauptsturmführer Franz NOVAK, working out of Adolf EICHMANN's office (Section IV B 4a). In the railway administration an official named Otto Stange was the person usually responsible for providing trains to transport the Jews to the camps; these trains were classified as *Sonderzüge* (special trains) and were part of the passenger service rendered by the Reichsbahn. Provisions were also made for the allocation of trains on a local basis, whenever the point of departure for the transports was inside the occupied country.

Section IV B 4a had branch offices in Paris, Bratislava, and Salonika, but no permanent branches of its own operating in the GENERALGOUVERNEMENT, in the occupied territories, or in the Soviet Union. In those areas it was the Sicherheitspolizei (Security Police) chiefs who, on behalf of the REICHSSICHERHEITSHAUPTAMT (Reich Security Main Office; RSHA), dealt with ordering the trains and preparing them for the transports. On the list of priorities that had to be drawn up, in view of the shortages caused by the exigencies of war, a relatively high place was reserved for the trains that took the Jews to the concentration and extermination camps.

In July 1942 the railway line leading to the SOBIBÓR extermination camp was closed for repairs. This coincided with the planned deportation from Warsaw in which three hundred thousand Jews were to be transported to the Sobibór gas chambers. On July 16, SS-Obergruppenführer Karl WOLFF, chief of Heinrich HIMMLER's personal staff, applied to Ganzenmüller for help. In reply, Ganzenmüller informed Wolff that as of July 22, a train for five thousand Jews would be available every day, to transport Jews from Warsaw to the newly constructed extermination camp at TREBLINKA.

In the bureaucratic records and dispositions the Jews were listed as human beings, but in fact they were shipped like cattle. As time went on, to save on engines and the frequency of journeys, the number of Jews per car on the "special trains" was doubled, from one thousand to two thousand, and, on relatively short rides inside Poland, was increased to as many as five thousand per train. The space on the trains per person was reduced to less than 2.15 square feet (0.2 sq m). The enormous weight carried by the trains slowed them down from 40 miles (65 km) an hour, for the average freight train, to no more than 31 miles (50 km) an hour, for the trains carrying the Jews. The "Jewish trains," moreover, were often sidetracked and had to wait for other trains to pass, and they were held up for long hours and days in stations along the way.

In descriptions given by the few survivors, the train ride to the extermination camps appears to have been one endless nightmare. The cars, sealed off and packed tight, were without air and had no food or water. In most cases, too, no food or water was doled out to the people waiting for long hours in the stations en route. The freight cars' small windows were sealed off or had barbed wire strung on them to prevent escapes from the train. Armed escorts shot any person caught trying to jump off the moving train to escape. In summer the cars were unbearably hot, and in winter they were freezing cold. Many deportees, especially the old and the very young, perished before the train reached its last stop.

From October 1941 to October 1944 the Reichsbahn transported millions of human beings to their death, and despite all the impediments and delays, not a single Jew was spared because of lack of transportation. The railway system's documented records contain no evidence that the Reichsbahn staff was aware of the fate in store for the human cargo that was being transported, but there is no doubt that the officials who routed the trains with hundreds of thousands of people to out-of-the-way railway stations must have known of the bitter end awaiting the Jews on these trains. The siting of the extermination camps in the vicinity of railway lines was known to the railway workers.

After the war the staff members of the various agencies that took part in implementing the "Final Solution" were put on trial, but not a single official of the German railway system was among them. Ganzenmüller was arrested in 1945 as a high-ranking official, and was held for a time by the United States Third Army, only to be set free. Other railway officials, including some who were involved in organizing the "special trains" in which the Jews were being deported, were raised in rank and promoted to key positions.

BIBLIOGRAPHY

Hilberg, R. *The Destruction of the European Jews.* Revised edition. 3 vols. New York, 1985.

ROBERT ROZETT

RASCH, EMIL OTTO (1891–1948), SS official and Einsatzgruppe commander (*see* EINSATZGRUPPEN). Born in East Prussia, Rasch was a lieutenant in the German navy during World War I, and from 1918 to 1923 studied at several universities, earning the degree of doctor of law and political affairs. For ten years he was an attorney and legal counselor for various companies. He became a member of the Nazi party in September 1931, and in 1933 joined the SS.

When the Nazis came to power, Rasch was appointed mayor of Radeberg and then of Wittenberg. In 1936 he was taken on the staff of Section I of the REICHSSICHERHEITSHAUPTAMT (Reich Security Main Office; RSHA). He became chief of the state police (Stapo) of Frankfurt am Main in 1938, and from March to May of that year he was also head of security for Upper Austria. For five weeks in early 1939, he headed the Sicherheitspolizei (Security Police; Sipo) and SD (Sicherheitsdienst; Security Service) in Prague, and after that became chief of the Sipo and SD in Königsberg, East Prussia, with the rank of SS-*Standartenführer.*

In May 1941, Rasch was appointed commander of Einsatzgruppe C. The next month his unit followed Army Group South on its way to the Ukraine, where it carried out numerous *Aktionen* in which tens of thousands of Jews were murdered, the bloodiest and most infamous *Aktion* being that of BABI YAR in Kiev.

In September of that year Rasch was ordered back to Berlin, owing, he later claimed, to difficulties he had had with the *Reichskommissar* for the Ukraine, Erich KOCH, and to differences with Heinrich HIMMLER. He became manager of the Continental Oil Company, a post he held until the end of the war.

After the war, Rasch was arrested and put on trial before the Nuremberg Military Tribunals (Trial 9, The *Einsatzgruppen* Case, July 3, 1947–April 10, 1948). He died (of natural causes) in prison early in 1948, before the case ended.

BIBLIOGRAPHY

Krausnick, H., and H.-H. Wilhelm. *Die Truppe des Weltanschauungskrieges: Die Einsatzgruppen der Sicherheitspolizei und des SD, 1938–1942.* Stuttgart, 1981.

SHMUEL SPECTOR

RASSE- UND SIEDLUNGSHAUPTAMT (Race and Resettlement Main Office; RuSHA), Nazi office for racial matters, established in 1931, that became an SS Hauptamt (Main Office) in 1935. Its original assignment was to deal with (1) research on race and the investigation of the "racial purity" of SS men and their wives; (2) the practical and technical aspects of settling SS men on the land and steering them to agricultural settlement, mainly near the cities; and (3) instruction in and study of racial issues, including special training courses on race for Nazi elite groups (*Blut-und-Boden Aristocratie,* or "blood-and-soil aristocracy").

RuSHA's first director, Richard Walther

DARRÉ, was removed from his post in 1938 because he was "too theoretical" for Heinrich HIMMLER; Darré was replaced by Günther Pancke. In 1940 Pancke was also replaced, and it was his successor, Otto Hofmann, who formulated RuSHA policy in the period of German territorial expansion and the war years. Richard Hildebrandt, appointed director in April 1943, was the last to hold the position.

As early as June 1939, RuSHA sent one of its staff, Oberführer Kurt von Gottberg, to Prague on a mission to dispossess landowners in the Protectorate of BOHEMIA AND MORAVIA of their estates and settle Germans in their place. In the Polish areas incorporated into the Reich, branch offices of RuSHA confiscated land owned by Jews and Poles. A plan was adopted in 1940 to "Germanize" Poles who were "found to have the required racial attributes," and RuSHA screened and classified prospective candidates—Poles who would be made into Germans. In November 1940 a RuSHA branch office was established in Łódź. Officials of this office, designated as *Rassenreferenten-Eignungsprüfer* (race experts and qualifications examiners), were dispatched to the transit camps where Poles who had been expelled from the German-annexed territories were being held, in order to select candidates for "Germanization." These examiners also checked the "racial value" and "racial purity" of persons who had been registered as ethnic Germans on the *Volksliste*. RuSHA took part in the removal to Germany of Polish children who had been designated for "Germanization" as part of the Lebensborn (Fountain of Life) program. There were also plans for the "Germanization," on a large scale, of Ukrainians.

In the course of the war, RuSHA took on a growing number of projects that involved uprooting farmers of various ethnic groups from their land and replacing them with Germans brought in from different countries. In its "Germanization" operations, RuSHA in some instances cooperated with other SS and Nazi party institutions, such as the REICHSKOMMISSARIAT FÜR DIE FESTIGUNG DES DEUTSCHEN VOLKSTUMS (Reich Commissariat for the Strengthening of German Nationhood), the Hauptamt für Volkstumsfragen (Main Office for Issues of Nationhood), and the Volksdeutsche Mittelstelle (Ethnic Germans' Welfare Office).

The expansion of racial operations and the increase in the number of institutions involved were accompanied by friction and infighting over jurisdiction and authority, as so often happened in the Nazi structure. As a result, RuSHA's status and the scope of its operations were gradually reduced. Some of the local Nazi governors, such as Albert FORSTER, *Gauleiter* of Danzig–Western Prussia, whose relations with Himmler were strained, obstructed RuSHA operations in the areas under their control. In the final two years of the war, when Hildebrandt was at the head of RuSHA, it was confined to secondary tasks assigned to it by the SS.

The RuSHA staff was made up of many ambitious young men with medical or other professional qualifications, some of whom were promoted to senior posts in the SS. Pancke became the *Höherer SS-und Polizeiführer* (Higher SS and Police Leader) in Denmark, and Gottberg and Hofmann were appointed to the same post in Belorussia and southwest Germany, respectively. In 1944, RuSHA had a staff of 284 at its head office in Berlin and in its various branch offices.

BIBLIOGRAPHY

Koehl, R. L. *RKFDV—German Resettlement and Population Policy, 1939–1945: A History of the Reich Commission for the Strengthening of Germandom.* Cambridge, Mass., 1957.

Polonski, F. "Rasistowskie przesłanki hitlerowskiej polityki zniemczania." *Studia nad faszyzmem i zbrodniami hitlerowskimi* 3 (1981): 167–193.

Weingartner, J. J. "The SS Race and Resettlement Main Office: Towards an Order of Blood and Soil." *The Historian* 34/1 (November 1971): 62–77.

ISRAEL GUTMAN

RATHENAU, WALTHER (1867–1922), German Jewish statesman. Rathenau earned a doctorate in physics, served in the German army, and after his father's death became president of the Allgemeine Elektrizitätsgesellschaft AEG (General Electric Company), in 1915. He eventually was a member of the board of seventy-nine German and twenty-one foreign companies. After World War I broke out, Rathenau established the efficient Kriegsrohstoffabteilung (Section for War-Essential Raw Materials) in the Ministry of War and became its chief.

Rathenau accepted the Weimar Republic when it was founded after Germany's defeat in World War I. In 1920 and 1921 he served as minister of rehabilitation in the Fehrenbach cabinet. When that cabinet resigned, the new chancellor, Dr. Josef Wirth, offered Rathenau the foreign-affairs portfolio. Rathenau represented Germany at the International Economic Conference in Genoa. He also signed the Treaty of Rapallo with the Soviet Union—a treaty that caused a tremendous stir in France, Britain, and Germany itself.

During World War I, Rathenau had evinced avid patriotism and worked on behalf of the German war effort. After the defeat he made efforts to revitalize the German economy and political system. But German racists could not forgive him for his Jewish origin, despite his fervent nationalism and dedication to Germany. Following a violent campaign with antisemitic overtones that was launched against him, Rathenau was murdered by nationalist fanatics, on June 24, 1922. In the words of Gordon Craig, "with the murder of Walther Rathenau, a border had been crossed, and Germany had entered a new and forbidding territory in which to be Jewish was more than a handicap or a social embarrassment; it was a danger and, not impossibly, a sentence to death."

BIBLIOGRAPHY

Bergler, P. *Walther Rathenau: Seine Zeit, sein Werk, seine Persönlichkeit*. Bremen, 1970.

Craig, G. *The Germans*. London, 1982.

Felix, D. *Walther Rathenau and the Weimar Republic: The Politics of Reparations*. Baltimore, 1970.

Joll, J. *Intellectuals in Politics: Three Biographical Essays*. London, 1960.

SEEV GOSHEN

RAUFF, WALTHER (1906–1984), Nazi official. Walther Rauff was a professional naval officer until a sordid divorce dimmed his career prospects and caused him to resign from the service in December 1937. He was then taken into Reinhard HEYDRICH's SD (Sicherheitsdienst; Security Service) and was eventually made head of the section for technical affairs (Gruppe II D) of the REICHSSICHERHEITSHAUPTAMT (Reich Security Main Office; RSHA). It was in this capacity that he supervised, in late 1941 and early 1942, the outfitting and dispatch of some twenty GAS VANS in which at least 200,000 people were murdered. Rauff left Berlin to lead an SD Einsatzkommando in Tunis in late 1942, and he became the district *SS- und Polizeiführer* (SS and Police Leader) for northern Italy when the Germans occupied that part of the country in September 1943.

After the war Rauff was held in a prisoner-of-war camp, from which he escaped in December 1946; he was hidden in a monastery in Rome for eighteen months. He then made his way abroad, eventually settling in Chile. In 1963, an extradition request made by the Federal Republic of Germany was rejected in the Chilean Supreme Court on the ground that the crimes with which Rauff was charged were beyond the Chilean statute of limitations. He died in Santiago, Chile.

BIBLIOGRAPHY

Browning, C. R. *Fateful Months: Essays on the Emergence of the Final Solution*. New York, 1985.

CHRISTOPHER R. BROWNING

RAUSCHNING, HERMANN (1887–1982), president of the DANZIG senate; Nazi politician who broke with Hitler. Born in Toruń, West Prussia, to an old Junker family, Rauschning studied history and music at Munich and Berlin. He served as a volunteer in World War I and was subsequently active in ethnic German organizations in Posen (Poznań). In 1926 he acquired an estate in the Free City of Danzig, and in 1931 he joined the Nazi party as one of the German conservatives who hoped to use the Nazis for their own purposes.

In 1932 Rauschning became president of the Danzig Agricultural League. In June

1933, when the Nazis won a majority in the elections to the Danzig parliament, he was appointed president of the Danzig senate and thereby head of the Free City of Danzig. He resigned in November 1934, disillusioned with Nazism after having become acquainted with Hitler and the local Danzig *Gauleiter*, Albert FORSTER. In 1936 Rauschning fled to Switzerland via Poland, and two years later the Danzig senate deprived him of his citizenship.

Rauschning then began to publish works that sought to reveal the true nature of the Nazi regime and to warn against its intentions: *Die Revolution des Nihilismus* (1938; published in English as *Hitler's Revolution of Destruction*, 1939) and *Gespräche mit Hitler* (1939; published in English the same year as *Hitler Speaks*). Both were enormously successful and influenced all subsequent writing on Hitler and Nazism, although doubts have been cast on the authenticity of parts of *Hitler Speaks*. However, the book is particularly valuable in revealing Hitler's obsession with "the natural wickedness of the Jew" and with the use of antisemitism as a political weapon.

In 1948 Rauschning left Switzerland for the United States. He continued to publish works dealing with German politics.

BIBLIOGRAPHY

Wistrich, R. *Who's Who in Nazi Germany*. New York, 1982.

LIONEL KOCHAN

RAVENSBRÜCK, concentration camp near Ravensbrück, a village on the Havel River two-thirds of a mile (1 km) from the Fürstenberg railway station and 56 miles (90 km) north of Berlin. On May 15, 1939, a concentration camp for women was opened there, and on May 18, 867 female prisoners were transferred there from the Nazi concentration camp at Lichtenburg (now Prettin, East Germany), together with the camp commandant, SS-Hauptsturmführer Max Koegel. Koegel remained in this post until the summer of 1942, when he was replaced by SS-Hauptsturmführer Fritz Suhren, who was commandant until May 1945. The prisoners' numbers began with 1,416, since a total of 1,415 prisoners had been transferred from Lichtenburg.

The camp structure was similar to that of other Nazi concentration camps, with 150 female supervisors (SS-*Aufseherinnen*) added to the men who served as guards and held administrative posts. The female supervisors were SS volunteers or women who had accepted the post for the sake of the better pay and work conditions it offered, compared to work in factories. In 1942 and 1943 Ravensbrück also had a training base for female SS supervisors; the 3,500 women who underwent training there served at Ravensbrück and at other concentration camps.

In late 1939 Ravensbrück had 2,000 prisoners, and by the end of 1942 the number had grown to 10,800. In 1944 another 70,000 prisoners were brought to Ravensbrück, from which most were transferred to one of the thirty-four Ravensbrück satellite camps. Some of these satellite camps were far away from Ravensbrück, in Mecklenburg, Bavaria, and the Protectorate of BOHEMIA AND MORAVIA. Most of the satellite camps were attached to military industrial plants, and one such plant was also put up near Ravensbrück itself. In 1944 the main Ravensbrück camp had 26,700 female prisoners, as well as several thousand girls in a detention camp for minors (*Jugendschutzlager*).

In April 1941 a concentration camp for men was established near the Ravensbrück camp, but officially it was a satellite of the SACHSENHAUSEN camp. Approximately 20,000 male prisoners passed through this camp during the years of its existence, 16 percent of them Jews. In early 1945, Soviet prisoners in the men's camp were recruited for Andrei VLASOV's army, while German prisoners were drafted into Oskar DIRLEWANGER's SS brigade. By early February 1945, 106,000 women had passed through the Ravensbrück camp. Twenty-five percent of them were Polish, 20 percent German, 19 percent Russian and Ukrainian, 15 percent Jewish, 7 percent French, 5.5 percent Gypsy, and 8.5 percent others.

From the summer of 1942, MEDICAL EXPERIMENTS were carried out at Ravensbrück. One such project, directed by Professor Karl Gebhardt, made use of sulfonamide to treat festering wounds and bone transplants. The victims of these experiments were some seventy-four prisoners, most of them young Polish women suspected of belonging to the underground. Another experiment, conducted by Professor Carl CLAUBERG, involved sterilization; thirty-five women were the victims of the experiment, most of them GYPSIES.

In the early stage of the camp's existence the method used for killing prisoners was to shoot them in the back of the neck. In 1942 the prisoners who were condemned to death were sent to institutions (such as Bernburg) that were involved in the EUTHANASIA PROGRAM, or to AUSCHWITZ; or they were later killed in Ravensbrück with phenol injections. Their bodies were cremated at the nearby Fürstenberg crematorium, but when the number of victims grew, in April 1943, Ravensbrück had its own crematorium installed, near the camp for minors. In late January or early February of 1945, gas chambers were constructed next to the crematorium, and by the end of April, 2,200 to 2,300 persons had been put to death in them.

In late March 1945 the order was given for Ravensbrück to be evacuated, and 24,500 prisoners, men and women, were put on the road to Mecklenburg. Early in April, 500 women prisoners were handed over to the Swedish and Danish Red Cross, and 2,500 German women prisoners were set free. On the night of April 29–30, Soviet forces liberated Ravensbrück, where they found 3,500 sick female prisoners being cared for by other prisoners.

BIBLIOGRAPHY

Arndt, I. "Das Frauenkonzentrationslager Ravensbrück." In *Studien zur Geschichte der Konzentrationslager,* edited by M. Broszat, pp. 93–129. Stuttgart, 1970.

Dufournier, D. *Ravensbrück: The Women's Camp of Death*. London, 1948.

Machlejd, W., ed. *Experimental Operations on Prisoners of Ravensbrück Concentration Camp*. Poznań, 1960.

Maurel, M. *Ravensbrück*. London, 1958.

Tillion, G. *Ravensbrück*. Paris, 1988.

SHMUEL SPECTOR

RAYMAN, MARCEL (1923–1944), French Jewish underground fighter. Born in Warsaw, Rayman emigrated with his parents to France, where he became active in the Communist Jewish Workers' Sports Club (Yidishe Arbeiter Sportishe Klub).

In June 1940, when Paris was occupied by the Germans, Rayman joined the Deuxième Détachement (Second Company), a Yiddish-speaking unit that was under the command of the Communist partisan organization, the Francs-Tireurs et Partisans (Fighters and Partisans; FTP). He participated in numerous attacks on German soldiers and army installations in Paris. When his company was liquidated by the French secret service, Rayman was put into the "Manouchian Company," a Communist partisan unit led by the Armenian poet Missak Manouchian. On September 28, 1943, Rayman took part in a daring operation in which SS-Obergruppenführer Dr. Julius von Ritter, the German official in charge of enlisting French laborers for work in Germany, was killed. Rayman fell into Gestapo hands a few days later and was one of the accused in a show trial, together with Manouchian and twenty-one other fighters, most of them Jewish. All of the accused, including Rayman, were executed.

BIBLIOGRAPHY

Diamant, D. *Les Juifs dans la Résistance française, 1940–1944*. Paris, 1971.

Ravine, J. *La résistance organisée des Juifs en France, 1940–1944*. Paris, 1973.

Rayski, A. *Nos illusions perdues*. Paris, 1985.

LUCIEN LAZARE

RAYSKI, ABRAHAM (Adam; b. 1914), Jewish Communist, active in the anti-Nazi resistance in France. Born in Białystok to a traditional middle-class family, Rayski was attracted to communism at an early age. He left for Paris in 1932 and within two years became a full-time journalist on the Communist newspaper *Neie Presse*. From July 1941 until the end of World War II, he served as national secretary of the Jewish section of the French Communist party. His articles in the clandestine press, his contribution to the establishment of the CONSEIL REPRÉSENTATIF DES JUIFS DE FRANCE, and his role in the development of the Jewish resistance played a major part in Jewish survival in France. Rayski published vivid autobiographical memoirs, *Nos illusions perdues* (Our Lost Illusions; 1985).

BIBLIOGRAPHY

Diamant, D. *Les Juifs dans la Résistance française, 1940–1944.* Paris, 1971.

Ravine, J. *La résistance organisée des Juifs en France, 1940–1944.* Paris, 1973.

Rayski, A. "We Fought Back in France." *Commentary* 1/4 (February 1946): 60–65.

JACQUES ADLER

RED CROSS, INTERNATIONAL. The International Committee of the Red Cross (ICRC), or Comité International de la Croix Rouge, founded in 1863, is a private humanitarian organization staffed entirely by Swiss citizens, the nationals of a neutral state. Its principal role is to maintain and develop the links among the national societies of the Red Cross, to act as a neutral intermediary between the belligerents in time of war, and, as an initiator of the first Geneva Convention of 1864, to monitor the application and development of humanitarian law. In World War II such law was mainly based on two texts signed in Geneva in 1929 by more than fifty states, including Germany. The first Geneva Convention aimed at protecting soldiers who were wounded or sick while on active service, and the second at ensuring correct treatment of prisoners of war.

The ICRC is mentioned only very marginally in these conventions, but according to its statutes it has the right to undertake humanitarian initiatives, such as those that it took before the war on behalf of political prisoners, that is, citizens who were being held by their own state. In this connection it visited prisons and camps a number of times, including those in Hitler's Germany. Carl J. Burckhardt made such a visit in 1935, and Guillaume Favre made another in 1938. As a general rule, the ICRC considers that in peacetime it is the responsibility of the national societies of the Red Cross to intervene with their governments on behalf of such prisoners.

Moreover, the ICRC sought to maintain the unity of the international movement of the Red Cross, despite the control exerted by totalitarian regimes—Soviet, fascist, and Nazi—over the national societies. It therefore relied on the German Red Cross to bring some relief to the prisoners in CONCENTRATION CAMPS.

World War II and Civilian Populations. When the war broke out in 1939, civilian populations were not protected by any international agreement. The so-called Tokyo proposal prepared by the ICRC had not yet been submitted to a diplomatic conference. It aimed at protecting civilians of enemy nationality being held on the soil of a belligerent nation at the outbreak of hostilities (that is, civilian internees), and civilians taken hostage by the enemy in the territories it occupied. Only for the first category did the ICRC succeed in obtaining treatment analogous to that required for prisoners of war. It was thus able to visit the internees' places of detention, to assure the passage of their correspondence, and to send to them the parcels allowed by both the Reich and the Allies who, between them, blockaded Europe.

The civilian internees, however, and the populations suffering from bombardments, cold, and hunger, were not the only groups of civilians who were victims of hostilities. The Germans, seeking to maintain order in the conquered countries, made massive arrests and carried hostages away to concentration camps, as provided in the Night and Fog Decree of December 1941 (*see* NACHT UND NEBEL).

Moreover, the war waged by the Reich had a secret and basic objective: the racial reorganization of Europe. For this to be achieved, the peoples of eastern Europe had to be crushed, and the Jews, above all, had to be made to disappear. From the autumn of 1939, the previous forced emigration was replaced by deportation, and from the summer of 1941, the Nazis began regrouping and concentrating Jews in the east with a view to their physical extermination.

The ICRC and the "Final Solution." The representatives of the ICRC were only very rarely witnesses of deportations. With the exception of two visits to Dutch civilian internees in BUCHENWALD in 1940 and 1941, and of an inspection of THERESIENSTADT that the SS carefully organized in 1944, they were never able to enter the concentration or extermination camps until almost the end of the war.

However, from 1939 onward, the representatives of the national societies of the Red Cross spoke of measures of expulsion, segregation, and isolation directed against the Jews, and, from 1941 onward, of acts of violence and massacres. These items of information were more than rumor. They did not yet indicate a plan of general extermination, but they were sufficiently precise and consistent for the heads of the ICRC, by the end of December 1941, to answer the cries of anguish and the questions they were being asked by envisaging the sending of assistance to the east.

From available documents it is not possible to know at which point the ICRC or its leading members became aware of the "FINAL SOLUTION." Carl Burckhardt, informed particularly by the representative of the World Jewish Congress, Gerhart Riegner, confirmed the rumors that had reached the United States consul in Geneva in November 1942. But ICRC members did not wait for a general massacre to initiate action and to decide, at the same time, on the amount of risk they were willing to take in coming to the assistance of the persecuted.

The ICRC at first kept to the arrangements that had been worked out before the war. In the autumn of 1941, it therefore addressed itself to the German Red Cross when it learned that this national society had suspended, at least for missing "non-Aryans," the tracing service it had provided for inmates of concentration camps and prisons. The president of the ICRC, Max Huber, nevertheless maintained that the ICRC could not propose to the belligerents that they should extend to political prisoners treatment analogous to that required for prisoners of war by the Fourth Geneva Convention of 1929. In addition, most of the Jews in German custody had either been handed over by their governments or were stateless, whereas the Geneva conventions only provided criteria for defining a victim as belonging to an enemy state, that is, as having nationality.

In the spring of 1942, when the first deportation trains left France, the ICRC was forced

French prisoners of war being repatriated on Red Cross trucks from a site near Erfurt, Germany. [CICR Archives]

to acknowledge the facts. The German Red Cross was no longer ready to assume the tasks expected of it, and the ICRC's usual interlocutors in the Oberkommando der Wehrmacht (Armed Forces High Command) and the Foreign Ministry withdrew assistance when ICRC representatives sought to discover the fate of deportees, especially Jews, or requested permission to give them aid.

The "Tokyo proposal," whose practical application the ICRC had been unable to achieve in 1939, did in fact provide a minimum of protection for hostages and enemy civilians brought into the territory of the occupying power. The ICRC, searching for possible ways to take action, decided to base itself on this text and to suggest to the Germans that they should grant to deportees of French and Belgian nationality who had been taken to concentration camps in the Reich, guarantees similar to those enjoyed by civilian internees. The Jews were not mentioned in this note, but they were considered in the instructions sent to Roland Marti, the representative of the ICRC in Berlin. Insofar as they belonged to nations hostile to the Reich, they entered into the category of the civilian internees on behalf of whom the ICRC believed it had the right to intervene. The German Foreign Office never responded to this initiative of September 24, 1942, prudently presented by Marti in an oral form, and at the end of the year the ICRC had to acknowledge the total failure of its attempt.

It has been suggested that the ICRC should have appealed to public opinion. It had made very few public appeals before then. A text was prepared during the summer of 1942 that did not directly concern the deportees or even the prisoners in the concentration camps, but dealt with the aggravation of methods of warfare of which civilians, especially, were victims. The text submitted to the ICRC, meeting in full session on October 14, 1942, did not specifically mention the Jews, who were included in the totality of prisoners, deportees, and hostages for whom the Red Cross asked, on the basis of international law, protection at least comparable to that provided by the conventions for combatants.

The majority of the twenty-three members present on that day favored a public gesture, but they were divided as to the form it should take. Moreover, the Swiss authorities feared the proposed initiative, coming at a time when the Axis was victorious on all fronts. This opposition, combined with the apprehension that the Reich might condemn the Geneva conventions, sealed the fate of the public appeal. At that time the ICRC apparently did not consider the idea of taking the matter up directly with the SS or the German Ministry of Justice, as Marti had suggested since the summer of 1942.

In that same year the ICRC attempted to assist the deportees, including the Jews, but it did so while subordinating its intervention to its traditional functions. Legally, it based itself on the "Tokyo proposal," although the Jews belonged only very partially to the relevant categories in this proposal. In any case, the ICRC did not wish to raise the question of racial discrimination as such in connection with the Geneva conventions. Thus, it failed to protest when it learned that, in the prison camps, the Germans had separated the French medical personnel of Jewish faith in order to transfer them to the eastern front. It was silent about this step, as it had been silent when Polish prisoners of war had become civilian workers, thinking it better to take specific action in order to provide concrete assistance. Finally, it did not seek—exploiting its right to take an initiative or basing itself on the general principles of humanitarian rights—to intervene on behalf of the Jews in general, intervention that might have taken the form of a protest to a competent (and presumably indifferent) representative of the German authorities, or of a demand for action from the western Allies.

There were several reasons, personal and institutional, historical and contemporary, for this restraint in matters of principle. The most important of these, from the point of view of the Red Cross, was its fear of endangering the tasks that the ICRC had assumed throughout the world in protecting and assisting prisoners of war and civilian internees, including the laborious and fruitless negotiations it had undertaken to improve the lot of the millions of prisoners of war on the eastern front.

Since the rescue of the Jews seemed impossible or unachievable, the ICRC, at the end of 1942 and the beginning of 1943, decided to act on two levels. It attempted to send assistance to the deportees, and at the same time, it intervened in a number of countries that were allies or satellites of the Reich. Unable to protect the victims, the ICRC sought to alleviate their suffering by sending food, clothing, and medicines. In 1941 the Joint Relief Commission of the International Red Cross was created for this purpose by the ICRC, together with the League of the Red Cross, but its possibilities for action remained limited, because it never succeeded in obtaining from the Allies the documents necessary to pass through the blockade. It was therefore unable to send provisions to the ghettos of the east and had to be content with sending a few shipments to the area of the GENERALGOUVERNEMENT and to a small number of camps, and with helping to supply provisions to the refugees in the south of France, among whom there were Jews. The parcels sent to the concentration camps, from the spring of 1943, very marginally affected the Jews, as they could be sent only to prisoners of whose place of detention the ICRC was aware.

Intervention Action. In the spring of 1943, an ICRC mission led by Edouard Chapuisat made a journey in southeastern Europe, meeting the heads of state and the leaders of the Red Cross and the church in Slovakia, Croatia, Hungary, Romania, and Bulgaria. The object of this journey was, among other things, to study the possibility of the Jews of the Balkans emigrating to Palestine. Each of the countries visited had perpetrated acts of violence and racial massacres. Each one followed an antisemitic policy, of their own volition or under Nazi influence, although sometimes in implicit opposition to the "final solution" of the Nazis.

The representatives of the ICRC who had been or would be assigned to these countries paid particular attention to the victims of racial persecution, sometimes with the assistance of certain local authorities, as the following examples show. Until September 1944, however, the ICRC itself did not change the priorities it had set in 1942.

The assignment of Charles Kolb to BUCHAREST in November 1943 gave a new impetus to the work of the International Red Cross in that city. He made a tour of inspection in TRANSNISTRIA and did his utmost to bring assistance to the survivors of the terrible massacres that had taken place there, but his main task in the spring of 1944 was to attempt to organize emigration to Palestine by way of the Black Sea and Turkey. In this he was supported by the Romanian Red Cross and Jewish organizations, diplomats such as the Swiss minister René de Weck, the WAR REFUGEE BOARD, and even the minister for foreign affairs, Mihai ANTONESCU. The ICRC headquarters, however, was still very cautious, regarding questions of emigration as impinging on the rights of states. The British did not wish to undermine the WHITE PAPER OF 1939, which severely limited Jewish immigration into Palestine, and the Germans, of course, would not agree to provide exit permits. All of Kolb's efforts came to nothing, owing to the interests of the various elements, and the emigration via the Black Sea remained clandestine, dangerous, and very limited.

Soviet prisoners of war evacuated from the Oranienburg camp receive Red Cross parcels. [CICR Archives]

Carl J. Burckhardt (right), president of the International Red Cross, visits prisoners of war in Germany (1945). [CICR Archives]

The concentration and deportation of the Jews of HUNGARY in the spring of 1944 gave rise to several humanitarian gestures. The ICRC, which had appointed a representative there several months previously, joined this movement at the beginning of July. After others had done so, the president of the ICRC asked the Hungarian head of state to suspend the deportations.

In the weeks following this suspension, the ICRC representative, Friedrich Born, organized the lodging and maintenance in BUDAPEST of thousands of Jews. It was hoped they would be saved from deportation through the granting of visas or emigration certificates, distributed by the Swede Raoul WALLENBERG and the Swiss diplomat Carl LUTZ, on their own responsibility. Here too, however, all hopes that the persecuted could reach a neutral territory were frustrated by Nazi intransigence. The Red Cross's task of assistance and protection therefore took on a new scope after the coup d'état of the ARROW CROSS PARTY in October 1944; these efforts made it possible to save several thousand lives before the liberation of Budapest by the Soviet army.

When Georges Dunand, representing the ICRC, reached SLOVAKIA at the end of the autumn, there were no longer many Jews left in that region. In September 1942, when the Slovak Red Cross had called for the assistance of the ICRC at the time of the deportations to AUSCHWITZ, the ICRC had responded by acknowledging its inability to act. Two years later Dunand, with the help of the Swiss consular authorities, tried to assist survivors who were in hiding, but by the end of 1944 he had achieved only poor results.

With the beginning of the liberation of France, there were political overtures. The Paris government asked the Red Cross in Geneva to intensify its efforts on behalf of French civilians, this time using the argument of reciprocity, since the French now detained German civilians.

On October 2, 1944, Max Huber, the head of the ICRC, suggested to the German foreign minister, Joachim von RIBBENTROP, that deportees of French, Belgian, and Dutch nationality imprisoned in the concentration camps be granted rights similar to those enjoyed by civilian internees. This was a repetition of the note of September 24, 1942, but on a higher diplomatic level and in totally different circumstances. On February 1, 1945, the

Friedrich Born, International Red Cross representative, in Budapest (1944).

Germans accepted the proposal on condition of reciprocity, and furthermore proposed negotiating exchanges of civilian detainees. However, even at this time, they still refused the Red Cross access to the concentration camps.

Final Attempt. By the autumn of 1944, leaders of the ICRC were hoping for a meeting at the highest level with the SS, which now controlled all the camps. A few months later, the Allied governments and the Jewish organizations, fearing a general massacre of prisoners of war, detainees in the camps, and deportees, pressed the Red Cross and SWITZERLAND, as a protecting power, to send in inspectors to exercise control until the camps were liberated by the victorious Allies. These suggestions fell on receptive ears in Bern, the Swiss capital, and in Geneva, the headquarters of the Red Cross. In northern Italy the ICRC representative, Hans Bon, already had made contact with SS General Karl WOLFF, who was negotiating secretly with the Allies to obtain the suspension of the deportations of the Jews. Carl Burckhardt—who on January 1, 1945, replaced Huber as head of the ICRC—agreed to meet Heinrich HIMMLER, who also met with the then vice president of the Swedish Red Cross, Count Folke BERNADOTTE. Meanwhile, the delegation in Berlin endeavored to obtain permission to visit and provision the camps from other SS leaders who were attempting, like Himmler, to extricate themselves from the deteriorating situation.

The top-level meeting finally took place on March 12, 1945, at the Arlberg Pass, near the Austrian-Swiss frontier, between Burckhardt and Ernst KALTENBRUNNER, head of the REICHSSICHERHEITSHAUPTAMT (Reich Security Main Office; RSHA). The guidelines were laid down for a policy of rescue that this time also involved the survivors of the Holocaust. In actual fact, the results were poor, for although Kaltenbrunner personally agreed to the entry into the concentration camps of representatives of the Red Cross and the protecting power, in reality this concession produced concrete results only in the MAUTHAUSEN camp and in the Theresienstadt ghetto. Supply columns were able to bring a few hundred prisoners out of RAVENSBRÜCK and Mauthausen, but ICRC representatives were also sometimes present, practically helpless, during the agonizing evacuations from ORANIENBURG, SACHSENHAUSEN, and Ravensbrück.

[*See also* Displaced Persons; Refugees, 1933–1945.]

BIBLIOGRAPHY

Arsenijevic, D. *Otages volontaires des SS.* Paris, 1984.

Ben Tov, A. *Facing the Holocaust in Budapest.* Geneva, 1988.

Comité International de la Croix-Rouge. *Documents sur l'activité du Comité International de la Croix-Rouge en faveur des civils détenus dans les camps de concentration en Allemagne (1939–1945).* Geneva, 1947.

Comité International de la Croix-Rouge. *Rapport du Comité International de la Croix-Rouge sur son activité pendant la Seconde guerre mondiale.* 3 vols. Geneva, 1948.

Durand, A. *De Sarajevo à Hiroshima: Histoire du Comité International de la Croix-Rouge.* Geneva, 1978.

Favez, J.-C. *Une mission impossible? Le CICR, les déportations et les camps de concentration nazis.* Lausanne, 1988.

JEAN-CLAUDE FAVEZ

RED ORCHESTRA (Rote Kapelle), name of a World War II spy ring run by the chief directorate of Soviet military intelligence (Glavnoe Razvedovatelnoe Upravlenie) in the occupied countries of western Europe. The name "Red Orchestra" was given to the network by the German security services when they first began tracking it down.

The network was established by Leopold Trepper, a Jew born in Poland in 1904. In 1924 he emigrated to Palestine and soon joined the Palestinian Communist party. At the end of 1929 he was expelled to France, where he became active among Jewish immigrants. In 1932 he went to the Soviet Union. There he attended the College for Party Activists in Europe, and on graduating from it worked as a newspaperman for the Yiddish daily *Emes.* In April 1938 he was assigned to Belgium, where he set up the foundation for an intelligence network, under the guise of a commercial firm.

Following the German occupation of France in 1940, the network moved its headquarters to Paris, establishing branches in Marseilles, Brussels, and the Netherlands. Non-Jews as well as many Jews were in the network, most of them members of the Communist party. The Red Orchestra also had contacts with the French Communist underground and with Soviet spy rings in Germany, among them the Schulze-Boysen group, which operated in the Air Ministry in Berlin. The network succeeded in penetrating central German offices in Paris and even in tapping the phones of the ABWEHR's branch in France. Among the Red Orchestra's achievements were the transmission of an advance report on the timing and the detailed plans of the German invasion of the Soviet Union and of German attacks on Moscow, on Stalingrad, and in the Caucasus.

The network came under German surveillance at the end of 1941, and in the spring of 1942 the first arrests were made among its members in Belgium. Some of those arrested broke down, and this enabled the Germans to liquidate the Dutch branch and, in August 1942, the branch in Germany. On November 19 of that year, the network's headquarters in Paris was liquidated (its cover had been that of a business firm named Simex). Trepper himself, whose code name was Jean Gilbert, was seized on November 24. On September 19, 1943, he managed to escape and go into hiding, where he remained until the liberation of Paris.

In January 1945 Trepper was flown to Moscow, where he was arrested on a trumped-up charge and kept in prison until 1955, when he was released and cleared. Two years later he moved to Poland with his family and became the head of the Jewish Cultural Society. After prolonged efforts to emigrate, he was permitted to go to Israel in 1973. He died there in 1982.

BIBLIOGRAPHY

Perrault, G. *The Red Orchestra.* New York, 1969.

Rothfels, H. *The German Opposition to Hitler.* Chicago, 1948.

Trepper, L. *The Great Game: Memoirs of the Spy Hitler Couldn't Silence.* New York, 1977.

SHMUEL SPECTOR

REFUGEE AID COMMITTEE IN ROMANIA. *See* Comisia Autonoma de Ajutorare.

REFUGEES, 1933–1945. Although political refugees have existed for most of European history, only since the mid-nineteenth century has the process of individuals' fleeing the land of their birth—as a result of political, social, or economic persecution—taken on the characteristics of a mass movement. This has been especially true of the Jewish migratory movements from eastern Europe that followed the Russian pogroms of 1881, 1882, and thereafter. Nevertheless, only as a result of World War I and the subsequent social and economic upheavals associated with the rise of the so-called successor states and totalitarian regimes in eastern Europe can a refugee problem be said to exist.

The First Wave, 1933–1938. Jews figured prominently in the first wave of refugees who fled GERMANY immediately after Hitler took power in January 1933. There are different estimates, based on many sources, of the number of Jews who emigrated from Germany during 1933. According to the 1938 report of the REICHSVERTRETUNG DER DEUTSCHEN JUDEN, 52,000 Jews left Germany in 1933 and 37,000 remained abroad. In November 1941 the Reichsvertretung submitted a report to the German authorities stating that 63,000 Jews had emigrated in 1933 but not indicating how many had remained abroad. Since the Jewish community kept records of only those emigrés who received aid from the community, and not of those who left on their own, the emigration figures are not conclusive. No official obstacles were placed in the path of those who wanted to leave, and government policy encouraged them to do so. The pace slowed somewhat in 1934 and most of 1935, but accelerated notably after the NUREMBERG LAWS of September 1935 deprived Jews of German citizenship and prompted extensive new exclusions from economic and public life.

Most of the emigrés went to neighboring countries. The principal destination was France, although substantial numbers also traveled to the Netherlands, Switzerland, Czechoslovakia, and Austria. Many antici-

Jewish refugees from Germany arrive in France (1936). [JDC Archives, New York]

pated that their exodus would be temporary, for there was widespread expectation that the Nazis would not remain long in power. Often only individual family members departed, assuming that it was in the family or personal interest for some to remain in Germany. Occasionally, emigrés returned on short visits, and some even came back to live in Germany, having failed to establish themselves abroad or having misjudged the situation at home, assuming that persecution had "stabilized." To block this influx, the Gestapo issued orders in 1935 to intern returnees in concentration camps.

Some Jews remained in Germany to avoid the increasingly heavy emigration tax (*Reichsfluchtsteuer*) and because strict regulations limited remittances of income from Germany. Up to 1938, the exodus remained limited; just over one-fourth of the 525,000 German Jews had left. Within the Reich, many Jews maintained their economic position until the end of 1937, and there were periodic indications—mistaken, as it turned out—that things might improve.

The Second Wave, 1938–1941. All this changed in 1938, when the flow of emigration quickened substantially, flooding neighboring countries with frightened, impoverished German Jews. The exodus became a mass migration, with entire families uprooting themselves and becoming refugees. During 1938, Nazi policy toward Jews clarified, focusing at this time on emigration: the objective, it was plainly said, was to rid Germany of its Jews. One reason for this shift was the incorporation into the Reich of the two hundred thousand Austrian Jews; with the ANSCHLUSS, the Nazis realized that expansion brought in more Jews than were removed by emigration. Their conclusion was to speed up the process by initiating forced expulsion. Berlin dispatched SS-Untersturmführer Adolf EICHMANN, groomed as an expert on such matters, to VIENNA to organize the exodus. Austrian Jews now knocked urgently at the gates of receiving countries. Between April and November of 1938, fifty thousand left the newly incorporated territory—over thirty thousand more than left Germany in the same period.

The German Jews also lost their fragile material position at home. With the recovery of the German economy and the end of unemployment, ARISIERUNG ("Aryanization," or the confiscation of Jewish property) intensified, with the object of removing Jews entirely from economic life. In addition, a new wave of violence throughout the Reich convinced many Jews that there was no future for them in Germany. In October, as a result of threats by the Polish government to denationalize eighteen thousand of its expatriates in Germany, Berlin expelled masses of Jews. Thousands of them were dumped in the Polish border town of ZBĄSZYŃ, their entry to Poland blocked by the Polish government. After KRISTALLNACHT, on November 9–10, 1938, departures intensified. To these refugees were added others from Czechoslovakia, part of which was absorbed into the Reich early in the following year.

In all, it has been estimated, about 150,000 additional Jews fled Germany after this turning point. Many more would certainly have done so had there been places where they could go. More would have left if the war had not broken out, in September 1939. The problem was to find precious space on a ship and to secure the rare entry visas and other documents necessary to travel abroad. Some 71,500 Jews left the Greater German Reich between September 1939 and the end of 1941, when all exits were finally sealed. These represented about a fifth of the Jews remaining in the expanded German state. Most of them went to Britain, to the Western Hemisphere, to SHANGHAI, or to Palestine. The least fortunate remained in western Europe, where many were again engulfed by Nazism in 1940.

Closing the Doors. Throughout Europe and America, immigration policies of the period were conditioned by severe economic depression. In this pre-Keynesian era, restrictions were everywhere seen as the antidote to the economic ills of the capitalist world. Governments attempted to curb the labor supply, reduce government spending, and prevent commitments to future expenses. Hard times practically everywhere brought to the surface currents of antisemitism, which were sometimes part of more extensive waves of xenophobia and racism. In consequence, barriers against immigration were hastily erected everywhere. Western European countries did so in the early 1930s. The Soviet Union, in the throes of Stalin's purges, remained cold and inhospitable to Hitler's victims, even when they were Communists. The British, faced with the Arab revolt in Palestine (1936–1939), began to limit entry just at the moment when Jewish refugees were prepared to go there in large numbers. In Canada and the United States restrictive policies governed Jewish immigration, with only a few thousand permitted to immigrate each year.

Before 1938, however, temporary havens certainly existed in Europe, and refugees managed to leave, giving formal assurance that they would not work in their host country and would eventually move elsewhere. But the international climate was cold and forbidding. The League of Nations, whose High Commission for Refugees (the Nansen Office) had done important work during the 1920s, had practically nothing to offer the refugees. A High Commission for Refugees (Jewish and Other) from Germany emerged from the League of Nations discussions in Geneva in 1933, and was separated from the parent agency in the hope that it could deal with Hitler's Germany. However, this body with a cumbersome name failed to make an impression on the policy of any state, and its director, James Grover MCDONALD, quit spectacularly in 1935, protesting the international failure to act against Germany. As the flow of refugees increased, so did the work and expense involved in facilitating their passage, a burden entirely borne by Jewish agencies. The American Jewish JOINT DISTRIBUTION COMMITTEE (JDC) was the largest of these. It worked closely with the Jewish Colonization Association, HICEM (an amalgam, established in 1927, of several Jewish emigration and immigration organizations), the Jewish Agency for Palestine, and other groups.

Restrictions everywhere hardened into firm barriers in the late 1930s, particularly after the Anschluss and the widely observed plight of the Austrian Jews, who faced furious Nazi pressure to leave their country. Those in charge of such questions now feared a totally unmanageable flood of unwanted refugees. Many of the fugitives from the Reich became stateless, having either lost their German nationality or been stripped of their Czech or Austrian citizenship after the absorption of their countries. An international conference at Evian in July 1938 (*see* EVIAN CONFERENCE) gave widespread publicity to the plight of the refugees, but failed to achieve any change in

A group of Polish Jewish refugees on board the Japanese ship *Hikawa Maru.* It set sail from Yokohama, Japan, on June 5, 1941, and arrived at Vancouver, Canada, on June 17.

the overall climate of restriction. The Jewish observers left the meeting feeling bitter and alone. An INTERGOVERNMENTAL COMMITTEE ON REFUGEES (IGCR) emerged from the deliberations, but this body had no ability to change national policy, which constituted the principal obstacle to refuge.

The Jews increasingly appeared on the international stage as mendicants, since they were now being driven virtually destitute from their homes. One resolution of the crisis was negotiation with the Germans, but this path was rejected by receiving countries, which feared that negotiation might encourage an even greater exodus. In 1933 the Nazis had negotiated the HAAVARA AGREEMENT with the German Zionist Federation and the Anglo-Palestine Bank, permitting German Jews who went to Palestine to take a percentage of their capital with them. After Kristallnacht some Nazi officials attempted to negotiate a similar arrangement with host countries in the West, but without success.

At the end of the 1930s, policymakers in the countries enacting further immigration restrictions did not have only Germany in mind. They were also concerned that, because an equally great danger existed for the Jews in eastern Europe, the tens of thousands of Jews from the Reich might soon be joined by millions from Poland, Hungary, and Romania. Behind such fear lay the deepening antisemitism in those countries, along with the severe impoverishment accompanying the Depression. Throughout the area right-wing regimes fanned the flames of popular antipathy toward Jews, which occasionally even broke into the open with violent attacks.

In 1939 the doors slammed shut in one traditional country of immigration after another. After the MUNICH CONFERENCE, governments in the West grimly prepared for the war they had so long hoped to avoid. With their WHITE PAPER OF 1939 (the MacDonald White Paper), the British placed severe limitations on Jewish access to Palestine, in practice raising a firm barrier. Panic-stricken Jews now sought any possible haven. Corrupt consular authorities sometimes sold entry permits to Latin American countries. About seventeen thousand German and Austrian Jews managed to reach the international port of Shanghai, practically the only place on the globe that required no visas or other docu-

Jewish refugee children who were smuggled out of occupied France to Lisbon in 1941. [JDC Archives, New York]

mentation for entry, and later a haven for many Polish Jews as well (*see* RESCUE OF POLISH JEWS VIA EAST ASIA). Other Jews, without legal means of staying in one country, had to continue moving from one place to another.

Wartime Refugees. About 110,000 Jewish refugees were spread across Europe when war broke out in 1939. In western European countries, Jewish fugitives from Nazism were often interned, though they were frequently released after it was recognized that they posed no threat. After the outbreak of war, Jews continued to flee the Nazis, with the greatest movement in eastern Europe. An estimated 300,000 Jews, almost 10 percent of the entire Polish Jewish population, fled German-held territory in western Poland and crossed into parts occupied by the Soviets. During the following months, close to two million Jews came under Soviet rule for the first time, in parts of Poland and Romania as well as in the Baltic states. Substantial numbers of these, deemed suspect and threatening to the new process of Sovietization, were uprooted and dispatched to the eastern regions of the USSR, along with many of their non-Jewish neighbors.

Meanwhile, in the areas of Poland held by the Nazis, hundreds of thousands of Jews were also on the move. Nazi plans involved a massive transfer of Jews from the German-incorporated parts of Poland to the rest of the country under Nazi occupation, known as the GENERALGOUVERNEMENT—a kind of reservation originally intended to be a vast dumping ground for the unwanted "ethnic refuse" of the Nazi-conquered east. Although these plans were halted after early deportations of Jews, the refugees continued to flow to towns and cities, dragooned by brutal occupation policies of ghettoization. Jewish refugees were jammed into every one of the ghettos created in Nazi-held territory. Evidence suggests that at least a million of Poland's three million Jews were torn loose from their homes by the effects of war and persecution during this period. Between 500,000 and 600,000 Jews—about one-fifth of Polish Jewry—died in ghettos and labor camps as a result of these Nazi policies.

For a short time in 1939 and 1940, Nazi strategists focused on the Lublin area, in the southeastern corner of the Generalgouvernement, as a concentration point for Jewish refugees who could not be accommodated elsewhere. This effort, subsequently known as the Lublin Plan (*see* NISKO AND LUBLIN PLAN), was seen as a temporary measure, following which its survivors would be dispatched even farther to the east, across Soviet territory. Tens of thousands of refugees were dumped into the Lublin region before Nazi priorities changed, and the plan was shelved. A year later the MADAGASCAR PLAN was considered by several German agencies, but no Jews were actually sent to that island in the Indian Ocean.

In the summer of 1941, during the weeks following the Nazi attack on the Soviet Union, many communities of Polish and Soviet Jews were overrun too quickly for their inhabitants to become refugees. Eventually, hundreds of thousands of them were massacred by EINSATZGRUPPEN and other Nazi forces. On the Nazi side of the former border, very few Jews escaped, but as many as ten thousand refugees hid in so-called family camps in the often inhospitable countryside (*see* FAMILY CAMPS IN THE FORESTS). About one and a half million Jews did manage to flee the German advance, ending up behind Soviet lines. Several hundred thousand were then scattered throughout the Soviet Union, where they suffered great mortality and privation during the war.

Other Jews fled elsewhere in Europe, pathetic eddies of humanity sometimes forgotten in the mainstream torrent of deportations and expulsions. Oddly, two Axis countries provided sanctuary to significant numbers of Jewish refugees. Italian forces protected Jews wherever Mussolini's armies found themselves in occupation—in parts of France, of Greece, and of Croatia. Hungary, although tied to Nazi Germany and committed to its own anti-Jewish program, nevertheless received Jewish refugees unofficially from neighboring Poland and Slovakia. Occasionally, Jews managed to leave from Bulgaria or Romania, departing on the Black Sea. Their ultimate objective was Palestine, but refugee ships with this destination had to stop at Turkey to refuel and take on supplies of food. Turkish policy, which sought to avoid the use of a Turkish port for stopovers, proved to be an obstacle in the refugees' path, and only a small number of Jews managed to land there. In 1941, for example, the Turks, urged on by the British, refused to allow passengers to land from the derelict Bulgarian steamer STRUMA, and forced it to leave the port of Istanbul. The ship, struck by a torpedo fired (in error) by a Soviet submarine, sank with great loss of life.

About 21,600 Jews managed to enter SWITZERLAND, but thousands more were turned back or deterred from attempting entry because of that country's harshly restrictive policy, tinged with antisemitism. Although its frontier was not officially open, SPAIN generally did not turn back those who made the perilous journey across the Pyrenees. Spanish policy made every effort to speed refugees out of the country, sending them on to the Portuguese port of Lisbon, from which thousands managed to leave for America. As many as 100,000 refugees passed through the Iberian countries during the war, a substantial number of whom were Jews. In the north, SWEDEN provided sanctuary for Jews from other Scandinavian countries, notably the 6,000 or so refugees from Denmark who fled quickly across the Øresund to Malmö in October 1943.

Outside Europe, obstacles remained in the path of Jewish refugees, despite the increasing availability to foreign governments of information about the extreme peril faced by the Jews in Nazi Europe. The gates to Palestine remained shut, and Jews who managed to enter, whether legally or illegally (smuggled into the country by ALIYA BET) numbered only

Jewish refugees in one of the "homes" established in Shanghai to house those who succeeded in escaping from Europe via East Asia in the 1940s. [Leo Baeck Institute, New York]

58,000. American policy remained restrictionist; the admission of Jews was strongly opposed by Breckinridge Long, the State Department official whose influence dominated policy (*see* UNITED STATES DEPARTMENT OF STATE). In April 1943, facing mounting public pressure in Great Britain and the United States, the Allies met at the BERMUDA CONFERENCE to discuss the refugee problem. The British and American governments were determined, however, that the gathering would alter nothing in their policies. The conference's results, therefore, were meager. In America, protest against inaction became louder, sparked particularly by young activists led by Peter Bergson (*see* BERGSON GROUP). Gradually the climate shifted, and Franklin D. ROOSEVELT finally agreed, on January 17, 1944, to establish an agency devoted to the refugee problem and to the rescue of imperiled Jews, the WAR REFUGEE BOARD. The board's representatives, both in the United States and abroad, set about their task with dedication and energy, and succeeded in saving many thousands of Jewish lives. Yet owing to the late establishment of the board, its work could not constitute much more than an afterthought.

Elsewhere too, the approaching end of the war brought about a loosening of restrictions and a greater movement of refugees. Swiss restrictions eased, and more Jews were now able to enter that country. The Swedes too became more willing to receive fugitives. Unfortunately, by this time few Jews were in a position to flee, and for millions it was already too late.

[*See also the entries listed under* Rescue.]

BIBLIOGRAPHY

Abella, I., and H. Troper. *None Is Too Many: Canada and the Jews of Europe.* New York, 1982.

Bauer, Y. *American Jewry and the Holocaust: The American Jewish Joint Distribution Committee, 1939–1945.* Detroit, 1981.

Bauer, Y. *My Brother's Keeper: A History of the American Jewish Joint Distribution Committee, 1929–1939.* Philadelphia, 1974.

Ben-Elissar, E. *La diplomatie du IIIe Reich et les Juifs.* Paris, 1981.

Edelheit, A. J., and H. Edelheit, eds. *Bibliography on Holocaust Literature.* Boulder, 1986. See chapter 13.

Feingold, H. *The Politics of Rescue: The Roosevelt Administration and the Holocaust, 1938–1945.* New Brunswick, N.J., 1970.

Marrus, M. R. *The Unwanted: European Refugees in the Twentieth Century.* New York, 1985.

Penkower, M. N. *The Jews Were Expendable: Free World Diplomacy and the Holocaust.* Urbana, Ill., 1983.

Sherman, J. *Island Refuge: Britain and Refugees from the Third Reich, 1933–1939.* London, 1973.

Wasserstein, B. *Britain and the Jews of Europe, 1939–1945.* Oxford, 1979.

Wyman, D. S. *The Abandonment of the Jews: America and the Holocaust, 1941–1945.* New York, 1985.

Wyman, D. S. *Paper Walls: America and the Refugee Crisis, 1938–1941.* Boston, 1968.

MICHAEL R. MARRUS

REICH ASSOCIATION OF JEWS IN GERMANY. *See* Reichsvertretung der Deutschen Juden.

REICH COMMISSARIAT FOR OSTLAND. *See* Reichskommissariat Ostland.

REICH COMMISSARIAT FOR THE STRENGTHENING OF GERMAN NATIONHOOD. *See* Reichskommissariat für die Festigung des Deutschen Volkstums.

REICH COMMISSARIAT FOR THE UKRAINE. *See* Reichskommissariat Ukraine.

REICHENAU, WALTER VON (1884–1942), German field marshal. Reichenau fought in World War I and served in the Reichswehr. He was the most ardent supporter of the Nazi party among the high-ranking officers of the German army. In his capacity as chief of a department in the Reichswehr Ministry, he was instrumental in the subordination of the armed forces under the Nazi leadership. He commanded an army in the attacks on Poland, France, and the Soviet Union. After the fall of France (June 1940), he was promoted to the rank of *Generalfeldmarschall.*

In December 1941, Reichenau rose to the

command of Army Group South in Russia. He issued a directive ordering and sanctioning the extermination of Soviet prisoners of war and Soviet citizens, in particular, Jews. It opened with the following sentences:

> There are frequent vague conceptions prevailing with regard to the behavior of the troops toward the Bolshevist system. The main object of the campaign against the Jewish Bolshevist system is the total destruction of their instruments of power and the elimination of the Asiatic influence from the cultural life of Europe. For this reason the troops are faced with tasks which far exceed mere soldierly routine. In the eastern sector the soldier is not only one who fights according to the rules of warfare, he is at the same time the exponent of an uncompromising ideology and the avenger of all the bestialities that have been inflicted upon German and racially related people. Therefore the soldier must fully understand the necessity of meting out severe yet fair retribution to the Jewish subhumans [*Untermenschen*]. This retribution will also result in nipping in the bud any uprisings in the rear of the army, which, as experience has shown, have always been instigated by Jews. . . . Only thus can we fulfill our historic task to free the German people once and for all from the Asiatic-Jewish danger.

Gen. Walter von Reichenau. [National Archives]

Hitler was greatly pleased with this order and directed that it be sent to all army commanders with a recommendation to issue similar orders. Reichenau died in Poltava on January 17, 1942, from a heart attack.

BIBLIOGRAPHY

Messerschmidt, M. *Die Wehrmacht im NS-Staat: Zeit der Indoktrination*. Hamburg, 1969.

Müller, K. J. *Das Heer und Hitler: Armee und nationalsozialistisches Regime 1933–1940*. Stuttgart, 1969.

JEHUDA L. WALLACH

REICH REPRESENTATION OF GERMAN JEWS. *See* Reichsvertretung der Deutschen Juden.

REICHSBUND JÜDISCHER FRONTSOLDATEN (Reich Union of Jewish Frontline Soldiers; RJF), Jewish war veterans' union founded on February 8, 1919, by forty Jewish ex-frontline soldiers led by Capt. Leo Löwenstein. The RJF's founders wished to counteract the widespread belief, prevailing in GERMANY after World War I, that Jews had avoided military service or held only office posts in the army. It manifested a political neutrality in internal Jewish political and religious affairs, but saw in the Zionists and their Jewish national aspirations the major opponent. From its inception, the RJF vowed its desire to integrate fully into German society, blurring the differences between Jewish and non-Jewish Germans and emphasizing that Jews had shared the war experience. It reiterated that since twelve thousand Jewish soldiers had given their lives for Germany in the war, the Jews had fulfilled their duty to Germany and had made the same sacrifices as their gentile comrades.

In 1933 the RJF had some thirty thousand members and fourteen thousand youngsters affiliated to 360 local branches, and it published a weekly periodical, *Der Schild* (The Shield). After Adolf Hitler's assumption of power in 1933, the RJF strove to protect the

A memorial ceremony held by Jewish veterans of World War I in the Jewish cemetery at Weissensee, 15 miles (24 km) north of Erfurt, in February 1937. [Bildarchiv Abraham Pisarek, Berlin]

interests of Jewish war veterans by preventing the extension of the segregation policy and seeking to obtain preferred treatment for its members. These attempts were supported by President Paul von HINDENBURG and were sustained until Hindenburg's death in 1934. Following the Nazis' racial legislation of 1935 (*see* NUREMBERG LAWS), the privileged position of the RJF was canceled.

BIBLIOGRAPHY

Pierson, R. "Embattled Veterans: The Reichsbund Jüdischer Frontsoldaten." *Leo Baeck Institute Year Book* 19 (1974): 139–154.

DAVID BANKIER

REICH SECURITY MAIN OFFICE. *See* Reichssicherheitshauptamt.

REICHSKOMMISSARIAT FÜR DIE FESTIGUNG DES DEUTSCHEN VOLKSTUMS (Reich Commissariat for the Strengthening of German Nationhood; RKFDV), an SS agency in charge of resettling ethnic Germans (VOLKSDEUTSCHE) who had been repatriated from foreign countries, particularly the Soviet Union. The price of Hitler's agreement with Stalin in August 1939 (*see* NAZI-SOVIET PACT) had been to concede Latvia, Estonia, eastern Poland, and Bessarabia to the Russian sphere, and a further agreement a month later conceded Lithuania as well. Gaining the Soviets' consent, Hitler moved quickly to repatriate the ethnic Germans in these territories. On October 7 of that year, he charged Heinrich HIMMLER with the dual task of resettling ethnic Germans from abroad and eliminating the harmful influence of alien populations on German soil. To carry out the first task, Himmler created the RKFDV, under SS-Gruppenführer Ulrich Greifelt, to organize the resettlement (*Umsiedlung*) of the uprooted *Volksdeutsche* on Polish territory being annexed to the Third Reich. Housing and employment were to be made available for the RKFDV's incoming ethnic Germans by accomplishing Himmler's second task—the expulsion, coordinated by Reinhard HEYDRICH's

REICHSSICHERHEITSHAUPTAMT (Reich Security Main Office; RSHA), of Poles and Jews from the incorporated territories. Ultimately, the RKFDV received about 500,000 ethnic Germans and resettled about 225,000 of them. The rest remained in temporary camps until the end of World War II.

In the spring of 1940 the RKFDV became involved in two further programs: (1) the compiling of the *Deutsche Volksliste*, the list of "discovered" ethnic Germans in Poland; and (2) "re-Germanization," that is, the selection of people deemed to have racial characteristics making them suitable for assimilation into the German race. The demographic engineers of the RKFDV helped to devise even more grandiose plans for population resettlement in eastern Poland and Russia, formulated in 1941 and 1942 and known as GENERALPLAN OST, but for the most part these proved unrealizable. Thus, the RKFDV was intended to be a crucial instrument for consolidating German LEBENSRAUM ("living space") through massive demographic engineering on a racial basis.

BIBLIOGRAPHY

Broszat, M. *Nationalsozialistische Polenpolitik, 1939–45*. Frankfurt, 1965.

Koehl, R. *RKFDV—German Resettlement and Population Policy, 1939–45: A History of the Reich Commission for the Strengthening of Germandom*. Cambridge, Mass., 1957.

CHRISTOPHER R. BROWNING

REICHSKOMMISSARIAT OSTLAND (Reich Commissariat for Ostland), one of the two major administrative units of the German civil administration in the occupied territories of the Soviet Union, headed by Alfred ROSENBERG, as Reich Minister for the Occupied Eastern [i.e., Soviet] Territories; the other was the REICHSKOMMISSARIAT UKRAINE. Reichskommissariat Ostland included the three Baltic states—LITHUANIA, LATVIA, and ESTONIA —as well as western BELORUSSIA (excluding Polesye), which until 1939 had been part of Poland, and the Minsk district in Soviet Belorussia. The transfer of authority from the military to the civil administration took place in stages, in the period from August to November of 1941, as the German forces advanced eastward. The remaining parts of Soviet Belorussia were not handed over to the Reichskommissariat and remained under military administration, since the German advance was halted at the approaches to Moscow and the Germans were forced to retreat westward. From 1941 to 1944, Hinrich LOHSE was Reichskommissar of the Eastern Territories.

According to the plans drawn up by the Germans for the future disposal of Soviet territory, the three Baltic states were to be settled by Germans and incorporated into the Third Reich; Belorussia was to be a separate territory, for colonial exploitation by Germany. Reichskommissariat Ostland was divided into four *Generalkommissariate* (General Commissariats), based on the previous political and ethnic division of the area (Lithuania, Latvia, Estonia, and Belorussia), each headed by a German *Generalkommissar*. The *Generalkommissariate* were divided into sub-units, called *Kreisgebiete* (districts) or *Gebietskommissariate* (district commissariats), each headed by a German *Gebietskommissar*.

Each of these administrative levels, in addition to the civil officials, had its own elements of SS, Sicherheitspolizei (Security Police; Sipo), and SD (Sicherheitsdienst; Security Service) units. In principle they were subject to the authority of the civil administration, but in practice they received their orders from the SS command, through its own channels.

In addition to the German civil administration, each *Generalkommissariat* also had a local administration, made up of collaborators from among the population who helped the Germans carry out their extermination policy against the Jews, terrorize the anti-German opposition groups, and exploit the economic resources in the area for the German war effort. This local administration had very limited powers. Municipal administrations were also established, with local inhabitants as mayors and village elders. A police force, consisting of volunteers, operated under the direct control of the German police. Local nationalist elements who collaborated with the Germans entertained the hope that in return they would at least be granted a form of national self-government. Much to their disappointment, no such self-government was accorded, nor were they given any promises for the future.

The extermination of the Jews in the Ostland was carried out by Einsatzgruppe A (in the Baltic states) and Einsatzgruppe B (in Belorussia), as well as by Sipo and SD elements attached to the civil administration, with wide-ranging assistance by volunteers from among the local collaborators. In the period from July to December 1941, the great majority of the Jews in the Baltic states were shot to death, close to where they had been living; the same fate overtook the Jews of Belorussia in the spring and summer of 1942. The last ghettos in the Ostland, including those of Vilna, Kovno, and Minsk, were liquidated in the summer of 1943. The entire Ostland, except for a small enclave in Latvia (Kurland), was liberated by the Soviet army in its offensive of the summer of 1944.

BIBLIOGRAPHY

Arad, Y. "Alfred Rosenberg and the 'Final Solution' in the Occupied Soviet Territories." *Yad Vashem Studies* 13 (1979): 263–286.

Dallin, A. *German Rule in Russia, 1941–1945*. London, 1957. See chapters 10, 11.

Toynbee, A. J., and V. Toynbee, eds. *Survey of International Affairs: Hitler's Europe*. New York, 1954.

YITZHAK ARAD

REICHSKOMMISSARIAT UKRAINE (Reich Commissariat for the Ukraine), the German civilian administration in the UKRAINE. Following the decision of the Germans to establish a Ministry for the Occupied Eastern Territories (Reichsministerium für die Besetzten Ostgebiete), under Alfred ROSENBERG, it was decided, at a meeting held at Adolf Hitler's headquarters on July 16, 1941, to divide the eastern occupied territories into two commissariats, REICHSKOMMISSARIAT OSTLAND and Reichskommissariat Ukraine. The latter was to be headed by the *Gauleiter* of East Prussia, Erich KOCH. In an order issued on August 20 of that year, Hitler made the first transfer of territories to the control of the Reichskommissariat Ukraine, to include the Soviet districts of Volhynia, Rovno, and Kamenets-Podolski, as well as the subdistricts of Brest-Litovsk (Brisk), Kobrin, and Pinsk. Further areas were added to the civil administration as the Germans advanced deeper into the Soviet Union. At the beginning of 1943 the commissariat encompassed 130,994 square miles (339,276 sq km), with a population of 16,910,003. Its administrative subdivisions are shown in Table 1. The Soviet districts of Chernigov, Sumy, Kharkov, Stalino (Donetsk), Voroshilovgrad (Lugansk), and the Crimea remained under military rule for as long as the German army was in occupation.

The commissariat's capital was Rovno. The *Höherer SS- und Polizeiführer* (Higher SS and Police Leader), Gen. Hans-Adolf PRÜTZMANN, was based in Kiev, as were the senior SD (Sicherheitsdienst; Security Service) and Sicherheitspolizei (Security Police) officer, Dr. Georg Thomas, and the military governor of the Ukraine, Gen. Karl Kitzinger. Einsatzgruppen C and D operated both in the Reichskommissariat Ukraine and in the part of the Ukraine that was under military administration.

TABLE 1. *Administrative Subdivisions of the Reichskommissariat Ukraine Early in 1943*

GENERALBEZIRK (GENERAL COMMISSARIAT)	SOVIET DISTRICTS CONTAINED THEREIN	NUMBER OF SUB-DISTRICTS	CAPITAL
Volhynia-Podolia	Volhynia, Rovno, Kamenets-Podolski, South Pinsk, Brest-Litovsk	24	Brest-Litovsk, Lutsk (from June 1943)
Zhitomir	Zhitomir, North Vinnitsa, South Polesye	29	Zhitomir
Kiev	Kiev, Poltava	26	Kiev
Nikolayev	Nikolayev, Kirovograd	14	Nikolayev
Dnepropetrovsk	Dnepropetrovsk, Zaporozhye	16	Dnepropetrovsk
Tauria	South Nikolayev, Zaporozhye	14	Melitopol

BIBLIOGRAPHY

Dallin, A. *German Rule in Russia, 1941–1945.* London, 1957.

SHMUEL SPECTOR

REICHSSICHERHEITSHAUPTAMT (Reich Security Main Office; RSHA), the combined headquarters of the Nazi Sicherheitspolizei (Security Police; Sipo) and SD (Sicherheitsdienst; Security Service). The RSHA was the central office through which the Nazis' fight against the "enemies of the regime" was organized in concert with the police and state bureaucracy. Embodying the SS ideology, the RSHA was the principal tool of the regime's ideological, political, and racial warfare against its enemies.

Antecedents (1931–1939). Several SS institutions that functioned in the period before the establishment of the RSHA may be considered its precursors. Chief among these was the SD and SS surveillance and intelligence apparatus, which was set up in 1931 by Heinrich HIMMLER and for which Reinhard HEYDRICH was responsible. Its primary tasks were to protect the Nazi leadership from the Weimar Republic's political police and to establish a secret espionage network to be used against party enemies, government agencies, and the party itself.

The second precursor to the RSHA was the GESTAPO, which was originally the political police of Prussia during the period of the Weimar Republic. In 1933 and 1934, the SD was instrumental in Himmler's successful takeover of the political police of all the German states. These were formally unified with the Gestapo in 1936, under the nominal authority of the Reich Ministry of the Interior. Characteristically, Himmler kept the SD itself outside this new state bureaucracy. Moreover, he encouraged competition between the Gestapo and the SD.

A third precursor to the RSHA was the KRIMINALPOLIZEI (Criminal Police; Kripo), under Arthur NEBE. Nebe served first in the Gestapo, and then, eager to centralize and to use methods forbidden in a state observing the law, took over the modern criminal police agencies of the German states and unified them to serve the new regime. In 1936, the Gestapo and Kripo were reorganized as the Sipo, and came under Heydrich's control as state agencies. Until 1939, the SD remained under his command as a separate SS main office (*Hauptamt*).

The RSHA from 1939 to 1945. On September 22, 1939, the SD and Sipo were merged to become the RSHA. When the selection of personnel was completed at that time, the instrument that would carry out future atrocities was readied. Under Heydrich, who maintained his title as chief of the Sipo and SD, the RSHA developed, between 1939 and 1941, into an enormous organization. It came to comprise seven departments (*Ämter*), as follows:

Amt I, under Bruno Streckenbach (who was to succeed Heydrich as acting RSHA chief for eight months following the latter's assassination in June 1942), was in charge of personnel.

Amt II, originally under Dr. Werner BEST and later under Dr. Neckmann, was in charge of organization and law, including legislation, passports, and budget.

Amt III, under Otto OHLENDORF, was essentially the former SD internal affairs department, and retained the same functions. Its main divisions dealt with economic matters, culture, and ethnic Germans.

Amt IV, under Heinrich MÜLLER, was the Gestapo, which was divided into fourteen divisions, plus the border police. The divisions dealt separately with political "enemies" (including Communists, Liberals, Catholics, and Protestants), and functionally with sabotage, counterintelligence, treason, and the like. Section IV B 4, under Adolf EICHMANN, combined two areas of responsibility, evacuations and Jews.

Amt V, under Nebe, was the Kriminalpolizei (Kripo), which had four main divisions.

Amt VI, officially under Heinz Jost and later under Walter SCHELLENBERG, was called SD-Foreign, and was the foreign intelligence of the SS. Its six divisions dealt with German spheres of interest in the West. In reality it was under the direct control of the chief of the RSHA.

Amt VII, under Professor Franz Six, was the "ideological" branch of the RSHA, in charge of collecting, evaluating, and disseminating ideological material, mainly concerning Jews.

Following the assassination of Heydrich, his temporary replacement by Streckenbach, and his subsequent permanent replacement by Ernst KALTENBRUNNER in early 1943, the basic structure of the organization remained the same. During Kaltenbrunner's era, the Gestapo department grew even larger. In the wake of the attempts on Hitler's life in 1944 and the subsequent breakup of the ABWEHR (the Wehrmacht's intelligence service) because of its alleged involvement in the attempts, the SD's foreign department also became significantly larger.

The regional structure of the RSHA in the Reich itself was under the often nominal control of the Sipo and SD inspectors in each military district. State police district offices (Staatspolizeileitstellen) in the larger cities, and Gestapo branches and SD main and sectional offices (Leitabschnitte and Abschnitte), were also theoretically subordinated to these inspectors. In reality, however, the Gestapo issued orders directly to its own branches. From 1941 on it often acted on its own against "enemies of the Reich," denounced and arrested citizens, and supervised foreign workers who had been brought forcibly to Germany to fill the manpower gap.

In the occupied territories, a similar control from Berlin was generally maintained. Here, the Gestapo, Kripo, and SD branches were under the control of the commanders of the Sipo and SD (*Befehlshaber der Sicherheitspolizei und des Sicherheitsdienstes*), although in the field the Gestapo, SD, and mobile killing units (EINSATZGRUPPEN) were largely autonomous. An alternate line of command was established by Himmler on May 21, 1941. The *Höherer SS- und Polizeiführer* (Higher SS and Police Leaders), whom Himmler had designated as his personal representatives on November 13, 1937, were given sanction to bypass the regular chain of command and issue orders in Himmler's name directly to the Sipo and SD commanders, cutting out the RSHA.

Regardless of their professional training, the RSHA's personnel were used for its tasks both in the occupied territories and the Reich itself. Thus, Dr. Ohlendorf, an economist, commanded Einsatzgruppe D; and the former SD man who became dean of the Faculty for Foreign Countries at Berlin University, Professor Six, commanded Vorkommando Moskau of Einsatzgruppe B.

The Gestapo was the formidable backbone of the RSHA, combining surveillance, denunciation, and torture with its power to imprison people in the concentration camps and execute them there. The primary victims of the Nazis, the Jews, became a special focus of RSHA activity under Eichmann's section, IV B 4. From late 1941 on, it directed the deportation of most of European Jewry to ghettos, slave labor, and extermination camps. The RSHA continued Hitler's extermination policies to the very end of the war.

BIBLIOGRAPHY

Delarue, J. *The Gestapo: A History of Horror.* New York, 1964.

Hohne, H. *The Order of the Death's Head: The Story of Hitler's SS.* New York, 1969.

Krausnick, H., et al. *The Anatomy of the SS State.* New York, 1968.

SHLOMO ARONSON

REICHSVEREINIGUNG DER JUDEN IN DEUTSCHLAND. *See* Reichsvertretung der Deutschen Juden.

REICHSVERTRETUNG DER DEUTSCHEN JUDEN (Reich Representation of German Jews), German Jewry's central organization. Its name was changed in 1935 to the Reichsvertretung der Juden in Deutschland (Reich Representation of Jews in Germany) on orders of the authorities, and in 1939, following changes in its structure and legal status, it became the Reichsvereinigung der Juden in Deutschland (Reich Association of Jews in Germany). (*See* Appendix, Volume 4.)

When Hitler came to power in 1933, German Jews did not have an overall representative body, but only a loose federation of *Landesverbände* (state unions), which had come into being in January 1932. It was not until September 1933 that a comprehensive representative body, the Reichsvertretung, was established, on the initiative of several Jewish communities in the western part of the country, in cooperation with the Berlin community board and the above federation. The new organization's task was to deal with the serious problems facing German Jewry under the new totalitarian regime, whose declared policy was anti-Jewish. Rabbi Leo BAECK was elected president, and the moving spirit in the organization was its chief executive officer, Otto HIRSCH.

The organization's activities were to include all aspects of the internal life of the Jews of GERMANY, and it was to act as their representative before the authorities as well as vis-à-vis Jewish organizations abroad. Its main spheres of operation, conducted through the ZENTRALAUSSCHUSS DER DEUTSCHEN JUDEN FÜR HILFE UND AUFBAU (Central Committee of German Jews for Relief and Reconstruction), were the following:

1. Education, which consisted of supporting and expanding Jewish schools and a wide network of adult education, the latter mainly by means of the MITTELSTELLE FÜR JÜDISCHE ERWACHSENENBILDUNG (Jewish Center for Adult Education);
2. Vocational training and retraining for the large number of Jews who had lost their means of livelihood, to prepare them for emigration;
3. Support for the needy, whose number was growing as a result of the ongoing impoverishment of the Jews, and for homes for the aged, hospitals, and so on;
4. Economic assistance, which included the establishment of employment offices and loan funds;
5. Emigration, which in the first few years was handled by the HILFSVEREIN DER DEUTSCHEN JUDEN (German Jews' Aid Society) and the Palestine Office (the latter dealt only with emigration to Palestine).

The widespread cultural activities were in the hands of the KULTURBUND DEUTSCHER JUDEN (Cultural Society of German Jews), which until the end of 1941 was an independent organization. The intensive work carried out by the Reichsvertretung enabled the Jews of Germany to cope with the severe problems that confronted them as a result of the regime's discrimination and persecution. Jewish relief organizations abroad were of great help to the Reichsvertretung, but its main sources of strength were the German Jews themselves, their communal spirit, and the help they extended to one another.

In its contacts with the authorities, the Reichsvertretung sought to safeguard the physical and moral existence of the Jews of Germany, and considered itself competent to react to major anti-Jewish measures, such as the NUREMBERG LAWS, passed in September 1935, or the terrorist actions and mass arrests that took place in the summer of 1938. In extreme cases the Reichsvertretung even resorted to special public actions, such as its protest against the blood-libel incitement (the accusation that Jews kill gentiles to obtain their blood for Jewish rituals) by the newspaper *Der Stürmer* in the summer of 1934 (*see* STÜRMER, DER), or the special prayers it composed, to be read out in the synagogues, in the wake of the widespread waves of anti-Jewish terror acts in the spring and fall of 1935. The authorities reacted sharply to such steps by the Reichsvertretung, which did not prevent it from making further protests against the growing terror of the summer of 1938, and even against the first mass deportations in 1940.

Unlike the Jewish communities that were its constituent members, the Reichsvertretung did not have a recognized legal status, but the authorities recognized it de facto, regarding the Reichsvertretung, in the SD's definition, as "the only representation of the Jews living in Germany acknowledged as such by the Reich government." In March 1938, when the legal status that the Jewish communities had had under the Weimar Republic was revoked, the Reichsvertretung embarked on a reorganization that was to convert it into a single, countrywide community. Owing to the KRISTALLNACHT events in November of that year, this process was not completed until February 1939, when the Reichsvereinigung der Juden in Deutschland came into being. It took the authorities until July 1939 to pass a special law in which it granted recognition to the Reichsvereinigung, authorizing it to deal with emigration, education, and welfare. In this new form, however, the Reichsvereinigung was put under the control of the Ministry of the Interior—(in practice, under the REICHSSICHERHEITSHAUPTAMT (Reich Security Main Office; RSHA)—and it had to accept as its members all persons whom the Nuremberg Laws defined as Jews.

As far as the composition of its leadership and the basic purposes of its operations were concerned, the Reichsvereinigung was the continuation of its predecessor, the Reichsvertretung, but the constant intensification of the Reich's anti-Jewish policies enhanced the significance of its activities. From the end of 1938 until its liquidation in July 1943, the Reichsvereinigung was the only organization in Germany dealing with Jewish survival. Its chief objective was emigration—now seen as meaning the saving of lives—and it kept up its efforts to enable Jews to get out of Germany even after the outbreak of World War II, in close cooperation with Jewish organizations in neutral countries. This continued until October 1941, when emigration was officially banned. When the last Jewish students were expelled from German public schools, at the end of 1938, the Reichsvereinigung expanded the Jewish school network, which remained in operation even when the mass deportations were in progress, until it too was closed down, in June 1942. When the Reichsvereinigung intensified its efforts on behalf of emigration, it provided additional facilities for vocational training and retraining. With the increasing pauperization of the Jews remaining in Germany—mostly old people—welfare gradually became the organization's major sphere of operations.

All these activities by the Reichsvereinigung were carried on under increasing pressure and terrorization by the authorities, which included the imprisonment and execution of several of the Vereinigung's top officials. Thus, in 1940, Julius Seligsohn was imprisoned following the protest issued by the Reichsvereinigung against the mass expulsion of Jews from Baden-Pfalz in southwest Germany. Other examples are the arrest of Otto Hirsch, followed by his execution in the summer of 1941, and the repeated arrests of his successor, Paul EPPSTEIN. A number of the staff members of the Reichsvereinigung were among the several hundred Jews who were seized as hostages and put to death in retaliation for the underground operations of the BAUM GRUPPE, in June 1942.

For many years after the war, the attitude of the Vereinigung and its role in the mass deportations constituted the subject of a controversy among scholars and the general public. An archive of the Reichsvereinigung discovered in the 1960s revealed that its leadership protested publicly against the first deportations in 1940, while from the fall of 1941 onward, the central leadership was not involved in the deportations. However, the Jewish communities in Germany, which were then functioning as branches of the Vereinigung, were in certain cases forced by the Gestapo to deliver the summonses to the persons who were to be deported and to ensure that they all reported to the assembly points.

The last of the Vereinigung's leaders, including Leo Baeck and Paul Eppstein, were deported to THERESIENSTADT in the first half of 1943. In July of that year the Reichsvereinigung was officially abolished, and its organ, the *Jüdisches Nachrichtenblatt* (which was the only Jewish newspaper in existence after *Kristallnacht*), was no longer published. The Reichsvereinigung was now replaced by the Rest-Reichsvereinigung (Residue Reich Association), which remained in existence until shortly before the fall of the Reich. It dealt mainly with Jews living in mixed marriages and their progeny, who were not being deported.

The overall evaluation of the Reichsvereinigung and its activities varied among its Jewish contemporaries in Germany, and these varying opinions are also reflected, to some degree, in research on the subject. In some quarters it was believed that the organization's work expressed the will to preserve and foster the authentic character of German Jewry and its basic values even under the totalitarian and racist regime. It is in this context that the definition of "moral resistance" is applied, especially with respect to schooling and adult education (the view of Ernst Simon). Others hold that it was precisely these expectations that were illusions and, indeed, a tragic error, which may perhaps have prevented sufficient emphasis from being placed on emigration efforts that could have saved lives (the view of Robert WELTSCH). Another aspect is the effect that the existence of this central Jewish organization in Nazi Germany may have had on Nazi policy with regard to Jewish leadership in the German-occupied countries. There are clear indications that at least at some stage, the Nazis considered it important that the Jewish representative bodies be made up not of their own puppets but of authentic leaders, who were recognized as such by the Jews, as for example when they set up the central organization of Czech Jews, the first Judenräte (Jewish councils) in Poland, and the UNION GÉNÉRALE DES ISRAÉLITES DE FRANCE.

BIBLIOGRAPHY

Gruenewald, M. "The Beginning of the 'Reichsvertretung.'" *Leo Baeck Institute Year Book* 1 (1956): 57–67.

Kulka, O. D. "The 'Reichsvereinigung' and the Fate of German Jews, 1938/1939–1943: Continuity or Discontinuity?" In *The Jews in Nazi Germany, 1933–1943,* edited by A. Paucker, pp. 353–363. Tübingen, 1986.

Margaliot, A. "The Dispute over the Leadership of German Jewry (1933–1938)." *Yad Vashem Studies* 10 (1974): 129–148.

ESRIEL HILDESHEIMER and OTTO DOV KULKA

REICH UNION OF JEWISH FRONTLINE SOLDIERS. *See* Reichsbund Jüdischer Frontsoldaten.

REIK, HAVIVA (Emma; 1914–1944), World War II parachutist and emissary of the Jewish Agency's underground military organization, the Hagana. Reik was born in a small

Haviva Reik.

village near Banská Bystrica, Slovakia. She was a member of the Ha-Shomer ha-Tsa'ir Zionist youth movement and in 1939 settled in Palestine, where she joined Kibbutz Ma'anit. At the time of the El Alamein battle she enlisted in the Hagana's strike force, the Palmaḥ. When her period of service was completed, Reik learned about the parachutists' unit for which volunteers were being sought and promptly joined, in the hope of being sent to Slovakia to help in the rescue of Jews in that country.

On September 21, 1944, Reik was dropped over Slovakia at a point near Banská Bystrica, which at the time was the center of the SLOVAK NATIONAL UPRISING. Her mission was to get to BRATISLAVA and there to establish contact with the leaders of the PRACOVNÁ SKUPINA (Working Group), Rabbi Michael Dov WEISSMANDEL and Gisi FLEISCHMANN. Reik had been preceded a week earlier by three other parachutists, Rafael Reiss, Zvi Ben-Yaakov, and Chaim Hermesh (Kassaf). At the end of September a fifth parachutist was dropped, Abba Berdiczew, who brought radio transmitters along for his colleagues. Reik and her group were unable to begin any activity on behalf of the Jews since, like their Slovak partisan friends, they were forced to fight for their lives against the Germans. They tried to set up an independent Jewish unit and succeeded in rounding up some forty Jewish partisans from among the general partisan units that were still operating against the Germans.

After the fall of Banská Bystrica, at the end of October 1944, Reik and her comrades from Palestine retreated into the Tatra Mountains, together with the Jewish partisan group. There, near the village of Bukovice, they set up a small camp, collecting weapons and trying to make the camp a stronghold. "Every day that we are still alive," Reik wrote in a letter, "is like a gift from heaven." On the sixth day of their stay in the camp, owing to inadequate security precautions, they were captured by a unit of the Ukrainian "Galicia" Waffen-SS division that was operating in the area against the Slovak rebels. Reik, Reiss, and Ben-Yaakov were among those taken prisoner, and on November 20, 1944, the Germans executed them at Kremnica. Kibbutz Lahavot Haviva, the postwar "illegal" immigration ship *Haviva Reik*, and the Israeli educational center Givat Haviva were all named after Haviva Reik.

BIBLIOGRAPHY

Benkler, R. "Haviva Reik: Heroine without Heroics." *Israel Horizon* 12/10 (December 1964): 15–19.

Ben Nachum, D., ed. *Like a Mother Sensing Rescue: The Mission of Haviva Reik*. Merhavia, Israel, 1965. (In Hebrew.)

Chermesh, C. *Operation Amsterdam*. Tel Aviv, 1971. (In Hebrew.)

GIDEON GREIF

RELICO. *See* Relief Committee for the Warstricken Jewish Population.

RELIEF AND RESCUE COMMITTEE OF BUDAPEST (Va'adat ha-Ezra ve-ha-Hatsala be-Budapest; known as the Va'ada), committee that began functioning in late 1941 to render aid to Jewish refugees in HUNGARY. In January 1943, in response to an appeal from Palestine asking it to be their conduit for relief and information in central Europe, the committee was officially constituted as a recognized arm of the Jewish Agency. Composed of representatives from the small, semilegal, and marginal Zionist groups, the committee's leadership included Ottó KOMOLY (General Zionists), the head of the Zionist Association of Hungary; Jenő Frankel (Mizraḥi); Ernő (Zvi) Szilágyi (Ha-Shomer ha-Tsa'ir); and Joel BRAND, Rezső (Israel) KASZTNER, and Samuel Springmann (Ichud). At the time of the German occupation of Hungary, on March 19, 1944, it expanded to include other youth leaders and refugees: Josko Baumer, Uziel Lichtenberg, Moshe Rosenberg, Siegfried (Stephen) Roth, Moshe Schweiger, and Dov Weiss. Although Komoly was the titular head of the Va'ada, its de facto leader was Kasztner. The original objectives of the Va'ada included rescuing Jews by smuggling them into Hungary, helping refugees within the country, and preparing for the self-defense of Hungarian Jewry.

The smuggling of refugees across the border

was the responsibility of the Tiyyul ("Excursion") section, headed by Brand. The operation was based on a well-developed network of daring individuals—Jews and non-Jews—who risked their freedom and lives for either humanitarian and idealistic reasons or for financial rewards. With the help of members of the Zionist youth movement and the Slovak-based PRACOVNÁ SKUPINA (Working Group), the Tiyyul activists managed to smuggle approximately 1,100 Polish Jews out of Poland before the German occupation; around 1,000 other Polish Jews succeeded in reaching Hungary by themselves. The Va'ada also helped support approximately 13,000 other Jewish refugees who were in Hungary. These came mostly from Slovakia (8,000) and Germany (4,000).

The Va'ada served as a vital communication link between the Jewish organizations of the free world and the oppressed communities of Poland and Slovakia. It maintained close contact with the Jewish Agency office in Istanbul, headed by Haim Barlas, and with the Swiss branch of He-Haluts, headed by Nathan Schwalb. It also worked closely with the Jewish leaders of Slovakia, especially the representatives of the Working Group, and with various Jewish underground groups in the southern part of Poland. In 1944 and 1945, these contacts were extended to include the representatives of the major Jewish organizations, among them the American Jewish JOINT DISTRIBUTION COMMITTEE, and the United States WAR REFUGEE BOARD in Switzerland.

These contacts involved not only the transfer of funds, but also the exchange of information and the transmission of letters, newspapers, and reports about conditions in the camps and ghettos. They were effected through a courier service that included persons who worked with the Hungarian Ministry of Foreign Affairs and the intelligence services of the German and Hungarian general staffs. As a result, the members of the Va'ada were among the best-informed persons in Europe regarding the ghastly details of the Nazis' "FINAL SOLUTION" program.

With the German occupation, the Va'ada leaders divided up their responsibilities in their attempt to save Hungarian Jewry. Komoly pursued the "'Hungarian line," establishing contact with and soliciting support

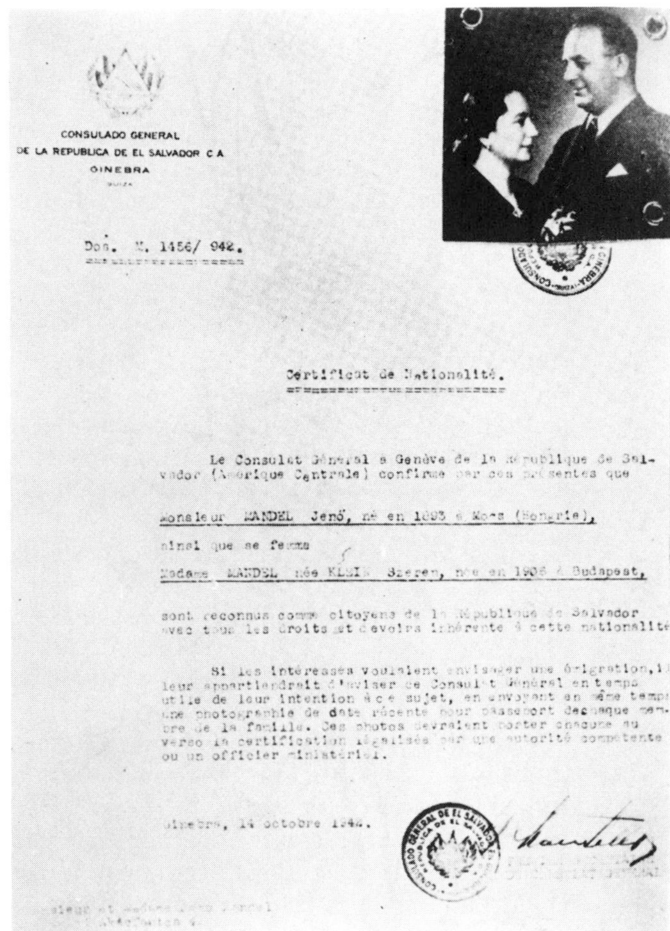

CONSULADO GENERAL
DE LA REPUBLICA DE EL SALVADOR C A
GINEBRA

Dos. N. 1456/ 942.

Certificat de Nationalité.

Le Consulat Général à Genève de la République de Salvador (Amérique Centrale) confirme par ces présentes que

Monsieur MANDEL Jenő, né en 1893 à [illegible] (Hongrie),

ainsi que sa femme

Madame MANDEL née KLEIN Szeren, née en 1906 à Budapest,

sont reconnus comme citoyens de la République de Salvador avec tous les droits et devoirs inhérents à cette nationalité.

Si les intéressés voulaient envisager une émigration, il leur appartiendrait d'aviser ce Consulat Général en temps utile de leur intention à ce sujet, en envoyant en même temps une photographie de date récente pour passeport de chaque membre de la famille. Ces photos devraient porter chacune au verso la certification légalisée par une autorité compétente ou un officier ministériel.

Ginebra, 14 octobre 1942.

Certificate of nationality issued by the Consulate General of El Salvador in Geneva, one of many thousands issued by the El Salvador government to Hungarian Jews. They were given to Carl Lutz, the Swiss representative in Budapest, who also represented Salvadoran interests. Lutz in turn was responsible for distributing the certificates. The text reads: "Certificate of Nationality. The Consulate General of the Republic of El Salvador (Central America) in Geneva hereby confirms that Mr. Jenő Mandel, born in 1893 in [?] (Hungary), and his wife, Mrs. Szeren Mandel, née Klein, born in 1906 in Budapest, are recognized as citizens of the Republic of Salvador with all the rights and obligations pertaining to this nationality. If the above-mentioned are considering emigration they must give sufficient notice of their intention to the Consulate General and must supply a recent photograph for each member of the family. These photos must be notarized on the reverse side by a competent authority or by a ministerial official. Geneva, October 14, 1942."

from Hungarian governmental, political, and church leaders. Kasztner and Brand took on the controversial task of dealing with the Germans.

The Va'ada leaders' first contact with the SS was apparently established on April 5, 1944. The rescue negotiations that followed were based on the EUROPA PLAN, which had been initiated by Rabbi Michael Dov WEISSMANDEL and other leaders of the Working Group in October 1942, following their ostensibly successful deal with Dieter WISLICENY early that year. The negotiations of the SS, including those conducted by Adolf EICHMANN and Kurt BECHER, had the approval of the REICHSSICHERHEITSHAUPTAMT (Reich Security Main Office; RSHA) in Berlin. The Nazis, it seems, hoped not only to extract the maximum economic benefits for the Reich, but also to assure the smoothest possible implementation of the "Final Solution." A corollary objective of their notorious "Blood for Goods" offer, according to which they expressed their readiness to exchange one million Jews for certain specified goods, was to split the western Allies from the Soviet Union so that the former could join Nazi Germany in the fight against the Communist forces. The Va'ada leaders used this opportunity to attempt to prevent or at least postpone the implementation of the Nazi program.

Brand departed for Turkey on May 17, 1944 —two days after the mass deportations had started—to bring the SS offer to the attention of the Allies. Subsequently, Kasztner, other members of the Va'ada, and Jewish leaders from the various strata of the community became preoccupied with one element of the negotiations. First broached by Wisliceny in April, the idea of allowing several hundred Hungarian Jews to leave Hungary by train for the West resurfaced in the context of Brand's mission. The Nazis called the transport a gesture of their goodwill, and the Jewish leaders realized that it might be a one-time chance for rescue that must be exploited fully. Not all the community agreed that the Nazis could be trusted; many Zionist youths who were offered places on the train declined to join it. Eventually, a transport of 1,684 Jews was organized, including Jews from all segments of Hungarian Jewry, as well as family members and friends of some of the Va'ada leaders. Both Kasztner and Komoly refused to join the group, believing they must remain in Hungary to further their rescue efforts. On June 30, 1944, the train left Budapest, and after a relatively short stay in the BERGEN-BELSEN camp, some 300 members of the transport were brought to Switzerland. At the end of the year the remainder joined them.

The negotiations with the SS continued until early 1945. Saly MAYER, the Joint Distribution Committee's Swiss representative, became an important participant in them from the summer of 1944. Accompanied by Becher and his associates, Kasztner traveled to Switzerland to discuss the bargaining with Mayer. The American War Refugee Board was apprised of these contacts, and its representative in Switzerland, Roswell McClelland, even met with Becher, on November 5. Mayer's strategy, supported by the War Refugee Board, was to lead on the Nazis without really giving them anything, since the Nazis' eagerness to come to terms and create alibis for themselves increased as it became clearer that they were losing the war. This stand brought Mayer and Kasztner into conflict with each other because Kasztner wanted to consummate an arrangement to rescue the remnants of Hungarian Jewry. Under Mayer's guidance, however, the discussions expanded into negotiations for the rescue of the remaining Jews in Nazi-dominated Europe.

Although a bargain was never reached, the negotiations did yield some significant results. A major achievement was the rescue of almost twenty-one thousand Jews, mostly from the southern and southeastern parts of Trianon Hungary, including Baja, Debrecen, SZEGED, and Szolnok. They were transferred to STRASSHOF, Austria, between June 25 and 28, 1944, to be "put on ice" pending Brand's return. While the physically fit were subject to conscription for labor in various industrial and agricultural enterprises, most of these Jews, including children and the elderly, survived. Another accomplishment was Heinrich HIMMLER's order of August 25, 1944, to stop further deportations from Budapest. In December, Becher and the *Höherer SS- und Polizeiführer* (Higher SS and Police Leader) in Hungary, Generalleutnant Otto Winkelmann, received permission from Berlin to maintain the Budapest ghetto, which was again under the threat of deportation, for the sake of the

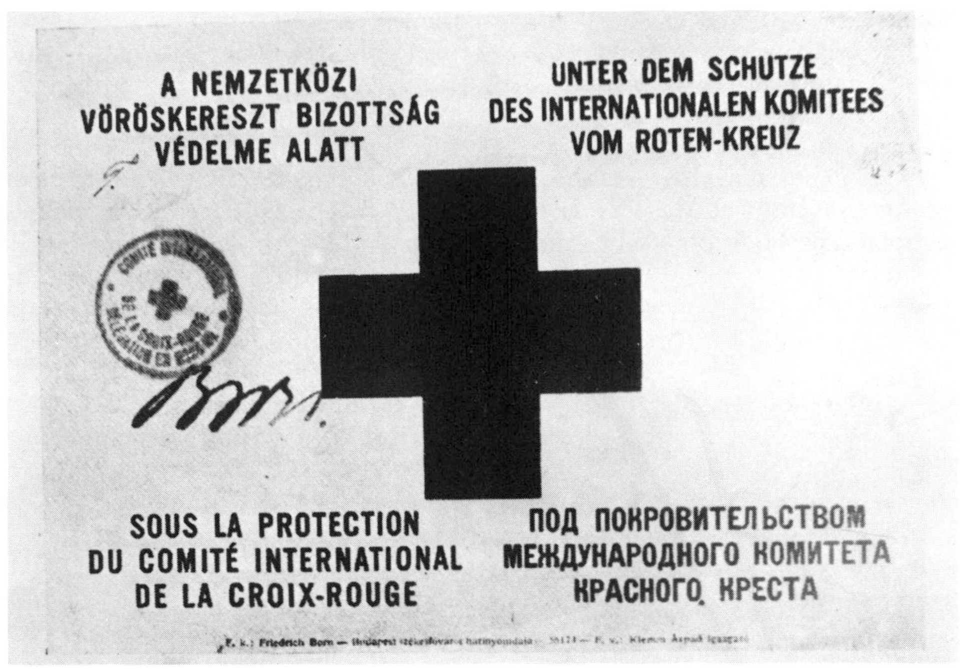

A sign outside the building of a children's home in Budapest indicating that the building was under the protection of the International Red Cross.

negotiations.

After the defeat of Hungary, Kasztner continued to travel around central Europe with Becher, and he continued to help Jews. He supplied food and medicines for the Strasshof group, aided Jews hiding underground in BRATISLAVA, arranged for a transport from Slovakia to Switzerland that included Rabbi Weissmandel, and apparently convinced Becher to use his authority to make sure that the NEUENGAMME and Bergen-Belsen camps were handed over to the Allies without resistance.

The rescue of the Jews via Bergen-Belsen also clearly resulted from the negotiations, but, coupled with Kasztner's testimonies on behalf of Becher and his staff after the war, it aroused great controversy and political confrontation in Israel in the mid-1950s. The transport and Kasztner's activities in relation to it became the core of a sensational trial. Judge Benjamin Halevi of the Jerusalem District Court concluded that Kasztner had "sold his soul to the devil" (June 22, 1955). In June 1958, the Israeli Supreme Court reversed by a split vote the lower court's judgment. Kasztner did not live to hear his vindication; he was killed by an assassin on March 15, 1957.

After the SZÁLASI coup of October 15, 1944, the Va'ada was involved in safeguarding Budapest Jewry in the city itself. Particularly important here were the activities of Komoly. Under the protection of the International RED CROSS representative in Budapest, Friedrich Born, Komoly headed Section A of the Red Cross offices in Hungary beginning in August 1944. Working mostly with Zionist youth movement members, but also with the help of Born, other neutral diplomats, and members of the Zsidó Tanács (Jewish Council), Komoly helped organize rescue activities that provided food, shelter, heat, and protection from rampaging ARROW CROSS PARTY men during the Szálasi regime. A major element of their work was the rescue of some five thousand Jewish children in special buildings. Komoly himself was abducted by the Arrow Cross early in January 1945 and murdered.

A striking aspect of the history of the Va'ada is that it was not the official leadership of Hungarian Jewry, yet as the period of the German occupation unfolded, the Va'ada became the dominant force in the Jewish community. Komoly, Kasztner, and the Zionist youth who worked with the Va'ada were outsiders, because of their age or social status, because they were refugees, or because they came from territories that were annexed to Trianon Hungary. Komoly was the closest to the official leadership group, but as a Zionist, even he stood at its periphery. Perhaps it was this status that allowed the Va'ada to try unconventional methods of rescue, that brought them to center stage, and that made them the de facto leaders of Hungarian Jewry at the most critical period of its history.

BIBLIOGRAPHY

Braham, R. L. *The Politics of Genocide: The Holocaust in Hungary*. New York, 1981.

Cohen, A. *The Halutz Resistance in Hungary, 1942–1944*. New York, 1986.

Landau, E., ed. *Der Kastner-Bericht über Eichmanns Menschenhandel in Ungarn*. Munich, 1961.

Rozett, R. "Child Rescue in Budapest, 1944–1945." *Holocaust and Genocide Studies* 2/1 (1987): 49–59.

Vago, B. "Budapest Jewry in the Summer of 1944: Otto Komoly's Diaries." *Yad Vashem Studies* 8 (1970): 81–105.

RANDOLPH L. BRAHAM

RELIEF COMMITTEE FOR THE WAR-STRICKEN JEWISH POPULATION (RELICO), organization established in Geneva in September 1939 by Dr. Abraham Silberschein under the auspices of the WORLD JEWISH CONGRESS. At first RELICO was devoted to the search for missing relatives and the provision of material and legal assistance to Jewish refugees from the countries of Europe, but Silberschein soon turned his efforts to refugee activities. When information reached him that the Germans were prepared to release Polish Jews from the SACHSENHAUSEN, DACHAU, and BUCHENWALD concentration camps on condition that they leave Germany immediately, Silberschein requested assistance from the Association of Jews from Galicia in the United States. As a result, several groups were enabled to leave Germany in 1940 and go to Bolivia and Palestine. RELICO was also instrumental in organizing the emigration of refugees from Vilna and Kovno to Kōbe, JAPAN; to SHANGHAI; and to the Dutch colonies. It also assisted Polish refugees in Romania, Slovakia, Hungary, and Italy, as well as refugees from the Netherlands, Belgium, and northern France, who reached the unoccupied zone of France.

RELICO generally worked in close cooperation with existing Jewish bodies, but in places where these organizations did not exist, such as Portugal, Spain, Tangier, and Casablanca, RELICO representatives were active, helping to liberate refugees from imprisonment and to resolve their legal status.

In all these activities, Silberschein used the services of the International RED CROSS and the consuls of Poland, Czechoslovakia, and the Netherlands in Switzerland, as well as the papal representatives, the Protestant Church Council, and the Quakers. They helped to convey information and deliver food parcels and medicines, especially in Poland and in the prisoner-of-war camps. For the transfer of money and letters, mainly to Zionist activists, Silberschein used special couriers. After the war it became apparent that some of them had been German agents. Because of its ramified contacts and its ability to convey information speedily, RELICO was among the first sources to inform the Jewish organizations and the world at large about the CHEŁMNO and TREBLINKA extermination camps, and it appealed for the intervention of the major powers to put a stop to the deportations. During the course of the war and immediately afterward, Silberschein published evidence of the forced-labor camps and the annihilation of Polish Jewry.

In addition to allotments from the World Jewish Congress, RELICO received financial support from the American Jewish JOINT DISTRIBUTION COMMITTEE, the RESCUE COMMITTEE OF THE JEWISH AGENCY IN TURKEY, and the Labor Zionist Movement in the United States and Britain, as well as the Jewish relief organizations in Switzerland.

Silberschein's accurate reading of the situation, and his independent and unconventional methods, often brought him into conflict with the World Jewish Congress representatives in Switzerland and the United States, and as a result, RELICO was divided into two sections. One section, headed by Silberschein, continued its relief activities for the Jews of Poland and of eastern and southern Europe, while the other section concerned itself primarily with searching for missing relatives, rescuing children from western Europe, and sending food parcels to the THERESIENSTADT camp.

Learning that the Germans were not sending persons holding South American passports to the extermination camps but instead relocating them to the Titmoning and VITTEL detention camps and to other camps, Silberschein set about obtaining the appropriate passports and sponsoring letters. Thanks to the consuls of Paraguay, Honduras, El Salvador, and other countries, who considered this operation a humanitarian one, rescue certificates were sent to about ten thousand public figures and intellectuals in the GENERALGOUVERNEMENT and Upper Silesia. However, in July 1943 Madone, the director of the United States consular division and representative of the Pan-American Alliance in Switzerland, undermined the operation, announcing that the documents, issued without the knowledge of the foreign offices of the countries involved, were not legal. As a result the South American governments declared that these passports were not valid. Silberschein explained that these were rescue documents, but he did not succeed in influencing the United States government, and through its intervention the governments involved withdrew their support of the operation. The Spanish embassy in Berlin, which represented the interests of the South American countries, informed the German government that the passports issued were invalid. On December 10, 1943, a German committee arrived at the Vittel detention camp and confiscated the South American passports from the majority of the Jews; in the middle of 1944 most of them, including the poet Itzhak KATZENELSON, were sent to Auschwitz, where they were put to death. During the same year RELICO also conducted rescue activities in behalf of the Jews of Hungary.

After the war, Silberschein continued to assist Holocaust survivors in Poland, Germany, Austria, and Italy, and he maintained contacts with associations of Polish Jews. He was active in the search for war criminals and in placing young survivors suffering from tuberculosis in convalescent homes in Switzerland.

After his death on December 30, 1951, Silberschein's rich archives were transferred to YAD VASHEM.

BIBLIOGRAPHY

Cohen, Y., and D. Sidan, eds. *Galicia Chapters: A Memorial Book for Dr. Abraham Silberschein.* Tel Aviv, 1957. (In Hebrew.)

Eck, N. "The Rescue of Jews with the Aid of Passports and Citizenship Papers of Latin American States." *Yad Vashem Studies* 1 (1957): 125–152.

Shulman, A. *The Case of Hotel Polski.* New York, 1982.

BRONIA KLIBANSKI

RELIEF ORGANIZATION OF GERMAN JEWS. *See* Hilfsverein der Deutschen Juden.

REPARATIONS AND RESTITUTION, collective indemnification paid by the Federal Republic of GERMANY (West Germany) to the state of Israel and the Jewish people over the period from 1953 to 1965, for the property stolen from the Jews of Germany and the Jews of countries occupied during the Nazi regime.

As early as the beginning of World War II, plans were made for restitution demands that the Jewish people would make to Germany for the Jewish property it had plundered. Such plans were prepared, almost concurrently, by Siegfried Moses in Israel, Salomon Adler-Rudel in Britain, and Nehemiah and Jacob ROBINSON in the United States. The plans called for indemnification of individual Nazi victims and for collective indemnification of the Jewish people for the unprecedented material damage they had sustained. These plans were discussed by Jewish institutions and gained the support of Jewish organizations all over the world. The demands raised while the war was still in progress were formulated before the extent of the Holocaust was known and they dealt with material damage only. But those that were raised in the postwar period were not essentially different, since it was clear that money could not compensate for the millions of lives lost and for the unspeakable sufferings caused by the Nazis.

First Official Claims. On September 20, 1945, Chaim WEIZMANN, on behalf of the Jewish Agency, presented to the governments of the United States, Britain, France, and the Soviet Union the first official claim for restitution of property and indemnification. Weizmann demanded that stolen property that could be identified be returned to the original owners if they had survived, or to Jewish organizations and institutions. Heirless Jewish property should be handed over to representatives of the Jewish people, to be used for the rehabilitation of Nazi victims, with a certain percentage of the indemnification paid by Germany to be given to the Jewish Agency for the rehabilitation of the survivors and their resettlement in Palestine. This was the basis for the reparations claim made by the state of Israel to Germany six years later.

Between 1945 and 1947, the Western occupying powers enacted legislation—each in its own zone—for the return of real estate. This legislation led to the creation of the Jewish Restitution Successor Organization in the American zone, the Jewish Trust Commission in the British zone, and a branch of the latter in the French zone. The three organizations demanded that heirless Jewish property be handed over to them. This was done, the property thus restored being valued at hundreds of millions of deutsche marks.

State of Israel. When the state of Israel came into being in 1948, it was obvious that the Jewish state, together with the major world Jewish organizations, would be the body authorized to submit the restitution claims on behalf of the Jewish people. In the course of 1950 the elements and principles of such claims were formulated in a number of memorandums, and on January 16, 1951, the government of Israel submitted to the four occupying powers a note on the restitution of Jewish property and indemnification. Stating that legislation passed by the occupying powers up to that stage was incomplete and inadequate, the note demanded that existing legislation be improved and expanded, that the government of the Federal Republic of Germany share the financial responsibility, and that the process of restoring property and transferring funds to claimants living outside Germany be speeded up. Israel based its claim on its absorption and resettlement of most of the DISPLACED PERSONS who had been in camps in Germany after the war, which had placed on it a financial burden that otherwise would have had to be borne by the Allied powers.

On March 12, 1951, Israel addressed a second note to the Allied powers, and it was this note that eventually became the cornerstone of the negotiations for reparations. In it the demand for collective indemnification (reparations) was set out for the first time in reasoned and detailed exposition. The basis for the demand was that the YISHUV (the Jewish community in Palestine before the state was established) and the state of Israel had absorbed 500,000 Jews who had been the victims of Nazi persecution. The costs of absorption were estimated at $3,000 per person, and accordingly the total amount asked for was $1.5 billion—$1 billion from West Germany and $500 million from East Germany. The value of the Jewish assets that had been plundered was estimated at $6 billion. The note emphasized that for the crime of GENOCIDE there could be no atonement by any form of material indemnification.

The Soviet Union did not respond to either of the two notes. The responses of the Western powers were couched in cautious and evasive terms, but nevertheless intimated that these powers would not make the payment of reparations by the Federal Republic of Germany to the Jews a condition for the establishment of diplomatic relations between them and the Federal Republic, and that a settlement of the issue would have to be negotiated directly by Israel and the Federal Republic.

German Considerations. West German government circles, and particularly the chancellor, Konrad Adenauer, were inclined to agree to the payment of reparations to the Jewish people. For Adenauer, who admitted Germany's guilt to the Jews, the personal and moral aspect was an important motive, and he was prepared to enter into negotiations with Israel and the Jewish organizations without waiting for pressure to be exerted on him by the Western powers. West Germany was also aware of the political benefits it could derive, affecting its renewed recognition by the West, even though under the circumstances prevailing at the time—the cold war and the Korean War—there was little doubt that it would become a Western ally, regardless of its policy on the reparations issue.

Those politically opposed to Adenauer, that is, the leaders of the Social Democratic party (SPD), also gave strong public support to the payment of reparations to the Jews. Kurt Schumacher, the party leader, was the first German political leader to emphasize that this was an obligation that Germany had to assume. In February 1951, SPD spokesman Carlo Schmid suggested that the Federal Republic of Germany propose to the Allies that Israel be recognized as the inheritor of heirless Jewish property.

In various quarters in West Germany the opinion was voiced that Germany should ask the Jewish people for forgiveness. In August 1951 Erich Lüth, a prominent Hamburg journalist, published an article under the headline "We Are Asking for Peace with Israel," and a similar piece was published by another newspaperman, Rudolf Küstermeier. No official ties of any kind existed at the time between the Federal Republic of Germany and Israel; this added great importance to the personal and unofficial ties with the top German leadership maintained by the European representative of the World Jewish Congress, Noah Barou.

Responsibility Assumed. Although Israel's note of March 1951 was not addressed to the Federal Republic of Germany, Adenauer was made aware of its contents and he decided to respond to it in positive terms. At a meeting of the Bundestag on September 27, 1951, he made a declaration on the restitution of Jewish property and reparations to the Jewish people. In the name of the German people, he stated, unspeakable crimes had been committed that obliged Germany to make moral and material amends for the harm that had been done to the Jews and the sufferings they had undergone. By this declaration the Federal Republic of Germany assumed responsibility for the crimes of the THIRD REICH. Adenauer promised that the Federal Government would take the steps necessary to expand existing legislation on restitution and ensure its implementation, but he added that there were limits to how far the Federal Republic could go, because of its economic situation and the burden it had assumed to repair the war damage and take in millions of refugees and expelled persons. Adenauer ended his speech by expressing his government's willingness to cooperate with representatives of Israel and of world Jewry in the attempt to reach a settlement of the reparations issue, and he accepted Israel's demand for $1 billion as a basis for the negotiations between the two countries.

At a meeting held in New York City on October 26, 1951, attended by representatives of twenty-two Jewish organizations (to which a twenty-third was added at a later date), the Conference on Jewish Material Claims against Germany (Claims Conference) was set up to support Israel's claim and to represent the claims of Nazi victims living outside the state of Israel. Dr. Nahum GOLDMANN was appointed chairman of the Claims Conference.

Controversy. In Israel, reparations from Germany became a highly controversial and divisive issue. Many of the survivors—among them the leaders of the Ghetto Fighters and Partisans Organization—were utterly opposed to such an agreement with Germany and gave vent to their feelings in mass demonstrations and meetings. There was also strong political opposition, from both the Right (the Herut party) and the Left (the Mapam party). The argument was that negotiations about indemnification and restitution should be held with the Allied powers, rather than with Germany; Germany and its representatives did not mean to repent and atone for the crimes. Instead, it intended to use the negotiations with Israel as a means to gain recognition and readmittance to the European community and a reconciliation of sorts with the Jewish people that it would buy and pay for. By negotiating with Germany, the Jewish people and Israel were being made into an instrument serving Germany's plans and purposes. Some quarters also had doubts whether Germany intended to carry out, in practice, the financial obligations that it would assume as a result of such negotiations.

Those who supported a reparations agreement, especially Premier David BEN-GURION and the Mapai (Labor party) leadership, argued that the Allied powers were not going to defend Israel's interests and rights, nor those of the Jewish people; that vast sums were required for the effort of reconstruction and rehabilitation of the survivors; and that it was only natural that restitution of property and reparations should be the source for these financial requirements. The Federal Republic of Germany would be a part of the postwar political and social structure, and there was no choice but to accept this state of affairs.

In January 1952 Israel's parliament, the Knesset, approved a government motion to enter into direct negotiations with the Federal Republic of Germany, by a vote of 61 to 50, despite a violent demonstration organized by the Herut party two days earlier, during the Knesset debate on the motion.

Negotiations Begin. Negotiations were opened on March 21, 1952, at Wassenaar, a town near The Hague, in the Netherlands. Three delegations took part: the Israeli delegation, headed by Giora Josephtal and Felix Eliezer Shinnar; the delegation of the Claims Conference, headed by Moses Leavitt; and the West German delegation, headed by Professor Franz Böhm and Dr. Otto Küster. At the same time, West Germany was negotiating in London the settlement of its prewar debts. The head of the German delegation in London, Hermann Abs, was one of the leading opponents of West Germany's assuming any further obligations at a time when he was attempting to reduce existing ones, and he put forward a demand to link the commitment to Israel to the outcome of the London negotiations. In protest, the two heads of the German delegation to Wassenaar submitted their resignations and the negotiations reached a deadlock.

On Adenauer's initiative and on the basis of contacts with Goldmann, an outline of agreements was worked out and negotiations were resumed, on June 22, 1952. On September 10 of that year, Adenauer and Israeli Foreign Minister Moshe Sharett met in Luxembourg to sign the Reparations Agreement between the two countries. Adenauer and Goldmann signed two protocols between the Federal Republic and the Claims Conference. It took until March 18, 1953, for the Bundestag to approve the agreement and the protocols (followed by the Bundesrat on March 21). The delay was caused by differences of opinion in the West German cabinet and to Arab efforts to block approval by threatening the Federal Republic of Germany with economic boycott.

Under the agreement, West Germany undertook to pay Israel, in the form of goods, over a period of twelve to fourteen years, 3.45 billion deutsche marks ($845 million), out of which Israel would pass on 450 million deutsche marks ($110 million) to the Claims Conference. Of the total sum, 30 percent was transferred directly to Britain, to pay for crude-oil shipments to Israel. The remaining amount was to be used for the purchase of capital goods to be invested in Israel's economy.

Agreement Aids Development. The Federal Republic of Germany carried out the Reparations Agreement fully and faithfully. The reparations were a tremendous contribution to Israel's economy. They saved the country from bankruptcy and played a decisive role in providing a firm base for its economy. Israel's merchant fleet—sixty ships, mostly freighters, including a floating dock—was constructed with reparations funds. By developing the country's water resources and providing the money for mechanization, reparations enabled Israel's agriculture to become highly modernized. A decisive advance was made in all branches of industry, and fourteen hundred industrial enterprises were able to renovate their equipment, thanks to reparations. A purchasing mission headed by Dr. Felix Eliezer Shinnar, representing the Israeli Ministry of Commerce and Industry, with Dr. Chaim Yahil of the Israeli Ministry for Foreign Affairs acting as his deputy, was established in Cologne to supervise and manage the implementation of the Reparations Agreement.

The funds allocated to the Claims Conference were used to assist hundreds of Jewish communities, institutions, and organizations in thirty-nine countries (mostly in Europe) to reestablish themselves. Financial assistance was also provided for education and cultural rehabilitation, and these contributions were increased when the Jewish communities grew in strength and were no longer in need of subsidies; some of these resources were made available for Holocaust studies and documentation and related institutions. In

1960 the Claims Conference decided that the funds still outstanding in 1964, when its function would come to an end, would be dedicated to the commemoration of the victims of the Holocaust. For this purpose, the Memorial Foundation for Jewish Culture was established, and it remains in operation to this day.

The Bundestag also passed a restitution law, applying to all parts of the Federal Republic and West Berlin, that went into effect on October 1, 1953. Like the Reparations Agreement, the Restitution Law was fully observed: as a result of ongoing negotiations between the Claims Conference and the Federal Republic, since 1956 a great many amendments have widened its scope and it now goes far beyond the original version. Restitution (unlike reparations) was to be made to individuals and was to compensate them for suffering, loss of property, loss of education and opportunity, and so on, resulting from German action in the Nazi period. The number of persons entitled to restitution grew steadily as new categories for such entitlement were created, and the size of the payments was also increased. In 1978 West Germany estimated that by the year 2000, a sum of 85 billion deutsche marks would have been paid out to the victims of Nazism. The German Democratic Republic (East Germany), on the other hand, has not even recognized the Jewish people's right to restitution and indemnification.

Payments to Israel under the Reparations Agreement ended in 1965, which was the year in which Israel and the Federal Republic of Germany agreed on the establishment of diplomatic relations.

BIBLIOGRAPHY

Balabkins, N. *West German Reparations to Israel.* New Brunswick, N.J., 1971.

Grossman, K. *Germany and Israel: Six Years of the Luxemburg Agreement.* New York, 1958.

Sagi, N. *German Reparations: A History of the Negotiations.* New York, 1986.

Shinnar, F. E. *The Burden of Necessity and Emotions on a State Mission: Relations between Israel and Germany, 1951–1966.* Jerusalem, 1967. (In Hebrew.)

NANA SAGI

REPRESENTATIVE COUNCIL OF THE JEWS OF FRANCE. *See* Conseil Représentatif des Juifs de France.

RESCUE. *For information on the overall issue of rescue, see* Refugees, 1933–1945. *Specific rescue proposals and operations are detailed in* Aliya Bet; Bermuda Conference; Europa Plan; Evian Conference; Exchange: Jews and Germans; Fort Ontario; Rescue of Polish Jews via East Asia; "Righteous among the Nations"; "Tehran Children"; Youth Aliya. *The differing responses in specific countries to the rescue issue are discussed in* Aid to Jews by Poles; American Jewry and the Holocaust; Australia, Jewish Refugees in; Great Britain: Jewish Refugees; Italy: Aid to Jews by Italians; Japan; Rescue of Children, United States; Shanghai; Sweden; United States Department of State; United States of America; Yishuv. *Organizations involved in the rescue of Jews include* Bergson Group; Comisia Autonoma de Ajutorare; Council for German Jewry; Intergovernmental Committee on Refugees; Joint Rescue Committee; Nonsectarian Refugee Organizations in the United States; Oeuvre de Secours aux Enfants; Pracovná Skupina; President's Advisory Committee on Political Refugees; Red Cross, International; Relief and Rescue Committee of Budapest; Relief Committee for the War-stricken Jewish Population; Rescue Committee of the Jewish Agency in Turkey; United Nations Relief and Rehabilitation Administration; Va'ad ha-Hatsala; War Refugee Board; World Jewish Congress. *See also the biographies of key individuals concerned with rescue during the Holocaust.*

RESCUE COMMITTEE OF THE JEWISH AGENCY IN TURKEY (Heb., Va'ad ha-Hatsala be-Kushta), delegation acting on behalf of the JOINT RESCUE COMMITTEE of the Jewish Agency that operated in Istanbul in 1943 and 1944. All Jewish political movements in Palestine took part in the delegation. The committee had a twofold task: to establish contact with the Jewish communities in the occupied countries of Europe and convey to them the abiding concern of Palestinian Jewry; and to carry out aid and rescue operations decided on by the self-governing institutions of Palestinian Jewry and initiate proposals of its own for the rescue of Jews in Europe.

The decision to set up such a mission in Istanbul was the outcome of the work already being done in Istanbul by representatives of the kibbutz (cooperative settlement in Palestine) movements and the Palestine Office that had been established by the Jewish Agency in Turkey. The representatives reported on the political contacts they had been able to establish with various elements in Istanbul (British intelligence agents, the staffs of the embassies and consulates of neutral governments and governments-in-exile, and businessmen traveling in European countries). These showed neutral Turkey to be an ideal location for making contact with occupied Europe and for advancing aid and rescue projects.

Turkey's proximity to the Balkans, the principal area that in late 1942 contained a large number of Jews who had not yet fallen into the murderous net of the "FINAL SOLUTION," enabled it to serve as an important base for rescue efforts on behalf of Balkan Jewry. The main object of these rescue efforts was to save the Jews of the Balkan countries from deportation to the Nazi extermination camps. The turn in favor of the Allies that the war had taken by early 1943 had its effect on the governments of the Balkan states and led them to reconsider their support of Germany, their policy on the Jews, and their readiness to respond to German plans and proposals concerning the fate of the Jews. These developments opened up new possibilities for help and rescue. Contacts via Turkey with the Jews in the Balkan states, it was thought, could also serve as a channel of communication and financial assistance to the Jews in Poland and the Soviet Union. The relatively short distance between Turkey and Palestine facilitated communications, and this added to the importance of Turkey as a base for the operations of these emissaries. Istanbul was also used for contacts with the centers of information and operations in other neutral countries, primarily in Switzerland, where an important contingent of Palestinian Jewish representatives had been functioning since the beginning of the war. The Istanbul committee's significance was also enhanced by the high quality of the persons who served on it, the plans they initiated, the methods they employed, and the assignments they were given.

The original core of the committee was made up of Zeev Shind, representing the ALIYA BET ("illegal" immigration) organization; Menachem Bader, from the kibbutz movement of the Marxist Ha-Shomer ha-Tsa'ir movement; and Venja Pomerantz, of the socialist Kibbutz ha-Me'uḥad movement. They were the first to establish contacts with the various elements and were in charge of the committee's finances and of organizing "illegal" immigration. At the time when this group of three arrived in Istanbul, in December 1942, two representatives from Palestine were already present in Istanbul: Haim Barlas, the official representative of the Jewish Agency, and Eliezer Leder, representing the Committee for Aid to Polish Refugees.

The second phase in the committee's consolidation came in March 1943, when it was officially established and Barlas was appointed as its head. In the course of 1943 it was joined by Joseph Klarman, representing the Revisionist (Zionist) movement; Yaakov Griffel of the ultrareligious Agudat Israel; David Zimend of Ha-No'ar ha-Tsiyyoni (a Zionist youth movement); and Akiva Levinsky, representing YOUTH ALIYA. Also attached to the committee for a while were Teddy Kollek and Ehud Avriel, representatives of the Political Department of the Jewish Agency, who were of great help in establishing contacts with British and American intelligence.

Following the committee's expansion, its pattern of work crystallized and a more formal procedure was established. This process was accompanied by strained relations among the representatives of the different political movements, as well as some clashes of personalities, with charges leveled that the kibbutz movements' representatives were giving priority in their rescue work to the members of their movements.

The internal tension was exacerbated by the fact that the committee had no legal status in Turkey. The Turkish government did not permit the transfer of foreign currency to and from Turkey, unless it was exchanged for

Turkish pounds at the official rate. The committee's contacts with couriers and double agents were against the law, and in every operation its enlarged staff ran the risk of being expelled from the country. Staff members posed as journalists or businessmen, with the sole exception of Barlas, who was a recognized representative of the Jewish Agency.

The division of labor agreed upon provided for Barlas to maintain the contacts with the Turkish government, as well as all official contacts with foreign organizations, including the International RED CROSS, the Catholic and Greek Orthodox churches, and the British and American embassies. Menachem Bader was the chief financial officer; Venja Pomerantz was in charge of contacts with couriers and agents and of correspondence with Jewish communities, on behalf of the committee as a whole; and Zeev Shind and Moshe Agami were in charge of "illegal" immigration operations. This inner circle discussed the ongoing operations and made the decisions. The other emissaries took part in general discussions, maintained contacts with members of their respective movements, and embarked on activities among the Jewish youth in Turkey. In the summer of 1944 Reuben Resnik and Herbert Katzki joined the committee as representatives of the American Jewish JOINT DISTRIBUTION COMMITTEE. Ira HIRSCHMANN, representative of the WAR REFUGEE BOARD, also attended some of the committee's meetings.

Senior leaders of the Jewish community in Palestine, such as Moshe Shertok (Sharett) and Eliezer Kaplan, regularly visited Istanbul for short stays. Chief Rabbi Isaac Halevi Herzog and Hebrew University president Judah L. Magnes also came on visits; Shaul Meirov (Avigur), the head of "illegal" immigration, came to Istanbul for extended stays.

The committee's work covered three areas of operations:

1. Contacts with Jewish communities in occupied Europe and in the satellite states, and exchange of information with them. The exchange of correspondence between members of the committee and various Jewish leaders in these countries was in itself a source of encouragement and support. The information transmitted and received served the decision makers, the leaders of the communities, and also the mutual contacts among the communities.

2. Transfer of funds for various purposes to the Jewish communities in the occupied countries and the satellite states. The leaders of these communities had the final say on the precise use to which the money would be put, although the committee spelled out the purpose of the transfer and the allocations to the various movements. Among the programs for which funds were transmitted were the EUROPA PLAN, conceived by Slovak Jewish leaders for ransoming Jews from the Nazis; assistance to Jews in the labor camps in Slovakia; the support of refugees in the satellite states; and the smuggling of Jews across the border from one European country to another where the Jews were thought to be safer, as from Slovakia to Hungary and, at a later date, from Hungary to Romania.

3. "Legal" and "illegal" immigration to Palestine—regarded as the most important and surest ways of rescuing Jews.

"Legal" immigration took the land route, by rail, from the Balkan countries to Turkey and then to Palestine. It depended on the willingness of the British to issue entry visas to Palestine on the basis of lists submitted by the Jewish Agency, and on the agreement by the Balkan states and Turkey to the transit of Jews across their territory to Palestine. The long negotiations required to make these arrangements, which involved a great deal of bureaucratic red tape, were handled by Haim Barlas; the Turkish government finally gave permission for a weekly quota of fifty families to pass through. "Illegal" immigration was fraught with danger, because of the shortage of serviceable boats, the conditions under which the boats had to sail, and the naval warfare in the waters that the boats had to traverse to reach their destination. Efforts to obtain "safe conduct" for the boats under International Red Cross protection proved to be in vain, and in the absence of legal arrangements for the continuation of the trip, the Turks would not permit the passengers to land in Turkey for transit. Despite all these difficulties, the Istanbul committee in the period from March to December 1944 arranged nine sailings, with a total of 5,250 passengers aboard the vessels.

The total sum transmitted by the Jewish Agency to the committee in Istanbul for aid and immigration was 523,547 Palestine pounds, half that amount coming from the Palestinian Jewish community's rescue fund. A total of 16,474 immigrants—"legal" and "illegal"—passed through Turkey in the course of the war, 5,500 before the committee came into being.

Following the Soviet occupation of Romania and Bulgaria, some of the committee's staff members concentrated on rescue and emigration to Palestine from these countries, and took part in organizing the BERIḤA escape routes and in establishing contacts with other eastern European countries that were being liberated. Menachem Bader and Ehud Avriel remained in Istanbul until the end of the war. By then the city had gradually lost its importance as a base for communication with Europe and immigration to Palestine.

BIBLIOGRAPHY

Barlas, H. *Rescue during the Holocaust.* Naharia, Israel, 1974. (In Hebrew.)

Ofer, D. "The Rescue Activities of the Jewish Agency Delegation in Istanbul in 1943." In *Rescue Attempts during the Holocaust.* Proceedings of the Second Yad Vashem International Historical Conference, edited by Y. Gutman and E. Zuroff, pp. 435–450. Jerusalem, 1972.

Porat, D. *Entangled Leadership: The Yishuv and the Holocaust, 1942–1945.* Tel Aviv, 1986. (In Hebrew.)

DALIA OFER

RESCUE COMMITTEE OF UNITED STATES ORTHODOX RABBIS. *See* Va'ad ha-Hatsala.

RESCUE OF CHILDREN, UNITED STATES. In the period from 1934 to 1945, about one thousand unaccompanied Jewish refugees aged sixteen and below reached the United States. Most of them were from Germany, and they traveled to the United States either directly from there or after spending some time in a third country, such as Belgium, the Netherlands, France, Spain, or Portugal. The first organization to deal with the project of bringing the children to the United States and settling them there was the German Jewish Children's Aid (GJCA), established in New York in 1934. Another twelve or so organizations eventually came to play a role in selecting Jewish children from Germany, bringing them to the United States, settling them there, and providing financial assistance for these purposes. Some of the bodies, like the GJCA, were set up for this purpose, while others were veteran organizations such as the American Jewish JOINT DISTRIBUTION COMMITTEE, the AMERICAN JEWISH COMMITTEE, and the United Hias Service, which decided to join this rescue effort.

Up to 1941, the GJCA, in cooperation with the children's emigration section of the German Jewish representative body, the Reichsvertretung der Juden in Deutschland (Reich Representation of Jews in Germany), and local American relief organizations, was able to bring 590 refugee children to the United States directly from Germany. The United States immigration authorities accepted the GJCA's undertaking to be responsible for the children, which relieved it of the need to find an individual guarantor for each child (to provide an "affidavit of support"). But in all other respects the children had to go through exactly the same immigration procedure as adults who sought to immigrate to the United States: submit an immigration application, enclose medical certificates and security clearances, and wait for their turn in their country's immigration quota. In addition to the rescue effort made on the organizational level, attempts were also made to have special legislation passed to facilitate the immigration of refugee children. In 1939, in the wake of KRISTALLNACHT, Senator Robert Wagner and Congresswoman Edith Rogers introduced a bill into Congress to enable 20,000 children—not necessarily Jewish—to enter the United States between 1939 and 1941, over and above the German immigration quota. After a drawn-out struggle, the bill was taken off the congressional agenda.

In the summer of 1940, when the Battle of Britain was at its height, the idea was broached of enabling British children to be brought to the United States on a temporary basis. Within a few weeks the UNITED STATES DEPARTMENT OF STATE was ready with a set of procedures that made it possible for the children to enter the country as visitors, and thus to circumvent the immigration regulations. Congress even passed a law permitting the children to be brought to the United States on American ships. This well-disposed attitude of the administration and the American public toward the transfer of British children to the United States contrasted sharply with their reservations about admitting refugee children from Germany. A special organization, the United States Committee for the Care of European Children (USCOM), was formed to deal with transporting the children from Britain and their absorption in the United States. By the fall of 1940, when the "evacuation project" was called off, USCOM had brought in 835 (838, according to another version) British children. The precise number of Jewish children among them is not known, but it may be assumed not to have exceeded 30 or 40.

In addition to the children who went directly from Germany and the ones from Britain, there were also Jewish refugee children who went to the United States after a stay in Belgium, the Netherlands, or France. Following the cancellation of the "evacuation project" from Britain, USCOM accepted the task of bringing these children to the United States. Between 1940 and 1942, volunteers from the Quakers (the AMERICAN FRIENDS SERVICE COMMITTEE) helped in selecting children from Jewish orphanages in France that belonged to the OEUVRE DE SECOURS AUX ENFANTS relief organization, and from internment camps for foreign nationals in southern France, and in bringing them to the United States; on arrival, these children were taken over by the GJCA. From the summer of 1941 to the end of the war, 350 Jewish refugee children arrived in the United States after transit in France and then in Spain.

On their arrival in the United States most of the children had to undergo treatment, including physical and psychological examinations, and were then handed over to foster parents. The criteria laid down by the American Children's Bureau for choosing the foster parents took into account their economic situation, their temperament and personality, and the reasons that had prompted them to apply to the local welfare office for a refugee child to be put in their care. There also had to be compatibility between the child and the foster parents from the religious aspect; United States law required that a child must not be placed in the care of foster parents belonging to a different religion. This meant that Jewish children were handed over only to Jewish foster parents, unlike the situation in other countries, where Jewish refugee children were put into the hands of any family that was prepared to accept them and care for them. According to research conducted during the war and afterward, most of these Jewish refugee children integrated rapidly and well into American life.

BIBLIOGRAPHY

Feingold, H. L. *The Politics of Rescue.* New Brunswick, N.J., 1970.

Morse, A. D. *While Six Million Died: A Chronicle of American Apathy.* New York, 1968.

JUDITH TYDOR-BAUMEL

RESCUE OF POLISH JEWS VIA EAST ASIA. The city of VILNA (Lith., Vilnius) and its environs, which had been part of Poland between the two world wars, was taken by the Red Army on September 19, 1939. However, on October 10 the Soviet government transferred that area to the independent republic of LITHUANIA. In the wake of this decision, approximately fourteen thousand Polish Jews fled to Vilna in the hope of escaping from Nazi or Soviet rule. They included such noted leaders as Menachem Begin, Moshe Sneh, and Zorah WARHAFTIG; approximately two thousand members of the Zionist pioneer movements (*halutsim*); and the rabbis and yeshiva students of more than twenty Polish yeshivas, including those of MIR, Kletsk, Radin, Kamenets-Podolski, and BARANOVICHI, headed by some of the most prominent rabbinic scholars.

In June 1940, the Soviets occupied Lithuania, and many of the refugees sought to emigrate at all costs. That summer, a rescue route for the Polish refugees in Lithuania opened up via East Asia, in addition to the emigration route to Palestine. Two Dutch yeshiva students obtained visas to Curaçao, a

Jews waiting outside the Japanese consulate in Kovno to obtain Japanese transit visas from the consul, Sempo Sugihara.

Dutch colony in the Caribbean, from Jan Zwartendijk, the Dutch consul in KOVNO (Kaunas), who subsequently agreed to grant such documents to other refugees. The refugees then asked the local Japanese consul, Sempo SUGIHARA, for the transit visas that would enable them to travel via JAPAN. Sugihara, on his own initiative, and later despite express instructions to the contrary, issued thousands of transit visas during the final weeks preceding his departure from Lithuania. (The Soviets closed down all the local consulates in Lithuania after its annexation.) The refugees, headed by Dr. Zorah Warhaftig, who was in charge of the local Palestine Office for Polish Refugees, then applied for Soviet exit permits and transit visas. After extensive efforts by refugee leaders to convince the Soviet authorities, the latter granted the refugees permission to leave the Soviet Union, and the first group arrived in Japan in October 1940.

Once it became known that exit permits were available, efforts were made to obtain the necessary documentation by many who had previously refrained from doing so. Thus, visas to Curaçao were obtained from A. M. de Jong, the Dutch consul in Stockholm, and Nicolaas Aire Johannes de Voogd, the Dutch consul in Kōbe, Japan. Japanese transit visas were procured from consuls in various Russian cities, primarily with the help of the Japanese N.Y.K. (Nippon Yusen Kaisya) shipping line, which provided visas to those for whom boat tickets had been purchased. Several hundred refugees who possessed visas to the United States, Palestine, and other countries traveled via Japan, leaving the Soviet Union by means of the Curaçao and/or Japanese visas; among them were such prominent rabbis as Aron Kotler, Reuven Grazowsky, and Moshe Shatzkes.

Beginning in the early spring of 1941, the Japanese attempted to halt the entry of Jewish refugees to Japan, but despite their efforts, more than 500 Jews entered between April and August. That summer, the Japanese sent those Jewish refugees who were unable to emigrate to SHANGHAI, where most remained for the duration of the war. During the period from October 1940 to August 1941, a total of 3,489 Jewish refugees entered Japan. Of these, 2,178 were of Polish origin, among them more than 500 rabbis and yeshiva students. In the spring of 1941, efforts were made to arrange for the entry of refugees from the Soviet Union directly to Shanghai, and the necessary permits were obtained. It is not known how many of these documents were actually utilized (apparently between 50 and 150).

BIBLIOGRAPHY

Bauer, Y. "Rescue Operations through Vilna." *Yad Vashem Studies* 9 (1973): 215–224.

Warhaftig, Z. *Refugee and Survivor: Rescue Efforts during the Holocaust.* Jerusalem, 1988.

Zuroff, E. "Attempts to Obtain Shanghai Permits in 1941: A Case of Rescue Priority during the Holocaust." *Yad Vashem Studies* 13 (1979): 321–351.

Zuroff, E. "Rescue via the Far East: The Attempts to Save Polish Rabbis and Yeshivah Students, 1939–1941." *Simon Wiesenthal Center Annual* 1 (1984): 153–183.

EFRAIM ZUROFF

RESETTLEMENT CENTRAL OFFICE. *See* Umwandererzentralstelle.

RESISTANCE, JEWISH, planned or spontaneous opposition to the Nazis and their collaborators by individual Jews or groups of Jews. In the Nazi system, within which Jews were faced with a process of dehumanization that ultimately culminated in death, any act that opposed that process can be regarded as resistance. In response to this system, Jewish resistance to the Nazis and their collaborators took many forms and worked on many different levels.

Organized armed resistance is regarded as the epitome of opposition to the Nazis. Since the end of World War II many instances of Jewish armed struggle throughout Europe have been documented, the most famous being the WARSAW GHETTO UPRISING of the spring of 1943. Virtually every attempt by Jewish fighters to confront Nazi forces ended in the defeat of the Jews. Still, the idea became widespread that if more Jews had fought, more would have survived the Holocaust. Most scholars of the Holocaust have come to the conclusion that even the majority of the fighters themselves generally did not regard armed resistance as a way to save significant numbers of Jews from death at the hands of the Nazis. Instead, Jews fought for various reasons, such as a wish to avenge the murder of other Jews, or so that future generations would know that Jews had resisted the Nazis with arms for the sake of Jewish honor.

Among the Jewish PARTISANS, however, fighting and survival went hand in hand. In addition to the partisan fighting units, in many places FAMILY CAMPS IN THE FORESTS were created for those Jews who had reached the partisans but could not fight; these camps were protected by the fighters. Rescue was an important factor in the SLOVAK NATIONAL UPRISING. The Jewish fighters taking part in it hoped that the remnants of Slovak Jewry would be saved through the ousting of the Nazi-oriented government from power.

In several camps, notably SOBIBÓR, TREBLINKA, and Birkenau (*see* AUSCHWITZ), Jewish members of the SONDERKOMMANDOs initiated uprisings. All were brutally suppressed. In Birkenau all the rebels were killed, but in Sobibór and Treblinka a small number managed to escape during the fray. The Jewish-initiated uprisings in the camps were the only organized acts of armed resistance carried out against the Nazis in the concentration and extermination camp network.

In most of the countries of central and western Europe, the focal point of Jewish response was rescue, with organized Jewish armed resistance essentially a marginal phenomenon. This was especially true for BELGIUM, the NETHERLANDS, HUNGARY, and GERMANY. In FRANCE, however, there was significant Jewish participation in organized armed resistance, along with rescue activities. During the summer and autumn of 1942, the Jewish underground crystallized and the united Jewish forces established the ARMÉE JUIVE (Jewish Army), which participated in many operations. It took revenge on traitors; attacked German airplanes, transport vehicles, and trains; and sabotaged factories producing materials for the Axis war effort.

In ALGERIA a defense group under the guise of a sports club was organized by young Jews. Along with other Algerian Jews they

JEWISH RESISTANCE
0 100 miles 200 300
0 kilometers 480
Greater Germany September 1939
N
FINLAND
SWEDEN
BALTIC SEA
Leningrad
Tallinn
ESTONIA
Riga
LATVIA
LITHUANIA
Front Line
Moscow
USSR
November 1942
Front Line
Stalingrad
November 1942
CASPIAN SEA
CAUCASIA
Vitebsk
Smolensk
Tatarsk
Starodubsk
Kovno
Vilna
Naroch Forest
Rudninkai Forest
Minsk
Naliboki Forest
Mogilev
Briansk
Lipiczany Forest
Mir
BELORUSSIA
GREATER GERMANY
Białystok
Baranovichi
Nesvizh
Kletsk
Wyszków Forest
Treblinka
Warsaw
Mińsk Mazowiecki
Łódź
Pinsk
Lachva
Parczew Forest
Sobibór
Lublin
Majdanek
Ostrowiec-Świętokrzyski
Kraśnik
Tuchin
Kremenets
Rovno
Zhitomir
Kiev
Kharkov
Częstochowa
Kruszyna
Będzin
Sosnowiec
Auschwitz
Tarnów
Kraków
Lvov (Janówska)
Dnepropetrovsk
UKRAINE
BOHEMIA AND MORAVIA
SLOVAKIA
Rostov-on-Don
Chernovtsy
AUSTRIA
Budapest
HUNGARY
Odessa
Kherson
CRIMEA
Simferopol
YUGOSLAVIA
ROMANIA
BLACK SEA

played a key role in facilitating the entry of Allied forces in November 1942, primarily by seizing and holding strategic positions in the cities.

The foundation of Jewish resistance, especially in the ghettos of eastern Europe and in the Nazi camps, was the struggle for physical existence. Jews responded to draconian Nazi economic and social measures, which made such existence increasingly difficult, by circumventing them. The smuggling of food, clothing, medicine, and other necessities helped many Jews to stay alive, at least for a while. Jews in ghettos, in forced-labor details, and sometimes even in Nazi camps also traded with gentiles whenever possible. In this way an active underground countereconomy was often established and maintained.

Also of great importance was spiritual resistance, called by the Jews "sanctification of life" (KIDDUSH HA-HAYYIM). Along with efforts to foster emigration, this was the focus of Jewish reaction in the Third Reich before the outbreak of the war. After the war began, Jews responded to their deteriorating circumstances and dehumanization with spiritual resistance, especially in the ghettos of Nazi-occupied eastern Europe and in the Nazi camps. The creation of Jewish schools, theaters, and orchestras helped Jews retain their dignity despite Nazi oppression in the ghettos. In VILNA, for example, the cultural achievements of the Jews were prodigious. Similarly, Jewish religious observance in the face of laws or rules that forbade it was an important aspect of the sanctification of life in ghettos and camps, as were the underground meetings of Zionist youth groups. On an individual level, as Primo LEVI has described in *Survival in Auschwitz*, merely keeping oneself clean in a place such as Auschwitz was an assertion of human dignity and the human spirit. Their preservation often aided camp inmates to retain the will to live, which was crucial to their survival.

In many of the ghettos, notably those of WARSAW and KRAKÓW, underground Jewish newspapers and pamphlets were printed and distributed, fulfilling a wide range of services. The press provided information about events and analyzed them; it buttressed Jewish morale by publicizing poems, fiction, and jokes; and, finally, it called for acts of armed resistance.

Other forms of resistance may also come under the heading of rescue, especially rescue activity that Jews initiated or in which they cooperated with non-Jews. Individuals and groups tried to escape from the Nazis by crossing borders to safer lands; with the use of false identity papers; or by hiding—with non-Jews, or in any place where conditions permitted. Some 350,000 Jews fled to Soviet territory from Poland in the wake of the advancing Nazi forces. Tens of thousands escaped from the Warsaw ghetto to the "Aryan" side of the city and were among the tens of thousands more who hid throughout Poland. Other tens of thousands of Jews fled from the western Soviet regions to the Soviet interior. Thousands of Jews fled from Slovakia to Hungary after the start of deportations from Slovakia, and thousands more fled Hungary after the Germans began their occupation there, going primarily to Romania. The entire atmosphere of rescue that was generated in BUDAPEST after the ARROW CROSS PARTY came to power on October 15, 1944—and in which some elements of the Jewish community played an important role—was also a form of resistance to the Nazis and their policies. Similarly, the rescue of Jewish children in France and Belgium, and the smuggling of Jews from France to Spain and from Italy to Switzerland—all operations in which the Jewish YOUTH MOVEMENTS took part—come under the heading of resistance as well as rescue.

Individual noncompliance with specific Nazi demands may also be regarded as resistance. Many Jewish leaders who refused to follow Nazi directives were killed for their defiance. The first chairman of the JUDENRAT (Jewish Council) of LVOV, Dr. Joseph Parnes, was arrested and killed by the Nazis for refusing to hand Jews over to them for forced labor. Moshe Jaffe, the last leader of the MINSK Judenrat, was ordered by the Germans to calm down the Jews they had gathered together during an *Aktion* in late July 1942. Instead, Jaffe told the Jews to flee for their lives, and was killed soon afterward. Instances have been recorded when individual Jews cursed their persecutors, spat at them, or attacked them with their bare hands, when it became clear that they were about to be deported or executed. In most cases the Nazi reaction was to swiftly kill the resisting Jew.

The documentation of Jewish resistance during the Nazi period that has been gathered since the end of World War II is great, and not all of it has yet been evaluated. But historians are coming to realize that Jewish resistance, in all its manifestations, was a widespread phenomenon. Jewish resistance activities contained a statement of the Jewish will to live and a reaffirmation of the continuity of Jewish survival. Despite the horrors of the Nazi regime, Jewish men and women sought to defend their lives and their dignity using whatever means were available. They lacked the power, however, to stay the Nazi machinery of murder.

ROBERT ROZETT

At the beginning of 1942, armed resistance came to be included in the operations of the Jewish underground organizations. Such resistance by Jews in the Holocaust years differed from the resistance offered in the oppressed nations of occupied Europe in World War II. Armed struggle by Jews was carried on under conditions in which the Jews were the object of general, absolute extermination. It was a struggle carried on by a population that was dispersed over hundreds of ghettos and hundreds of camps, none of which had any contact with the other, and by underground groups that had very few possibilities open to them to make preparations for an armed uprising. The Jews had to enter into armed confrontation with the Germans without having had a chance to train for it, at a time when German might was at its height, and to do so without any external support. The timing of the resistance actions was dictated by the dates fixed by the Nazis for the transports of Jews to extermination camps.

Armed Resistance in the Ghettos. In approximately one hundred ghettos, in Poland, Lithuania, Belorussia, and the Ukraine, underground organizations came into being whose purpose was to wage armed struggle, that is, to stage an uprising in the ghetto or to break out of the walled-in ghetto by the use of armed force in order to engage in partisan operations on the outside. In many instances the two forms combined, the uprising being followed by an escape from the ghetto. There were also cases in which the uprising was spontaneous or improvised.

The clandestine groups in the ghettos faced extremely difficult problems, such as smuggling arms into the ghetto, training the fighters under ghetto conditions, and establishing a method for putting the fighters on battle alert in case of a surprise action by the Germans. No less difficult was the task of gaining the ghetto inmates' support for the fighting underground. It was clear to all that the insurgents did not have the slightest chance of forcing the Germans to put a stop to the extermination, and it was equally clear that only a handful of fighters could actually succeed in breaking out of the ghetto and joining partisan units in order to continue the fight against the Germans. This made the ghetto underground the only organization of its kind in recorded history to call for an uprising whose primary purpose was to offer resistance for its own sake. As a result, in some ghettos there was a clash between the concept advocated by the fighting underground —to rise up against the Nazis—and that of the Judenrat, which based its policy on the hope that at least a few of the ghetto prisoners had a chance of being saved by working in German enterprises, a policy that was incompatible with armed resistance.

Warsaw ghetto uprising. The largest single revolt by Jews was the Warsaw ghetto uprising in April and May of 1943, the echoes of which reverberated all over the world. On August 28, 1942, the Zionist youth movements set up the ŻYDOWSKA ORGANIZACJA BOJOWA (Jewish Fighting Organization; ŻOB). By the time the mass deportation came to an end, on September 13, the ŻOB had succeeded in carrying out several military operations, but these had no effect on the deportation process. In October and November of 1942 most of the underground political parties and movements in the ghetto—the Zionists, the BUND, and the Communists—joined the ŻOB. The new body was now able to begin preparations on a relatively large scale for a future uprising. By then, 300,000 Jews had either been murdered on the spot or deported to Treblinka, and no more than 60,000

Jews were left in the ghetto. The ŻOB, owing to contacts with the Polish underground, found new avenues by which to acquire weapons, and it also undertook the manufacture of Molotov cocktails in the ghetto itself. Emissaries were dispatched from Warsaw to other ghettos to urge them to follow the Warsaw example and take up armed resistance. The Revisionist movement, which never integrated into the ŻOB, set up its own fighting organization, the ŻYDOWSKI ZWIĄZEK WOJSKOWY (Jewish Military Union; ŻZW).

On January 18, 1943, the Germans resumed the deportations from the Warsaw ghetto. The ŻOB decided to react, despite the small store of arms at its disposal, and for the first time there was street fighting in occupied Warsaw. On January 21, the Germans called a halt to the deportations. The two Jewish military underground organizations, the ŻOB and ŻZW, utilized the respite to speed up the preparations for the revolt, and the civilian population set up underground bunkers where they planned to hide and hold out against attacks. Close to the date of the planned attack, the two groups coordinated their respective plans of action.

German forces entered the ghetto in strength on April 19, 1943, in order to resume the deportations to extermination camps. Meeting with well-organized resistance by the Jewish fighters, the Germans were forced to retreat from the scene of the fighting. Two elements took the Germans by surprise: the ability of the Jews to create a military force capable of holding its own, despite the conditions prevailing in the ghetto; and the length of time it took to quell the uprising, despite the incomparable superiority of the German force, whose firepower exceeded that of the ghetto fighters by a ratio of 100 to 1.

On May 10, dozens of survivors managed to escape from the ghetto through the city sewers. They reached the Wyszków Forest, where they tried to link up with partisans in order to keep up their fight against the Germans. Inside the ghetto, which by now was destroyed, several small groups maintained resistance throughout the month of June 1943.

Jewish fighting organizations in other ghettos. Several other ghettos in Poland also formed Jewish fighting organizations of their own, largely inspired by the ŻOB in Warsaw and on a similar basis, that is, a union of various organizations, mostly Zionist youth movements, but also Communists and the Bund. In the smaller ghettos, preparing a force for a revolt was much more difficult than in a large place like Warsaw; it was harder to keep the preparations secret, undetected by the watchful eyes of the Germans who surrounded the ghetto; it was also more difficult to maintain contact with the non-Jewish underground. Despite these difficulties, a Jewish fighting organization was formed in several ghettos that rose up in arms against the Germans or broke out of the ghetto in order to take part in partisan operations on the outside.

The BIAŁYSTOK ghetto revolt, which broke out on August 16, 1943, made a profound impression abroad (although not on the scale of the Warsaw ghetto uprising). It went on for several days, in the course of which most of the fighters fell in battle, among them the commander of the Jewish fighting organization in the ghetto, Mordechai TENENBAUM. Several dozen fighters battled their way out of the ghetto and were able to continue the struggle on the outside, mostly with Kadimah, the Jewish partisan unit that operated in the area.

During the liquidation of the ghetto in CZĘSTOCHOWA on June 25, 1943, the local Jewish fighting organization, commanded by Mordechai Silberberg, offered armed resistance. It was a short battle because the Germans took the Jewish fighters by surprise. Some of them, however, were able to escape and join partisan operations in the area.

Local Jewish fighting organizations also rose up in armed resistance in BĘDZIN and SOSNOWIEC (August 1, 1943) and in TARNÓW (September 2, 1943).

In Kraków, the Jewish fighting organization gave up the idea of staging a revolt inside the ghetto, maintaining that under the circumstances it did not stand a chance. Instead, even before the liquidation of the ghetto, the organization decided to move the fight against the Germans to the "Aryan" side of the city, and it launched several attacks against the Germans in the streets of Kraków. Of these, the most famous was the raid on the Cyganeria, the German officers' club in the city, on December 22, 1942.

In several ghettos the local military underground organization went under a different name but in its composition resembled the Warsaw ghetto ŻOB. The first and most important of these was the FAREYNEGTE PARTIZANER ORGANIZATSYE (United Partisan Organization; FPO) in the Vilna ghetto, which became active as early as January 1942. The FPO was not content with local operations and made great efforts to stir up resistance in wide areas of eastern Europe. It was from Vilna that Abba KOVNER made his famous appeal for armed struggle against the Nazis. The FPO did not succeed in staging a revolt inside the Vilna ghetto, but it did manage to get several hundred fighters out to join the partisans' struggle in the Rudninkai and Naroch forests.

Similar to the FPO in style and action was the Antifascist Organization, which came into being in the KOVNO ghetto in January 1942 and operated until the liquidation of the ghetto in the summer of 1944. There, too, no open revolt took place inside the ghetto, but many fighters were able to join the partisans in the area, where some joined fighters from the Vilna ghetto.

In Minsk, the capital of Belorussia, the local fighting organization engaged in a variety of underground activities, among the most important of which was enabling fighters to leave the ghetto to join up with the partisans' struggle in the area. The Minsk fighting organization began its operations in December 1941, and within a short time was able to bring out the first group of fighters to join the partisans.

Organized uprisings took place in many of the small ghettos, in some instances on the spur of the moment because of the pressure of time (of impending deportations to extermination camps) and sometimes after a short interval of preparation, during which the ghetto population was organized (not necessarily on the basis of their previous political affiliations).

On October 25, 1941, when the Germans were about to put up ghettos in Starodubsk and Tatarsk, in the Smolensk district, they were met with armed resistance by the local Jews. There were no survivors in this fight, and the events that took place came to be known from Nazi records only. On July 21, 1942, the Jews of Kletsk rose up in revolt, setting their houses on fire and breaking out of the ghetto by force. On the same day, the Jews of Nesvizh rose up; on August 9, 1942, the Jews of MIR; on September 3, 1942, the Jews in the LACHVA ghetto; on September 9, 1942, the Jews in the Kremenets ghetto; and on September 24, 1942, the Jews in the TUCHIN ghetto.

Uprisings in the Camps. For the Jewish resistance movement, the Nazi camps were an extraordinary place in which to fight. Conditions there posed far greater problems for organizing and preparing resistance and for actual fighting than in the ghettos. The ghetto population, in relative terms, enjoyed freedom of movement within the confines of the Jewish quarter, whereas the concentration camp inmates had only their barrack or place of work in which to move and keep in touch with one another—and even there, they were almost constantly under the supervision of the camp administration.

Conditions for resistance varied greatly in the different types of camps that the Germans had created—EXTERMINATION CAMPS, CONCENTRATION CAMPS, forced-labor camps, and prisoner-of-war camps—but they also all had certain features in common.

One enormous difficulty faced by the resistance movement was the incredible terror to which the inmates were exposed. They had no means at all of defending themselves, and they were completely in the hands of the camp administration, its guards, and its officials, and at the mercy of their capriciousness. Any prisoner could be subjected to the most brutal torture and murder for even the slightest offense, or without having committed any offense at all. The possibility of offering resistance was severely limited, far more than in the ghettos, by chronic starvation and the prevailing conditions, which robbed many prisoners of their strength and led to their physical degeneration.

Another factor that stood in the way of resistance initiatives was the principle of "collective responsibility" applied to the prisoners. This meant that when prisoners committed some "wrong," it was not only those who had taken part who were punished, often with their lives, but also other prisoners, who had not been involved. Moreover, the success of one group of prisoners—for instance, in breaking out of the camp—in most cases led to the punishment of other prisoners. The civilians outside the camps were subject to the death penalty, more often than not without trial, for assisting a prisoner to escape or offer resistance. This made it extremely difficult to establish contact with the civilian population living in the vicinity of the camps and receive any help from them.

There was no single system for fencing in and guarding the camps. All the systems, however, had in common a network of fences and roadblocks that not only cut the whole camp off from the outside, but also separated different parts of the camp from one another. There was a dense array of guard towers and searchlights to ensure effective visibility in the camp and its environs and prevent individual escapes, and the entire camp was covered by machine guns, to be used in case of a general uprising.

Despite all these difficulties the prisoners succeeded in organizing uprisings in a number of camps, and in several dozen camps organized escapes to join partisan operations in the area. The best-known instances of Jewish uprisings took place in three extermination camps: Treblinka, Sobibór, and Auschwitz II (Birkenau).

The uprising in Treblinka broke out on August 2, 1943, and was preceded by several months of preparation. Plans were worked out for the uprising, and "cold" weapons—axes and knives—were accumulated, to be used in an assault on the camp personnel, primarily on the Ukrainian guards; there was also a plan to break into the arms store used by the Germans and the Ukrainians. Some six hundred prisoners took part in the uprising. Most of them fell in battle, during the breakout from the camp, or when they were being pursued by the Germans; but several dozen prisoners did escape and some of these kept fighting the Germans up to the day of liberation.

The uprising in Sobibór, which had been well prepared, took place on October 14, 1943, with the rebelling prisoners killing ten SS men and seizing their weapons. As in Treblinka, most of the rebels fell in battle, either during the breakout from the camp or in the pursuit that followed. Dozens of prisoners did make their escape and joined partisan units, one of them the Jewish partisan company commanded by Yehiel Grynszpan, operating in the Parczew Forest.

The uprising of Jewish prisoners in Auschwitz II (Birkenau), the largest extermination camp of all, took place on October 6 and 7, 1944. The rebels belonged to a Sonderkommando, a special detachment in which they were forced to work cremating the corpses of the murder victims. The rebels killed several SS men and destroyed one of the crematoria, but they all fell in battle. The uprising had been made possible by the explosive devices provided by female Jewish prisoners working in the nearby Union factory. Four of these women, led by Roza ROBOTA, who were members of the underground in the camp, were seized and hanged in public.

Other uprisings took place in the following camps: the uprising in Kruszyna, on December 16, 1942; the resistance offered in MIŃSK MAZOWIECKI, on January 10, 1943; the uprising in Krychów, on August 16, 1943; and the rebellion in JANÓWSKA, on November 19, 1943. There was an exceptionally successful escape from the prisoner-of-war camp in LUBLIN, in the wake of which partisan operations were organized. Other successful escapes that were followed by partisan operations took place in Kraśnik, MAJDANEK, and Ostrowiec-Świętokrzyski.

SHMUEL KRAKOWSKI

BIBLIOGRAPHY

Arad, Y. *Ghetto in Flames.* New York, 1981.

Cholawski, S. *Soldiers from the Ghetto.* New York, 1980.

Gutman, Y. *Fighters among the Ruins.* Jerusalem, 1988. (In Hebrew.)

Gutman, Y. *The Jews of Warsaw, 1939–1943: Ghetto, Underground, Revolt.* Bloomington, 1982.

Jewish Resistance during the Holocaust. Proceedings of the Conference on Manifestations of Jewish Resistance. Jerusalem, 1971.

Krakowski, S. *The War of the Doomed: Jewish Armed Resistance in Poland, 1942–1944.* New York, 1983.

Levin, D. *Fighting Back: Lithuanian Jewry's Armed Resistance to the Nazis.* New York, 1983.
Spector, S. *The Holocaust of Volhynian Jews, 1941–1944.* Jerusalem, 1986. (In Hebrew.)
Suhl, Y., ed. *They Fought Back.* London, 1968.

RESTITUTION. *See* Reparations and Restitution.

REVEL. *See* Tallinn.

REVISIONISM. *See* Holocaust, Denial of the.

RHODES, southernmost of the Dodecanese islands in the Aegean Sea, southwest of Turkey. Rhodes was under Italian control from 1912. Its Jewish population, numbering 3,700 in 1934, was halved as a result of the Italian anti-Jewish policies introduced in 1938; 55 recent immigrants were banished, and another 1,300 left in 1939 and 1940. The famous Rabbinical College was closed and Jews were segregated. In July 1942, Adm. I. Campioni replaced the anti-Jewish Cesare Maria de Vecchi di Vol Cismon as governor, and the conditions of the Jews improved.

The B'nai B'rith Anti-Defamation League's fourth "Courage to Care" Award, given by the agency and its International Center for Holocaust Studies to honor gentiles who helped Jews during the Holocaust. Here, it is presented to Selahattin Ulkumen, who, as Turkish consul on the island of Rhodes in 1944, saved forty-two Jews from deportation to Auschwitz by claiming them as Turkish citizens. He is shown with Mathilde Turiel, one of the Jews he saved. [B'nai B'rith Anti-Defamation League, New York]

The Germans occupied Rhodes in September 1943. British raids on February 2 and Passover (April 15) 1944 killed a number of Jews. That June, Adolf EICHMANN's assistant, Anton Burger, went to Rhodes to organize the deportations of its Jews. On July 13, Generalleutnant Ulrich Kleemann, commander of the 999th Division (he reported to Generaloberst Alexander Löhr, commander of Army Group E), designated Rhodes (the town), Trianda, Cremasto, and Villabona as assembly centers where Jews had to report by July 17. The Jews were ordered to assemble on July 19 behind the palace that was the former headquarters of the Italian air force commander in the town of Rhodes.

On July 20, the male Jews were arrested. Their women and children joined them, and on July 24, 1,700 were shipped to Athens on two coal barges with no food or water; 120 Jews from the island of Kos were added to the transport. On arrival in Athens, they were imprisoned in the notorious Haidar prison. This transport reached AUSCHWITZ on August 17; 400 Jews were selected for hard labor and the rest were killed. Only 150 survived the war. Several Jews had escaped the roundup and joined the partisans.

The Turkish consul, Selahattin Ulkumen, succeeded in saving forty-two Jews who either held a Turkish passport or were married to the holder of one, by claiming them as Turkish citizens. The Mufti of Rhodes kept the Torah scrolls from the synagogue in safe custody until the end of the war.

BIBLIOGRAPHY

Angel, M. D. *The Jews of Rhodes: The History of a Sephardic Community.* New York, 1978.
Ben, Y. *Greek Jewry in the Holocaust and the Resistance, 1941–1944.* Tel Aviv, 1985. (In Hebrew.)
Franco, H. M. *Les martyrs juifs de Rhodes et de Cos.* Elisabethville, France, 1952.
Galanté, A. *Appendice à l'histoire des Juifs de Rhodes, Chio, Cos etc. et fin tragique des communautés juives de Rhodes et de Cos, œuvre du brigandage hitlérien.* Istanbul, 1948.

Molho, M., and J. Nehama. *The Destruction of Greek Jewry, 1941–1944*. Jerusalem, 1965. (In Hebrew.)

STEVEN B. BOWMAN

RIBBENTROP, JOACHIM VON (1893–1946), foreign minister of Germany from 1938 to 1945. Ribbentrop spent four years working in Canada before returning to Germany in 1914. After World War I he became an exporter of wines and spirits. He also secured use of the noble prefix "von" before his name by paying a lifelong annuity to a relative who had no male heirs.

Ribbentrop was introduced to Hitler in August 1932 when the latter expressed interest in someone able to read the foreign press. Ribbentrop made his Dahlem villa available for some of the meetings in January 1933 that led to Hitler's appointment as chancellor. He quickly gained a position as Hitler's foreign-policy adviser, and was appointed ambassador to England in 1936 and foreign minister in February 1938.

An early advocate of a pro-British foreign-policy orientation, Ribbentrop shared and encouraged his master's growing anti-British attitude in the late 1930s. He reached the apogee of his career with the signing of the NAZI-SOVIET PACT in August 1939. His influence and importance rapidly diminished thereafter, as war and conquest replaced diplomacy. Ribbentrop's preference for a "continental policy" in continued alliance with the Soviets did not sway Hitler from his invasion of the USSR in 1941.

Ribbentrop was notoriously incompetent and excessively vain, and was despised by the other Nazi leaders (with the partial exception of Heinrich HIMMLER, who found him a useful ally), but he was not a fanatical antisemite. It was only in late 1942 and early 1943 that he fully perceived the importance that Hitler attached to "solving the Jewish question." Only then did Ribbentrop throw himself into personal diplomacy on behalf of the "FINAL SOLUTION," most notoriously when he told the regent of Hungary, Adm. Miklós HORTHY, in April 1943 that "the Jews must either be exterminated or taken to concentration camps. There is no other possibility."

Joachim von Ribbentrop speaking to an enthusiastic crowd in Königsberg on his way to Berlin from Moscow, where he signed the Nazi-Soviet Pact on August 23, 1939.

For crimes against peace as well as crimes against humanity, Ribbentrop was condemned to death by hanging at the NUREMBERG TRIAL.

BIBLIOGRAPHY

Browning, C. R. *The Final Solution and the German Foreign Office: A Study of Referat D3 of Abteilung Deutschland, 1940–1943.* New York, 1978.

Jacobsen, H. A. *Nationalsozialistische Aussenpolitik 1933–1938.* Frankfurt, 1968.

Michalka, W. *Ribbentrop und die deutsche Weltpolitik 1933–1940: Aussenpolitische Konzeptionen und Entscheidungsprozesse im Dritten Reich.* Munich, 1980.

CHRISTOPHER R. BROWNING

RIBBENTROP-MOLOTOV PACT. *See* Nazi-Soviet Pact.

RICHTER, GUSTAV (b. 1913), Nazi official; one of Adolf EICHMANN's aides. A lawyer by profession, Richter joined the SS, serving in

Eichmann's department in the REICHSSICHERHEITSHAUPTAMT (Reich Security Main Office; RSHA) with the rank of *Hauptsturmführer.* In April 1941 Richter was sent to ROMANIA as adviser for Jewish affairs, with the task of guiding the Romanian government in the formulation of ANTI-JEWISH LEGISLATION on the same lines as that in force in Germany. In May 1941 Richter submitted a report on his plan of action to the German delegate in Bucharest, Manfred von KILLINGER, and requested that the latter have every "Romanization" law (every law for the despoliation of Jewish property and rights) examined before it was submitted for the approval of the Romanian dictator, Ion ANTONESCU.

After a short stay in Romania, Richter was returned to Germany, since at that time the Romanian government excelled in confiscating Jewish property, organizing pogroms, and massacring tens of thousands of Jews in BESSARABIA and BUKOVINA without the aid of a German expert. In September 1941, at the request of Mihai ANTONESCU, Richter resumed his post as adviser for Jewish affairs at the German legation in Bucharest, where he remained until the Romanian surrender in August 1944. In his activity he was assisted by the head of Jewish affairs in the Romanian prime minister's office, Radu LECCA, who was his agent and personal friend. Richter at times grossly interfered in these affairs, infringing on established diplomatic procedures and creating tension and sometimes even reactions adverse to his mission.

Richter's personal pressure led to the disbanding of the Federatia Uniunilor de Comunitati Evreesti (Union of Jewish Communities), the veteran Jewish organization headed by Wilhelm FILDERMAN, and to the establishment of a JUDENRAT (Jewish Council), called, on his recommendation, the CENTRALA EVREILOR (Jewish Center). Richter's candidate, the apostate Nandor Ghingold, was placed at the head of the Jewish Center, reporting directly to Richter on the center's activity and on the policy of the Romanian government in Jewish affairs. A census of persons with Jewish blood was organized, and preparations for ghettoization began. The Jews were ordered to wear yellow badges, confiscation of Jewish property continued, the Zionist organization was disbanded, and all Zionist activity was banned; large-scale emigration of Jews from Romania to Palestine was prevented.

The climax of Richter's activity was the written agreement he received from Mihai Antonescu for the deportation of all the Jews of Romania to the BEŁŻEC extermination camp. Richter elaborated a detailed plan, which included the methods of camouflage and deceit to be used, for deporting the Jews by train to the GENERALGOUVERNEMENT, beginning on September 15, 1942. In the end, however, Richter was unsuccessful in achieving his object, and the Jewish Center increasingly became an organization dealing with the special problems of the Jewish population, aid to the deportees, and support for Jews affected by the antisemitic legislation and mobilized for forced labor.

The antisemitic Romanian government, on its own initiative and without Richter's guidance, enforced the policy of despoiling Jewish rights and property, as Romanian antisemites had demanded as early as the nineteenth century. In June 1941 some 40,000 Jews were evicted from villages and small towns, but despite the preparations, ghettos were not established in Romania, apart from those in CHERNOVTSY and Bessarabia. Filderman's efforts led to the abolition of the yellow badge, which was to have been the first step before ghettoization and deportation. Richter's plan for the deportation of 300,000 Jews from Romania to the Bełżec camp was thwarted by the stubborn struggle of the underground Jewish leadership, and by the complex situation existing in German-Romanian relations. After the failure to implement Richter's deportation plan, Romania gradually changed its policy on the extermination of the Jews, and under pressure of the events at the war front attempted to withdraw from the alliance with Nazi Germany.

For a long time Richter managed to prevent the immigration to Palestine of deportees, and in particular of the orphans from TRANSNISTRIA, in accordance with the detailed instructions he received directly from Eichmann and the German Foreign Ministry. Richter's importance gradually decreased, and his influence was limited to the field of antisemitic and anticommunist propaganda.

On August 23, 1944, Richter and all the German embassy personnel were seized by the Romanians and handed over to the Soviet army. After ten years in prisoner-of-war camps in the Soviet Union, he was sent back to Germany after Chancellor Konrad Adenauer's 1955 visit to Moscow. Preparations for Richter's trial began in Germany in 1961, but the trial did not open until December 1981. The basis for his conviction was the plan, signed by his hand, for the deportation of Romanian Jewry. In early 1982 Richter was sentenced to four years' imprisonment.

BIBLIOGRAPHY

Ancel, J. "The Romanian Way of Solving the 'Jewish Problem' in Bessarabia and Bukovina, June–July 1941." *Yad Vashem Studies* 19 (1988): 187–232.

Carp, M. *Transnistria.* Vol. 3 of *Cartea Neagră.* Bucharest, 1947.

JEAN ANCEL

RIEGNER CABLE, cable sent on August 8, 1942, by Dr. Gerhart Riegner, the representative of the WORLD JEWISH CONGRESS (WJC) in Geneva, to Stephen S. WISE in the United States and Sidney Silverman, member of Parliament, in Britain. The cable read as follows:

> Received alarming report that in Führer's headquarters plan discussed and under consideration according to which all Jews in countries occupied or controlled Germany numbering 3½–4 million should after deportation and concentration in east be exterminated at one blow to resolve once and for all the Jewish question in Europe. Action reported planned for autumn; methods under discussion including prussic acid. We transmit information with all necessary reservation as exactitude cannot be confirmed. Informant stated to have close connections with highest German authorities and his reports generally speaking reliable.

It is now known, after many years of investigation, that the information on which the cable was based was transmitted by Eduard Scholte, a Leipzig businessman who had official business in Switzerland and used the opportunity to transmit information to the western Allies. He contacted a Swiss intermediary, who in turn informed Dr. Benjamin Sagalowitz, a Jewish journalist who ran the Swiss Jewish press agency. Sagalowitz conveyed the information to Riegner on August 1.

The sources on which Scholte based himself are not known. The information was inaccurate: mass murder of Jews had been going on since June 1941, and gassings (first in GAS VANS, with carbon monoxide, and later in GAS CHAMBERS) had been taking place since September 1941. The cable spoke of a future "blow" under "consideration," whereas the extermination that had been begun was an ongoing process. Moreover, the cable itself indicated that the information may not have been true. The last sentence had been introduced into the cable at the insistence of Dr. Paul Guggenheim, a senior member of the WJC living in Geneva. Nevertheless, the cable was a breakthrough, because it confirmed seemingly inconclusive information about the mass murder that had reached the West previously.

The cable was transmitted through the British legation to Silverman, and Howard Elting attempted to transmit the message through the American vice-consul in Geneva to the UNITED STATES DEPARTMENT OF STATE. The State Department refused to inform Wise, in view of the apparently unsubstantiated nature of the information. However, Silverman sent the cable to Wise from London, and it reached him on August 28. On September 2, Wise sent the cable to Under Secretary of State Sumner Welles, who invited Wise to meet with him, asking that he not publish the cable until it had been confirmed. Wise agreed, but he informed a number of Cabinet members; President Franklin D. ROOSEVELT, through Supreme Court Justice Felix Frankfurter; and Christian clergymen. On September 3, Jacob Rosenheim, president of Agudat Israel (the ultra-Orthodox Jewish movement) in New York, received a similar cable from Isaac STERNBUCH of VA'AD HAHATSALA in Switzerland. As a result, Wise approached Rosenheim and formed a temporary emergency committee of Jewish leaders to deal with the situation. On November 24, when the American government finally became convinced of the fact of the mass murder of the Jews, Wise broke the news of the cable, together with much supporting information, to the press.

BIBLIOGRAPHY

Bauer, Y. "When Did They Know?" *Midstream* 14/4 (April 1968): 51–58.

Gilbert, M. *Auschwitz and the Allies*. New York, 1981.

Laqueur, W. *The Terrible Secret: An Investigation into the Suppression of Information about Hitler's "Final Solution."* London, 1980.

Laqueur, W., and R. Breitman. *Breaking the Silence.* New York, 1986.

Wyman, D. S. *The Abandonment of the Jews: America and the Holocaust, 1941–1945*. New York, 1984.

YEHUDA BAUER

RIGA, capital of LATVIA. Riga was founded in the thirteenth century; at different times it was under German, Polish, Swedish, and Russian rule. From 1918 to 1940 it was the capital of independent Latvia. In June 1940 it was annexed to the Soviet Union with the rest of Latvia, and became the capital of the Latvian Soviet Socialist Republic.

Jews first settled in Riga in the seventeenth century. They were expelled from the city in 1742, but a few decades later Jews were again living there. In 1935 the Jewish population of Riga was forty-three thousand, about half the total number of Jews in Latvia and 11 percent of the city's total population. Riga was the political and cultural center of Latvian Jewry. It had Jewish schools with Hebrew, Yiddish, Russian, or German as the language of instruction; seminars for kindergarten teachers; a rabbinical academy; a "people's university"; a theater; several hospitals and welfare institutions; and three Yiddish dailies and several periodicals in different languages.

On July 1, 1941, nine days after their invasion of the Soviet Union, the Germans occupied Riga. Several thousand Jews—among them soldiers serving in the Red Army—managed to get out of the city when it was being evacuated, but many Jews from other places who had taken refuge in Riga were caught there.

On the first day of the occupation, Latvian volunteer units began arresting Jewish males by the thousands and imprisoning them in the Centralka and Terminka jails, in police headquarters, and in the cellars of the headquarters of Perkonkrust (Thundercross), the Latvian fascist organization. After a few days of torture and beatings, the prisoners were killed in the nearby Bikernieki Forest. A German report put the number of Jews who had been shot by July 16 at twenty-seven hundred, with another two thousand being held in prison at that point. These Jews, too, were murdered, except for the doctors among them and a few skilled artisans, who were released. Several thousand more Jewish males were shot to death during the course of July, in the Bikernieki Forest and at other locations, but the precise number is not known.

At that time a pogrom was launched inside the city. Jews were rounded up for forced labor, subjected to assault and rape, chased away from the food distribution lines, and denied treatment in the hospitals. Many Jews were driven out of their homes to make room for Germans, and their money, furnishings, and valuables were confiscated. On July 4 the Latvian volunteers set fire to the city's central synagogue (the Chor synagogue) and later burned all the other synagogues, leaving only the Pietstavas synagogue standing, since the adjacent buildings were inhabited by Latvians.

Between July and October 1941 the Germans issued one anti-Jewish decree after another. Jewish property was confiscated, and Jews had to register and to be identified by a Star of David. They were not allowed to use public transportation, walk on the sidewalk, frequent public places, attend any educational institution, or practice a profession (except for doctors, who were permitted to have Jewish patients only). Ritual slaughter was outlawed, Jews were permitted to purchase food in only three stores, and they suffered from discrimination in the allocation of food rations. Any property still owned by Jews was put under tight control, and conscription of Jews for forced labor was made official. In mid-August a decree was enacted ordering all Jews into the ghetto, which had been set up in the Moscow quarter, a suburb north of Riga populated by Jews and poor

Russians. By the time the ghetto was sealed off, 29,602 Jews were concentrated there—15,738 women, 8,212 men, and 5,652 children. (Another estimate puts the number of Jews in the ghetto at 32,000.) A high fence was erected around the ghetto, and Latvian guards were posted at its gates to supervise exit and entry. The ghetto covered an area of 96,875 square feet (9,000 sq m) and was extremely congested; most of the houses were dilapidated, and sanitary conditions and water supplies were totally inadequate.

Even before the ghetto was cut off from the rest of the world, an Ältestenrat (Council of Elders) was appointed, chaired by Michael Elyashov, and a JÜDISCHER ORDNUNGSDIENST (Jewish ghetto police) was formed, with Michael Rosenthal as its commander. The Council of Elders and its sections and committees made efforts to improve living conditions in the ghetto, establishing a hospital, a medical clinic, and a pharmacy; a home for the aged; a laundry; a shoe repair shop; and a variety of other services in which handicapped persons were put to work. A labor exchange supplied the Germans with Jewish forced labor: the unskilled were employed in backbreaking work, and the skilled artisans, in their regular occupations. A few Jews with special technical skills were given preferential treatment. The women were employed in kitchen and cleaning jobs. Occasionally groups of Jews were sent to work outside the ghetto, in peat bogs, on farms, or on the construction of the Salaspils concentration camp, which was being set up on a nearby site. On the eve of the ghetto's liquidation four thousand men and one thousand women were listed as workers, out of a total of eight thousand and sixteen thousand, respectively.

On November 19, 1941, the Germans separated the working Jews from the rest of the ghetto inhabitants, moving them to a fenced-in area in the northeast corner of the ghetto, which three days previously had been cleared of its inhabitants. This area came to be known as the "small ghetto."

On the night of November 30 the western section of the "large ghetto" was surrounded by German and Latvian guards, and the Jews inside were gathered into groups, each group numbering a thousand persons. The next morning the groups were taken to the RUMBULA Forest, 5 miles (8 km) from Riga, where they were shot to death, next to large pits that had been prepared beforehand. On that day, and continuing on December 8 and 9, the entire population of the "large ghetto" was killed, including most of the members of the Council of Elders, the historian Simon DUBNOW, and Rabbi Menahem Mendel Zak, the Chief Rabbi of Riga. In these two stages of the *Aktion*, twenty-five thousand to twenty-eight thousand Jews were murdered in the Rumbula Forest.

Some four thousand Jewish men were left in the "small ghetto," as well as several hundred Jewish seamstresses who had been removed from it on the eve of the *Aktion*. The women were brought back there and put up in several separate buildings, which came to be known as the "women's ghetto." Having emptied the "large ghetto," the Germans now proceeded to repopulate it with Jews whom they had deported from the Reich

Young Jewish girl from Munich who was deported to Riga.

(Germany, Austria, and the Protectorate of BOHEMIA AND MORAVIA). They set it up as a separate ghetto, with its own institutions, that came to be known as the "German ghetto." Between December 1941 and the spring of 1942, sixteen thousand Jews from the Reich were brought to the "German ghetto"; most were killed in subsequent *Aktionen*.

The "small ghetto" was reorganized under A. Kelman, who had been one of the leaders of Maccabi, the Jewish sports organization. A small proportion of the ghetto inhabitants were employed in the ghetto institutions, but most of them worked outside the ghetto. Some of these outside workers began living at their places of work. Large groups of Jews from the ghetto were sent on seasonal jobs outside the ghetto, mainly to the peat bogs. The official food rations were too meager to live on; they were augmented by supplemental rations handed out at the Jews' places of work and, primarily, by food smuggled into the ghetto. The smuggling—which also included medicines and fuel—continued all the time, even though it was strictly prohibited and was punishable by imprisonment, flogging, or even death. On February 8, 1942, 380 Jews from Kovno—men, women, and children—were deported to Riga, and another 300 Jews, also from Kovno, arrived on October 24. The new arrivals set up a clandestine grocery and bakery and helped organize classes for the few children left in the ghetto. A school and a special kitchen for the children were established, and a program of cultural events was introduced.

In early January 1942 the first steps were taken to organize an underground, which eventually became a network of twenty-five secret cells, with a total of two hundred to three hundred members. Twenty-eight of the ghetto's forty policemen were in four special cells. The ghetto underground organization contacted underground groups on the outside in the hope of joining the partisan fighters. The underground members' principal endeavor was to acquire weapons, mostly by having them smuggled in by Jews working in the German storehouses of captured weapons; they also trained in the use of the arms.

On October 28 of that year, the first group of ten underground members left the ghetto in a truck driven by a Latvian, heading for the Belorussian border in order to join the partisans there. The group fell into a trap, and in the ensuing exchange of fire most of the Jews were killed; only two were captured alive by the Germans. The German security authorities, having encountered the underground, lost no time in taking punitive action against the "small ghetto." That very day large numbers of suspects were arrested; on October 31, 108 Jews who were classified as "unfit for work" and who had nothing to do with the underground were executed. The Jewish policemen were summoned to the ghetto commandant, lined up, and shot on the spot. Several Jews who had succeeded in escaping the slaughter were caught and killed.

On November 1, the "small ghetto" ceased to exist as a separate entity and was incorporated into the "German ghetto." Henceforth Riga had only one ghetto, divided into two sections: section "R" for the Jews from the Reich, and section "L" for the Latvian Jews. The latter had one representative on the joint ghetto council. The Jewish police from the two ghettos were unified into a single body, commanded by a German Jew but consisting, for internal purposes, of two platoons, made up of German and Latvian Jews, respectively. (A new Latvian Jewish police force was formed after the murder of their predecessors.) These changes had the effect of further aggravating the existing tension between the Jews from the Reich and the Latvian Jews.

In the wake of the underground's exposure, more and more Jews began living at their places of work. Each such place became a separate unit with its own internal leadership. The ghetto was gradually emptied of its inhabitants, and there was only tenuous contact among the different groups. In the summer of 1943 the Germans further thinned out the ghetto, transferring some of its inhabitants to the KAISERWALD camp and others to their places of work or to labor camps that later became Kaiserwald satellite camps. That November the Germans carried out large-scale *Aktionen* in what was left of the Riga ghetto and in the places where Jews were employed. In December, when the process of clearing the ghetto of its inhabitants had been completed, the Germans returned the area to the Riga municipality.

In 1944, with the Soviet army advancing

toward the Latvian border, the Germans launched an operation designed to obliterate traces of the crimes they had committed. Special groups (Sonderkommandos) of Jewish men were ordered to reopen the pits containing the mass graves and burn the corpses; on completion of their assignment, the Sonderkommando men were liquidated. In June, by which time the Soviet army had reached the Latvian border, the Germans launched *Aktionen* in which they killed many of the Jewish prisoners in Kaiserwald and its satellite camps. The remaining Jews were sent to concentration camps outside Latvia, chiefly to the STUTTHOF camp, near Danzig. On October 13, the Soviet army liberated Riga. A few days later some one hundred and fifty Jews, among them a few children, came out of their hiding places.

After the war the Soviet authorities encouraged citizens from the Soviet interior, including a large number of Jews, to settle in Riga. In 1947 Riga had a Jewish population of 10,000, which by 1959 had grown to 30,267, representing 5.01 percent of the population. Some were remnants of Latvian Jewry who had taken refuge in the Soviet Union, or had survived concentration camps or exile in Siberia, but the majority were new "immigrants" from the Soviet interior. In 1970 the Jewish population of Riga was 30,581, or 4.18 percent of the total.

In late 1962 a group of Riga Jews sought to have a special memorial set up for the Jewish victims of the Holocaust on the field of slaughter in the Rumbula Forest. Their efforts were successful, and the site became a garden with a memorial to the murdered Jews, where commemorative meetings take place several times a year.

In the late 1960s and the early 1970s Riga was one of the centers of the Jewish national reawakening in the USSR and of the struggle for emigration permits to Israel. The emigration sharply reduced the Jewish population of Riga, and in the late 1980s twenty thousand Jews lived there.

BIBLIOGRAPHY

Levin, D., ed. *Latvia and Estonia*. In *Pinkas Hakehillot; Encyclopaedia of Jewish Communities.* Jerusalem, 1988. See pages 242–295. (In Hebrew.)

Schneider, G. *Journey into Terror: The Story of the Riga Ghetto.* New York, 1979.

ESTHER HAGAR

"RIGHTEOUS AMONG THE NATIONS," title for non-Jews who risked their lives to save Jews during the Holocaust. The name comes from a Hebrew phrase, *hasidei ummot ha-olam,* used by the rabbis of the Talmud, who stated: "The righteous among the nations of the world have a place in the world to come." The Martyrs' and Heroes' Remembrance (Yad Vashem) Law, passed by Israel's Knesset (parliament) in 1953, charged the YAD VASHEM Remembrance Authority with perpetuating and establishing a memorial to "the Righteous among the Nations who risked their lives to save Jews."

The perpetuation of the events and uprisings of the Holocaust would be incomplete without the inspiring chapters—unique points of light—recorded by individuals within the nations under Nazi rule, whose conscience did not let them stand aside and accept with indifference the fate of the Jews. In comparison with the needs of the masses of Jews requiring aid and rescue in occupied Europe, the "Righteous among the Nations" were few. Yet the acts of those few show that aid and rescue were possible, with effort and sacrifice, and that more could have been done had there been more high-minded people who saw assistance to fellow beings in danger as a human obligation.

Since the early 1960s a public committee for recognition of the "Righteous among the Nations" has worked under the aegis of the Yad Vashem Remembrance Authority in Jerusalem. The committee is made up of public personalities, including jurists, most of whom are themselves Holocaust survivors, and is headed by a supreme court judge. In the first years of its activity, the committee was presided over by Justice Moshe Landau, subsequently president of the Israeli Supreme Court. Every instance of a rescuer being submitted for recognition as a "Righteous among the Nations" is debated and carefully examined by the committee, after prior gathering of information in Yad Vashem's Department for Righteous among

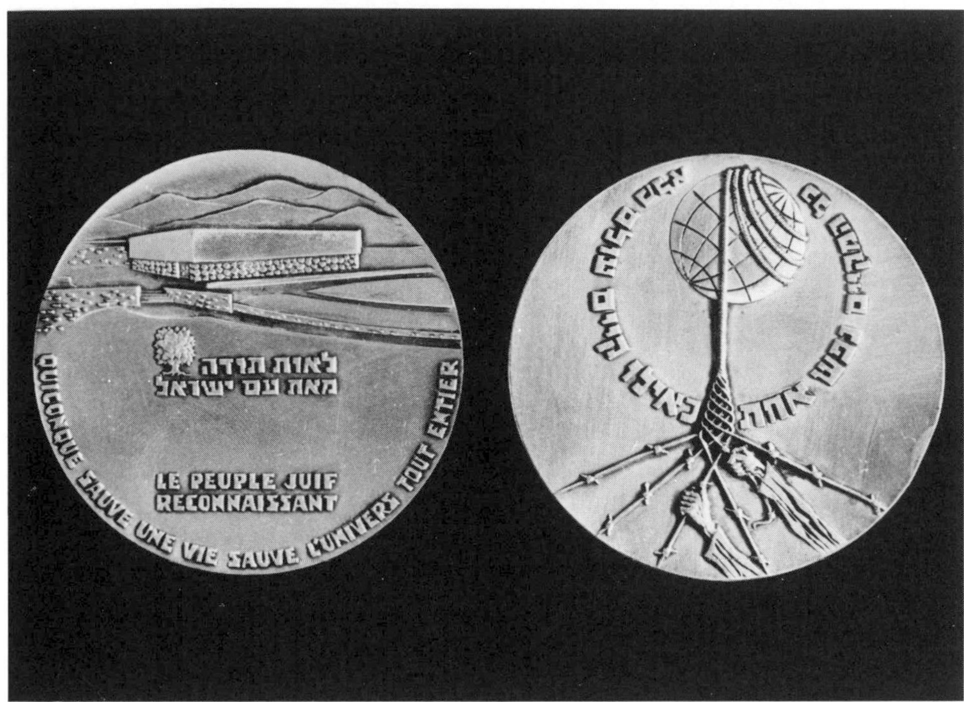

The medal awarded to the "Righteous among the Nations," designed by Israeli artist Nathan Karp. The text, in Hebrew and French, reads: "In gratitude from the Jewish people. Whosoever saves a single life, saves the entire universe."

the Nations and the taking of evidence from the survivor or survivors involved, or—when this is impossible—of declarations and testimonies before Israeli consular delegations in the country where the survivor lives. The committee is sometimes aided by authentic documentation from historical institutions of countries in Europe in determining the course of events described by the survivor.

The law did not give a precise, detailed definition of the term "Righteous among the Nations"; in general, it is intended to apply to a moral personage who in time of trouble and trial extended sympathy, kindness, and assistance to Jews. However, in the context of the Martyrs' and Heroes' Remembrance law, it is clear that loftier requirements were required to qualify as "Righteous among the Nations who risked their lives to save Jews." Hence, the rank of "Righteous among the Nations" in the sense of the law is due to those who risked their own lives in rescuing a Jew.

Although by virtue of Nazi law anyone hiding or assisting a Jew endangered his life, certain cases came before the committee in which the question of danger aroused problems of interpretation. Examples are the cases of people with diplomatic immunity who defied the instructions of their governments and gave entry visas for free countries to persecuted Jews: the Portuguese consul in France, Aristides de SOUSA MENDES; the Japanese consul in Kovno, Sempo SUGIHARA; or the Swiss police captain Paul GRÜNINGER, who allowed hundreds of fleeing Jews to enter Switzerland. Owing to their special status, these people did not actually risk their lives, but they lost or suffered damage to their well-being and their professional and even civil status because they violated official instructions and listened to the dictates of their conscience. Diplomatic immunity did not help the legendary Raoul WALLENBERG, who saved tens of thousands of Hungarian Jews. In such prominent cases, the committee interpreted the legal definition in its broadest sense. There were many instances, however, when the aid proffered was conditional on payment, for the most part of large sums, and not only to cover maintenance expenses. Anyone who offered aid in return for financial remuneration is not considered worthy of the title "Righteous among the Nations" in the sense of the law, even if he endangered himself in saving Jews. There are thus three main criteria for recognition of a rescuer as a "Righteous among the Nations": (1) a concrete rescue action or aid in rescue; (2) rescue carried out at personal risk; and (3) remuneration neither requested nor received by the rescuer for the action or aid.

The number of Holocaust survivors saved thanks to the assistance given by citizens of European countries under Nazi rule is not known, and it is not easy to locate all of them. Both survivors and rescuers are dispersed throughout the world. Some Jews, aided by a rescuer who endangered himself, died later during the war, and no one remains to give testimony, while some rescuers lost their lives along with the Jews they hid. Other rescuers wished to remain anonymous even after the war, and since Israel's relations were severed with the Communist countries, it became difficult to obtain reliable information from there. Unfortunately, many survivors did not trouble to inform Yad Vashem of the details of the aid received, and their rescuers received no appreciation for their noble acts. Taking into consideration an unknown number of rescue acts about which information is not available, together with those recognized by the committee, the number of "Righteous among the Nations" reaches perhaps ten thousand or twenty thousand. Everyone recognized as a "Righteous among the Nations" is entitled to plant a tree in his name along the avenue on Har ha-Zikkaron (the Yad Vashem Memorial Hill).

By early 1989 about eight thousand "Righteous among the Nations" had been recognized. Each was awarded a certificate of honor and a medal engraved with his or her name and the Talmudic maxim "He who saves one life is considered as having saved the whole universe." As one of its commemoration activities, Yad Vashem decided to issue a lexicon of "Righteous among the Nations," giving a brief description of the rescue act of each of them. The importance of this project transcends the aim of commemoration: no less important is the public dissemination of the stories of rescue and self-sacrifice, so that future generations will be educated to understand the significance of the term "humanity."

The majority of the rescues involved concealment in the home or yard of the rescuer, most often by building a bunker within the house or a warehouse; those in hiding had to remain there for weeks, months, and even years, usually without seeing the light of day. The food supply was a special problem in the wartime conditions of scarcity, and at times the needy rescuer shared a scant slice of bread with the people he was concealing. This kind of rescue was perhaps the most dangerous, because of the long period of concealment, the frequent searches for people in hiding, and, at times, denunciation by collaborators with the Germans. Others found a

תעודת כבוד

Certificate of Honour

THIS IS TO CERTIFY THAT IN ITS SESSION OF 23 DECEMBER 1987 THE COMMISSION FOR THE DESIGNATION OF THE RIGHTEOUS, ESTABLISHED BY YAD VASHEM THE HOLOCAUST HEROES & MARTYRS' REMEMBRANCE AUTHORITY, ON THE BASIS OF EVIDENCE PRESENTED BEFORE IT HAS DECIDED TO HONOUR

Arno & Gretel Bach; Alfred & Lisel Gruesman; Fridel Loessel

WHO, DURING THE HOLOCAUST PERIOD IN EUROPE, RISKED THEIR LIVES TO SAVE PERSECUTED JEWS.

THE COMMISSION, THEREFORE, HAS ACCORDED THEM THE MEDAL OF THE RIGHTEOUS AMONG THE NATIONS AND HAS AUTHORIZED THEM TO PLANT A TREE IN THEIR NAME IN THE AVENUE OF THE RIGHTEOUS AT YAD VASHEM ON MOUNT OF REMEMBRANCE, JERUSALEM.

Jerusalem, Israel
19 DECEMBER 1988

ON BEHALF OF YAD VASHEM DIRECTORATE

ON BEHALF OF THE COMMISSION FOR THE DESIGNATION OF THE RIGHTEOUS

WHOEVER SAVES ONE LIFE IS AS THOUGH HE HAD SAVED THE ENTIRE WORLD

The Certificate of Honor awarded to "Righteous among the Nations."

way to rescue by providing forged papers that allowed a Jew to live as a non-Jew outside the ghetto or camp, or by helping to smuggle Jews over the border to another area or country (such as unoccupied France, Spain, Portugal, and Switzerland). One teenage girl working in a munitions factory deprived herself of a slice of bread every day, month after month, giving it to the Jewish prisoner working next to her.

For the most part the "Righteous among the Nations" worked as individuals, each one guided by the dictates of his conscience, out of purely humane motives, and at times from profound religious convictions. In several cases, as in Norway and the Netherlands, and to a certain extent in France and in Belgium, the anti-Nazi underground also helped persecuted Jews in different ways, mainly by finding hiding places. A unique and unusual instance of a collective rescue activity took place in the Dutch village of Nieuwlande. In 1942 and 1943 the village inhabitants resolved that every household would hide one Jewish family or at least one Jew. Given the collective nature of the activity, the danger to the village was small; there was no fear of denunciation since all the village dwellers were partners to the "crime." All 117 inhabitants of that village were recognized as "Righteous among the Nations." The other known case of collective activity was in the village of LE CHAMBON-SUR-LIGNON in France, where many Jews also found a hiding place and aid, thanks to the initiative and activity of the pastor, André Trocmé. The greatest collective activity was in DENMARK, where over 7,000 out of the nearly 8,000 Jewish inhabitants of the country were transferred, in a specially organized operation, in small boats to Sweden, while at the same time ships were waiting at Copenhagen to transport them to the extermination camps. The rescue was made possible by the universal willingness of the Danish population to take part in the operation.

Some individuals also developed broad rescue networks, saving many endangered Jews. The bold enterprise of Raoul Wallenberg in Hungary is one of the most famous; his passion to rescue was boundless. His initiatives were designed to prevent continuation of the deportations of BUDAPEST Jews to AUSCHWITZ, and they were largely successful. Wallenberg was always present where assistance was required and spared no activity to reduce the suffering, also encouraging others with his initiative. Georg Ferdinand DUCKWITZ attempted to prevent the deportation of Danish Jewry, warning the Danish underground and sounding the alarm for the rescue operation in boats to Sweden, which was completed in three nights. Oskar SCHINDLER took under his aegis about twelve hundred Jews working in his factory, made their living conditions easier, and looked after them until the liberation by the Red Army. Berthold Beitz, director of a kerosene works in DROGOBYCH, in the Ukraine, treated his thirteen hundred Jewish workers humanely, protecting them from deportation for as long as possible and enabling many to survive the war. In the Nazi nerve center of Berlin, Elisabeth ABEGG courageously extended aid to persecuted Jews, concealing them in her apartment, close to the Nazi command headquarters. Irena ADAMOWICZ, a member of the Catholic scout movement in Warsaw, worked for the pioneering youth movement underground, traveling to many ghettos on dangerous missions. In 1942 she reached even the distant ghettos of Lithuania, where she reported on events in the Jewish communities throughout the occupied countries in eastern Europe. In her devotion and deep identification with the fate of the Jews she won their trust, and prompted some of the members of her movement to work for the Jewish underground.

The thousands of rescues effected by the "Righteous among the Nations" in the countries of occupied Europe show that in all places and in all circumstances, even in the extermination camps themselves, rescue was possible, although difficult and dangerous. Herman Langbein and Ludwig Worl, themselves interned at Auschwitz, came to the aid of Jewish prisoners there, working to ease their wretched conditions. Julius Madritsch and Raimund Titsch manifested concern for the Jewish internees employed in the factories at the PŁASZÓW camp, obtaining food supplements for them and defending them from the ill-treatment of the commandant, Amon GOETH, and his murderous helpers. The French doctor Adelaide HAUTVAL was sent to

Auschwitz as punishment for protecting Jews who were to be deported; arriving at the block where experiments were carried out on Jewish girls, she refused to participate in murder and cared for the Jewish prisoners with great devotion.

By their acts the "Righteous among the Nations" saved not only Jewish lives but the honor of humanity in the terrible period of the Holocaust.

BIBLIOGRAPHY

Bartoszewski, W., and Z. Lewin, eds. *Righteous among Nations: How Poles Helped the Jews.* London, 1969.

Bauminger, A. L. *Roll of Honor.* Tel Aviv, 1971.

Bejski, M. "Righteous among the Nations and Their Part in the Rescue of Jews." In *Rescue Attempts during the Holocaust.* Proceedings of the Second Yad Vashem International Historical Conference, edited by Y. Gutman and E. Zuroff, pp. 627–647. Jerusalem, 1977.

Friedman, P. *Their Brothers' Keepers.* New York, 1979.

Oliner, S. P., and P. M. Oliner. *The Altruistic Personality: Rescuers of Jews in Nazi Europe.* New York, 1989.

Rittner, C., and S. Myers, eds. *The Courage to Care.* New York, 1986. See pages 99–119.

MOSHE BEJSKI

RIJKSINSTITUUT VOOR OORLOGSDOCUMENTATIE. *See* Documentation Centers: Rijksinstituut voor Oorlogsdocumentatie.

RINGELBLUM, EMANUEL (1900–1944), historian and Jewish public figure; founder and director of the clandestine archive ONEG SHABBAT. Ringelblum was born in Buczacz, Eastern Galicia, into a middle-class merchant family. In World War I the family suffered economic setbacks and moved to Nowy Sącz. In 1927 Ringelblum was awarded a doctorate by the University of Warsaw for his thesis on the history of the Jews of Warsaw in the Middle Ages. From an early age, Ringelblum was a member of Po'alei Zion Left and was active in public affairs. For several years he taught history in Jewish high schools. In 1930 he took on part-time employment with the JOINT DISTRIBUTION COMMITTEE and established close working relations and personal ties with Yitzhak GITTERMAN, one of its leaders in Poland, which he maintained in the war years as well. In November 1938 the Joint sent Ringelblum to the ZBĄSZYŃ camp, where six thousand Jews were gathered—Polish citizens who had been expelled from Germany at the end of October. The five weeks that Ringelblum spent there, as the person responsible for the fortunes of the refugees, left an indelible impression on him.

In his professional capacity Ringelblum belonged to the third generation of historians of the Jews of Poland, a generation educated and trained in independent Poland. In 1923 a number of these historians formed a group, with Ringelblum as one of its outstanding scholars and organizers, that eventually was associated with YIVO (Yidisher Visenshaftlikher Institut; Institute for Jewish Research). Ringelblum was one of the editors of the publications issued by the group—*Yunger Historiker* (1926–1929) and *Bleter far Geschichte* (1934, 1938). In his research work Ringelblum concentrated on the history of the Jews of WARSAW, which he planned to bring up-to-date. Most of his writings are based on original archival material and cover a wide range of subjects; by 1939 he had published 126 scholarly articles.

During the war, Ringelblum was engaged in four spheres of activity in the Warsaw ghetto: (1) working in an institute for social self-aid among Warsaw Jews (Żydowska Samopomoc Społeczna; also known as Jüdische Soziale Selbsthilfe); (2) working in the political underground, with emphasis on its cultural affairs sector; (3) establishing and administering the clandestine Oneg Shabbat Archive; and (4) keeping an up-to-date chronicle of events, including articles on specific subjects, concerning the life of the Jews during the German occupation of Poland, especially Warsaw, covering the period from the beginning of the war up to his own arrest, on March 7, 1944.

Ringelblum was in charge of the "public sector" in the self-aid organization. He ran a network of soup kitchens for the desperately impoverished Jewish population and organized and promoted the growth of "House

Committees" (Komitety Domowe), made up of volunteers with no previous experience of public activity. These committees eventually became a dynamic instrument for dealing with the growing distress.

Ringelblum and his associates made the soup kitchens—in which tens of thousands of soup portions were dispensed every day—into clubs, under the auspices of the political underground. Together with his friend Menahem Linder, Ringelblum founded in the Warsaw ghetto a society for the promotion of Yiddish culture (Yidishe Kultur Organizatsye), which arranged lectures, observances of anniversaries of Jewish writers, and meetings with writers and scholars in the ghetto.

Ringelblum's outstanding achievement was the secret Oneg Shabbat Archive, which he launched in the first few months of the war. In the initial stage, Ringelblum and a small group of friends concentrated on collecting testimonies and reports on events by Jews who came to Warsaw from the provinces in order to solicit aid from the self-aid organization. Ringelblum was aware that there was no precedent for what was happening to the Jews under the occupation, and believed that "it was important that future historians have available to them accurate records of the events that were taking place." He attracted a large circle of friends and activists to the archive, and succeeded in gaining the support of writers and underground activists representing the various political shadings. As reported by Hirsch Wasser, the secretary of the underground archive (and the only surviving member of the team): "Every item, every article, be it long or short, had to pass through Dr. Ringelblum's hands. . . . For weeks and months he spent the nights poring over the manuscripts, adding his comments and instructions."

During the last stages of the ghetto's existence, Ringelblum and his associates collected every document and piece of evidence relating to the deportations and the murders and passed them on to the Polish underground, which in turn transmitted the information to London. This was how the Polish underground and London learned for the first time about the CHEŁMNO extermination camp and came in possession of a detailed report on the deportation of 300,000 Jews from Warsaw.

Emanuel Ringelblum.

The archive also put out in the ghetto a bulletin, *Yediot* (News), which enabled the underground to keep abreast of events. The ghetto archive—also known as the Ringelblum Archive—is the most extensive documentary source that we have about Jews under the Nazi regime.

Ringelblum himself kept a running record of events and important items of information, at first on a daily basis (until July 1942) and then on a weekly and monthly basis. It was not a diary but rather a chronicle of events, augmented by the author's own appraisals and the historical associations that the events brought to his mind. Ringelblum's notes abound in abbreviations and allusions; he obviously regarded them as the raw material for a comprehensive work that he would write after the war. After the mass deportation, Ringelblum's method of writing underwent a change. He no longer put down information in the form of a digest, but instead dealt with the broad and pressing issues of the time, in an attempt to evaluate the events he was witnessing and fathom their meaning, and his writings convey his bitter resentment and fear. He also composed biographical notes on many of the outstanding Jewish personalities who had gone to their death in the deportations and the struggle, with details of their accomplishments and of their fate under the occupation and in the ghetto. He dealt extensively with the lives of Yitzhak Gitterman, Mordecai ANIELEWICZ, Ignacy (Yitzhak) SCHIPER, Meir Balaban, and Janusz KORCZAK. Ringelblum continued writing up to the last months of his life, which he spent in hiding with Poles. It was in that period that he wrote his work on Jewish-Polish relations, an attempt to encompass a multifaceted subject without the help of written sources or reference materials.

The sum total of Ringelblum's writings represents the most extensive effort made by any person to transmit information on the events that were taking place and to cope with their significance. Ringelblum's works have been translated and published, in full or in part, in Yiddish, Polish, English (*Notes from the Warsaw Ghetto*; 1958), Italian, French, German, and Japanese. He was the model for the hero of John Hersey's *The Wall.*

After the great deportation Ringelblum became an advocate of armed resistance, and the archive was put under the aegis of the civilian arm of the ŻYDOWSKA ORGANIZACJA BOJOWA (Jewish Fighting Organization; ŻOB). In March 1943 Ringelblum accepted the invitation that he had repeatedly received from the Polish side, and with his wife and thirteen-year-old son left the ghetto and went into hiding among the Poles. On the eve of Passover 1943 he entered the ghetto on his own and walked straight into the uprising. What happened to him during the deportation and the fighting is not known, but in July 1943 he was found in the TRAWNIKI labor camp. Two members of the Warsaw underground—a Polish man and a Jewish woman—got him out of Trawniki and took him to Warsaw, in the guise of a railway worker. Together with his family and another thirty Jews, he hid in an underground refuge—and continued writing. A Jewish team that had set itself the task of rescuing Jews who were hiding among the Poles sought to enlist Ringelblum for their operation and to utilize his non-Jewish appearance. On March 7, 1944, however, before Ringelblum had decided whether to leave the hideaway, the place was discovered and all the Jews and Polish-protected persons who had taken refuge there were taken to Warsaw's PAWIAK PRISON. According to one report, Jewish prisoners who were working in the prison as skilled craftsmen proposed that Ringelblum join their group, but when he came to the conclusion that there was no chance for his family to be saved, he rejected the offer. A few days later Ringelblum, his family, and the other Jews who had been with him in the hideout were shot to death among the ruins of the ghetto.

BIBLIOGRAPHY

A Commemorative Symposium in Honor of Dr. Emanuel Ringelblum and his "Oneg Shabbath" Underground Archives. Jerusalem, 1983.

Kermish, J., ed. *To Live with Honor and Die with Honor! Selected Documents from the Warsaw Ghetto Underground Archives "O.S." (Oneg Shabbath).* Jerusalem, 1986.

Ringelblum, E. *Polish-Jewish Relations during the Second World War,* edited by J. Kermish and S. Krakowski. New York, 1976.

Ringelblum, E. *Writings from the Warsaw Ghetto,* edited by J. Kermish and Y. L. Peretz. 2 vols. Tel Aviv, 1985. (In Yiddish.)

Sakowska, R., ed. *Archiwum Ringelbluma Getto warszawskie, Lipiec 1942–Styczeń 1943.* Warsaw, 1980.

Shatzki, Y. *Menahem ben Feibush Ringelblum (1900–1944).* Buenos Aires, 1953. (In Yiddish.)

ISRAEL GUTMAN

RISHA. *See* Rzeszów.

RJF. *See* Reichsbund Jüdischer Frontsoldaten.

RKFDV. *See* Reichskommissariat für die Festigung des Deutschen Volkstums.

ROA. *See* Russkaya Osvoboditelnaya Armiya.

ROBINSON, JACOB (1889–1977), jurist and Jewish public figure. Born in Seirijai, Lithuania, and a graduate of the law faculty of Warsaw University, Robinson was the founder of the Hebrew *Gymnasium* (secondary school) of Virbalis and its director from 1919 to 1922. He was a member of the Lithuanian parliament from 1922 to 1926, representing the Zionists, and was the chairman of the Jewish faction in the parliament. Robinson served as legal adviser to the Lithuanian government and was its representative at the Hague International Court. When World War II broke out, he was appointed to head the Jewish committee that was formed to care for the refugees from Poland.

In 1940, Robinson left for the United States, where he became the head of the Institute of Jewish Affairs; he also lectured on international law at Columbia University. In 1945 he served as an adviser to the United States prosecutor at the NUREMBERG TRIAL. He acted in a similar capacity at the EICHMANN TRIAL in Jerusalem. As a result of that trial, Robinson published a book, *And the Crooked Shall Be Made Straight* (Jerusalem, 1966), which was his reaction to Hannah Arendt's *Eichmann in Jerusalem* (*see* ARENDT CONTROVERSY).

Robinson was an outstanding historian of the Holocaust; in particular, he conducted research on behalf of YAD VASHEM as editor of the Holocaust section of the *Encyclopaedia Judaica*. He died in New York.

DOV LEVIN

Roza Robota, Jewish underground activist in Auschwitz-Birkenau.

ROBOTA, ROZA (1921–1944), Jewish underground activist in the AUSCHWITZ-Birkenau camp. Born in Ciechanów, Poland, Robota was a member of the Ha-Shomer ha-Tsa'ir Zionist underground in the town. In 1942 she was taken to Auschwitz, together with a transport from Ciechanów, and was among the first prisoners to be put into the women's camp in Birkenau. A Jewish underground group set up in Auschwitz in 1943 contacted Robota, and she became the channel through which the group was able to win support in the Birkenau women's camp.

In 1944, with Robota's help, minute quantities of explosives were smuggled out of the Union ammunition factory in the camp. They were handed over to the underground in Auschwitz I and to the SONDERKOMMANDO men employed in the Birkenau crematoria. In the wake of the investigation held after the Sonderkommando mutiny of October 1944, Robota and three other young female prisoners working in the Union factory were arrested. Robota was the only one who knew the names of the core group that ran the operations of the underground and its channels of communication, but despite the torture that she underwent, she did not reveal a single name. On January 6, 1945, just a few weeks before the camp was evacuated, Roza Robota and three comrades —Ella Gartner, Tusia, and Regina—were hanged.

BIBLIOGRAPHY

Gutman, I. *People and Ash: The Auschwitz-*

Birkenau Book. Merhavia, Israel, 1957. (In Hebrew.)
Kagan, R. *Hell's Office Women.* Merhavia, Israel, 1947. (In Hebrew.)

ISRAEL GUTMAN

ROGATIN (Pol., Rohatyn), town in Galicia, now in the Ukrainian SSR, north of Ivano-Frankovsk (STANISŁAWÓW); in the interwar period it belonged to Poland. On the eve of World War II, it had a Jewish population of three thousand. In September 1939 Rogatin was occupied by the Red Army and incorporated into the Soviet Union, together with the rest of eastern Poland; subsequently, several hundred Jews from the German-occupied part of Poland took refuge there. After the German invasion of the Soviet Union, on June 22, 1941, several dozen young Jews succeeded in escaping from Rogatin and making their way east into the Soviet interior.

Rogatin was taken by the Germans on July 2. Four days later, Ukrainian militiamen rounded up several hundred Jews in the market square to harass and beat them. On July 12, five hundred Jews were concentrated in the synagogue, where they were abused, beaten up, and otherwise humiliated. Jews were also seized at random and sent on forced labor, and Jewish property was plundered.

At the end of July 1941 a JUDENRAT (Jewish Council) was set up, headed by Shlomo Amarant. In August the Germans ordered the Judenrat to collect a fine and hand it over to them. That fall, the Judenrat was ordered to provide groups of workers for the labor camps in the area. Toward the end of the year, Rogatin Jews were confined to a ghetto, which also had to take in Jews from the nearby townlets of Potok, Zalipie, Cherche, Babintse, and Podkamen. Cut off from the outside world, the ghetto inhabitants had a hard time obtaining the minimum requirements of food. The starvation and overcrowded conditions caused the spread of contagious diseases, from which many died.

On March 20, 1942, a massacre took place. The German and Ukrainian police rounded up the Jews and assembled them in the market square. Several dozen who tried to escape were killed. That same day, the Jews were taken from the square to pits that had been prepared in advance near the railway station, to be shot to death there. A total of two thousand Jews were killed. Ukrainian peasants robbed the victims of their clothes and other possessions. That spring, Jews from Burshtyn, Kniginiche, and Bukachevtsy were brought into the Rogatin ghetto. Another *Aktion* was carried out on September 2, culminating in one thousand Jews being taken to the BEŁŻEC extermination camp.

In October and November 1942, remnants of the Chodorov and Bolshovtsy Jewish communities were brought into the Rogatin ghetto. On December 8 another fifteen hundred persons were sent to Bełżec, while the elderly and infirm were killed on the spot. Sporadic killings continued throughout the first half of 1943. With the population shrinking in this fashion, the ghetto area was reduced. In May 1943 a group of young Jews organized and left for the forests to investigate the possibilities of fighting the Germans and their Ukrainian helpers. Unable to obtain arms, most of the group returned to the ghetto.

The liquidation of the Rogatin ghetto was launched on June 6, 1943. The Germans and Ukrainians set fire to the houses in the ghetto to force out any Jews who were hiding there. The remnants of the Jewish community were murdered in pits at the cemetery. The hunt for survivors who had gone into hiding went on even after the liquidation of the ghetto, and when the Germans discovered such hiding places they encountered armed resistance. All Jews who were caught were killed. On July 24, 1944, Rogatin was liberated by the Soviet army and some thirty survivors emerged from hideouts, having eluded the German search. A short while later most of the survivors left the town.

BIBLIOGRAPHY

Amitai, M., et al., eds. *Rohatyn: The History of a Jewish Community*. Tel Aviv, 1962. (In Hebrew.)

AHARON WEISS

Ernst Röhm.

RÖHM, ERNST (1887–1934), chief of staff of the SA (Sturmabteilung; Storm Troopers). Röhm was born in Munich into a family of officials. He served in World War I, reaching the rank of captain. Finding no place in the postwar world, he joined the Freikorps, led by Franz Xaver Ritter von Epp, and took part in the overthrow of the Munich soviet government.

Röhm became acquainted with Adolf Hitler in 1919 and joined the German Workers' party. In 1923 he participated in the Munich Beer-Hall Putsch, which led to his dismissal from the Reichswehr. The following year he took over a sector of the SA. He became estranged from Hitler, whose legal tactics in the post-1924 period Röhm despised. In 1929, after a series of unsatisfying jobs, he left Germany for Bolivia as a military adviser. In the fall of 1930, following the spectacular Nazi successes in the Reichstag elections, Hitler recalled Röhm to take command of the SA, which rapidly grew from 70,000 members in 1930 to 170,000 in 1931 and 4.5 million in 1934. The SA served as Hitler's private army in the increasingly violent street fighting of the last years of the Weimar Republic.

The collapse of the republic and the Nazi seizure of power in 1933 soon brought Röhm and the SA into conflict with the new regime. By the end of that year, SA members were disillusioned with their lack of material improvement. Röhm, now not only SA chief of staff but also minister without portfolio and minister of the Bavarian state government, made himself the spokesman for "a second revolution" that would take over the state, renounce compromise with industrialists, landowners, and others, and displace the existing class structure—on which, however, the Nazi regime still depended. Moreover, Röhm hoped to transform the SA into a people's army, a plan that disturbed the Reichswehr generals on whom Hitler also depended.

The friction between Röhm and Hitler eventually led to the killing of Röhm, together with about seventy other leading Nazis and at least a hundred others, on the *Nacht der langen Messer* ("Night of the Long Knives"; June 30, 1934). Röhm was posthumously charged with treachery and accused of engineering a plot to overthrow the government.

BIBLIOGRAPHY

Bracher, K. D. *The German Dictatorship: The Origins, Structure, and Effects of National Socialism.* London, 1971.

Fest, J. *The Face of the Third Reich: Portraits of the Nazi Leadership.* New York, 1970.

LIONEL KOCHAN

ROMANIA. [*The first of these two articles,* General Survey, *traces the modern history of Romania through the end of the Nazi era. The second,* Jews during the Holocaust, *chronicles the destruction and survival of Romanian Jewry.*]

General Survey

During the period between the world wars, Romania covered an area of 115,830 square miles (300,000 sq km). Its core was the Regat, consisting of the two former principalities of Walachia and Moldavia, which in 1859 had united to form a single principality, under Ottoman suzerainty. Romania became an independent kingdom in 1878. In 1913 it annexed southern Dobruja—until then a part of Bulgaria—and after World War I it took over from Hungary the province of Transylvania (largely populated by ethnic Romanians); from Austria, the province of BUKOVINA; and from Russia, the province of BESSARABIA. These territorial gains enlarged the area of Romania by about half its previous size, but they also created grave internal and external difficulties: an enormous minority problem inside the country, and the aspirations of Hungary, Bulgaria, and the Soviet Union to recover their former territories. In the face of these goals of three of its neighboring states, Romania in 1921 associated itself with two of its other neighbors, Czechoslovakia and Yugoslavia, in the Little Entente, an alliance based on French support. In addition, it forged an alliance with its sixth neighbor, Poland, which also had close ties with France. This system of alliances was Romania's principal base of political support between the two world wars.

A third of Romania's population belonged to minorities. Before World War II more than 80 percent of its population was rural, but many of the villages did not possess the minimal plots of land they needed. The country's economy was backward. The lack of internal political stability provided a fertile breeding ground for right-wing nationalist movements, such as the IRON GUARD. The parliamentary regime was greatly weakened, and in February 1938 King Carol II suspended the constitution, dissolved the political parties, introduced strict censorship, and established a dictatorial regime under his leadership. In late November of that year several leaders of the Iron Guard were murdered on Carol's orders, including Corneliu Codreanu, the leader of the Guard, who had sought to bring Romania close to Nazi Germany.

On April 13, 1939, France and Britain issued guarantees for Romania's independence and territorial integrity. Romania's position, however, had already been weakened in the wake of the MUNICH CONFERENCE in September 1938, which had truncated the territory of Romania's ally Czechoslovakia. This was followed by a further deterioration in March 1939, when Germany occupied BOHEMIA AND MORAVIA and Germany's ally Hungary took over Czechoslovakia's eastern province of the TRANSCARPATHIAN UKRAINE. That same month Romania was forced to sign a trade agreement with Germany, which was followed by several more such treaties that placed the Romanian economy at the mercy of the Third Reich. In the Ribbentrop-Molotov Pact (*see* NAZI-SOVIET PACT) of August 23, 1939, Germany gave its agreement to the annexation of Bessarabia by the Soviet Union. The following month, Germany and the Soviet Union occupied the territory of Poland, another ally of Romania; also in September, Iron Guard members assassinated Romania's prime minister, Armand Calinescu, and the Iron Guard leader, Horia SIMA, and some of his men were given political asylum in Germany.

With the fall of France, Romania was left without any international political support. On June 27, 1940, several days after the French surrender, Romania was compelled to cede Bessarabia and northern Bukovina to the Soviet Union, faced as it was with a Soviet ultimatum and German pressure to yield. Two months later, on August 30, Germany imposed on Romania the second Vienna Arbitration Award, under which it had to cede northern Transylvania (*see* TRANSYLVANIA, NORTHERN) to Hungary. A week later (September 7), Romania had to transfer southern Dobruja to Bulgaria.

The collapse of Romania's external position also put an end to the king's dictatorial regime. On September 5, Carol II was forced to ask Gen. Ion ANTONESCU to set up a new pro-German cabinet. The next day Carol fled the country; his son became king (Michael I), and Antonescu, now the country's dictator, appointed a fascist government made up of Iron Guard members and army officers, with Horia Sima as deputy prime minister. Romania was declared a "National Legionary State," and the last vestiges of democracy—the parliament, the Crown council, and the trade unions—were abolished. A Legionary police was formed, based on the model of the SS in Germany, which operated in addition to the regular police, concentrating on the Jews and enemies of the regime. Antonescu became a prisoner in the hands of the German legation in Bucharest and of a regime that was being run by Nazi elements in the country.

In November 1940 members of the Iron Guard murdered sixty-seven Romanian political figures, officials, and police officers, including two former prime ministers who while in office had suppressed the Guard. Some of the victims had an antisemitic inclination but were opposed to the alliance with Germany, such as Professor Nicolae Jorga, a historian, writer, and politician who jointly with Alexandru CUZA had formed Romania's first antisemitic political party and who had served as minister of education and prime minister. This spate of murder aroused the

ROMANIA, Autumn 1940

anger of broad circles who in the past had opposed the Iron Guard and were against the pro-German political orientation.

Opposition to the Iron Guard was also aroused by the chaos it created in the economic life of the country, as a result of the actions its men had taken against the Jews (see below). The German attitude toward the emerging struggle for primacy in the Romanian regime was of crucial significance. On Romanian soil there were twelve German army divisions, which had entered the country in October 1940. This was in fact a garrison force, although according to Hitler's directives it was not to be regarded as an army of occupation, but as an extension, of sorts, of the German military mission that he had dispatched to the country on September 7. Hitler's desire to maintain a facade of Romanian independence derived from his awareness of the country's key position in the Balkans and the undesirable effect that its occupation would have on Germany's allies in the region, and on the Italians and the Soviets. Although the murder of the sixty-seven Romanian leaders had Heinrich HIMMLER's blessing (in a letter he sent to Sima), Hitler decided to give his support to Antonescu and the army in their struggle with the Iron Guard. During Antonescu's visit with Hitler, on January 14, 1941, Hitler divulged his plan for the invasion of the Soviet Union and assured Antonescu of his support, promising that the German forces in Romania would not intervene in any violence that might erupt between the Iron Guard and the Romanian army.

A week later, between January 21 and 23, the Iron Guard rose in revolt and tried to seize power in the country. The army foiled the attempted coup and suppressed the Iron Guard with bloody force (although the German legation rescued the Guard's chiefs and transported 300 of them to Germany in German military trains). Antonescu consolidated his dictatorial fascist regime and abolished the "National Legionary State" (February 17), but he became increasingly dependent on Germany. German forces continued to flow into the country, and by March 330,000 German troops were stationed there, seizing all the vital points and manning the borders with Bulgaria and the Soviet Union. The German ambassador to Romania, Manfred von KILLINGER, came to wield great influence on Romanian policy. The gendarmerie, the police, and a special intelligence unit suppressed those opposing the regime, especially the Communists and also the Jews. Among the main figures of the regime were the "Leader" (Conducator), Ion Antonescu; his deputy, Mihai ANTONESCU; Minister of Defense Hano Pantazi; Minister of the Interior Dumitru Popescu; Undersecretary of Police and Public Security Ion Popescu (succeeded by Constantin Vasiliu); Commissar for Jewish Questions Radu LECCA; Gen. Alexandru Rioşanu, Gen. Corneliu Calotescu, and Cornel Dragalina, successive govenors of Bukovina; the governor of Bessarabia, Gen. Constantin Voiculescu; and the governor of TRANSNISTRIA, Gen. Gheorghe Alexianu, succeeded by Gen. Gheorghe Potopaenu.

When the Germans attacked the Soviet Union on June 22, 1941, the Romanians joined them, in the hope of regaining the territory they had been forced to cede to the latter. On December 6 of the same year Britain declared war on Romania; Canada, New Zealand, Australia, and South Africa followed suit, as did the United States (the last on June 4, 1942). Because of its size and its natural resources, Romania was Germany's most important ally in eastern Europe. A Romanian contingent of nearly a million men fought fiercely on the eastern front. Eventually the Romanians sustained heavy losses, especially in the battle for ODESSA and at STALINGRAD. In 1941 Romania regained the territories that the Soviets had annexed in 1940 and in addition seized a part of the southeastern Ukraine; in the course of the war, however, the Soviets reoccupied all these territories.

Wide circles in the country had opposed the war from the beginning. Most of them objected to Romania's economy being hitched to the German war machine and to the ensuing deterioration of living conditions in Romania. Many also hated Germany for having forced Romania to make territorial concessions to its neighbors. On the eve of the invasion of the Soviet Union, Antonescu dismissed fifty generals and eighteen colonels who had opposed Romania's entry into the war, among them a former defense minister and the chiefs of the general staff. Nevertheless, the anti-German faction did succeed in preventing another 220,000 troops from being sent to the Russian front. In the political arena, Social Democrats, members of the Peasants' party, members of the National Liberal party, the Communists, and the king himself opposed the war. Throughout the period of Romanian participation in the war on Germany's side there was social unrest at home, expressed by antiwar memorandums, strikes, and acts of sabotage.

From the German (and Romanian) defeat at Stalingrad in early 1943 until the Romanian coup that took place in August 1944 (see below), the specter of a German defeat in the war brought the Antonescu government more and more in line with the opponents of the war. The Romanian government established contacts with the Allies and negotiated with them, with the object of ending Romania's subservience to Nazi Germany. Such contacts were pursued zealously in Rome, at the Vatican, and in Bern, Lisbon, Madrid, Stockholm, Ankara, Cairo, and Bucharest. In the initial stage the Romanians hoped to achieve a separate peace with the western Allies, but when this hope waned, Antonescu pressed for an armistice that would include the Soviet Union and would enable Romania to join the Allies. A national consensus was reached on this position, and on June 20, 1944, the National Democratic Bloc was formed, with the participation of the Communist party, the Social Democrat party, the Peasants' party, and the National Liberal party. The Soviet Army's entry into Moldavia in August was an additional incentive to come to terms with the Allies.

On August 23, 1944, an antifascist rebellion broke out in Romania. The National Democratic Bloc, with the aid of a few generals, overthrew the Antonescu regime and formed a new government in its place. That evening, King Michael I broadcast an address to the nation, in which he proclaimed that the new government had accepted the armistice terms offered by the Allies and that Romania would join the fight against Nazi Germany. A similar declaration was made by the new prime minister, Gen. Constantin Sanatescu, who also expressed the hope that the Vienna Award would be nullified and northern Transylvania would be returned to Romania. The new government lost no time in enacting two important laws—one abolishing all detention camps, and the other releasing all antifascist prisoners, restoring their civil and political rights, and annulling all discriminatory racial laws. The Romanian army rallied to the new government and committed itself to its control. On September 12, Romania and the Soviet Union signed a formal agreement in Moscow that put the seal on Romania's exit from its alliance with Nazi Germany.

The Romanian turnabout had significant repercussions. It contributed to the disintegration of the German military hold on southeastern Europe, especially by depriving Germany of the much-needed Romanian oil supplies. It also had its effect on Bulgaria, Hungary, and Croatia, encouraging these states to try to extricate themselves from their membership in the Axis.

BIBLIOGRAPHY

Ceausescu, I. *A Turning Point in World War II: 23 August 1944 in Rumania*. Boulder, 1985.

Roberts, H. L. *Rumania: Political Problems of an Agrarian State.* New Haven, 1951.

Seton-Watson, H. *The East European Revolution.* London, 1961.

Vago, B. *The Shadow of the Swastika: The Rise of Fascism and Antisemitism in the Danube Basin, 1936–1939.* Farnborough, England, 1975.

Webster, A. F. C. *The Romanian Legionary Movement.* Pittsburgh, 1986.

CRISTIAN POPISTEANU

Jews during the Holocaust

Jews were living in Romania as early as the second century, but knowledge of continuous Jewish settlement dates from a later period. The fate and history of Romania's Jews have differed from one region to another. In the fourteenth century they settled in the principalities of Walachia and Moldavia, and in the sixteenth century they were joined by Sephardic Jews. When the two principalities merged in 1859, their combined Jewish population was 135,000.

At the 1878 Congress of Berlin, the participating powers—Germany, Great Britain, Austria-Hungary, Russia, and Turkey—made the grant of equal rights to Jews one of the conditions for Romania's independence, but in practice the Romanian government made it extremely difficult for Jews to obtain citizenship. Only 2,000 Jews had gained that status by 1914, out of a Jewish population that by then had grown to 240,000. Romanian Jewry suffered from persecutions and economic restrictions, and antisemitism was widespread, among the educated as well as the general population. From time to time Jews were the victims of violent attacks. Their depressed economic situation caused numerous Jews to emigrate from the country, many to the United States. Romanian Jews were among the first to live in Palestine in the modern settlement, beginning in the early 1880s.

In the post–World War I period, since Romania had made large territorial gains, its Jewish population almost trebled in size, and in 1930 it numbered 760,000 (4.2 percent of the total population). The great powers imposed upon Romania a treaty on minority rights that was to ensure the status of the country's minorities, including the Jewish minority. In practice, however, the Jews were not granted full equality, and the rising tide of Romanian nationalism expressed itself first and foremost in hostility toward the minorities, especially the Jews. Giving in to pressure by university students, the authorities introduced a Jewish quota at the universities; Jews suffered from discrimination in certain professions, and government service was virtually barred to them. The "Jewish party," which had been formed after World War I, fought to establish and maintain Jewish rights and was represented in parliament, but its efforts met with only limited success. An independent Jewish educational system existed in the interwar period, and Jewish culture flourished in literature, poetry, and journalism in Yiddish, Hebrew, and Romanian. Zionism became a mass movement, and Zionist youth movements and agricultural training facilities for pioneers preparing to settle in Palestine developed an intensive program of activities.

Two major antisemitic organizations were in operation in Romania during the 1930s: the League of National Christian Defense (Liga Apararei Nationale Crestine) and the IRON GUARD. These movements played a major role in creating a negative, even demonic, image of the Jews. They provided the ideological justification for expelling the Jews from Romanian society, and for removing existing inhibitions to the achievement of that goal. The Nazi rise to power in Germany in 1933 and internal processes taking place in Romanian society strengthened the two antisemitic movements and transformed them from marginal political parties, devoid of any real power, into popular mass movements that gained in strength from year to year, as evidenced by the parliamentary election results. Before the Nazi assumption of power, Britain and France had provided the ideals of government. But Nazi Germany's successes and the feeble response to them by the Western democracies reinforced the existing inclination toward a dictatorial regime in Romania, the more so because the constitutional monarchy suffered from many defects and had never observed the principles of individual rights, democracy, and equal opportunity for all.

In the 1930s, and especially after the Nazi seizure of power in Germany, antagonism toward Jews—indeed, sheer hatred of them—rose to the surface in Romanian public opinion and in all strata of society, hand in hand with a growing interest in Nazi Germany. The Nazi party's Foreign Policy Office, headed by Alfred ROSENBERG, established ties with the two major antisemitic parties in Romania and sought to persuade them to merge. As a result of the Foreign Policy Office's endeavors, Octavian GOGA's National Peasants' party merged with Alexandru CUZA's League of National Christian Defense, a union that in late 1937 led to the formation of an antisemitic government, the Goga-Cuza cabinet—the second such government in Europe, after Germany. This was a great success for Germany, since the Goga-Cuza party advocated an alliance with the Third Reich.

The Goga-Cuza Government. When their two parties had merged, Goga and Cuza undertook to amend the constitution. Political power would be confined to "Romanians who had pure Romanian blood in their veins"; the Jews would be removed from the press; Romanians would have priority in all economic enterprises and cultural institutions; and

Jews would be barred from government service. The two antisemitic leaders also committed themselves to the expulsion from the country of Jews who had entered it by illegal means; to an amendment of the nationality law that would deprive the Jews of their citizenship; to the confiscation of Jewish urban and rural property; and to steps ensuring that the nation's cities had a "national Romanian" character.

During the forty days that Goga and Cuza were in power, their government did its best to translate its antisemitic principles into practice. The three existing democratic newspapers were closed down on the pretext that they had "sold out to the Jews." The gravest of the anti-Jewish measures was a law enacted on January 22, 1938, to review the citizenship of Jews. As a result of this review, a quarter of a million Jews—about one-third of the total Jewish population—were deprived of their rights as citizens. Among the Romanian population there were some instances of resistance to the legislative and administrative terror tactics employed by the Goga-Cuza government.

Under the dictatorial regime instituted by King Carol II in February 1938 (with himself as dictator), which lasted until September 1940, the deterioration in the situation of the Jews that had begun under the Goga-Cuza government continued. In a vain attempt to block the growing ideological, economic, and political influence of Nazi Germany, Carol pursued a vacillating policy that—without help from abroad—was doomed from the start. The weak stance of the Western powers had an immediate impact on the internal situation of Romania and on the status of its Jews. The first cabinet in the king's regime was headed by Patriarch Miron Cristea, head of the Orthodox church of Romania. A series of decisions and statements that were made in this period, and of laws and amendments to laws that were enacted, intensified the ongoing process of excluding the Jews from society and ostracizing them. This trend went on at the same time that the king was trying to outlaw the activities of the Iron Guard, which had allied itself with Germany and was furthering German interests in Romania.

The new constitution promulgated in 1938 contained several sections that provided for racial discrimination, their stated purpose being "to expel from the country all persons who do not possess citizens' rights." The exclusion of the Jews from membership in the National Renaissance Front, the government party (and only legal political party), further extended the process of removing the Jews from the country's life, since only party members were eligible for posts in government service or administrative positions in the economy. The new legislation coined a new legal term, "ethnic Romanian," which was used to gradually exclude Jews from all public activities and occupations.

A further grave turn in the situation of the Jews came in the summer of 1940, when Romania was forced to give up Bessarabia and Bukovina. Antisemitic agitation reached new heights, and in some parts of Bukovina and northern Moldavia the withdrawing Romanian troops went on a rampage against the Jews, in which they were joined by local villagers. On June 30, 200 Jews were killed in DOROHOI by a Romanian infantry battalion, and hundreds of Jews were murdered in villages on both sides of the new border. In the first few days—before the Soviets withdrew permission—thousands of Jews fled to Bessarabia. A Jewish refugee problem arose on both sides of the border. At this stage, in an attempt to please the Germans, a special law, the Statute of the Jews, was passed on August 8, 1940, which in effect canceled the citizenship of most Jews and prohibited mixed marriages. The Jews, as a body, were charged with responsibility for all the disasters that had befallen the Romanian people and nation, since, as alleged Communists, they had served the interests of the Soviet Union. As a result of territorial annexations by the Soviet Union and, later, by Hungary and Bulgaria, only 342,000 Jews remained in Romania.

Following the installation of the "National Legionary State" in September 1940, the predicament of the Jews took another, and even more dramatic, turn for the worse. Iron Guard members, who now manned the government on all levels, launched a terrorization and intimidation campaign against the Jews; their purpose was to seize Jewish property by force, beginning with Jewish-owned shops, enterprises, and factories. The new government conducted its anti-Jewish operations on two levels: "legal" (that is, according to laws based on the constitution) and illegal (following measures not based on the constitution). The three major legislative measures against the Jews passed by the Ion ANTONESCU–Horia SIMA government were (1) a law providing for the confiscation of Jewish property in rural areas, including land and equipment, passed on October 5, 1940; (2) a law that confiscated Jewish-owned forests, distilleries, and sawmills, passed on November 17; and (3) a law, passed on December 4, that confiscated sailing vessels in Jewish possession (the vessels were transferred directly to German hands). These laws affected only a small number of Jews, whereas the "Romanianization" of the economy—the measures designed to exclude Jews from the country's economic and commercial life (which were illegal and not based on any section of the constitution)—struck at the great majority of the Jewish population.

Before long the Legionnaires' campaign of terror created chaotic conditions in numerous sectors of the economy and industry, to an extent that worried even the Nazis. Antonescu was dissatisfied with the methods adopted by his partners in the government and demanded that law and order be maintained. His position on the seizure of Jewish property and the displacement of the Jews from the economy differed from that of the Iron Guard; it called for a gradual process that would avoid shocks to the economy and provide for qualified replacements for the Jews who were being ousted. The trade unions, to cite one example, had expelled their Jewish members without waiting for the special laws to be put into force. Jewish property was plundered and pillaged, enriching yet another stratum of Iron Guard members and their supporters. It was not only the legionaries who robbed the Jews; their regime made it possible for many Romanians to disregard the law and overcome moral inhibitions, and it rendered Jewish property—and sometimes Jewish life as well—free for the taking. The Iron Guard rebellion, which took place from January 21 to 23, 1941, was accompanied by anti-Jewish riots. Members of the Guard—together with gangs of thugs, riffraff from the suburbs, and Gypsies—attacked the Jewish quarters, robbed and destroyed Jewish shops and apartments, and killed Jews and seized their belongings. One hundred twenty-seven Jews were tortured and brutually murdered in the focal points of the uprising.

"Legal Antisemitism" (February to June 1941). The months that elapsed between the expulsion of the Legionnaires from the government and the outbreak of the war against the Soviet Union are regarded as an intermediary period, an interval between "illegal" measures against the Jews and the introduction of a "legal" antisemitic policy. Antonescu's one-man regime was helped in the implementation of this policy by the German Foreign Office, which in March 1941 sent a special adviser on Jewish affairs to Bucharest, in the person of Gustav RICHTER, from Adolf EICHMANN's office. Richter's official task was "to advise the Romanian government on legislation against the Jews, similar to the kind of laws that have been enacted in Germany." It was in this period that the Law for the Protection of the State was passed (February 5, 1941), which provided that for the same offense, Jews would be given double the punishment meted out to Christians. Another law, dated March 27, enabled the antisemites and the Antonescu regime to see an old dream come true: it provided for the confiscation of Jewish-owned dwellings by "legal" means, and under its authority 40,758 houses and apartments were seized. Many of the Jews who had already been dismissed from their jobs were now also thrown out of their homes and made destitute.

A National Romanianization Center was set up that, on the basis of the antisemitic laws and special regulations, applied official terror against the Jews, expelling most of them from their homes overnight and assigning these residences to government officials, army officers, disabled war veterans, war widows, and Romanian refugees from the territories annexed by the Soviet Union or by Hungary. In this manner, hundreds of thousands more Romanians profited from the confiscation of Jewish property. A great many more laws were put into force and further measures were taken to complete the "Romanianization" plan, whose final goal was the total removal of Jews from Romanian life. One of these laws—an important one, dated May 15, 1941—was aimed at "labor for the common good"; it deprived the Jews of the last vestiges of legal protection and provided that they be drafted for forced labor.

When the war against the Soviet Union broke out, forty thousand Jews were expelled from villages and towns, on Antonescu's orders, and their property was confiscated. Some were put into detention camps and others were transferred to other cities or towns, where they became welfare cases. This step was also part of an old dream of the Romanian antisemites, that of "purging" the villages of their Jews. The Antonescu regime was convinced that it would have the chance to "solve the Jewish question." Antonescu and his confidants regarded the war as an opportunity to rid Romania of what they regarded as an enormous burden. Unlike other fascist regimes, however, the Antonescu regime used two different methods in its treatment of the Jews—one applied to the Jews of Bessarabia and Bukovina, and another to the Jews of the Regat (Romania in its pre–World War I borders) and southern Transylvania.

"Solution of the Jewish Question" in the "Liberated Areas." On June 12, 1941, Hitler revealed to Antonescu his solution to the problem of the "Jews of the east." It stands to reason, therefore, that Antonescu was influenced by Hitler to embark upon the "solution of the Jewish question" in Bessarabia and Bukovina by allowing mass murder to take place there. The army was ordered to imprison the Jews living in the cities, and the gendarmerie was assigned the task of killing every Jew found in the rural areas. In actual fact the annihilation of the Jews in both city and countryside was carried out by German and Romanian army units, assisted by SS killing squads of Einsatzgruppe D. In the first phase of the operation 160,000 Jews were killed, with local Ukrainians and Romanians taking part in the slaughter. On September 15, 1941, Antonescu ordered the surviving Jews—some 150,000—to be expelled to TRANSNISTRIA, the area between the Bug and Dniester rivers. En route to this destination, tens of thousands of Jews died, either shot by their Romanian escorts or perishing from hunger, thirst, disease, maltreatment, and total exhaustion. Transnistria became a mass grave for Romanian Jews, 90,000 meeting their death there in the period when it was under Romanian control, from the fall of 1941 to the spring of 1944.

The Romanian army and gendarmerie also took part in the killing of tens of thousands of Ukrainian Jews. The formal pretext for the action was the need to "purge" the area of its hostile Jewish element, which had collaborated with the Soviet occupation in 1940 and 1941, and had conducted itself in an "anti-Romanian" manner during the Romanian withdrawal in late June 1940. In October 1941 it was the turn of the Jews of southern Bukovina, who could not be accused of having collaborated with the Soviets. Ion Antonescu gave the order in person, adding that Bessarabia would henceforth be *judenrein* ("cleansed of Jews"); of Bukovina's Jewish population of ninety thousand, only ten thousand would remain, and these only because they were indispensable to the economy of the region. The Germans had no need to pressure Antonescu on this issue, since as far as the Jews were concerned he implemented the Nazi plans of his own free will.

The "Solution" in the Regat and Southern Transylvania. Antonescu was willing to cooperate with his dangerous ally with all his heart and in every respect, including the treatment of the "Jewish question." But this was so only for as long as he could hope that—in return for his pro-German and antisemitic policies and the sacrifices that Romania was making in behalf of Germany—northern Transylvania, with its millions of Romanians, would be restored to Romania. By late 1941, however, Antonescu had lost some of his confidence in the eventual victory of the Reich, and during the course of 1942 he became increasingly doubtful of the outcome. The Romanian dictator and his deputy, Mihai ANTONESCU, came to realize that the Germans had no intention of forcing Hungary to return northern Transylvania, and they also noted the first signs of an impending defeat on the Russian front and the heavy losses that the Romanian forces were incurring. Other factors at play were the subjugation of Romania's economy and natural resources to the interests of Germany, and the unfriendly attitude manifested by the German minority in the country.

The combination of these factors, together with the determined struggle that the Jewish leadership was putting up in behalf of the Jews, led to the cancellation of the next phase to which Antonescu had agreed—the deportation of the greater part of the country's remaining Jewish population of 292,000. (This figure, the result of a special census taken in May 1942, was based on racist criteria and included thousands of converts and their offspring.) The cancellation of this German-conceived plan was not made all at once. The Nazis did not expect the Romanians to pose any problems, since it was the Romanians who had initiated and participated in the extermination drive in Bessarabia, Bukovina, and Transnistria. In November 1941 Mihai Antonescu still agreed to the deportation to the extermination camps of Jews who were Romanian nationals living in Germany or German-occupied countries, and several thousand of these Jews were in fact deported and killed. In August 1942 Mihai Antonescu even gave the Germans, in writing, his agreement for launching the deportation of Romanian Jews. However, weighty political considerations by the Romanian leaders—together with growing demands by the Germans for supplies of oil and food, and for additional Romanian forces on the eastern front—caused the Romanians first to hesitate and finally to reject the Nazi plan to deport Romania's Jews to the BEŁŻEC extermination camp.

The courageous and unceasing efforts made by the Jewish community's traditional leadership, headed by Dr. Wilhelm FILDERMAN, also had their effect. That leadership created an underground Jewish Council (in which Misu Benvenisti, president of the Zionist Organization, also took part), which made use of the confusion within and outside the Antonescu regime to play upon the Romanians' patriotic sentiments. The council gained the support of the opposition, headed by Iuliu Maniu, chairman of the National Peasants' party, and Constantin Bratianu, chairman of the National Liberal party; of court circles, notably Queen Mother Helena; of some clergymen, especially Archbishop Balan, a close friend of Antonescu's; and of the Swiss minister, René de Weck, among others. It enlisted their help for the protection of Romanian Jewry and for aid to the deported Jews in Transnistria, as well as for the cancellation of the existing plans for the extermination of the Jews.

Chief Rabbi Alexander SAFRAN, who maintained contacts with the clergy and the royal court, also gained the support of the papal nuncio, Archbishop Andrea Cassulo, who was the doyen of the diplomatic corps in Bucharest. On several occasions Cassulo interceded with Mihai Antonescu on behalf of the Jews, the Romanian official assuming that what the nuncio was telling him represented the wishes of the pope. The newspaper issued by the German legation in several instances denounced the actions taken by the Jews in preventing the deportations, and also condemned the Romanian officials and other figures who had been instrumental in canceling the deportations. In its issue of October 11, 1941, the paper warned that these Romanians would be called to account for their actions.

In March 1943 Ion Antonescu, on a visit to Hitler, was again subjected to pressure, this time by Nazi Foreign Minister Joachim von RIBBENTROP, to agree to the "resettlement of the Jews in the east." Antonescu rejected the demand. In the winter of 1942–1943, the Romanian regime reached the decision that the solution to the "Jewish question" lay in the emigration of the Jews from Romania, and give its agreement for 70,000 Jews to emigrate, in return for a large payment. Such a plan had very little prospect of succeeding, since the departure of the Jews from the country depended on German goodwill (the Germans were in control of the land route to Istanbul and the Black Sea). Eichmann did all he could to make sure that the plan would not be implemented. Two boats with "illegal" immigrants (to Palestine) aboard were indeed sunk. On December 12, 1941, a Soviet submarine sank (apparently by error) the STRUMA near Istanbul, with 769 Jews aboard whom the British government in Palestine had refused entry into the country. In August 1944 the Germans sank the *Pekora*, with 320 immigrants on their way to Palestine, among them orphans rescued from Transnistria.

The sum total of immigrants from Romania to Palestine during the war years did not exceed five thousand. Despite their modest dimensions, however, these operations involved great effort; they were a beacon of hope and a boost to the morale of the beleaguered Jews. They represent only a small part of the aid and rescue work carried out by the Zionist organization in Romania, especially by the underground Haluts (pioneering) movement. The latter, in the fall of 1943, added a new chapter to its story when it was joined by parachutists from Palestine (*see* PARACHUTISTS, JEWISH) who had been dropped into Europe.

Repatriation of Deportees and Orphans. Once the extermination plan was abandoned, all the Jewish organizations in Romania, including the Jewish Council, conducted a long, hard struggle for the repatriation of the Jews who had been deported to Transnistria, or, at least, of the thousands of orphans who were imprisoned there. This struggle had its vicissitudes. It was only in late 1943, when the battlefront was fast approaching the borders of Transnistria, that the first of the deportees—two thousand orphans and a few thousand adults (mostly from Dorohoi and its vicinity)—came back. The rest, some fifty thousand Jews, were repatriated only in 1945 and 1946, after the Soviets had liberated the area and occupied Romania. The prolonged delay in the repatriation was caused by the resistance of the governor of Transnistria, Gheorghe Alexianu; by the Nazis' adamant opposition; and, apparently, also by Antonescu's unwillingness to admit the failure of his policy on the Jews. In late 1943 and early 1944, the Jewish policy of the Antonescu regime underwent a profound change. The leaders of the regime became convinced that by protecting the Jews from the Nazi demands and by ameliorating the Jews' situation, they would project a positive image of themselves to the Allies; this would have a beneficial effect on the conditions to be imposed on Romania by the postwar peace conference.

Throughout its existence, Antonescu's fascist dictatorial regime applied laws and took other steps that led to the pauperization of the Jewish community. Jewish manpower was exploited in forced-labor battalions and other economic enterprises. The levies and taxes imposed on the Jews, and especially the "special levy" of 4 billion lei that Antonescu decreed in May 1943, impoverished the Jews to the extent that when they were liberated, more than half of the Jews of Romania (some 150,000) were totally destitute, with nothing to eat and no clothes to wear. The anti-Jewish discriminatory policy was in effect during this entire period, from 1940 to 1944.

Owing to a number of circumstances, however, the fate of Romanian Jewry (in the Regat and southern Transylvania) differed from that of the other Jewish communities in eastern Europe, both in the conditions under which the Jews lived during the war, and in the number and percentage of survivors. This difference was the result of the specific texture and ideology of the Romanian regime, the problems engendered by Romania's own war aims, Romania's distrust of its German partner, and the intercession of major Romanian figures who abhorred the Nazi methods and showed concern for the plight of the Jews. The different fate experienced by Romania's Jews stands out particularly when compared with that of the Jews under the fascist regime in Hungary. From Hungarian-ruled northern Transylvania, 155,000 Jews were deported to Auschwitz in April and May 1944, whereas in southern Transylvania the entire Jewish population of 40,000 survived the war.

After the War. Some 420,000 Jews who were living on Romanian soil in 1939 are estimated to have perished in the Holocaust. This figure includes the Jews killed in Bessarabia and Bukovina in July and August 1941; the Jews who died during the deportation to Transnistria or after their arrival there; the victims of the pogroms in Iaşi and other places in Romania; and the Jews of northern Transylvania who were deported to Auschwitz and killed there. Not included are the Jews who had been living in the Soviet territory that Romania occupied during the war and who also perished in the Holocaust.

After the liberation Romania had a Jewish population of 350,000, which included the Jews repatriated from Transnistria—that is, about half the number living in the country in 1930. Worst off were the Transnistria survivors, who were repatriated in 1945 and 1946, and the Jews of Moldavia, who had been maltreated by the Romanian military administration there in the last few months before the surrender.

The overthrow of the Antonescu regime enabled the Jewish organizations that had been outlawed in 1938 to resume their operations. The Federatia Uniunilor de Comunitati Evreesti (Union of Jewish Communities) replaced the CENTRALA EVREILOR (Jewish Center), and the Zionist movement with all its component organizations, the UNIUNEA EVREILOR ROMÂNI (Union of Romanian Jews), and the American Jewish JOINT DISTRIBUTION COMMITTEE all resumed their functions. Prior to this development, the Jewish Communists attempted to seize the leadership of all the non-Zionist Jewish organizations in order to dissolve them or to recruit them for the Communist party's struggle against the king and the veteran Romanian political parties.

The Jewish organizations lost no time in embarking upon a drive for the restoration of Jewish rights and the property of which the Jews had been robbed. The new regime was in no particular hurry on this issue, and it was not until December 19, 1944, four months after the liberation, that the antisemitic legislation was abolished. Most of the property taken from the Jews was not returned to them, since this would have affected the large number of Romanians who had been the principal beneficiaries of the confiscation. The state did not pay any indemnification to the Jews, and took its time before restoring civil rights to those Jews who had been stripped of them.

In the ensuing period, between the liberation of Romania and the final victory over the Nazis, the Jewish organizations, under the leadership of Dr. Wilhelm Filderman, were largely successful in preventing the draft of Jewish youth into the antisemitic Romanian army. Antisemitism, both in its old form and under a new guise, again reared its

Jewish refugees from Romania, assisted by the Joint Distribution Committee, find temporary shelter in Budapest during the first stage of their journey to displaced-persons' camps in Vienna and then to Israel (1948). [JDC Archives, New York]

head in the country, owing to a combination of various factors: the difficult problems facing Romania, the Soviet occupation, the pillage and confiscation of property by the Soviet army, the fierce rivalry between the Soviet-supported Communist party and the traditional political forces in the country, and the large number of Jewish members of the Communist party. Every attempt by the Jewish population and its organizations to obtain reparation for the wrongs done to them served only to further reinforce antisemitism. In the elections, the Jews had no choice except to vote for the Communist party, since it was the only political force that condemned antisemitism outright.

In 1945 the Comitetul Democrat Evreesc (Jewish Democratic Committee), a Jewish Communist organization, was formed. It employed unconventional methods, such as threats, vilification, and arrests, to curb the growing Jewish support of the Zionist movement, which was fast becoming widespread. The strained economic circumstances in Romania helped create a strong desire for emigration to Palestine. This, however, could not be realized, owing to the British WHITE PAPER policy then in force, which restricted Jewish immigration there. In the first few postwar years the Romanian government did not interfere with Jewish emigration; it even aided it, in view of the internal situation and the strong antisemitic sentiments prevailing among the general population. Since legal immigration to Palestine was not possible, illegal immigration and a BERIḤA (escape) movement were launched, by way of Yugoslavia and Hungary. In 1947 some twenty thousand Jews fled Romania in the "hunger flight," an unorganized and spontaneous movement given that designation because hunger and the grave economic situation of Romania's Jews were among the causes of the headlong departure.

The war years and all that had taken place during them—antisemitic legislation, deportations, evacuations, forced labor—changed the structure of Romanian Jewry for the worse, and the conditions that prevailed after liberation did not hold out the promise of an early improvement. Successive Romanian governments did not acknowledge any obligation to restore to the Jews their possessions or to indemnify them for damage caused to them by the state. The enormous task of rehabilitation became the exclusive responsibility of the Jewish organizations, and the solutions they were able to propose were not commensurate with the dimensions of the problem. These groups kept up their work until the moment that the monarchy was abolished and the Communist party seized full control, in 1948. At that point, as in other countries of Eastern Europe, the conclusion of the struggle for power also put an end to the continued existence of the established Jewish organizations.

Following the creation of the state of Israel, the vast majority of Romanian Jewry moved there. This process was interrupted from time to time by the authorities, and then resumed. By the end of the 1980s, only a small number of Jews were to be found in Romania.

[*See also* Comisia Autonoma de Ajutorare; Trials of War Criminals: Romania; Youth Movements: Romania.]

BIBLIOGRAPHY

Ancel, J. "Plans for Deportation of the Rumanian Jews and Their Discontinuation in Light of Documentary Evidence (July–October 1942)." *Yad Vashem Studies* 16 (1984): 381–420.

Ancel, J. "The Romanian Way of Solving the 'Jewish Problem' in Bessarabia and Bukovina, June–July 1941." *Yad Vashem Studies* 19 (1988): 187–232.

Ancel, J., and T. Lavi, eds. *Rumania.* 2 vols. In *Pinkas Hakehillot; Encyclopaedia of Jewish Communities.* Jerusalem, 1969, 1980. (In Hebrew.)

Carp, M. *Cartea Neagră.* 3 vols. Bucharest, 1946–1948.

Lavi, T. *Romanian Jewry in World War II: The Fight for Survival.* Jerusalem, 1965. (In Hebrew.)

JEAN ANCEL

ROMANIAN JEWS, UNION OF. *See* Uniunea Evreilor Români.

ROME. The Roman Jewish community is the oldest in the Western world. As early as 59 B.C., Cicero referred to its numerical importance and its influence in the popular assemblies. Today, more than two thousand years later and decades after the Holocaust, it still functions as the largest and most vital Jewish community on the Italian peninsula, with nearly half of ITALY's thirty-five thousand Jews.

According to the special Jewish census of August 22, 1938, 12,799 persons of Jewish "race" lived in Rome. When Benito MUSSOLINI was overthrown five years later, there were still about 12,000, despite the anti-Jewish laws enacted by the Fascist regime. Until Italy's surrender to the Allies (September 8, 1943), Hitler made no attempt whatever to force his murderous policy on his ally; it was only after Marshal Pietro BADOGLIO's "betrayal" that he finally decided to extend the "FINAL SOLUTION" to the Italian peninsula. On September 12 Obersturmbannführer Herbert KAPPLER, head of the Gestapo in Rome, received a telephone call from Hitler's headquarters at Rastenburg informing him that the *Reichsführer-SS,* Heinrich HIMMLER, wanted to proceed with the roundup and deportation of the Roman Jews. The telephone call was followed by a secret cable requesting Kappler "to take without delay all preliminary measures necessary to ensure the swiftness and secrecy of the operation to be carried out in the territory of the city of Rome." On September 24 (the day after the establishment of Mussolini's Fascist puppet regime), Himmler's office in Berlin dispatched a top secret message to Kappler, calling for a "final solution" to the "Jewish problem" in Rome: all Jews, regardless of age, sex, citizenship, and state of health, were to be arrested and sent to the Reich "for liquidation."

The planned operation was considered objectionable by the German military and diplomatic representatives in Rome, who feared complications with the Vatican and Italian public opinion. On September 26 Field Marshal Albert Kesselring, commander of Army Group South, refused to give his approval to the projected *Judenaktion* (*Aktion* against the Jews), being unable to spare a single soldier for this purpose. Kappler thereupon decided on an action of his own—the imposition of a levy of fifty kilograms of gold on Roman Jewry, to be paid within thirty-six hours. On September 28 the gold was duly delivered to the Gestapo, and the Jews of Rome heaved a sigh of relief. The relaxation of tension, however, was short-lived. The very next morning, September 29, a party of SS men confiscated the files of Jewish names and addresses at the main synagogue. At the beginning of October, Hauptsturmführer Theodor DANNECKER arrived in Rome at the head of a team of forty-four SS men, armed with a document empowering him to deport the Jews of Rome. This was "a definitive authorization, containing an order to the local police commands to furnish all aid requested by Dannecker," signed by Gestapo chief Heinrich MÜLLER. Consul Eitel Friedrich Möllhausen (then in charge of the German embassy in Rome) thereupon requested the Reich foreign minister and the Vatican to intervene, but in vain.

On October 16—a Sabbath and the blackest day in the long history of Roman Jewry—the signal was given at 5:30 a.m., and the *Judenrazzia* (rampage against the Jews) began. Wherever Jews lived in Rome, they were brutally seized, regardless of age, sex, and state of health, and taken to the Collegio Militare. After two days, they were sent to AUSCHWITZ. Of the 1,060 Roman Jews listed for departure on the Rome-Auschwitz train, at least 1,035 were actually deported. Kappler informed Obergruppenführer Karl WOLFF, commander of the SS in Italy, that participation by the Fascist police "was not possible, given their unreliability" and that the behavior of the Italian population "was outright passive resistance, which in many individual cases amounted to active assistance. . . . The antisemitic section of the population was nowhere to be seen during the action, only a great mass of people, who in some individual cases even tried to cut off the police from the Jews."

Dannecker's *Razzia* (roundup) horrified the Curia, the Catholic clergy, and the overwhelming majority of the Italian people. Himmler and his aides, on the other hand, were displeased to learn from Kappler that for every Roman Jew seized by the SS, eleven others had escaped. In January 1944 Dannecker was recalled and replaced by Sturmbannführer Friedrich Robert Bosshammer, Adolf EICHMANN's Italian-affairs expert. Subsequent *Razzien* resulted in the arrest of another 1,084 Roman Jews at the hands of the

Germans and their Italian accomplices.

On June 4, 1944, after nearly nine months of anguish, Rome was liberated by the American Fifth Army, and the Jewish fugitives came out of their hiding places. On the following day the anti-Jewish laws were repealed, and a liberation ceremony was held in the main synagogue, attended by Jewish members of the Allied forces. The nightmare was over; but Roman Jewry had suffered a blow from which it never recovered.

BIBLIOGRAPHY

Katz, R. *Death in Rome.* New York, 1967.

Michaelis, M. *Mussolini and the Jews: German-Italian Relations and the Jewish Question in Italy, 1922–1945.* Oxford, 1978.

Zuccotti, S. *The Italians and the Holocaust: Persecution, Rescue, and Survival.* New York, 1987.

MEIR MICHAELIS

ROOSEVELT, FRANKLIN DELANO (1882–1945), thirty-second president of the United States. Roosevelt's unprecedented four-term administration (1933–1945) began with the end of the collapse of the world economy known as the Great Depression, and ended with the events of World War II, which witnessed the destruction of European Jewry. He was the world leader in the best position to attempt the rescue of the Jews of Europe, but, according to many historians, his actions fell short of what might have been done.

For American Jewry that failure was a special disappointment since they supported Roosevelt enthusiastically. The shift of Jews to the Democratic party, which began in earnest in 1924, brought them closer to Roosevelt, whose political career up until then was confined to that party's New York State branch. In the presidential elections of 1932 and 1936, Jews gave him an overwhelming percentage of their votes, and by the 1940 election nine out of ten Jews were casting their ballots for him.

Roosevelt's New Deal program matched the social-democratic proclivities of the majority of Jewish voters and accounts for their great loyalty to him. But this unity of outlook was not present when it came to the specific Jewish interest in a more effective rescue policy during the Holocaust period. It is true that Roosevelt instructed American consuls, who made the final judgments on who should receive visas, to show "special concern" for Jewish refugees, and that he called home his ambassador to Germany in a gesture of dismay after KRISTALLNACHT (November 9–10, 1938), then permitting those Jews who had entered the United States on visitor's visas to extend their stay. Yet he did not generally alter the administration of the "Likely to Become Public Charge" (LPC) provision of the immigration law. This directive, introduced by President Herbert Hoover, was so rigidly enforced that in most depression years there was a net loss of immigrants. Only in 1939 were the applicable quotas fully utilized. More important, the policy of doing nothing concrete to help the Jews of Europe created a momentum for inaction that continued into the phase when they were being subject to mass killings. In that period, virtually every suggestion—including the sending of food packages, retributive bombing, changing the designation of camp inmates to that of prisoners of war, and filling the holds of empty ships returning to the United States with refugees—was rejected. These rejections emanated from the State Department (*see* UNITED STATES DEPARTMENT OF STATE) and War Department in particular, as well as from smaller government branches such as the Office of War Information.

After the ANSCHLUSS, Roosevelt made a halfhearted attempt to solve the growing refugee problem at its source. In July 1938, thirty-two nations were invited to meet at Evian-les-Bains. But Jewish rescue advocates watched in dismay as the delegations refused to accept any responsibility for the problem. The American delegation, headed by Myron Taylor, announced that its own restrictive immigration laws were sacrosanct and that no differentiation could be made between an ordinary immigrant and a refugee in dire need of a haven. Although Roosevelt had called the refugee conference, the United States declined to set an example that other nations might have followed.

The two agencies that grew out of the EVIAN

CONFERENCE, the INTERGOVERNMENTAL COMMITTEE ON REFUGEES (IGCR), designed to coordinate the international effort, and the PRESIDENT'S ADVISORY COMMITTEE ON POLITICAL REFUGEES (PAC), set up to coordinate the domestic effort, remained totally ineffective throughout the crisis and were monuments to the Roosevelt administration's "politics of gestures." The conference was designed more to placate the rescue advocates than it was to save the victims of the Holocaust.

The Roosevelt administration supported a policy of mass resettlement, giving publicity, for example, to a scheme to resettle thousands of European Jews in the Dominican Republic through the Dominican Republic Resettlement Association (DORSA). It supported British efforts to settle Jews in British Guiana, a locale of previous failures to do so. Hundreds of other areas, usually unsuitable or unavailable, were investigated by various agencies in the administration, and all but DORSA came to naught (DORSA succeeded in resettling 500 Jews in the Dominican Republic).

When public pressure in face of the "FINAL SOLUTION" reached a crescendo in the early months of 1943, Roosevelt joined with the British to convene a second refugee conference, on the island of Bermuda, in April 1943. The BERMUDA CONFERENCE was a particularly bitter experience for rescue advocates. As with previous gatherings, its results were virtually nonexistent and were dismissed by rescue advocates as a "hollow mockery."

Only in January 1944 did Roosevelt permit some deviation from wartime priorities to make a modest gesture in the cause of the rescue of the Jews. As a result of a special plea by his secretary of the treasury, Henry MORGENTHAU, Jr., who presented evidence of the State Department's systematic sabotage of the rescue effort, the WAR REFUGEE BOARD (WRB) was established. That agency's sometimes imaginative but often reluctant efforts to save the Jews of HUNGARY, the only sizable Jewish community remaining in Europe, came too late to make an appreciable difference. In April of that year, there occurred at Roosevelt's behest a circumvention of the supposedly immutable immigration laws. More than nine hundred predominantly Jewish refugees were admitted and housed in FORT ONTARIO, at Oswego, New York. But this was a symbolic rather than a substantive victory, and only demonstrated what could have been done had there been a will to save lives.

President Franklin D. Roosevelt. [Zionist Archives and Library, New York]

There were, of course, many reasons why Roosevelt chose not to act, but behind them all was his failure to fathom what the Holocaust signified for his own time in history. Preoccupied with the war and in failing health, Roosevelt was only peripherally aware of the destruction of European Jewry, which he perceived simply as an unpleasant fact.

President Roosevelt (left) meets with Prime Minister Winston Churchill at the Casablanca Conference (January 12–23, 1943). The conference dealt mainly with military matters. A statement was also issued by the two leaders announcing the policy of "unconditional surrender."

BIBLIOGRAPHY

Feingold, H. L. *The Politics of Rescue.* New Brunswick, N.J., 1970.

Feingold, H. L. "Roosevelt and the Resettlement Question." In *Rescue Attempts during the Holocaust.* Proceedings of the Second Yad Vashem International Historical Conference, edited by Y. Gutman and E. Zuroff, pp. 123–181. Jerusalem, 1977.

Wyman, D. S. *The Abandonment of the Jews: America and the Holocaust, 1941–1945.* New York, 1984.

Wyman, D. S. *Paper Walls: America and the Refugee Crisis, 1938–1941.* Amherst, Mass., 1968.

HENRY L. FEINGOLD

ROSENBERG, ALFRED (1893–1946), Nazi ideologist and head of the Nazi party's foreign-policy department. Born in Revel (now Tallinn) in Estonia, Rosenberg came from a family of Baltic Germans. He studied architecture at the universities of Riga and Moscow. Fleeing to Germany in 1918, he settled in Munich, where he associated with White Russian reactionary emigré circles and joined the ultranationalist and semi-occult Thule Society. He was already becoming known for his antisemitic and anti-Bolshevik views through such works as *Die Spur der Juden im Wandel der Zeiten* (The Track of the Jews through the Ages) and *Unmoral im Talmud* (Immorality in the Talmud), both published in 1919.

Rosenberg joined the German Workers' party in the wake of Adolf HITLER, whom he impressed with his theories of a Judeo-Bolshevik-Masonic conspiracy constantly engaged in "undermining the foundations of our existence." In 1921 he became chief editor of the party newspaper, the *Völkischer Beobachter*, and was one of the principal disseminators of the PROTOCOLS OF THE ELDERS OF ZION, a forgery of the tsarist police that appealed to Rosenberg's belief in the active working of occult powers to subvert civilization. He participated in the abortive Munich Beer-Hall Putsch of November 1923 and was protected by Hitler from the attacks of other leading Nazis, who were affronted by Rosenberg's Baltic origins and his intellectual arrogance.

Rosenberg's role as chief Nazi ideologist was enhanced by his founding, in 1929, of the Kampfbund für Deutsche Kultur (Fighting League for German Culture) and, above all, by his major work, *Der Mythus des 20. Jahrhunderts* (The Myth of the Twentieth Century; 1930). As an expression of Nazi philosophy this book had an influence comparable to that of Hitler's MEIN KAMPF. It was enormously popular, and by 1942 had sold over a million copies. The book incorporated the racial theories of Joseph-Arthur de Gobineau and Houston Stewart CHAMBERLAIN, proclaiming that race was the decisive factor determining art, science, culture, and the course of world history (*see* RACISM). The Teutons represented the "master race" of "Aryans," whose task it was to subdue Europe. This belief was combined with denunciation of Judaism and Christianity, whose ideals of compassion and charity must yield to the neo-pagan Teutonic sense of honor. The swastika was the symbol of blood and soil, and denoted the worship of Wotan and the ancient Norse gods. The Jews had subverted the ideal of race with their internationalism and a religion of humanity destructive of the Teutonic spirit. With doctrines such as these, Rosenberg's *Mythus* sought to systematize Nazi ideology.

In 1930 Rosenberg was elected to the Reichstag as Nazi deputy for Hesse-Darmstadt, and he made a rapid ascent to positions of influence after 1933. In 1934 Hitler appointed him the "Führer's delegate for the supervision of the whole intellectual and philosophical education and training of the National Socialist party." From 1933 to 1945 he also headed the party's foreign-affairs department, which gave him access especially to fascist parties in eastern Europe and the Balkans. In 1939 he established in Frankfurt

Alfred Rosenberg.

the Institut zur Erforschung der Judenfrage (Institute for the Investigation of the Jewish Question). Rosenberg declared in his inaugural address there that the "Jewish question" would be considered solved "only after the last Jew has left the Greater German living space." The institute's principal task was to ransack the libraries, archives, and art galleries of European Jewry in order to promote its "research." After the fall of France, EINSATZSTAB ROSENBERG (Operational Staff Rosenberg) seized French art treasures and sent them to Germany.

In November 1941 Rosenberg was appointed *Reichsminister für die Besetzten Ostgebiete* (Reich Minister for the Occupied Eastern Territories), where his policy differed in detail but not in principle from the extermination policy perpetrated by Heinrich HIMMLER, Reinhard HEYDRICH, and the REICHSSICHERHEITSHAUPTAMT (Reich Security Main Office; RSHA). Although he had always regarded the Slavs as subhuman, Rosenberg regretted the policy of Germanization, believing it politically harmful; however, he found no support for this view. Condemned to death at Nuremberg as a major war criminal, he was hanged in 1946.

BIBLIOGRAPHY

Cecil, R. *The Myth of the Master Race: Alfred Rosenberg and Nazi Ideology*. New York, 1972.

Fest, J. *The Face of the Third Reich: Portraits of the Nazi Leadership*. New York, 1970. See pages 163–174.

Nova, F. *Alfred Rosenberg, Nazi Theorist of the Holocaust*. New York, 1986.

LIONEL KOCHAN

ROSENBERG OPERATIONAL STAFF. *See* Einsatzstab Rosenberg.

ROSTOV-ON-DON (Russ., Rostov-na-Donu), city and administrative center of Rostov Oblast (district), in the southern part of the RSFSR (Russian Soviet Federated Socialist Republic). On the eve of World War II the city had a Jewish population of over 27,000, out of a total population of 510,253.

On November 21, 1941, after heavy battles, Rostov was occupied by the Germans, but a week later, on November 29, the Soviet army recaptured it. The Germans took Rostov for the second time on July 27, 1942. By then, most of the Jews had left or had been evacuated, and only a few thousand were left in the city, mostly women, children, and the elderly.

In the first few days of their occupation of Rostov, the Germans appointed a Jew named Lurie as Elder of the Jews (*Evreyski starshina*). On August 4, an announcement was published over Lurie's signature, ordering all Jews to register. Three days later another announcement followed, in which all Jews were told to report to a designated assembly point on August 11 and to bring along their clothing, the valuables in their possession, and the keys to their apartments. For their own security, the proclamation stated, the Jews were going to be moved. On that day, two thousand of Rostov's Jews were taken by truck to the "snake ravine" (Zmieva Balka) just outside the city, where men of Einsatzkommando 10a from Einsatzgruppe D killed them. Several dozen Jews who were caught later were gassed in GAS VANS.

Rostov was liberated by the Soviets on February 14, 1943.

BIBLIOGRAPHY

Ehrenburg, I., and V. Grossman, eds. *The Black Book of Soviet Jewry*. New York, 1981.

SHMUEL SPECTOR

ROTE KAPELLE. *See* Red Orchestra.

ROTTERDAM, city in the NETHERLANDS, the second largest in the country and the largest port. Rotterdam was founded in the thirteenth century; Jews have been living there since the seventeenth century. In the 1931 census Rotterdam's Jewish population was 10,357, or 1.7 percent of the total of 590,000. In a census taken on January 10, 1941, on orders of the German administration and based on the NUREMBERG LAWS, only 8,368 Jews were counted, plus another 2,738 persons classified as Jews under the racist laws who had not been regarded as Jews in the earlier census. This meant that the percentage of Jews among the population had dropped to 1.4 percent in spite of the large influx of Jewish refugees into Rotterdam in the late 1930s (4,326 in 1939).

The decrease in the size of the Jewish population had several causes. On May 14, 1940, the Germans bombed Rotterdam, inflicting tremendous damage on the city. Among the places destroyed were synagogues and prayerhouses, the building housing the rabbinate and the Jewish community offices, the old Jewish cemetery, and many houses in the Jewish quarter. Following the air raid many of the residents fled the city, among them a relatively large number of Jews. The Jewish population decreased further in September 1940, when the German administration decided to clear the Netherlands' coastal strip of any German Jews living there, and some seven hundred German Jewish refugees were forced to leave Rotterdam.

In late 1940 a local branch of the Joodse Coördinatiecommissie (Jewish Coordination Committee) was formed in Rotterdam. In cooperation with the Jewish community board and under the leadership of the Chief Rabbi of Rotterdam, Aaron Issachar Davids, it accomplished much in the social and cultural sphere, such as manufacturing ritual articles, making the ritual bath available as a bathhouse for general use, and distributing food among the Jewish population.

There was relatively little anti-Jewish activity by local Nazi elements in Rotterdam. About one hundred members of the Dutch NATIONAAL SOCIALISTISCHE BEWEGING (National Socialist Movement) launched a drive to post "No Entry for Jews" signs in the city, but they met with only partial success. Jewish community life continued, within the strictures imposed on all the Jews of the Netherlands, unimpeded by any special occurrences. In the fall of 1941 three Jewish elementary schools, a secondary school, and several vocational schools were opened for the Jewish students, who had been expelled from the public school system. At this time, too, Jews were called up for forced labor, to take part in the rebuilding of the city.

Deportations of Jews from Rotterdam began on July 30, 1942. Some 1,400 Jews were summoned to report for the first draft, but only 1,000 responded. In August, 900 Jews were summoned, with only 300 reporting, and in the third call-up only 520 reported, out of a total of 2,000 who had been summoned. On the night of October 2–3, the families of all the Jewish males of the Netherlands who were on forced labor, including those of Rotterdam, were arrested and deported to the extermination camps, by way of the WESTERBORK camp. The German police conducted several searches in the city, to fill the required quota of Jews and seize the Jews who had gone into hiding. The Rotterdam chief of police, Dr. D. J. de Jong, resigned in protest against the involvement of the police in these searches. The Germans nevertheless managed to find most of the Jews, and had help in their drive from a thirty-member Dutch detective squad that specialized in ferreting out Jews in hiding. Hundreds of Jews were given refuge in the homes of non-Jewish families. Altogether, 1,400 Rotterdam Jews were saved: by hiding, by being protected, or by surviving in the extermination camps.

A member of the Rotterdam city council, Dr. Krop, had managed to remove the Jewish community archive, the ritual articles, and other items from the Jewish community building, which the Germans had sealed off. The community continued to exist clandestinely, and the cantor, who was able to move about freely with forged papers, organized undercover religious services and even arranged a wedding ceremony for a young local couple. As late as the last winter of the war, the underground Jewish community was still distributing 225 food rations daily in the city. On May 1, 1945, public religious services were resumed for the first time, in the Lev Yam (High Seas) Synagogue, the only one left standing. In 1954 the city council honored the memory of Chief Rabbi Davids by naming a city square after him, and on October 21, 1981, in the presence of Queen Beatrix of the Netherlands, a memorial was unveiled in memory of the Jews who had perished in the Holocaust.

BIBLIOGRAPHY

De Jong, L. *Het Koninkrijk der Nederlanden tijdens*

de Tweede Wereldoorlog. Vols. 1–13. The Hague, 1969–1988.

Michman, J., et al. *The Netherlands*. In *Pinkas Hakehillot; Encyclopaedia of Jewish Communities*. Jerusalem, 1985. See pages 388–403. (In Hebrew.)

Presser, J. *The Destruction of the Dutch Jews*. New York, 1969.

JOZEPH MICHMAN

ROVNO (Pol., Równe), city in the northwestern UKRAINE, capital of the oblast (district) of the same name.

In the interwar period, Rovno belonged to the Volhynia (Pol., Wołyń) district of Poland. Jews had been living in the town since the sixteenth century. On the eve of World War II, it had a population of nearly 57,000, of whom about 25,000 were Jews. In September 1939 Rovno was occupied by the Soviet Union, and thousands of Jews from German-occupied Poland found refuge there. By June 1941, the Jewish population had grown to over 30,000.

In the battle for the city following the German attack on the Soviet Union in June 1941, the city center and the railway station were bombed and shelled and were heavily damaged or destroyed. Three thousand to four thousand people were killed, many of them Jews. Several thousand Jews fled the city to the east, either during the mobilization and general flight or in the evacuation organized by the local Communist party secretary.

On June 28, six days after the invasion, Rovno was occupied by the Germans. In the course of July and August, some three thousand Jews were murdered under various pretexts. By order of the military government, a JUDENRAT (Jewish Council) was set up whose members included men active in community affairs during the prewar period. Two of the appointees to the Judenrat—the chairman, Dr. Moshe Bergmann, and a lawyer, Leon Sukharchuk—committed suicide rather than become the Nazis' helpers. The Jews were ordered to wear an armband with a blue Star of David on a white background (later replaced by a yellow badge; *see* BADGE, JEWISH); they were sent on forced labor and had to hand over their valuables and pay a ransom, in large sums of money and in gold.

On September 1, 1941, the Ukraine was put under the control of the REICHSKOMMISSARIAT UKRAINE. The *Reichskommissar*, Erich KOCH, established his headquarters at Rovno, and apparently for this reason he sought to speed up the purge of its Jews. The planning of the *Aktion* was in the hands of Höherer SS- und Polizeiführer Friedrich JECKELN of Army Group South. Its implementation was entrusted to the SD (Sicherheitsdienst; Security Service) forces in Rovno—members of Einsatzkommando 5 and ORDNUNGSPOLIZEI (Orpo) Battalion 320—as well as to Ukrainian auxiliary police (*see* UKRAINISCHE HILFSPOLIZEI). The German military administration also took part.

On November 5, the Rovno district *Kommissar* informed the Judenrat that Jews who had no work permits would be moved to other locations for work. Notices to this effect were posted in the streets, ordering the Jews to report on November 7 with a minimum of luggage. On November 7 and 8, twenty-one thousand Jews were rounded up and taken to a pine grove at Sosenki, 4 miles (6 km) away, where they were all shot standing next to trenches that had been dug in advance for their burial.

About 80 percent of Rovno's Jews were murdered in this operation. In postwar reports published by members of the Soviet underground the claim was made that, having learned from Soviet prisoners of war of the trenches that were being dug, the underground tried to warn the Jews of their fate, but the Jews would not believe what they were told. There has been no confirmation of this report by any Jewish source.

The five thousand surviving Jews were moved into a ghetto set up in the Wola quarter of Rovno, with seven families to an apartment. Though the ghetto was not sealed off from the outside, the inhabitants were severely restricted in their movement and in effect were confined to the ghetto area. They were assigned to forced labor, with several hundred working for the Jung construction firm, whose manager, Hermann Friedrich GRÄBE, endeavored to alleviate their plight. The daily bread ration of Jews who were put to work amounted to 100 grams (3.5 oz).

The murder of Jews, singly or in small groups, went on uninterruptedly until the final destruction of the ghetto. Occasionally, individual Jews offered resistance, sometimes even using firearms. In one case four Jews—Syma Gimberg, Isaac Schneider, Nyonya Kopilnik, and a woman by the name of Dvoricz—fought a group of Germans and Ukrainians face to face, killing some and themselves falling in the battle. A few Jews belonged to the Soviet underground in the city; one of them, Liza Gelfand, the wife of a Soviet officer, took part in the bombing of a restaurant reserved for German officers. In the *Aktion* of July 1942 (see below), there was also some resistance. Gräbe, who went into the ghetto to take out the Jews working for his firm, later testified, at the Nuremberg trials and afterward, that they had blocked the doors of their houses and ignored German orders for them to come out; the Germans had to force their way in by the use of hand grenades and other explosives.

On July 13, 1942, the ghetto was surrounded by Ordnungspolizei and Ukrainian auxiliaries. Force was used in rounding up the Jews, who were taken to the railway station. All of them—some five thousand people—were packed into freight cars and sent northeast, in the direction of Kostopol. When the train reached its destination, a wood northwest of the town, the Jews were taken out, lined up along prepared trenches, and shot.

While the ghetto was under siege, dozens of its inhabitants tried to flee; there were also some who jumped off the train while it was in motion. Most of the escapees were young people, who formed into groups or roamed the woods on their own. Before long they joined up with Soviet partisan units, such as the Medvedev unit in the Rovno group, under the command of Maj. Gen. Vasily Begma.

On February 5, 1944, Rovno was liberated in a combined operation of the Soviet army (Thirteenth Army and Eighteenth Cavalry Corps) and the partisan forces under Begma, who made their assault on the city from the west. The number of Jewish survivors in the city did not exceed a few dozen, but they were joined by survivors and returnees from small towns in the district, where their lives had been endangered by Ukrainian nationalist partisans of the UKRAINSKA POVSTANSKA ARMYIA (Ukrainian Insurgent Army; UPA). The Jewish partisans obtained permission to es-

tablish a religious community and were given a building for a synagogue, which they made into a center where all new Jewish arrivals in the city reported and were given food and clothing.

In the summer of 1944, on the initiative of Zionist activists, the brothers Abraham and Eliezer Lidowski, a clandestine organization was set up to establish escape routes to Palestine. The organization contacted a similar group in Vilna and devised a joint plan to move the Jews in the direction of Bucharest, where the pro-German regime had fallen in August 1944. After this plan misfired, the Rovno and Vilna groups concentrated their efforts on central Poland, encouraged by the fact that an official repatriation program of Polish nationals—among them many Jews—had just been launched. By the fall of 1944, as many as twelve hundred Jews had gathered in Rovno. Most of them left the city, moving toward destinations in the west.

BIBLIOGRAPHY

Avtihi, A., ed. *Rowno: A Memorial to the Jewish Community of Rowno Wolyn.* Tel Aviv, 1956. (In Hebrew.)

Spector, S. *The Holocaust of Volhynian Jews, 1941–1944.* Jerusalem, 1986. (In Hebrew.)

SHMUEL SPECTOR

ROWECKI, STEFAN (1895–1944), Polish officer; commander of the ARMIA KRAJOWA (Home Army). In the underground, Rowecki was known by the code name Grot ("arrowhead"). During World War I he fought in the ranks of the Polish Legion, commanded by Józef Piłsudski, and after the war became an officer in the Polish army, reaching the rank of colonel.

In the fighting of September 1939 Rowecki was in command of an armored brigade. When the Polish forces in besieged Warsaw surrendered at the end of that month, Rowecki, on the orders of the Polish general Juliusz Karol Rommel, went underground to create and head a secret resistance organization engaging in anti-German actions. Subordinate to the authority of the POLISH GOVERNMENT-IN-EXILE, it was first named Służba Zwycięstwu Polski (Service for the Victory of Poland); in 1940 it was renamed Związek Walki Zbrojnej (Union for Armed Struggle), and as of 1942 was called Armia Krajowa. It became the strongest and most important element of the Polish underground.

In 1940 the Polish government-in-exile appointed Rowecki to the rank of brigadier general. He developed the concept of restricting actual fighting against the Germans and instead worked to strengthen the underground so as to prepare it for an uprising that would take place when the German army in Poland was on the verge of collapse. This concept failed to prove itself when the test came. Rowecki decided to cooperate, within limits, with the ŻYDOWSKA ORGANIZACJA BOJOWA (Jewish Fighting Organization; ŻOB) in the Warsaw ghetto and to supply it with some assistance. On June 30, 1943, Rowecki was arrested in Warsaw by the Germans, taken to the SACHSENHAUSEN concentration camp, and murdered. His memoirs, *Wspomnienia i notatki, czerwiec-wrzesień* (Recollections and Notes, June–September), were published posthumously in Warsaw, in 1957.

BIBLIOGRAPHY

Korbonski, S. *The Polish Underground State.* New York, 1969.

SHMUEL KRAKOWSKI

RÓWNE. *See* Rovno.

RSHA. *See* Reichssicherheitshauptamt.

RUDEL, HANS-ULRICH (1916–1982), German World War II air ace. Born in Silesia, Rudel entered a military school at Wildpark and was later trained in the use of Stuka and reconnaissance aircraft. As a bomber pilot in the Luftwaffe he enjoyed unprecedented success, sinking a cruiser and severely disabling a battleship. On the eastern front, he flew 2,530 sorties and he and his squadron destroyed 519 Soviet tanks. He was the most highly decorated officer in the Wehrmacht. Rudel was shot down in 1944 and captured by the Soviets but succeeded in escaping. In 1945 he was again shot down and had his right leg amputated.

After the war Rudel fled to Argentina, where he helped form a Nazi community in exile and also maintained contact with Nazi supporters in Lower Saxony. Returning to Germany in 1951, he sponsored a rightwing nationalist organization, Freikorps Deutschland. His memoirs, published in Buenos Aires under the title *Trotzdem* (Nevertheless), revealed a continuing admiration for Hitler. Rudel also propagated the cause of the neo-Nazi Socialist Reich party. His identification with neo-Nazism was indirectly responsible for the dismissal in 1976 of two air force generals, who had failed to prohibit officers of the Bundeswehr (the German army) from attending a reunion in Rudel's honor.

BIBLIOGRAPHY

Hereth, M. *Der Fall Rudel oder Die Hoffähigkeit der Nazi-Diktatur: Protokoll einer Bundestagsdebatte.* Reinbek, West Germany, 1977.

Overy, R. J. *The Air War, 1939–1945*. London, 1980.

LIONEL KOCHAN

RUDNINKAI FOREST. *See* Partisans.

RUFAJZEN, OSWALD (Shmuel Rufeisen, later Brother Daniel; b. 1922), wartime activist. Rufajzen was born in Zadziele, a village in the Kraków district, and during his studies joined the Akiva youth movement. In 1939, when World War II broke out, he fled to Vilna, where he joined the *halutsim* (members of the Zionist pioneering movements) who had gathered there. In June 1941, when Vilna was occupied by the Nazis, Rufajzen succeeded in obtaining an "Aryan" document certifying that he was a VOLKSDEUTSCHE (ethnic German) named Josef Oswald. He moved to MIR, where he became the interpreter of the gendarmerie commandant, gaining his complete confidence. After a while he was appointed police commander for the area.

In Mir, Rufajzen met two of the *halutsim* with whom he had become acquainted in Vilna; both were organizers of the ghetto underground. Oswald (the name by which Rufajzen now went) regularly passed information on the activities of the Germans to his friends in the ghetto underground, and on more than one occasion saved those in the ghetto from falling into traps engineered by the police, such as a sham "sale" of weapons to ghetto Jews by a local farmer. Oswald's friends told him of their determination to resist a German *Aktion* by force, and asked him to supply them with arms. Over a period of time he provided the ghetto with twelve rifles, two submachine guns, eight pistols, thirty hand grenades, and thousands of rounds of ammunition. At Oswald's suggestion the underground altered its plan to escape from the ghetto in the course of the *Aktion*, by advancing the date for the escape. On August 6, 1942, he informed the ghetto underground commanders of the date that had been fixed for the liquidation of the ghetto (August 13) and the date on which he would be taking the town police on an "antipartisan patrol" (August 9). On that day, with the town empty of police and Germans, 180 Mir Jews fled the ghetto and took refuge in the forests.

Following the flight, Oswald was arrested and interrogated by the German commander, Schulz, on suspicion of having provided the Jews with arms and helping them to flee. He managed to escape from the place where he was being held and found refuge in a monastery, where he remained for the next sixteen months. When the search for him intensified, Oswald fled once more, this time to the forest. The partisans thought he was German and placed him under arrest, but he was saved by Jewish partisans from Mir who interceded on his behalf.

When the war was over Oswald took part in the efforts to apprehend local inhabitants of Mir who had collaborated with the Germans. He then left for Kraków, where he was baptized and given the name of "Daniel, the son of Miriam." Later he went to Israel and joined the Stella Maris monastery on Mount Carmel.

BIBLIOGRAPHY

Cholawski, S. *The Jews in Belorussia (White Russia) during World War II*. Tel Aviv, 1982. (In Hebrew.)

The Jewish Partisans. Vol. 1. Tel Aviv, 1958. See pages 469–475. (In Hebrew.)

SHALOM CHOLAWSKI

RUMANIA. *See* Romania.

RUMBULA (also Rumbuli), site of a massacre, in a wooded area near the railway station of that name, 5 miles (8 km) from RIGA, the capital of Latvia. From November 29 to December 9, 1941, thirty-eight thousand Jews were murdered at Rumbula: twenty-eight thousand from the Riga ghetto and ten thousand who had been transported by train from Germany, Austria, and the Protectorate of BOHEMIA AND MORAVIA.

After World War II the site was neglected, and there was no sign to commemorate the

Temporary monument erected at Rumbula. The text reads: "Away with fascism!"

massacre that had taken place. In 1962 a group of Jewish activists placed a wooden sign there that read: "On this site the voice of thirty-eight thousand Jews of Riga was stilled, November 29–30, 1941 to December 8–9, 1941." The Soviet authorities, disapproving of any memorial sign that specifically mentioned Jews, removed it from the site. After persistent public pressure, a memorial stone was erected with inscriptions in Russian, Latvian, and Yiddish: "To the memory of the victims of the Nazis, 1941–1944."

The site has since become a place of Jewish assembly, particularly on the anniversaries of the Rumbula massacre and the WARSAW GHETTO UPRISING, and on the Jewish high holidays. These gatherings have also become, to some extent, an expression of the national rebirth of the remnants of the Jewish population in Soviet Latvia.

BIBLIOGRAPHY

Michelson, F. *I Survived Rumbuli*. New York, 1979.

Perach, M. "The Meetings in Rumbuli." *Yalkut Moreshet* 13 (June 1971): 5–16. (In Hebrew.)

DOV LEVIN

RUMKOWSKI, MORDECHAI CHAIM (1877–1944), chairman of the JUDENRAT (Jewish Council) in ŁÓDŹ. Born in Ilino, a village in the Velikie Luki district of Russia, Rumkowski at an early age settled in Łódź and tried to make his way in commerce, without much success. For several years he was director of the Jewish orphanage at Helenowek, in the northern suburbs of Łódź. In 1937 he was elected to the Jewish community board, on behalf of the General Zionist party, but he fell out with the party, refusing both to accept its authority and to relinquish his seat on the board.

When the Germans occupied Łódź on September 8, 1939, they dissolved all the Jewish community institutions, as was their policy throughout Poland. In their place they appointed a Judenrat, which in Łódź they called an Ältestenrat (Council of Elders). On October 13 the Germans appointed Rumkowski *Älteste der Juden* (Elder of the Jews), the official title of the chairman of the Łódź Judenrat. Rumkowski retained the post throughout the ghetto's existence, until its liquidation in August 1944.

As Judenrat chairman, Rumkowski was directly responsible to the German ghetto administration (Gettoverwaltung), headed by Hans BIEBOW. The German authorities gave Rumkowski wide powers in all areas related to the day-to-day life of the population imprisoned in the ghetto, such as the establishment of factories, food distribution, sanitation services, housing, and appointments to available positions. Rumkowski had at his disposal a Jewish ghetto police (JÜDISCHER ORDNUNGSDIENST), which had the job of keeping "law and order" in the ghetto.

For the Germans the ghetto was a source of very cheap labor, in addition to the benefits they derived from it by robbing the Jewish inhabitants of their possessions, a process that began on the first day of the occupation. Rumkowski was given the task of setting up factories (*Arbeitsresorte*, or work sections, in the Germans' terminology), from which the German ghetto administration came to reap substantial profits. In Rumkowski's eyes the factories were a means of overcoming unemployment and the mounting food shortage. A total of 120 factories were established, all working for the ghetto administration.

Rumkowski displayed great zeal and organizational ability in running the factories and the internal life of the ghetto. He exploited to the full the wide powers given to him and did not give veteran leaders and Jewish public figures any role to play in the affairs of the ghetto. In addition, manifested domineering and self-promoting tendencies.

At the end of 1941, when the CHEŁMNO extermination camp had been established, the German authorities forced Rumkowski to organize the deportation of part of the ghetto population, ostensibly for resettlement elsewhere. While nobody in the ghetto, including Rumkowski, was aware of the existence of the extermination camp, the danger inherent in the expulsion operation was felt by one and all. Rumkowski tried in vain to persuade the Germans to reduce the number of persons to be deported. In the period between January and May 1942, fifty-five thousand Jews were taken from the ghetto and deported to Chełmno, where they were all killed. The Germans left to Rumkowski and his Ältestenrat staff the task of deciding who was to be included in the deportations, thus giving him an authority that earned him the hatred of most of the ghetto population. Among the starving and helpless ghetto inhabitants, however, there was no other public body or underground political group that saw any possibility of resisting the deportation or of forcing Rumkowski to seek an alternative mode of action.

From September 5 to 12, 1942, the Germans carried out another partial deportation, this time using speedier methods, without the direct involvement of the Ältestenrat. Substantial German forces entered the ghetto, blocked off one section after the other, and, with great brutality, seized twenty thousand persons—men, women and children—and transported them to Chełmno, where they were killed. After this deportation there was a period of relative quiet in the ghetto, which reinforced Rumkowski's belief that his policy of working for the ghetto administration and maintaining peace was the only way to save the remaining Jews in the ghetto.

In the late spring of 1944, when the Soviet army was drawing near, the Germans decided on the final liquidation of the ghetto. Once again they made Rumkowski organize the deportation, on the pretext that because of the advance of the Soviet army, the factories in the ghetto were being transferred to Germany. In the period from June 23 to July 14, 1944, seven thousand Jews were taken from the ghetto, according to lists prepared by the Ältestenrat, and transported to Chełmno, where they were killed. In the hope that liberation was near at hand, the ghetto population offered considerable passive resistance during these roundups by refusing to report to the deportation stations. Consequently, the rate of deportations did not meet the German expectations. Because of the resistance, and the accelerated advance of the Soviet army, the Nazis resolved that the liquidation of the ghetto had to take place immediately, with the SS and German police accomplishing the task. In early August of 1944 all the factories were closed and the Ältestenrat institutions were dissolved. The destination of the deportation transports was changed from Chełmno to AUSCHWITZ.

At an assembly called by the German ghetto administration, both Biebow and Rumkowski urged the ghetto inhabitants to obey the orders they had received to report for the deportations. The ghetto population, however, ignored these appeals and made desperate efforts to avoid being deported, in the hope that Łódź would soon be liberated. The halt in the Russian advance in late July 1944, however, enabled the Germans to complete the liquidation of the ghetto, using house-to-house searches in the process. Under the conditions existing in the ghetto there was no chance of thousands, let alone tens of thousands, going into hiding, and with the exception of a few hundred persons, the remaining Jews in the ghetto were seized by the Germans and deported to Auschwitz. Most of them died in the gas chambers, and the rest were sent to concentration camps to perform forced labor. Rumkowski and his family as well were deported to Auschwitz, on August 30, 1944, and were killed there. Five months later, on January 19, 1945, Łódź was liberated by the Soviet army.

Within the ghetto, Rumkowski had succeeded gradually and with great determination in shoring up his position. In 1940 and 1941, when riots and strikes broke out in the ghetto, the starving people turned their wrath against Rumkowski and the Ältestenrat. Rumkowski overcame the opposition with the aid of German intervention and by introducing an evenhanded system of food distribution. At first he consulted with representatives of the various political groups in the ghetto to assure himself of their support, but as time went on he strengthened his position and was able to rule with an iron hand without having to take into account the opinion of community leaders. The few who dared to speak up against Rumkowski or organize resistance to him ran the risk of his taking revenge, which in some extreme instances meant being included on the lists of candidates for deportation.

The figure of Rumkowski, more than that of any other Judenrat leader, has attracted the attention of historians and writers, and opinions about him, his behavior, and his accomplishments range from one extreme to the other. In the view of some of these writers and historians, Rumkowski was a traitor and a collaborator. Others believe that his policies—toward both the Jews and the Germans—helped extend the life span of the Łódź ghetto, which remained in existence when all the other ghettos in Poland had been liquidated. Those who hold the latter opinion point out that the five thousand to seven thousand survivors of the Łódź ghetto constituted, in relative terms, the largest among all the groups of Holocaust survivors in Poland.

BIBLIOGRAPHY

Bloom, S. F. "Dictator of Lodz Ghetto: The Strange History of Mordechai Chaim Rumkowski." *Commentary* 7/2 (February 1949): 111–122.

Dobroszycki, L., ed. *The Chronicle of the Lodz Ghetto, 1941–1944*. New Haven, 1984.

Friedman, P. "Pseudo-Saviors in the Polish Ghettos: Mordechai Chaim Rumkowski of Lodz." In *Roads to Extinction: Essays on the Holocaust*, edited by Ada J. Friedman, pp. 333–352. Philadelphia, 1980.

Huppert, S. "King of the Ghetto: Mordecai Haim Rumkowski, the Elder of the Lodz Ghetto." *Yad Vashem Studies* 15 (1983): 125–157.

Rudnicki, A. *Kupiec łódzki*. Warsaw, 1963.

Trunk, I. *Judenrat: The Jewish Councils in Eastern Europe under Nazi Occupation*. New York, 1972.

SHMUEL KRAKOWSKI

RUSHA. *See* Rasse- und Siedlungshauptamt.

RUSSIA. *See* Soviet Union.

RUSSKAYA OSVOBODITELNAYA ARMIYA (Russian Liberation Army; ROA), name of two divisions of Russians serving in the German army. The first, established on December 1, 1944, was commanded by Gen. Sergei Buniachenko, and the second, formed on January 23, 1945, was commanded by a General Zverev. The army as such was under the command of Gen. Andrei VLASOV. Both divisions surrendered to American army units; most of their men were handed over to the Soviets.

SHMUEL SPECTOR

RUTHENIA. *See* Transcarpathian Ukraine.

RZESZÓW (Risha, in Jewish usage), district center in southern POLAND, about 93 miles (150 km) east of Kraków. Jewish settlement in Rzeszów dates back to the fifteenth century, and the first synagogue was built in the seventeenth century. In 1765 Rzeszów had a Jewish population of 1,200, which by the end of the eighteenth century had grown to 3,375, representing 75 percent of the total population. In 1900 the Jewish population was 7,000, but its percentage of the total had dropped to 40. On the eve of World War II,

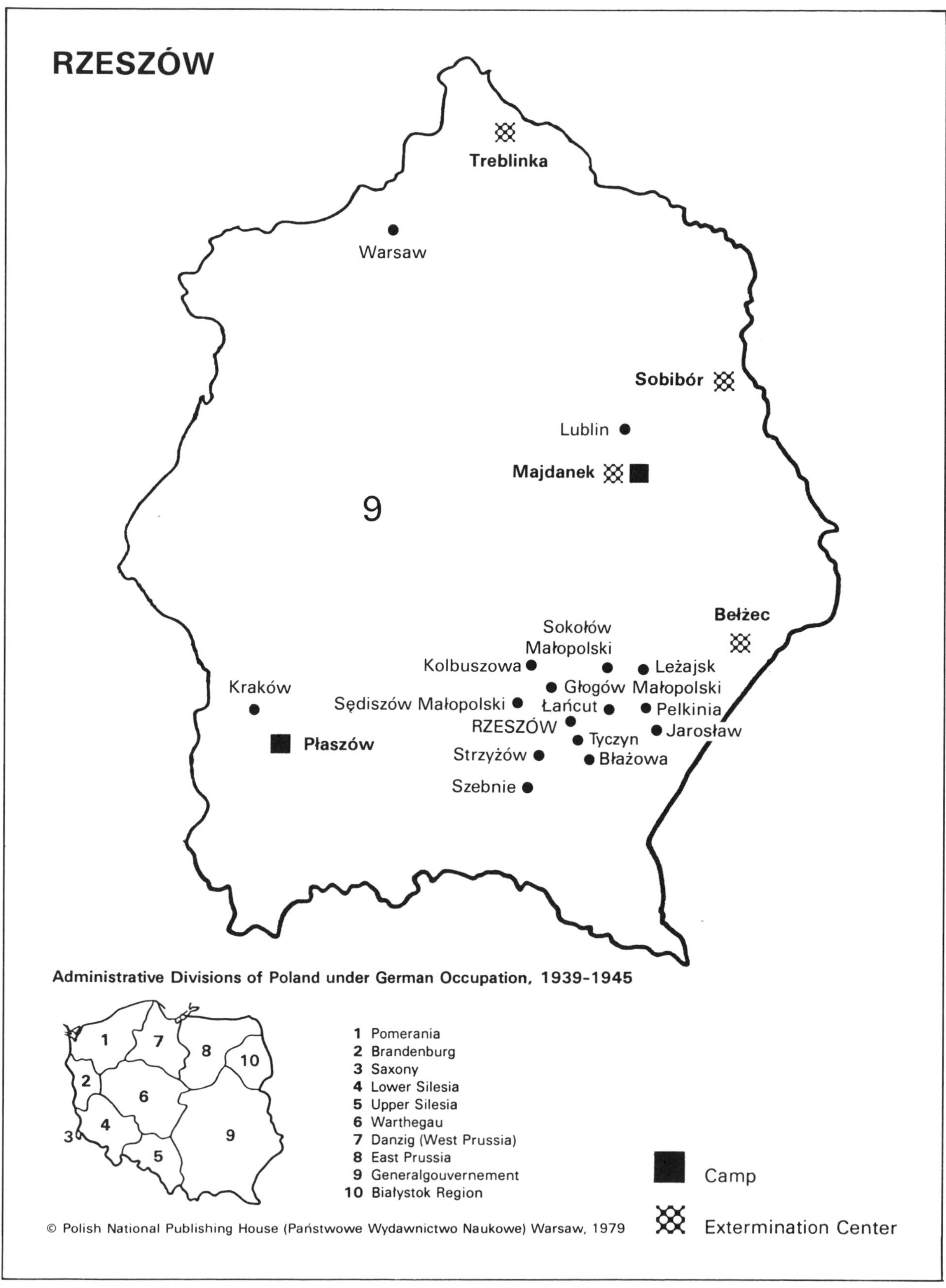
RZESZÓW
Treblinka
Warsaw
Sobibór
Lublin
Majdanek
9
Bełżec
Sokołów
Małopolski
Kolbuszowa
Leżajsk
Kraków
Głogów Małopolski
Sędiszów Małopolski
Łańcut
Pelkinia
RZESZÓW
Jarosław
Tyczyn
Płaszów
Strzyżów
Błażowa
Szebnie
Administrative Divisions of Poland under German Occupation, 1939-1945
1 Pomerania
2 Brandenburg
3 Saxony
4 Lower Silesia
5 Upper Silesia
6 Warthegau
7 Danzig (West Prussia)
8 East Prussia
9 Generalgouvernement
10 Białystok Region
Camp
Extermination Center
© Polish National Publishing House (Państwowe Wydawnictwo Naukowe) Warsaw, 1979

14,000 Jews, one-third of the city's total population, were living in Rzeszów.

The Germans occupied Rzeszów on September 10, 1939, and immediately began to persecute the Jews. In late September they destroyed the synagogues and Batei Midrash (houses of study and prayer) in the city. The worst cases of harassment in this initial phase took place during the Jewish high holidays. The Germans confiscated the apartments of hundreds of Jewish families, and Jews were prohibited from using the main thoroughfares (Trzeciego Maja and Zamkowa streets). A new name, Reichshof, was given by the Germans to the city, which was subjected to all the anti-Jewish decrees issued in the GENERALGOUVERNEMENT.

In October the German authorities appointed a JUDENRAT (Jewish Council), headed by a lawyer, Dr. Kleinman; only a few weeks later, however, in January 1940, Kleinman and other members of the Judenrat were executed. Benno Kahana was appointed Judenrat chairman in Kleinman's place.

In December 1939 and January 1940, 6,000 Jews were deported to Rzeszów from areas that had been incorporated into the Reich, mainly from ŁÓDŹ, Kalisz, and Upper Silesia. Subsequently, several thousand Jews—permanent inhabitants and refugees—left Rzeszów, making their way to Warsaw, to Soviet-occupied parts of Poland, or to other places in the Generalgouvernement. On December 17, 1941, a decree was issued announcing the establishment of a ghetto, and on January 10, 1942, the ghetto was closed off, with 12,500 Jews imprisoned inside. As a result of overcrowding and starvation an epidemic broke out in the ghetto, from which hundreds of persons died.

On April 30, 1942, the Gestapo carried out a terror action, describing it as an "anti-Communist operation," in the ghetto; thirty-five persons were taken out of their homes and shot to death. In June, twelve thousand Jews from the vicinity were forced into the ghetto, mostly from the towns of Łańcut, Leżajsk, Kolbuszowa, Sokołów Małopolski, Głogów Małopolski, Strzyżów, Tyczyn, Sędziszów Małopolski, and Błażowa, raising the population of the Rzeszów ghetto to twenty-three thousand.

From July 7 to 13, the Germans carried out the first deportation to the extermination camps. In the course of this *Aktion*, 360 persons were shot to death in the ghetto streets, another 2,000 were taken to the nearby Rudna Forest (between Rzeszów and Głogów) and shot to death there, and 14,000 Jews were taken to the Staroniwa railway station, where they were loaded into freight cars and dispatched to the BEŁŻEC extermination camp. Following this *Aktion* the ghetto area was considerably reduced in size.

On August 8, a second deportation *Aktion* took place. About one thousand women and children were removed from the ghetto, taken to the Pelkinia forced-labor camp near Jarosław in the Lvov district, and after a short stay there, transported to Bełżec. A third deportation *Aktion* was carried out on November 15, 1942, in which two thousand Jews were removed from the ghetto to Bełżec. While this operation was going on, a large force of Gestapo men under the command of Paul Lehmann, SS-*Scharführer* of the Kraków Sicherheitspolizei; (Security Police), combed the entire ghetto area for any remaining children, taking those they found from the arms of their parents and killing them.

During the deportations, activists of the ghetto underground, mainly from the Ha-Shomer ha-Tsa'ir Zionist movement, made attempts to engage the Germans in partisan warfare in the vicinity of the ghetto, but they were all killed after a short fight. The November 1942 deportation *Aktion* left no more than three thousand Jews in the ghetto, whose area was further reduced. It was now divided into two separate parts, and each became a camp. The part that lay east of Baldachowska Street was called Camp A and housed persons on forced labor; its official designation was *Jüdisches Zwangsarbeitslager* (Forced-Labor Camp for Jews). The second part, Camp B, lying west of Baldachowska, was used to house the families of the forced laborers. The prisoners referred to it as the *Schmelzgetto* ("melting ghetto"), that is, a ghetto for persons who were designated to be killed. The chief of the JÜDISCHER ORDNUNGSDIENST (Jewish police) in charge of the Jewish prisoners, Gorelik, tried to organize rescue efforts, but he was caught in the act by the Gestapo and killed.

In September 1943 most of the prisoners in Camp A were moved to the Szebnie forced-labor camp, about 80 miles (129 km) southeast of AUSCHWITZ. In early November some of these prisoners were taken to a forest near the village of Dobrucowa and shot to death; the rest were transferred to Auschwitz, where most of them perished. The prisoners in Camp B were all taken to Auschwitz-Birkenau that month and killed in the gas chambers.

By July 1944 only about six hundred prisoners were left in Camp A. Some of them escaped to the forests, where they hid out until the liberation of the area by the Soviet army the following month. The Germans transferred several hundred prisoners to Auschwitz before their own withdrawal, and most of them perished there. Jewish life was not resumed in Rzeszów after the war.

BIBLIOGRAPHY

Yaari-Wald, M., ed. *Rzeszow Jews' Memorial Book*. Tel Aviv, 1967. (In Hebrew, Yiddish, and English.)

SHMUEL KRAKOWSKI